LATINOS

By Earl Shorris

FICTION

Ofay

The Boots of the Virgin

Under the Fifth Sun: A Novel of Pancho Villa

In the Yucatán

NONFICTION

The Death of the Great Spirit: An Elegy for the American Indian

The Oppressed Middle: Scenes from Corporate Life

Jews Without Mercy: A Lament

Power Sits at Another Table: Aphorisms

While Someone Else Is Eating (editor)

Latinos: A Biography of the People

*A Nation of Salesmen: The Tyranny of the Market
and the Subversion of Culture*

New American Blues: A Journey Through Poverty to Democracy

Riches for the Poor: The Clemente Course in the Humanities

*In the Language of Kings: An Anthology of
Mesoamerican Literature—Pre-Columbian to the Present*
(with Miguel León-Portilla)

LATINOS

A BIOGRAPHY

OF THE PEOPLE

EARL SHORRIS

W·W·NORTON & COMPANY

NEW YORK   LONDON

Portions of this book, in different form, have appeared in *New York Times Book Review, Harper's Magazine, The Nation, El Nuevo Herald* (Miami), *New York Newsday,* California Chicáno News Media Association's *Tribute to Rubén Salazar, El Observador,* and *San Juan Star.*

The text of this book is composed in
10.5/12.5 Berkeley Old Style Book
with the display set in Gill Sans Bold Extra Condensed,
Gill Sans Bold Condensed, and Gill Sans Condensed.
Composition by Allentown Digital Services Division of RR Donnelley & Sons
Book design by Margaret M. Wagner

Library of Congress Cataloging-in-Publication Data
Shorris, Earl, 1936–
Latinos / by Earl Shorris.
p. cm.
Includes bibliographical references and index.
1. Hispanic Americans—History. 2. Hispanic Americans—Biography.
I. Title.
E184.S75S5 1992
973'.0468—dc20 91-39720
ISBN 0-393-03360-0
ISBN 0-393-32190-8 pbk.

W. W. Norton & Company, Inc.,
500 Fifth Avenue, New York, N.Y. 10110
www.wwnorton.com

W. W. Norton & Company Ltd.,
Castle House, 75/76 Wells Street, London W1T 3QT

1 2 3 4 5 6 7 8 9 0

Grateful acknowledgment is made to the following for permission to reprint from previously published material:

The Los Angeles *Times*: "A Chicano is a Mexican-American with a non-Anlgo image of himself . . ." by Ruben Salazar. Copyright 1970, Los Angeles *Times*. Reprinted by permission.

Arte Publico Press: Excerpt from "Simplemente Maria" by Tato Laviera, published in Revista Chicano-Riqueña Año X, 1982. Copyright 1982, Arte Publico Press. Reprinted by permission.

Arte Publico Press: Excerpt from "Refugee Ship" by Lorna Dee Cervantes published in Revista Chicano-Riqueña Año III, 1975. Copyright 1975, Arte Publico Press. Reprinted by permission.

Jorge Valls: "Where I Am There Is No Light" by Jorge Valls. Reprinted by permission of the author.

Bilingual Press: Excerpts from "Trumpets from the Islands of Their Eviction" by Martin Espada. Copyright 1987, Bilingual Press/Editorial Bilingue, Arizona State University, Tempe, AZ. Reprinted by permission.

Cecilio García-Camarillo: Excerpt from "El Ex-Pinto Todo Contento," published by El Norte Publications. Copyright 1982. Reprinted by permission of the author.

To my brother-in-law Larry
and my friend Rubén,
two Latinos,
a cop who was killed
and
a reporter who was killed by a cop;
que descansen en paz

Contents

THE PLAN OF THE BOOK

Latinos, who will soon be the largest group of minorities in the United States, are not one nationality, one culture, but many. This book describes the origins of the main groups, their history in the Americas and in the United States, and their situation at the close of the twentieth century. The method is largely biographical; that is, once the foundation of facts has been laid down and distinctions have been drawn among people of different national origins, the book proceeds through telling of the lives of individuals and families, including my own family. At the conclusion of the main body of the book, oral histories of two families, one Caribbean (Cuban) in origin and the other mainland (Mexican), are provided to enable the reader to meet Latinos with very little interference by the author. Some theories—about family, education, economics, politics, language, racism, art, poverty, and the effects of history and culture upon the process of immigration—are developed along the way, but it is finally a book about people, a biography, sometimes critical, but always with affection.

THE NAME OF THE PEOPLE

One summer afternoon in Los Angeles I asked Margarita Avila, "If you were writing this book, what would you want it to say?"

"Just tell them who we are and that we are not all alike," she said, distilling into a single sentence what I had heard from people in Florida, Texas, New York, and other parts of California. Before I could begin, there was a word to be chosen, a name to be given to the noun represented by "we."

It was hot that afternoon and there was no breeze. Margarita Avila and Sylvia Shorris had been chatting easily in their Mexican-accented Spanish, discussing their sons in a style no Anglo-Saxon mother could understand. They spoke in the shadow of the evil eye, never daring to exhibit pride, characterizing Harvard and Yale as distant places, cold stone, strangers into whose care they had given their sons. They indicated great successes by speaking of little troubles, for the rule of the evil eye is that immodesty will be punished; it is the enforcer of humility. Both women knew the etiquette of the evil eye; each one listened carefully to what the other did not say.

Later, over lunch, I asked Mrs. Avila, whose interest in language leads her to keep four dictionaries in her house, what she had meant by the pronoun "we." She smiled, the grandmother of adolescents, still girlish, pretty in her white summer suit. "Mejicanos," she said.

"Yes, but there is a larger group," I insisted, hoping to learn what word she would prefer.

"We are Mejicanos," she said again, laughing now, looking over at her husband and then at Sylvia for confirmation. Everyone laughed. She had left the problem to me. No matter which other, more inclusive noun I chose, it would blur the distinct character of Mejicanos, and she was unwilling to do that. As the Avilas explain in the oral history of their family, which serves as part of the Epilogue to this book, culture, the nuances of language, history are important to them.

Mrs. Avila knew all the other, less specific nouns and preferred not to use them. I think the variety of them must have pleased her, however, for she once said to me that the difference between English well-spoken and Spanish well-spoken is in the propensity in Spanish for what H. W. Fowler, the arbiter of English usage, called "elegant variation."

"Hispanic?" I asked.

"Mejicano," she said.

"Mejicano," he said.

And Sylvia nodded too.

"Hispano, Latino, Latin, Spanish, Spanish-speaking."

"Mejicano," she said. And even I laughed then.

Gently, but very firmly, with laughter, but without permitting argument, she had made her point. No other word was acceptable, not because there were no other nouns or adjectives available, but because any less specific, more encompassing word was damaging: To conflate cultures is to destroy them; to take away the name of a group, as of an individual, is to make pale the existence of the group.

Unfortunately, I do not have the luxury of taking Margarita Avila's advice. To carry out the mission of this book requires that the people have a name. But what?

"Tell them that we are not all alike" is good advice, but once that is done, what name should be given to the set of people who share—with many exceptions—a common language, some customs, and some ancestors? Any set that can be defined can be named. There must be one name, a single word that is not objectionable.

Leobardo Estrada, the demographer at UCLA, told me that in 1980 the U.S. Census was on the verge of choosing *Latino* as the correct word when someone said that it sounded too much like *Ladino,* the ancient Castillian now spoken only by descendants of the Spanish Jews who went into exile in the fifteenth century. *Latino* was replaced by *Hispanic* in the census. The battle was joined immediately on all sides. Political, racial, linguistic, and historical arguments were advanced; some were serious, a few were petulant, and at least one was offered as a joke.

Geographically, *Hispanic* is preferred in the Southeast and much of Texas. New Yorkers use both *Hispanic* and *Latino.* Chicago, where no nationality has attained a majority, prefers *Latino.* In California, the word *Hispanic* has been barred from the Los Angeles *Times,* in keeping with the strong feelings of people in that community. Some people in New Mexico prefer *Hispano*.

Politically, *Hispanic* belongs to the right and some of the center, while *Latino* belongs to the left and the center. Politically active Mexican-American women in Los Angeles are fond of asking, "Why *HISpanic?* Why not *HER-Spanic?*"

Historically, the choice went from *Spanish* or *Spanish-speaking* to *Latin American, Latino,* and *Hispanic.*

Economically, Rodolfo Acuña, the historian, is correct when he says that *Hispanic* belongs to the middle class, which seems most pleased by the term. Anglos[1] and people who oppose bilingual education and bilingualism prefer *Hispanic,* which makes sense, since *Hispanic* is an English word meaning "pertaining to ancient Spain."

I have chosen to use *Latino/Latina* for linguistic rather than political, geographic, or economic reasons: Latino has gender, which is Spanish, as opposed to Hispanic, which follows English rules. Although the linguistic connection to culture in the group name may eventually be killed, I choose not to be among the assassins.

[1]I have accepted the usage common among Mexican-Americans to describe any person who is neither Latino nor black. "Anglo" carries no derogatory baggage; it is merely descriptive. Some Latinos refer to non-Latino Caucasians as Americans, which is confusing. Since Latinos may have African origins, I have chosen to use black rather than African-American to avoid confusing those blacks who are Latinos with those who are not.

LATINOS

1

INTRODUCTION: RUBÉN, BIENVENIDA, AND JAMES

I.

When Bienvenida Petilón got lost on the subway, her sour daughter Alegre (which means *happy*) was beside herself, for there was hardly anyone in New York who spoke Spanish in those days and Bienvenida did not speak one word of English. Fortunately, that was a gentler time, and Bienvenida, toothless and terrifying, all in black, found her way back to the Bronx and her haven of gossip, coffee, and the Spanish language.

Language held a special place in Bienvenida's life, beginning with her name; as the eighth child and the first daughter, she was called Welcome. She continued the policy with her children by Petilón the fisherman; in addition to the inappropriately named Alegre, she had an olive-skinned daughter whom she named Blanca, the fair.

Although Bienvenida was not old when she came to the United States, she held on to her language and culture as if they were life itself. Indeed, when she died, it was not of illness but of English, for she had been condemned to a nursing home where no one spoke Spanish. Until that time, Bienvenida had determined the language spoken in her presence. She had also done her best to fend off the culture of the new country. According to her granddaughter, Bienvenida never accepted the concept of such things as recorded music. When she heard the voice of a singer on the radio before breakfast, she mused to her granddaughter Sylvia that it seemed strange for someone to be so happy in the morning.

Bienvenida was often an embarrassment to her daughter and grand-daughter. If she didn't approve of a suitor who brought her daughter home after dinner or a party, Bienvenida waited at the window for him to come into range, then rained bananas on his head. She filled the rooms of the apartment with the evil eye, black stars, and the misinterpretation of dreams. In the practice of medicine she excelled at the use of garlic, which she hung around Sylvia's neck in clusters before sending her off to school. It was a very long time ago, when New York was still welcoming to immigrants, but even so it must have been very difficult for a little girl with a Buster Brown haircut, a strange Spanish name, and a necklace of garlic to attend a public school in the Bronx.

A generation later, Assistant District Attorney James Sasson Shorris, Sylvia's son and Bienvenida's great-grandson, paced the worn-out floor of a Manhattan courtroom, questioning a witness who spoke only Spanish. In high school James's weakest subject had been Spanish. His mother had met often with his instructor to try to find a way to coach a bright young man in the language one of his ancestors had used to write poetry in the city of Toledo at the beginning of the fourteenth century. She had spent years of evenings cajoling her son into the world of Spanish verbs and vowels, but the effort had been entirely in vain; the assistant district attorney who looked as if he should be working in Madrid or Mexico City spoke to the witness through an interpreter.

The process of assimilation, the core issue of this book, is more dramatic in the Sasson-Petilón family than in most, for they are Spanish Jews, people who left Spain at the end of the fifteenth century, but who so loved the language and the culture that it was still their first language 450 years later. Why were James and his brother Anthony, the great-grandsons of Bien-venida and the grandsons of Ernesto and Blanca, the first generation to lose the language?

It might appear to someone looking at the family from a distance that the loss was due to the first out-marriage of either a Sasson or a Petilón in four-and-a-half centuries of living among speakers of foreign languages, but I think there were other reasons. The language really began to lose its grip on the families with the courtship of Ernesto and Blanca, for they wrote to each other in French rather than Spanish, seeking to make something like love out of an arranged marriage.

She succeeded. We do not know about him, because he died suddenly at the age of twenty-eight, but there is no reason to believe that he was not also in love. In French. And Spanish and Italian and Turkish and Greek, and eventually in English. For Ernesto and Blanca the Spanish language fell into equality. Multicultural and multilingual, they did not cling to any one language, but to languages. Ernesto, a romantic, believed Esperanto was the solution to the punishment of Babel. Blanca, being more practical, changed her name to Blanche, and limited her reading to novels in French.

Sylvia, among the first generation born in the United States, was apprenticed to Bienvenida, who knew several languages but lived in Spanish. Although it was uncomfortable being Spanish in schools filled with Goldbergs and Murphys, Sylvia did not abandon the language. On the contrary, she went to Mexico,[1] where she felt so comfortable that she stayed for years, living and working in a Mexican world. Arriving in Mexico, she said, was like coming home.

Her brother, who was much younger and not in the thrall of Bienvenida, limited his Spanish to the few nouns required to get through dinner and dessert. He was a portly Don Quixote in appearance and character, but he spoke with a Princeton accent, drawling the words through a very Spanish nose. His rejection of the language of his ancestors was so complete that it affected the way he chose to make his living; he taught English.[2]

The lesson of the Sasson-Petilón family is one of the axioms of Latino culture: *Las viejitas* rule the world. The language survives for one generation beyond the last little old lady who spoke it, and neither bilingual education nor English-only initiatives can change that. The difference between Sylvia and her brother was Bienvenida, who reached over a generation to speak to her granddaughter. Otherwise, the last Spanish-speaking Sasson-Petilón would have been Blanca.

No other factors appear to have had much importance in the transmission of language. Both of Bienvenida's great-grandsons spent their early years on the Mexican border; James was born in El Paso, Texas. James's parents both spoke Spanish, one like a *chilanga*[3] and the other like a *pachuco*[4] with Alz-

---

[1] An aunt and her husband moved to Miami to live and work among Cubans. An uncle married a Puerto Rican woman and lived in her world in New York. Apparently, Sylvia was not the only one who understood language as the defining characteristic of Latinos.

[2] Like Quixote, Larry had an ironic life; he worked on weekends as an auxiliary highway patrolman. In that job, while wearing his beloved boots and leather jacket, armed with nothing more than a walkie talkie and a nightstick, he was killed. Although he had escaped to a small town near Princeton, New Jersey, he died in the Bronx, where he was born.

[3] A resident of Mexico, D.F.

[4] A tough guy, a gang member, a person from El Paso, Texas, which is known on the streets as El Chuco. The etymology of El Chuco as well as *pachuco* is uncertain. One version is that *pachuco* is a contraction of *para* El Chuco (to El Paso).

NOTE TO THE READER: Words that may be unfamiliar to some readers are defined in footnotes. When such words appear more than once, the reader will also find them in an abbreviated glossary at the back of the book. Some words that may be familiar to most readers, but not all, appear in the glossary.

heimer's. The babysitters who cared for him until he got through the first two years of school spoke no English. He ate tortillas before he ate bread, but he did not ingest the language, not even when he tried.

The last test of Bienvenida's influence came with the 1990 U.S. Census forms. Her granddaughter, Sylvia, identified herself as Hispanic, but her great-grandsons simply checked the box marked white and went on with their lives.[5]

According to some people, mainly on the political right, the progression from Latino to Anglo of the descendants of Bienvenida was inevitable; the melting pot, which excludes blacks, will not exclude Latinos. Perhaps—but I wonder what would have happened to Bienvenida and her family if they had arrived in New York just twenty years ago or even yesterday. Bienvenida would not have gotten lost on the subway, which is a bilingual monster now; the commonness of her language might even have led her to feel, like Sylvia arriving in Mexico, that she was at home, and that would have changed everything.

2.

When I was a small boy in El Paso, Texas, I did not like Mr. Salazar's son, Rubén, very much. Because of him I had to wear my knickers up so high that the waistband touched the pockets of my shirt. The knees were an even greater embarrassment, bunched up, held there with a rubber band to keep them from falling down to my ankles. I looked at a photograph of myself in that ancient Cub Scout uniform recently; nothing fit properly but the nekerchief. The face between the cap with the tuck taken in the back and the gigantic collar was not a happy one.

Not all of this was Rubén's fault. Nature had caused him, in my view, to grow too tall and too wide, but not nearly so tall as the watchmaker's son, Junior Rojas, whose uniform was also passed down to me. Mr. Salazar, Mr. Rojas, and my father all worked together in a jewelry store in downtown El

---

[5]Ethnicity was a different kind of issue for them when they applied to colleges and law schools. They decided not to seek admission under affirmative action programs on the grounds that neither they nor their parents had been denied economic or educational opportunities in the past. When he was named a commissioner in the New York City government, Anthony chose not to be counted among the mayor's minority appointees, although he was always pleased to say that his mother was Spanish and from the Bronx.

The decision neither to deny their heritage nor to exploit it unfairly suggests an interesting approach to affirmative action: an economic and educational means test, like the one Anthony and James imposed upon themselves, in addition to ethnic or racial identification. Redress should be granted only to those who have been wronged.

Paso. Mr. Salazar was the head of the silver department, and my father was the watchmaker's assistant.

Rubén was older and went to Lamar, a slightly more middle-class institution than the old Morehead School on the north edge of the downtown district where I sang the Texas state anthem every morning. Although I followed in his footsteps (literally, in his kneesocks), we didn't really know each other until we worked together on the El Paso *Herald-Post*. Rubén was the newspaper's star reporter, the darling of E. M. Pooley, a crabby, opinionated Scripps-Howard man who used his newspaper to advance the cause of Mexican-Americans and Mexicans. Pooley attacked the Immigration and Naturalization Service (INS) relentlessly for its mistreatment of Mexican nationals, and in local politics he was largely responsible for the election of El Paso's first Latino mayor and the promotion of Latinos to positions of authority in the police department.

With Pooley's blessing, Rubén had himself arrested and sent to the city jail. His exposé of the conditions in the jail made the front page of the paper for a week. Eight months later, after Rubén had helped me to get a job at the paper, he asked if I wanted to go undercover to report on the failure of the police to correct any of the conditions he had described. "You're small and dark, and you talk like a damn *pachuco*," he said; "you'll be okay."

He arranged for two detectives to pick me up on Mesa Street not far from my parents' house. I was to wear old clothes, boots, bluejeans, and a western shirt and not carry anything that would identify me as a reporter. Shortly before six o'clock on a Friday evening, I left my parents' house and walked down the hill toward Mesa Highway. I was almost at the corner when my father came running down the street. Since I had never, in my entire life, seen him run, I thought it must be something important. "Rubén's on the phone," he said; "he has to talk to you."

I ran back up to the house. "You can't go," Rubén said. "They know about it. They're going to kill you." It seemed a bit melodramatic. I even wondered whether Rubén might not have changed his mind about helping another reporter to repeat his great success.

A few months later, on the occasion of Rubén's departure for California, a detective in the El Paso police department told me about the reporter who wanted to duplicate Rubén Salazar's expose. "It was a setup. They were gonna throw him in the tank and turn their backs. Shit, I don't think he would have come out alive." He laughed, "Cause of death: *pendejismo*."[6]

Rubén went on to California, quickly moving up to the Los Angeles *Times*, which sent him to Mexico and Vietnam. When he came back to Los Angeles, he persuaded the paper to give him a column, to permit him to become a

[6]stupidity

voice of the people from the east side. From the outset, it was a troublesome column for the *Times*. Rubén had learned from Ed Pooley that a newspaper could affect the politics of a city, and he did not hesitate to use his column for that purpose. When he moved from the *Times* to KMEX-TV, he told me, "Chandler let me keep the column." Somehow I got the impression, which I am told now was wrong, that the *Times* was not entirely sorry to see him leave. Rubén made trouble; he thought that was part of the job description.

While he was still at the *Times*, I telephoned him from San Francisco, where I was working on *Scanlan's Monthly,* the short-lived successor to *Ramparts* magazine, to ask if he would consider writing a series of articles on Latinos in the United States. It was a curiously comfortable conversation after so many years. "How's your dad?" we asked each other, as if to reestablish our roots. I said how much I admired his work. He said he had read one of my books. We talked about our kids, his Rubita,[7] my Sylvia. He was beginning to get complaints about the column by then; the sheriff of Los Angeles County had accused him of "stirring up the Mexicans."

"What are you going to do?"

"Keep writing," he said.

"Pos, andale, mano."

He laughed at the street talk encouragement. He said he would think about the magazine pieces, what to say, how to organize them, how to make time to do the work. We agreed to meet soon, either in Los Angeles or San Francisco.

We talked several times about the series, but it was a busy time for Rubén. He was moving over to KMEX, still writing the column, being a husband and father. Then, in the late summer of 1970, he telephoned to ask a favor: He had been invited to teach a class on Saturday mornings at the University of California in Berkeley; could he stay over at my house on Friday nights, beginning on the first Friday in September?

"Mi casa es tu casa."

We talked for a while. Things were going well for him, although he had been getting more complaints about the column from the sheriff of Los Angeles County. The sheriff had actually threatened him.

"Be careful," I said, advising the man who had taught me to distrust the police that he should distrust the police.

He laughed. There would be time to talk on Friday night, he said. I asked if he would be in San Francisco in time for dinner. He said he didn't think so, but he would let me know.

On the last Saturday in August, 1970, in Los Angeles, there was a great march against the war in Vietnam. It was clear by then that the numbers of

---

[7]Blondie, an affectionate name for his wife.

minorities drafted, sent overseas, wounded, and killed were entirely out of proportion. Vietnam was turning out to be a black and Latino war against an Asian enemy. In East Los Angeles the march for peace turned into a riot. To get away from the chaos in the streets or perhaps just to have a cold beer Rubén went into the Silver Dollar Bar. There was shooting outside on the street. Deputies from the Los Angeles County Sheriff's Department moved into the Silver Dollar, firing as they came. They shot Rubén in the head with a tear gas projectile.

Sylvia and our two sons and I were in our car driving north to visit a friend in Sebastopol, California, when we heard that someone had been killed in the riots in East Los Angeles. "It's Rubén," she said.

"What makes you think it was Rubén?"

"It was," she said.

A few minutes later, the dead person was identified as a reporter.

All afternoon, as we drove through the brown, late summer hills of Marin, the news kept coming in, getting closer and closer to him until they finally said his name. It was time to tell my sons about him, what he had done as a writer, how we were connected as people. I said that I owed him something.

It was a long drive home and very quiet. For some reason I thought more about the beer we had consumed together than about his accomplishments as a reporter. I remembered the afternoon we had gone to the bullfights in Juárez with two other reporters. We drank tequila until four o'clock, then sat in the sun drinking beer while six weary bulls died slowly and shamefully in the Plaza Balderas. Afterward we headed for our favorite bar only to find it had been closed and padlocked for selling American cigarettes without a license. Outraged, we decided to enter the bar anyway. We lifted up one of our colleagues, who was stiff with drink, and attempted to use his head as a battering ram. A policeman convinced us it was a bad idea.

Later, after the giddy moment of denial had passed, I thought about his life, what might have been. It was one of the sorrows of an early death that he had not written the series of articles before he was killed; they would have become a book, of course, a rallying point, the next step after Carey McWilliams's *North From Mexico*. Rubén was a good, clear writer, not a fussy writer, but a reporter who had not lost his passion in boredom or a bottle. He was not the first Latino reporter or even the first Latino columnist, but he was the best and the bravest.

———

There are many monuments to Rubén Salazar, parks and libraries and ironies. One of the ironies is a housing project on the south side of El Paso. It is separated by a freeway from the middle-class part of the city, a ghetto by design. There have been riots in the projects and shootings. The gang that currently runs the social life of the young people in the Salazar Projects, Los Blue Diamonds, does its best to force the *tecatos*[8] to move out, but it is difficult. People who live in the projects must sometimes steal to feed themselves and their families. Everyone who comes from the projects wears his or her origins like a scarlet letter or a yellow star.

On one of the walls in the projects a large mural has been painted. A giant cartoon bearing some resemblance to Rubén Salazar looks out over the repetitions of low brick buildings and old cars, down the empty sidewalks, past the graffiti of Los Blue Diamonds to the gang members flattened against a wall, half-hidden from the street, difficult targets for a shooter passing by. Even the *veteranos*, the members of the old Flaming Angels, barely remember the story of the man whose face looks down at them every day of their lives. Los Blue Diamonds know that he was killed, but they do not know where or how. The Cypress Scorpions, the next generation of gangsters, know nothing about the life of the man for whom the projects were named; for them he is no one, not even a myth, but his name has become a burden they will carry all their lives. "There's stereotyping," they say. "People who come from here are nothings. They don't got a chance."

In East Los Angeles there is another place that should be a monument to Rubén Salazar and the sixties and the chicano movement, which is also dead now, turned into ritual handshakes and a few catch phrases. I went to that place one night with Ron Catana, the composer of the cabaret operetta *Joaquín*. We had been at First and Boyle talking to the mariachis who gather there every night in imitation of the Plaza Garibaldi in Mexico City. It was a good time in summer, full of noise and car fumes and people tuning guitars and warming up their chops with little horn solos. There were *norteños*[9] with their little concertinas and men from Guadalajara in *charro* costumes. A group of Salvadoreños who had studied the music as adults, hoping to earn a living by it, chatted about nuances with an old man in a sleeveless undershirt who sat in a canvas chair, joking, advising, pontificating with wisecracks.

As the mariachis drifted away, going to their jobs, heading for nightclubs in Santa Monica or parties in El Monte or Beverly Hills, a depressing quiet came over the island at the intersection where the musicians had gathered. It was time to leave. "Do you want to go to the Silver Dollar?" Catana asked. "We could drive by there, see what you think."

I had put off the visit a dozen times; until we went there that evening, I did not know why.

There were two pool tables and two jukeboxes in the Silver Dollar. One jukebox worked; the other bubbled and shone in a fluorescent way, but made no sound. Between the pool tables, in a small open space, men with big

[8]Heroin addicts
[9]Northerners

mustaches and billed caps danced with the barmaids, all thick and shiny women who sweat like bottles of Budweiser. They held each other carefully, keeping some distance between them, courtly country people, Mejicanos still too mannerly for East Los Angeles. In a corner, exiled from the vivacity of short skirts and dimpled thighs, an old couple danced together, moving to a more sedate rhythm. He was thin and stooped; she had no more shape than laundry stuffed into a bag. The other dancers and the boys in cutoff shirts shooting pool averted their eyes from the aged pair, as if they were the unavoidable future come to stand like sorrows at the edge of the evening.

And Rubén, was he any longer part of this time or that? "Do you know Rubén Salazar?" I asked a barmaid. She said she had only been in Los Angeles for two months. None of the others knew him, had ever heard his name. "I don't think he comes here anymore," a barmaid said.

I asked them all, all the barmaids and all the people who stood at the bar.

Then the manager appeared, wanting to know what I was asking. Was there a problem? "Ah, Rubén Salazar, the journalist. Yes, they made a play about him and performed it here. I have the program somewhere; would you like to see it?" He rummaged in a drawer behind the bar until he found a folded sheet of paper. It was the program of the play that had been performed twice in 1987 in the Silver Dollar. "Here, take it," he said; "it's the last one."

"But it's the only one."

"Keep it," he said. Then he excused himself and went back into the room at the end of the bar.

There were no other signs, not a picture or a plaque. Catana pointed out three holes in a post. "Bullet holes," he said.

"Perhaps."

A group of mariachis came in. They walked the length of the bar, stopping before each barmaid, asking the man who sat across from her if he would like them to play something. They were *norteños,* men with long sideburns and cowboy hats. One man loomed above the rest. He wore black, and his face, which was as serious as an axe, drew everyone's attention. The man in black hung back from the others; he did not solicit customers.

No one ordered a song. The mariachis left, and Catana and I followed them out of the bar. Our business in the Silver Dollar was also finished. We watched the four men cross the street, heading toward another bar.

"There was nothing," I said. "That's why I never wanted to come here; I was afraid of the portent."

"It used to be a chicano bar. If it was still a chicano bar, there would have been something."

"That was a long time ago."

"Yes," he said, "the end of the sixties."

3.

Along with life experience, an assumption informs this book. It seems a simple-minded, obvious concept upon which to build, but there are doubters—egoists, idealists, and utopians—who believe that people can be fitted into a single form and that pluralism is merely an aberration along the way to perfection. The world tells us otherwise. History governs. Culture exists.[10] Pluralism endures. A person is born a tabula rasa and within a few years becomes a library of history and language, of tastes, smells, feelings, fears, relations, rhythms, rhymes, gestures, stories, dreams. Culture is real, distinguishing and determining. Whenever cultures are conflated, forced into the prisons of paradigms, they must either deceive the theorists or die.[11] Most have died; more are dying.

In an age of universal electronic communications, the history of the Olmec, Taino, Anasazi, and a thousand other cultures may be repeated on a global scale. But it will take a long time for that to happen, and the resistance to extinction may be more fierce than anyone expects. Those who accepted the idea of the melting pot, embracing a kind of cultural suicide, have found that despite their efforts, culture steered them through the soup to a place of their own: the Poles here, the Jews there, the Irish and the Germans and the Italians somewhere else. Even intermarriage is not necessarily murder; the mix is new, but everything is not lost.

As a result of racism in the United States, some groups have not been permitted into the mythical melting pot. Others, from Mennonites to Gypsies to black Muslims to Hasidic Jews, have stubbornly resisted the comfortable life of the assimilated.

Most people who come to the United States will, over some number of generations, assimilate, but the patterns of assimilation will not all be the same; culture persists and, because it persists, determines how people live in new circumstances. Moreover, it determines the circumstances; no culture is immune from loving infection by its neighbors.

Although the name of this book is *Latinos,* the theory of it is that there are no Latinos, only diverse peoples struggling to remain who they are while becoming someone else. Each of them has a history, which may be forgotten,

---

[10]For a definition of culture see Kroeber and Kluckhohn, *Culture.* They cite 164 different definitions in their work, first published in 1952. Since then, one would expect at least another hundred, or at least another sixty-four, to have been published.

[11]If the structuralist theory of homologous minds is correct, the homologies are still made of details so specific that only the genius of Claude Lévi-Strauss could find them less than unique.

muddled, misrepresented, misunderstood, but not erased. Every people has its own Eden, and there are no parallel tracks.[12]

4.

Every season, for the last twenty years, I have expected the appearance of this book. If not Rubén, someone else should have written it by now. But a generation has been born and a generation has died, and the book has not been written. Rodolfo Acuña, Mario T. García, Alejandro Portes, and others have written fine, useful books, but not a book about Latinos.

Perhaps they know something. Perhaps no Latino writer can write a book about Latinos. On the other hand, this is no task for tourists. Who then? What writer can both be and not be a tourist? The purpose of this introduction is not to claim that I have defied the law of the excluded middle, but to tell you where this book begins so that you can make adjustments to compensate for the author's prejudices and other failings.

This is not a travel book. I wrote it because I could. I have no distance from the subject, no space in which to cool memories, perceptions, feelings. As objectivity is a pretense of innocence, this is worldly work.

[12]For an enlightening explanation of the creative, democratic value of pluralism, see Isaiah Berlin, *Vico and Herder: Two Studies in the History of Ideas* (New York: The Viking Press), 1976.

2

WELCOME TO THE OLD WORLD

We are ordinary people,
we are subject to death and destruction,
we are mortals;
allow us then to die,
let us perish now,
since our gods are already dead.

Colloquies of 1524, transcribed by Fray Bernardino de Sahagún

A small group of Dominican artists and intellectuals met in Manhattan in the closing days of 1989 to plan the attack. It seemed less than serious at first, an idea born over drinks and a little smoke in a dark room, whispered, enjoyed, explored over the sound of drums and an old piano. They laughed. Later, the next day and the day after, it became more than an amusement. They hated the imperialists, their whiteness, the soft dough feel of them, their thin hair hanging. And they hated Christopher Columbus most of all.

This was the plan: When the ships arrived to recreate his landing in celebration of the five hundredth anniversary of the discovery of Hispaniola, and all the weaklings, all the ass-lickers, rushed out to greet them, the true Dominicans, hundreds of them in native dress, would rise up out of their hiding places and attack the white invaders. With spears and stones, they would drive the Europeans back to their ships and away from the island of Hispaniola forever.

The Dominicans had overlooked history; they had permitted the symbolism to become confused. No one remembered that by 1570 only the imperialists and their African slaves were left; the genocide of the native population of Hispaniola was virtually complete. It did not occur to the little group of angry romantics in Manhattan that it was themselves they planned to drive away, for the Columbus Day conspirators were the children of conquest, doomed to a life of unendurable irony—Latinos.

Any history of Latinos stumbles at the start, for there is no single line to trace back to its ultimate origin. There are many Edens, a thousand floods, discoveries and conquests in numbers beyond the capability of human memory. Only the smallest fragment of this history survives. We shall never know the Olmecs or read the Mayan books the Spaniards burned; no more is known of the mind of Chief Hatuey of Hispaniola than what a Spanish friar heard; the grandeur of the Yoruba pantheon was not recorded during its reign.

Latino history has become a confused and painful algebra of race, culture, and conquest; it has less to do with evidence than with politics, for whoever owns the beginning has dignity, whoever owns the beginning owns the world. So every version has its adherents, for every human being wishes to be at least equal in his own mind: the African to the Spaniard, the person of mixed blood to the fair-haired descendant of Europeans, the Indian to the person of mixed races, the darker to the lighter, the one with kinky hair to the one with the softly curled hair of Europe to the one with the straight black hair of the Americas.[1]

For some the choice of beginnings is obvious. Imagine a family descended directly from Indians who lived in the Mexican state of Oaxaca: If the family concedes that Columbus "discovered" a New World, they accept the notion that whites (Europeans) come from a superior civilization. On the other hand, if the descendants of Indians say that Latino history began with the Toltecs or the Maya or with the emergence of people from the earth in a place called Aztlán, they raise the value of their own ancestry, making themselves at least equal and possibly superior to the whites.

The choice becomes more difficult for a person of mixed ancestry for whom those small conceits of identity, which are the ordinary rules of chauvinism, do not apply. Should a woman in Chicago who traces her family back to both Chihuahua and Castile identify with Europe or the Americas? According to the rules of conquest, the blood of the conquered dominates, but the rules are not profound; they are written on the skin. If the woman in Chicago appears to be European, she will have to choose where Latino history began, who were the subjects—the ones who acted, the dignified ones—and who were the objects—the people whom the forces of history acted upon.

---

[1]In 1990, Kirkpatrick Sale offered a fascinating revision of the European version of the history of the Americas in *The Conquest of Paradise*. His humanistic, thoughtful work contrasts sharply with a restatement of the old ethnocentric white European view published a year later by Mario Vargas Llosa. As the quincentennial celebration of the Voyage of Columbus drew closer, books, films, television programs and articles appeared in ever-increasing numbers. The Sale and Vargas Llosa books remained at the opposite poles of opinion.

Her decision will not be frivolous; it will determine her vision of herself, the face she sees in the mirror as well as the one she presents to the world. Her politics, left or right, Democrat or Republican, may be affected by what she considers the beginning of history; she may even choose to speak and dress and cook according to how and where she thinks Latino history began. The name by which she identifies herself—Hispanic, Latino, Spanish, chicano, Mexican, Mejicano, Mexican-American—will depend upon her understanding of the past.

The history of Latinos was not always a difficult one. Until 1920 it was understood that Columbus had discovered the "New World" and begun the process of civilizing its savages and exploiting its natural resources. It was also understood that other savages had been imported from Africa, enslaved, and used to replace the American natives who died in such enormous numbers in the fields and mines of the Caribbean. But the end of the Mexican Revolution of 1910, after almost ten years of war, brought with it the need to integrate the rural Indians into the political economy of the nation. The task was given to one of Mexico's leading intellectuals, José Vasconcelos, who was appointed minister of education. With three words, he proclaimed the integration of the Indian into Mexican society at the most profound level: *la raza cosmica.*

To explain the notion of this cosmic race to people who could not read, Vasconcelos turned to Mexico's painters. He commissioned Diego Rivera, José Clemente Orozco, and David Alfaro Siquieros, among others, to paint murals depicting Mexican subjects, and he gave them complete artistic freedom, which they used to attack the government, the colonialists, the capitalists, and the Spanish conquerors. A new version of Mexican history appeared on the walls of public places. For the first time in four hundred years a large number of people began to see the conquest in a different light: Instead of the discovery of a dark, savage continent by intellectually, technologically, morally superior white men, the muralists portrayed the destruction of the glorious civilizations of the Americas by the brutal Spaniards.

After Vasconcelos and his muralists, the victory of the Indianists would seem to have been assured. But there were doubts, even in the mind of the minister of education himself. Vasconcelos wrote that the "blood and soul" of Mexico were Indian, but the language was Spanish. And even more pointedly, the civilization, he said, came from Spain.

Mexico cannot seem to shake off the idea of the civilizing of the savages. The sense of a dark continent, however subtle, exists even in the work of Miguel León-Portilla, the author of the brilliant study *Aztec Thought and Culture.* When the Indianist anthropologist León-Portilla writes of "the discovery of the New World," it is a sign that history has not yet triumphed over power, and the complex beginning of Latino history remains at the center of the politics of the people who came here from Puerto Rico, Cuba, the Dominican Republic, Mexico, Guatemala, El Salvador, Honduras, Nicaragua, and all the other countries of Central and South America and the Caribbean, as well as Spain.

—

The objective truth has little influence; nevertheless, it may be useful to consider some of the facts and how they are used by different groups of people. If the idea of a Promethean Europe can be set aside and the arrival of Columbus considered as the coming together of cultures—greedy, violent, murderously cruel, but still a confluence—the various streams can be traced back to their origins. Latino history then begins in Africa, Asia by way of the Americas, and Europe.

Spain, separated by a great mountain range and profoundly influenced by Middle Eastern and North African cultures, is the least European of the countries of Europe. To locate the beginning of Latino history there requires looking back to the Paleolithic cave painters. Then come thousands of years of wars, conquests, and genetic and cultural intermarriages. The Spaniards who sailed to the Americas were themselves the mestizos of Europe: the natives, children of the painters, mixed with Celtic tribes, Phoenician sailors, soldiers and settlers from Carthage, Greeks, Hebrews, Romans, Visigoths, and Moors.

By the fifteenth century the geographic area that is now Spain was divided into Castile and several other kingdoms. Compared to northern Europe, the peninsula was backward, lacking in industry, underdeveloped agriculturally, usually at war. In Castile, agriculture was severely hampered by the Mesta, a guild of sheepowners who were permitted to move their flocks from summer to winter pasture over cultivated land. Armed shepherds protected the animals as they ate their way across the Spanish dinnertable.

Isabella claimed the Castilian crown in 1474, but she was not acknowledged without five years of bloody war. Her marriage to Ferdinand, the king of Aragon, united the peninsula, but did not solve its economic problems. There was simply no money in Spain—credit could be obtained only from Jews and *conversos*[2]—the capital that would enable Spain to become the most powerful country on earth only a few decades later was nowhere on the horizon. Isabella and Ferdinand, rulers of a nation without great prospects, turned much of their attention to otherworldly matters; they were the Catholic kings.

How the conquest of the Western hemisphere aided Spain in its rise to

[2]People who had become Christians during the forced conversions of 1391, but were still exempt from laws forbidding moneylending

power can best be demonstrated by Alexander von Humboldt's estimate of the wealth, mostly in silver, gold, and pearls, brought out of the hemisphere by the Spaniards and the Portuguese. In 1803, he put the value at 5.7 billion pesos. Clearly, the Western hemisphere, including its human population, was viewed in Europe as a natural resource to be exploited. It took fifty years from the time they sighted land in the hemisphere for the Spaniards to grant the remaining native population the status of human beings, with some protection from the crown.

The *New Laws of the Indies,* published in 1542, grew out of a debate between Bartolomé de las Casas and the theologian Juan Ginés de Sepúlveda. The Catholic bishop Las Casas had argued against the mistreatment of the natives of the hemisphere, claiming in 1522 that the Spaniards had already killed fifteen million. Sepúlveda responded that Indians were as different from Spaniards as monkeys were from men. By the time the Catholic kings resolved the debate in favor of Las Casas, the destruction of the native population in the Caribbean was nearly complete. Of perhaps a quarter of a million indigenous people who had lived on Hispaniola, only 500 were left alive to enjoy the new laws.

To locate the beginning of Latino history in Spain revives the argument between Las Casas and Sepúlveda. Humanity becomes a matter of genealogy or simply the color of one's eyes. If Spain is the beginning, the black-eyed professor of philosophy in Houston, descended from men who worked in the Spanish silver mines of Zacatecas, must prove to himself in the secret cells of his own mind that he is not a monkey.

For the green-eyed and the fair, the Spanish connection is a way to separate oneself from the painful daily life of many Latinos, to escape the suffering of the stereotyped. A Cuban woman in California speaks of visiting her Spanish grandfather; a Puerto Rican psychologist in New York builds a house in Spain; an advertising copywriter in Miami recalls a childhood memory of leaving Cuba for sanctuary among distant relatives in Asturias; a member of the Mexican delegation to the United Nations wears a tiny rosette indicating that he has no Indian blood. All of them call Spain *la madre patria,* the beginning, the mother of countries, the teacher of culture, the source of civilization. Sepúlveda's argument appalls them; like Las Casas, they believe that by knowing God the Indians will become the happiest people in the world. They do not forget, however, who brings the knowledge of God to whom; they are the Europeans, the discoverers of the New World.

Latino history also began in Africa at Ife with the creation of the earth by Oddudúa, the great god of the Yoruba. Since the history of everybody appears to have begun in Africa, the Yoruba version may be the safest choice. Yoruba society developed in the forests of West Africa, where the people became adept at living in large communities, farming and producing metalwork of extraordinary sophistication. The quality of Yoruba craftsmanship was so high that European scientists said for many years that it must have been learned from Greeks who had ventured into Africa; how else, they argued, could black Africans have produced such elegant metalwork using the lost wax-method of casting?

Little is known about the Yoruba past other than the speculations of archeologists, for the Yoruba have an artful rather than a scientific history, one based more in myth than fact. They produced a rich oral literature and an elaborate pantheon. Unfortunately, in the Western hemisphere and perhaps even in Africa, the pantheon has become fused with Christian ideas, making it difficult to separate the attributes of Olofi, for example, from the crucified Christ.

The Yoruba were not the only people whose descendants came to the West. There were also large numbers of Bantus, who are associated with the Mayombé religion,[3] and some people from the interior as well as the east coast. But it is the highly developed culture of the Yoruba that points back to the specific African origin of Latinos.

The U.S. educated Dominican poet who heads the United Nations Project on Women in Latin America, Chiqui Vicioso, said she learned to understand and to value her own origins while working in Africa. Vicioso now connects herself to Oshún, the water goddess and the Venus of the Yoruba. Because of her African awakening, the daughter of middle-class Dominicans, who once wished to look European, has embraced her own past, even letting her hair grow out into two African wings.

One of the leading educators in New York City, Awilda Orta, a Puerto Rican, did not need a trip to Africa to understand her origins; she quotes an old saying of the island, "Si no es Dingo es Mandingo."[4] Jorge Valls, one of the intellectual leaders of the Cuban revolution and now, after his release from prison, the discomfiting conscience of the Cuban exiles, has no outward sign of African heritage; in fact, he could not look more European, but Valls is careful always to say that there are blacks among his ancestors, for in his mind he could not otherwise be Cuban.

In Latino neighborhoods where people of Caribbean origin live, the botánicas[5] that are found on virtually every commercial street exist as open opposition to European mores. The Afro-Christian religion known as Sant-

---

[3]In Esteban Montejo's *Autobiography of a Runaway Slave,* the author remembers the distinctions between Lucummi and the Congolese religion. Lucummi, he said, had more to do with divining and Mayombé with casting spells. He also described the skin colors of various tribes: The Mandinga were reddish-brown, the Congolese (Bantus) were black, and so on.

[4]If you are not a member of the Dingo tribe, you are a Mandingo; in other words, if your ancestors don't come from one African tribe, they come from another.

[5]Stores that sell herbs, incense, statues, and books connected with folk medicine.

ería for which the *botánicas* provide herbs and icons places Latino origins squarely in Africa. Santería, based largely on Yoruba medicine, empowers its adherents through magic; a santero can divine the future, hurt or kill an enemy, enchant a lover, cure the sick. But the political empowerment of Santería is even more useful to the person who looks in the mirror and sees the face of Africa; Santería is a connection to the time before slavery, proof that Africans are at least equal and in arcane ways, perhaps in the most profound ways, superior to the native people of the Western hemisphere and to Europeans.

Through the calculus of self-preservation, many people, especially Cubans, who place the beginning of Latino history in Africa, consider themselves partners of the Spaniards in the New World. They know that not all blacks in the New World were slaves, confined to the mines and fields; African freemen explored the hemisphere along with Europeans. These Latinos understand the distinction between the discoverer and the discovered, between the survivors and the ghosts. If Latino history did not begin in Africa, they ask, whose hands are making music on the drum? Who is dancing? What is the origin of the rhythms in the sauce?[6]

An Asian origin for Latino history is a kind of academic amusement, a game played upon an imaginary land bridge across the Pacific. If Latinos are of indigenous origin, the beginning of their history is difficult to locate. There is a myth of a chthonian origin somewhere in what is now the southwestern United States, a place called Aztlán, but it is one of many such myths. In the Popol Vuh[7] of the Quiché Maya, the first people were manikins made of wood; "they had no blood, no lymph. They had no sweat, no fat. Their complexions were dry, their faces were crusty." These experimental humans were destroyed in a flood, according to the Quiché myth. Only later, after the flood, were real humans created.

The Caribbean origin myth transcribed by the Spaniards has the first humans coming out of caves on the side of a mountain called Canta. The Aztec creation myth recorded by Bernardino de Sahagún,[8] the father of modern ethnography, tells how all the other gods "died that the sun might come into being." There follows a description of the miraculous conception by Coatlicue, the mother of the gods. Whether her descendants, the Toltecs, were humans or gods is uncertain and not of great importance here; the immaculate conception of her son, Huitzilopochtli, is fascinating. It may have been the homologous relation of the Christian and Náhua conceptions that showed the Spaniards how to meld the two sets of beliefs.

---

[6]"Sauce" is the literal translation of *salsa*, a popular musical form and dance.

[7]Translated most recently by Dennis Tedlock

[8]A magnificent translation direct into English from the Náhuatl has been made by Arthur J. O. Anderson and Charles E. Dibble. A twelve-volume limited edition is published by the School of American Research and the University of Utah.

The archeological history begins with the formation of villages in what is now the Mexican state of Puebla some time after 5,000 B.C.[9] A pre-Classical period, lasting from 1,500 to 200 B.C., saw the establishment of ceremonial sites and the refinement of agriculture and various crafts.

The Classical period, which lasted only from 200 B.C. to 900 A.D., included the rise and unexplained decline of the Mayan theocracy in the south of Mexico, Guatemala, and Honduras and the great advances in both art and technique of the Toltecs, whose civilization spread south from central Mexico. The florescence of Classical civilizations in Mexico during that period included monumental architecture, brilliant artistic achievements, mathematics more sophisticated than those of Europe at the time, highly accurate astronomy, and the development of an unwieldy but functional form of writing.

The post-Classical period, the most familiar one, belongs mainly to the Aztecs. It began with the invasion of the Chichimeca, the barbarians from the north, and after the arrival of the Aztecs in the Valley of Mexico, enjoyed a period of astonishing political and military activity. In a brief time, the wandering tribe from somewhere north and west conquered the Valley of Mexico, built one of the great cities of the world, and managed to achieve political and military hegemony over the entire region.

By 1532, nothing remained of the three thousand year development of civilization in the Americas but relics, ruins, and dying languages. The Spaniards had killed off the populations of the Caribbean islands, burned the paper books that contained the treasures of the Classical period in the Yucatán Peninsula, destroyed Tenochtitlán. And Pizarro, with only 180 men, had shattered the glorious Inca civilization of Peru.

Two coincidences describe the temper of the opposing worlds at the end of the fourteenth century. The landing of Columbus and the destruction of the Indians of the Caribbean were entirely expected, according to Fray Ramón Pané's *Account of the Customs of the Indians*. He wrote that a *cemí* (an idol representing one of the gods of the Taino pantheon) had predicted that the Indians "would see in their country a clothed people who were to rule over them, and slay them, and they would die of hunger. At first, they thought these would be the Caribs, but reflecting that the Caribs only plundered and fled, they believed that it must be another people. Wherefore, they now believe it was the Admiral [Columbus]."

The explanation for the Aztec response is more elaborate. Motecuhzoma II reigned over a deeply troubled nation. Surrounded by hostile tribes, many of whom paid debilitating tribute to Tenochtitlán, Motecuhzoma II—sybaritic, neurotic, dependent upon soothsayers, signs, and myths for information and advice, apparently in the thrall of the priests—was unable to deal

[9]The bones of a woman found at Tepexpán in Mexico may be several thousand years older.

rationally with the arrival of the Spaniards. The reports of strange men on the Gulf coast were preceded by a spate of disturbing omens, according to the histories, but the omens had little effect compared to what is now said to be the myth of Quetzalcóatl.

There are many versions of the myth, particularly of the loss of innocence of Quetzalcóatl, the good monk of Tula. One version has it that Quetzalcóatl, who is the culture-bearer in Aztec mythology, lived a life of innocence, without sin, when Tezcatlipoca, the evil god, tricked him into drinking an intoxicating liquid. While Quetzalcóatl was drunk, he committed the worst of sins, he slept with his sister. Upon awakening, he realized that he had been drunk and remembered what he had done. Unable to bear the thought of anyone seeing his face, which was now the ugly, puffy face of a sinner, a drunkard, one who had committed incest, Quetzalcóatl put on a jade mask and sneaked out of the city of Tula. He walked all the way to the sea, where he built a boat of paper and sailed out onto the water. When he was far from the shore, he set the boat afire, and from the flames the most beautiful bird arose, the sacred Quetzal.

The last part of the myth predicts the return of the good monk. It was said that one day he would come back from the place where the sun rose, and he would have yellow hair, even on his face; he would come riding on the back of a deer, and he would be wearing spurs.

When the man with yellow hair on his face came riding, not on the back of a deer, but on a larger beast, unlike anything ever seen in the Aztec Empire, it was noted that he even wore spurs, as in the legend, and he was greeted as if he were a god. The destruction of Tenochtitlán was assured, and the relative value of the cultures was established in the minds of the conquerors and the conquered.

Homologous legends may simply be a coincidence, or they may reflect the structures of the human mind, but I think it is more likely that they indicate how the Spaniards reached back in time to extend their conquest to the very history of the inhabitants of the hemisphere. The treatment of the Aztec goddess, Tonantzin (Our Mother or The Mother of Gods) is the best example of the process of revising a culture.

In 1531, Juan Diego, a newly converted Indian, went to Tepeyac where there had been a shrine to Tonantzin. In that very place he had a vision of the Virgin, but not exactly the Virgin the Spaniards knew. Juan Diego saw a Virgin with skin the color of his own, a brown-skinned Virgin. From that fortuitous miracle the Virgin of Guadalupe, the patron saint of Mexico, emerged and the identity of the Aztec goddess disappeared into the person of the new Mother of the Gods.

The archeological history of Mexico, as well as the testimonies written down by Sahagún and others, shows that the Aztecs and the Toltecs before them followed similar patterns of conquest: defeat the enemy in battle, destroy the surviving adult males, and breed with the women, creating a new race of mixed bloods who can be integrated into the conquering society through the acceptance of the gods of the victors.

The Spaniards were even more thorough than the Aztecs. They extended their conquest to every military, cultural, and economic institution. Languages disappeared, a system of mathematics based on ten was instituted, old methods of agriculture were replaced, the diet changed, people were required to wear European clothing, and all the gods that could not be assimilated were broken and buried.

Since the 1960s there has been a continuing exhumation of the gods who lived at the Indian beginning of Latino history. It is not an organized effort such as Vasconcelos made, and it lacks painters of the stature of Rivera or Siquieros. No codified politics belong to this attempt to locate a beginning. The writers of it take uncertain steps; most make poems with an Aztec image here and there, a name in Náhuatl, less frequently in Quiché, Cakchikel, or Mixtec.

I saw the origins of Latino history dreamed alive once in Watsonville, California, on a Sunday in the summer of 1989 before the earthquake destroyed so much of the town. First, came the drumming, ancient rhythms sounded in the streets of a cannery town, reverberating from the walls of the old Wells Fargo bank building, touching the windows of the shops and restaurants that looked east into the morning sun, their rooms already shaded, cooling at four o'clock in the afternoon. Then the flutes and whistles began, shrill sounds, more excited than musical, more ancient than the drums—Indian, like the men who leaned against the sides of the buildings or wrapped their arms around parking meters; brown men with toothpicks in their mouths, straw sheriff's hats pulled low over their eyes; Indians in cowboy clothes; cannery workers, migrants, men who bent their backs in strawberry fields and oceans of tomatoes; men who waited all week to spend Sunday in the shade.

After a while, the men who stood with their legs crossed, balancing on the heel of one boot and the toe of the other, accepted the invitation of the whistles and drums; they moved across Main Street to the *placita*. A crowd had gathered there on the very green grass in the shade of the trees. The drumming rose out of the crowd; it dominated the July afternoon in Watsonville. The whistles pierced the air, so many thin sounds, a competition of thin sounds, wind blown through the hollow bones of birds.

Above the bank building, in the light westerly breeze that came from the ocean, the U.S. flag spread and fell, a creature of the breeze; beside it, the California bear danced slowly on a white background. Cars passed in the street. A fire engine hurried by.

In the center of the *placita*, hidden from the street by the crowd, forty dancers leapt and twirled according to the directions of three great drums. The dancers wore feathers and breastplates, bracelets, breechclouts, rattles, and bells. They carried gourds, which they shook to the rhythms dictated by the drums. They stomped their feet and leapt into the air; the bells and rattles attached to their ankles sang in keeping with the drums.

The crowd had grown to more than a hundred and was dotted with children, infants, old women, a drunkard in a pink fedora, men wearing the tasseled straw hats of Michoacán, tattooed motorcyclists and their gaudy girls. Only a few people knew that the names of the dance troupes were Tonantzin and Xipe Totec. The sound of the names was familiar to them, but they could not connect Tonantzin with the Virgin of Guadalupe or Xipe Totec with the hope for a rich harvest. "Indian names," they said, "from ancient times."

At the end of each dance the onlookers applauded politely, but without enthusiasm. A woman admired the long feathers in the headdresses of the dancers; she said they were graceful. When the dancers came close to the crowd to rest between the dances, everyone could see that their breastplates and bracelets were identical, mass produced tin stampings painted in bright colors. One dancer wore eyeglasses; the bare feet of a young woman showed the callouses and corns of the shoes of Western civilization.

While the Aztec dancers rested, a new troupe entered the open space. They wore grass skirts and headdresses that looked like inverted pots. A short, very fat man, with many tattoos, led them into the circle. His dancers were of all ages, and their costumes were not so formal as those of the Aztecs; they had the look of poor relations or primitives. They danced around in a circle for a moment or two, then stopped while the fat man spoke to the crowd. He said he was from the Alona[10] tribe, which had lived around Watsonville before the white man came. He sang an Alona song. Then he shouted a speech about the theft of their souls by the whites.

Some people in the crowd knew the self-proclaimed medicine chief of the Alonas. He had been a Brown Beret[11] during the sixties, they said, but in recent years he had become more interested in his Native American ancestry. They listened impassively while he spoke of sacred things, spiritual things, of the power of Alona medicine, which the whites could not take away from them. He spoke for a long time, in English and Spanish. Then he announced a friendship dance. The medicine chief of the Alonas, brown,

---

[10]No one in the crowd understood the name ironically; there may well have been a tribe known as the Alonas, however, the major tribes in the area were the Costanoans, Salinans, Chumash, and further inland, the Yokuts.

[11]A group of radical Mexican-American youngsters patterned after the Black Panthers

tattooed, a fat man in a grass skirt with a pot on his head, beckoned to the crowd, to "all the *raza*," to join him. People came out of the crowd onto the grass; they were self-conscious, laughing nervously; they took the hands of those nearest them and danced.

In Mexico, the dances of anthropology are held almost every afternoon and evening at the site of the great pyramids of Teotihuacán as part of a light and sound show. In Mexico, the Indian origins of Latino history can be overwhelming; a Mexican-American who stands before the statue of Coatlicue in the Anthropological Museum finds his origins in a work of awesome power, embodied in a creature who exists between life and death, terrifying and grand, made of the heads of serpents and the claws of an enormous bird, dressed in skulls and living hearts, transcending worlds. She is the matriarch of the pantheon, the mother of movement, the progenitor of the sun. She is greater than Spanish queens or Roman popes; to be descended from her, merely to worship her, is to be a personage, somebody in the world.

Coatlicue and the other gods of Mexico appear everywhere in California: in San Francisco alleyways and under the freeways of Los Angeles. Farmworkers claim descent from the kings of Texcoco and Tenochtitlán. Poets scarcely compose a stanza without some reference to the Aztec past. Children have begun again to bear the names of the gods, as they did after the Mexican Revolution. Aztlán, the name given to the American Southwest during the sixties, provides the title for books and political movements. A young painter in Los Angeles has even made a map of Aztlán, with symbolic warriors drawn on the various states. The faces of the warriors are shown in profile, as in the ancient carvings, but their headdresses are the bandannas worn by *cholos*.[12] To give his map greater authenticity the painter has covered it with marks that look like glyphs, but careful examination reveals that they only resemble the glyphs drawn by Aztec writers; these marks are merely designs, utterly without meaning.

A textbook history of Mexico, written by an Anglo, identifies Aztlán as an island off the west coast of Mexico. A collection of writings edited by Rudolfo Anaya, a novelist and teacher from New Mexico, places the origin of Latinos somewhere in the neighborhood of Albuquerque. The reality of Aztlán has no importance for Anaya, just as it had no importance for the political activists of the sixties. But the idea of Aztlán stands in opposition to the concept of discovery; if the emergence of human beings from the earth at Aztlán is the seminal event in the development of the Western hemisphere, the arrival of Columbus remains important, but only as a moment on the time line of Latino history.

The problem of the mestizo is that the place of origin changes. He is

[12]Hoodlums, sometimes members of gangs

chicano one day, Hispanic the next, pushed by politics and economics to be what he needs to be in order to survive, to forget Spanish, study Yoruba, love the barrio, build a home in the hills, do something with his hair. Even the improbable miracle, the end of racism in the United States, will not solve the mestizo's problem; he is condemned by the complexity of his nature to an endless examination of his own blood.

3
THE SECOND CONQUEST

I thought how noble it would have been to see her free by her own efforts, and how sad, and crushing, and shameful it was to see her change from one master to another, without ever being her own.

Eugenio María de Hostos upon leaving Puerto Rico[1]

Puerto Rico is in America, according to the Nuyorican gang girls in *West Side Story*, who may be as good an authority as any on the political status of the island. It would have been helpful, though, if they had been a bit more precise. Puerto Rico is definitely in the Americas, but whether the island is spiritually, socially, culturally, and linguistically part of the United States of America is a far more difficult question.

Whatever its future status, Puerto Rico has belonged to somebody else for almost five hundred years. When the Spaniards left in 1898, it became a U.S. territory. It became slightly less owned and more incorporated in 1951 when its status was changed to a U.S. commonwealth. Since then, however, the question of the exact location of Puerto Rico has become an issue: There are 3.5 million Puerto Ricans on the island and 2.5 million on the mainland.

Part of the population would like the island of Puerto Rico to become independent, another part wants statehood, and a third group favors continued status as a commonwealth. In addition to tax considerations, transfer payments from the U.S. government, and the problem of whether the island could survive as an independent country after five hundred years of ownership, there is a serious question about who should decide the fate of whom. The U.S. Congress? Island residents? Puerto Ricans on the island and on the U.S. mainland, or perhaps people on the island plus those who live on the

---

[1]From his diary entry of September 13, 1898, quoted in *The Puerto Ricans* by Karl and Olga Jiménez Wagenheim.

mainland and come back now and then or who plan to come back or who own property on the island? What are the political rights in Puerto Rico of an old woman in Queens who whispers to her great-grandchildren that she wants to go home to die and to be buried in the welcoming earth of the shining star of the Caribbean?

For the old woman there are no issues but land and language; she looks back. It is more difficult for those who look ahead. To be Puerto Rican is to walk on uncertain ground, the object always of some grander politics, the student of an intractable history. If the arrival of Africans on the island, even though they first came as slaves, was a form of conquest, statehood for Puerto Rico may be the third conquest—or the fourth.

In 1512, a bishop arrived in Puerto Rico, assuring that the souls of the inhabitants, white and native, would be saved. He did not bring much help to the natives in this world, however. They continued to die or commit suicide at an astonishing rate. Less than a year after the arrival of the bishop, the first black slaves were brought in to augment the native labor force.

There followed, in slightly more than a quarter of a century, the great moral victory of Las Casas: the first of what were to be many proclamations emancipating the natives of the West Indies. It had the effect of increasing the number of slaves imported from Africa, since the surviving Indians could not be exploited in quite the same murderous fashion. Despite its labor problems and occasional raids by hostile Caribs, the colony continued to grow. San Juan was made the capital, and construction of La Fortaleza, now the governor's mansion, was begun in 1533.

San Juan took its first census in 1673; there were 1,791 inhabitants. The figure included whites, blacks, and free mulattos, but there is no mention of the indigenous population. Intermarriage between Spaniards and natives had been permitted from time to time, and the progeny may have been included as mulattos, but the best evidence is that most of the Indians had been worked to death, killed outright, had committed suicide, starved, or died of disease long before the census. Where the remaining Tainos went is uncertain. One need only look at the physical characteristics of present day Puerto Ricans to know that some survived, at least genetically. The language is gone, but artifacts remain, and there are vestiges of the culture in reality and in dreams. The Tainos are the romance of Puerto Rico, the legend that binds people to the land.

No other island in the Caribbean has even the slight shadow of Indian character that distinguishes Puerto Rico. The area mainly served as a meeting ground for Spain and Africa, a jumping off point for both races and cultures in the hemisphere. With few natural resources, no remaining native population, and relatively little arable land, the greatest value of the islands was strategic: Whoever controlled Cuba, Hispaniola, and Puerto Rico in the sixteenth century controlled the gateway to Mexico and Central and South America. The strategic value of the islands remained undiminished through the middle years of the twentieth century. After the Cuban Missile Crisis of October 1962, however, technology combined with world events to diminish their importance.

—

The first Latinos did not settle in the continental United States until 1598, when Juan de Oñate established a small colony at Santa Fe in what is now the state of New Mexico. As always, the soldiers and the priests went first, and the settlers followed. The priests understood the natives as gentiles or heathens, and since the priests were in control, much of the work of the colonies was devoted to the conversion of the native population. The Church, however, did not have a monolithic view of the natives: Theological arguments ranged from a view of Indians as the lost tribe of Israel to Sepúlveda's cockeyed version of evolution in which Indians were compared to monkeys. Still, the Indians found few allies in the Church or in the Spanish government, despite the pleadings of Bishop Las Casas in the sixteenth century.

Conflicts between the Old World and the New, the conservative and progressive elements in the Catholic Church and in the Spanish character were played out in the life of a Spanish priest in Taos during the loss of the New Mexico territory to the North Americans in the nineteenth century. Willa Cather made Father José Antonio Martínez the villain of *Death Comes for the Archbishop,* characterizing him as a hideously ugly man, tyrannical, possessed by lust, a betrayer of the Indians, and a rebel against the United States. But the research of playwright E. A. Mares and others provides a more likely history.

The Church did not slip comfortably into control of New Mexico. In 1680, the Pueblo Indians, who were somewhat less peaceful and unemotional than the people described in Ruth Benedict's classic work of comparative anthropology, *Patterns of Culture,* rebelled against the replacement of their traditional religion by the Spanish Church. They killed most of the priests and drove the rest of the Spaniards south. But the confederation of Pueblos that had come together in revolt could not hold together in victory. The old intertribal wars returned, leaving the Pueblos vulnerable to an effort by the crown to retake Santa Fe. By 1696 Spain was once again in control of New Mexico, but never again to sit quite so comfortably in the territory.

When José Antonio Martínez was born in Albuquerque in 1793, Spain controlled the territory, but not without the memory of the Pueblo Revolt. Relations between the Church and the Pueblos were not like those of separate states observing a peace treaty; the Indians maintained their distance from the Church, but they were eager to trade with the Spanish merchants.[2] José Antonio, the son of a merchant who traveled from Taos to the major cities of Mexico, grew up with a special view of relations between ethnic groups.

After his wife died in childbirth, leaving him with an infant daughter, José Antonio turned to the Church, entering a seminary in Durango in 1817. It was an extraordinary time in Mexico. The two great Indianist priests, Hidalgo and Morelos, had been defeated and executed by Spanish troops during the wars for independence, but the battle between their mestizo nation and the white colonialists had been joined, and it was not to end until Spain relinquished control of the country. A liberal tradition had been born in Mesoamerica, and the young novitiate from Taos found it to his taste.

Martínez was a political priest, a worldly man who made speeches, represented the interests of those he deemed his constituents, and served in both the Mexican assembly and the U.S. territorial assembly. In 1837, when the territory was part of the new Republic of Mexico, he made several speeches opposing new taxes. The people of the town of Chimayó, perhaps as a result of his speeches, revolted. They attacked Santa Fe, took the city, and executed the governor. In early spring of the following year, loyal Mexican troops marched north from Albuquerque, retook the town, killed some of the rebels, and sent the rest fleeing back to their farms and ranches.

The political priest went home to Taos to teach, but he again became caught up in events of the time. Following the opening of hostilities in the Mexican War, U.S. troops occupied the New Mexico territory and installed a military governor. The Mexicans in Taos, probably at the direction of their priest, refused to accept the new government. Once again, a crowd of angry farmers and cowboys marched on Santa Fe. Although the insurrection was brief, the U.S. governor, Charles Bent, was killed. Martínez was accused of fomenting the revolt and participating in the assassination of the governor, but there was no formal indictment, and the priest returned to his work.

In 1851, Jean-Baptiste Lamy, a conservative priest from France by way of Baltimore, Maryland, was appointed bishop of the Archdiocese of Santa Fe. Lamy was ambitious and openly racist; he said the Indians and Mexicans were poor, childlike creatures, given to gluttony, thievery, and wild sexuality. Either on their behalf or to further his own career, he demanded heavy tithes and taxes in support of his plans for an expanded role for the Church in public education. Martínez saw a different role for the Church, one which

[2]In the history of Mesoamerica merchants enjoyed a special situation; they were able to pass safely through hostile territories carrying goods and news and, using this immunity from harm, act as the diplomatic corps of the Indian empires.

included separation of church and state, and he let it be known through his writings and homilies. The conflict went on for several years, brown against white, liberal against conservative, the people against the power structure. Lamy finally excommunicated his liberal adversary, but Martínez refused to give up his vocation or his ministry, continuing to serve the poor, the Indians, and the mestizos of New Mexico until he died.

The life of the priest of Taos as metaphor would not be complete without Willa Cather's book. In 1927, when *Death Comes for the Archbishop* was published, Mexicans were presumed to be docile people, a supply of cheap unskilled labor, useful as domestics or to keep wages low in agriculture and industry. By transmuting the active defense of the political and economic rights of the Indians and mestizos into beastly acts against the established world, Cather punished the politics of resistance; it was a literary lesson in who was boss.

—

Latino history followed a similar course in Texas and California. The Spaniards conquered and converted the Indians, setting up missions, forts, and farms, and then lost the territory to independent Mexico, which, in turn, sold or ceded the land to the United States. However the Spaniards did it, by kindness or cruelty, their language and culture were firmly established in California when the gold rush brought waves of Anglo immigrants to the Pacific coast. The Californios, who resented the imposition of U.S. rule during the Mexican War, now suffered the economic, political, and cultural consequences of massive immigration. Racial conflicts that had been smoldering for years came to the surface. Anglo politicians, crooks, and fortune hunters tried to steal the wealth of the rich Californios, while merchants and entrepreneurs from the East made money from the working people as well as the rich and the forty-niners. The Californios tried to maintain their language in the schools, but the Anglo immigration overwhelmed them.

In an attempt to accommodate both cultures the town of Santa Barbara tried bilingual education in the public schools in 1855. Neither side liked the situation, which was resolved only when the Spanish-speaking families took their children out of the public school and sent them to a parochial school where they could study in Spanish. The victory of the Anglos was quick and cruel. In less than a quarter of a century California changed from Spanish to Anglo. The Mexicans lost their lands, their language, and their culture; bullfights were stopped, celebrations were interrupted, their income per capita went down, and their infant mortality rate went up—the people who had taken the Pacific coast from the Native Americans lost it to the Anglo-Americans.

The extent to which racism was employed in the cultural and economic conquest of California is exemplified by the Greaser Law, an anti-vagrancy statute passed in 1856, which actually referred to people "known as greasers."

From the passage of a Greaser Law to lynch mobs and shanty towns filled with imported laborers and their families was but a short step. Working-class Mexicans, now more properly known as Mexican-Americans, were virtually leaderless, unable to defend themselves. Even the grand old Californio families put up no resistance; as their lands and fortunes were taken away, the one-time aristocrats accepted the Anglos as friends and sons-in-law. All the granddaughters of General Mariano Vallejo, who had been arrested, mistreated, and imprisoned at Sutter's Fort by Americans under the command of John C. Frémont, married Anglos.

The Anglo domination was so ruthless and so thorough that any other response would have been futile. By 1859 there were 100,000 people in California of whom only 13,000 were Mexican. Ironically, it was through the use of the new democratic practices of the United States that the once dominant population group was excluded from having any voice in the government. Anglo legislators passed tax and land-use laws designed to wrest the huge ranches away from the rich Californios and to take the modest homesites of the poor. A class of men, known as desperados,[3] offered the only real opposition.

Juan Flores, Joaquín Murietta, Jacinto Treviño, and Tiburcio Vásquez, sometimes working alone, sometimes at the head of gangs of twenty or thirty men, made war or revolution or simply harrassed the rich Anglos and Californios. They were poor men, with little hope of success against either the ricos[4] or the Anglos, but to the Mexicans of California they became romantic figures, dark and elegant, men who wore masks and rode magnificent horses as they held up stagecoaches or boldly robbed the rich haciendas. When they were killed or captured, it was usually by Mexicans who sided with the rich and the Anglos. The folk history is filled with stories of betrayal, proof to those who wish it that the desperados could not have been caught without the help of spurned women or misguided Mejicanos.

Like the priest of Taos, these men reflected the Mexican political tradition begun by Hidalgo and Morelos—a tradition that would result, in 1917, in the world's first socialist constitution. And like Father Martínez, they were changed by Anglo fictions into something more acceptable: in this case, Zorro of Hollywood, the caped swordsman who defended the poor Mexicans against the rich, cruel, and unscrupulous Spanish/Mexican upper class, los

---

[3]From desesperado, without hope

[4]Literally, "the rich," but in this case the wealthy families holding land grants from the Spanish crown

ricos, not against the Anglo-Americans who brought democracy, justice, and egalitarian notions to the rigid class system of old Spain.

The Mejicanos knew better. They were shoved into slums, Californios and newcomers alike. They worked in factories,[5] in foundries, and on the railroad. When the Anglos took the cattle ranches, there was no place for the Mejicanos to work but in the fields or at the lowest paying jobs in the cities. The women washed clothes and cleaned houses. The conquerors of California now lived on the scraps the Anglos left. Murietta and Treviño and Vásquez were vital components of the last vestiges of self-esteem left to them by the Anglos; had the bandits not existed, it would have been necessary to invent them.

But the existence of a few daring resistors could not overcome the effects of a racist society. The Mexicans had been defeated in war, politically and economically disenfranchised, forced to turn on each other in service of the desires of the dominant population. Despite the Treaty of Guadalupe Hidalgo, which promised citizenship, freedom to choose their religion and their language, maintenance of their lands, and so on to the Mexicans who lived in territories ceded to the United States after the Mexican War, the Californios suffered the effects of conquest. For those whose ancestors had been conquered by the Europeans in the sixteenth century, there may perhaps have been too many gods in the eastern sky; to survive a second conquest was a serious test of the resilience of the human spirit.

The gold rush began in Texas in 1537 with Alvar Núñez Cabeza de Vaca's report to the king of Spain on his travels in the country north of Mexico. Although he brought back fascinating tales of the land and its inhabitants, it was neither geography nor anthropology that interested most of Cabeza de Vaca's countrymen. The information that caught their fancy was contained in a single paragraph in the published version of the report, which appeared in Spain in 1542. Cabeza de Vaca wrote (probably about the Pima Indians):

> The people gave us innumerable deerhide and cotton blankets, the latter better than those of New Spain, beads made of coral from the South Sea, fine turquoises from the north—in fact, everything they had, including a special gift to me of five emerald arrowheads such as they use in their singing and dancing. These looked quite valuable. I asked where they came from. They said from lofty mountains to the north, where there were towns of great population and great houses, and that the arrowheads had been purchased with feather bushes and parrot plumes.

[5]Alejandro Morales offers an excellent portrait of life in nineteenth-century California in his historical novel, *The Brick People.*

Although his name was Head of a Cow and he got so lost on his trip to Florida that he traveled six thousand miles through North America, losing 296 of the 300 men in his expedition along the way, hardly anyone doubted his tale of emerald cities. It didn't even matter that he had left the emerald arrowheads on the ship that took him home to Spain. Cabeza de Vaca had seen the proof: The Seven Cities of Cibola were not a dream; somewhere north of Mexico men lived in cities of gold.

Coronado and De Soto led expeditions in search of Cibola, but found only a vast country populated by strange people, shaggy, humpbacked beasts, and often inhospitable vegetation. No permanent settlement was established in Texas until the Pueblo uprising of 1680, led by the black Indian Popé,[6] drove the Spaniards south from Santa Fe to the long established missions of El Paso. There, in the strategic pass between the Rockies and the Sierra Madres, they started a town.

East Texas was settled in 1690, but only briefly. The Spaniards founded the settlements to keep the French from claiming the territory, but the hostility of the Indians proved to be worse than the threat of the French. By the end of the century, the Spaniards closed the missions and abandoned East Texas. In 1714, the appearance of a French explorer renewed Spanish interest in the Texas territory, and they established three permanent towns, including San Antonio.

For the next hundred years, Texas remained a quiet northern outpost of Spain in the New World. At the beginning of the nineteenth century, there were fewer than seven thousand Latinos in the territory. Then, in 1821, following the Mexican independence, Stephen F. Austin received a land grant in the Texas territory from the new government. It was as if the Mexicans had turned on a spigot that poured American settlers.

In fifteen years, the foreign population increased to thirty thousand, while the number of Mexicans remained stable at around seven thousand. Intimations of trouble in Texas were heard in Mexico City, but Texas was very far away, and there were other, more pressing problems: a quick succession of presidents, a new constitution, the organization of the country into states and territories, including the state of Coahuila y Texas, a Spanish invasion, a firing squad for former president Vicente Guerrero, the rise to power of General Antonio López de Santa Anna, and yet another constitution and another reorganization of the states, this time into military departments.

---

[6]The evidence is uncertain, but Popé probably had African as well as Native American and Spanish ancestors. He spread the story that the god Poheyemo had come to him in the kiva at Taos and told him he had chosen a tall black man as his earthly representative. Although their influence was not strong in New Mexico, there was a significant African or Afro-Spanish population in the colony by the middle of the seventeenth century.

Despite its problems at home, the Mexican government made some efforts to control the Anglos. The abolition of slavery in 1829 was aimed at Texas, the only place in Mexico where it was an important factor. President Guerrero's action irked the American colonists, but they found a way to circumvent the law by changing the status of slaves to lifetime indenture. Immigration was officially halted in 1830, but Americans kept coming in. Meanwhile, the U.S. government tried again and again to buy Texas from Mexico. The key to the independence movement in Texas, however, may have been Santa Anna's suspension of the Constitution of 1824 and with it the end of all state's rights.

On March 2, 1836, the Texans declared their independence, naming David Burnet president of the republic and Lorenzo de Zavala, a Mexican liberal and former minister to France, vice-president. It was merely a formality. General Santa Anna had formed an army in Mexico in December of 1835 and marched north. He crossed the river into Texas in February and arrived at San Antonio de Béxar at the beginning of March. The town fell quickly, except for a small garrison inside a sturdy old Franciscan mission.

—

There are many versions of the siege of that old mission. Of one thing, however, there can be no doubt: John Wayne fought and died there. And that is a problem Latinos have had to live with for over a hundred fifty years. The true history of the Alamo has no meaning; only John Wayne counts, for only John Wayne conforms to the dream of the founding of the United States. The theory of the nation cannot include alternatives to the courage of the defenders of the Alamo and the cowardice of the Mexicans. In any description of the battle of the Alamo, the odds must be stacked in favor of the Mexicans: The Americans must be outgunned as well as outnumbered, and the Mexican troops must be as disciplined and terrible as Hessians. All acts of courage must be committed in full knowledge of the consequences by a cadre of roughhewn Texas ethicists.

To walk through the Alamo today, passing the displays of curios and courage, stopping in a small room with a low ceiling and a few uncomfortable chairs to watch a slide show about the defense of the old mission, is to see the battle and the events leading up to it through Texas eyes wearing Disneyland spectacles. Every man who died at the Alamo died a hero, clear-eyed, blue-eyed, and handsome. Texans died there, fine men, farmers and cattlemen, settlers, civilizers. Americans. Protestants. Pioneers. In that vision of the men and the circumstances of their death, the Alamo is a shrine to anti-Mexican sentiment, the ultimate symbol of the triumph of the moral character of white over brown.

What really happened at the Alamo is more interesting, although not so useful as the nationalist allegory. Lorenzo de Zavala, representing Mexican liberals, had advised the Americans in Texas to secede from Mexico. Santa Anna's suspension of the Constitution of 1824 was as intolerable to the Mexicans as to the American settlers in Texas. In fact, the only Texans who died defending the Alamo were eight Mexican citizens who opposed Santa Anna's highhanded politics. Most of the others—the Anglos—were recent arrivals, many from New York and Philadelphia and other eastern cities, men who had been in Texas for only a few weeks or months when the battle started.

Santa Anna's army was not the well-equipped, superbly trained and disciplined invasion force pictured in films and textbooks used in Texas schools. The general raised an army through conscription. Some sources claim that many of his troops were Indians from the south of Mexico who couldn't speak Spanish, didn't understand military discipline or tactics, and didn't even know where they were going or for what purpose. Santa Anna may have been lucky to get them to San Antonio at all. It is a long hike from Mexico City to San Antonio, and even though most of the walk is downhill, there are some bumpy roads along the way. The four, five or six thousand Mexican troops who camped in front of the old mission had been in the field for three-and-a-half months when the siege began.

The Mexicans were two thousand miles from home, fighting in hostile territory, using old-fashioned, inaccurate weapons. They had half as many artillery pieces as the Texans, and they had to fight from the open field against an enemy protected by thick adobe and stone walls. Although the Mexicans outnumbered the defenders of the Alamo by twenty or thirty to one, Santa Anna and his troops must have known it was going to be a terrible battle.

Of the four to six thousand Mexican troops who attacked the Alamo, at least a thousand and perhaps as many as sixteen hundred were killed. Like most of the men inside the mission, they died bravely and were buried far from home.

What happened inside the Alamo is pure conjecture. Did William Barrett Travis really draw a line in the dirt with his sword and say that every man had a choice: Whoever wanted to fight should step over the line and join him, and the rest could go? How brave was Davy Crockett during the last hours of his life? Texas myth has it that he killed Mexicans with his bare hands even as he lay dying. Mexican myth says he was one of the few who surrendered and was executed.

As a schoolboy in West Texas I heard the story of the Alamo almost daily. It seemed to be there, hidden in the lyrics, every morning when we sang "Texas, Our Texas." There was an odor of gunpowder in the room, the glint of a bowie knife, an accent of Tennessee by way of Louisiana and Texas.

Somewhere across the river, near Cristo Rey or in the back streets behind the cathedral, the troops of Santa Anna waited, resplendent in their nineteenth-century finery, the cruel, invincible army, the crack troops of an entire nation poised to descend on the Alamo. In that daydream of history the Alamo was no larger than a single classroom in the Morehead School, while the massed troops of Santa Anna were an entire army on parade. They could have been Hessian mercenaries or British grenadiers at Bunker Hill or Valley Forge. They bore no relation to the poor people of Juárez or Agua Prieta; they did not look like the fathers and brothers of my classmates. In the dream song history it was the Mexican invaders who were powerful, cruel, the foreign oppressors.

In light of the battle of the Alamo, the poverty of the Mexicans and the good fortune of the white Texans was simple justice. The allegory permits the whites to oppress the brown-skinned people of Texas without the nagging unpleasantness of guilt. In San Antonio itself, the Alamo was the moral enabler of the Good Government League, an avaricious combine of powerful white interests, which forced the Mexican-Americans of the city to live with poor housing and education on the west and south sides of town, where for more than a century after Santa Anna took the old mission, the streets flooded and people drowned almost every spring.

In allegories there is no difference between history and deceit. Allegory is neither a motive nor an end; it is merely a means. For the sake of allegorical clarity most of the political issues surrounding the battle of the Alamo have been omitted from the popular history. They are complex and confusing, and it is far easier to cut through to the heart of the matter by uttering the battle cry of the republic: Remember the Alamo!

The Alamo is a special problem for the large number of Tejanos[7] who must somehow accommodate their Texas history to their Mexican ancestry. "We never crossed a border," these Tejanos are fond of saying, "the border crossed us." It is a witticism that describes a tragedy, the second conquest from which many Tejanos have not yet recovered. In the slums of San Antonio, spread-eagled on the floodlands west of the place where the river turns through the town, there has been no reward for being one of the first Tejanos. The descendants of those early residents are often among the poorest people in the state. After five or six generations many of them still don't speak English comfortably. They work at the lowest paying jobs; some still take to the road when times are tough in San Antonio.

All of the older people who worked as migrants remember buying food at the back doors of restaurants, traveling through towns looking for a Mexican

---

[7]Mexican-Americans in Texas, especially those whose families have been in the state for several generations, refer to themselves proudly as Tejanos.

restaurant where they could go inside and sit down. As children they thought it was fun, like a picnic, to climb out of the truck and sit by the side of the road while they ate. When they grew older and realized that no one would have them, that they ate in the open, using only their hands, and relieved themselves in the woods because there was no choice, because they were "spics" or "greasers" or "skins," they suffered. But it was a long time before the irony of their situation came to them. Not until the sixties, when the radicals put on brown berets and made threats that were empty of danger but instructive in self-esteem, did it occur to the descendants of those who had been crossed by the border that it was the children and grandchildren of foreigners who now rejected them in their own land.

The Mexican War of 1846 is often said to have produced the word "gringo" from the phrase "green grows" in a song the Americans sang as they rode to war. In addition to that useful epithet, the Mexicans gained a reputation for courage in battle. The U.S. troops under the command of Major General Winfield Scott were better trained and better armed. They had destroyed Vera Cruz, killing hundreds, perhaps a thousand civilians in a relentless bombardment. At Cerro Gordo, they had outflanked Santa Anna's troops and routed them. The people of Puebla turned the city over to Scott without a fight. He rested his troops there, then took them, fresh and fed, up to the capital.

Churubusco was the first surprise. The Mexicans refused to surrender their position outside the capital. The battle came down to hand to hand fighting before U.S. troops were finally able to overrun the Mexican positions. Still, the Mexicans would not surrender their capital. Scott waited. A little more than two weeks later, at Molino del Rey, Scott's cavalry charged the Mexicans, with the U.S. infantry following on, firing as they came. But the swift stroke did not succeed. The Mexicans held on. Molino del Rey became a slaughterhouse. Three thousand men died there, before the fighting moved on into the city, where the Mexicans set up their last line of defense at Chapultepec Castle.

Why they chose to continue the war, with nothing left to defend in all of Mexico but a castle on a hill in a captured city, is impossible to understand, but a thousand troops and the corps of cadets waited there for Winfield Scott's army. The battle began with an artillery barrage, then came the attack. The first U.S. troops to enter the castle used crowbars to tear the stones out of the walls at ground level. It was war in an ancient form, castle walls breached, men on ladders fighting hand to hand on the battlements. The last defenders left alive were the cadets, the brave boys who would not surrender, especially the one who, at the very end, after the battle was done and the war was lost, mounted the ramparts of the castle, wrapped himself in the

Mexican flag, and leapt to his death rather than give up to the gringos. The last defenders were an echo of an earlier battle for the city, when it was called Tenochtitlán. The character of these *niños héroes* was the only Mexican victory in the war.

On the U.S. side, character was the only battle lost. In the north of Mexico, Zachary Taylor was unable to maintain order among his volunteers. Two officers who fought under his command, Ulysses S. Grant and George Gordon Meade, wrote that the U.S. volunteers and the Texans were out of control, stealing, murdering "with no object other than their own amusement." To Grant and Meade they were cowards, uncivilized men.

The artillery bombardments were terrible everywhere: Hospitals and churches were destroyed; women and children died more often than soldiers. The destruction of captured territory had no military value, yet town after town was left ruined, blown apart and burned to the ground. Some of the U.S. troops, appalled by the treatment of priests and nuns and the desecration of churches, deserted, formed their own unit and fought alongside the Mexicans at Churubusco.

Such wars leave scars that cannot ever be overcome. Racism is compounded by history and the economics of land forever lost. Rage ebbs into nostalgia and regret. The bitter taste of 1848 affects all intercourse between Mexicans and Anglos, and it lives in every encounter between Mexicans and the U.S. descendants of Mexicans. *Agringado* is the ugly word Mexicans use for brown-skinned people whose Spanish lacks the grace and complexity of the mother tongue. After the Treaty of Guadalupe Hidalgo, their ancestral home was no longer a haven for Mexican-Americans; official Mexico welcomed them and their dollars, but shoe clerks, waiters, landlords, poets, and philosophers examined their pedigrees as well as their pocketbooks and told them to go back up north.

Although it seldom occupies a major place in U.S. histories or histories of Mexico published in the U.S., the importance of the treaty cannot be overemphasized: On February 2, 1848, for $15 million the Mexican government ceded California, Texas, Nevada, and Utah, and parts of Arizona, Colorado, Kansas, New Mexico, Oklahoma, and Wyoming to the United States. The Mexicans had not been able to settle or administer the territory, but it was theirs, and it comprised more than half the total area of their country. After the Treaty of Guadalupe Hidalgo there was no longer any possibility of Mexico becoming a world power or even a major force on the continent. It was a loss not only of land and power, but a devastating loss of face.

From that time forward, despite the defeat of the French by the Juaristas and the brave, bloody years of revolution and counterrevolution at the beginning of the twentieth century, Anglos would speak of Mexicans as docile, manageable workers, and Mexicans would speak of themselves as a people who were able to endure.[8] To correct those perceptions has been the first task of every Mexican-American social and political activist since the signing of the Treaty of Guadalupe Hidalgo.

———

Spain held on to its conquests in the Caribbean until the end of the nineteenth century. Only then, after the wars of independence had forced her to find a new relationship with Cuba, did Spain finally leave the hemisphere. The immediate cause was the sinking of a U.S. battleship in Havana harbor. The Hearst newspapers demanded war: Remember the *Maine!* When the Spanish government refused to make reparations for the *Maine*, claiming it had no part in the explosion that sank the ship, President McKinley had the excuse he needed in the Caribbean. The United States had harbored ambitions in the West Indies since Thomas Jefferson first described it as a likely part of his "empire for liberty."

At the end of the war, the United States granted freedom, with certain conditions specified in the Platt Amendment, to Cuba and declared Puerto Rico a U.S. territory. Although the Platt Amendment limited some aspects of sovereignty in Cuba, giving the U.S. naval bases on Cuban territory, disputing ownership of the Isle of Pines, and granting the United States the right to intervene to maintain "a government adequate for the protection of life, property, and individual liberty," Cuba had finally gotten out from under Spanish domination and achieved its independence. Puerto Rico had gained nothing; instead of a Spanish-speaking owner across the ocean, it now had an English-speaking owner next door. The island had been conquered again, this time by treaty.

Yet another distinction between Puerto Rico and Cuba occurred during the nineteenth century. Cuba produced one of the great romantic figures of the hemisphere: José Martí.[9] With a black general, Antonio Maceo, beside him, Martí fought a civil war not only for the independence of Cuba, but for the true emancipation of the African in the Americas. In his essay, "My Race," he argued that there were no races; men were alike in matters of the soul; their vices and virtues were the same in the African desert as in a Scottish cathedral. "With what justice can the white racist, who believes his race to be superior, complain of the Negro racist who considers his race

---

[8]*Aguantar* is the word in Spanish. The concept will be discussed at some length later, for it is central to the behavior of Mexican-Americans and Mejicanos.

[9]In 1890, José Martí founded a revolutionary movement in New York City. It included a school and a newspaper. He lectured to Cuban workers in New York and Florida, organizing them into a revolutionary cadre.

specially privileged?" he wrote, anticipating by a century the new problems of racism. "How can the Negro racist, who insists on the special character of his race, complain of the white racist?"

José Martí affected the politics of his country forever, but in a man such as he it is the moral influence that is, in the end, profound. With the man who wrote, "Keats gives birth to that painful struggle of the English poets who fight as if against an insurmountable force, to awake a love for impalpable beauty and the spiritual intangibles in a public that rejects everything that does not woo, flatter or lull its senses," for a national hero, Cuba developed a strong intellectual tradition. Alongside the famously aggressive, entrepreneurial character of the Cuban, there is a ruminative aspect; the man who does business all day may read philosophy at night. In Cuba politics takes on meaning beyond the practical—it has an otherworldly side, for Martí blurred the distinctions between politics and theology, and after the man on the white horse, no Cuban has been able to extricate the soul from the worldly associations of men.

The failure of Martí was that he was never able to promote General Maceo into the company of redeemers; Cuba remained a racist society, dominated like the rest of the Caribbean by colonialist political, social, and economic policies. Philosophy had not changed this world. Living conditions for blacks and mulattos, the laboring class of Cuba and the rest of the Caribbean, did not improve. In matters of health and nutrition they may actually have grown worse. Eric Williams, in his history of the Caribbean, listed some of the conditions endured by agricultural workers in Cuba and Puerto Rico during the 1920s and 1930s:

- In a small Puerto Rican town the daily expenditure on food for a family of six was twenty-three cents.
- Pay for a Puerto Rican rural laborer was twelve cents a day, while the cost of food for one adult male was thirty-eight dollars a year.
- On average 30,253 cases of malaria were reported each year between 1932 and 1936 in Puerto Rico. However, tuberculosis was the principal cause of death on the island during that period.
- In 1934 nearly half of all the doctors in Cuba lived in Havana.
- Puerto Rico bought 10 percent of all the food exported from the United States during that period, more than any foreign country except Britain and Canada.
- Of the people in Cuba 46 percent were illiterate in 1917. The illiteracy rate in Puerto Rico was 35 percent in 1935.
- In 1933 over half of the children of school age were not attending school in Cuba. Nearly 67 percent of those enrolled in elementary school were in the first two grades.

• There was not a single high school in any of the forty-five rural municipalities (containing 40 percent of the population) of Puerto Rico in 1931.

The economic lives of the poor of Cuba and Puerto Rico were setting the stage for two enormous migrations that would take place in the 1950s, the Puerto Rican exodus to New York City that began the decade and the Cuban exile in Miami and New Jersey at its close.

In Mexico, colonialism took a different form. Although the country had been politically sovereign since the defeat of the French and the restoration of the republic in 1867, it was an economic colony of foreign investment, mainly from the north. At the beginning of the twentieth century, the Mexican dictator Porfirio Díaz said of his country, "Poor Mexico, so far from God and so close to the United States." Díaz could not be blamed for the geography, but the economic and political situation that grew up under his reign, known as the Porfiriato, put the Mexican rural poor in an intolerable situation. As in the Mexican proverb, the rich left the poor like dishes at an inn, face down and scraped clean. They appropriated what little land was left to the farmers, paid starvation wages to their workers, and enjoyed the protections of a brutal police state. During the Porfiriato, unions were destroyed, and union organizers were either imprisoned or forced into exile. Mexican political organizers and intellectuals fled to the United States. The Revolution of 1910 was fomented and planned in San Antonio, St. Louis, El Paso, and Los Angeles, as well as in Monterrey, Mexico, D.F., and Anenecuilco.[10]

Large numbers of Mexicans did not begin coming to the United States until the serious depression in the Mexican economy of 1906. The rate increased with the start of the Revolution of 1910. Over the next ten years more than a quarter of a million people crossed the northern border into Texas. Others went to Arizona, New Mexico, and California. Most of the emigrants were poor, but at least 10 percent of the people who moved to Texas were members of the Mexican elite, people who had somehow managed to get their fortunes out of the country before the revolution or who had enough political influence to get out with at least part of their wealth during the war. The refugees went everywhere in the southwest: A colony of wealthy Mexicans was started in San Antonio, while the poor settled into the slums on the city's west side; the Porfiristas of El Paso welcomed their wealthy political allies from the interior, at the same time that hundreds of poor Mexicans moved into shacks along the river.

---

[10]Among others, the Flores Magón brothers, whose writings had a deep effect on the Mexican revolutionary movement, were chased from city to city and finally imprisoned in the United States. Ricardo died in a federal prison.

For rich Mexicans life outside their country was ordinary business; many had been educated at Harvard or the Sorbonne or the École Militaire. For the poor the problems were impossible to overcome; they had no skills, little or no education, and they could not speak English; they were forced to work for the lowest wages in the worst jobs. Nevertheless, it was better than life in Mexico during a civil war in which the population of the country was decimated.[11] Between 1880 and 1929 over a million people crossed the border from Mexico into the United States.

With few exceptions, the pattern of emigration from Latin America would be repeated throughout the century: At first, only a small number of poor people are driven to emigrate; the economic situation worsens, and there is a revolution; the left leads the revolution; the rich and well-educated elite flee the leftists; as the revolution goes on, the middle class and the poor follow the rich vanguard out of the devastated country. Education proves to be the most portable wealth, even more valuable than capital; the intellectually rich and the barely literate poor have entirely different experiences in the United States.

The history and geography of the hemisphere place Latinos in a unique situation; they are both sojourners and citizens, more resistant to the melting pot than any major immigrant group in the history of the nation. The question that will be raised again and again is whether a democratic society, which promised the right to social mobility as one of the chief tenets of its founding, can accommodate the whole spectrum of Latino immigrants. In the course of seeking that accommodation the limits of the American experiment will be tested, for the right to cultural diversity is only implied in the Constitution, and, as Martí and Tocqueville noted about English-speaking democracies, the tendency of the nation is to crush diversity in all its forms.

[11]The population of Mexico was about 15 million at the beginning of the revolution. Between 1 million and 1.5 million of those were criollos (those who were or who claimed to be of pure European stock) and the rest were mestizos and indigenous peoples. At the end of the decade, the population was estimated at 14 million. Considering the rate of population growth, and even accounting for emigration, losses during the war were somewhere between 1 and 2 million.

4

CHRISTOPHER COLUMBUS
AT THE TACO BELL

Two Tibetans were standing at the corner of 48th Street and Madison speaking in their native language when a New Yorker passed by and chanced to overhear them. "For Chrissake," he said, "you guys're in New York now: speak Spanish."

A joke told in New York City in 1990

In my childhood I lived in the cultural future of the United States. There were no gringos in southern Arizona or West Texas then. Although many people had blond hair and blue eyes and spoke English without a trace of the soft vowels and musical endings of sentences born on the border, there were no gringos. Not the kosher butcher, nor the car dealer's daughter, who was elected queen of the Sun Carnival, nor even Sheriff Chris P. Fox, the leading racist in town, was truly a gringo.

That pure Protestant Anglo-Saxon sense of self, the attitude of the civilized stranger in a world of foreign savages—adopted by Germans, Poles, Italians, Austrians, Russians, Turks, and the French when thinking of Mexico or things Mexican—simply did not exist in the Southwest then. These Europeans, including Anglo-Saxons, failed to satisfy many of the criteria of the true gringo.

A gringo is one who cannot bear the dust of the desert or the cactus's thorny will to survive. A gringo cannot soften a vowel or countenance a jalapeño in his stew. A gringo is always in the process of getting diarrhea, having diarrhea, or recovering from diahrrea. Gringos drink directly from the bottle and eat tostadas with a fork. They address waiters as "Sir" and grandmothers as "Miss." The male of the species is always in search of a whorehouse, while the female looks for a live-in maid. Both are sunburnt.

Half a century ago, everyone in El Paso ate chiles and crossed the border every week, if not every day. The best place for lunch was the Café Central, which provided a meeting place for retailers and bankers from both sides of the border. The Central, in Ciudad Juárez just over the international bridge, had been a famous place for lunch since Pancho Villa and Pascual Orozco dined there together after taking the city in the first major victory of the Revolution of 1910. No one ever called it the Central Café; they always said "Central," with a Spanish *a* and the accent on the last syllable.

The town had two cultural lives. The bullfights at the Plaza Alberto Balderas in Juárez were advertised in the El Paso *Herald-Post* and *Times*. Children in elementary school went to the music room to learn "Git Along Li'l Dogie" and came out singing "La Golondrina" and "Cielito Lindo" as well. The first time boys and girls held hands and danced together there was a small sombrero on the floor between them. In the plaza in the center of town where all the buses stopped, an old man sat on a bench all afternoon with a gutstring harp between his knees and played Mexican folk songs. After dark a man played "Chiapas"[1] on the ocarina.

Rich Anglo children learned Spanish from the women who raised them; the poor ones studied border slang (Caló) in the schoolyard. Most Anglos spoke Spanish badly, generally in the present tense, certainly without the subjunctive, but they knew enough to sell a shirt or buy a roast, shorten a dress, admire a child, or inquire after the health of a grandmother.

To be a gringo was inefficient. Prejudice and exploitation took place in Spanish; anybody can be a racist, but the subtleties of de facto segregation require a talent for communication. To keep the Mexican-American poor on the south side of town, crammed into adobe tenements, three, five, seven people to a room, sometimes with only one toilet for the entire tenement was straightforward stuff; low pay and poor education were usually sufficient. The more difficult task was to explain to a person with a middle-class salary that he and his family would not be comfortable in a middle-class house in a middle-class neighborhood.

To maintain a system of exploitation without state sanction—Jim Crow laws existed in Texas but both Anglos and Mexican-Americans considered people of Mexican descent members of the white race—required the ethnic majority to develop many of the characteristics of the overseer. It is the overseer who must be both anthropologist and psychologist, who must understand the slaves or indentured workers well enough to get maximum effort from them without pushing them to the point of rebellion. Some Anglos, including political bosses, were able to hire Latinos as overseers, but most were forced to act as overseers themselves.

In employment, the problem for the overseer was how to manipulate the Mexican-American worker's attachment to his family and, at the same time, to play his feelings of pride and stoicism, the conflicting aspects of his sense

[1]A folk song from the state of Chiapas in southern Mexico

of dignity, off against each other. The intent was to paralyze him emotionally so that he could be shoved from place to place to break a strike or keep wages low.

The sophistication of the system, when judged from the distance of time, was extraordinary. Mexicans and people of Mexican descent are recognized now as prepared by their culture to work very hard; they are frequently likened to the Koreans in this respect. According to Orange County supervisor Gaddi Vasquez, executives of a large corporation asked whether they could count on a labor force of semi-skilled Mexican workers before they would commit to building a manufacturing facility in the county. During the first ninety years of this century, however, the Mexicans were almost always described as lazy, more interested in their siestas than their jobs. The ploy worked perfectly; it downgraded the value of Mexican labor, giving their bosses an excuse to pay low wages, and it spurred the Latinos on to work harder to overcome the stereotype.

The Mexican sense of *familia* was widely known to Anglo as well as Mexican-American bosses who used the desire to provide for one's family as a means of disciplining employees. It was not the fear of personal poverty or even hunger that drove the Mexican and Mexican-American workers; it was the thought that their children might be hurt. As a result, the Latino worker with a family suffered from an overabundance of machismo in his personal life and was easily manageable on the job; he gained a reputation for docility.

Retailers, who are anthropologists by instinct and accountants by preference, used the same kind of knowledge, selling toys and expensive children's clothing on credit. Bridal shops sold dresses far too expensive for the people who bought them. Chain stores altered their mix of merchandise for the border, learning from their local managers that business with Latinos was skewed toward the children.

The economic position of the Latino was impossible; he had no choice but to develop debilitating work habits to meet the demands of his situation: The Latino husband worked all day at one job, all evening at another, and nights and weekends at yet another. So many Mexicans and other Latinos who came to the United States during the twentieth century worked at two or more jobs that psychologists now recognize the inability of the male head of the family to spend a significant amount of time at home as the root cause of the breakdown of the Latino family.

The irony of the situation is that the cultural victories of Latinos in the Southwest made them more vulnerable to exploitation. The more the Anglos knew them and were like them, the easier it was for Anglos to adopt the methods of the wise, cruel overseer. With no capital and no secrets, Mejicanos were easy pickings.

But all the while, Mejicanos and the other Latinos in New York, Florida,

California, and Illinois, were changing the nation in which they lived; by the seductive charm of their culture and by sheer numbers, they created the foundations of a new American ethnicity. While others leapt gladly into the melting pot, the Latinos refused. Instead of transforming themselves into poor imitations of Anglo-Saxons, they engaged in a kind of cultural commerce, bartering words for food, attitudes for music, history for history, art for art.

A snapshot of America taken now, in the last decade of the twentieth century, would reveal strong Latino influences in language, cuisine, music, and entertainment. These are not signs of conquest, however; history is not a matter of repetitions, and cultural vengeance is an absurd notion. Civilization need not be a zero sum game; the victories of Latino culture are victories of pluralism, additions. Nothing is taken in return for this enrichment; it is, by definition, a gift.

I.

The Latino influence on American English began around the ninth century, perhaps earlier, when the Arawakans on the mainland of South America developed a method for making small but seaworthy boats capable of carrying them from the mainland to the islands of the Caribbean. The name they gave these little log boats was passed from the original Arawakans to the Tainos to the Spanish and then into the English language: canoe.

English is notorious among languages for borrowing, but the borrowing slowed greatly when the English speakers came to North America. The language continued to change, of course, gaining new words from technology, social situations, errors that were incorporated, and so on. But it gained surprisingly little from European immigrants as the westward migration of humanity delivered its last great wave to America in the early part of the twentieth century. North American English gained very little from Russian, Polish, Czech, any of the Slavic languages. With the exception of words connected with food, Italian had most of its influence on the language long before the southern Europeans migrated to the United States; it was a gift from ancient Rome rather than Little Italy. French and German and Greek, which have had such a pronounced influence on the English language, also had their influence early. By the turn of the century, the new direction of linguistic influences was firmly established: American English was generating its own new words, giving far more than it was getting.

It was, after all, the American Century. But the American century had begun long before 1900. America was the world of the new. The cotton gin, the steam engine, the airplane, mass production all came from America. So did new elements of languages. Immigrants in the United States had no interest in bringing their Old World words with them; they had left them on the other side of the ocean. Only the Latinos deviated from the pattern. Like the old Tejanos of San Antonio, many of them felt they had not crossed the border, the border had crossed them. More important, however, for making additions to the language, they knew what they were talking about. Having gotten here first, the Latinos—Indians, Africans, Spaniards—were obliged to name the things they found and the way they lived. English-speaking Americans adopted and continue to adopt the way of life and the words that go with it, as in these familiar examples:

adios The *Random House Dictionary* includes this deist farewell, but the *Oxford English Dictionary,* which has an article on *adieu,* does not.

adobe *Santamaria's Diccionario de Mejicanismos* says that adobe was a building material used in what was a part of Mexico "in ancient times," but is now North America.

amigo *Random House* has an article on amigo and the *OED* doesn't. In many instances, however, the situation will be reversed, the *Random House* being a small, sporty mess in comparison with the *OED*. The absence of a precise pattern suggests that the criteria for inclusion of words given to English by Latinos have not yet been clearly established.

bronco There were no wild horses in England.

burro Donkeys are British.

cantina The *OED* quotes Hemingway among others.

casa At home in the Southwest

chile or **chilli** Originally a Náhuatl word, like *tamal*

cigar Cigars are called *puros* in Spanish, but the word cigar and its diminutive are Spanish imports.

coca and **cola** The two words now most closely associated with U.S. cultural imperialism are both of Latino origin. Coca was taken by the Spanish from *cuca,* a word used by the natives of Bolivia and Peru. Cola came to the Indies from West Africa; the cola nut was thought to have some of the narcotic properties of the cuca leaf.

contra A new import from Nicaragua

coyote *Coyotl* to the Náhuas

gringo The origin is unclear. It probably comes from "green grows." Supposedly, U.S. troops sang a song containing those words during the Mexican War. *Gringo* also means gibberish in Spanish, but I do not know whether that meaning preceded the singing soldiers of General Zachary Taylor, because Spanish dictionaries are not based on historical principles.

guerrilla Modern warfare is apparently a Latino invention.

hacienda Home, the way we'd like it to be

hombre Usually with bad or tough

hurricane From the Tainos, who must have been surprised by their first

junta Now generally made up of bad hombres

lariat and **lasso** Synonyms, one derived from two Spanish words, *la reata*, and the other borrowed as is

loco The word joined the English language as a description of the weed that made horses and cattle behave crazily.

macho From the Náhuatl word meaning "to be known," which casts an interesting light on the concept

maize A Cuban contribution, originally Arawakan

marijuana A story of the Mexican Revolution of 1910: Maria Juana is said to be the complete name of the Juana, the generic name for a camp follower. Marijuana was widely used by Constitutionalist forces during the fighting. It has an honored place in one of the best known battle songs:

> La cucaracha, la cucaracha
> ya no quiere caminar;
> porque le falta, porque no tiene
> marijuana que fumar.

mesquite Náhua botany

mosquito The miserable little fly of "the New World"

padre A sixteenth century addition

peon Colonialism needed such a word.

pinto Horses and beans

plaza In the New World the Spaniards made the Indian market into a place for hangings and the auto-da-fé. Virtually every town in the southwest was built around a plaza intended for gentler uses.

poncho An Arawakan cloak

ranch A *rancho* north of the border

rio A word that lost its accent in English

rodeo Pronounced as a Spanish word on the eastern seaboard and as a Drive in Beverly Hills, and with a cowboy *ee* in the rest of the country

savvy The word came to English from two directions: the U.S. southwest and black English; slaves are said to have used a word like savvy, which was brought to the United States from the Caribbean, where it derived from either the Spanish or the French verb "to know."

sombrero A hat that gives a lot of shade

tomato An Aztec vegetable

tonto Racist wit: The name of the widely known Native American character on radio, on television, and in the movies is the Spanish word for stupid.

vista A nice view or prospect, which could also be from the Italian

Yanqui Borrowed from English and returned tarnished

As the Spaniards explored and settled the Southwest and Florida, they did future generations the favor of naming rivers, mountains, and deserts, flora and fauna, and every place in which they built a mission or a town. In some parts of the country, particularly along the border between the United States and Mexico, the names are pronounced with a full or partial Spanish accent. In California, the Spanish accent has disappeared almost entirely, which sometimes causes confusion.

The pronunciation is better in New Mexico, which runs from the Llano Estacado (Staked Plain) in the southeast corner to the Mancos (Oarless Boats) River at the northwest corner. Texas has Carthage, Paris, and Palestine, but it also has Sabinal, San Angelo, San Antonio, San Augustine, San Benito, San Diego, San Juan, San Marcos, San Saba, Santa Anna, Santa Rosa, and Sarita. Florida runs from the Perdido (Lost) River in the northwest to the Keys, with Key Vaca (Cow) being about as far east and south as one can get without leaving the United States. Going north from the Mexican border in California, one passes from San Diego to Santa Ana, Los Angeles, Santa Barbara, San Luis Obispo, Monterey, Santa Cruz, San Jose, San Francisco, Marin County, and up to where the state ends in Del Norte County. If one were to travel up the central San Joaquin Valley from Los Angeles to the state capitol at Sacramento, three of the biggest cities would be Fresno, Modesto, and Merced. *Sierra, canyon, arroyo,* and *montana,* are all Spanish words. *Nevada* is a Spanish word meaning "snowy"; hence, the Snowy Mountains or Sierra Nevada.

The point of all of this, of course, is that Latinos made their mark on American English a long time ago. The nation is, at least linguistically, on its way to becoming bicultural. Those who urge that the United States adopt an English-only policy are the Quixotes of racism, pursuing in comic fashion a notion of a past that never existed. It is simply too late for the United States to ban the Spanish language. What would we call the Grand *Canyon?* Or the *Sierra Nevada?* Arizona, Colorado, California, Florida, Nevada, Montana, and New Mexico would have to change their names immediately. If an English-only law were adopted and enforced, the names of so many cities, towns, rivers, roads, mountains, canyons, gullies, washes, creeks, parks, schools, colleges, streets, avenues, boulevards, alleys, highways, airports, lakes, inlets, keys, and bays would have to be changed that the United States would seem to most of us like a foreign country—with no tomatoes.

2.

The chef at Drexel, Burnham was an American and the assistant
chef was a Mexican. They served guacamole almost every day in the
dining room. And a couple of times a week they had this pie with
layers of meat and dough, like a tamale pie. Then one time I made
Puerto Rican rice and beans and put it out on the buffet, and they
made me come and take it away.   Yvonne Ortiz

If cooking had to do with hunger, we would make our meals to fit our sizes and our lives, and go on to other business. But in a rich country eating is more personal than the mere satisfaction of hunger; the belly is among the least important of its beneficiaries. Dinner for the rich, a class that begins for culinary purposes with those who can choose between rice and wheat, is a way of dealing with one's appetite for symbols. It is especially so in a place like the United States where the national cuisine has less to do with what is cooked than how one cooks it: thaw, add hot water, or microwave are the three basic kinds of North American cooking.

When the process is more important than the palate, the foods that are the easiest to prepare and eat become the most popular. Neither the hot dog nor the hamburger is likely to be displaced, but the potato chip, once the nation's favorite snack food, is in real danger of losing out to a foreign invader: the toasted triangle of tortilla dough known as the Frito, Tostito, taco chip, corn chip, and so on. The taco chip, if that is the generic name, apparently can accept more interesting seasonings than the potato chip, holds up as well on the shelf, and can be produced using various oils, thus raising or lowering the amount and kind of fat in each portion. And corn is cheap.

But more than cost and convenience count in the choice of foods. Chips can be made of almost any grain and even some starchy fruits, like plantains. The popularity of Mexican food or some approximation of Mexican food in the United States may have more to do with the special relationship of Latinos to North Americans than with the food itself. There are, after all, finger foods, stews, and snacks available in every cuisine.

It might be argued that Mexican food is actually the true American food, in the sense that it is a pre-Columbian cuisine. Even the names of most of the dishes are of Náhuatl origin. Unfortunately, the variety of the cuisine has disappeared in the United States and most of Mexico. Virtually all tamales, for example, are made of ground beef or chicken now, but there were many other varieties, and they were made in many different shapes at the time of the conquest, as Bernardino de Sahagún's Aztec informants told him:

The tortilla seller, the food seller [is] an owner of tortillas or a retailer. He sells meat tamales, turkey pasties, plain tamales, barbecued tamales, those cooked in an olla—they burn within; grains of maize with chili, tamales with chili, burning within; fish tamales, fish with grains of maize, frog tamales, frog with grains of maize, axolotl with grains of maize, axolotl tamales, tadpoles with grains of maize, mushrooms with grains of maize, tuna cactus with grains of maize, rabbit tamales, rabbit with grains of maize, gopher tamales: tasty—tasty, very tasty, very well made, always tasty, savory, of pleasing odor, of very pleasing odor; made with a pleasing odor, very savory. Where [it is] tasty, [it has] chili, salt, tomatoes, gourd seeds: shredded, crumbled, juiced.

He sells tamales of maize softened in woodashes, the water of tamales, tamales of maize softened in lime—narrow tamales, fruit tamales, cooked bean tamales; cooked beans with grains of maize, cracked beans with grains of maize; broken, cracked grains of maize. [He sells] salted wide tamales, pointed tamales, white tamales, fast foods, roll-shaped tamales, tamales with beans forming a seashell on top [with] grains of maize thrown in; crumbled, pounded tamales; spotted tamales, pointed tamales, white fruit tamales, red fruit tamales, turkey egg tamales; turkey eggs with grains of maize; tamales of tender maize, tamales of green maize, adobe-shaped tamales, braised ones; unleavened tamales, honey tamales, beeswax tamales, tamales with grains of maize, gourd tamales, crumbled tamales, maize flower tamales.[2]

Sahagún also describes the bad tamales that are offered in the marketplace—filthy, gummy, sticky, old, and cold—before he goes on to tortillas, sauces, and the wheaten bread made from "Castilian flour."

Elsewhere he notes that tamales were also made of worms and insects. The Aztecs, lacking herd animals and living in a densely populated city, had a problem with finding sufficient proteins. Fowl, reptiles, insects, and various mixtures of grains and legumes, which are known to produce amino acids, supplied most of their needs. Some anthropologists argue that they practiced ritual cannibalism to supplement the other proteins in their diet. If so, they didn't make their victims into tamales, at least according to Sahagún's Aztec informants.

The number and location of Mexican restaurants in the United States is astonishing. Los Angeles has the most, Boston the fewest. Francisco García-Rodríguez, an attorney for the Mexican American Legal Defense and Education Fund, said that when he was an undergraduate at Harvard he and a few other chicano students found a good Mexican restaurant in New Hampshire.

[2]*The Florentine Codex,* Book X, Chapter 19.

They couldn't imagine why a man would start a Mexican restaurant in New Hampshire, unless he was an undocumented Mexican national who thought he would be safe up there.

Mexican restaurants originally followed the railroad lines north and then east across the United States. Gringos liked the food once they tasted it, and the restaurant owners had a captive customer group in any Mexican or Mexican-American workers or travelers who passed by, for most other restaurants in the Southwest and Midwest refused to serve them.

Meanwhile, the cuisine degenerated into a stew of sauteed beef, pinto beans, tomato sauce, and red chili powder, heavily influenced by southern cooking and the fast-food style of the open range. The tortilla was replaced by the soda cracker in chili parlors, and the tamale sellers who wandered the streets of poor neighborhoods wrapped their food in paper instead of corn husks. Mexican food in its Texas disguise became the quintessential American food, rough and ready, associated with the open range and the wild west, manly; in fact, real Americans use salsa—more often than catsup. There was, after all, no other uniquely American cuisine. Southern cooking was different, but not a complete cuisine, and as it moved west and south toward New Orleans it became mixed with French and Spanish styles.

Like every cuisine, Mexican food moved up the economic ladder—from the slums, pool halls, and railroad workers' canteens to Main Street—but unlike most other styles of cooking it didn't become expensive. The conception of the Mexican in the Anglo mind is such that diners won't tolerate a high-priced Mexican restaurant. Even in New York City, where the prices in midtown restaurants are larcenous, Mexican food remains comparatively inexpensive. For an Anglo to eat Mexican food then is to profess loyalty to America and at the same time to reinforce class distinctions. If the customer has any doubt about the class question, it can be resolved in the California style by mispronouncing the names of the foods and addressing the waiter as "señor."

Were Mexican food to return to its pre-Columbian variety and subtlety, it would not only cease to be a ruggedly American food, its class status would change. Anglos who partook of Aztec haute cuisine would have to look up to it, as they do to French or Mandarin Chinese cooking. They would be discomfited by every mouthful, not because of the texture or flavor, but because food is a soup of symbols, and for the Anglo Mexican food is still a symbol of the adventure of conquest. In a Mexican restaurant or even when eating a Mexican prepared-food from a grocery store, every Anglo is a colonialist exercising his power.

The rules of these symbols are so rigid that in Zarela, a Mexican restaurant in midtown Manhattan, the waiters are not Mexican but East Indian. Mexicans were apparently in short supply when the owner, a Mexican woman, staffed the restaurant, but she understands her business well enough to know that she must hire dark-skinned people to maintain the symbolic comfort of her customers. The prices are higher at Zarela than at most Mexican restaurants, but it survives because it is still only a medium-priced restaurant and its decor is tacky. Elegant Mexican restaurants don't do as well; two have opened in the United States, one in the Time-Life Building in Rockefeller Center and the other in Ghirardelli Square in San Francisco; both have long since gone out of business.

——

Puerto Ricans can't sell their food to Anglos at any price. There are no Puerto Rican restaurants in midtown Manhattan and only a few counter places on the southern and northern fringes of the island, Tasa de Oro on 14th Street and Del Pueblo on 116th Street and Third Avenue. In fact, there are very few Puerto Rican restaurants anywhere on the U.S. mainland. Most places that serve Puerto Rican dishes prefer to call themselves Spanish or to say that they serve *cuchifritos* (fried pork entrails) or *comidas criollas*.[3]

There are a lot of bodegas in Puerto Rican neighborhoods, but as in most places where people are poor, restaurants don't do well: Eating out is a middle-class pleasure and an upper middle-class addiction; the poor, even the foolish poor, usually eat at home. However, the lack of interest in Puerto Rican food has less to do with economics than with symbols.

Puerto Rico has no connection with dreams. U.S. colonialist actions in Puerto Rico have taken place offstage, knowledge of the island is limited, and familiarity with Puerto Rican culture is confined to revivals of *West Side Story*. Anglos who visit Puerto Rico understand it as another vacation spot in the Caribbean, a place to gamble or enjoy the sun in winter. It is not American (U.S.) in their minds, but it isn't foreign either. The island of Puerto Rico has no symbolic value at all. Puerto Ricans on the mainland are simply the unwelcome poor.

To eat in a Puerto Rican restaurant does not recall the open range, the Alamo, Pancho Villa, or the triumph of manifest destiny; it is dinner with the doorman, a janitor's repast, the flavor of failure. In New York City, which has the largest concentration of Puerto Ricans on the mainland, only two statistics have any importance: cash and crime. Puerto Rican food symbolizes little of one and an overabundance of the other.

Even on Manhattan's Loisaida, a name that mixes the old Lower East Side and Loíza, a town in Puerto Rico named for a Taino princess, there are several Mexican restaurants, but not one that offers Puerto Rican food.

Symbols may be only part of the problem. It could also be argued that Caribbean food has failed to become popular because it lacks the alternatives

---

[3]Used to indicate Latin American or Caribbean food; home cooking

to hot dogs and hamburgers provided by tacos and tamales. *Cuchifritos* joints sell food that can be eaten like a hot dog, but not with great success. Most Puerto Rican dishes require crockery and eating utensils; the fritters, which are the closest thing to finger food, need a napkin or two or three.

Curiously, the few real restaurants that serve Puerto Rican dishes are owned by Cubans or Dominicans. In these places Puerto Rican food is served along with traditional Spanish, Cuban, and Dominican dishes, raising the question of whether a sufficiently distinct Puerto Rican cuisine exists.

At the most basic level all Caribbean food is similar: suckling pig, plantains, sweet potatoes, yuca (manioc), rice, and various kinds of beans. Dominicans say that Puerto Rican food is all deep fried and very greasy, which is a fairly accurate picture of the fare of the *cuchifritos* joints. Cubans claim a closer kinship with Spanish cooking. There are differences: Puerto Ricans and Dominicans don't make pressed and toasted Cuban sandwiches. Only Puerto Ricans cook *mofongo,* which is made of plantains, beans, and pork and served with a lightly seasoned soup used as a sauce. No one but the Cubans serves *ropa vieja* (old clothes), which is a stew of shredded beef in a tomato sauce. Everyone serves *lechón,* including Puerto Ricans who often roast the pigs over open fires in empty lots in New York City. Cubans stuff and deep fry *boniato,* the Cuban version of a potato. Everyone eats *flan,* Spanish caramel custard, for dessert.

The most Puerto Rican of dishes, other than *mofongo,* are the little boiled pies called *pasteles.* The dough is made of *platano* and *yauta* (plantain and a root vegetable) and filled with spiced pork, then wrapped in leaves or waxed paper, tied with a string, and boiled. One can usually buy *pasteles* in a *cuchifritos* joint, but they often don't taste good and they can't be eaten while walking down the street.

Moros y Christianos, beans and rice, are eaten in one form or another everywhere in the Caribbean. Cubans have a variation in *arroz moro* and Puerto Ricans have another in rice cooked with two kinds of beans and seasoned with *sofrito,* a seasoning paste of peppers, oregano, cilantro, and other spices. Everyone makes *tostones,* green plantains in varying degrees of ripeness fried, pounded, and fried again, and everyone in the Caribbean seasons them with garlic.

Neither the Caribbean cuisines, nor the food of Spain, is a high cuisine, with the subtlety and variety of Aztec cooking. But Cuban and Spanish restaurants succeed where the others don't, an indication that in the symbolic world of foods Cubans and Spaniards are brothers in the Anglo mind, fair-haired, European, cultured, colonialists themselves in the New World. One wonders whether a restaurant run by Cubans of African descent, serving only foods with a strong African influence, would do as well; or would the color of the proprietor's skin change the symbolic value of the food?

And now that Nicaraguans, Guatemalans, and Salvadorans have begun to open restaurants in their own barrios it will be interesting to see how the symbols-play out for them. Will they be considered American, symbolic of ruggedness and the West, like the Mexicans? Will an Anglo enjoy the egotistical thrill of the colonialist in a Salvadoran restaurant? Will the refugees from Nicaragua achieve the same middle-class equality as those from Cuba, or will the newest Latino groups join the inglorious poor, dark-skinned and familiar, dangerous and unromantic, like the Puerto Ricans?

3.

The old man who stood at night in the San Jacinto Plaza of El Paso, Texas, with the metal collection cup suspended from his belt, playing folk songs on his ocarina, while the buses came and went and the great flying insects of the high desert landed on his head and shoulders as if he were a tree, was, in the charitable eyes of nostalgia, in show business.

Like the kitchen and the battlefield, show business is a meeting place for cultures. But it is not often a meeting of equals. Since class determines the relations between cultures, it is almost always the poor who entertain and the rich who are amused, as it was in ancient Rome and Tenochtitlan.[4] The ocarina player told the fair-haired people—they also rode buses in those long ago evenings—about his world; unknowingly, without ever being introduced, they danced together. He wore metal thimbles on all his fingers, and he could make rhythmic patterns with them to accompany the primitive whistle of his ocarina. The fair haired people tapped their feet to his music. They did not move their hips or allow their shoulders the freedom to dance back and forth in time with the music. It was a long time ago, and although they were fair-haired people from the Southwest, not so distant from the ocarina player that they could not hear him, they were not close enough to allow the dancing to be anywhere but in their heads.

The old ocarina player and the man with the tiny straw hat who sat on a bench in the plaza and played his gutstring harp belonged to the generation of imports. They influenced U.S. culture only in that they created a tolerance for their own form of entertainment. None of the fair-haired people who heard the ocarina's whistle or the tapping of the thimbles was inspired to repeat the performance or even to invite it into their vocabulary of songs and rhythms. The entertainer and the audience did not exchange roles, nor did the entertainer succeed so well at his work that he became rich enough to join the audience. The limits of the dance in that desert town were as severe as the line between shadow and sun.

[4]The vast sums paid to a few successful athletes and performers are a cruel and debilitating exception.

In the beginning, all the Latino music was like that of the ocarina player. The tango belonged more to Hollywood and an Italian-American actor, Rudolph Valentino, than to Carlos Gardel and Argentina. When Valentino dressed as a gaucho and danced American women into spasms of sighing, he was an erotic dream, not a man. Like the Frenchmen of fantasy, he was the perfect stranger, a man from so far away that he could be permitted anything, for it was always fantasy, always safe. Lupe Velez and Dolores del Rio were the female counterparts of Valentino, dreams in a darkened theater, movement in black and white, symbols for the night. With the tango, Valentino, Velez, del Rio, Ramon Navarro, the dancing remained inside the head of the listener.

Then Xavier Cugat appeared with a Chihuahua dog in his hand, Carmen Miranda showed up with a salad of fresh fruit for a hat, and the dance moved from the heads of the listeners to their feet. Conga, rhumba, mambo! Latin American music came north. Desi Arnaz sang out the name of a Yoruba deity connected with the cure of disease, and African rhythms, first imported through jazz, found another route into the United States. A nightclub called El Chico opened in Manhattan. Matrons from Kansas City traveled to Mexico to buy Chihuahua dogs. Conga lines formed in Elks Lodges in Illinois and Michigan. Men with ruffled sleeves and maracas in their hands were in demand everywhere. Businessmen from Atlanta, at the behest of their wives, took rhumba lessons at Arthur Murray dancing schools.

Where the tango had been arcane, slightly sinister, the conga was the perfect party dance: Valentino danced the tango, Van Johnson joined the conga line. The rhumba was a good time dance; the samba made everyone laugh. Nothing broke the ice of the icy fifties like Latin music. Yet the music was still foreign. It was Latin, not Latino; Latin American, not North American. There had been no marriage; a guest had been invited into the house to sing and dance to marimba, drums, and guitar.

The only fusion of musical cultures in the post–World War II era came through Latin jazz. It is said to have begun in the late thirties, in Cab Calloway's band, when Mario Bauza hummed a few bars for Cozy Cole and Dizzy Gillespie. But it was not until after the war that Cal Tjader and others mixed Caribbean rhythms with American jazz forms to create a distinct style and sound, a mixture of blue-eyed cool and Afro-Cuban fire that pleased the seemingly emotionless jazz fans of the period. There was also some importation of jazz forms into Caribbean music, but it remained essentially a meeting of African rhythms and Spanish tones. A strong German influence came into the music in the northern states of Mexico, but the creation of Tex-Mex or Tejano *conjunto* and *orchesta* music was not a blending of North American and Latin music, not then, not in the beginning; it came direct from Europe to Mexico.

Not even in Vikki Carr or Joan Baez or Linda Ronstadt—all of whom are Latinas or have a Latino parent—do the musical cultures marry. They sing in Spanish or English, they are Mexican or American, never Mexican-American. Perhaps the closest to a blending of cultures in a popular singer comes in the style of Eydie Gormé, in whose long, very slightly nasal notes one can hear overtones of the Moorish or ancient Hebrew ancestors of Spanish flamenco music. Curiously, the sound of Spain is less evident when she sings in Spanish.

At the end of the 1980s true integration had begun in Miami and Texas. Gloria Estefan and the Miami Sound Machine fused Afro-Cuban music, rock and roll, and jazz into a big band sound that was equally successful with Latino and Anglo audiences. In the Southwest, Johnny Canales could be seen every week on Spanish network television, telling his audience, in English, "You got it!" and giving them what they wanted, three-fourths in Spanish and the rest in repeated English phrases. Canales brought Tex-Mex groups from little Rio Grande Valley towns to television, and he gave narrow but national exposure to such Tejano stars as Esteban (Steve) Jordan, the thin, devilishly dark accordion player with the black eyepatch and the silver rings on all his fingers.

Perhaps Steve Jordan and Gloria Estefan will break the pattern of foreignness. The others did not. The conga, mambo, rhumba, tango, samba are all gone now, rhythms of nostalgia; salsa and Tex-Mex music are narrow bridges to the future.

———

When the faces of actors were our faces as we would like them to be, Latinos found work in films. It was so before films were able to speak. In fantasies Latino faces served the movies well; they were lovers and spitfires, never accountants or physicians; neither the banker nor the banker's daughter had dark eyes and black, curled hair. In the movies before the movies spoke, Latinos had a slightly higher body temperature than anyone else, which made them impetuous; the women, especially the women, could not control their passions. Every Anglo knew that the color of virtue was pale; in the realm of goodness, the blue hint of a vein could always be discerned beneath white, translucent flesh.

Latinos stopped representing fantasies of the dark, erotic side of human nature when the movies began to speak. At that juncture the primacy of language over appearance asserted itself. The dark-eyed lover became a comic figure, a simpleton who could not speak English. It was not a case of Don Quixote turning into Sancho Panza. High-minded motives had never been attributed to Latinos and the new persona had no worldly wit. The Mexican accent became a joke.

Actors like Gilbert Roland, the son of a bullfighter, born in Ciudad Juárez, Mexico, and once a leading man, had difficulty finding work. In 1959, just before Roland was to go onstage at the Plaza Theater in El Paso, Texas, an aspiring actor asked him for help getting started in the movies. "Leesen, keed," Roland answered in the accent that had limited his career after sound came to the movies, "I'm having enough trouble keeping my own head above wadder."

In the next generation Latino actors who spoke proper English worked as Anglos (or Saxons). José Ferrer played Cyrano de Bergerac. Anthony Quinn played Gauguin. John Gavin played only Anglos. Rita Hayworth and Raquel Welch never appeared as Latinas. When Mexicans played Mexicans in the movies they were always simpletons or comic creatures, even when they were bandits, like Alfonso Bedoya in *Treasure of the Sierra Madre*. If an Anglo played a Mexican, the character was either a crazed or gallant child: Wallace Beery as Villa or Marlon Brando as the illiterate naif in Hollywood's great insult to Mexican history, *Viva Zapata!*

Movies have become more sophisticated, but Latinos remain childlike. *La Bamba, Salsa, Stand and Deliver* are all movies about children or adolescents. *West Side Story* was about adolescents. Even a socially conscious film like *El Norte* described the journey to Los Angeles of a young man and woman from Guatemala as an odyssey of children.

The revelation of the treatment of the characters in *El Norte* is that the childlike character and the savage have much in common. The Latino, deprived of the haven of silence, became subhuman, a savage, who could behave either foolishly or dangerously, but always irrationally. When the savage had emotions, they were always out of control: love, sentimentality, rage. The beautiful Dionysian creature of the silents had become the feckless, but still Dionysian creature of the talkies, the comedy of bathos. In the role of savage the Latino was able to endure insults, privations, suffering, and pain that would be unbearable for civilized human beings.

Without language, the Latino was not human. Claude Lévi-Straus is correct; it is not the opposable thumb but the word that distinguishes the species. The movies were every bit as adept at anthropology as he; they put the speechless Latinos into the part of brutes, a role from which they have not yet been able to escape. There are no middle-class Latinos in the movies.

Television presented the brute—either moronic or dangerous—as the Latino contribution to culture. Bill Dana, an Italian-American, invented a character he called José Jimenez, a stereotype of the Latino played so broadly it was not clear whether he was Mexican or Caribbean. José Jimenez was not only a simpleton, he was a venal, greedy simpleton whose stupidities often arose out of character flaws as well as childlike shyness. Steve Allen, a professed political liberal, presented Bill Dana regularly on his television programs. Audiences from the 1950s through the 1980s, who would have been appalled by the presentation of a shuffling stereotypical black, laughed uproariously at the brute with the vacant stare from the moment he opened his mouth to introduce himself in his fool's accent: "My na'an José Jimenez."

Edward James Olmos, an actor of Hungarian and Mexican descent, represented the other aspect of the brutish Latino on television. He rarely spoke. The theme of his dark, pockmarked face was carried out through his dark suits and ties. In his best known role, as a police lieutenant in charge of the Miami vice squad, he pitted himself against the other savages, the Latino criminals, mainly drug dealers, who died violently every week on the program.

In both instances the evidence of brutishess was linguistic: Dana could not speak properly and Olmos could hardly speak at all. If these linguistic brutes had a place in the United States, it was not in the general society, for the rule of society, as given by Lévi-Strauss, applies exactly to their situation: "Whoever says man says language, whoever says language says society." Without language there could be no social life for the Latinos: Television separated them from the rest of society. In the electronic approximation of reality they were not part of the civilized world. The politically liberal viewer of Steve Allen's shows or the "Miami Vice" series could watch Dana or Olmos and the Latino villain with no discomfort, for the people on screen were separated from his species as effectively as if they had been portrayed without an opposable thumb.

An enormously popular exception in the 1950s and 1960s was the husband of Lucille Ball. Desi Arnaz, a bandleader and drummer from Cuba, married the comedienne and then appeared as her husband on the television situation comedy. Arnaz could not, of course, get rid of his accent, but he could make it a foreign accent rather than brutish speechlessness. As Ricky Ricardo, Arnaz was middle-class, married, the father of a small child, and a man who had a successful band. Playing off the Mertzes who lived in the same apartment building, the Ricardos were clearly part of middle-class society. In the combination of Desi and Lucy, it was Lucy who played the clown and Desi who was amusing—after all, it was a comedy show—but not a clown.

Desi Arnaz's accent, because he was middle-class and married to an Anglo, was a human voice. The program made it clear that although he was Cuban, he was white, not black or Indian. He was a Latino, but he was also a European in the context of the show.

Unfortunately, Desi Arnaz did not bring Latino culture into the U.S. mainstream. He was not a brute; he was an exception. The authors of the programs gave Ricky Ricardo North American, middle-class values, not Cuban values. He did not even behave like a musician; Ricky Ricardo's band could have been a hardware store.

Freddie Prinz, half–Puerto Rican, half–European Jew, wanted to bring Latino values into U.S. culture through television, but the producers of his program kept him in the ghetto. Prinz, who had a long history of drug use, killed himself at the height of his career.

By 1990, the comedian Paul Rodríguez was able, at last, to overcome the language barrier and mix cultures, but only on Spanish television. His program, a standard potpourri of interviews, skits, and music, was conducted in Spanish, but often had English-speaking guests. Rodríguez, who is bilingual, spoke with his Latino guests in Spanish and with his Anglo guests in English. After every paragraph of Spanish conversation, he translated for the Anglo guests.

By doing so Rodríguez turned the cultural tables. The Anglos were the strangers; they had to struggle with the dominant language on a program produced and broadcast in the United States. Rodríguez, ordinarily a funny fellow who trades on jokes about stereotypes of Latinos, became the hero of his program by virtue of his ability to speak both languages. It gave him control. Rather than being viewed as a brute because of his lack of English, Rodríguez was the most civilized person on the program; his ability to use two languages made him more social than the others, while his monolingual guests seemed ignorant, helpless, isolated from society: What may well be the future of U.S. culture was adumbrated on television by a clown.

5

FULANO DE CUBA

Fulano is a very old Spanish word for someone of uncertain identity, a so-and-so, that less than memorable person the English call a bloke or a chap, the one known in American English as a guy or you-know (as in whatsisname). Fulano, zutano, mengano play the role of Tom, Dick, and Harry or the butcher, the baker, the candlestick maker. Fulano isn't real, no one bears that name; fúlano doesn't play first base or marry your niece; he pays no taxes, eats no food, and leaves no mess behind; he's nobody.[1] If by some error of madness, alcohol, or utter failure of the imagination, a child were named Fulano, his life would be a trial, for he would be no one and everyman, rich and poor, short and tall, Colombian, Cuban, Dominican, Mexican, Puerto Rican, Spanish, and so on. In the case of fulano the wound is minor, one person obliterated. "Latino" is another matter, a deed, a name into which millions disappear.

Since the nationalities that make up the ethnic group known as Latinos are not randomly distributed across the United States, but tend to cluster in certain areas, most Anglos think of all Latinos as being like the people who live nearby. In the Northeast, for example, Latinos are thought to be Puerto Rican. The identification of Puerto Ricans with New York City is so strong that they are sometimes referred to as Neoricans or Nuyoricans. In Miami, Latinos (who prefer to be called Hispanics there) are thought to be Cuban,

[1]In some parts of Latin America, "fulano" has taken on an opposite meaning, as in "Es un fulano," He's a somebody.

although the Nicaraguan refugees may broaden the definition by the end of the 1990s. Californians and Texans think of Latinos as Mejicanos or Mexican-Americans or chicanos. Chicagoans have a problem, for that city has neither a Mejicano nor Puertorriqueño nor Cubano majority; it is a city with a large Latino population.

Salvadorans live in Los Angeles, San Francisco, and Hempstead, N.Y. Cubans and Puerto Ricans have moved into New Jersey in roughly equal numbers. Even in New York City, once the capital of Puerto Rican immigrants, perhaps half a million Dominicans have moved in, along with a huge Colombian colony, and a growing number of Central Americans and Mexicans. There are also sizable communities of Spaniards and Sephardim (or Spanish Jews) in the city. In every city, even Miami (which is dominated by Cuban exiles) and Los Angeles (which would rank as one of the largest cities in Mexico if one simply counted the number of Mexican citizens living there), other nationalities have made their presence felt.

To many Latinos drawing the distinctions among the nationalities constitutes a kind of game, like a quiz program. Everyone has a theory about everyone else. Some are amusing, all are accurate, and every nuance is important. A few people are better situated than others to draw the distinctions. Raymond del Portillo, who headed up San Francisco's initial effort at bilingual education, is the son of a Cuban father and a Mexican mother. On the Cuban side his great-grandfather wrote the Cuban national anthem. On the Mexican side his grandfather crossed the Sierra Madres three times while fighting with the Villistas during the Mexican Revolution of 1910. His wife, Carlota, is Puerto Rican, raised in Puerto Rico and New York.

From his unique viewpoint del Portillo offers these observations about the cultural extremes of the three nationalities. "Cubans," he said, "are aggressive, assertive, and sometimes appallingly arrogant. There is a steadfastness and loyalty among Mexican-Americans, but their docility is sometimes disappointing. And the feistiness of the Puerto Rican is understandable. They're tough, very tough, either because of life on the island or prejudice in New York; they're tough, but not bitter."

Leobardo Estrada, a demographer at UCLA whose work takes him to every Latino community in the country, says that a visitor must prove himself in different fashion for each group. For the Cubans, the litmus test is language: One must not only speak Spanish, one must speak the language well, with a vocabulary of synonyms and the ability to use arcane verb forms. Puerto Ricans judge a person by his or her familiarity with the island; one must know not only the cities, but the towns and villages as well. To establish oneself with Mexican-Americans, it is necessary only to be a professor, so great is the reverence for education in the Mejicano and Mexican-American culture.

A young woman in New York offers a somewhat different view. To Rose Vega, who left an executive position in New York City government to attend law school, Puerto Ricans and Dominicans, the dominant groups in New York, are quite different. "Puerto Ricans just want to party all the time," she said. "Dominicans are smooth talkers; they're full of lavish compliments." Vega, whose parents are Puerto Rican and Spanish, finds Spaniards, like her father, stern and very proud, particularly when it comes to language: The Spaniards frown upon both Puerto Rican vocabulary and pronunciation.

—

The difference between stereotypes and cultural distinctions is sometimes very subtle. Instead of relying on my own judgment, I asked people from the various nationalities to describe their own cultures. Guarione M. Diaz,[2] executive director of the Cuban American National Council, said in response to the challenge to convey in a word the essence of the Cuban character, *"Atrevimiento,"* which means bold or daring. Others, lacking the precision of Diaz, said "aggressive" or "hard-working," but the tone was always the same.

A few people tried to draw distinctions between the early Cuban refugees and the Marielitos, who came out much later and were said to have been undesirables, criminals and lunatics that Fidel Castro wanted to get rid of. But it became clear after a while that the real distinction between the two waves of emigrants was mainly in the level of their education and the color of their skin; many of the Marielitos were black, while almost all of the first wave of emigrants were white.[3]

About 10 percent of the Marielitos were actually criminals, but all of them were painted into convict's stripes. Still, six or seven years after arriving here, they were climbing the Cuban economic ladder, following the same

---

[2] I have followed each person's choice in the use of accents in proper names. Díaz is spelled without the accent on his business card. Guarione is an Indian name which has several variant spellings.

[3] The difference in class origin between the first and last (Mariel) waves was profound.

In the first wave, 1959–1962, 31 percent were professional, technical, and managerial (compared with 9.2 percent of the entire Cuban population); 33 percent clerical or in sales (compared with 13.7 percent of the entire population); 8 percent were semiskilled or unskilled, 7 percent were service workers, and 4 percent were agricultural workers. Only 4 percent had less than a fourth grade education (compared with 52 percent of the entire population), and 36 percent had completed high school or had some college (compared to 4 percent for the entire population).

By 1967, only 18 percent of the Cuban immigrants were professional, technical, and managerial, and when the Marielitos arrived thirteen years later, the number had fallen to 8.5 percent. The Mariel group included large numbers of machine operators, transportation operators, and people who simply classified themselves as laborers.

pattern of daring and evincing the same confidence in their ability to solve problems. There is a story in Miami about *atrevimiento* and the plumbing in many of the houses. It is said to be unlike the plumbing anywhere else in the world. The reason is that Cubans who came over in the sixties took whatever work they could get. When there was work for plumbers, they said they could do plumbing, and they did, but an autodidact is not necessarily a successful plumber. Most of the work they produced is apparently so strange and convoluted that when it breaks no real plumber can figure out how to repair it.

The most poignant description of exile life is contained in the story of the Cuban dog, a wretched little thing, with a short, ragged tail, thin haunches, and sorry, splayed paws. As it was walking down a Miami street it came across a group of large American dogs, with big tails and shiny coats. "Look at that bedraggled beast," the American dogs said. They laughed at the little Cuban and insulted him for being so small and powerless. The Cuban dog endured the insults for a few moments, then he said, "Go ahead, laugh. You see me as I am now, but in Cuba I was a German shepherd."

It is not a humble tale. No Mexican would tell such a story. The Cuban dog knew who he was, and he knew the transitory nature of power. It is really a story about the failure of American dogs to recognize one of their own, perhaps even a member of a superior culture. Unlike other Latinos, the Cuban has nothing of the supplicant in his culture; he has been wronged, and he means to set the world aright. The nature of the immigrant is to flee the past; the exile seeks only the return of his former glory; he wants only the opportunity to act upon his nostalgia.

The wit of the Cubans, which is often self-deprecating, the classic survivor's sigh in the form of a joke, helps to overcome the aggressiveness in business, social, and cultural life that is almost universally ascribed to them. Although Cuba has historically had a taste for philosophy, the exile has favored practical life. Eating and paying the rent became paramount for people who left their homes with nothing but the powers of mind for capital.

The middle class is resourceful, but anxious; there is no theory of property that denies the comfort of capital. The nature of the bourgeoisie is to understand economic reverses as a fall from grace. Hell is doing without, and the lowest circle of Hell is watching one's children do without. In exile, the hungers of the Cuban middle class took precedence.

Andrea Camps, the elegant doyenne of Latino society in Houston, remembers coming to the United States. Her husband, a physician, was in Central America. She and her children lived alone in Miami on welfare payments of $100 a month. "Rent was $67.50," she said. "We had to live on the rest. I suffered from hunger, because the food was for the children. I drank water to fill myself up." She laughed, "It was not so bad, really; I lost a lot of weight, and because there was no money for cigarettes, I gave up smoking." The little laugh, the gallantry, are not fraudulent: she typifies the exile at her most successful; she keeps her sorrows to herself.

No one seeing her now could imagine Andrea Camps poor, moving in 1963 to Detroit for several years because she could not bear the discrimination against Cubans in Houston. She sits at a conference table in the little mansion that houses the Hispanic Cultural Institute of Houston, a woman of perfect fingernails and solemn coif, clothed by Saks, tough-minded and tall, elitist, still sensual, a woman. Yet something about her style doesn't work as she would like it to; her hair is red, her skin is olive, an unsuccessful mix, too far from nature's intent, yet not far enough. Her husband delivers sixty babies a month, she has a perfect grasp of style; she can leap over all but one hurdle on the way to the U.S. upper middle class—she cannot extirpate the sun from her skin.

But she will try. It is the Cuban way. As Andrea Camps, who brought a Ph.D. with her from Cuba, said, "We Cubans are aggressive, progressive. We make the opportunity; it is not given to us."

She and her husband and children came back to Houston in 1977. Detroit was a success for them. She taught at Wayne State University, her husband did well in his practice, their children attended the exclusive and expensive Cranbrook Academy. But there is still prejudice, she feels. "They resent us, the Cubans, here, because we are successful. A lady said to me, 'I can't believe you are Cuban. You don't even speak like a Cuban. You are not very loud.' They also call us the Jews of the Caribbean, but they say it in a pejorative way. I think that they think we are too concerned with money, but maybe we had to learn. The Cubans are very generous with money. For a Cuban, the problem is not to have money, but to be able to make money."

In Houston, as in Los Angeles, the Cubans rose quickly to become an elite among Latinos. Most of the Latino doctors are Cuban. The Hispanic Cultural Organization is run by Cubans, and when they have an annual ball, complete with king and queen and their court, it is the Cubans who invite one of the more social Anglo families to reign over the ball, for the Cubans wish to move out into Anglo society in East Texas. They do not understand themselves as Latinos, but as citizens of the world. Cuba was a crossroads, a place where justice winked, a palimpsest of racism, the only place in the hemisphere in which sophistication and evil made an Old World arrangement.

But Cuba was then, now the Cubans are also fulanos, the inheritors of new responsibilities, especially when they live outside Miami. Señora Camps sees their role in Houston as bolstering the entire Latino community. "The Mexicans who come here . . . have given the Anglos their version of Hispanics. They are people who go to bad schools, who get a feeling of pessimism.

We are trying to present them with role models; we are trying to prove to them that their pessimism is wrong."

She remembers Cuba fondly, but return is not an option for her. "We Cubans cannot go back," she said, "we have to go forward." Then she sighed, and the tensions that give pace to her life disappeared for a moment. She looked away, and when she turned back toward me, I saw for a moment the children, the hard years, the toll it takes of a woman when she refuses to fail. "To leave Cuba," she said, "is a spiritual liberation, because we have lost our fear of the future.

—

To be a Cuban in Miami is to live in a special country, somewhere between the United States and history. Miami and Cuba have been tied together culturally and economically since Cuba dominated the hemisphere in the sixteenth century. Eighth Street, now known as Calle Ocho, began changing from a predominantly Jewish neighborhood to the Cuban section in the 1950s. That was when my wife's uncle opened a restaurant there. It was a tiny place, but comfortable; business was conducted entirely in Spanish. They did not seek English-speaking customers. The advantage of Miami, the pleasure and the opportunity of Miami, was that they didn't have to speak English.

The entire city changed after the refugees began coming out in the early sixties. Although they were poor at first—every Cuban, especially those who became rich, has a tale to tell about the struggle of those first few years—they were given asylum, the right to work, and financial assistance from the federal government. More than anything, the right to work legally gave them the chance to use their skills. The professional class took some time to get licensed to practice and the businessmen had to work day and night at difficult jobs to get the capital to go into business, but they managed.

They followed the Cuban system of doing business known as *socios* or *socioismo*,[4] an exaggerated form of the old boy network. In the system of *socios* one does not approve a loan or accept a contract based upon objective criteria, as U.S. businessmen are supposed to do; knowing the person, being a friend or even an acquaintance, is more important than a Dun & Bradstreet rating. The system worked, helped along by the high level of education and the willingness to take on any challenge, the daring Guarione Diaz talks about, and what he calls a lack of reverence for persons or position. The Cuban exiles, primarily middle- and upper middle-class, soon became middle- and upper middle-class again.

Never before had there been a group of exiles quite like them, not even

---

[4]Castro coined the word to condemn the establishment professionals and businessmen of prerevolutionary Cuba.

the White Russians who carried out more royalist baggage than worldly capabilities, not even the German Jews who came to the U.S. in the nineteenth century; no group of newcomers in the United States had ever moved so quickly from penury to prosperity; Fidel Castro had given the middle-class engine of the Cuban economic system to his worst enemy.

Exiles are not emigrants, however. They come to the new country laden with bitterness. Although time and comfort bank the fires of what might have been, action turns into a rage of words, and danger dies slowly into nostalgia. Ambition is the exception, the only barrier to a happy old age. And even ambition tires of action in old men; it turns to dominoes or politics. It isn't easy to find a bomb thrower in Miami anymore. The members of the Brigada 2506, those brave and foolish men who landed at the Bay of Pigs, have opened a museum.

The Greeks understood exile as a form of capital punishment: not travel, relocation, or emigration, but death. Nothing else radicalizes a person quite so thoroughly, nothing makes one quite so daring, as to be already dead. Thus, the politics of Miami in the first quarter of a century of exile were those of the risen dead. What many interpreted as a sinister quality in the exiles was merely the freedom from morality of those who are already in purgatory. These angelic exiles threw bombs, landed at the Bay of Pigs, worked for the CIA, ranted on the radio.

But exiles grow old, even when they consider themselves the risen angels of righteousness. The hands of the once dead warriors tremble; they are better at business or dominoes. The celebration of anniversaries drains their radicalism now. Real death will soon replace the symbolism of exile. Their backs ache; they know more doctors than arms merchants. The Cuban American National Foundation, once a junta of fanatics, jockeys for influence with political contributions and the promise of votes and appeals to the guilt of the host country that sent them naked onto the beaches of the Bay of Pigs.

The right wing, which was motivated by bitterness and nationalism in the beginning, is driven now by the wildest ambition. Jorge Más, a charming businessman, who unquestionably loves both Cuba and the United States, expects to be the first democratic, or at least the first non-communist, leader of Cuba after the Castro regime finally falls. He denies that, of course, but not with much vehemence.

As an anti-Castro fanatic, Más was not a dangerous man. He was a leader of the Cuban right, which supplied lunatics to the CIA and the Nixon Administration. As some people pointed out, in soft voice, it was not healthy for the image of the Cuban community to be in the business of leasing loonies to government and quasi–government agencies. But Más and his Cuban American National Foundation have recently learned that it is better to be in charge of the asylum. And in the United States, they learned, that can be done with cash contributions and a few votes.[5] He and other officials of the foundation told me that they don't throw bombs anymore, and I believe them.

It is very difficult to disbelieve anything that Jorge Más says. He is a round faced man with a receding hairline, hospitable and informal, but crisp, quick, scheduled. When my wife and I visited with him, he served Cuban coffee for the digestion and straightforward responses for the tape recorder. He had been warned by his staff at the foundation that my politics were liberal-left,[6] and I warned him again before we spoke. He seemed to like the idea, to be pleased at the thought of combat.

Only once during a long conversation did he stray from the reasoned clarity that is so surprising in a man who leads what is often described as the radical right fringe of Cuban-American politics. And even then his response to a question about bombs was only a jesuitical kind of madness: He said that the people who had bombed the Cuban leftists in Miami were agents of Castro intent upon discrediting the actions of the anti-Castro right.

The thought disturbed him. It led him into paths of mind that were bizarre. He spoke of people who sent clothing or money or food to relatives in Cuba. They were all agents of the Castro government, he said. It was a trick, this sending of money to relatives, these cash payments for burials and such. Castro needed the hard currency. For an instant he saw agents everywhere. Then the telephone rang. He had a cryptic conversation in Spanish. "I

[5]The extent to which political action committee money and personal donations from Cuban exiles, as well as votes, have penetrated two morally corrupt administrations—those of Ronald Reagan and George Bush—was revealed in the summer of 1990 when the U.S. government, under intense pressure from the Bush Administration, released the terrorist pediatrician, Orlando Bosch from prison. An editorial in the *New York Times* of July 20, 1990, concluded:

"In the name of fighting terrorism, the United States sent the Air Force to bomb Libya and the Army to invade Panama. Yet now the Bush Administration coddles one of the hemisphere's most notorious terrorists. And for what reason? The only one evident is currying favor in South Florida."

In the classic pattern of exile thinking, Cuban moderates in Miami saw a more complex plan behind the freeing of Bosch. They believed the government had given Bosch to the right in exchange for a promise to react mildly to the opening of dialogue with the Castro government. As usual in Latin American politics, the moderates were wrong.

[6]The use of the term left in speaking of Latin America and the United States presents serious problems, because the left in the United States is more like the center in Latin America. The continuing rightward drift of the U.S. Supreme Court as well as the executive branch makes drawing the distinction even more difficult. It is not my impression that the anti-Castro Cuban-exile rightists are necessarily economic rightists. Marilyn Kalusin and Rene Silva of the CANF deal with Democrats as well as Republicans. Silva described the complexity of Cuban views with a joke: "When there are two Jews, you have three opinions; when there are two Cubans, you have three organizations."

can't give you any details now," he said, "but we are buying one of the oldest and largest businesses of its kind in Florida."

He had been rescued by business. He was charming again, although still intense, the man who was shown in the photograph with President Ronald Reagan, the man who had access to the office of the Secretary of State of the United States of America, one of the few who saw Secretary James Baker without appearing on the public calendar. He smiled and drank his tiny coffee. The informality returned. We spoke of family, of Cuban things, not politics. He recalled his early years in exile.

It was difficult, listening to the ordinariness of the man, to remember that the Mercedes Benz parked outside beside the Porsche had not always belonged to Jorge Más; it had been the personal armored car of Anastasio Somoza of Nicaragua. There was no craziness apparent in the man; he did not look at us with a fanatic's glare. He looked like the person who had been photographed in Angola, dressed in a bush jacket, inspecting the situation as if he were a head of state, not merely the enemy of Fidel Castro who had sent troops there.

He spoke of freedom, of his appreciation of dissent. He said he had contributed $10,000 of his own money, "the legal limit," to the campaign of the liberal, Senator Howard Metzenbaum. In his voice there were hesitations, a quality of fulmination that came more from his frustration with English than from his temper. He had been generous in the contest between us, giving away the advantage; we spoke in my language, not his.

In Joan Didion's book on Miami, Jorge Más is a part of the sinister paranoia of the radical right. And I think she was partly correct, but ill-served by her own humorlessness. The Cubans who came in the first wave of exile are more Spanish than Caribbean, and it must be remembered that there are two Spains: the Spain of the Inquisition and that of Miguel Cervantes, the inventor of Don Quixote, a Spain of certainty and irony, of paranoia and hope, of death and laughter. There was a time in Miami when the foundation ran an inquisition; whoever did not oppose Fidel Castro wholeheartedly was suspect, to be ostracized, tortured in a social sense, destroyed in business, in a political auto-da-fé. And Jorge Más Canosa was the Grand Inquisitor.

He was also the knight from the plain of La Mancha. When a commissioner of the city of Miami insulted him, Más challenged the commissioner to a duel! "Yes, I did," he said. "It's what I was referring to you about the emotions and the passions. Yes, I did."

"Can you tell me about that?" I asked.

"This is nothing new. This is something as old as mankind. We were living in a society here where people used to offend each other every day and call names on each other. And I had never gone into that situation. This man used a very unfortunate situation which had nothing to do with politics to offend what I think was my honor.[7] And I said, 'Look, I don't want to debate with you publicly. I don't want to exchange names, that's up to you. If you feel that I have offended you or I feel that you have offended me, I will challenge you in a duel. Let's clean your name, your thinking that I have hurt you, and we'll clean mine. Let's see who comes out the winner, period, that's it.'

"He didn't accept. I will do it. I don't have any problem with that. I have a lot of respect for many presidents and vice-presidents of this country who did it before, statesmen around the world; there's nothing new to it. It's all out of fashion, yes, but you know, all fashions always find a way to come back. Nowadays there's pants with cuffs and polyester coats, there's nothing new. I didn't invent that.

"We were going to do it in Central America. It's forbidden here in this country. I'm a law-abiding citizen.

"He turned it down immediately, and he quit right there and it was over. Can you find a better way to do something better to the community? Otherwise, we would have been throwing mud back and forth for weeks and weeks and weeks forever. This way, it's only two hours.

"It's just to show you, I'm not a conventional guy."

Like the other son of Spain who wished to return to the time of good knights and great deeds, Jorge Más sees grandeur where reality is something less. He did, in truth, challenge the offending commissioner to a duel. But the commissioner did not decline. He accepted.

"Choose your weapons," said Más in the grand tradition of the duel.

"Water pistols," the commissioner answered, with the ferocity of a real windmill, "at twenty paces."

———

The tragic side of the Spanish character also exists in the Cuban exile community of Miami. There is in Little Havana a portrait photographer, Ketty Gort, a woman whose utterly deliberate smile frames the tragedy of civil war and exile. "I am divorced," she said. "I had, how could you say it, a political divorce." She is a grandmother now, a woman of business, but when she spoke of her marriage, her voice became that of the little bride, the young mother. "We were in the beginning political exiles from Batista. That's how we came to this country.

"We were living in New York then. We had our two kids, but we went back in 1960. I thought it was fine. I went to Cuba, and I stayed about a year. For me it was a contrast, because I was already used to the way over here,

[7]The cause of the argument was a real-estate deal between the commissioner and Más. When the deal went sour, Más accused the commissioner of being a communist.

and I started seeing things that I didn't like, but I never said anything to him until I came here to the States to see my folks. While I was here, that's when he called me, and he said, 'You better come back right away, because if you don't come back everything is finished. I feel socialista, Marxista, Leninista.' "

She is a little woman who wears big eyeglasses; she is sturdy and as realistic as small business or a two-line telephone. But for a moment she was possessed by tears. She seemed to stagger. "He was in favor of the revolution, and he'd like to stay in Cuba. What am I supposed to do?

"It was very difficult, because I married with my first fiancé, my first love in life. I was very much in love with him. It was very hard; it was a decision you have to make between really being a wife and a woman or saving your kids.

"I don't like people who start complaining that Castro took this, this sugar cane plantation or took a house, took this. For me, he didn't take any money, any material thing, but he did something very bad for me: He destroyed my marriage; he took away the father of my two sons."

Her granddaughter, who was born in 1980, is more practical than Ketty Gort. The girl refuses to say the name of Fidel Castro, as if it were a dirty word; she indicates with coy pointing that he belongs in Hell. The girl has learned the lesson of reaction early. But the woman who lost her husband to Marxism is a Democrat, which she says is not a popular position in Little Havana. If she has a hero in the community, it is not a rightist, but Jorge Valls, the socialist who spent twenty years and forty days in Cuban prisons and emerged with his leftist politics and Catholicism intact. They have never met, although they are both in Cuban Miami and they are both among the few who understand that a revolution is also a civil war. For her, exile and tragedy provided the strength to raise her sons; for him, "Exile is worse than a sentence of death, much worse. Exile is like trying to breathe and not finding enough air. But exile is also one of the greatest experiences."

—

Like everyone who has studied the exile community, Lisandro Pérez, a sociologist at Florida International University, focuses on the first wave. Data on the Marielitos, Castro's castaways, is still fragmentary. (The oral history of Ivan Orta, a Marielito, appears in the Epilogue of this book.) Moreover, they don't please the earlier exiles, whose reputation and statistics they have sullied.

"Here, selectivity of migration draws disproportionately from middle and upper-middle strata," Pérez said, speaking of the first wave. "High aspirations for social mobility—Cubans also had high expectations." He notes that Cuban women work to help the family, calling them "instrumental, not career oriented."

"Cubans are not fatalistic," he said. "Cubans are a take-charge sort of people." He relates much of this aspect of Cuban character to the role of the Catholic Church in pre-Castro Cuba. "In the 1950s churches were popular because one priest would give the homily while the other proceeded with the ceremony in Latin. So the service was over in fifteen minutes and people could go on with their business.

"The challenge to the Church in 1960–61 took place before Vatican II. The Church opposed the government, but had no effect. The Church was weak as a political institution. However, the Church has been important here in the refugee movement, very important in the beginning."

Those with the other view of the Catholic Church's power in Cuba argue that Castro has recently attempted some rapprochement with the Church because he understands how the Church affected the work ethic in prerevolutionary Cuba. The very fatalism that Pérez says does not exist in the Cuban culture is the element Castro seeks to bring back, for the Cuban communists have apparently decided that only a fatalistic person can work hard for little earthly reward. And the fuel of fatalism is the afterlife.

Pérez said Cuba was "a secular rather than an insular society, a collection of ports," a crossroads of culture and commerce. And he is, of course, correct about the effect of Cuba's geographic and economic position upon the educated class of Cubans, many of whom came to the United States.

For those who remained behind, largely the less affluent, Castro's sociologists have made what amounts to an interesting self-criticism: The Cuban economy depended upon the promise of an afterlife to maintain high levels of productivity despite the disparity in wages and living standards. However, during the glorious years of success and foreign aid Castro and the middle- and upper middle-class intelligentsia who helped him overthrow Batista forgot that one needs a reason to suffer life on the edge of absolute misery; people must make excuses to their children for giving them less than they need.

It was a form of what Lisandro Pérez and others term arrogance, but what I think is closer to self-deception, following the Greek view that *apate,* (deception) is a result of human blindness and *logos.* Although it is sometimes difficult to remember, given all the turmoil around his Marxist-Leninist ideas, Fidel Castro is a Cuban, and it is his perfectly Cuban combination of daring and self-deception that has led to his successes and his failures. I have no doubt that on his deathbed, when the inward debate of soul takes precedence, Fidel Castro will call for a priest.

In other areas, language for one, Lisandro Pérez has a penetratingly amusing view of the Cuban exile in America. The English-only movement, in his view, is moot for the Cubans. "To learn English is consistent with the notion of social mobility." He gives as an example the Belen Jesuit School, now in Miami, recalling that Fidel Castro attended the Belen School in Cuba. The institution has been moved whole to Miami, but "they teach in English: They have only one hour of Spanish every day. It is a Cuban institution in English."

He believes that "all ethnic communities have an expiration date. Cultures do change." At the same time he refers to the enclave theory of Alejandro Portes: "You can live here," he says, "without speaking English; the Spanish community is institutionally complete."

The differences between Cubans and other Latinos, which are greater than the differences among all other groups, are apparent to Pérez. "There is an absence of minority-group orientation. Cubans have a very high self-concept—at times there is a certain arrogance—that's very different from the self-concept of Mexican-Americans and Puerto Ricans." He offers an anecdote to make his theory concrete: At a meeting a Mexican complained of being unable to get a bank loan because he was Mexican. Surprised, a Cuban businessman said that when he started his business he couldn't get bank loans because he was poor, not because he was Cuban. The Cuban said, "Now, I own twenty stores and everybody wants to lend me money, and I'm still Cuban."

Lisandro Pérez is a big man, ursine, bearded; he overflows his tiny office. A small, sharp nose comes out of his soft, round face, a surprise—insight leaping out of caution. Perhaps that is not so good for him; he must be careful. Florida International University is not a place that appreciates daring; its president, Modesto Maidique, has cowered publicly before the demands of the political right. Lisandro Pérez has nothing to say about the Cuban American National Foundation. I cannot blame him for his caution. He has a wife and children, and although he does not say it, he cannot help but be aware of the inability of the Cuban exile community to grasp the concept of freedom in the United States. It is a community of old people, and the institutional completeness of which he speaks has kept the Cubans from experiencing much of the best of America.

Pérez said, "I'm not sure that Cubans feel a brotherhood with other Latin Americans. The Cuban connection was more with Spain and the U.S." Unfortunately, much of that connection was with the worst of the United States: the mafia, the government that supported Batista, the plantation owners who were glad to exploit Cuban labor, the racists who came to have sex with the mulatas populating the hundreds of whorehouses that existed in Havana on the eve of the revolution. Even the most sophisticated exiles have not learned to appreciate fully the United States's concept of political protection for the minority, the loyal opposition.

Younger Cubans are quite different. They have virtually no interest in island politics. For them Miami has become what Cuba was to their parents. Diana Campoamor lives in San Francisco with her teenage son, who thinks of Miami as home. That's where his grandparents live, where he spent his first few years, where his roots are. Christina Gelabert went to Boston College, worked in communications in New York and Europe, married, had two children, and then brought her non-Cuban family back to Miami with her. Although I have known her for many years and still think of her as a little girl with dimples, she has grown into a strikingly beautiful woman, tall, slim, and still with the Gelabert dimples. Her life in Miami has nothing to do with politics. She earns her living in Miami, as she did in New York, as a writer. Christina was born in Cuba and raised partly in Spain, but she is fond of saying, "I don't write with an accent." And she doesn't. Nor does she live with an accent, except perhaps for her closeness to her family, all of whom (both parents and her brother and sister) are architects.

Diana Campoamor is politically liberal; she worked for the Mexican American Legal Defense and Education Fund in California. Christina Gelabert, who is a few years younger, is apolitical. Both are divorced, which is, according to social scientists at the Cuban American Council, typical; they claim that Cuban women have the highest divorce rate of any identifiable group in the United States.

The second great distinction in the Cuban community, even greater than age, is class. Despite the popular misconception, all Cubans are not rich, even though they are more affluent as a group than other Latinos. Those who came from a working-class background in Cuba do not have the same "high self-concept" as the richer and better educated first wave. They say that most people think of Cubans as loud, always having to let everyone know they're around. And the burden of the Marielitos has fallen very heavily on them.

The work ethic has not deserted these Cubans, but they work at different kinds of jobs. They drive trucks or wait on tables or do the routine tasks of factories. And they do not live in elegant beachfront homes; they live in apartments in New Jersey or bungalows in Hialeah. Their expectations are lower, but they are not without dreams. They want to move out of Little Havana, where the crime rate is high and the good stores have mostly closed and gone to the suburbs. Little Havana belongs to the old people now, and Nicaraguans and Salvadorans are moving in. The effort to rejuvenate the neighborhood may not succeed. It is the new areas that fill the dreams of the working-class Cubans, and they are determined to find some way to get there. Generally, it will mean that every member of the family works: both parents, perhaps even a grandparent, and all the children who have finished school. In such families of strivers, it is not out of the ordinary for most of the working family members to have more than one job; thus a family of two parents, two grown children, and two high-school age children might have eight or ten jobs between them.

Older Cubans say they will return to Cuba as soon as Castro dies or is deposed. The younger generation is interested only in going back to visit. How many older Cubans really would go back is impossible to gauge. Meanwhile, the pain of the exile does not recede. Arturo Rodríguez, a painter who lives in Little Havana, continues his series of dreams of exile, producing works in which he always sees himself with a missing or disjointed limb.

Rolando Fernández, a young psychiatrist in Miami, treats many old people. Perhaps he does so because he has the cherubic smile and good humor of the grandson every old man or woman dreams of. Perhaps it is simply that the community is old and the supply of patients is determined by demographics. Every day, Dr. Fernández, the patron of avant-garde painters and writers, cousin of Roberto Fernández, one of the exile's more imaginative novelists, goes to his office to minister to the old angels of exile, the dead who are dying again, quietly now, forever now.

He tells of one of his patients, an old woman who had not seen her daughter, who remained behind in Cuba, for more than twenty years. Under an agreement that permits brief visits to the United States by relatives from Cuba, her daughter came to Miami. The old woman, who had been depressed, was happy during the visit of her daughter, but when the daughter had to return to Cuba, the old woman fell into a deep depression and was hospitalized.

Dr. Fernández does professionally what has become the familial vocation of many of the children of the exile—he comforts the dying. There are so few children and so many old people that the burden weighs heavily in the community of memories.

Massive changes will be coming to the exile community soon. Relations between the United States and Cuba will eventually improve, with or without the fall of Castro. But even more certainly the time of the old exiles is coming to an end. The new generation is not much interested by ancient wars. They are Miami people, and they are not like the old Cubans; they want to be free to make their own way in the world, yet they know that cannot happen until the exile is resolved in politics and time.

6

MENGANO DE PUERTO RICO

la tierra prometida
eres
tú[1]

Clemente Soto Vélez

I.

Life in New York City is full of famous woes. Everyone in the city is
afflicted with dreaming and gossip: Nothing private endures; the truth has
no purchase on what is known; everything is made to fit the expectations of
the market. No more cruel or democratic place exists or was ever imagined.

The tragedy of the Puerto Ricans began the moment they chose New
York. It condemned them to live as the objects of invention even as it set
them to furious dreaming. They ceased to be who they were. They became
words and music. In Puerto Rico they had been conquered by force of arms
and politics; in the new city they fell victim to disappointment and the *Daily
News*.

One of the first books about being Puerto Rican in New York was *Island in
the City* by Dan Wakefield, written in 1957. Wakefield used Spanish only
three times in the book, and twice he was in error—"buenos noches" instead of *buenas noches* and "tu sabe" instead of *tú sabes*. Those mistakes
would never have been tolerated in French or German, but Spanish was so
foreign to the well-bred and well-educated in New York in 1957 that neither
he nor his copy editor bothered to find out the gender of the night or the
familiarity of the verb.

[1]you
are
the promised land

77

If Wakefield was liberal, distant, and kind, Stephen Sondheim and Leonard Bernstein were liberal, close, and unkind. The characters in *West Side Story* were based on Romeo and Juliet, but Sondheim and Bernstein had taken them down the social scale from minor nobility to street killers. The musical was about immigrants of a decidedly lower cultural and moral level than the immigrants and immigrants' children who sat in the audience. Writers like Piri Thomas drove the point home in autobiographies of crime, drugs, and poverty. In the media capital of the world, the Puerto Ricans got plenty of coverage, and it was all bad.

The capstone was Oscar Lewis's enormously successful book on Puerto Ricans and the culture of poverty, *La Vida*. It was not a novel of righteous anger or an autobiography of painful experience in the classic Christian literary tradition, with its loving sense of the nobility of the poor. Lewis produced a book of explicit sexual detail—enough so that it would become a best-seller—and ubiquitous amorality. There was no sense of the possibility of redemption through suffering, as in Dostoyevsky's novels. His Puerto Rican men were lazy, stupid louts who lived off women or welfare, beat their wives and girlfriends, and then left them penniless and pregnant. His Puerto Rican women were whores, without exception. There was no sense of a human soul in the characters as presented by the omnipotent editor. Lewis called his work anthropology, science. The intellectual world adored the book, for it confirmed everything they thought they saw on the Upper West Side of New York: The women were hot, and the men were bums. No matter what Lewis had set out to do, he had ended up with a racist's dream, the truth and value of which were confirmed by Michael Harrington, the *New York Times, Newsweek, The New Yorker,* and the *National Book Award*.[2]

No defense of Puerto Ricans had a similar effect. A stereotype was created and internalized in a single generation. The grace of island life could not survive in the brusque middle European culture of New York—the Puerto Ricans had to change or be physically destroyed by life in the city. They chose not to die or rather to die slowly, to be defined from without, stereotyped, defeated in their persons, enduring yet another conquest. This time,

---

[2]Lewis, an Anglo anthropologist with an interest in things Latin American, also produced several books about Mexicans living in poverty. The Mexicans did not fare much better than the Puerto Ricans.

As an epilogue to this book I have included oral histories of two Latino families. Although both families have known difficult times, they are, I think, more typical of the character of Latinos than the wretched people put forward by Lewis.

I had planned to include an oral history of the López/Rojas family (the matriarchs are sisters), who came to New York from Puerto Rico, as well as another Mexican family and a Dominican family. The taping was completed, but for reasons of length I limited the number of families to one from the Caribbean and one from Mexico.

however, it was to be the last wounding of a battered bastard culture; this time it was to be the end.

Oscar Lewis would picture Puerto Ricans dying in small, hot rooms, on beds with no sheets, sweating, lubricious, third time fourth time fucking while the children waited in grandma's house, unattended by the old whore. And as if to be sure they are dead, to kill them forever, Linda Chavez, former executive director of the U.S. Commission on Civil Rights in the Reagan administration, a woman who claims to be of Spanish and Irish descent, wrote a book[3] in which, she told me, she said that "Hispanics are the same as any other ethnic group statistically, if we remove the Puerto Ricans from the category."

In fact, death is hunting the Nuyoricans on winter mornings when it is still dark and the Dominican who just bought the bodega on the corner has refused further credit. Death goes shivering into the stone cold of the subway, chasing the man who worked until three A.M. and must now begin again, riding the subway, then the train to New Jersey, two hours to work, ten hours on the job, two hours to home, and then for as long as he can keep his eyes open working again in his cousin's uncle's shop.

Whites do not open the door to dark-skinned people for any reason other than to use them. New York is a business town, a plantation; the Puerto Ricans came to work—but not to live. New York killed them; it took their health and their hopes; it locked them up in dark rooms; it gave them to the landlords for a gift, a sacrifice. Even worse, it told them who they were and made it impossible for them not to accept that external definition. The Puerto Ricans became objects, people who were not the center or the beginning of anything. In such circumstances the present time and place were unbearable. There was no comfort for them but the past. Nostalgia became the dominant factor in the Puerto Rican character; the island achieved mythical status, became the Golden Age of King Muñoz Marín and the Knights of Operation Bootstrap.

2.

They get one pat on the back here, and when they go outside they get ten slaps in the face.

Antonia Rodríguez, Principal,
Bilingual Bicultural Art School, District 4,
New York City

[3]It is a common practice among Latinos from New Mexico, like Ms. Chavez, to describe themselves as Hispanos, people with no Native American ancestors.

By the end of the 1980s statistical proof of the extraordinary pain of life for mainland Puerto Ricans became widely available: ASPIRA, a Puerto Rican social and political organization, announced that the poorest people in New York City were Puerto Rican single parent families—in 1988, they lived on an average of $205 a week. Oscar Lewis had been correct in one respect, the Puerto Ricans were poor. Even Linda Chavez had to be conceded her point: If Puerto Ricans were dropped out of the statistical sample, the profile of Latinos would look very different. Perhaps there was a culture that was no culture but poverty; perhaps the Puerto Ricans were not anybody, just fulano the poor, nothing more, nothing. I thought of Julia Arana. If anyone was condemned to the amoral life of the culture of poverty, it was Julia.

Julia lived on First Avenue and 114th Street in New York City. It is a block populated by a few remaining Italians (one of whom owns the building in which Julia and her five children live), the dregs of the Marielitos, and a mixture of Puerto Ricans, Dominicans, and perhaps a Mexican or two. Julia's tenement apartment faces a huge complex of gray housing projects. There is a small altar in front of the projects in the middle of the block. It was built by the mother of a boy who was shot to death in the street there just below Julia's third floor window. There are often shots fired in the night on 114th and First Avenue. Julia says that whenever she and the girls lie down together to sleep in the big bed beside the window they expect the sound of gunfire. When she hears the shots, she tells the girls not to stand up, to lie on the bed and keep their heads down, because a wild shot could come in through the window.[4] It is not paranoia. She watches the news on television; it has happened.

I first met Julia at a Christmas party in Upper Manhattan. She was not a member of the group that gave the party. I don't know how she got there, not that she was unwelcome. She was good humored, dressed like what used to be called a tomboy, in bluejeans and tee-shirt and a puffy, downfilled jacket. She didn't wear lipstick or perfume. I remember thinking when she sat down next to me that her face was so open I could read her dreams.

She had a tough guy's way of talking, full of gravel and street sounds born in Brooklyn. I was surprised when she said she had five children, for there was no sign of motherliness about her. She was small and slightly muscular, like a gymnast, and her conversation had a sports fan's enthusiasms. "You think that's a good school, you should see the school where my daughter goes. No, she don't go to bilingual. You got to speak English if you want to do good. I know the principal real good, because I'm helping out there. I'll get you an interview with her. When d'you want to go?"

---

[4]In the space of a few weeks in 1990 six children in New York City were killed or gravely wounded by stray bullets.

Then we shook hands. She said her name was Julia Arana. She wrote it for me on a page of my notebook: Arana. It means a trick or a swindle, Mrs. Trick.

After that, I saw her often; somehow she was always around when there was a major function in the school district in which I had arranged to observe bilingual classes for the year. We always had a moment to talk. We became pals. Julia was forever sending me somewhere, explaining something, my semi-official and for a while my official research assistant. She introduced me to the principal of the school attended by two of her daughters. I introduced her to the head of bilingual education for the district: "This is my friend, Julia Arana." She smiled. She liked to hear her name said with an English j. I said it that way.

One day she said, "Aren't you gonna interview me?"

We set a time. I told her I would ask my wife to join us. On the appointed day it was very cold. The sun goes somewhere south of Brooklyn in winter, too far from the barrio to warm the streets. No one was outside on First Avenue that afternoon. The street belonged to the wind.

Julia lives in one of the ancient tenements that line the east side of the avenue. A few of these brick buildings have been abandoned, boarded up, and left for dead. No one knows who climbs in and out of the windows and doorways behind the plywood or metal sheets. Julia says they make and sell rock cocaine in one of the buildings.

The mailboxes have been broken open in Julia's building, but the buzzer system still works. A boy carrying a brown paper bag rushed past us, hurrying up the steps, taking them two at a time, not even bothering to touch the old iron banisters. We followed him, walking two generations slower. At apartment F on the third floor Julia greeted us. She wore the usual short-sleeved knit shirt. This one had a collar and three open buttons at the throat. I thought I detected the color of cosmetics on her mouth, but it may have been the flush of excitement.

"Where are the cameras?" she asked.

I reminded her that I wrote books. Had she ever seen me with cameras? Had we ever talked about cameras? She shook her head. She said nothing, but I saw the sigh of disappointment pass through her body. Behind her on the table in the kitchen area she had laid out cold cuts and meatballs and whitebread and mustard. There was enough for the cameramen, too.

She took our coats, and in a room the width of a hallway we sat down on a couch covered with a brown blanket. I had failed her, I knew, but I did not know how. How had she made up the dream of the cameras? How? I knew why, but I did not know how.

She sat on a low chair, a child's chair, opposite us. The children gathered around. There was a homemade crèche to her left, a schoolchild's work, and to her right, on a battered metal cart, a television set and a videotape machine. It was comfortable in the apartment, but there were not enough places for Julia and her guests and all five children to sit.

The early years of Julia's life were not so different from those of any poor immigrant. Her parents came from Puerto Rico to New York. Her father was sickly, asthmatic at first and then suffering from heart disease. He worked as a carpenter when they first settled in Brooklyn, but he always liked to bake at home. Julia remembers him putting pastries on the window to cool. She filched them from the window sill, as children do in fairy tales of domestic life.

When he became ill and could not work at carpentry, life became difficult for his family. When he died, it became still more difficult. Her mother made cakes or sewed or worked as an aide at the school to add to their public assistance checks. They moved from the house of good memories in Brooklyn to the barrio (Spanish Harlem) and then to the South Bronx. Julia had two brothers who helped with the bills. The Aranas did not starve, but they did not have much. Her mother was forty-one when Julia was born. She was a very traditional woman, Julia said, one who tried to instill traditional values in her children.

At sixteen, when she was a student at Benjamin Franklin High School, which was one of the worst, most violent high schools in New York City, Julia stopped eating in the school lunchroom. She got a job in a Greek restaurant during her school lunch hour. Sometimes she worked there after school too.

It was 1970, near the end of the Vietnam War. Julia met a young marine and got pregnant. She went down to South Carolina to marry the Marine, who said he had permission from his commanding officer, but when she got there the commanding officer refused to allow them to be married. She had three children with the marine. They lived together until he beat her up, and she took her children and left. He never helped her much after that, although he did stay in touch with the children.

Julia lived briefly with her putative mother-in-law, but they did not get along. The mother-in-law put Julia and her children out into the street. Those were bad years. There were times when they did not have enough to eat. Julia said, "I thought of selling my body to get food for my children. I knew other women who did it, but I remembered how my mother brought me up, and I got through it some way without doing that.

"I didn't use no drugs. I mean I tried a little when I was young, but I didn't do it, heroin. A girl I knew, she was beautiful as a model; she got into heroin, and she was so thin, like a skeleton. I don't know why I didn't. It was the tradition from my mother."

She moved to Manhattan, lived with a Dominican, and had two more children. When he beat her up, she threw him out. The worst years followed. With five children, she moved from Queens to Manhattan, from apartment to apartment, always late with the rent, often with not enough to eat. She had a job and lost a job when she stayed home with her sick child. As the years went by, she became closer and closer to the children.

The illnesses of the children have been a terrible burden for Julia. Her second child was born with a defective heart and mismatched legs. The girl's legs were broken and shortened to make them the same size. Her heart was repaired in a very difficult operation. Then the girl had a series of convulsions, for which she was given heavy doses of phenobarbital. Now, the convulsions have passed, but she has problems with both her muscular and nervous systems.

At one point, four of Julia's five children were ill. She knows doctors, hospitals. She can recommend a heart surgeon or an orthopedist. The doctors have become her friends. The heart surgeon is interested in her children. The family that takes one of the girls every summer as part of the Fresh Air Fund has become attached to her.

Julia doesn't go out often now. She saw a Cuban man for a while, but after a few dates, she said, he wanted to move in to her house and take over, bringing his own family with him. She thinks about going out. "I get all dressed," she said, "and I even go downstairs, but when I get down there, I think about my children, and I come back up and put on my jeans and we eat some junk food and watch TV. We make a party, put out the lights, and I get some popcorn, and we watch TV like it was our own movie."

There is tragedy everywhere in her family. Her brother's child fell from a fifth floor window. When the baby's mother reached the yard where he had fallen, she picked him up, and by lifting him in her arms she caused the bones of his broken neck to sever his spinal cord and killed him. After that, two of her brother's small children were hit by cars in the street. Julia's brother left his wife then, taking the remaining children with him.

Julia's daughters by her first man have been going to New York Prep, which is one of the most innovative schools in the city. Her oldest daughter wants to be a doctor or, if not a doctor, a writer. She and a friend write plays together. Agustina, the one who had heart surgery and the operation on her legs, said she likes to write too; she always gets check plus on the stories she shows to her teacher. Julia's son, Luis, who is a gentle child and close to his mother, wants to join the marines when he finishes high school. He would like to be an architect—drawing is his talent—but he goes to a technical school, where they teach him the printing trade.

The liveliest of the children is the third daughter, the first child by the Dominican. She is pretty and plump and given to misbehaving. It is clear that she is her mother's pet, for of all the children she is the best dressed and combed, fixed up like a prize. A chocolate-skinned child, whose hair falls in thick curls, she prances and pouts and shows off her dress, which is not of winter afternoons in tenement rooms but of sunny store windows where dreamgirls in organdy make a fuss.

When the children go to school, Julia goes to beauty operator's college. Half the cost of the course is paid for by a federal grant, the other half by a bank loan guaranteed by the government. "They treated me very good when I applied," Julia said, "but now they got my money, they slam the door in my face when I ask a question. I didn't go all last week. I might not go back the way they treat me." And then she pronounces her motto, the one consistent rule in her life: "I don't take nothing from nobody."

Julia was born Puerto Rican, but that was a long time ago. She is Nuyorican now, scrappy, streetwise, tough, and crazy with dreams. "Things are getting better. I don't want to hurt it by saying so, but things are going good lately." The rent is paid. Her mother helps. The children usually eat at *Abuela*'s[5] house. The telephone is in *Abuela*'s house. Puerto Rico is in *Abuela*'s house. Hope and help are in family. Julia's brother has moved to Florida where he has a little carpentry business. "It's going good. He has two part-time helpers. I'm going down to see him right after the first of the year. I got the money already for the ticket. Maybe I'll move to Florida with my brother. Not Miami. Orlando. Orlando is where it's at."

Maybe she'll take the children with her when she goes to visit her brother to see about moving. If they miss a few days of school, it will be all right. She tells the children they can take a day off from school now and then to see a movie. "Unless they take a day off sometimes, they'll just be sleepy in class."

Julia was raised a Roman Catholic, but she went to the Pentecostal Church for a while. "I went to a meeting one day and they were collecting for a sister who didn't have nothing to eat. I was surprised when they gave the money to me—thirty-one dollars. I was really happy. We needed that money for food." She doesn't go to the Pentecostal Church anymore, although she still sees the brothers and sisters on the street. She has returned to the Catholic Church.

At the end of the afternoon, Julia sent Luis to the refrigerator to get "the special thing." It came in a brown paper bag. "Here, it's for you," Julia said, "a New Year's gift."

I protested, but Sylvia took the wine. She examined it and praised the maker. It was a kind we liked very much, she said. And when Julia offered some of the *albondigas* she and the girls had made, saying that there was too much, we should take a few of the meatballs home, Sylvia accepted those, too, all with grace and gratitude.

After many *abrazos*,[6] Sylvia and I left. Luis walked to Second Avenue with

---

[5]Grandmother
[6]Embraces

us. He had not spoken much all afternoon, but on the brief walk west and north to 116th Street, he had a lot to say. He worried about his mother, his sisters, the way she never let the girls out of the house. He worried about the gunfire in streets. Would they be safe after he left home to join the marines? He had a list of worries, a litany. Luis was seventeen, his mother was thirty-three. When he becomes a marine, he said, he would send money home.

—

The Florida trip did not work out. Luis did join the marines. Julia quit the beauty operator's school, which kept her money. There was a scene. She said again, "I don't take nothing from nobody." Now, Julia is gone. I don't know where; I haven't seen her for a year. No one answers the phone at her mother's house. There is a new principal at P.S. 206. All the connections are gone.

I should have expected that. Julia does not stay with anyone or anything for long. Nothing lasts for her but family—and culture.

For a long time I did not know how to think about Julia. To say that hers is the culture of poverty is to misunderstand completely the nostalgia of Puerto Ricans on the mainland. Their longing for the golden age of island life connects them not only to language, music, food, and custom, but to place. The Puerto Rican golden age is not a dream; it is a tree, a hill, a house open to the breeze, a culture reified in nature, art, and artifact. A mountain is not poverty. Oscar Lewis missed the point: His Puerto Ricans have no memory; his book did not contain a tree.

At night, in the near darkness of First Avenue, Julia Arana and her girls lie together on the big bed beside the only window in the herniated corridor that is their flat. And they are all rich and safe together. Julia did not abort them when she was pregnant; she did not avoid their births when she lay with their fathers. Family is wealth. It does not disappear in the bodega or the Laundromat. Every morning it is new again. Julia is never alone, never bored. She is five times fulfilled: teacher, mother, sister, nurse. She entertains and is entertained. She teaches the value of the moment and the truth that the moment is not all. She loves and is loved.

Julia does not give her blessing formally, as the older generation did; there is no hand for her children to kiss in thanks for the blessing, but the sense of *bendición* binds mother and children. It is love's orthodoxy, the nucleus of culture. Hope is not out of the question.

—

Among Latinos, the sad distinction of Puerto Ricans is that so many of them live in New York City, which is very far from paradise and no longer close to possibility. In New York City, there is no social or economic peace; there are no plateaus, no places to rest. It is never now in New York City;

tomorrow and its anxiety control the day and make an incessant and irregular noise in the night. In such a city, the gentleness of Puerto Ricans and their overdeveloped sense of loyalty is less successful every year. There are no *dichos*[7] to explain the murderous social and economic competition.

A Puerto Rican woman, a friend of many years, said she thought the failure of Puerto Ricans in New York City was due to the lack of a Puerto Rican criminal organization: "We don't sell drugs, we use them. The Italians, the Jews, the Irish, the Cubans, and now the Dominicans each established effective, highly organized criminal operations. The Puerto Ricans have not. That's been our problem. Crime gets you into this society. It gets you the money to lend to your own people at exorbitant rates, but that enables them to start small businesses. It gets you into legitimate businesses, lets you hire lawyers and accountants, and it gives you political clout. We have none."

She is a woman of accomplishment and great self-awareness; her comment on life in American cities is a bitter one, an inner-city, bottom-up perspective, but it is not to be dismissed. It reflects much of the frustration and envy of the Puerto Rican community in New York and the sense of being a minority among minorities, different somehow, without much luck. *"Bendito,"* the Puerto Ricans say, but with an ironic overtone, for there are few Puerto Ricans who believe they are blessed. Life has been too difficult; the winters have been too cold.

The other side of the criminal theory is a curious, inside out version of conservative social theory: If the other immigrants succeeded, it must be because they are bad; therefore, the Puerto Ricans failed because they are good. Underlying the theory is the lack of aggressiveness of many Puerto Ricans—the fatalism that psychologists sometimes call depression—of the generation of people who came in the first wave of migration at the end of World War II.

Many Puerto Ricans say now of themselves, "We just get the worst ones here, for the welfare.[8] On the island, it's not so poor. The Dominican Republic is poor, not Puerto Rico." The distinction such people draw between rich and poor is elemental and accurate: Running water, electricity, and television are the signs of development. Many who leave the Dominican Republic for Puerto Rico, where they mix in with the rest of the population on the way north to New York, come from towns where water and electricity are uncertain. They risk a dangerous ocean crossing to Puerto Rico, but it is worth the risk to them, for the life of the poor in the Dominican Republic is dreadful. During the great wave of northward migration from Puerto Rico it simply was not so; people were poor, but life was not unbearable.

---

[7]Sayings, proverbs

[8]The impression is not correct. Puerto Ricans who moved to the mainland during the 1980s and early 1990s were better educated and of higher economic status than ever before.

The immigrant histories differ in tone from those of other groups. Puerto Rico is a U.S. commonwealth. It was, and remains, at a lower level of development than the rest of the country, but it could not be described accurately as an underdeveloped country. One cannot make statistics of the dreams of immigrants, but many of their personal histories follow a pattern. When Domingo Figueroa left Santurce for New York, he was the owner of eight houses and a yard-goods store. Why did he leave the solidity of that life for unknown New York? His children charge him with ambition: "When a man has something, he always wants more."

He came alone, leaving his family in Santurce. His wife ran the store; his children grew up. But life in New York did not produce more for Domingo Figueroa. Instead of riches, he found a grim job, and out of the job came an industrial accident that ruined him. Cleaning solution splashed into his eyes. He went to a doctor, who apparently did not wash his eyes with the proper antidote. He went to more doctors. The illness devoured the houses and then the store. The doctors removed one of his eyes, then the other. At the age of ninety-four, without eyes, he waited out his time in a government hospital, visited by his children and grandchildren. They said he was still a strong man, one who did not let his blindness deter him from dancing whenever he heard music.

Edward Rivera, the novelist, writes of such families, men who are never late to work, but who eventually suffer betrayal by their bosses and their bodies. Rivera's picture of Puerto Rican life in New York City is not sensational, but it is perhaps the most accurate picture available, far more reliable than the work of Piri Thomas or Oscar Lewis. Nicholasa Mohr's novels produce the same picture: people with working-class or lower–middle-class values whose hopes are frustrated by city life. Puerto Ricans in New York City have suffered from the diseases of stress and loyalty. Heart disease, strokes, accidents, ulcers, and cancer take away their health, their livelihood, and eventually their lives, and through it all they remain loyal to the employers who betray them.

The story of the layoff of a longtime, loyal employee that Rivera tells in *While Someone Else Is Eating* is so common to Puerto Ricans in New York that were it not for the wealth of detail in his writing the life of the man he calls Segundo would be a commonplace. It happens again and again: Puerto Ricans work in marginal businesses; they have no unions, no benefits, nothing but the weekly paycheck, from which social security may or may not have been deducted and paid; the employers milk the business, transferring every cent out of the little corporation into their private accounts; when the marginal business goes broke after a few or even many years or when the owners decide to liquidate the business and retire, the loyal Puerto Rican employee, fulano, is left with nothing, literally and figuratively out in the cold.

Lacking money, medical insurance, and hope, the Puerto Rican man set-
tles into patriarchy and machismo; he plays dominoes and sings songs, and
sometimes he drinks. If the break in his life plan comes early enough, the
affront to his manhood of betrayal and broken dreams will excite his machismo, and he will become an abusive husband before his wife throws him
out.

In the 1970s the Puerto Rican community—relieved of the pressure of
the Cubans, who came to the barrio, established businesses, made some
money, and moved out—was enjoying a renaissance. The stranglehold of
the old ethnics on the school system had finally been broken, and Puerto
Rican teachers, many of them bilingual, were moving into teaching and
supervisory positions. Nuyoricans were graduating from two- and four-year
colleges and professional schools. The stores and shops in the barrio were
owned by people who lived in the barrio. La Marketa (or Marqueta) was
thriving on Park Avenue under the railroad tracks; many of the stalls had
been rented to Puerto Ricans. Barriers seemed to be breaking down everywhere in the good feeling carried over from the sixties; Puerto Ricans were
marrying into the immigrant strivers groups of the city. The most famous
marriage was that of Herman and Irma Badillo, a Puerto Rican who was
elected to the U.S. House of Representatives and a scrappy New York Jew. In
Spanish Harlem, the superintendent of School District 4, Anthony Alvarado,
was creating a successful experiment. Awilda Orta, the principal of Interme-
diate School 99, informally known as Jailhouse 99, had taken over one of the
sloughs of the city's educational system and turned it into a place where
teachers taught and students were anxious to learn.

The single greatest sign of health in the community was the establishment
of the Museo del Barrio in a storefront on Third Avenue. One exhibition
consisted of a series of installations depicting life in the barrio. In the centerpiece a conical orange nose adorned the grotesquely predatory face of the
Statue of Liberty. A battered suitcase lay at her feet. Dollars emerged from her
dress. In one hand she carried a large electric light bulb and with the other
she offered brochures in Spanish and English explaining the food-stamp
program. In the rooms around her, human brains were sold on the cheap,
defaced political posters and advertisements for salsa concerts crowded the
walls; a shrouded body, that of a recent murder victim, lay on the floor of a
dark corridor; a Caribbean forest held altars and *cemíes,* the stone gods of the
Tainos. A window looked in upon a narrow bed and a crucifix in a dimly lit
room. The exhibition was a series of confrontations: Arrive at the moment of
being able to look at yourself, laugh, and go on, the artists urged.

Since no one came to the barrio to review the show, the artists looked to
the community to learn how their work was received. In the office of the
storefront, on a three-legged desk, they put out a guest book. A group of

them gathered around to read the comment left by an old woman who laboriously wrote out a single sentence: "It lacks only the smell of rice and beans and the *pillo* [literally, "the mischief," but in the barrio an illegal tap on the wires of the hated Consolidated Edison]."

The series of installations in the storefront museum and the old woman's comment about them pointed to the strangling connection of the Puerto Ricans to governmental and quasi-governmental institutions. If the exhibits or the *pillo* left any doubt about the nature of the relationship, José Antonio Vázquez, a young photographer, clarified it. "The young people call the Welfare the Gestapo, because they're like the Nazis in the movies; they don't even look up at you, they just say, 'Papers, let me see your papers.' "

As the recession and the Reagan administration—combined with the arrival of the aggressive Dominican population—drove the Puerto Rican community backwards by every social and economic measure, the truth of what the artists and the old woman thought was borne out: Like no other newcomers in the history of New York City, the Puerto Ricans were at the mercy of their government. And it was more than economic dependence that weighed on them: They were psychological prisoners of the state.

3.

One cannot observe Puerto Rican life close up without reaching the conclusion that every form of tutelage is morally degrading. As long as sovereignty does not reside in us, there will be genuflections and degradations before those in whom it does reside. This is the political illness of colonial Puerto Rico, and its only cure is a dose of unadulterated sovereignty.   Luis Muñoz Marín

When I asked Puerto Ricans to define their essence in a word, the answer that came most often from ordinary people was, "partying." Two other answers amplified that notion and further separated Puerto Ricans from other Latinos: "struggling" and "conquered." The notion of a people who are interested in partying (if that is a word) conforms with the opinion other Latinos hold of Puerto Ricans. There is nothing pejorative in that view, as there is in the idea that Puerto Ricans come to the mainland for no other purpose than to get welfare checks; it describes a happy-go-lucky attitude toward life, one that can be enormously attractive, although difficult to live with or to do business with.

Unfortunately, in this instance partying probably has more to do with despair than happiness; "happy-go-lucky" isn't so much rooted in love of the present as fear of the future. The partying mentality is often exhibited by troops expecting to go into battle or men in very dangerous jobs. To say that two-and-a-half million Puerto Ricans on the mainland have the same world-view as men about to go into combat implies a tragic essence. It can be heard in the comment of William López, a young Puerto Rican corporate executive: "I'm worried. Things are just going too good. Everything's falling into place. It's just too good. I'm really starting to worry." The sense of impending disaster so affected a Puerto Rican investor that he took to buying gold, expecting a recession. When I reminded him that buying gold is considered good protection against inflation rather than recession, he said I didn't understand how bad things could get: "You can always barter gold, get food with it, if you need it." When I asked what kind of terrible disaster could cause gold to be useful that way, he said, "You'll see."

Struggle in the Puerto Rican world is not a struggle to succeed in business or other practical aspects of life; it is an Aristotelian struggle against fate, the classic situation of the tragic hero in literature. When the murderous cuts in social programs were instituted by the Reagan administration, many people in the Puerto Rican community shrugged—it was to be expected—but one man I know of jumped out the window of his fifth floor apartment when he could no longer pay the rent; not everyone from Puerto Rico is happy-go-lucky.

"Conquest" describes the Puerto Rican character for fewer people, and it may be that they mean to speak of a cause rather than an effect, but that is not what they say. "Conquered," is the answer to the question about essence not about history. Few nations, if any, in human history have not been conquered at one time or another, but to be conquered and to have been conquered are entirely different situations. Puerto Ricans consider themselves conquered now—not occupied, not defeated, but conquered. Occupied nations live in the expectation of overthrowing the enemies on their land, defeated nations hope to fight again, but those who are conquered have niether the wherewithal nor the will to overcome their situation; they live in hope that some external force will free them—gods, spirits, Russians, the lottery, or death. A conquered people cannot be other than fatalistic.

"Struggle" seems, at first, to describe the opposite of conquered, but that interpretation does not hold up to scrutiny; "struggle" in the context of the Puerto Rican character means the struggle to survive, the attempt to overcome one's fate. Without the aspect of struggle, the Puerto Rican character would be dolorous rather than tragic, the partying an expression of despair rather than a rage against the past. Without partying, the Puerto Ricans would not be wounded, they would be dead.

Almost all serious thinking about Puerto Rico and Puerto Ricans devolves from the ideas of Luis Muñoz Marín. Muñoz was not only the political leader of the island from 1940 through 1968, as senator, governor, and power behind the governor, he was the discoverer of the dangerous effect of colonialism on the character of the people. Like José Martí, he spent his youth in New York City where he first made his reputation as a writer. Muñoz Marín, the son of the man who won Puerto Rico's independence from Spain, was a poet and a good one. He was known affectionately in Puerto Rico as The Bard, El Vate.

When El Vate chose to enter politics in Puerto Rico, he encountered an island in poverty. It was one of the poorest places in Latin America, exploited by agricultural interests and despised by the country that controlled it. Puerto Rico was divided by race and class. Blacks were excluded from clubs and even political parties. The poor *jíbaros* who lived up in the hills were undernourished, illiterate, often unemployed, not even part of the sugar economy. Muñoz made them his special concern. In his famous political campaign as head of a new party, he went up into the hills to meet the voters. *¡Jalda arriba!* was the description of his campaign as well as his slogan. He went up the hill to the voters, and he intended to bring Puerto Rico up the hill to development and prosperity.

He was elected governor in 1948, and by the time his party was voted out of office twenty years later he had transformed the island from the poorest to the richest place in Latin America. He had used a mix of socialism and capitalism to increase per capita income from $118 in 1940 to $1,200 in 1970. He used public funds to build the cement plants to create the roads for the infrastructure necessary to industrialization, and then he used the tax advantages of Operation Bootstrap to bring industry to the island. The irony of his success did not escape El Vate, however. It had been his hope to maintain the character of the *jíbaro* in an industrialized society, and in that he had failed; by 1968 the man who had developed the island's economy was campaigning for serenity. He said the noise level was too high in the cities, literally beyond the point at which it was said to cause pain to human beings; he fought to bring back the tranquil culture of the *jíbaro,* and his Popular Democratic party was defeated.

The psychologist and director of the Roberto Clemente Family Guidance Center on the Loisaida of New York, Jaime E. Inclán, finds Muñoz at the very center of the Puerto Rican character. He agrees with Muñoz that the chief issue in the Puerto Rican character is the problem of self-esteem, which Muñoz called by its more meaningful name—self-respect—and that the Spanish and U.S. conquests weigh heavily in Puerto Ricans' judgment of themselves. Inclán goes beyond the question of colonialism to the role of

Muñoz Marín himself in Puerto Rican psychology. He reasons that the first generation Puerto Ricans came to the mainland full of the dreams of success taught by Muñoz. El Vate had created an atmosphere in which anything seemed possible for Puerto Rico and Puerto Ricans. When the first wave of migrants, which Inclán calls the "beachhead generation," came to the mainland, Puerto Rico was in the bloom of development.

They found no such opportunity in New York City. Within a few years they became known as "the Puerto Rican problem." Landlords gouged them, employers took advantage of them, nothing worked for them, and they sank into a mire of self-doubt; the job of succeeding in New York was given to their children. Of these first two generations Inclán writes: "Puerto Ricans were able to survive marginally and to channel towards the self the blame and the anger that took the place of the shock. Muñoz Marín's rhetoric could not reach New York. The delusion of the man and the Island could persist, frozen like the myth of the return in memory and hope. Immediate reality was harsh and stagnant: wages low, racism rampant, winter months returned. It was not the time for 'our place in the sun.' Muñoz Marín retired from island politics in 1968 and exiled himself to Europe until his death in the summer of 1980. Ironically, second generation Puerto Ricans who hardly knew Muñoz the man, but who were expected by their parents to live his dreams, had the job, unbeknownst to them, of mourning him."

He goes on, "The low self-esteem and self-blame of the current second generation of Puerto Ricans is alarming to other Hispanics, who caricature Puerto Ricans as the only Latins who condemn themselves, reject their own peoples and products as inferior, and 'prefer' to work for others rather than for themselves—as demonstrated by the lowest percentage of businesses owned by themselves. One can only speculate that the over four hundred years of colonialism, as well as the attacks on nationalist sentiments by the left and right during the last fifteen years, must have significantly contributed to this depressive dynamism of collective and personal self."

The crisis, in his view, occurs in the third generation of Puerto Ricans, "who symbolically can be said to [have been] born in the summer of 1980, with the death of Muñoz Marín." As a prescription for the third generation, Inclán calls for "the rechanneling on to external objects of an anger that is addressed to the self." To do this he sees a need for the anger to be legitimized by political leaders in the community, but not, he argues, following "the patriarchal models of centralized control of power á la Muñoz Marín."

———

On a humid summer night in the New York City barrio the streets smell like a slaughterhouse. The customers in El Caribeño are mixed Puerto Rican and Dominican, but the owner and all the waitresses are Dominicans. The dishes on the menu are Dominican or vaguely Spanish, but there is a sign on the refrigerator advising that they have mavi, a Puerto Rican drink made of tree sap. Although it is not on the menu, the mofongo is magnificent, fresh and rich with little pieces of pork. At the next table a Dominican woman is dousing her tostones with catsup instead of dipping the fried plantains in garlic sauce. Two Puerto Ricans watch the act of culinary sacrilege with a mixture of pity and disgust. The jukebox plays only merengues. High above the door to the kitchen, next to the shelf on which the television set rests, is a statue of Santa Barbara and a votive candle to honor the great goddess of Santería. The manager of the restaurant comes in late, after the summer rain has passed and the water in the streets has turned to steam. He is light-skinned, dressed in a guayabera,[10] a slim man with a fierce Spanish nose and Caribbean laughter. The dark-skinned waitresses attend him. He crackles with efficiency, importance. Everyone notices the owner.

Outside, on the next corner, under the awning of the bodega, four men play dominoes, holding the board on their knees, keeping it twice as steady as a four-legged table. The men are young, in their thirties; it is a surprise to see such young men playing dominoes on a weekend night. They drink beer, concentrate, clack, clack, clack, clack-clack, clack. Game. Curse. Chat. English. The losers turn the dominoes over the moment the score is counted. They stir the pieces. Each man picks seven and puts them in the small wooden stand in front of him. Double six, clack, clack, clack—Faster than bridge or poker or gin rummy, every man counts every number on the board, estimating the points in each hand, the lead players speaking to each through the choice of plays—clack, clack-clack, clack. The sign above the bodega is yellow; the streets stink and shine. The youngest man wears white sneakers and shows a stylish haircut, short on top and long at the neck. Clack, clack. Game. Curse. English chatter. Turn and mix. Double six. Clack, clack. Drink. Clack.

Two blocks away, next to the funeral home, down the street from the Pentecostal church, the neighborhood social club has opened for the night. Couples drift in. They are middle-aged and older. One man wears a cap to hide his baldness; another man shows his full head of white hair. The women have thickened. Two couples meet for the first time, introduced by the woman in the pants suit who serves dollar beers and talks to the customers in her thick voice. The couples ask the Puerto Rican question of each other: Where are you from?

"The capital."

"Oh, the capital! Santo Domingo!"

"I'm Puerto Rican. Born in the capital. And you?"

---

[10]A loose-fitting shirt, usually white, worn outside the trousers

"Camagüey."

"Ay, Camagüey!"

They sit down together, order beer, and talk loudly. The man with the white hair dances the merengue with a woman who is surely his wife; their little steps are as practiced as budgets or breakfasts.

The social club is one room in a basement with a homemade bar at the near end facing a television set and a fan across the room twenty-five feet away. There are two toilets, each with the same hand-printed sign: "No más una persona en baño. No more than one person in bathroom." In the Spanish version of each sign someone has made a carat and written in the article "el" before "baño." The English remains uncorrected.

Every social club has the same purpose: partying. In this club, all the preparations have been made for every possible kind of party. The ceiling and the walls are hung with crepe paper decorations, ribbons, and signs: hearts for Valentine's Day, jack-o'-lanterns for Halloween, posters for Puerto Rican cultural celebrations, and suspended from the low ceiling dozens of ribbons bearing the words, "HAPPY BIRTHDAY." Partying and Puerto Rico, homesickness and the moment, the limits of the world in which there is no tomorrow.

Outside, on the streets, the people have begun to come out after the rain. Unadorned women and their children gather in front of the Pentecostal church; something is going on in the funeral home. Near the corner, in a doorway, a young man dressed in dark clothing and gold jewelry beckons. An abandoned building has been closed with metal shutters and padlocked. Two doors down a boy puts a radio on a milk crate beside the stoop, flicks the switch, and lets salsa blare. The slaughterhouse stench of the streets grows with the heat that comes back at the end of the rain. Two men in their early twenties hurry home to their fifth floor walkup apartment. They are first cousins, Puerto Ricans, but not from the city. The barrio frightens them. They avoid walking down deserted streets; they stay out near the curb, in the light, away from the doorways. They are young, middle-class men with middle-class ambitions, still subtle, still flexible, without the Nuyorican bluntness; they will live in the barrio until the first day on which they can afford to leave.

7

ZUTANO DE MEXICO

Mejicanos and Mexican-Americans differ from other Latinos by duration and number, as well as by character. Most Latinos in the United States, perhaps two-thirds or more, are of Mexican descent. Some are here temporarily, part of the labor force that fills the lowest paying, most onerous jobs; others have been here for generations. If one includes some of the early settlers of the Southwest who came from Spain via Mexico as Mexican, the Mexican-American community is moving toward its sixth century in what is now the United States. Unlike the Cubans, mainland Puerto Ricans, and other Latinos, most of whom arrived in the second half of the twentieth century, the Mexican-Americans live in the light of their own history in the United States.

Several scholars, among them Mario García and Rodolfo Alvarez, have begun to break down this long history into distinct periods of development. Alvarez, writing in 1973, described four generations: "The 'Creation Generation,' characterized by economic subjugation and being the object of race and ethnic prejudice, appeared in 1848 when the Mexican-American people were created as a people by the signing of the Treaty of Guadalupe Hidalgo. By 1900 the majority of Mexican-Americans were members of the 'Migrant Generation' who left a lower-class status in Mexico to enter a lower-caste status in the United States. Around the time of World War II there developed another state of collective consciousness termed here the 'Mexican-American Generation.' This generation moved to the cities, experienced some upward mobility, and managed to establish their claims as bonafide citizens of the United States in the eyes of only one of the social psychologically relevant populations—themselves. Finally, in the late 1960s, a new consciousness began to make itself felt among the Mexican-Americans with the emergence of the 'Chicano Generation.' "

García adds a fifth generation, which he calls "post-chicano." He says of this current generation, "Mexican-American leadership on the whole has seemed more disposed to conform to the conservative temper of the times. Mexican-American leaders, besides pursuing a reduced agenda on the civil rights front, have allowed government and the mass media to define them as 'Hispanics' and thus obliterate or disguise the historically based effort by Mexican-Americans at self-definition.

". . . To regain . . . momentum this new political generation will need to discard the historical amnesia of the 1980s, so well revealed in Richard Rodriguez's classic statement of the decade, *Hunger of Memory,* and instead recapture a 'memory of history'—a history of uncompromising dedication and struggle for full equality with other Americans."

Events in Mexico at the beginning of the twentieth century created a special cohort of Mexican-Americans, less than a generation but more than an anomaly: the educated and often wealthy families who left the country during the Revolution of 1910. These exiles were much like the people who came from Cuba in the 1960s and the first wave of Nicaraguans who left after the overthrow of the Somoza regime in the 1980s; they quickly established themselves as an elite. Most of them planned to go back to Mexico as soon as political and economic conditions returned to normal, and indeed many of them did eventually reclaim lands and lives temporarily lost to the revolution that degenerated into a civil war. Those who stayed did not become immigrants until long after they arrived in the United States.

During the sixties it was proper for people who called themselves chicanos to think of the Mexican-American generation as docile, assimilationist, utterly bourgeois in its goals and attitudes. In fact, as Mario García has demonstrated in two volumes of Mexican-American history, the parents of the chicanos were not all *vendidos;* although many did sell out, or attempt to sell out, others fought for change. There was a union movement, particularly among the mine workers in West Texas and New Mexico. In California there was a radical faction allied with the Communist party, if not controlled by it. An intellectual tradition was growing in New Mexico and Texas, and LULAC, the League of United Latin American Citizens, although middle class to a fault, was fighting against segregation in schools, theaters, and swimming pools. It was a difficult time. The word "Mexican" was so connected with prejudice that the members of LULAC decided to call themselves Latins in an attempt to improve their status.

Consciousness of the United States as a deeply racist nation, one that used racism for purposes of economic exploitation, came during the generation of World War II veterans. Measured by the number of Medal of Honor winners who were Mexican-American and the rate at which Mexican-Americans suffered casualties, no other racial or ethnic group served with greater courage. According to Raúl Morín, who wrote *Among the Valiant,* 25 percent of the U.S. soldiers on the Bataan Death March were Mexican-Americans. Yet in June of 1943 in California, hundreds of young Mejicanos and Mexican-Americans were beaten and stripped of their zoot suits by Anglo soldiers and sailors. The Los Angeles police provided no protection for the Latinos; instead of arresting the rioting soldiers and sailors, they arrested hundreds of their victims. According to some historians, it was only the intervention of the military police that stopped the Zoot Suit Riots from becoming a full-scale mutiny by the military. In Los Angeles, the Latinos found no allies in local government or in the press; when Eleanor Roosevelt blamed the riots on "longstanding discrimination against the Mexicans in the Southwest," the Los Angeles *Times* took her to task for her views.

The veterans came home angered and disillusioned by the riots, but there was worse news to come. In Three Rivers, Texas, a funeral parlor refused to bury Félix Longoria, a Mexican-American soldier who had been decorated for heroism in World War II. Rage over the Longoria case (he was finally buried in Arlington National Cemetery) led Dr. Hector García of Corpus Christi to found the American GI Forum. It was exactly what the vets had been looking for. Within a few months, there were a hundred chapters. As the name implies, its members wished to obliterate any distinction between themselves and the rest of society.

World War II, more than any other event, changed the character of the Mexican-American. A people that had won more Medals of Honor than any other racial or ethnic group during the war could not feel quite so humble at home. The private machismo of the man who suffered humiliations in public was no longer the only solace for the Mexican-American husband; a public expression of anger was possible. War had also given Mexican-Americans the chance to serve as commissioned and noncommissioned officers. Men who had commanded Anglo troops in battle did not cringe before them in civilian life; the experience of command and of observing others in command taught them that they did not have to resort to the role of overseer in order to have power. Sergeants and captains and buck privates turned into professional men and entrepreneurs; the vets no longer felt like intruders in a strange country. They were Americans, men who had fought for *their* country. It was a melting-pot army, one in which Mexican-Americans had often been treated as white ethnics. Nearly half a million Latinos, most of them of Mexican descent, came home from the war with one idea in mind: They had been Americans; they could be Americans; they didn't want to be Mexican anymore.

Until the war, few Mejicanos or Mexican-Americans had gone beyond high school. Language problems, segregated schools, and economic pressures made it almost impossible for them to go to college. Furthermore, parents were reluctant to see their children, especially daughters, go far from home. Junior college or the local branch of a state university was all that was available even to the few students who could overcome the economic barriers. The GI Bill and the independence from family pressures learned in years away from home during the war suddenly made it possible for thousands of Mexican-Americans to earn college degrees. The burden of violent necessity had been lifted from an entire generation; World War II ended a hundred years of feudalism in the American Southwest.

If any one person embodied the change that came over the Mexican-American community after the war, it was a young veteran from El Paso, Texas, Raymond L. Telles, who had joined the army as a private and been discharged with the rank of major. His family had been involved in local politics, but no one had dared to run for office until they persuaded Raymond to take the chance. In 1948 he was elected county clerk. Nine years later he ran for mayor. There had not been a Mexican-American mayor of a major city in the Southwest in the twentieth century when Raymond Telles entered the Democratic primary.

The El Paso newspapers were split on his candidacy. The *Times* supported the establishment candidate in the Democratic primary, which was the only contest in Texas in 1957. The *Herald-Post,* edited by E. M. Pooley, sided with Telles. I knew Pooley slightly, having worked for him as a reporter during that period. He was the most unpleasant decent man I ever met. The city editor, a gentleman who wore a green eyeshade, was terrified of him. The only young reporter he ever showed any interest in was Rubén Salazar. Pooley was crotchety, miserable, opinionated, and on the decent side of almost every issue. He fought like a lion for the election of Raymond Telles. He defended him against charges of cronyism and communism. He lauded Telles and excoriated his opponent day after day, partly because he believed in Raymond L. Telles and partly, I think, because he hated the owner and the editor of the extremely conservative morning paper.

Telles had another important ally in the race. As part of his ticket, he had chosen Ted Bender, the popular television weatherman and the host of the town's only talk show on radio. Bender had a phenomenal memory for facts, which somehow convinced his audience that he was a man of great wisdom. Since the majority of the citizens were Latino, but the majority of the voters were Anglo, Bender's willingness to support Telles by running on the People's party ticket with him may have been the deciding factor.

Whatever combination of factors gave Telles the election, on April 1, 1957, he became the mayor of El Paso, Texas. It was a victory for the liberals, for LULAC, for the VFW and the unions. Raymond Telles, a tall, thin man, an officer and gentleman in his bearing and his language, had come home from the war and won self-respect for every Mexican-American in Texas.

At the same time, in the same town, another man named Tellez (the names were pronounced the same although spelled differently) had become the leading radio and television personality. Rudy Tellez[1] was also a veteran. Unlike the mayor, who went to business college, Rudy Tellez had a real bachelor's degree from Texas Western College (now the University of Texas at El Paso). Although he was fluent in Spanish, he spoke English with a network announcer's accent and precision. At KTSM he was the guy with show business connections, a mixture of Hollywood and New York, interested in politics, music, and theater, the most up-to-date man in town. And when we jumped into his Triumph sports car and went across the border to a tiny homestyle restaurant in Ciudad Juárez to have the *comida corrida,* he was as comfortable with the Mexican version of the blue plate special as any person in the room.

—

A third Mexican-American reached prominence at the same time: In the El Paso police department Arturo Islas[2] was promoted to lieutenant and then to captain. When he joined the department in 1942, he was only the seventh Mexican-American on the force. Thirty years later, long since retired with the rank of inspector, he remembered the difficulties of getting ahead in the department. He spoke of the other Latinos as men who were still uncomfortable going into downtown restaurant to have a cup of coffee. They were men who were satisfied with being in the department; they didn't even take the examinations for promotion—not Islas. When he was passed over for sergeant in favor of an Anglo who scored lower than he did on the test, he complained. He didn't get anywhere, he said, until Ed Pooley "interceded with the powers that be" on his behalf.

Islas achieved near legendary stature as a policeman. He was known as

---

[1]Rudy and I worked together for several years. He and his wife, Yvette, and my wife and I were close friends. When Rudy and his family moved to San Francisco, we followed in a few months. Rudy and I had plans to go into business together, but we had little capital and less luck. He stayed in broadcasting, eventually becoming the producer of the "Tonight Show" on the NBC network.

[2]He is the father of the novelist Arturo Islas, Jr.

the smartest detective, the toughest cop, the best diplomat with other law enforcement agencies. He had a certain lack of finesse, however, in dealing with superiors in his own department: When he felt he was ill-treated in some way, he said, he did not hesitate to advise the person who had wronged him to "kiss the Mexican side of my ass," even if that person was the chief of police.

Going into the 1960s, the Mexican-American generation seemed to have won its rightful place in El Paso, the traditional starting place for Mexicans in the United States. Rubén Salazar was a trouble maker, but a brilliant reporter. Ray Sánchez was the sports editor of the *Herald-Post,* Raymond Telles was the mayor of the town, Art Islas was the best known cop, Rudy Tellez was El Paso's favorite son, and Ed Pooley assured Mexican-Americans a public voice in the English-language media. The Anglos still had all the money, but the Telles election had proved that, despite the poll tax, Mexican-Americans would vote in larger numbers than anyone expected and that Anglos did not necessarily vote along straight ethnic lines.

The first year of the new decade gave even more hope to the generation of assimilationists: A Roman Catholic was elected president of the United States, and he owed his victory, in part, to the Mexican-American vote in Texas. The poll tax was dead. Passage of some sort of civil rights act was possible. Federally funded health care for the poor was promised. On the left, there was a different view: While there had been some outstanding Latino successes in towns like El Paso during the fifties, the systemic problems had not been overcome. The number of employed people in the city of El Paso doubled during the decade, but per capita income actually fell. In San Antonio, half of the Mejicanos and Mexican-Americans were living without indoor plumbing. Economic conditions in South Texas were worse.

In Los Angeles, Edward Roybal had been elected to the city council in 1949, the first Mexican-American to sit on the council since 1881. But Edmund G. Brown, Sr., the governor of California during most of the sixties, named only thirty Mexican-Americans among his first five thousand appointees, arguing that there were no qualified Mexicans in the state. Mexican-American children who could not speak English when they entered California schools were still put into classes for the mentally retarded. It was the same everywhere: The Mexican-American generation had made history, they had proved that change was possible, but they had not created a revolution. For most Mejicanos and Mexican-Americans in the United States in 1960 life was still miserable.

The chicano generation began in the late 1960s and lasted about six or eight years, dying slowly through the seventies. Nothing remains of it now but a handshake practiced by middle-aged men. Some people still call themselves chicanos, but the definition is vague and the word has lost its fire. Six months before he was killed, Rubén Salazar wrote a column for the Los Angeles *Times* in which he attempted to define the chicano concept for both Mexican-Americans and Anglos. This concept emerged early in the movement, and it had strong assimilationist overtones. It is of historical value to reprint the column here, for it was a bridge between the Mexican-American and chicano generations, a moderate position.

Salazar, who was born in Chihuahua, should have known the original meaning of the word chicano.[3] If not, he could certainly have asked his father. Perhaps he did, and then chose not to use the answer in his column for fear of giving ammunition to the enemy. The column, reprinted below, has a few of the oversights common to daily journalism. The history of the newspaper demanded that Rubén write with some discretion, for the Los Angeles *Times,* which had been overtly anti-Mexican since it began publishing in the nineteenth century, was just beginning to learn under Rubén's tutelage that Latinos were sentient creatures. The style reflects the short paragraphs and simple sentences taught by Rubén's mentor, Ed Pooley, who railed against fancy writing and posted notes on the city room bulletin board about the sixth-grade reading level of newspaper readers.

A chicano is a Mexican-American with a non-Anglo image of himself.

He resents being told Columbus "discovered" America when the chicano's ancestors, the Mayans and the Aztecs, founded highly sophisticated civilizations centuries before Spain financed the Italian explorer's trip to the "New World."

Chicanos resent also Anglo pronouncements that chicanos are "culturally deprived" or that the fact that they speak Spanish is a "problem."

Chicanos will tell you that their culture predates that of the Pilgrims and that Spanish was spoken in America before English and so the "problem" is not theirs but the Anglos' who don't speak Spanish.

Having told you that, the chicano will then contend that Anglos are Spanish-oriented at the expense of Mexicans.

They will complain that when the governor dresses up as a Spanish nobleman for the Santa Barbara fiesta he's insulting Mexicans because the Spanish conquered and exploited the Mexicans.

It's as if the governor dressed like an English Redcoat for a Fourth of July parade, chicanos say.

[3]In Chihuahua, a chicano was a *marrano* or small pig, according to Joaquín Avila, Sr., and others. The very poor and people who labored at the lowest level were known as chicanos. Although the word was derogatory, it was the mildest of insults. Nevertheless, many older people continue to be appalled at the use of the term to describe people of Mexican descent.

On the issue of capitalization, I have not used an initial capital letter, just as I would not use an initial capital for black, brown, gringo, or white.

When you think you know what chicanos are getting at, a Mexican-American will tell you that chicano is an insulting term and may even quote the Spanish Academy to prove that chicano derives from chicanery.

A chicano will scoff at this and say that such Mexican-Americans have been brainwashed by Anglos and that they're Tio Tacos (Uncle Toms). This type of Mexican-American, chicanos will argue, doesn't like the word chicano because it's abrasive to their Anglo-oriented minds.

These poor people are brown Anglos, chicanos will smirk.

What, then, is a chicano? Chicanos say that if you have to ask you'll never understand, much less become a chicano.

Actually, the word chicano is as difficult to define as "soul."

For those who like simplistic answers, chicano can be defined as short for Mexicano. For those who prefer complicated answers, it has been suggested that chicano may have come from the word Chihuahua—the name of a Mexican state bordering on the United States. Getting trickier, this version then contends that Mexicans who migrated to Texas call themselves chicanos because having crossed into the United States from Chihuahua they adopted the first three letters of that state, Chi, and then added cano, for the latter part of Texano.

Such explanations, however, tend to miss the whole point as to why Mexican-American activists call themselves chicanos.

Mexican-Americans, the second largest minority in the country and the largest in the Southwestern states (California, Texas, New Mexico and Colorado), have always had difficulty making up their minds what to call themselves.

In New Mexico they call themselves Spanish-Americans. In other parts of the Southwest they call themselves Americans of Mexican descent, people with Spanish surnames or Hispanos.

Why, ask some Mexican-Americans, can't we just call ourselves Americans?

Chicanos are trying to explain why not. Mexican-Americans, though indigenous to the Southwest, are on the lowest rung scholastically, economically, socially and politically. Chicanos feel cheated. They want to effect change. Now.

Mexican-Americans average eight years of schooling compared to the Negroes' ten years. Farm workers, most of whom are Mexican-Americans in the Southwest, are excluded from the National Labor Relations Act unlike other workers. Also, Mexican-Americans often have to compete for low-paying jobs with their Mexican brothers from across the border who are willing to work for even less. Mexican-Americans have to live with the stinging fact that the word Mexican is the synonym for inferior in many parts of the Southwest.

That is why Mexican-American activists flaunt the barrio word chicano—as an act of defiance and a badge of honor. Mexican-Americans, though large in numbers, are so politically impotent that in Los Angeles, where the country's largest single concentration of Spanish-speakers live, they have no one of their own on the City Council.[4] This, in a city politically sophisticated enough to have three Negro councilmen.

Chicanos, then, are merely fighting to become "Americans." Yes, but with a chicano outlook.

The movement had no official beginning. It may have started in the mid-sixties with the Brown Berets or in 1967 with the publication of the epic poem *I Am Joaquín,* by the former professional boxer, Rodolfo "Corky" Gonzales. The chicanos showed their power for the first time in Los Angeles in March of 1968 when ten thousand students walked out of barrio high schools. The Brown Berets were cited by some public officials and journalists as the organizers of the walkout. In reality, the Brown Berets were a poor imitation of the Black Panthers, and, like the Panthers, they were wildly romanticized in the newspapers. The leaders of both organizations exhibited the style of charming ferocity required of radicals in America, but their followers were platoons of children, many of them seeking to overcome some physical or emotional handicap by wearing the appropriate headgear and marching in line, if not in step.

No one noticed the reality of the Brown Berets. The myth of resistance, of an army of Mejicanos as politically pure as Zapatistas and as tough as Pancho Villa's Division del Norte, fed the spirit of Chicanismo. The Brown Berets were the dream marines of the movement, Mejicanos who scared the gringos. There were more walkouts.

Chicano students protested in Colorado, Texas, and Arizona. The complaints were always the same: poor facilities, racism, cultural bias, and a tracking system that prepared Latino students for the worst, lowest-paying jobs. Lewis Terman, the foolish psychologist from Stanford, had put the academic imprimatur on racism, supporting the idea that Mexicans could not compete intellectually with Anglos. As a result, schools all over the Southwest expected Mejicano and Mexican-American students to drop out. And they did. The dropout rate for Latinos was about 50 percent, which was an improvement over the early years of the twentieth century, when the dropout rate was about 90 percent in towns like El Paso: Of those who graduated from high school between 1898 and 1920, 812 were Anglos and 22 Latinos, even though more than 60 percent of the elementary school students during that period were of Mexican descent. San Antonio packed

---

[4]Edward Roybal was then serving in the U.S. House of Representatives.

Latinos into poorly staffed, crumbling schools, according them half the space and less than half the facilities given to Anglo students. In 1968 there was no city or town in the United States in which Latino students were educated according to constitutional guarantees of equality of treatment under the law.

The Los Angeles walkout, which began as a demand to be educated as well as blacks and Anglos, turned into the linchpin for a national movement. It was the single largest, most concerted action in the brief history of Chicanismo. The United Farm Workers boycotts were the most broadly based actions and the Crystal City, Texas, overthrow of the Anglo power structure was the most successful, but nothing equaled the 1968 walkout as a demonstration of the will of the people. Political and student groups were formed, among them La Raza Unida party, the Mexican-American Youth Organization (MAYO), United Mexican-American Students (UMAS), and El Movimiento Estudiantil Chicano de Aztlán (MECHA). William (Willie) Velásquez, the son of a butcher in San Antonio, founded the Southwest Voter Registration and Education Project, and McGeorge Bundy, then president of the Ford Foundation, sent money to a small legal services organization with the proviso that it take on important cases in the style of the NAACP, which changed the Mexican American Legal Defense and Education Fund from a poverty law office into an effective civil rights organization.

On August 29, 1970, in the aftermath of an anti-war demonstration that had turned into a riot, Rubén Salazar was killed and Chicanismo lost its clearest voice. There were other marches, other riots, other writers, but the killing of Rubén was the beginning of the end of the movement. He did not become a martyr; his death became a different symbol. The sheriff had threatened him, and the sheriff's deputies had killed him. No one was indicted in the killing; no one was reprimanded. The Los Angeles *Times* and a few of the radical weeklies of the sixties protested briefly, but there was no uprising by the media over the killing of one of their own. Within a few months the newspapers and television stations in Los Angeles returned to speaking for the police in any confrontation with chicanos. The voice of the resistance was gone.

In all the history of the Mexica[5] the pattern had been the same. A man rose to prominence and led the people in war. He was killed in ambush or in battle, and he was neither replaced nor remembered in anger. The Mexica believed in heroes but not in martyrs. Conquered cities did not rise again; destroyed temples were not rebuilt. The Náhua poet asked, "Is it true that we pass this way but once?"

For these ancient reasons, the killing of Rubén Salazar was a Mexican

---

[5]The people commonly known as Aztecs referred to themselves as "Mexica" (pronounced "Mesheeka"), hence "Mexico."

death. As in the past, some people survived, but the spirit of the civilization died. Of those who survived, some were used as slaves and servants by the conquerors; others in their worldly wisdom chose to become like the conquerors and prospered. Soon it was the 1980s and Ronald Reagan was elected president of the United States. His California cadre called out to the crowd, "Viva!" and the crowd answered, "Olé!" Never before had so many Mexican-Americans voted for a Republican presidential candidate.

2.

We must gently obey and endure the laws of our condition. We are subject to grow aged, to become weak, and to fall sick, in spite of all physic. It is the first lesson the Mexicans give their children. When they come out of their mothers' wombs, they thus salute them: My child, thou art come into the world to suffer; therefore suffer and hold thy peace.   Montaigne, *"Of Experience"*

How quickly the world learned about the Mexicans! In France, in the waning years of the sixteenth century, Montaigne admired that aspect of character which the older generation of Mejicanos and Mexican-Americans still say is most important in their world-view. Answering the challenge to describe their character in a single word, they say, *"Aguantar."* The verb means to bear, to endure, to stand, to tolerate, to put up with. The noun formed from it, *aguante,* means fortitude, patience, endurance, resistance to toil or fatigue. In the lexicon of the bullfight, *aguantar* means to stand firm. The sign of courage (defined as overcoming one's fear) in the bullring is to hold one's ground when the bull charges. "Aguantar la vara como venga" means to bear whatever comes, as the bull must bear the *vara* used by the picador.

Aguantar is thus not entirely Mexican; under certain circumstances it is Spanish as well. In the mestizo character of Mexico, the fatalism of the Indians combined comfortably with the Spanish willingness to endure danger and suffering. Thus, *aguantar* came to mean enduring one's fate bravely and with a certain style. The Mexican *aguantar* differs from Faulkner's concept of what poor blacks in the South do—"and they endure"—in that the Mexicans do not mean merely to live long without dying, but to have fortitude, to consider endurance a virtue.

In Mexico, the concept of *aguantar* enabled the conquerors to make use of the poor, particularly the Indian poor, as cheap labor. The North Americans were quick to learn from the criollos.[6] Based on the Mejicano's willingness to endure, the Anglo decided that Mejicanos were docile, easily managed. *Aguantar,* the virtue, betrayed Mexican immigrants in labor negotiations, education, housing, every aspect of life in the United States. Because of the Mejicano's willingness to endure danger, intolerable working and living conditions, and so on, the Mejicanos became the safety valve for labor in the Southwest, low-paid casuals, relegated to the worst jobs, and hired and fired almost capriciously as a means of maintaining stable employment in the best jobs for Anglos.

Mejicanos still hold to the virtue of *aguantar.* Among Mexican-Americans only the old generation promotes the heroics of fatalism; younger people say the single word that best describes the character of the Mexican-American is *respeto,* which means respect, but also has overtones of deference and awe. *Respeto* is more than the tone of social relations; it is the relation of one person to another, child to parent, student to teacher, citizen to police officer, worker to boss, and neighbor to neighbor. Ideally, *respeto* does not operate in only one direction; ideally, *respeto* serves as a brake on the driving individualism of Anglo society and makes a person more familial, more communal in his orientation. In reality, *respeto* may combine with the notion of *aguantar* to produce passivity.

Latino educators find that the rule of *respeto* too often leaves Mejicano and Mexican-American students so passive they seem almost to be asleep. Emily Cole, a Latina who had recently become the principal of Jefferson High School in Houston, lamented that "Latino kids will allow an adult to talk down to them. Culturally, we don't defend ourselves. Kids just accept anything anybody tells them. They respect adults too much.

"The teachers like that. Some teachers[7] who are assigned to honors classes complain that the kids ask questions. And the teachers can't handle that."

Almost all of the children in Jefferson High School are Latinos. Recently, some Salvadoran refugee children have joined the Mexicans, Mejicanos, and Mexican-Americans. Ms. Cole, who prefers the role of realist to that of apologist, gave the painful statistics of Jefferson High: in the entering class, 650; in the tenth grade, 300; in the graduating class, 200. By her straightforward calculation, the dropout rate is almost 70 percent.

[6]People of European descent

[7]The teachers in Jefferson High School were mainly Anglo, men and women who did not understand the Mejicano and Mexican-American culture sufficiently well to teach the children within the context of their own culture. This problem of the failure of Anglo and Mexican-American teachers to work effectively with children who bring the values of *aguantar* and *respeto* to the classroom will be discussed in the chapters on education.

She also finds the idea of *aguantar* a danger to the children. They endure whatever happens to them. In many cases children are asked to drop out of school to work or to take care of other children at home, and they do so uncomplainingly. Neither the children nor their parents are willing to speak out in defense of themselves.

On the other hand, when the concept of *respeto* is absent, as in some of the very poor children now coming across the border in West Texas, there is nothing in the culture to replace it. Teachers in Socorro, a small town in the Lower Valley of eastern El Paso County, find the new immigrant children uncontrollable, different from the children they have come to know in decades of working there in the Lower Valley. The new immigrants are often children of homeless people or the squatters who live near the garbage dump in Ciudad Juárez. How their lack of *respeto* will affect their lives is uncertain. According to the teachers in the Socorro schools, the children arrive in the United States with virtually no skills in Spanish, and they are not emotionally or intellectually capable of learning in English or in bilingual classes.

The origin of the concept of *aguantar* is very old. It is an Indian way of understanding how to live in the world. Claude Lévi-Strauss compared this "savage" way of thinking with modern Western thought and found the "savage mind" complex, brilliant, and very much the equal of the modern mind. For the Belgian anthropologist the difference came with writing and the accumulation of knowledge, which led to a linear mode of thinking, the modern replacement for the neolithic vision of time and the world as circular. Lévi-Strauss compared the two modes of thinking to a train and a clock. With homage to Rousseau, he wrote lovingly of the "youth of the world" and agreed that modern man is its "decrepitude."

The problem of *aguantar* is that in a modern, acquisitive society the character of the person who acquiesces to nature is out of step. Neolithic man has no greater wish than to be in harmony with nature, while modern man wishes to control nature. The irony of the Mexican tie to neolithic thinking is that both the Aztec and the Mayan societies were on the verge of modernity. Both had begun to accumulate knowledge, although they still believed, in the neolithic way, that everything could be explained through myth and religion.

When people bring fatalistic views with them to a society intent upon controlling its own fate, the newcomers find accommodation extremely difficult. The aims of the new society make no sense to them: Nature has a built in sense of limits, which the mestizo world-view accepts, but the same world-view staggers before the failure of a civilization that often lacks any sense of limits. *Aguantar* and *respeto* are concepts perfectly suited to the view

of the world as a circle, a view in which any break in the circle is cata-
strophic. In Aztec mythology, for example, the sun renews itself in fifty-
two-year cycles; if the sun fails to renew itself and the circle is broken, the
world will end.

Living according to the concepts of *aguantar* and *respeto,* one can get
along perfectly well in a small, very stable society, in a village culture. To
compete, to be acquisitive, to be selfish, the traits valued in a modern capitalist society, have no place in a village culture. It is a gentler but more formal
place, one in which the rules of society, which accommodate themselves to
the laws of nature, are observed more carefully than in a tumultuous modern
urban setting.

Anglos and other Latinos encountering Mejicanos and Mexican-Americans who still hold on to the old values find them gentle, charming, passive,
easy to manage, docile, and they are quick to take advantage of them. The
Mejicanos who suffer from being used by modern Anglo society react in
several ways; they adopt Anglo values, they sink into passivity, or they resort
to machismo, with all of its attendant interpersonal and social problems.
During the late sixties and early seventies the chicano movement attempted
to find a middle ground in which one could retain the value of *respeto* while
shedding the fatalism of *aguantar,* picking and choosing the best and most
useful aspects of both cultures. The movement did not survive, but there can
be no doubt that for many people it did shift the world-view toward *respeto,*
but a healthy *respeto,* without the overtones of awe and deference, engendered by the unifying character of culture rather than the divisive power of
class.

In those Mexican-Americans who have succeeded best in the United
States the quality of *aguantar* seems largely to have disappeared. Robert
Ortega, who heads CMA Construction, is the antithesis of the fatalistic vil-
lager who lived by the whim of nature, yet Ortega demonstrates the closeness to his family and community of *respeto.* The combination of the two sets
of values produces some interesting contradictions in Ortega: Although he
considers himself a Republican, he is a major funder of a radical community
action group.

Vilma Martínez, who was general counsel of the Mexican American Legal
Defense and Education Fund (MALDEF), grew up in a small town in Texas,
where her high school counselors advised her not to waste her time preparing for college. *Aguantar* required that she accept the judgment of the school
and prepare for the barefoot and pregnant life of a rural Mejicana, but she did
not put up with what seemed to be her lot in life. Although her family was
Mexican, culture did not determine her behavior. She chose her life. After
graduating from law school, she worked at public interest law, becoming

president and general counsel of MALDEF, then moving to a private firm,[8] Munger, Tolles, & Olson.

Although she is more gracious and far more informal than most members of prestigious law firms, even in Los Angeles where she practices, one does not become a regent of the University of California and a member of the board of directors of Anheuser Busch through fatalism; Vilma Martínez continues to choose her own path. The practice of law in the United States, particularly public interest law, requires character traits opposite to those of *aguantar*. A particularly individualistic world-view is required of a former public interest lawyer who defends a corporation against charges of discrimination against Mexican-Americans; although she was criticized for it by some of her former allies, Ms. Martínez took on such a case.

A highly trained lawyer or a successful businessman seems to have moved beyond the cultural determinism that wounds so many Mexican-Americans. Or is it a wound? Concha Saucedo, who heads the Instituto La Raza Familiar in San Francisco, argues in favor of cultural determinism. She sees refugees and many poor people for whom the old culture is the best and the only grip on life. "People who have made it here," she says, "have paid a high price. I see many who are suffering, who have had to turn off part of themselves. I see them here as patients."

Saucedo, a psychologist, said she named the clinic on the advice of *las viejas,* for the old women are very wise and very influential. She knew after talking with them that if she simply translated the English phrase and called it *salud mental,* no one would come to the mental health clinic. All of her work is based in the old culture. She keeps an altar in her office, and she wears jewelry of jade and silver.

Although she is small physically, her presence, in her office or across the table in a restaurant, is commanding. It is possible, her face says, that she knows something, which is required of psychologists who practice the healing system of the youth of the world. What she knows was learned partly in school and in studying with a well-known psychiatrist, but it was also learned partly in the old way. "I went with my father who was a *maestro*—we didn't use the word *curandero* then. I went with him when he treated people. In the last eight years I've spent time in the mountains of Oaxaca learning from a woman there. I don't talk much about that. We're usually asked not to."

Everything in the Instituto is rooted in Latino culture. Concha Saucedo's

---

[8]Joaquín Avila, who succeeded her at MALDEF, followed a different path when he left the organization. His career is described in Chapter 24 and in his own words in the oral history of the Avila Family in the Epilogue.

speech is laced with Spanish; the Virgin of Guadalupe appears in her office on the altar along with things found or given to her by patients: a curled glass tube meant to hold a flower, tiny decorated pots, a small feather, a painted card about peace. The altar is more like the contents of a medicine bundle on display than the altar of a Western church. She is Indian, descended from Yaquis, Coros, and Huicholes, and the holder of an advanced degree from UCLA. Her medicine is not much of this time. On the walls outside her office the brief biographies under the photographs of the members of the board of directors of the instituto tell their names, family names, nationalities, and "favorite pastimes," but give no information about profession or employment; in Mejicano culture a job does not define a person. Everything about the work of Concha Saucedo is rooted in Indian or mestizo culture, the culture of *aguantar,* but the *curandera* is also a psychologist from UCLA; she treats patients in the real world of California, not in the mountains of Oaxaca. "To be healthy," she said, "means to have power over your own life."

8

TIME'S FATE

It is impossible to know what time it is in the Latino world. So many theories have been advanced by philosophers and psychologists, ranging from Octavio Paz to Peggy Lee, that no one knows for certain whether it is yesterday or today. The only assurance given by every scholar is that tomorrow is not under consideration.

To complicate matters, Arthur L. Campa, the folklorist, has argued that, in the Mexican mind, today is followed by yesterday. The present is so heightened for Mexicans and Mexican-Americans, Campa wrote, that they live every moment twice—first as present, then as past.

Peggy Lee, in a popular song, "Mañana," also attributed the character of people of Mexican descent to their concept of time. Using a cruel parody of a Mejicano accent, she sang: "Mañana, mañana ees soon enough for me." In the song, a poor Mejicano tells how his house, his life, his whole world is falling down around him and concludes each verse with the philosophy of mañana; that is, he will attend to his business in the lazy man's tomorrow, the tomorrow that never comes.

To the Mexican-American veterans of World War II who were, at the height of the song's popularity, attempting to move into the middle class, "Mañana" was an almost physical barrier to be overcome in applying for a job or a business development loan. No stereotype could have been more damaging than the slothful simpleton portrayed by Lee.

Mañana actually has several distinct meanings in Spanish, among them "morning," "tomorrow," "the future," "an aperitif," or "the first drink of the day," the one known in English as "the hair of the dog." In Spanish, one says tomorrow morning as "mañana en la mañana," and it is true that "Mañana en la mañana es en la mañana." That is, tomorrow morning is in the future. From this evidence it would seem that either the future is very close in the Latino mind or tomorrow is very distant. The distinction determines the moral sense of the culture.

If tomorrow is so distant that it cannot be considered, actions have no consequences. A culture with no sense of the future is sociopathic. It produces people like those in Peggy Lee's song, men and women as rooted in the present as animals. They can live in squalor, kill without fear of punishment, breed like animals. If one cannot imagine the coming of rain, what is the use of repairing the roof? If one cannot think forward to law courts, prisons, Hell, what is the use in letting an enemy live? A sense of the future is a requirement for social life; without it, no law, no taboo has meaning. When the lack of a sense of future is attributed to people, the real meaning is that they are less than human.

Unfortunately, there are people in the Latino community who do have an incomplete sense of time. In east Los Angeles, a boy of fifteen, more or less in high school, a gang member, not a killer, but the best friend of a killer, said he could not imagine the future. "In the future you might be dead," he told me. He said he could think about the next day, but never beyond that; he had no interest in anything after the next day.

Being Mexican-American did not steal his sense of the future; it was not culture that killed his moral life. He was the victim of a situation in which the real future was so grim that he could survive only by refusing to consider it. In his neighborhood all the young men went to jail, which was not the worst of prisons, just a formal variation on life in an east Los Angeles housing project. For him, a life without the future is preferable to a life of utter despair. If he were to focus on his real prospects as represented by the people around him—single parents, drug addicts, people living on welfare, the victims of racism, violence, poverty, poor health care, and ineffective education—he would go mad.

With no sense of the future, and certainly no sense of control over the future, fatalism takes hold. As the Greeks understood fate, it was a force beyond the gods, the foundation of natural law, the springboard of ethics. The man who sought to oppose his fate was guilty of hubris. Fatalism, which appeared with the Stoics, differs from the classical Greek notion of fate in that it absolves man from thinking. Fatalism does not admit the notion of hubris, nor does it allow man to seriously contemplate the morality of his actions, for what is fated will happen no matter what he thinks or chooses; in fatalism everything is predestined, man's will is useless. Fate made the rules of cause and effect inevitable, fatalism makes them irrelevant. Greek tragedy portrays the hubristic effort of a man to overcome his fate. Fatalism does not allow a man to confront his fate; he has no choice but to bear it *(aguantar)*. In the Greek notion fate makes the consequences of actions as immutable as natural law; in fatalism the consequences of actions cannot be known; everything is according to the will of the gods, man's actions have no meaning.

Is it the strict moral life of one who believes the consequences of actions are ineluctable that the thinkers mean to ascribe to Latinos, or do they argue that Latinos lack a sense of future and so must be fatalistic? In the case of Latinos, there is something to be learned from the *dichos* (aphorisms) that are always on everyone's lips. The Latino version of "As ye sow, so shall ye reap"—El que la hace, la paga; quien mal anda, mal acaba—lets one know that a life lived badly will end badly. On the other hand, there is hope: Mañana oscura, tarde segura, which is a little like "It's always darkest just before the dawn."

Most Spanish *dichos* could have been spoken comfortably by St. Augustine, but on the Indian side of Latino culture the case is not so clear. The Mexican anthropologist Miguel León-Portilla argues passionately for a sense of free will among the *tlamatinime* or "wise men" of the Aztecs, but he must do handsprings in his exegesis of the old texts, particularly the Florentine Codex, to make his point. The Aztecs were more concerned with divinations, the "conjunctions of the stars" that Augustine scorned. At the birth of an Aztec child, the book of divinations or horoscopes, the *tonalámatl,* was consulted. Other Aztec works say that a man could ruin his good destiny by bad behavior, which gives credence to León-Portilla's argument. However, the idea that the Aztecs had a moral sense anything like that of Western civilizations is belied by their behavior. The Aztecs deviated from fatalism mainly in that they thought the gods could be influenced by prayer or sacrifice; they had not reached the stage of development at which philosophy becomes codified. Other tribes in the Caribbean and on the mainland were at even earlier stages. Whatever contribution was made to the theory of the individual and free will at the time of the conquest came from the West.

How fatalism and fate balanced in the Western mind was demonstrated by the marriage of two old Spanish families who came to the Western hemisphere only in the twentieth century: The Petilón family lived near the bottom of the economic scale; the men were fishermen and the women worked as domestics; the Sasson family was affluent, educated, involved in business and real estate development within a few years after arriving in the United States. One family believed in divination, and the other put its faith in a kind of Fabian socialism. Fatalism was the philosophy of the poor, while the heavy moral hand of fate fell on the shoulder of the affluent.

Control over the past taught the Petilón and Sasson families about control over the future. Neither family held entirely to one view of the world, but the degree to which they believed they controlled their own destiny depended upon experience as much as culture, for they came from different strata of the same culture. The fisherman and the real-estate speculator also lived at different removes from nature, positions based almost entirely on economics. The real-estate speculator took the long view, while the fisherman believed that fish should be taken now and eaten soon.

It may seem too delicate a distinction, but the sense of time of different economic and social levels within the same culture leads to the theory that there is no culture of poverty, only a philosophy of poverty. People who live entirely in the present have learned that they cannot control the future. Culture does not teach this view or it would be embedded in the language. Oscar Lewis, following Ruth Benedict and Margaret Mead in the classical anthropological tradition, passed through a culture too quickly and misinterpreted what little he saw. The philosophy of presentness, the set of observed principles that makes fatalists of great numbers of people in the modern world, does not have deep roots.

Presentness is no more profound than a transaction at a bodega. The poor person cannot put away money for the future; hunger is now. The bodega owner, a sociologist who wears an apron and keeps a pencil behind his ear, offers his poor customers food and drink, soap and toilet tissue, now. *"Apuntelo,"* they tell him, and he writes down the amount of the sale. *Apuntelo*— the word is always said pridefully, imperiously, as if the credit of the borrower were unlimited. *Apuntelo,* the buyer says, with no concern for the price-gouging of the bodega owner, *apuntelo!* Credit captures the moment. The bill will come due later, and it will devour the paycheck so that it will be necessary to write down the amount of the first purchase after payday, continuing the cycle of credit, but for now the bodega belongs to the borrower.

Latinos do not have a culture of poverty, but those who are poor use presentness as a practical way to live with misery. It is a philosophy of life based upon what they know and expect. If the real estate speculator and the domestic worker thought of the world in the same way, one of them would have been mad or at the very least foolish.

A person's sense of time is not a result of culture but a response to conditions. While cultures change slowly, the sense of time, an either/or proposition (there is or is not a future to be considered), changes abruptly. No one would accuse Vilma Martínez, who sits on the board of directors of a major corporation and the board of regents of the University of California, of having the same sense of time as a woman from south Texas who lives in a colonia (unincorporated housing development generally without water, drainage, or sewerage).

They are about the same age and may have had similar early experiences of prejudice in a largely segregated society. However, the view from the window of a homemade house in the dusty colonia, with its unpaved roads and outhouses, and the view from a law office high above the city of Los Angeles lead to different senses of control. To one woman the cause and effect of fate must seem a comfort, a proof of order in the world, a defense of reason; to the other the thought that she is living the consequences of her actions in the world could not but be a disaster, a repudiation of her every act. To one the future is a promise, to the other it is even less bearable than the present.

Culturally, the two women have begun to diverge. The culture of one is greatly enlarged from the place where it began; the other woman's culture has, if anything, grown narrower, more focused on the present. Both are Mexican-American, both are bilingual, both exhibit the grace and generosity to strangers so characteristic of the culture, both have children. They differ in that the woman in the colonia had her second child before Vilma Martínez completed high school. The woman in the colonia did not marry until her second child was in school, then had two more children before her husband left. Recently, she married again, this time an old man who had retired from a job in a factory near the colonia. The old man said of his marriage to her, "At last, she started to think of the future. When I'm dead, that's when her future will be."

No future presented itself to the woman who lives in the colonia, so she lived entirely in the present; she describes her life as hedonistic, careless. When Vilma Martínez was told by her elementary school teacher in San Antonio that she would be more "comfortable" at a technical high school rather than one that prepared her for college, Martínez rejected her destiny; with human hubris the little girl insisted that she could determine her own future.

It was not culture, but an aspect of culture, a philosophical view, that gave the young Martínez such hubris. Culturally, she and the woman in the colonia were almost identical. Martínez said she could read and write when she started school, having been taught by her paternal grandmother, but she could read and write and speak only in Spanish. The woman in the colonia reads and writes less well than a graduate of Columbia University Law School, but she is literate in English and she, too, spoke only Spanish when she started school. Both women are the children of literate parents, although both were raised partly by grandmothers. They are different psychologically and philosophically, but they are products of the same culture. The poor woman's fatalism, which is the forerunner of presentness and its attendant hedonism, was determined by her economic condition. Had it been determined by culture, both she and Martínez would have held the same view of time.

The politics of presentness derives from the theory that poverty is a separate culture and from its corollary: Since presentness is cultural, that is, not learned from experience but held a priori, it cannot be affected by improving the material conditions of the poor. This error in thinking is vicious, for it means that presentness and its consequent hedonism and amorality are virtually immutable: The poor will always behave the same way no matter what is done to change the conditions in which they live; they are incurable.

Then to ascribe this presentness to all Latinos or to all Puerto Ricans and Mexican-Americans is a paradigm of prejudice, whether it is done by an Anglo (Oscar Lewis or Peggy Lee) or a Mexican-American (Arthur L. Campa), for it is not true and it is demeaning and injurious. But the argument has been made and generally accepted; because of it every Puerto Rican or Mexican-American who has a normal sense of time and therefore a normal ethic must argue that he or she is an exception, which is a burden and an invitation to loneliness.

The unique sense of time common to Latinos is not presentness, but uncertainty. The grammar of the Spanish language reveals this unique aspect of the culture by the importance it places upon the worrying tense, the subjunctive. The tense itself hesitates, ponders, questions the correctness, safety, sanity, sensitivity of every thought and act. Unlike the French thoughts on the stairs, the subjunctive suffers beforehand, while going up the stairs, rather than in the descending afterward; it is never depressed, only anxious.

The subjunctive has no memory; it lives entirely in apprehension, married to conditions for its very existence. On the battlefield of life the subjunctive asks, "If the wine were poured, must it necessarily be drunk? And if I were to drink it, then what?" The subjunctive is a disease of anxiety. The psychiatrist Rolando Fernández sees it in his practice in Miami; he said that his Latino patients suffer from anxiety while the Anglos drown in depression. Dr. Murray Persky, a psychiatrist practicing in San Francisco, made a similar observation about his Latino patients.

In speaking of the future only the subjunctive can ward off the evil eye. Any less tentative expression invites bad luck, for hubris is no more acceptable to the Spanish-speaking mind than to the ancient Greek. Only the humble tense, the one that can never get beyond the fork in the road, can be said safely. Nothing more daring will do. Poor subjunctive, with its pitiable, stammering sense of life! How strange that the masters of the subjunctive, the people who see not one future, but many, are said to live only in the present!

The truth about the people of the subjunctive is that they know exactly what time it is, but they are so aware of the rules of fate that action often eludes them. Hesitant, gripped by the moral mood of infinite contingency, they seem docile as they suffer, trapped in the present, made anxious to the point of passivity by the kaleidoscopic, unpredictable future. They are timid until they burst.

9

SHAKESPEARE, CERVANTES, & CO.

> My brain I'll prove the female to my soul,
> My soul the father. . . .
>
> *Shakespeare, Richard II*

As an observer in bilingual classes in schools around the country I had often heard the struggles of small children, the sound of a strange language filling up their mouths like water surprising a swimmer's gasp. It had come to seem more like war than education, a battle between English and the mother tongue. The phrase struck me. Could there truly be a mother tongue, an all-encompassing gender? What clues to character are contained in the variations on the structure common to all languages? What meanings are hidden in the sounds themselves? I did not know how to begin thinking about the questions until one night in London, walking back to my hotel after a performance of Richard II, *I was struck by Shakespeare's idea of a male and female of souls, brains, words. Perhaps there was an all-encompassing gender; it seemed unlikely, but I hoped that consideration of the idea might lead to some interesting speculation about the difference between Anglo and Latino culture.*

___

The English language is more changed by the voice of the speaker than Spanish, which in each of its nationalities, has a permanent speed and does not vary so much in volume. Spanish is not such a good language for whispering as English; it wants more opportunity for the tongue.

Tradition is everything in language, which is why North Americans must read and hear Shakespeare. Latin Americans must know not only Cervantes, but García Lorca and Jiménez and Neruda and García Márquez, for they have no Shakespeare from whom to learn the full range of a language as it invents them; they must piece together the description of themselves from several sources.

My Anglo friend who loves Shakespeare claims the language of the bard shimmers; that is, the meaning of the words is not precise so much as poetic. My friend does not know Spanish or he would know that the Spanish language also shimmers, but more in the construction of the sentences than in the meaning of the individual words.

Spanish brings blessings, welcomes, precisions, hopes, love, and songs, but there is no Spanish Shakespeare.

God is not an Englishman, but God's best speakers have been Englishmen; they have spoken even better than Greeks or Romans, certainly better than the French, Germans, or Russians, but even Shakespeare did not sing so well as Spaniards do, for Spanish at its best is a serenade.

Spanish is not a good language to be spoken by women; only a man and one with a deep voice can roll the rs with courage. Even the best women singers of Spanish have deep voices, like the Mexican women who sing *ranchera* songs.

English is a good language for both men and women, but it is not androgynous. There are two sexes in English; it can change from the voice of a man to that of a woman. As the actor Derek Jacobi interprets the sentences, Shakespeare sometimes uses woman's English for Richard II; he does this so the king will not be forced to draw his sword. Bolingbroke speaks only man's English, which is why Richard and Henry seem not to be able to understand each other.

There is no linguistic rule which decrees that the gender of the speaker and his or her language must be the same. Clearly, English is a better language for conquerors than Spanish, for it is so difficult that no man can speak it fluently without changing his soul. Spanish invites guests by its very orderliness; the streets of Spanish run north and south, with only the boulevard of an irregular verb here and there to cut across the logic of its terrain. One may therefore easily visit the Spanish language; the traditional welcome is accurate: Mi casa es su casa. This welcome to Spanish consists of a communal singing in which any person can move his lips or at least strum his vocal chords with deep breaths.

Children sing pleasantly in either tongue, but children cannot be proprietors of a language, for they do not know enough words, nor can children say precisely what they think, since no language has yet abducted them from nature.

Spanish loves sweet sentences, because it has a Latin mother. English has no mother, it behaves like the child of a German father, one who demanded to be understood and informed exactly, because he was away at war or business most of the day and into the night, leaving him only a little time with his child. The Latin mother was very kind to her child, whom she imagined a son, a soldier gone to war: Thus her son does not weep, but growls in nearly every sentence.

To be away from Spanish creates a loneliness peculiar to motherless children; it leads the sons to barbarism and the daughters to sad submissions.

English does not appear ever to die, but only to increase over time and distance. The language prevented the British from marrying their conquests. English speakers lived apart. The Spanish conquered by inverting their own welcome: Your house is my house, they said.

In most places there was only one Spanish language that spanned all economic classes, until the proximity of English taught distinctions to the speakers, leading the poor to eat the heads and tails of words, as if they were so starved for food and affection they could not help but nibble their thoughts.

English does not love bastards; it legitimizes all its children. Spanish lets the bastards be—what do mothers care? They love all their children, even the nameless and the dying.

The Spanish language came like a mother's son seeking a wife, advised by his mother to conquer by creating a family; those it does not kill, it marries. English arrived as the father's son; those it does not conquer, it kills.

A mother's son marries late; a motherless son does not marry at all.

English has rhythms, dynamics, sonorities, but few melodies. Although there are more words in English, it is not a singer's tongue and cannot produce great operas, only well-spoken translations.

Shakespeare said the mind of an Englishman was dioecious, the result of a two-sided language. Cervantes spoke with a single, male voice; it is his characters who are two-sided (real and dreamed), not his voice.

Adages are best in Spanish; English, being two-sided, wants to analyze its wit.

English has the fewest coups and revolutions, because of the father's discipline; the mother of Spanish did not teach the same lesson to her errant sons.

Although anyone may speak two languages, no man or woman, no child can dream in more than one. Therefore, the logic of the proponents of bilingual education is indisputable: A child sitting at a schoolroom desk in Spanish Harlem or a kindergarten table in Texas is in danger of losing hope, unless that child is permitted, in the moonlit gardens of the soul, a serenade.

10

TRUE REVOLUTION

*The happy and the powerful do not go into exile and there are
no surer guarantees of equality among men than poverty and
misfortune.*

Tocqueville

There was no fire. In its place the Tlacolulenses had put a desk lamp on
the floor in the center of the circle. The metal shade was bent low, close to
the floor, so that the fluorescent light was dim, absorbed by the carpeting. All
around the lamp, dark-skinned people, darker for the lack of light, sat on
kitchen chairs and couches. The walls of the apartment in Santa Monica,
California, were bare, except for a large cartoon of Cantinflas. Benito Antonio, a short, thick man with full-blown cheeks, conducted the weekly
telephone call to Oaxaca. He listened solemnly while the people at home told
the news.

After a while, he passed the telephone to the person next to him. The
conversation was intense; the people in the circle were concerned. A few
months before, there had been a confrontation in Tlacolula. The FUCHI
people had made trouble and so had the FUDT and ORO. All the acronyms
had risen up against the PRI,[1] for they believed the elections had been
dishonest. The women had carried stones instead of food down to the square
in their marketbaskets. Led by the women, the FUCHI people had made war
on the PRI.

The FUCHI people threw stones and shot firecrackers out of a tube, which

---

[1]FUCHI (Frente Unida de Chicharroneros) also means filth in the language used by chil-
dren. FUDT is the Frente Unico Democrático de Tlacolula. PRI is the Partido Revoluciónario
Institucional. The Pristas have been the ruling party in Mexico for generations. ORO is the
Organización Regional de Oaxaca.

the Pristas said was a bazooka supplied by the Russians. Finally, the Pristas got hold of some machine guns and fired on the FUCHI people. They did not hit any of the women, but several of the bullets ricocheted back toward the machine gunners, wounding three of their own.

Since their defeat by the Mexica in the fifteenth century, the Zapotecans of Tlacolula and the other peoples of the state of Oaxaca had steadily deteriorated militarily, socially, culturally, and economically. By the last part of the twentieth century there was very little left to them. Their lands were not fertile, their schools were not good, their children were not healthy, their culture was fading; every year fewer people could speak Zapoteco or do the most intricate dances. The worst problem, however, was the inflation that had gripped the country, making it almost impossible for the people of Tlacolula to buy adequate food and clothing. To solve this problem they followed the lead of other towns and sent forth workers, young men with strong arms who spoke Spanish well; their mission was to earn money for their families and for the town.

The place where the Zapotecans were sent was very far north, across the river into California, where there was money to be earned. Only the young men went, then some of the women followed, bringing their children with them. Almost every town sent a separate group of workers, and all the groups were organized by the leaders of the towns. The Tlacolulenses who came to Santa Monica, west of Los Angeles, were originally organized in the colonial fashion. The leaders of Tlacolula appointed a presidente, secretario, tesorero, and three vocales (councilors) to manage the affairs of the Tlacolulenses in Santa Monica.

At first, the organization worked well. Control rested in Tlacolula, money was sent home regularly, the radical activities of the FUCHI people and FUDT and ORO were subsidized by the people who worked in Los Angeles. Although the Tlacolulenses were not pleased with the kind of work they were able to get, they settled in and gave themselves a name and an acronym, COTLA (Comité Tlacolulense de Los Angeles). They lived and worked in accord with the oldest Zapotecan customs; life in the United States was a form of *tequio,* an Aztec word now meaning a donation of work to help the community, although it originally meant servitude.

When the Tlacolulenses in Santa Monica saw how the officers of COTLA behaved, they began to resent them: The appointed leaders strutted but did not work; they communicated with Tlacolula but contributed nothing. The members of COTLA revolted. A new, consensual organization was formed. Other groups from Oaxaca, less sophisticated than the Tlacolulenses, continue in the old colonial structure. Every town has its own *comite,* which belongs to a larger organization that coordinates the activities of the tens of thousands of Oaxaqueños in Los Angeles.

Each person sends money home to his family in Oaxaca, but there are also communal needs. To buy a tractor or build a warehouse the *comites* hold dances to which all the other Zapotecans are invited. On a winter evening the Comité Tlacolulense de Los Angeles worked to organize its next dance.[2] Benito Antonio telephoned the leader of a band that played both the *jarabes* and *sones* of Oaxaca and popular Latin American music. While the others listened to his side of the conversation, Benito Antonio discussed the hours and the number of musicians, finally arriving at a fee of four hundred fifty dollars for the job.

Next, there was the raffle. They had chosen an enormous boom box for the prize, but they did not know how to show it on posters and flyers. "We will need a Macintosh," the baker who had become a hospital worker said; "who has access to a Macintosh?" Electricity and its uses enchanted them. They taught the ancient customs of the Zapotecans to their children by showing them videotapes made at festivals in Tlacolula.

In one tape the Zapotecos danced *jarabes* and the great dance of the feathers, then the young cousin of Audencio Hernández Santiago, who is said to have been killed by government forces, recited a poem about the town. Other tapes show all the eight *sones* that must be danced at the major festivals and the little dramas made in Oaxaca to teach the children in the United States to think and act like Zapotecos. None of the members of COTLA knows what to do about holding on to the old ways. Even at home the language and the culture are fading. Last year, in Galala, Oaxaca, they included gringos in the *sones*. The gringos were people from the village dressed in sunglasses and carrying video cameras. In other dances, the Zapotecan versions of fashionable young women appeared, wearing lipstick and short skirts, but in these dances the roles of the women are played by men from the village, because it would be immodest for a Zapotecan woman to dress that way.

After the layout of the poster for the dance was agreed upon, the leaders of the reorganized COTLA sat around the fluorescent fire and talked. Benito Antonio and his wife were leaving soon, moving to Chicago. He had been a teacher in Tlacolula; now the only work he could get was at MacDonald's. "They discriminate against us here and in our country," he said. "In our poor country we go to the north of Mexico, then here."

A salesman who had been a campesino in Oaxaca said, "My family is still in Tlacolula, because I have two children. I don't want them to learn about

[2]Rina Tamayo, a young Mexican woman who worked at UCLA, helped the Zapotecons organize into *comites*. Her method is interesting; she is a saintly gadfly. She will not tolerate inefficiency or unfairness, but there seems to be no limit to her energy and nothing she will not do to help them.

drugs here in the United States. They come to visit me, but I don't want them to live in an apartment in Los Angeles, where they can't make noise because of the neighbors. In Tlacolula they live in a big house, with a patio, and they can play freely; they do not have to be afraid of the street, because there is no traffic in Tlacolula."

The Zapotecos believe that the best way to keep their children free of drugs in Los Angeles is to maintain their culture and to involve them in athletics. Although they seem ill-suited physically, their favorite sport is basketball, which they play with wild enthusiasm at every opportunity. The various *comites* field teams that play against each other individually or in large Zapotecan tournaments.

The salesman let out a sigh, saying that he had been away from his family for a long time, long enough to have received amnesty under the Immigration Reform and Control Act. "I am lonely," he said, "but it is worth the loneliness to keep my children away from the drugs and violence in Los Angeles. I went only to the sixth grade, but my children will do better, because I am here and I can provide for them. My children will finish high school. Maybe they will go to the university." He would be seeing them soon, he said, for spring was coming and he went home every spring when it was time for planting.

César Lievana, who serves as the theoretician of COTLA but not as the leader, was a student at the University of Oaxaca before he came to the United States. He is serious and comic, airier than the others, slimmer, tense, moving at the speed of Hollywood. "The United States," he said, "is a mole de todos los chiles."[3] Lievana worked as a gardener but he also parked cars, which gave him peasant's hands and a wiseguy's strut. He said he was educated in politics by Marxist groups in Oaxaca. As if to prove his education, he explained how the people of Oaxaca would triumph: "It is dialectical. The repression of the people will be followed by the autonomy of the people. I am confident of the future of the people.

"Us, here, we are *delitos* [criminals] because we cross the border. And *delitos* are like delinquents, so here in the U.S. we are delinquents. But we work hard, we aid the economy of the richest state, California, and we live *sin techo* [literally, without a roof over our heads]. And look at the Mixtecos who live in San Diego! They have no houses; they dig holes at the base of a tree and live there.

"We will be successful eventually, because we are men. And we know that to be a man means more than merely being with a woman; to be a man means to defend the people."

---

[3]Literally, a ground up mixture of all the chile peppers.

In that nearly dark room, sitting around the fluorescent fire, the miracle of immigration seemed clear enough, raised to high relief by the contrast of videotape and *jarabes,* Macintosh and Tlacolula. The pattern defined the United States, which is, as John F. Kennedy wrote in 1958, "a nation of immigrants." The Latinos were but the next wave to reach the shores. Or were they?

Senator Kennedy had written his little book with a master politician's eye for popular appeal. The idea of a nation of immigrants pleased nearly everyone, because it gave coherence to a society in which English was no more than the lingua franca and no one country or culture served as the ancestral home for a majority of the people. Within the grand category, pluralism was more or less acceptable, for immigrants in the abstract had similar histories and intentions. There may not have been a melting pot at the most personal level, but as the Archimedean point was moved away, the myriad of nationalities appeared more and more like a single nation. The original error of the Nathan Glazer and Daniel Patrick Moynihan book, *Beyond the Melting Pot,* was that when the Archimedean point was far enough away from the object, at an academic distance, ethnic experiences and the national experience appeared to be isomorphic; that is, all the patterns looked the same. There was no need to think through the meaning of various kinds of movement across borders: If all patterns of immigration were the same, the only questions were about the rate of assimilation and upward mobility. The book argued that there was not a melting pot, and then proceeded to prove that there was.

As a view of the United States in the middle of the twentieth century, the theory could not have been more comforting. It promised domestic tranquility, national unity, and a generally rosy ethnic future. If some groups were still poorer than others, they had only to wait for the metamorphosis that would fit them into the pattern of the American dream. A few years later, the authors realized they had failed to consider history: A century before the publication of the book there had been a civil war in the United States, and one of the issues in the war had been the uniqueness of people who immigrated under special circumstances. A second edition of the work graciously admitted the first error and went on to make another: It introduced the concept that later came to be known as "blaming the victim," especially the victim who was willing to complain about his circumstances. But the thesis of the revision was fairly clear: Blacks were the exception to the pattern, and Latinos were probably going to be an exception too.[4]

---

[4]In *The Newcomers,* published four years before *Beyond the Melting Pot,* Oscar Handlin, continuing his profound understanding of the process of immigration, recognized that the

Glazer and Moynihan and their readers had good reason for wanting the United States to be a nation of immigrants. They agreed with Tocqueville's observation that immigrants were ideally suited to live in a constitutional democracy, especially one with an expressed preference for equality. Since immigrants generally came from low social and economic strata, they understood equalitarianism as an improvement in their standard of living. Many were also escaping from political and religious oppression into a new situation in which they could attend whatever church they chose and vote for anyone who appealed to their newfound sense of freedom and equality.

The immigrants did not come from a Lockean political tradition, but no immigrant is a tabula rasa; they came with a taste for political liberalism built in. If they didn't know Locke's theories, they could learn them from the realities of life in the new country. In America it was possible to own property by attaching one's labor to it. A penniless immigrant could stake a claim to unoccupied land or get forty acres of government land just by working it. Success in the cities was not so clearly connected to the state of nature, but hard work did produce wealth, and there was plenty of hard work to be had. In a young, still expanding country, theories of property and politics based upon man's relation to the state of nature made practical sense.

Immigrants quickly embraced the liberal political ideas that improved their lives. If the subtleties of Locke eluded them, they understood the more elemental notions of Rousseau. To Locke's liberalism they added the belief in a compact between themselves and all the people who had come before. The general will made sense to them; something like it had propelled them by the thousands to leave their homelands and cross the ocean to America. All the urges that had informed the framers of the U.S. Constitution existed in these immigrants, although they could not articulate them. They voted as soon as they could, for they recognized the control the people exercised over their government. They understood, however imperfectly, the power of the legislative branch and the checks on the executive. People who had experienced despotism, poverty, and instability believed the rule of law and the emphasis on equalitarianism in the United States was a kind of miracle. They had come

---

blacks and Puerto Ricans of New York were probably not going to follow the pattern of previous immigrants. He wrote of the "genuine, ominous possibility" that they were going to remain "especially vulnerable to the dangers of the city." In the conclusion to the book, he named the conditions that would enable the newcomers to New York City to follow the immigrant pattern: "Communal institutions, under responsible leadership that will give order and purpose to their lives, and the reduction of prejudice and the expansion of opportunities . . . [are] essential to such development." His last point, was that "Negroes and Puerto Ricans are likely to continue, as they have in the past, to depend more on governmental services. . . ."

to a place beyond their dreams; they had found a government of immigrants, by immigrants, for immigrants here on earth.

Until the middle of the twentieth century, the United States remained a nation of immigrants. There were some exceptions—the natives, those who came over as slaves,[5] several groups of Latinos—but immigrants and the descendants of immigrants made up the vast majority of the population. After World War II, the character of the newcomers began to change. Sojourners came, and exiles, and there were many others, all the conquered peoples in the hemisphere who did not immigrate, but simply migrated from one trouble to another.

Among these newcomers were the displaced persons of Europe, mainly Jews, and the great waves of Latinos, from Mexico, Puerto Rico, then Cuba, the Dominican Republic, Chile, Central America, Colombia, Ecuador, Peru; from wherever there was trouble or hunger they came, and there were millions, and they were not like the immigrants who had come before. The displaced persons were the last vestiges of the great westward migration of man; after hundreds of years, the direction of the world had changed.[6]

Along the southern borders of the United States, where the change of direction can be seen in the faces that pass by on the street, the philosophers and the politicians have begun to speculate. In the Dade County school district in Florida they wonder about the great northward migration. They do not doubt that it is happening, but they do not know why, for it is not a movement of people who know about the United States; it is something more. The people are coming down out of the mountains and from the black jungles, heading north, almost blindly, navigating like the birds and the fish, pushed or drawn by some genetic compass, heading toward some place, they know not where, so long as it is north.

Nestor Rodríguez, of the University of Houston, has seen the same movement, but he has a less mystical view. He assigns reasons for such movements: politics, hunger, ambition. In his visits to food lines and refugee camps, he interviews the newcomers. "I met an eighty-four-year-old man on a bread line here," Rodríguez said in the course of describing the range of people coming into the United States from Central America. "He said that he never expected to be here asking for food at this age. The old man said he had looked at the earth here in Houston and found it was no good. At home,

---

[5]Here again, Oscar Handlin was much more aware than most of his colleagues of the uniqueness of the problems of immigrating in slavery.

[6]Since the nineteenth century, there has been some immigration from Asia to the United States, and it continues, but the number of Asian immigrants, although large, is dwarfed by the northward movement of Latinos.

he walked on *la tierra*. Here, he walks on concrete. He knows *la tierra*, he knows earth, but he knows nothing of the city."

The old man came north, yet he did not know what he would find. It was the same for many Puerto Ricans who saw the tall buildings, crowded streets, and endless machines of the city for the first time as they passed through San Juan on their way to the mainland. In his memoir, *Family Installments*, Edward Rivera wrote, "Chuito took an oxcart with us to San Juan, then a bus to the airport. . . ."

Mixtec Indians living in the hills near Oceanside, California, come north to live, for there is not much work in the south of Mexico and what little there is goes to the mestizos and a few rich criollos; nothing is left for the Indians. But how they find their way down out of the mountains to the towns, then to the buses, across the border, and up into the California hills is unimaginable. They come first for a season, then another and another. The old man, Méndez, who works four days a week in a slaughterhouse in San Diego County, speaks no English and only rudimentary Spanish; his first language is Mixteco. To arrive at the slaughterhouse he had to descend seven thousand feet and cross two cultures.

A lonely man, forty-seven years old, who lives with a crowd of twenty-five other people in a one bedroom apartment in Los Angeles, used to work as a *carbonero* in El Salvador, collecting firewood and preparing charcoal from it for cooking fires. When I asked him what sort of work he expected to find in the middle of Los Angeles, he shrugged. *"No hay leña,"* he said solemnly, as if the lack of firewood to be found and gathered up in the center of the city was a discovery of some importance. Speaking of his life in Los Angeles, he said, "Sometimes they say to come and you think they want you to go. Sometimes they say to go and you think they want you to come. It's hard to understand them. One man said he couldn't figure out how I managed to get here."

Jorge Valls, who lives in Miami, where the sense of a great migration is most acute, has developed a thesis: "Now, what causes the migration from the south to the north?" he asks. "No one really knows why a massive population moves from one part of the world to the other. You have an immediate cause, in the economical structure or invasion or war, but this is the accident. The reality is of the normal tendency of man to move from one region to the other. Now, we are living in the last thirty years, forty years, an enormous migration from the south to the north that every year becomes greater, so it is a natural tendency. The psychological reasons are the success of the North American state and the deficiency of the structures of the South, the changes of population, that is, the growth of the population of the South, less growth of the North. The United States has, I think, fifteen inhabitants per square kilometer, Cuba has eighty-three. There are many things that move people from south to north, and after it starts, it is contagious. That is, the first one who comes decides, the second one imitates, and the third one simply goes with the flow. This is what happens with many people in the south who go north as it has become a collective attitude. They don't decide why they go north.

"For many Cubans it is that they have to go out, they have to go out, they have to go to the United States, go to the United States. They could go much better economically to other places, but this is unconscious. They move because a whole bunch is moving. It's not just the Cubans. This is, let us say, the substructure of the emigration current. This means that most of the people who come are not conscious of why they are moving."

Perhaps it is too soon to know the reason behind the change in the axis of immigration; what seems now like a collective unconscious may be revealed in fifty or a hundred years to be the result of a change of climate, a response to the infant mortality rate, or some hitherto undiscovered biological sense of survival. Perhaps the sociobiologists will find the reason for the new direction of the world in the habits of ants. For the moment, the method of communication beyond the immediate stimuli of economics and politics is unknown, although something is surely going on, something draws the people down out of the mountains and sends them into a world they could not have dreamed. The pattern is clear; it has been observed; the people are coming north.

On this different axis there are no oceans to cross; often a bus will do to make the trip, or one can walk—people come on foot from El Salvador or Nicaragua to Texas. The air fare from San Juan, P.R., to New York City is only $150.[7] Coyotes smuggle people across the California border for $100. At Brownsville or El Paso, Texas, the Charons of the Río Grande row people across the river in rubber rafts for less than fifty cents a head.

Because of this change of direction, the current newcomers differ from most of those who came before. They are southerners come to the cold, rural people come to the city, dark-skinned people come to a white world. Nor is the new, northern world they enter the same one that greeted the Europeans. The great geographic and economic expansion is over; the United States is a mature country. The form of its economic life has undergone transformations; there are no longer the farmlands in the Midwest that welcomed the Scandinavians and the Dutch; there are no more factories and foundries waiting to be manned. The strength of a man's arm, the body he was willing

---

[7]American Airlines' published lowest one-way fare, autumn 1990. Half of the lowest published round trip fare is less than $150, and a travel agent can arrange to split the ticket.

to attach to the rhythms of the machine, the broad, muscled back he was willing to bend to the demands of the assembly line are no longer the wants of industry.

There will always be a place for cheap labor—there will always be the dangerous jobs, the disgusting jobs no one else wants to do—but most of the work available to North Americans now requires language and computational skills far beyond the fifth grade education the average newcomer brings to this country. The high-paying manufacturing jobs are treasured by trade unionists who bar entrance to newcomers, especially blacks and Latinos. Nothing is impossible, some succeed, but it has become more difficult to leap from the mountain village to the suburb. The Tlacolulenses must learn to use a Macintosh while keeping the drug dealers away from their children and sending money home to buy tractors, build drainage ditches, and feed their families.

Oscar Handlin saw the barrios of the nineties foreshadowed in statistics gathered at midcentury. ". . . Movement from within the United States was more likely to be a source of disorder than movement from outside it," he wrote, although it was too soon then to see the rotation of the axis of the continuing human migration and far too early to begin questioning which movements were from within and which were from outside. Clearly, Handlin was on to something, for within a few years of his writing, the geographic and economic changes would force newcomers to behave differently. New forms of accommodation would be added to the patterns of the past. Latinos, who were the single largest group of recent newcomers, would comprise five distinct categories, only one of which behaved like the newcomers of old:

- Immigrants—the hopeful poor who come to the U.S. willing to abandon their national culture, because they have no intention of returning to their native country;
- Transporters—failed immigrants, the unfortunate poor, who come hoping to change their life situation, but end up repeating it in new surroundings;
- Sojourners—the distrustful poor who hold on to their national culture, because they intend to return to their native country;
- Exiles—the angry rich who maintain their national culture as a sign of defiance of the current regime in their native country and to foster the plan or myth of return;
- Ghosts—the embattled poor who left their home and culture without leaving their native country.

Among Latinos each nationality tends toward a single category, but the lines are not sharply drawn, the categories are not exclusive, and people of

Mexican descent, the largest group, are so diverse they fall into several categories.

I. IMMIGRANTS AND TRANSPORTERS

Before a person can become an emigrant, he must first become expert in the study of his own condition, for emigration is made of despair and dreams, despair over life at home and dreams of life in another place. These dreams of emigrants are of times and places so distant that they pass through abstraction to become real again, as do fairy tales or visions of gold.

The first travelers to North America, a pack of Spaniards, green-eyed men with noses as sharp as scimitars, went in search of heaven on earth. For some of them heaven was Çibola, an array of seven golden cities just beyond the desert, on the other side of the mountains, somewhere ahead. The more practical sought the fountain of youth, with its promise of eternal life.

Nothing they imagined ever appeared. Disappointed, Cabeza de Vaca, Ponce de León, and Coronado all abandoned the swamps and deserts, the savages and impossible beasts, and went home to more hospitable country. It was not until a full century after the arrival of Christopher Columbus that Juan de Oñate set up housekeeping in what is now New Mexico and became the leader of the first group of immigrants in North America since some Asians crossed over the land bridge to Alaska.

Oñate and his colonists differed from the explorers by the nature of their dreams. The explorers went to find something they could bring back; Cibola was not a place to live but a city to loot. Oñate was commissioned to found a colony; the people who went with him had earthly dreams, which are engendered by the realization that home presents no hope. Unlike the adventurers who preceded them, the colonists had no intention of turning back; they immigrated.

For the next three hundred fifty years the earthly dreamers came to North America. The stories of streets paved with gold persisted through the beginning of the twentieth century, but by then most immigrants understood the tales as metaphor: It was to the land of opportunity they went, and viewed from their circumstances, opportunity was as good as gold.

Immigration represented far more than a change of physical surroundings; it was an attempt to turn the world upside down. The hungry came to get fat, the poor came to get rich. The homeless and the outcast of Europe designed bungalow palaces in their dreams. The goal of every immigrant was to overthrow the established order of the world. They were not travelers, but revolutionaries. To make the revolution they were willing to sacrifice their native language, the culture of their forefathers, their names, everything, even their lives; for immigration is a form of exile, the civilized society's sentence of death. To immigrate is the truest revolution. There is no more radical act.

The symbol of immigration is the ocean, the space between the old order and the new. In the mythology, immigrants embark from poverty, carrying bundles of clothing and battered suitcases, reeking of the old world, and after days of storm-tossed travel in the terrible darkness of the lowest hold of the ship, they find their way up to an open deck to stand at the railing and behold the Statue of Liberty and the skyline of lower Manhattan bathed in brilliant light. The trip is the battle that forges the revolutionary spirit; immigration is the end of the old world, the destruction of the Homeric myth of return.

Those who crossed the waters came to a new social and economic order. They were prepared for democracy, which was in their eyes the empowerment of the poor, and for equalitarianism, which was the defeat of the rich. The social contract they made with their new nation was a simple exchange: language for liberty, culture for equality. They were the answer to Karl Marx's famous question about Rousseau's doctrine: Who signed the social contract? At their citizenship ceremonies, they not only signed the contract, they swore an oath of allegiance to it.

Optimism was the only choice for the immigrants who came across an ocean. A few returned to Europe, having come in search of Cibola, which they were either unable to find or from which they looted a few precious stones and an urn of myrrh. For the rest, it was sink or swim, and they swam furiously.

Only a small percentage of Latinos in the United States have been able to live the immigrant experience fully. For various reasons the rest have failed to get the new social contract that makes the classic pattern of U.S. immigration possible. Racism exemplifies the failure of the new country to sign the contract. For the newcomer who plans to stay only briefly, like the explorers of old, it is the sojourner himself who chooses not to sign. A new social contract is not an option for the migrant. And the exile is concerned only with the contract offered by his former home.

Whoever gets a new social contract succeeds in the world, almost as if the contract were a guarantee, if not for this generation then for the next. When there is this sense of a new contract, the Latino family behaves in the classic immigrant pattern. The parents struggle; the children go to college; the family joins the middle class. Social mobility is understood as a clause in the new contract, the prophecy is self-fulfilling. There are tens of thousands of such families now, and more appear every year. A magazine, *Hispanic,* is devoted to the celebration of social mobility. Another, *Hispanic Business,* is devoted to the methodology.

Professional organizations for Latino lawyers, engineers, teachers, and so on reinforce the immigrant mentality. The membership in these organizations and in the Latino middle and upper middle class is mainly Mexican-American, because two-thirds of all Latinos are of Mexican descent. It is not proportionally Mexican-American, however. Cubans dominate. People from South America, especially Argentines, are represented in disproportionately large numbers, as are those from Spain. There are, of course, many reasons for immigrating, and distance from home is one of them, but the most common one among successful families is the next generation. Immigrants are optimists, whether they cross an ocean or a river to get to the new country.

Perhaps more Mexicans would have immigrated if they had been able to enter the United States legally. Those who came without papers were not offered a social contract; on the contrary, they were barred from any contract, any stability, by law. That many lived for years in the United States with no contract other than the one they made for their children, and still behaved as immigrants, is testimony to the hubris of parents.

Those who crossed the border legally, seeking a contract with the new country, also needed hubris to become immigrants. They had to drag the contract out of a racist society, one which preferred for economic reasons to keep a pool of people available at the economic margin. To make such a contract, to will it in spite of the other party, was more than most people could manage. Those who failed to get a contract, the disappointed, abandoned hope for themselves and their children. Successful immigrants became a separate group in their eyes.

David Moquel, a graduate student at Harvard, whose father came to the United States from Yucatán, illustrated the difference between those who have successfully immigrated and those who could not get a contract. When he was an undergraduate at Stanford, he taught summer school in nearby San Francisco. He had trouble with one of the students, a third generation Mexican-American. They got into a shoving match, and the boy hit Moquel. A few days later, at Moquel's insistence, the boy's mother came to school to talk about her son's behavior.

The woman, a single parent who worked in the post office, spoke no Spanish. Moquel compared her to his own father, a short-order cook at the Hilton Hotel in downtown Los Angeles. He said the woman and his father were of the same economic class, but the woman was crude, with antiestablishment values, lower class values. By contrast, his father was a man who knew how to put off gratification, sacrificing the VCR and plush car to educate his children.

During their conference, Moquel said the woman became angry and lashed out at him. "You goddamned gringos," she said, "you make life impossible for us."

After the woman left, Moquel thought he should have responded by telling her that he was able to speak Spanish, he knew his culture, he was more chicano than she would ever be. Only much later did David Moquel, who is of Mayan descent on both sides, a slim young man, with teeth so small and features so delicate he looks as if he might be made of glass, realize the meaning of the encounter.

———

Immigration occurs in the first generation or it may not occur at all. When the first generation lives in the bitterness of a failed revolution, recovery is difficult, if not impossible. Instead of immigrating, the newcomer transports his despair to the new nation; instead of the dream turning into reality, the dream dies. In that event, the second generation—the hope of the immigrant, the generation in which the great social and economic leaps most often occur, the dream incarnate—is born dead.

The gulf between those Latinos who are able to immigrate and those who are not is greater than the gulf between Latinos and Anglos, as the student's mother taught David Moquel. With each generation, the difference between those who immigrated and those who merely transported their despair becomes greater. Both groups are increasing at an amazing rate, but with a high-school dropout rate of more than fifty percent and a sudden increase in fatherless families, the number of Latinos for whom the revolution has failed is, tragically, the faster growing group.

2. SOJOURNERS

The Tlacolulenses brought no dreams to the United States, they sought no new contract; the revolution that interests them is in the Mexican state of Oaxaca. Although they cannot resist the basketball games and electronics of Santa Monica, they use the devices to try to stave off the exchange of culture for equality. They do not trust the culture of the United States; their view of its effect on their children is completely opposite that of the immigrant.

On the other hand, there is very little left for them to return to in Tlacolula. Inflation, repression, poverty, a broken culture, and the probable loss of their land are not happy prospects. Many of the Tlacolulenses will stay in Los Angeles or Chicago. Some have already received amnesty under the Immigration Reform and Control Act. Yet, when I asked them to think of themselves as anthropologists and tell me what they saw in the United States, they spoke only of drugs and rock and roll, crowding, noise, danger, traffic, a *mole* made of all the *chiles*. They saw nothing positive, nothing to give them hope. Although many of them were in the United States to stay, they could not bring themselves to say so. They despaired not of the old place but of the new; they were sojourners, people for whom success meant going home.

Sojourners do not buy houses or open businesses. Some live in trailers or trucks or cars or in the fields, not only because they cannot afford the rents of decent housing, but also because they do not want the permanence. When sojourners do return home, their adventure, unlike that of Cabeza de Vaca or Coronado, often leaves them better off than before. In a sense, they do find Cibola, and with money brought home from there, they buy land or farm implements or education for their children. Only the sojourners who do not return home find themselves worse off.

In addition to the foragers, like the Tlacolulenses, most refugees come to the United States as sojourners. They arrive with no papers, no money, nothing more than the name of a friend, a distant relative, the address of a sanctuary, and sometimes they come starkly alone, like leaves torn from a tree. Sojourners do the dirtiest work; they stoop over strawberries or crawl in dark manure-filled rooms where mushrooms grow. It was the sojourners of California who bent like pitiful land crabs over the short-handled hoe until it was finally declared illegal, inhuman, a crippling torture of the spine.

The sojourner has few defenders, no place to call home in the United States, no hope for the next generation here. In San Francisco, thousands of Salvadorans came to wait for peace in their own country. One of them, Guillermo Chacón, is twenty-seven years old and he has no papers, no home, nothing permanent in his life but the civil war in El Salvador and the refugee problem in San Francisco. He is a nationalist without illusions, a chauvinist without a horse, an altar boy made into a whirlwind by the war. Guillermo Chacón speaks propaganda and raffles off postcard pictures of home to people who wait in the basement of a church for distributions of food; he organizes, cajoles, demands, pleads, and makes alliances with the most attractive young women who work for the good of the refugees. He is paid three hundred dollars a month. If he had more than he needed to feed himself and pay the rent, he would send the remainder home to El Salvador.

Chacón, who handles food distribution for a Salvadoran refugee relief agency in San Francisco, said the credo of the sojourner is: "It may be illegal, but we want to make a U-turn." He tells everyone who asks that he wants to make a U-turn; it is his best joke, his Yanqui joke. "I arrived in the Big Apple," he said. "New York is a tough city. I lived in the Bronx. For me it was a big shock. When I went to the South Bronx, I couldn't believe it. Our image was the U.S. was the richest country. I ask why is it so poor in parts of the country here?"

Chacón is an organizer, a charmer, expert at politics, publicity, and professions of love for his country. He recalls the deaths of friends in El Salvador, the day the National Guard came for him. "They came to my home. I was in a retreat house in San Salvador. They told my mother and father I was a communist and they want me.

"My father was very nervous. He was not crying, but his eyes were shining. He said, 'The National Guard was looking for you.' My mother was in bed. She had a nervous attack. She fell down.

"My father said, 'I was talking with other relatives, but nobody wants you.' Everybody was afraid to help me. My father was angry.

"I went to one of my teachers from the school. I stayed there for a month. I stayed in her house for a month. I never went outside. She didn't tell her children why I was there. She was pregnant. Her husband was killed four months before I got there. He taught in Apopa and in a very small village.

"When I arrived, I was shaking, nervous. I was thinking a lot about the past, about close friends I lost, about Rafael. I was thinking about Roberto, about Jaime, about Sonia. We did things together. We went to the beach. I thought of why I was not home when the National Guard came to the house.

"Every night I could hear the guns. The teacher said some people in the neighborhood asked who I was. She is very white and I am very brown. She said I was her cousin, but people were starting to make speculations.

"She said, 'It's hard for me to tell you, but you have to leave, for your own security.' She was more concerned for me than for herself. I asked her to buy me sunglasses. I was very well known, because of my work with Father Rafael. I went to the bus terminal. The National Guard was there. I remember my heart was beating fast and my hands were wet. I thought of the Scriptures. 'La mejor expresión de amor por un Christiano es dar la vida por hermanos y hermanas.'[8] I went to the bus, bought the ticket, and left."

Chacón is the speaker, the dealmaker, the quick one of the refugee group. When a pretty Anglo girl appears to help with the work, she becomes Guillermo's girl. When a dispute must be settled, Guillermo charms the contestants into compromise. He moves, he hustles, he survives. "You do many things when you leave your country," he says. One thing he has not done is adopt his new country. The distribution of its wealth displeases him, and its foreign policy enrages him. "Your government does many bad things in our country. You don't have to be an expert to know your government is making the biggest errors in history in Latin America. You provide the guns, and we provide the bodies.

"We have dignity, but we have poverty. We have no children's hospital in the whole country, but your government gave us seventy helicopters. Nobody can eat a helicopter, believe me."

Every year, the lives of the sojourner Salvadorans grow worse in San Francisco. When there were not so many of them, they found work as gardeners, maids, babysitters, dishwashers. Churches helped; food was donated by restaurants and markets. EMPLEOS, an employment cooperative, was able to find jobs for twenty or even a hundred people every week.

---

[8]The best expression of love for a Christian is to give his life for his brothers and sisters.

Local churches cashed the checks with which the undocumented people were paid. But time weakened the will of the charitable, and the threat of fines and other sanctions frightened the people who employed the refugees. Drugs crept into the community. Some of the women turned to prostitution. Gangs formed.

A peace accord has been reached in El Salvador between the government and the guerrillas. But the refugees have heard of peace agreements, cease-fires, amnesties, and democracy for many years. The question of return is not simple. There are economic as well as political factors to consider, and for the sojourner there is always the question of when. "The majority of our people want to go home," Guillermo said, "but say you were a campesino, you never have the possibility to buy a car, own a home, have a boss who says to you, 'You do a good job.' What are you going to do?"

Word of the sojourner experience has spread south from San Francisco and Los Angeles to San Salvador. At Casa Romero, the sanctuary named for the Catholic Bishop who was murdered by the Salvadoran military, three young Salvadorans lolled on the porch outside the small office of the camp, waiting until they could find a way to get bus fare to Los Angeles or Washington, D.C. It was winter in Brownsville, warm, shirt-sleeve weather. The young men had been out of the Immigration and Naturalization Service processing center at Bayview for only two days. They had papers in English, which they could not understand, instructing them in what they were permitted to do, where they had to report and when, until their requests for political asylum came before the courts. The boy who was going to Washington was lost, very frightened. The one who was going to Los Angeles wore white basketball shoes with the laces untied and tossed his head to rearrange his long, shining hair when it was mussed by the breeze.

"Do you know anyone in Los Angeles?" I asked.

"Brothers."

"Family?"

"Amigos."

"Many?"

"The crowd."

"A gang?"

"Mara Salva Trucha"[9]—he smiled. Although he was still trapped in a sanctuary run by nuns and Anglo women volunteers, he could strut his

---

[9]"The Salvadoran Wiseguys" is a reasonable translation of the name, but it has many puns and resonances. *Mara* means "the crowd" in Salvadoran slang, but Maravilla is the name of a section of Los Angeles. *Salva* refers to El Salvador, but a *salva* is a salvo or an oath, both important concepts in gang life. *Trucha* literally means "trout," but as an adjective it means "alert," "aware," "quick-witted."

connections, for there is no tougher Latino gang in Los Angeles than Mara Salva Trucha. In the neighborhood they control, west of downtown Los Angeles, drug dealers run out into the street at midday to stop passing cars, desperately competing to sell marijuana, cocaine, heroin, PCP.

"Ask them for bus fare to L.A."

"I'm going by airplane," he said. "Te, doble oo, ah, the best."

The sadness of sojourners falls most heavily on the young, who cannot know where to commit their political and cultural loyalties. They come to the United States, and within a few years they lose the sound and smell of home. After that, they are trapped, unable to move in any direction. If they go back, they find themselves derided as half-breeds, renegades. If they stay, they find themselves passed by, having waited too long to commit to their new country, not immigrants, with no hope of becoming immigrants, victims of their own social paralysis. Sojourners who stay must live with the knowledge that they did not chance a revolution. Regret becomes companion to despair; they live in squalor; they are the home workers and the sweatshop workers. They are sojourners who stand on the streets of Los Angeles waiting for someone to pick them up and take them to a day's work on a construction site or in a garden. The young Salvadoran at Casa Romero knew; he did not expect to be offered a social contract, he came to the United States to be an outlaw.

3. EXILES

You take a tobacco
plant and you plant
it here, it's not
the same as Cuba.

Arturo Rodríguez

It was almost midnight when the Secretary's car left the compound. He sat behind the wheel himself. He trusted no one now, not even his chauffeur. As he drove through the dark streets of the capitol, he made several brief calls from his mobile telephone, never speaking more than a few sentences, never calling from so great a distance that his message could be intercepted. When Maritza Herrera, his former student and the daughter-in-law of Tacho's personal paymaster, answered the telephone, the Secretary said, "Take your children and go."

Maritza sat for a long time in the darkness. Should she go? Should she be-

lieve the Secretary? The young Herreras were among the lucky ones; they had connections to the regime on both sides. She was already well placed in the Central Bank; he was on his way to becoming one of the most important scientists in the country. Tacho was still in control of the army and the radio stations. There had been fighting in the mountains, but the city was calm. Whom could she ask? Whom could she trust?

Maritza's husband was more than two thousand miles away, at the University of Colorado; she could not risk a telephone call to him. Her father was back in Matagalpa, probably out in a cantina with one of his women. She could not tell her younger sister, who had ties to the revolutionaries. Her brother was an officer in the army, a fanatic, like her father; she could not betray the Secretary by telling her brother. She did not even dare to tell her personal maid, the little Indian woman who called her Doña.

She had no one to turn to, no godmothers, no old friends. The family had never been comfortable in Matagalpa. They were northerners, from Jinotega, and even though Maritza's father had done well as an importer and wholesaler of food, the community had not accepted them. Perhaps some of this isolation was due to the women her father took and the children he had by them; perhaps the community did not like the way he treated his wife. He was a difficult man, one who put his children to work in the warehouse as soon as they were able to read and do accounts. Because of him, Maritza had determined to be an independent woman, one who could do business.

She studied accounting at the university, then took a job administering funds from the U.S. Agency for International Development (AID). As the person behind the loans, she was something of a heroine to the small business people of Managua, especially the taxi drivers, who had never even dreamed of owning their own cars. But they were only taxi drivers; they could not help her now.

When her husband completed his M.S. in plant pathology, she planned to go to business school in the United States. But in the middle of the night, in the quiet of the sleeping household, such dreams no longer mattered. She had to do as the Secretary advised. The family was tied too closely to the government; there were too many military officers, too many business arrangements. She could not stay. She could not wait. She packed two suitcases. For some reason she would never be able to remember, she put an old lamp in one of them.

On the day the regime collapsed Maritza Herrera was at the airport in Houston, Texas, with two suitcases, her four-year-old daughter, a baby who had diarrhea, and no disposable diapers. Her brother was already in a revolutionary prison, where he would commit suicide. Her father would also go to prison, although a month later his radical daughter would bribe the new regime to release him and allow him to cross the border into Costa Rica.

But Maritza and her babies were in America. She was among the first of the first wave of exiles from Nicaragua.

Her husband stayed in school, and Maritza Herrera went to work. In two years she won a prize as the best Mary Kay Cosmetics salesperson in America. With her earnings and the money her husband began to bring in after completing his degree, the Herreras bought a house in a suburb southwest of Miami.

By then, thousands of Nicaraguan refugees were coming into Miami every month. There was no place for them to stay, no work for them to do. They lived in a baseball park, in every kind of shelter the city could find for them. Maritza Herrera opened a social service office. She took over a decrepit city building in one of Miami's worst neighborhoods and turned it into a school, an employment office, and a center for people seeking asylum in the United States.

Dressed in pants suits and made up to sell Mary Kay Cosmetics, she raised her children, ran the center for Nicaraguan refugees, and, working out of the office of a tortilla factory owned by Nicaraguans, helped Mexican farm workers in Homestead to apply for amnesty under the provisions of the Immigration Reform and Control Act. Less than ten years after going into exile she had returned to the middle class. In the social service center and the tortilla factory and the migrant worker camps of South Florida, Maritza Herrera enjoyed the role of *patrona;* she had recreated Managua in Miami.

It is the Cubans, even more than the Somocistas, who exemplify the life of the exile. They left in anger, the rich suddenly made poor in everything but their ability to prosper. Unlike the immigrants of Tocqueville's America, the Cuban exiles came with no taste for equalitarianism; they were utterly unprepared for the political philosophy of the United States. In defiance of Castro, they refused to become immigrants, knowing that as long as they remained exiles his victory was incomplete. Those who hadn't known English learned it, but they did not forget Spanish. They judged people by how well they spoke Spanish and how much they hated Castro.

The part of Miami where the Cubans settled quickly became Little Havana. On Calle Ocho, once known as Eighth Street, the restaurants sold *ropa vieja, arroz moro, bacalao, maduros,* and Cuban sandwiches. Men played dominoes on street corners, and businesses vied with each other to see who could serve the best cup of Cuban coffee.

Everything about Havana that could be reproduced in the United States appeared in Miami: schools, educational methods, businesses, even the *quinceañera,* the gaudy celebration of a girl's fifteenth birthday. In the country of exile culture takes the place of the state as the focus for politics, so that an institution like the Cuban Museum of Art and Culture becomes a cause instead of a gallery. The actions of its directors achieve the status of affairs of state.

Human rights, the Spanish language, and Cuban culture are the three stones on which the boiling pot of the exile sits. However, the sinister view of Miami and its Cuban community portrayed in Joan Didion's bestseller is simply wrong. A community in exile needs a few lunatics or even better, some news stories about lunatics. In that way, the Didion book served the exile well. But exiles as a class are not crazies; bomb throwing is not a bourgeois activity, but it is the bomb throwers who enable the majority of the Cubans in the United States, who are working class or lower middle class, to think and act like members of the bourgeoisie. The function of the bomb thrower in exile is to support the psychological commitment of the other exiles to maintain their cultural identity in their temporary residence; the arrogance of the shoe clerk and the daring of the entrepreneur both depend upon the willingness of the bomb thrower to give up his freedom or even his life for *patria y libertad*.

Without the bomb thrower, the exile becomes a sojourner, so every now and then, someone sets off a tiny bomb in the streets of Miami. The bombs are not serious anymore; no one gets hurt. The bombers are still adept at assembling their oversized firecrackers, but they are too old to throw them now; they make their weapons with trembling, arthritic fingers and set them with long fuses, for the knees that carry the bombers away from their targets are not what they used to be in the good old days of CIA stipends and the Watergate break in.

Without the bomb thrower, the exile would lose its middle-class standing. Opposition to the government rather than flight from poverty or chaos gives one the psychological power to separate oneself from the ordinary poor. The self-concept of the exile is of one too rich, too wise, too well-armed with education and character to tolerate or be tolerated by the evil regime.

Maintaining exile is more difficult for those who cannot remember the revolution. The Cuban-Americans, those born here and those who came as young children, don't concern themselves with Cuba. Yet their parents' insistence upon exile rather than immigration makes assimilation difficult for them. Andrea Camps said her children, now in their thirties, have no clear identity. She recalls one of them coming home from the Cranbrook Academy in Detroit saying, "My definition is 'I am not.' I am not American and I am not Cuban. I am nothing." Perhaps to clarify their world even more than her own, Camps said she does not intend to return to Cuba, no matter what happens to Castro.

In the end, it is the poor Cubans more than the rich who need the concept of exile. Bernardo Benes, a Cuban exile banker whose wish to open a dialogue with Castro has cost him dearly in both the social and economic spheres in Miami, tells all the reporters who interview him that the Cuban community in the United States cannot have as its raison d'etre the idea that Castro is a son of a bitch. For Benes, a garrulous, cigar-smoking, red-haired bull with spectacles, exile was an economic nuisance. He had no need of bomb throwers or CIA connections; he would have done as well or better without them. Benes brought his wealth with him, in education and business experience. He belonged to the system of *socios* on the day he left Havana and on the day he arrived in Miami. The United States was not a strange country to him or anyone of his social and economic class; his class did business in the United States; they sent their children to U.S. prep schools and universities.

Either Benes does not understand or, more likely, does not wish to concede that hatred of Castro, the sine qua non of the exile mentality, helped the poor Cubans more than the rich. The rich didn't need bomb throwers—they carried their wealth in their heads—but fanaticism made shopkeepers of the poor. Jorge Más, the 2506th, Radio Mambi, TV Martí, *Diario las Americas,* and all the madmen and Faustian schemers of the extreme right did what liberals could only dream about: They gave self-respect, even a touch of arrogance, to the working class, the aged, the lonely, and the unemployed. In return, they asked only undying, irrational loyalty to the exile credo, which is that Fidel Castro Ruz is a son of a bitch.

4. GHOSTS

no, not yet, no, not yet,
i will not proclaim myself
a total child of any land,
i'm still in the commonwealth
stage of my life, wondering
what to decide, what to conclude,
what to declare myself?

Tato Laviera

After the announcement by President George Bush in 1990 endorsing a plebiscite to determine the political future of Puerto Rico, four issues were debated: statehood, which Bush and the party associated with the Republicans[10] favored), "enhanced commonwealth status," which was favored by the island Democrats; independence, which was supported by its own Independence Party; and the question of whether Puerto Ricans living on the U.S.

[10]Representatives of all three parties, appearing on a television program broadcast in New York City (September 16, 1990), said they favored voting rights for Puerto Ricans who lived on the mainland. In Puerto Rico, only the Republican pro-commonwealth party favors that policy.

mainland should be eligible to vote in the plebiscite. Since the results of the plebiscite were not binding upon the U.S. government, but could be overturned by Congress, vetoed by the president, and then tied up in the courts for many years, much of the debate centered on the question of who should be able to vote; that is, who is a Puerto Rican.

Under U.S. law, neither a person born in Georgia and living in New York nor a person born in New York of Mexican descent would be permitted to vote anywhere but in New York, yet all three Puerto Rican political parties agreed that Nuyoricans were a special case; and indeed they are different from other Latinos, since they are neither immigrants nor exiles nor sojourners, they are not hopeful, they are not barred from returning to Puerto Rico, and they are forced by circumstance to shed their island culture.

Puerto Ricans most resemble migrants, who travel to find work, without any hope of change in their lives, doomed to repeat their woes in different places and times. But the Nuyoricans differ from them, too. The *jíbaros* who came down from the mountains wound up in high rise tenements, the farmers were turned into factory workers, and the keepers of little shops and the working class ended up on welfare. Only those who moved from the slums of San Juan to the slums of New York and New Jersey repeated their lives in a different place; all the rest found new problems in an old country.

The Puerto Ricans bear no resemblance to the immigrants who preceded them in New York. They follow a pattern similar to that of the blacks who came north after World War II. Like the blacks, they were members of a racial minority from an economically depressed area, poorly educated and with a colonial history, but to make matters worse, they couldn't speak English.

—

No personal revolution, no triumph of the spirit occurred when the Puerto Ricans arrived on the mainland. No exile arrogance propelled them to economic success. It was not the rich young island boys, educated at Groton and Yale, who came to New York; after school they went back home to run family businesses, just like the rich young men from Mexico, Venezuela, or Peru. It was the less fortunate who moved to New York. Those who arrived first say that the newcomers are less educated, less sophisticated, *jíbaros* and slum dwellers who come to get the welfare. Those who came most recently say that the old Nuyoricans think of welfare as a way of life. "My mother-in-law, she's of the old New York school," said a woman who came to the mainland recently after earning a degree from the University of Puerto Rico. "From the day I got married she started putting money in a treasure chest to pay for a divorce. She hates the idea that I work. She thinks I should stay home and collect welfare like a good Puerto Rican woman."

Neither group has anything good to say about the other. The first thing that comes to the minds of Puerto Ricans in New York is the stereotype of Puerto Ricans in New York: welfare. The conversation then invariably turns to crime. Like blacks, Puerto Ricans have internalized the outsider's view of them. Immigration or exile, which might have permitted them to reinvent themselves, did not take place. The old social contract, the one which had been such a rotten deal for them, remained in effect; they were what the others said they were.

How Spanish-speaking people from the Caribbean could have moved to the mainland United States without experiencing the sense of change that creates the true revolution is one of the cruelties of colonialism. As the debate over who is a Puerto Rican and therefore eligible to vote shows, colonialism is more than a matter of residence; it is an occupation of the mind as well as the land, a portable prison.

Since Puerto Rico has been a colony for almost five hundred years, the people of the island have no other view of themselves, no other history. The period before conquest was neolithic; history began with the conquest. In no remembered, recorded time did the people of Puerto Rico control their destiny; they have always belonged to someone, been a possession, nothing more. Had they been able to escape the monolith of their history by coming to the mainland, they might have freed themselves from the prison of colonialism, but coming to the mainland was not an act of immigration. The Puerto Ricans merely migrated: they remained Puerto Ricans; they remained colonized.

Every Puerto Rican who survives and succeeds to any degree on the mainland is a miracle of love and will. Every one who does not live according to the self-hatred of the colonized knows the distinguishing cause in his or her life:

"The Sisters helped me."

"It was *las viejitas* who saved me after I dropped out from high school; every day they prayed, all the time. *Oramos para ti,* they said."

"My mother, she worked in a sweatshop all day and then she cleaned other people's houses to make extra money so we could stay in school. We girls couldn't go out alone with boys; she was so strict with us, just like Puerto Rico."

"The army."

"My father was a postman."

"My math teacher helped me; she gave me extra work, she let me tutor the other children. We went midtown together. She bought me dresses, she got me this scholarship."

Every year, more Puerto Ricans break the rules of colonialism, but they are still exceptions. The extent to which Puerto Ricans on the mainland have been unable to overcome their colonial status is revealed in the word they use for other mainland people; they call them Americans. That is why José Luis Morín, a young Puerto Rican attorney who was born on the Lower East Side of New York and educated at Columbia University and New York University Law School, went before the United Nations Special Committee on the Implementation of the Resolution on the Granting of Independence to Colonized Nations and Peoples to plead the case of Puerto Rico. He compared the island to Namibia, asking that the United Nations treat it in the same fashion.

Like all colonized peoples, the Puerto Ricans have no home, no streets, no land, nothing that really belongs to them. Since they cross no border when coming to the mainland, they cannot become Americans, cannot become at all; nothing changes for them—they remain Puerto Ricans, they remain colonized. The argument in favor of mainland Puerto Ricans voting in the plebiscite is profound; it recognizes that no Puerto Rican can escape colonialism in the United States. For that reason there are no Puerto Rican leaders in New York City or anywhere else on the mainland. The dilemma of the Puerto Rican is nightmarish: Of all the Spanish-speaking peoples of the hemisphere, only the Puerto Ricans are U.S. citizens, and only the Puerto Ricans are barred from the United States.

As long as Puerto Ricans cannot immigrate, they remain the poorest of the poor, ghosts floating above the streets of the cities, prohibited by their very nature from touching down and rooting themselves in the culture and the economy. As long as Puerto Ricans cannot immigrate, they remain immutable, wooden people on whom the outer vestments of culture can be changed, but who are fixed by the morticians of colonialism in timeless imitations of party-goers.

Of the three solutions to the problem of Puerto Rico's status—statehood, enhanced commonwealth status, and independence—only one, the almost certain winner in a plebiscite, will not enable the Puerto Ricans to escape their ghostly existence. Enhanced commonwealth status changes nothing. Even statehood will leave the Puerto Ricans no better off than the black migrants, perhaps a little worse off because of the language problem. Only independence, the dangerous alternative, offers the possibility of immigration, a real life at last for the ghosts of Chicago, Boston, New Jersey and New York.

11

RACISM AND RACISMO

Until I came to New York,
I didn't know I was black.

Chiqui Vicioso, Dominican poet

Until I came here with my
Spanish, I didn't
know what it meant to be
a woman of color.

Dr. Liliana Rossi, Argentine psychologist

I.

At the end of summer there is a festival on Third Avenue in that part of Harlem known as El Barrio. The unofficial theme of the festival is Latin pride, and while there may be some pride in the streets, there is a lot more marketing. The musicians on the bandstand at the north end of the street wear shirts emblazoned with the brand names of breweries, and all the booths that line the street have sponsors, from 7-Up to cigarettes to social service agencies. When the festival is held during an election year, many of the candidates walk through the crowd, white candidates and black, men and women, all flanked by their brownest minions, walking as if on parade. Although people dance in the streets only on Third Avenue, the festival extends beyond the police barricades to 116th Street, where it curls west along the shady side of the street, past the storefront racks and sidewalk salesmen, to Park Avenue.

I was surprised and pleased to find Francisco, a student in the fifth grade bilingual class of P.S. 7, at the festival. He was strolling down the center of the street, dressed as always in a clean, long-sleeved shirt just slightly too tight across the belly, black oxfords, white socks, and perfectly pressed slacks. He looked prosperous and well fed except for his homestyle haircut, which leaves him with a cap of black hair shaped like a bowl. The bangs, cut straight across his forehead, accentuate the staring quality of his eyes, which

146

are very dark and still slightly too large for the rest of him. He appears to be slightly bemused, as if he were waiting for the arrival of puberty to clarify his life and thoughts.

We had become pals during the year in which I observed his class at P.S. 7. Francisco, who was born in Mexico, was fatherless and something of a stranger in a class of mostly Puerto Rican children, and I was also a stranger, the one who sat in the back of the room watching and being watched. When he told me he was from Mexico and his name was Francisco, I offered to bring him a book about another Francisco from Mexico, Francisco Villa. Suddenly, he threw his arms around me in the most profound *abrazo,* then stepped back, smiled, and said, "You're my friend."

At the festival we had hot dogs, sodas, and candy and talked about Miss Ojeda's class and Francisco's great triumph. He had gone from a less than mediocre student to being one of the stars. Instead of remaining with his class for the coming year, he had been chosen for a special fast track sixth grade class; the system had decided, almost at the last moment, that Francisco was destined to succeed.

We sat on a bench in the shade of the projects and ate and talked about his stepfather, who was a dishwasher in a restaurant in Chinatown, about his mother, the caretaker and domestic servant of a very important *babalawo*[1] in the barrio, and about school. Then we went for a tour of the festival. At the various booths they were giving away hats and pens and cups and buttons, and Francisco thought we should stop by and get ours before they ran out.

At almost every booth there was a sign explaining that the "free gifts" were only for people over eighteen. Francisco needed a front man, and I was perfect for the job. Within half an hour, we had two hats, a cup, a mug, a pocketful of discount coupons, and a banner.

The first time it happened was at the AIDS Prevention booth. A black woman in a white nurse's uniform handed me a pamphlet. "It's in Español," she said. Her accent was lovely; never had the word Español been drawled more sweetly. "Very importante. SIDA[2] very bad."

"Thank you very much," I said. "I shall take the proper precautions."

She was surprised, but only for a moment. She lowered her eyes and bowed her head slightly, as if in recognition of the error. "I'm sorry," she said. "We have them in English too."

Francisco wanted to walk up to 116th Street to tell his mother that he would be home in an hour. He lives there, near Second Avenue, in a tenement occupied entirely by Mexicans. On the way, we passed the babalawo,

---

[1]Priest in the Santería religion

[2]The acronym for the Spanish translation of Acquired Immune Deficiency Syndrome (AIDS).

who was being attended by Francisco's older sister. The woman sat in a wood and canvas chair that had been brought out to the street for her. She was gigantic, a mound of many Henry Moore sculptures; the fat was piled liked thighs on her shoulders. She wore Caribbean plantation clothing, the handkerchief upon her head, and leaned on a thick bamboo cane. Beside her, Francisco's sixteen-year-old sister was like a butterfly on a thread, fluttering around the babalawo, desperate to join the dancing, but unable to escape.

The babalawo looked up at us. In the heat of the afternoon, on the street without shade, sweat shone on her face. Francisco moved closer to me. I felt him take my hand. The babalawo pointed to his head. "Give me that cap," she said. He removed the hat and handed it to her. She examined it, then let it fall into her lap.

I looked down at Francisco. His lower lip stuck out. I could not tell whether he was angry or afraid.

"I'm hot," the *babalawo* said, looking up. "Bring me a beer."

It took a moment before I realized she had given the order to me. Then I said flatly, "No."

Our glances met. I was wearing dark glasses, but I was certain she saw through them. What I saw in her face was nothing, neither anger nor surprise, only opacity; her eyes, which were of the softest brown, did not even betray interest. She merely looked in my direction. I returned the gaze. I smiled at her. She made no response; she had dismissed me from the world—with malice.

On 116th Street, Francisco and I moved through the weekend crowd. Although there were many cuchifritos joints and dozens of sidewalk vendors of fritters and *lechón*,[3] the street was strangely odorless, except for the occasional stench of rotted food rising from a subway grating or a gutter. Even the garlic dip for *tostones*[4] seemed not to escape into the air on 116th Street.

Near the corner of Third Avenue we passed a table filled with newspapers, books, and pamphlets from the Socialist Workers party. A thin man, with dirty blonde hair and rimless spectacles, and a lumpy woman dressed in layers of prints and stripes stood behind the table. The man noticed that I was examining the papers and handed a broadsheet to me. I took the paper, but said nothing.

"We with poor people," he said, pointing with his forefinger to his breastbone.

Francisco smiled.

"So-shull-ees-ta Wor-kerr-zzz par-tee," he said, in a voice so loud it could be heard for twenty or thirty feet in every direction.

[3]Suckling pig
[4]Fried plantains

I nodded.

"Workers and union together," he said slowly and even more loudly. He exaggerated the movements of his mouth, as if I might be able to read his lips. He had steel-colored dental work, and his teeth were brown near the gums.

"So-shull-ees-ta with poor people," he said, making a fist of his right hand. He held the fist out to me and shook it. I drew back. As we turned away, Francisco and I laughed aloud.

At the "Just Say No" booth, a white woman with a gentle face and that special mix of dark brown and white hair which somehow signals good will said to me that I could take any of the pamphlets on drugs. When I made no motion toward the table, she pointed to Francisco. "For boy," she said loudly. "Take for boy. Save!"

After we left the booth, Francisco said, "You're a good reporter."

"Thank you, sir."

Suddenly, I heard the voice of the Anglo again, this time from my pal. "You are well-come, Seen-yore."

2.

The complex of racial, cultural, and linguistic relations of an afternoon in the barrio cannot be ignored; it hovers over everything, enters every conversation, appears on every page, dances every dance. It is not a hierarchy, but a matrix; obvious, yet unclear. To sort out the threads may be impossible, for the matrix exists in at least six dimensions: language, color, economics, education, citizenship, and national origin.

The problem has a history going back to the colonial period in Mexico when there were many attempts to codify racism. Santamaria's *Diccionario de Mejicanismos* reproduces two of these efforts, the first from the National Museum and the second from a series of numbered paintings in Michoacán.

Español con India—Mestizo.
Mestizo con Española—Castizo.
Castizo con Española—Español.
Español con Negra—Mulato.
Mulato con Española—Chino.
Chino con India—Salta atrás.[5]
Salta atrás con Mulata—Lobo.[6]

[5]Skip backwards
[6]Wolf

Lobo con China—Gibaro.[7]
Gibaro con Mulata—Albarazado.
Albarazado con Negra—Cambujo.
Cambujo con India—Zambaigo.
Zambaigo con Loba—Calpamulato.
Calpamulato con Cambuza—Tente en el aire.[8]
Tente en el aire con Mulata—No te entiendo.[9]
No te entiendo con India—Torna atrás.[10]

1. Generación de español y de india produce Mestizo.
2. De español y de mestiza produce Castizo.
3. De español y de castiza produce Español.
4. De español y de negra produce Mulato.
5. De español y de mulata produce Morisco.
6. De español y de morisca produce Albina.
7. De español y de albina produce Tornatrás.
8. De español y de tornatrás produce Tenté en el aire.
9. De indio y de negra produce Cambujo.
10. De chino cambujo y de india produce Lobo.
11. De lobo y de india produce Albarazado.
12. De albarazado y de mestiza produce Barnocino.[11]
13. De indio y de barnocina produce Zambaigo.
14. De mestizo y castiza produce Chamizo.[12]
15. De mestizo y de india produce Coyote.
16. De dicha y de indios gentiles (sic).

The Cuban system had only nine variations, which should not be taken as a reflection on the Cuban capacity for racism or subtlety. Since the native population of Cuba was destroyed very early in the conquest, the Cubans were left with only two variables, black and white, from which to fashion a hierarchy.

A new category of variable was added in what is now New Mexico when a class of former Indian slaves, the Genízaros, was defined. Soon afterward, Mexico declared its independence, and national origin became a variable, especially in the Catholic Church, where the European clergy placed itself on

[7]Compare to *jibaro* and *guajiro*, the former used in Puerto Rico and the latter in Cuba to designate a person from a rural area.
[8]Flaps in the air, hummingbird
[9]I don't understand.
[10]Throwback
[11]Varnished
[12]Thatched

a level far above the criollos and the mestizos who had been trained in Mexican seminaries under the influence of the Indianist radicals, Hidalgo and Morelos. After the Texas War and the Treaty of Guadalupe Hidalgo, citizenship became a variable. Literacy, which had been confined to the Españoles and a few mestizos, spread to the other castes, becoming an issue within each caste. Those who could not read suffered one kind of stigma; those who could read Spanish but not English suffered yet another.

Intermarriage between Latinos and Anglos produced still another caste, until finally surname, skin color, familiarity with English, accent in English, and place of origin were sliced so fine that people from one neighborhood or those who had attended one grammar school considered themselves different from those who had lived on the next block. As people arrived from countries other than Mexico, national origin became yet another factor. And there was always money, but money couldn't buy whiteness or perfectly accented English.

The relation of each variable to all the others is so complex (there are at least 46,656 possible permutations) that it is necessary to construct a hierarchy of variables just to maintain order among injustices. The problem for every Latino is to find his or her place within the bifurcated hierarchies of racism in the Anglo world and *racismo* among Latinos.

The problem exists at the most basic level: Should Latinos be considered a racial or an ethnic group? The confusion of race and ethnicity in any definition of Latinos was illustrated in an article in the *New York Times*.[13] In explaining the connection between race and the propensity to suffer certain ailments, the *Times* offered several examples, including this: "Research also suggests that Chinese and Hispanic women face significantly greater risk of developing diabetes during pregnancy than comparable blacks or whites." The statement defines groups racially rather than ethnically, so it must refer to an inherited rather than an acquired trait. Since some Hispanics or Latinos are black and some are white, but most are mestizos, the assertion borders on nonsense.

Similar nonsense occurs in the census. The forms once asked whether people were white, Negro, Oriental, or other. Now, in addition to white and black, there are Asians and Hispanics. It is an interesting idea, but it is also a category error. As the ingenious racists of colonial Mexico knew, there is no Hispanic or Latino race. The spectrum of races is the American spectrum, although the proportions are different: There are many more mestizos and Amerindians, because the Spaniards were as willing to marry as to exterminate the native populations.

Given the cultural diversity among the people called Latinos or Hispanics,

---

[13]"Uneasy Doctors Add Race-Consciousness to Diagnostic Tools," September 25, 1990.

the name comprises many ethnic groups rather than describing one, so ethnicity as it is generally understood, cannot be the determining factor. All that is left is the Spanish language, the salient quality among all Latinos, which now comes forward with every wave of immigration and fades with the birth of every new generation.

In the midst of such complexity one is tempted to repeat Sartre's error about Jews; that is, to say that Latinos are defined from without, made Latino by exclusion, a creation of prejudice. But the truth lies elsewhere. Diversity provokes racism, it does not result from it. Latinos existed before anyone despised them, and they continue to exist in places where they make up the majority. In the Western hemisphere they were the inventors of racism, the champions of ethnocentrism, the sponsors of the caste system, and now they are the victims of their own invention.

Although racism began in the Americas in an internecine way (racismo), the layers of it peel away more easily from the outside, starting with the way Anglos treat Latinos (racism). Felix Fraga, the director of Ripley House, a complex of social service agencies in Houston, Texas, recalled the way racism worked when he was a boy:

"I remember my older brother was the first one to ever have a friend that was an Anglo. It was 1940, I guess, because he dropped out of high school to go to the war. It was an unusual thing for us to see an Anglo befriend a Mexican. Up to that point, any acquaintance we had would have been a Mexican. Before the war, even soon after, it was hard to mix Anglos and Mexicans here. All through the forties, you'd run across many signs that said, 'No Mexicans allowed.'

"LULAC had to come in and take the school district to court, because they had schools where—no matter if you lived in front of it, you had to go to the Mexican school and not to the Anglo school. We went to our own parks and swimming pools, a little of what the black goes through, except it was harder for us, because at least they knew where they stood; we never knew. You'd go to a place and you'd wonder whether they'd tell you 'No' or 'Yes,' 'you can stay' or 'you can't stay.' "

Racist policies were entrenched in Texas before Felix Fraga was born. Mario T. García documented the policies in El Paso, Texas, during the early part of this century. In 1900, the ratio of Mexican to American laborers in the work force was 15 to 1. The ratio dropped to 6 to 1 in 1920 as the number of people identified as laborers decreased, then by 1940 when the overall percentage of laborers was the same, the ratio had gone back up to 11 to 1. As the total number of laborers declined, the number of service workers increased, and that's where the Mexicans went.

Meanwhile, the ratio of "Americans" to Mexicans among professionals and managers in El Paso grew steadily worse: from 4 to 1 in 1900 to 5 to 1 in

1920 all the way up to 7 to 1 in 1940. The situation was no better in Los Angeles, where in 1917 over 90 percent of all Mexicans and Mexican-Americans worked in blue collar jobs. The extent to which racism accounted for the low status employment of Mexicans was documented by LULAC's founder, M. C. González, in 1920. He listed five types of discrimination: segregation in the schools, segregation in public facilities, whiteman's primaries, housing covenants barring Mexicans from buying in white neighborhoods, and the failure to permit Mexican-Americans to serve on juries.

As if Gunnar Myrdal's theory of the economic basis of racism in *An American Dilemma* needed further proof, the most explicitly racist statements about people of Mexican descent surfaced during the Depression. Rodolfo Acuña's history of chicanos includes part of a report prepared for U.S. Representative John Box of Texas by Dr. Roy L. Garis of Vanderbilt University. "Garis reported to the congressional committee as an authority on eugenics that 'the following statement made to the author by an American who lives on the border seems to reflect the general sentiment of those who are deeply concerned with the future welfare of this country:

Their [the Mexicans'] minds run to nothing higher than animal functions—eat, sleep, and sexual debauchery. In every huddle of Mexican shacks one meets the same idleness, hordes of hungry dogs, and filthy children with faces plastered with flies, disease, lice, human filth, stench, promiscuous fornication, bastardy, lounging, apathetic peons and lazy squaws, beans and dried chili, liquor, general squalor, and envy and hatred of the gringo. These people sleep by day and prowl by night like coyotes, stealing anything they can get their hands on, no matter how useless to them it may be. Nothing left outside is safe unless padlocked or chained down. Yet there are Americans clamoring for more of this human swine to be brought over from Mexico.

It wasn't until 1970 that a federal district court defined Mexican-Americans as an "identifiable ethnic minority." Three years later, the U.S. Supreme Court, describing the problems of Mexican-American students in Denver, said that "Negroes and Hispanos" suffered identical patterns of discrimination. By the time the courts finally concluded that ethnic minorities as well as racial minorities could and did suffer discrimination, generations of Mejicanos and Mexican-Americans in the Southwest had been lost and the wounds of racism had been built into the heart of the Latino community.

As always, the cruelest effect of racism was on school-age children, where the damage is often irrevocable. Eleuterio Escobar, who headed the LULAC education committee for many years, led the battle against discrimination in the schools of San Antonio, a city that had been Latino from its beginnings, where intermarriage between Anglos and Latinos had not been uncommon, one of the few places in the Southwest to have developed a Latino elite that mirrored in many ways the arrogance, exploitative practices and exclusionary policies of the Anglo rich. During the Depression, there were twelve thousand students in San Antonio's twenty-eight white schools and the same number squeezed into eleven overcrowded and underfunded Mexican schools. Two of the Mexican schools in San Antonio at the end of World War II had no furniture in their cafeterias; the children ate off the floor. Another school, Sidney Lanier, had a cafeteria that seated 120 of its 1,700 students.

Almost half a century later, James B. (Jimmy) Vásquez, superintendent of the Edgewood School District in San Antonio, saw the Texas State Supreme Court rule that there had to be some equity in funding for schools in the same city. The court battle over equalization had taken years. There were sixty-eight school districts and many lawyers involved in winning the case, but Albert Kauffman of the Mexican American Legal Defense and Education Fund and Jimmy Vásquez were on the point. The case carries the name of the Edgewood School District because of the boldness of its superintendent, a man who looks like anything but a schoolteacher and a math teacher at that.

Jimmy Vásquez is a short, powerfully built man with the clean, masculine features coveted by political candidates. He exudes so much energy sitting behind a desk that he seems somehow to be moving from place to place, grappling physically with the ideas and memories that pour out of him:

"The Cubans came to South Florida and they own South Florida. We've been here four hundred years and we don't own crap in this state. I tell everybody I'm a fifth generation Texan. Never crossed a goddamn boundary in my life, but I'm still called a Mexican by everybody who knows me. And I say, I didn't cross the boundary. Several boundaries crossed me. But you've got somebody swimming the border at this very minute who's probably the poorest of the poor, and in Miami you've got the educated, the rich.

"Cummins[14] says that when you have a truly bicultural society is when the second language is held in the same esteem as the first language.

"Did you ever notice all the Hispanic militants who married Anglo women?[15] What does that tell you about self-concept? Did you know that big school systems, Hispanic systems in Texas, have Anglo superintendents? Del Rio, Brownsville, all of them have Anglo superintendents; they have to, because the people believe the Anglos are smarter than they are. And those systems are 80 percent chicano.

[14]Jim Cummins is a Canadian author of many works on bilingualism and bilingual education.

[15]Not all, but many militants, both men and women, have married Anglos. Of the three presidents of MALDEF, for example, only Joaquín Avila married a Mexican-American. Rubén Salazar married an Anglo, and so on.

"You won't find a single Anglo district that has a Hispanic superintendent. Why would Brownsville bring in a West Texas Anglo that *tawks lakh tha-a-at*? Why would Edinburgh [Texas] bring in a North Texas Anglo who can't even pronounce García and Vásquez? Why?"

Vásquez is full of angers, anecdotes, and statistics, all pointing to the years of racism Latinos have suffered in Texas. He grew up in a home in which his father, a man with little formal education, treasured the works of Victor Hugo, frequently quoting from them. There was a piano in the living room so the house could always be filled with music, a place of culture, where education was valued. But the Vásquez house was not common in San Antonio. "When I graduated from elementary school," Jimmy Vásquez said, "in my class only four of us graduated from high school. And there was never any talk about dropouts. It wasn't until the sixties that we dug up the statistics that we had an 80, 90 percent dropout rate here."

He sees no change in attitudes over the last thirty years.[16] "People think society can do well without us, so what's the difference if we drop out of school?" he said, speaking of the battle over the equalization issue. He recalls the opponents of equalization saying it was just a coincidence that "among the two hundred poorest schools in the state 90 percent of the students were black and Hispanic." To explain the meaning of the case he points to Europe, where the equalization victory was understood "as another statute of enslavement in the South removed."

The victory won by Vásquez and MALDEF in 1990 threw the Texas legislature into turmoil. How could it be implemented? How could money be transferred from rich school districts to poor ones? How could the Anglos be prevented from abandoning the public school systems for private schools, as they had in other southern states and in the large cities of the Northeast? While the Texas legislature argued over how it would implement the court decision, other lawsuits demanding equalization were filed. Meanwhile, public school systems serving largely Latino populations in the Southwest continued to operate at a level so far below U.S. norms that some were being threatened with loss of accreditation.

A still more difficult issue hangs over the schools, one that is not discussed: When does defining a culture cross the boundary into racism? In theory, it is important for children to know that they need not all be the same in order to be equal, but as the differences are stressed, how can children be

---

[16]A study by the National Opinion Research Center done in 1989 confirmed Vásquez's view. Of thirty-seven racial and ethnic categories ranked by "social standing," Mexicans, Puerto Ricans, and gypsies were, respectively, thirty-fifth through thirty-seventh, with Puerto Ricans scored twenty per cent lower than blacks on a nine point scale. The study was reported in the *New York Times*, January 8, 1992, in an article headlined, "Study Points to Increase in Tolerance of Ethicity."

taught not to associate certain characteristics with race rather than culture? At various times during the last several hundred years Anglo educators and social scientists have said that Latino children are intellectually inferior. The most damaging of them was Lewis Terman of Stanford University, who announced in the early 1930s that Latino children were unable to compete intellectually with Anglos. Based in part on Terman's statement, the racist policies of the first decades of this century were justified: Latinos were expected to do poorly in school and then to drop out. Those who stayed on past elementary school were consigned to trade schools. Children who had difficulty with English were treated like the feeble-minded in schools from Texas to California. Harry Gamboa, an art critic, playwright, and one of the founders of Asco, a group of Latino artists and writers in Los Angeles, said, "I'm sure I was one of the last students in public education to have a dunce cap put on with a little lapel pin that said Spanish." Bill Melendez, whose animated films of the cartoon characters from *Peanuts* are enjoyed by millions of American children several times a year, arrived in Los Angeles from Mexico by way of Douglas, Arizona, when he was eleven years old and was promptly put into kindergarten, because he didn't speak English well.

The confusion of race, culture, and capability is more subtle now, but there are still psychologists offering racist views of intelligence. Lloyd Dunn wrote in a monograph entitled *Bilingual Children on the U.S. Mainland: Review of Research on their Cognitive, Linguistic, and Scholastic Development* (1987): "While many people are willing to blame the low scores of Puerto Ricans and Mexican-Americans on their poor environmental conditions, few are prepared to face the probability that inherited genetic material is a contributing factor."[17] Like Terman before him, Dunn is the author of psychological tests used to determine how children should be educated.

Two professors in the Education Department of the University of Texas at El Paso recently enjoyed a demonstration of the complexity of race and culture for Latinos in the United States. One of them, Norma Hernández, is a native El Pasoan. Her skin is brown, but she speaks English with the excellent diction of a woman who taught school for many years before moving to the Education Department at UTEP.[18] Jorge Descamps is a Cuban, a priest who left the Catholic Church while still in Cuba. His skin is very fair, but he speaks English with a heavy Cuban accent. Descamps too was a teacher in the public schools before joining the faculty at UTEP.

---

[17]Needless to say, Dunn's racist conclusions have been disputed and discredited.

[18]Although we didn't remember each other, Norma Hernández and I went to the same elementary school during the same years. Hernández explained, with only a hint of a smile, that perhaps we didn't know each other in school, because her parents and aunts often advised her, "We're a little bit different. We're of a different class. We don't socialize with people in this neighborhood."

Hernández and Descamps are the moral and philosophical lights of their department, perhaps of the campus; they are two professors in middle age with all the enthusiasm of students in the 1960s. When they attempted to raise money from Christian Churches to buy materials for poor schoolchildren, they had their lesson in the rules of racism. If Descamps telephoned a church, asking in his heavily accented English for donations, no one paid attention to him. When Hernández telephoned the same church, she got an excellent response. However, when they called on the churches in person, the very fair Jorge Descamps got good responses, but the brown-skinned Norma Hernández didn't do well at all.

A few miles south of the campus, in the area known as Segundo Barrio, racism has determined virtually everything since the barrio was founded. There is, for example, no playground for the children who live in the neighborhood. Since the people who lived in Segundo Barrio have been poor from its beginning, the city fathers assumed that the living conditions of poor people in the nineteenth century were still acceptable to residents of the barrio in the last decades of the twentieth century.

For more than a century U.S. citizens in that part of El Paso have lived without sanitary facilities or with only one toilet for an entire building. The city never enforced its housing code in the barrio. There was, in truth, no civil law in Segundo Barrio.[19]

In every Latino neighborhood in the United States, with the possible exception of some parts of Miami, police treat all children, especially adolescent boys, as if they are criminals. It is not uncommon in east Los Angeles[20] to see a group of boys and girls kneeling on the sidewalk or in the middle of the street, handcuffed, responding as best they can to the questions and insults of the police. And while Los Angeles may be the worst town for such behavior, it is not alone. The rousting of young Latinos in New York is so common that Phillipe Bourgeois, an anthropologist who was living in the barrio to study the drug culture, wrote in the most matter-of-fact way in the

---

[19]When political activists finally prodded the city into enforcing its codes in the 1980s, the rules were applied without concern for the welfare of the people who lived in the barrio, many of whom were forced to relocate, often without any help from the city. The only people to profit by the changes in the barrio were the developers who repaired their buildings with government money, then raised the rents. As a result of redevelopment and strict enforcement of the housing code, large families could no longer live in the apartments in the barrio, and even those with small families couldn't pay the new rents. The carelessness with which the city government treated the people in the barrio produced a classic double bind: For your sake and that of your children, your apartment will be brought up to code and then you won't be allowed to live in it.

[20]The barrio, often referred to as East L.A. There is also a town, East Los Angeles within the east Los Angeles area. The town of East Los Angeles receives most of its services from the County of Los Angeles, while the rest of east Los Angeles is served by the city.

New York Times Magazine of how the police stopped him and made him stand against a wall while they patted him down in a search for weapons or drugs. The young anthropologist did not comment on the fact that he and his postadolescent informants had been singled out because they were (or appeared to be) Latinos.

Latinos who seek help from the federal government to overcome the problems of racism may find more irony than assistance. In 1988, a group of 311 agents took the Federal Bureau of Investigation to court, claiming a long pattern of discrimination. Judge Lucius D. Bunton of the U.S. District Court in Midland, Texas, ruled in favor of the agents. He ordered the bureau to address the question of promotions for Latinos, but he did not set either quotas or a timetable for promotions. In 1990, Latino agents claimed the bureau had retaliated against them for bringing the case, and they took the FBI to court again.

Because the suit involves the Federal Bureau of Investigation, an agency that is often employed to develop evidence in civil rights cases, it serves as a signal to Latinos everywhere that the government cannot be counted on as an ally in cases of discrimination, for the government itself is morally corrupt: The Department of Justice cannot or will not recognize injustice.

Parochial schools are not immune from racism even though the Latinos are the last great bastion of the Roman Catholic Church in the United States. Barbara Carrasco, the muralist, said, "I went to Catholic school from the first grade to the eighth grade. I resented the nuns a lot. I could see at a very early age that the white students were treated better." The irony for Carrasco, who grew up in the tough housing projects of Culver City, is that she was born with the face of Europe and all through her childhood she bore the burden of her skin: She was the gringa, and she was made to suffer for it.

Most Latino children still suffer from the essential confusion of race and ethnicity pointed out by Jimmy Vásquez: No matter how long their families have been in the United States, no matter how deep their roots, even after the language has been lost and all the *viejas* wear pastel pants suits and running shoes, they will be called Mexican or Puerto Rican or Cuban. By whatever name they will be called "Different."

A surname, the shape of an eye, the summer sun beneath the skin, history—any of these can give one the name Different. The rules of racism applied to Latinos follow most closely those applied to Jews, for like Jews, Latinos are not an identifiable race. Colonial Mexico and Nazi Germany followed similar strict rules of genealogy. In the confusion of race and ethnicity, neither the first intermarriage nor the second nor the third is sufficient to spare a person from the stigma of racial inferiority. In neither case is there a sense of the genealogical majority as a determinant of race; to speak Spanish or Yiddish or even to be the child or grandchild or great-grandchild of one who spoke Spanish or Yiddish is enough to taint the blood. An eighth was sufficient for the Nazis. In the United States Jimmy Vásquez is five generations distant from Mexico, and he is still called Mexican. The truth of racism is that the power to define belongs to the racist.

They write the definition into the very marrow of their victims, even when the victims are civil rights lawyers. It always startles me to see José Luis Morín, the young attorney who spoke before the United Nations in defense of Puerto Rican independence, because he and my younger son look more alike than most brothers. They are about the same age, both lawyers who depend on fierce mustaches to look older and more serious. José Luis and James Sasson both stand about five feet eight or nine inches tall, speak very softly but with an unmistakable edge of contentiousness, wear suits designed for old bookkeepers and young lawyers, and have no language but English. James has straight hair, dark, almost black, just touched with gray, and José has tightly waved Spanish or Semitic hair, but James is not so fair as José, especially in summer. Between these young men who look so alike there is one great difference: José thinks of himself as Puerto Rican and James thinks of himself as American; they walk differently in the world.

One evening, after dinner, José Luis said to me that he had always been different, felt different because he was Puerto Rican in the United States. His conversation turned silly with vehemence; he could not concede that New York was on the mainland of the continent and Puerto Rico was an island. He pronounced the name of the island with rs rolled like Gatling guns at war. Suddenly, he said, "I went to a meeting of lawyers last week, and they thought I was there to clean up."

3.

Racismo is the shadow of Spain in its former colonies, sixteenth-century arrogance transmuted, turned upon itself. The face of it can be examined in the plazas of Madrid or in the cafetérias along the Gran Vía; one need only say a Mexican phrase—*papa* for *patata* or *platicar* for *conversar*—in the presence of a waiter or a clerk to see that peculiarly Spanish remark, the sneer enveloped in a smile. No bullfighter, no singer, no mogul in the New World has the arrogance of a Spanish peddlar or civil servant. *Racismo* has not arrived at such refinement yet in Latin America, not even in Argentina or Cuba. Yet *racismo* determines relations among Latinos to such an extent that it spills over into the outside world, influencing the way Anglos and blacks value them.

No definite hierarchy, like that of colonial Mexico, has been published in the Spanish-language press or broadcast on television; the complexity of *racismo* makes that impossible: How should one picture a game of six dimensional chess? But within each variable the hierarchy follows the well-known rules of racism:

rich / poor
light / dark
English / Spanish
educated / ignorant
citizen / newcomer

The most complicated individual variable is country of origin, which is related to one's sense of a beginning—in Europe, Africa, or the Americas. However, Cubans go beyond the genesis theory in their estimate of themselves, as do Argentines, Costa Ricans, and some Mexicans. At the other extreme, no people are more humble than the impoverished Indians of the south of Mexico. To illustrate the complexity of the hierarchy, one might ask whether, in the eyes of a Puerto Rican, a poor, black Cuban who completed high school stands higher or lower than a middle-class, third generation Mexican-American who speaks no Spanish and attended a community college for one year?

If patterns prevail, the Cuban will think the Mexican-American is not very bright or aggressive, was maleducated, and should be embarrassed by his inability to speak Spanish. The Mexican-American will apply the race rules of the Old South to the African heritage of the Cuban, assume that he is a fascist, mock his accent, and be appalled by the Cuban's money-grubbing pushiness.

With so many factors to choose from, almost every Latino can find a way to use *racismo* to his or her benefit, but the most finely honed *racismo* belongs to the Cubans.[21] The novelist Roberto Fernández said that in his home town in Cuba 30 percent of the population was black, but all save one of his schoolmates were white. Fernández, whose novel *Raining Backwards* is filled with a kind of personal and murderous wit, recalls the Cuban saying, "The black will never be brave and the tamarind will never be sweet." To drive his point home further still, he recites a little poem about the deaths of José Martí and the mulato Antonio Maceo, which ends by asking, What difference does it make if a black is lost?

[21]The Cuban Revolution was a white, middle-class action against the government of a mulato. Batista's army was largely black and mulato, while Castro's revolutionaries were mostly white. Only one of Castro's officers was a mulato.

During the early years of the revolution Castro never spoke of the race question. Not until long after the white middle class began to desert him did Castro turn to the blacks and mulatos for support.

Loly Espino, a Cuban born social scientist, says that, in Cuba, one always found out about the bloodlines of a family when they were engaged in a feud with another family in the same town. The first thing the feuding families did was to investigate each other's genealogies to find out whether there were blacks in their background.

Cuban *racismo* also follows another track. Not only do light-skinned Cubans feel superior to blacks, but they also greeted the arrival of Central American refugees in Miami as "the Indian invasion." The black Cuban babalawo who employed my pal Francisco's mother and sister controlled the Mejicanos by insisting that wealth and national origin come before color in the hierarchy of *racismo*. In the schools of Homestead, Florida, Cuban teachers taunt the Mejicano farmworkers and their children by using common Cuban words that are considered obscene by Mexicans. *Coño,* which is as common to the Cuban vocabulary as "Wow" is to a North American, means "cunt" to a Mexican. Mejicano parents complained about the Cuban teachers, but the practice continued. Exasperated, the farmworkers took their children out of school.

One evening in Hialeah, the almost entirely Cuban suburb of Miami, sitting around the dining-room table with two famous and famously charming Cubans and their children, I was astonished to hear this joke:

"This guy comes to a friend and says, 'I have the latest Puerto Rican joke.'

And there's a Puerto Rican standing right there, who says, 'Hey, listen, I'm a Puerto Rican.'

And the first guy says, 'Okay, I'll tell you later. Slowly.'

Up until that moment, it had been the most pleasant of evenings, everyone talking at once in a mixture of English and Spanish, laughing, reciting poetry, eating the best homemade flan I have ever tasted, laughing and telling stories, looking at old pictures, laughing. Then our host went on. "The Puerto Ricans from Puerto Rico are good people, noble, but the Puerto Ricans from New York and Miami are something else. The Puerto Ricans here don't even know how to tie their shoes. [He illustrated the old joke by picking up his right foot, then leaning over very far to tie the shoe on his left foot, which was still on the floor.] I think the trouble with the Puerto Ricans is their diet. Their brains don't develop. It's a very poor country, and they don't get proper nourishment, not like us. In Cuba, we have Spanish food, a complete diet, not just rice and beans."

Mexicans were not to be spared. "Look at a country as big as Mexico," he said, "adjacent to the United States! The children still have to wash in the lakes and streams. They just don't get anywhere in the world. They're Indians and Indians don't work. The Indians are loafers. In Cuba, you don't see Indians; the Spaniards killed them all."

When Carlos Alberto Montaner, the widely read Cuban journalist, said on the Univision program, *Portada*,[22] "... There is a grave family problem in the Puerto Rican ghettos of the United States, where there are thousands of single mothers, very young, who try to escape poverty through welfare or through new partners who then leave, and leave behind other children to worsen this problem," his ugly sociology was described as *racismo*. Montaner's column was dropped by *Diario/La Prensa* in New York, Goya Foods withdrew its advertising from the New York City television station that broadcast the program, and many Puerto Rican community leaders, some of them self-proclaimed, demanded that Montaner be fired by Univision. The reaction was to *racismo* rather than to the remark itself. Cubans had long been perceived by other Latinos as arrogant, identifying with Europe rather than the Americas, with Anglos rather than Latinos, defending themselves socially and economically with *racismo;* the Montaner statement gave Puerto Ricans an opportunity to vent angers they had been storing up for nearly thirty years.

The discomfort of Puerto Ricans in Texas was described by David and Dolores Colmo,[23] a young couple who live in a housing project on the northern edge of Spanish Harlem. David is fair-skinned, Dolores—dark. On the surface they are a sweet young couple fighting to get ahead in New York City. Dolores was the president of the PTA at her daughter's school; David is a doorman in a relatively expensive building on the East Side of Manhattan.

Dolores works as a nurse's aide in hospitals and conducts Santería ceremonies. She charmed everyone at her daughter's school, but after she became the head of the PTA she exhibited an overbearing, abusive side of her character, cursing and insulting the principal, intimidating the other members of the PTA, and generally causing trouble until she was removed from the position by the principal.

Neither David nor Dolores has had an easy life; as a result, they take what they can get in this world; they are proud and strangely merciless people. Dolores was an abused child. David lived in the home of a macho autoworker, a man who beat his wife, who expressed his displeasure over the way a meal was cooked or served by throwing the plateful of food against a wall. When David was a young man, he saw his father holding his mother up against a wall, strangling her with her own braided hair. He attacked his father to save his mother's life. David left home after the fight, not returning until his father died.

Despite all their problems, the Colmos live in a comfortably furnished apartment in a mixed income project. Their children are pretty and polite. When an uncle comes to visit, the children kiss his hand and ask his blessing in traditional fashion. But things never go well for the Colmos in Manhattan.

[22]On November 5, 1990
[23]Not their real names

They are dreamers, mystics: Dolores prescribes potions and casts spells; David orders videotapes of ancient Egyptian secrets that he sees advertised on television; lifesize statues of the saints of Santería occupy the hallways and corners of their apartment.

Racismo, as well as racism, fouls their world. One afternoon, in conversation with David and Dolores and David's older brother, Jorge, who is also a doorman, the question of the future came up, as it always does with the Colmos, for they live in expectation of miracles, although they feel they are victims. Jorge, a big man, shambling, with affectations of the English countryside in his demeanor and dress, told of a black supervisor who had destroyed his career as head of the mailroom in the central office of a national department store chain.

Jorge: The blacks, everything's always "my civil rights." I mean, "I don't have this, I don't have that."

David: I don't understand it. They weren't the only slaves in this world. Practically everybody been slaves. I say, what is their problem? Marching, complaining, you see them in the street every time, complaining, "We don't got this." When have you ever seen a Hispanic running for president? You got Jesse Jackson running for president; what more you want? Look at the Hispanic community. Where they at? Nowhere! The blacks are ahead. They have politicians in office, more than Puerto Ricans.

Jorge: There were Jews, slaves in Puerto Rico. The thing is, Puerto Ricans, maybe because we're so comfortable with Americans, the United States, we don't have no get up and go. You got the Dominicans coming in, the Mexicans coming in. The jobs we wouldn't take at the minimum wage, they take. They want a better life. They take away our jobs. But we don't want the minimum wage, we know there's better.

David: There's another thing I don't understand. A lot of foreigners come to this country. They go for a bank loan; immediately they got it. Open a small business, even the Chinese, but if we go for a loan like that, we can't get it.

Jorge: The Dominicans are taking over the bodegas, but have you ever noticed the Puerto Rican bodegas? They're not well maintained. The Puerto Rican businessmen never maintain their business well, they have too many people hanging out, domino playing. You have cats and dogs in the damn fruits. Now, you got the Orientals, the Dominicans, they make it decent. We don't care. The Puerto Ricans, they go on that welfare line and that's it. Because we have the American citizenships. That's why we've gotten fat on our laurels, because we're citizens. On the TV, you had a report on generations on welfare, three or four generations on welfare now. That's ridiculous, Puerto Ricans.

David: We went out to Texas and it didn't work out. There was racism out there. I went to fill out a job application. I was never called. These Mexicans, they know you speak perfect English and like that, they figure you're going to take a job away from them.

Dolores: Mexicans! They hate Yankees!

David: They used to call me gringo, some shit like that. They used to call her *majeta*,[24] something like that. Like a black woman. They used to speak Spanish in front of us about us.

Dolores: They didn't think I was Spanish, they thought I was black.

David: They called me gringo. They thought I was an American, a white man.

Dolores: If I would walk into a store, they would say, *"Mira esta mujer."* They thought it was a different thing. I used to go up to the counter and say, *"Cuanto es esto?"* On some occasions, I had trouble. I would have to say, *"Yo soy Español."* We had a very rough time.

David: Cubans are another race. They wild people. They are. Dominicans, the same way. They like they greedy, they want everything for themselves. Cubans are nasty, greedy. Jorge used to say, 'If a war ever come out in Puerto Rico, we go. It could be against Cubans, Dominicans, Russians, we fight.' The Dominicans they talk so bad about our country, I ask them sometimes, why they be here? Colombians, we call them the Colombian drug farm.

Dolores: When my husband was out of a job and we had to go on public assistance, I saw all Colombians and Dominicans, and I said to my husband, "We don't belong here," and he went out and got a job and I went to school. I went through some hard times in my life. I say to him, God's truth, if it wasn't for him, I would be a druggie or a prostitute.

The *racismo* the Colmos found in Texas is not so different from the prejudice Mexican-Americans and Mexicans find among their own people. In a nation devoted to celebrating its Indian heritage the terrible irony is that Indians are despised. Every mestizo household has its rules of behavior based upon despising the Indian in Mexico. "Don't behave like an Indian," children are told. Girls are still taught not to shave the hair on their legs so they will not be smooth-skinned, like Indians, but as hairy as Spanish nuns. Good children, *de casta,* prefer tortillas of flour to those of corn, if they must eat tortillas at all; corn is Indian, wheat came from Europe.

The Indians of Mexico who come to the United States to live and work find the pain of racism added to *racismo* a devastation of their morale. The Mixtecos, Zapotecos, and Triquis of the southwestern mountains of Mexico, once among the great cultures of the world, now find themselves among the

---

[24]Probably *mayate,* a derogatory term for black.

poorest and most despised. There is some anger in the Zapotecos—one hears it in their ironies. But if the Mixtecos have been changed by suffering, their new character has not yet emerged.

It is unbearable to look into the dark brown eyes of a Mixteco and see the shimmer of memories, tears not yet fallen, wounds not yet healed. They describe themselves now only as others see them: short, dark, with big bellies. They say in their orotund way, speaking very carefully, as if words still had power, that they are the despised of the earth, despised among Mexicans and in the United States for their physical appearance, their poverty, their language, their nationality, and especially for their gentleness. And then they say, in the same voice, ancient rhetoricians speaking, what suffering they have endured, from the time the drought began in their mountains and they became migrants, first to a rich valley in Sinaloa, then to Hermosillo, to Mexicali, and on to the no man's land that was San Quintín, Baja California.

The suffering of the Indians in Mexico and the United States cannot be overstated. People have lost their lands to swindlers backed by corrupt government officials. They have been robbed at every turn by the Mexican police. Many of them have gone to work in the fields of San Quintín, living like slaves in the gigantic camp run by international agricultural interests connected to the Japanese and East Indians in California. In San Quintín, people are forced to live eighteen to a room, with no medical care and few sanitary facilities, and all to work for low pay. The unions that take part of the people's pay are a mockery; the government is so corrupt that it permits the Japanese owners of San Quintín to lock the inhabitants behind barbed wire fences during the growing season.

No one suffers *racismo* so much as the Mexicans and Mexican-Americans. During the last days of the amnesty offered under the Immigration and Reform Act, Maritza Herrera, the woman who had left Nicaragua only hours before the overthrow of the Somoza regime, helped Mexican migrant workers in Homestead, Florida, to fill out their papers. On weekend afternoons she used the offices of a tortillería owned by Nicaraguans in Homestead to interview people applying for amnesty. Although she was not an attorney, she had received a license from the Immigration and Naturalization Service that enabled her to do the work.

At two in the afternoon Maritza Herrera took her place behind the reception desk in the office. Her hair had been "done," her nails had been polished, her pants suit showed not one wrinkle. She smiled: She wore the ornate frames of her eyeglasses for a mask. Her arm lay across the desk. The black hair, the European hair, was exposed; there could be no doubt.

On the chairs lined up against the wall the farmworkers waited. The sun had painted them. They reeked of earth. Their hands had curled into claws;

they could not write, they made thumbprints on the paper, pictures of callouses and scars. Each one, in his turn, approached her, politely, bent as if to bow, hat in hand, papers at the ready: money orders, birth certificates, proof of residence, work records, letters from employers. Maritza Herrera hardly glanced at the men. She had come to do the papers; it was the last day of the last extension of the last part of the amnesty.

She had no patience with them. She insulted them, bossed them, treated them as if they were children. All the men backed away from her, apologized to her. She gave no quarter. She humbled them. "Where are your papers? Didn't I tell you to get your papers? Didn't you write for your birth certificate? How can I help you if you don't do as you're told?" On and on, she insulted one man after another. All the men had the smell of earth on them, not sweat, but earth, humus, damp clay, and sand. Only one could write.

It went on and on. She reduced them from men to children, from children to animals. She thought they were quaint, interesting, amusing, simple Indians from Mexico. It appalled her that the two Cuban doctors in Homestead were charging the Mexicans exorbitant rates to provide them with the medical tests required to apply for amnesty. Yet she humbled every man who stood before her, for they were Mexicans, Indians, illiterates, unfortunates, migrants, and she had attended universities, she had been the student of an intimate of Tacho Somoza. She told them this with her voice, her fingernails, her painted, primped face.

Without her, they had no hope for amnesty, could not remain in the United States. On the streets of Homestead they made way for Maritza, they tipped their hats, they smiled; their children waved to her. She was their *Somocista* saint.

—

Racismo enters every mestizo family, delineating the value and the place of the children according to their color. The darkest one may become the pet or the outsider, the success or the troublemaker—if there is a rule, I cannot discern it—but the darkest one will always be singled out. The darkest one will always get a pet name based on color: Negrito, Prieto, Chango, Indio. Ron Arias, the novelist, said he carried the nickname "Ink Spot."

In Latino society a fair-skinned mate is a prize, a fair-haired fair-skinned (*güero güero*) Anglo mate is an even greater prize. Yet the rules of race argue that sexual prowess belongs to darkness: The Mexicans say, Las prietas, hasta las mulas, son buenas ("The dark ones, even if they're mules, are sexy"), repeating the feelings of sexual fear and jealousy that have complicated relations between black and white since Solomon and Sheba.

Every Latino group suffers from it. A young Puerto Rican executive in midtown Manhattan said that if he were to bring a dark-skinned girl home to his parents, both of whom are very fair, "They would throw me out of the house." The issue of skin color affects every aspect of the New York Latino community, particularly politics: Dark-skinned people do not get elected or appointed to political posts. It is whispered in the Puerto Rican community that Awilda Orta, one of the city's most exciting educators, was moved out of the central office of the Board of Education partly because her skin is dark.

Two Latinos have been appointed to run the huge New York City school system; both are fair-skinned men. Joseph Fernández, who returned home from his great success in Miami to take over the New York system in 1990, looks like the proprietor of a successful haberdashery in Spain, and northern Spain at that. Anthony Alvarado, who held the job earlirer, is less expansive, a compressed man of pale, clerical mien. Florida has a similar record of electing and appointing fair-skinned Latinos. In Texas, the fair skin of Raymond Telles played a major role in his election as mayor of El Paso. Two decades later, the election of Henry Cisneros in San Antonio and Tati Santiesteban in El Paso indicated that education and social position were more important than skin color. Cisneros and Santiesteban are handsome men, tall, slim, the color of old wood. Cisneros is quiet, elegant; his eyes and his demeanor are Indian, almost Oriental. Santiesteban is older, a fast-talking good ole boy Texican politico, but he is quick to tell everyone he meets that his mother was Spanish. Henry Cisneros, who was educated at the best eastern universities, is the son of a civil servant. Santiesteban, an attorney, was the first Latino president of the student body at the University of Texas at Austin. In California, so few Latinos have been elected to public office that a pattern has not been established.

Racismo occurs in a curious form in New Mexico. A large group of people, who claim they are descended from the early Spanish settlers of the area, call themselves Hispanos. They insist that their Spanish ancestry distinguishes them from Mexican-Americans, whom they consider racial and cultural inferiors. Their history proves the practical value of *racismo*. By insisting that they are not Mexican, they were able to elect Hispanos to local and state office, and even the U.S. Senate, long before other Latinos could get past gerrymandering, ward politics, and "at-large" elections. Some Hispanos were able to avoid the racism practiced by Anglos in New Mexico by claiming to be Europeans, children of the *conquistadores* rather than Mexican mestizos. In many parts of New Mexico only an Anglo or an Hispano could get a haircut in a public barbershop before World War II; Mexicans had to go to a Mexican barber or have their hair cut at home.

Almost every writer, from Carey McWilliams to Rodolfo Acuña, who has looked into the Hispano argument has found it ludicrous. The case against racial purity is simple and incontrovertible; there were no female *conquistadores* and no recorded cases of parthenogenesis. The cruelties resulting from the *racismo* of the Hispanos are not so widely discussed. In the externalities of life in New Mexico, the barbershop and beauty parlor, the restaurant and ballot box, the effects of the Hispano hoax have largely disappeared, but *racismo* does not die easily; it merely burrows under the skin, where it waits, working in whispers rather than public places. *Racismo* lives inside the world of intimacies, in marriages, love affairs, families, and failed friendships.

A young woman, born of a mixed Anglo-Latino marriage, took an Hispano lover who taught her the private rules of *racismo*. "We spoke of the damn Mexicans," she said, "always the damn Mexicans this and the damn Mexicans that." Later, it was revealed that the father of her "Hispano" lover had been born in Mexico. *Racismo* had been a problem for the father, because his wife was the daughter of a gallego; the son tried to save himself from the shame of racial impurity by pretending he was Hispano.

Racismo did not originate in Albuquerque or Santa Fe; it dominates the history of Mexico, beginning with the wars of conquest that established the Toltec and Aztec hegemonies. In those wars and again in the vicious nineteenth century wars between the criollos and the mestizos almost every major engagement ended in a slaughter. Race war gives no quarter; it is a battle over blood; nothing can satisfy it but blood, and the Spanish taste for it is virtually insatiable.

In the United States, the Spaniards and the first wave of Cubans are now viewed by many Mexican-Americans as users of the advantages of color, culture, cash, and education in the struggle to dominate the Latino community. The situation erupted into a public conflict over the management of the Los Angeles Spanish-language television stations in 1989. Pickets appeared outside Channel 52 to protest the replacement of the Mexican-American anchorman on the news, Bob Navarro, by a Cuban. In a letter to *La Opinion,* the venerable Los Angeles Spanish-language newspaper, Graciela Villanueva complained about "TV Martí en Los Angeles." the headline over the letter included a neologism that was to become the focus of the debate: *Cubanización.*

As a result of the replacement of Navarro, many questions were raised about control of the local affiliates and of the two networks, Telemundo and Univision. Raúl Ruiz of MAPA (Mexican American Political Association) told the newspapers that the firing "demonstrated the insensibility, prejudice, and racism against the Mexican community." People began asking aloud why the programs came out of studios in Miami instead of Los Angeles. Finally, the question of color was broached: Why were so many people on Spanish television blue-eyed blonds? Joaquín Blaya, the president of Univision, explained to the *New York Times* that dark persons were never seen on Mexican television. Blaya, a Chilean-American, continued: "By the way, we have some very beautiful Mexican-Americans on the air. The anchor team on our national news is Mexican. They are both blond with blue eyes. It has to be said, without being afraid, that television as well as movies is a business for beautiful people. It's entertainment."

The public confirmation of *racismo* by the president of the largest Spanish-language television network north of the equator created no additional furor. Latinos, particularly Mexican-Americans, had lived with this ulceration at the core of the culture for so long that most of them accepted it as part of the natural order; the only answer to it was *aguantar*. Only the younger generation, those who had grown up with the sense of *coraje*[25] inspired in Los Angeles by Rubén Salazar and everywhere by the United Farmworkers and the chicano movement, revolted; the true meaning of the word "brown" was that *respeto* and *racismo* could not coexist.

A new kind of *racismo* grew up on the border between Mexico and the United States, and spread north and south. Like most forms of *racismo,* this chauvinistic variant is reciprocal: The Mexicans and the Mexican-Americans have learned to despise each other. A famous victim of this form of *racismo* in Mexico, the novelist Carlos Fuentes, was attacked in the Mexican press simply because he grew up in Washington, D.C., where his father was stationed by the Mexican foreign service.

The accusation against Fuentes, even though it was made by his enemies on the political right, carries great weight in Mexico, for there are few failures of the spirit more damning to a Mexican than to have become a pocho. The word itself has no good connotations. It probably originated with the Yaquis of northwestern Mexico, for whom it meant "stupid." Among the other early meanings were "small," "squat," and "discolored." Now, pocho means a Mexican-American, one who has traded his language and culture for the illusory blandishments of life in the United States.[26] Nonstandard uses of Spanish by people who live on the border are known as pochismos, as are examples of bad manners.

Pochismo may provide Carlos Fuentes with much of the internal conflict that drives his literary work; it is surely the impetus behind *The Old Gringo,* and it may also have provided the objective view of Mexican society and history that produced *Where the Air Is Clear,* as well as the brilliant transformation of politics into literature in his portrait of a morally bankrupt revolutionary, *The Death of Artemio Cruz.* Fuentes is the heroic pocho, the man who overcame his fate. The ordinary Mejicano or Mexican-American has to make do without the novelist's talent for turning conflict into art, art into success,

[25]Righteous anger.
[26]In *Ni Sangre, Ni Arena,* an early Cantinflas movie, Pedro Armendariz was cast as a rich fool, a *pocho* who used English words in conversation.

and success into social acceptance. The pocho lives on the cultural and racial line, a profoundly homeless person, utterly unprotected, despised on every side: too Mexican for the Anglos and too *agringado* for the Mexicans. In Mexico, the pocho is the butt of a thousand jokes:

> "My name is John Sánchez," the pocho tells the border guard on his way in to Mexico.
> "And what is your occupation?" the border guard asks.
> "I am a Latin lover."
> The border guard laughs. "A Latin lover?"
> "Yes, when I walk down the street in my *patria chica*, Phoenix, Arizona, the gringos all say, 'Here comes that fucking Mexican.' "

The purpose of the joke, of course, is to reassure the Mexicans who remain in Mexico that they have made the right choice. Wherever the pocho goes in Mexico, he is treated badly, worse than a gringo or a Mexican of similar economic and social standing. The pocho gets the table closest to the kitchen in a restaurant and the room over the airshaft in a hotel. He is a pariah, a renegade, and a fool. Every Mexican knows that when pochos go home to the United States, their Anglo neighbors will assume that the men are gardeners and the women are maids. And no amount of worldly success will change the situation for the pocho on either side of the border.

A logical response to the bitter combination of racism and *racismo* was invented by pocho political activists in the late 1960s and early 1970s: chicanismo. The public posture of the chicanos was to call Mexican nationals "brothers," but the truth is that chicanismo was as much a response to the *racismo* from across the border as to the racism directed toward chicanos by Anglos and blacks. It was the classic answer to being left out in the United States: the third party.

Anyone who has read Tocqueville and *The Federalist* knows that in the United States the third party option, although logical, is foolhardy, destined never to be more than a gesture. But the pochos needed a gesture, anything, some kind of cultural safe house in which they could rest for a while from the endless war on two fronts. Beyond that momentary solace, the logic failed; chicanismo was a form of cultural alchemy, an attempt to create a culture out of the absence of culture. The political notion of the creation of states does not apply to cultures. A culture is not a commonwealth. As an attempt to supplant pochismo with a positive alternative, chicanismo had no effect; the Mexican attitude toward pochos has only worsened over the last quarter of a century; *racismo* has always thrived on economic difficulties. As a response to racism, however, chicanismo remains an option.

The ability of the pochos to seek emotional and economic recompense from their Mexican neighbors plays an equally important role in the matrix

of *racismo;* the pochos along the border tend to mistreat newcomers, especially those who have come without papers. It is always astonishing to hear
Mexican-Americans refer to undocumented people as *mojados, pelados,*[27]
wetbacks or *pollos.* Economic and political rationalizations accompany the
epithets: "They take our jobs away, because they'll work for less," or "We
worked for so long to get our rights, and they come over here and get
everything we've worked for the minute they cross the border."

This hatred of the newcomer is a common cruelty, but by no means is it
universal. The widely publicized sanctuary movement is headed by Anglos,
but the real quotidian work is done by Latinos, who bring soup and beans to
the shelters and sanctuaries and always follow the rules of *familia,* taking in
any relative, no matter how distant the connection. It is an uneasy relationship, even within the family, but not unusual. Compared to the poor Mexicans who come across the border in search of work, the pochos are rich, and
the first order of business among the rich of the world is to hold on to their
wealth and increase it, which can happen only at the expense of the poor.

4.

Class differences exist among all immigrant groups, but *racismo* in all its
complexity is peculiar to Latinos, for no other identifiable group comprises
so many races and nationalities. The effect of *racismo* on the ability of Latinos
to survive and prosper in the United States is complementary to that of
racism. Both serve the dominant society by slowing or stopping completely
the ordinary newcomer's ability to compete economically and socially; racism and *racismo* are the real gates that must be opened if one is to achieve the
status of immigrant in the United States.

Racismo prevents entry into the society by demoralizing the newcomers
so that they do not dare to seek a new social contract. Racism prevents
newcomers from making a new social contract no matter what concessions
they are willing make; it is the dominant society's refusal to negotiate, a
lockout. Racism and *racismo* are the great counterrevolutionary forces ar-
rayed against every Latino who seeks to establish a new social contract in the
United States. They are the dream killers, the death of the future tense; in the
grasp of prejudices one can summon no greater expectations than the timid
subjunctive allows. Against that eternal anxiety the limitations of living in the
present must be preferred. Middle-class life, the unremarkable dream upon
which the dreamer may depend, is put out of easy reach by the *racistas* and
the racists. In such a world, all victories are fragile.

[27]Wets, bums. The literal meaning of *pelado* is hairless, but it is generally used for ill-
mannered people, those of the lower class, petty thieves, and so on.

12

LATE ENTRY, EARLY EXIT

Sabemos que aquellos que dominan más de un idioma tendrán
mayor opportunidad de avanzar en la vida.[1]

Coral Way Elementary School, Miami, Florida, Julia Menendez, Principal

*I told my father I want to establish a school for people like myself who want
their children to learn Spanish. There is a market—all the people who
went to Harvard and Yale, like me. My father said, "You can't do that.
That's not your culture, that's mine."*   David Moquel

I.

"When I went to the first grade," Awilda Orta said, "I had a vision that the
room was split. There were no lights on my side of the room. I sat in
darkness. Many years later, I went back to visit the nuns, and I saw the room
again. On the side where I sat, there were floor-to-ceiling windows; the room
was bathed in light. I realized then that I felt myself in darkness, because I
spoke no English."

Sylvia Sasson (Shorris), who entered school speaking some English, was
the only child with a Spanish surname in her class. "I remember the sound of
the other children's names," she said. "I was so different. The lunches my
grandmother fixed for me were an embarrassment. I never got peanut butter
and jelly like the other kids. For a while, I wanted to be anything but Spanish;
at one time I thought of telling people I was Estonian." Synesthesia for her
was of a better-known kind: Every morning, before going to school, she was
sick.[2]

---

[1]"We know that those who become proficient in more than one language will find more
opportunities to advance in later life." The statement is taken from the Bilingual School Organization and Parent Signature form distributed by the school in 1989.

[2]Carlota del Portillo reported a similar situation in Puerto Rico when the nuns taught
English by asking the students to march around a table, naming each of the objects laid out
there. She thought the room in which they studied was exceedingly hot, yet when she visited

Submersion, the method of learning a language endured by Sylvia Sasson and Awilda Orta, has generally been the American experience. At various times during the history of immigration, the submersion method has been replaced by a less traumatic variant known as the immersion method. In both methods classroom instruction is entirely in English, but in the immersion method all of the children come to class speaking only a foreign language.[3]

Immersion uses the coercive value of the peer group; submersion depends on shame. In the submersion method children learn to devalue their culture as well as their language. Sylvia Sasson wanted only to be named O'Brien or Goldberg or Perini, like the other children in her class. Awilda Orta prayed to be in the light. Richard Rodriguez, whose autobiography, *Hunger of Memory,* can be read as the experience of submersion writ large, wished to shed the "private" language of his home and family for a "public" language and the life that accompanied it. The shame of submersion has led other Latino children to try to change themselves into African-Americans or to throw away their lunches of tacos or burritos rather than be seen eating a foreign meal.

How to learn a new language and adopt a new culture would seem to be a thoroughly understood process in a country often described as a nation of immigrants. It is not. On the contrary, as observers from Tocqueville to the present have noted, a state lacking in some of the qualities of a nation overcompensates for its youth and diversity by requiring the highest degree of conformity from all of its citizens. During its relatively brief history the United States has shown varying degrees of acceptance of foreign-language speakers. Until the last decade of the nineteenth century most states permitted private "nationality" schools, which carried out what are now known as maintenance programs in languages other than English. Ten years later, most states had outlawed such schools. During World War I, nationalistic and patriotic feeling led to legal xenophobia: A town in Ohio fined people twenty-five dollars for speaking German in public. Not until 1923 did the Supreme Court strike down laws prohibiting private schools from teaching

---

the school many years later, she found the room well-ventilated, made comfortable by ocean breezes.

The method of instruction may have been borrowed from St. Augustine's idea for a naming game based on the way he believed he had learned to speak.

[3]English for Speakers of Other Languages (ESOL) uses the immersion method to relieve the pressure of submersion. Children who do not speak English are usually taken out of class for one or more periods for ESOL instruction.

In the complex politics of bilingual education, English as a Second Language (ESL) has been changed to English for Speakers of Other Languages to satisfy those who believe English should never be described as a second language in the United States.

in languages other than English. Even so, children were forbidden to speak Spanish in the classroom or the schoolyard in the Southwest for most of this century.

The Bilingual Education Act was passed in 1968 and strengthened and clarified by amendments in 1974 and 1978. Its survival was assured by the *Lau v. Nichols* decision of the Supreme Court in 1974, which held that under the provisions of the Civil Rights Act of 1964 children who could not understand the language in which they were being taught were not offered equal education. Yet by the end of 1980, the law that made Spanish, as well as English, an official language of Dade County, Florida, was voted out, and in the realm of commerce, the federal courts had upheld a ruling that an employer could prohibit the use of a foreign language in the workplace. As the Latino population increased and bilingual instruction became more widespread, the Reagan administration cut funding for bilingual programs and English-only laws were passed in sixteen states, including Florida and California.

For most of its history the United States has feared bilingualism and biculturalism as impediments to the forging of a nation. Assimilation or destruction have generally been the choices offered to those who differed from the majority; the brutality inherent in democracy made it so. And the Constitution, which has served well in mitigating the dangers of raw democracy in most areas, has few explicit views on culture. On such matters as an official language, for example, the intentions of the framers must be discerned from their omissions. With interpretation left to the Congress and the courts, the effect of the Constitution on pluralism has been less consistent and less salutary than one might have hoped for. Only during brief peaks of liberal toleration have the pluralistic implications of the Constitution been allowed to moderate the nation's politics.

As a rule, the educational arguments for and against bilingualism have been less important than the general willingness in the nation to tolerate the eccentricity of a second language and a nonstandard culture. Economics have almost always been the determining factor. The Depression years, when as many as a million people of Mexican descent were deported, had a devastating effect on biculturalism in the United States. Spanish-language theaters, newspapers, and publishing houses closed. Hard times produced xenophobia and exacerbated racism; Latinos, being both racially and culturally different, were easy targets. The desire then among Latinos for racial, cultural, and linguistic assimilation was overwhelming. Everyone wanted to be reborn in the melting pot; in a troubled democracy, it was the only safe response to xenophobia. So LULAC preached assimilation and insisted that people of Mexican descent were white, and children who were caught speaking Spanish in the classroom were punished in school and then pinched at home. Spanish became the grandmother's tongue.

In retrospect, the melting pot theory was coercive, illiberal in the extreme, but probably a necessary part of creating a nation in the unique circumstances of the United States. Whether a stable political and economic union could have been made of a population Balkanized by language and culture is an academic question; one theory serves as well as the next. However, the seemingly endless ethnic violence in every part of the world argues that the melting pot is as necessary politically as it is damaging culturally.

No educational method so perfectly mirrors the experience of the melting pot as submersion; it is the street of strangers brought into the school. After two weeks in the barrio, an eleven-year-old girl from Ecuador described New York as *frío y corrumpido,* and she made it clear that the cold and corruption did not end when she entered the schoolroom. Merely to survive physically the submerged student must learn to communicate; otherwise, she may never find the lunchroom or the bathroom. But elemental communication is one thing, education by submersion another; the student can get through the educational system without learning and can even succeed by manipulating the definition of success.

The choice of how to respond to the new environment must be made quickly. In the first days and months of school the submerged student is faced with making or accepting a series of definitions and then making decisions about them. The pressure is terrible, for it is mostly negative, a demand to rebel against the newly imposed culture, yet the children know, perhaps instinctively, that they cannot do well in the world either by maintaining their old culture or by adopting the culture of rebellion. The conflict leaves some of them paralyzed, mute in the classroom, raging in the schoolyard. I have heard many teachers describe these children as "the dead."

Although submersion seems a murderous system,[4] examples of survival and success run into the millions. The economic and intellectual prowess of the United States, it could be argued, is a direct result of the effectiveness of the submersion method of education. Of the three children described at the beginning of this section, all of whom had difficult submersion experiences, none failed. Sylvia Sasson, who fared badly in the early grades, won the English prize by the time she graduated from a prestigious high school and became a published writer in English. Awilda Orta, who sat in the emotional dark, became a brilliant teacher and educational administrator. Richard Rodriguez went on to earn a Ph.D. in Renaissance literature and to write an autobiography so preciously English it used single quote marks in the British style.

[4]Many studies (by M. Swain, and others) have been published validating the view that immersion is a better way to teach students with limited English proficiency (LEP) than submersion. The problem is the Nobel Prize winner or the chairman of the board who learned by submersion.

One factor common to all three is their facility for language. They are astonishingly verbal people and almost equally at home speaking or writing. Sasson and Orta are bilingual; only Rodriguez does not speak Spanish. Perhaps their natural ability enabled them to overcome the trauma of abruptly converting to a new language. Perhaps it was the schools they attended that brought them through. Orta and Rodriguez both went to Catholic schools; Sasson attended a girls' high school noted for its rigorous academic program. Perhaps they are merely anomalies.

On the other hand, if the sampling were done at a prison in New York or Texas or California, the conclusion would be very different. Most pintos[5] did not have successful school careers. Joan W. Moore reported in her book *Homeboys*, based on research gathered by the Pinto Project under grants from the National Science Foundation and the National Institute on Drug Abuse, that the educational level of chicano prisoners in San Quentin in the 1960s was so low the majority of them were prohibited from attending vocational training programs. A few years later, a study of 146 ex-pintos found only 2 percent had completed high school. The curious thing about ex-pintos is that they are not comfortable either in English or standard Spanish; they speak Caló, which has a vocabulary of between a thousand and fifteen hundred words and is used in conjunction with standard and non-standard English and Spanish.

Caló is a renegade language, a code; it creates a world at war with that of people who speak standard languages. Although it has been used by poets to enrich the standard English of their work with overtones of the streets and prisons of the Southwest, Caló is not an enrichment in daily speech, where it does not have the same ironic value. As in any argot, many of the words serve the function of clichés; that is, they are true but hackneyed, easy but almost always slightly off the mark, comfortable but never intimate. People who speak Caló or Spanglish, its East Coast equivalent, either lack the facility with language to overcome the distressing elements of the submersion method or have abandoned that facility to conform to another definition of prestige and success.

In the end, submersion performs a kind of social triage. Enough succeed to keep the method from being thrown out, but most fail, enabling the majority, who control the educational system, to maintain their social and economic advantages. Submersion functions like a sieve, which can be made coarse or fine by adding or subtracting such things as ESL classes, counseling programs, and orientation classes.

Submersion, which is a spur to the few, is too cruel for the many. The Chinese, French, Germans, Jews, Poles, Russians, and Scandinavians of ear-

[5]Caló for prisoner

lier times knew enough to save their children with schools and newspapers in their own languages, ethnic clubs, religious clubs, counseling, anything they could do to mitigate the Darwinian cruelty of the submersion system. Since the passage of the Bilingual Education Act, public schools in the United States have been attempting to help children with limited english proficiency (LEP) learn to listen, speak, read, and write in a new language in the most efficient way. But so far, bilingual education has not, of itself, solved the educational problems of Latino children. If submersion caused them to fail, bilingual education has not caused them to succeed.

Meanwhile, more Latino children enter kindergarten and fewer finish high school. And the country, which once embraced men and women who could work with their hands and arms, wants people who can use their minds; a new immigration law, passed in 1990, makes provision for people with skills to enter the country on a priority basis. The immigrants of the early part of the twentieth century, who could grunt or nod while they attached themselves to machines, levers, tools, whatever needed the strength of an arm and a human reflex to operate it, lived to enjoy union wages without adopting much of the new language or culture.[6] It is not so easy now. The Latino population is burgeoning at a difficult time. Too many Latinos have no English when a little English is not enough.

2.

So far, no one has produced the one study that proves now and forever whether bilingual education works. The studies are inconclusive, in part, because they do not adequately define the goal of bilingual education. According to *Life with Two Languages*, Francois Grosjean's introduction to bilingualism, there is no universally acceptable definition of the word. He writes:

> I have avoided up to this point the very complex question of describing a person's bilingualism. Researchers in the area have proposed a variety of definitions of bilingualism, and lay people also have rather precise ideas

[6]In 1975 I interviewed a first level manager in a General Motors foundry. She told me that so many of the people she supervised were functionally illiterate that she had to give instructions to them one at a time, putting her mouth next to each person's ear and shouting in order to be heard over the noise of the machinery. Less than a decade later, General Motors had become the largest privately owned educational institution in the United States. To work in a modern automobile plant required not only literacy, but in many instances what the trainers called computer literacy. The functional illiterates who earned fourteen dollars an hour in the foundry in 1975 could not be hired in 1990.

about the subject. Fluency in two languages has often been proposed as the main criterion, and psycholinguists have used ingenious methods to test this. However, I ... argue ... that far too much weight has been put on fluency, to the detriment of other factors such as the regular use of two languages, their domains of use, and the bilingual's need to have certain skills (reading and writing, for instance) in one language but not in the other.

The minimum definition of bilingualism is to be able to listen to someone speaking another language and understand what the speaker is saying. Such a definition, however, might mean that understanding kitchen Spanish makes one bilingual. Maybe speaking is a better skill to use as a minimum, but speaking about what? lunch? love? logarithms? literature? The quality and complexity of the conversation will have to be considered. Or should one be required to read and write two languages in order to be considered bilingual? And if so, how well? As well as Conrad? And didn't Conrad speak with a heavy Polish accent?

The most demanding definition insists that one be accepted as a native in speaking, listening, reading, and writing two languages. The *Oxford English Dictionary,* in the supplement published in 1987, states that bilingualism is the "ability to speak two languages; the habitual use of two languages colloquially."[7] Assuming that either of the two definitions in the *OED* is acceptable and that the failure even to hint at standards of literacy betrays carelessness and not despair, is bilingualism the goal of bilingual education? Or is the goal to convert children to monolingual English speakers?

Before addressing the social and political goals of bilingual education, the question of how people learn two languages and how they think after they have learned a second language needs to be considered. If educating people to have the ability to speak two languages is relatively easy and not harmful to their thinking in either language, that goal would appear to be a good one.

But what if speaking, listening, reading, and writing two languages fluently leads people to think more slowly, to have just a little bit less facility than they might have had with only one language? Research can be found to prove the "jack of all trades, master of none" theory of language acquisition. And there is an enormous amount of research proving that bilingual education lowers performance (test scores) in English.

[7]The definition is not clear. Does the semicolon signal an explanation? an alternative? a second level of bilingualism? The writers of the *Random House Dictionary* define the adjective "bilingual" even less rigorously: "Ability to speak one's native language and another with approximately equal facility." Perhaps they did not know the old joke, "I been spake six language, Ainglesh best."

Unfortunately, every statement about bilingualism and bilingual education requires an "on the other hand." For every paper proving the "jack of all trades" theory, there is another defending the notion that whoever doesn't know two languages doesn't know one. When the two sides meet, as in the 1989 debate between Judith Stern Torres of the New York City Board of Education and Keith Baker of U.S. English, most of the argument focuses on statistics, and the best anyone seems to be able to say about the statistics is that they "suggest" something or other. Nobody is quite sure what. As Jim Cummins wrote in *Bilingualism in Education*, "It is clear, then, that there is little consensus as to the exact meaning of the term bilingualism, and that it has been used to refer to a wide variety of phenomena. Research associated with bilingualism reflects this semantic confusion. It is essential, therefore, in reconciling contradictory results associated with bilingualism . . ."

Meanwhile, the question of the goal of bilingual education remains unresolved. All Latino parents want their children to learn English, and all proponents of bilingual education agree that in the end the children must be able to speak, listen, read, and write in English. The survival of English is not at issue, only the death of Spanish. With the question unresolved, the monolingual Spanish student entering school in the United States participates in a linguistic lottery: Depending on which public school, even which class, the child attends, he or she may encounter a method ranging from instruction entirely in Spanish to one in which the teachers and students do not use any language but English.

The tragic aspect of the lottery is that the number of losers far exceeds the number of winners; for Latinos, especially those who enter school speaking no English, the educational system is not a good bet. Optimists put the dropout rate for all Latino children in the U.S. at 35.8 percent. Realists think the national rate is over 40 percent. At Jefferson High School in Houston the raw numbers[8] show 70 percent fewer in the graduating class than in the entering class. To gauge the extent of the tragedy, it is probably useful to compare the Latino dropout rate to that of other groups. The *Washington Post*, which provided the 35.8 percent figure in 1989, estimated that the dropout rate in the same year for whites was 12.7 percent and for blacks—14.9 percent.

There is no standard by which the education of Latino children in the United States can be considered adequate, fair, or morally acceptable. If one of the goals of the Bilingual Education Act was to educate Spanish-speaking children as well as English-speaking white or black children, the act has failed. If the goal was to improve the education of Latino and other language-

---

[8]These figures do not take into account transfers to or from other schools, children returning to Mexico or Central America, those coming from Mexico or Central America, etc.

minority children, there is still not much evidence to support its success. Mario García says the dropout rate for Latino children in West Texas was close to 100 percent in the 1930s. By 1968, when the Latino students walked out of the Los Angeles schools, the dropout rate there was estimated at 50 percent. After more than twenty years of bilingual education, the most optimistic estimate nationwide is 35.8 percent.

An investigation of how the rate came down might prove embarrassing for supporters of bilingual education. Children who attend night school or take only one course are not considered dropouts anymore. People who return to any kind of school for even an hour a week are not considered dropouts. Children who can't be found are presumed to have left the school district, and so are not counted among the dropouts. In other words, that blunt, ugly number reported for the Houston high school, the kind of number that was used until quite recently to determine who finished high school and who didn't, has been discarded in favor of more sophisticated methods of counting dropouts, methods that seem always to improve the performance of the schools.

The issue of who is an educated adult has been discussed widely in the United States, but when it comes to children, a few standardized tests are thought to be enough. Rarely, if ever, is the moral character of the child considered part of his education. Rarely does anyone ask what happens to the values of one culture when that culture is denigrated by the teaching of a new one. A superbly educated Latino professional man said to me about his parents, "They speak broken English," but it did not occur to him to add that they speak beautiful Spanish. In America, the old culture dies easily; the tragedy, as the Zapotecos of Santa Monica said, is that it is replaced with drugs, violence, and rock and roll.

The late nineteenth- and early twentieth-century schools set up by the Germans, Italians, Jews, Norwegians, Poles, and Swedes and the more recent schools run by the Chinese and Japanese have endeavored to help their students retain the old culture as much or more than the language. The founders of those schools, many of whom were tied to the religious center of the community, feared the new or different or modern morality, which they understood as no morality at all. In many instances the conservation of values undoubtedly led to serious emotional conflict. The literature of the early part of the century is filled with such cases. Writers from Dreiser to Fitzgerald to Roth told stories of the clash of cultures.

Now the clash is different, no longer between opposing sets of values, but between values and the violent vacuum. The substitute for culture presented to newcomers was invented at the conjunction of entertainment and advertising; it may still be called culture, but neither Rambo nor Madonna has the character required to get a troubled child through the night. If submersion, which sets out to destroy every vestige of the old language and culture, is to be supplanted, bilingual education will have to offer something beyond words, or it will be no more than a mask to hide the old method.

The nature of the beginning, Spanish or English, bilingualism or submersion, early exit (transition) or late exit (maintenance), will determine how children understand school. If it is a place of failure and ridicule rather than comfort and hope, the child may choose to play dead. Merle Navarro, a dedicated teacher at Bowie High School in El Paso, Texas, danced, sang, told jokes, and imitated Jerry Lewis, all to get the attention of her students, to raise them from the dead. She succeeded better than most, but by the time the children get to high school they have been too long dead; the work will have to be done sooner. It will have to begin at the beginning—or the year before.

3.

> . . . When the home language is different from the school language
> and the home language tends to be denigrated by others and selves
> . . . , it would appear appropriate to begin initial instruction in the
> child's first language, switching at a later stage to instruction in the
> school language.
>   . . . Where the home language is a majority language valued by
> the community . . . then the most efficient means of promoting an
> additive form of bilingualism is to provide initial instruction in the
> second language.   Jim Cummins, Bilingualism in Education

The Bilingual Education Act, even with a tuck taken here and there to make it fit the politics of the interested, does not deal with the problem of the death of the Spanish language. This death hides behind the myth of the Promethean immigrant who bears his language in a basket, another treasure hidden among his few belongings. It is only a myth, no more than that, yet it has sustained the faith of those who love the sound and soul of Spanish. In reality, many Latinos now speak Spanish only to their parents or grandparents, if at all. Most newcomers live in the worst of the social and economic world, where the only middle-class Latinos they have contact with are shopkeepers or the grim officials who try to keep order among the crowds at the bottom of the social scale. To depend on continuing waves of newcomers, many of whom speak ungrammatically, using the tiniest vocabulary, is to ensure the death of the language. Third or fourth generation Latinos who live in suburbs of Minneapolis or Atlanta have no more reason to know Spanish than Polish-Americans need to know Polish or German-Americans to know German.

Spanish probably would go the way of French, German, and Italian in the United States, unless one thinks of it rather than English as the lingua franca of the hemisphere. And that is where the practical, political, and economic difference lies. Miami was the first city to make a business decision to maintain Spanish. So much of the city, its banking and export sectors, is concerned with Latin America that Spanish has become the preferred language of business. Everyone speaks English, of course, but it lacks the comfort of Spanish; it is not at home in Panama or Peru.

Latino businessmen in Texas, New York, California, and Illinois make the same argument. And if the hemisphere is declared a free trade zone early in the next century, as everyone expects, the practical value of Spanish will increase tenfold or a hundredfold or more.

In the battle between maintenance and transition, late and early exit from bilingual programs, the emotional issues of nationalism and the arguments for cultural enrichment may eventually give way to the business proposition expressed at Coral Way Elementary: People who know two languages have a better chance of getting ahead in life. If that is so, however, why should Anglos be denied the opportunity to succeed? Shouldn't bilingual education at the maintenance level be available to everyone who wants it? Wouldn't that begin to overcome some of the deficiencies in U.S. culture? Wouldn't that make the United States a more formidable competitor in the world?

Children in Latino neighborhoods could all learn Spanish as well as English. Where the Chinese language is strong, they could learn both Chinese and English, and so on. In larger cities, with several ethnic populations, children or their parents might be permitted to choose between many languages. Cummins explains exactly where to begin for both Anglo and Latino children. His method is not radical, but practical, the homely logic of a man hoping to avoid the wars of chauvinism.

Coral Way Elementary in Miami put Cummins's notion into practice. In bilingual schools the Anglos learn Spanish as a second language, attending special immersion classes from the earliest grades, just as their Latino counterparts attend immersion ESL classes. Before long, all the children are fluent in both English and Spanish. To continue the process after the elementary grades, high school students may take courses in Spanish after school for extra credit. If they do well in both their English and Spanish studies, those who take the extra courses are awarded a second diploma from a high school in Spain.

—

It is not a sentimental system; Dade County doesn't operate that way. Nor is it racist or ethnocentric. The method grew out of a sense of the equality of languages, cultures, and economic capabilities. It worked. Whether it will continue to work will be the test. When the federal government first provided money for a bilingual program at Coral Way Elementary in Little Havana in 1963, the students were the children of middle- and upper middle-class Cuban exiles. They arrived with great facility in Spanish, most of which was easily transferable to English. Many of the Cubans have moved away from Little Havana now. The newest immigrants are poor people who fled the war in Nicaragua or the death squads in Guatemala and El Salvador. Miami has become much more like prerevolutionary Havana. The wealthy Cubans send their children to a private school named for the best private school in remembered Havana, the one attended by Fidel Castro Ruz. The middle class has moved to the suburbs. The poor people and the people of color are left to struggle in the inner city public schools.

The Spanish-speaking teachers and the administrators at Coral Way Elementary are still Cuban, and their methods have not changed: They still believe that the maintenance of two languages is the proper form of bilingual education. It is still the culture of the school that accommodates the child, rather than attempting to force the child to learn in an alien environment. Only the students are different. Some of them come to school not knowing how to hold a pencil, never having touched a book, speaking only rudimentary Spanish, emotionally wounded by the experiences of war or drug addiction. This new cohort stands in terrible contrast to its predecessor, as if in one famous bilingual public school a test of the relative importance of school and home had been devised and the lives of the children had been committed to it.

Unfortunately, many of the children who do not learn Spanish well do not become proficient in English either. The failure of schools to teach English to Latino children by any method—submersion, immersion, transition, or maintenance—is so common in the United States that almost every successful Latino in business or the professions attributes part of his or her success to the ability to read, write, and speak English, a set of skills that second-generation European-Americans took for granted. Their view of the basis for success emphasizes the true horror of the education of Latinos in the United States: The system destroys one language, but does not replace it with another, creating a great class of mutes, victims who cannot even speak of their pain.

13

IN SEARCH OF ORDINARINESS

GUIDELINES FOR SCHEDULE OF SUBJECTS AT CORAL WAY ELEMENTARY 1988–1989

GRADE I

English

PE 20 minutes during A.M. *MUSIC* 20 min twice a week during A.M. *ART* 50 min per week during A.M.	1 hour & 30 min Language Arts in English	Reading, Spelling, Handwriting, Composition, ESOL (included)
Change classes at 11:50 A.M.	40 min	Science, Social Studies, Health* (with an ESOL approach when needed)

Spanish

	45 min Math	30 min in English, 15 min in Spanish
	1 hour Language Arts in Spanish	Lectura, Escritura, Composicion, Orthografia
	25 min	Ciencias, Estudios Sociales, Salud*

*Alternating Science, Social Studies, and Health in English and Spanish.

I.

The eggs had been given into the care of the teacher, while the boy, who was the father of the eggs, delivered a note to the office. It was not an unusual occurrence. No one paid much attention to the eggs resting together in their small, criblike basket on the corner of the teacher's desk, each egg half covered with a tiny blanket, its infant face staring up at the ceiling. There were many eggs in the class, all of them in their baskets, tucked in, cosseted by their parents, as eggs must be. In one basket the eggs were identical twins. In some baskets there was only one egg, which lay alone. There was something sad about those baskets with only one egg; the eggs in them appeared forlorn, abandoned. In all the baskets with only one egg a sense of loss was somehow said, tragedy was implied. And in one basket there were no eggs at all. But there had been eggs; the form of them was impressed upon the tiny blanket; there were signs in the stiffness of the bedding that something terrible had occurred, as final as a death.

All day and all night the eggs stayed with their child parents. Every night, at three A.M., the parents of the eggs awakened to the rudeness of an alarm clock, as if the bell or buzz were the voice of an infant child crying. At the lunch hour the parents of the eggs had to find babysitters for their delicate wards or they could not go to lunch. Day after day, night after night, the eggs exacted their demands upon their eleven- or twelve-year-old parents, relentless, delicate, and as irreparable as Humpty Dumpty.

The teachers at Coral Way Elementary, who have the bustling practicality of exiles, think the exercise of the eggs will teach their students something about the responsibilities of parenting. They have instituted the program because their students first begin to get pregnant in the sixth grade, and the teachers think it is the responsibility of pedagogues to educate children in the world. In this work they are as unforgiving as reality; the eggs in the baskets have not been cooked—if one should fall, its tiny face shatters and the yellow heart and clear, viscous body ooze through the wounds to die in the unrelenting world. The manicured pedagogues of Coral Way teach the tragic view of life, they give lessons in death; the teachers are the Spanish aunts of their students.

—

On a late winter afternoon, Coral Way Elementary bathes in the gentlest of ocean breezes. The building—constructed in 1936, now blurred slightly in the middle age of edifices, wearing too many coats of paint, decorated with the second, third, or fourth growth of foliage, and even that beginning to get tired—is overcrowded, operating at double its physical capacity and more, yet the school goes about its business in a hush, as if in awe. In the center court of the building, the grass is very tired, awaiting spring, and the covered walkways around the inner perimeter of the building are too deeply shaded for the season, almost cold. The architecture belongs to the Spain of the tropics, as if the architects knew that twenty-seven years after their work was done the role of the school would be to attract the children of the newly exiled, to be the first place in which they put down their intellectual roots in the United States.

If there is a secret to the success of the school, some say it is in the influence of Mrs. Rosa Inclán, who is the supervisor of bilingual/foreign language training for the Dade County schools. She is the teacher of teachers. Her influence is everywhere in the bilingual programs, and it is deeper than supervision, for many of the best teachers and administrators in the Dade County schools first studied education[1] in Cuba with Professor Rosa Inclán. She says there are no secrets to bilingual education: "Coral Way is so good because it has always been an ordinary school, with ordinary faculty, not special."

She gives a clue to the meaning of ordinariness when she speaks of one of her former students, Mrs. Julia Menendez, now the principal of Coral Way. "She was a fourth grade teacher," Mrs. Inclán said, "a beautiful teacher!"

Since ordinary teachers do not merit the enthusiasm Mrs. Inclán showed about her former student, she must not mean ordinary in the sense of mediocre; rather, she must be talking about normality, a school in which the students, teachers, and methods are as common to the culture as hot dogs, Mom, and flan. In her wish to make bilingual education unexceptional, she may have found the key to making it work. Pluralism, of course, depends upon those who are different still being ordinary; that is the essence of a multiracial, multicultural society. Under no other circumstances can such a society ever be just or fair.

Applied to bilingual, bicultural education, ordinariness requires equality; it is the quotidian practice of the most high-minded concept of a democratic society. It is as if Mrs. Inclán read Tocqueville's criticism of democracy in the United States, with its crushing demand for conformity, and found a solution, at least in the classroom. No one and nothing strange can be in her idea of a school. The faces in the classrooms of Coral Way reveal histories in Spain, Scandinavia, Africa, the Mediterranean, and the highlands of Guatemala. A fifth grade teacher there said, "I have children in this class from fifteen different cultures." The goal is to make them all ordinary, not common, not slow, not average, but ordinary, comfortable with who they are, accepted by the others as equal, similar, human.

[1]At a small private university, Santo Tomás de Villanueva.

With the days divided as in the schedule for the first graders, who can say which language dominates, which culture has the greatest value? Spanish and English live side by side, sometimes in the same classroom on the same subject. In mathematics the children switch from one language to the other every day, in every class. At the end of their time in Little Havana, when the children leave Coral Way to enter junior high school, Spanish and English have attained the highest cultural level in the minds of the students: Both languages have become ordinary.

When most of the students at Coral Way were the children of middle-class Cubans, in its glorious days, test scores were high, ordinariness was the Cuban exile sense of achievement, and there were few students who did not go on to finish high school at the very least. Now, only 79 percent of the children are Latino, and few of those are Cuban. There are exiles—a boy in the first grade who walked from Nicaragua impresses the teachers, some of whom remember the ordeal of leaving Cuba—and immigrants and many children who have no legal status in the United States. The principal, Mrs. Menendez, is impressed with the task-orientation of the Chinese students and depressed by what she calls the low literacy level of the children from Mexico. Many of the Nicaraguans, she said, have few social or literacy skills; they are campesinos who came out of the back country.   .

The astonishing aspect of the school is the willingness of its faculty to make any situation ordinary. If the children do not understand the seriousness of parenting, they will be handed personified eggs and told to care for them. If they come without language skills and no English at all, they will begin school when they are four years old, and a teacher whose energy surpasses even that of her preschool pupils will teach them about Tricky Turkey's two toes and their own teeth and tongues. Since the students are no longer motivated at home as they were in the beginning, Coral Way has established its own dropout prevention program, identifying potential dropouts in the earliest years of school and starting to work on their problems then, when they can make some difference.

Mrs. Menendez exemplifies the character of the school. She bustles. She wears gold chains and bracelets, and her hennaed hair is pulled back tightly and tied with a long black scarf at the beginning of her pony tail. She organizes; she administrates. Teachers must change classes if they aren't bilingual. English in the morning, Spanish in the afternoon, working out the 60/40 English to Spanish split. And the building itself interests her: She accepts its age, the crowding of temporary buildings at the back and sides to accommodate the overflow of students, but she will accept no graffiti; if the custodians find writing on the walls of the open building on Monday morning, they paint it out before noon.

Walking across the brown grass to a temporary classroom, Mrs. Menendez, whose ample figure balances on tiny feet and high spike heels, stops suddenly to pick up a piece of paper lying on the ground. It is a scrap, hardly noticeable, but she bends carefully, balancing on her tiny feet and heels, careful about the rising of her skirt, and picks it up, then crushes the scrap in her hand, and moves on. More than test scores or order in the classrooms, the bending of the principal to pick up a scrap of paper signifies an effective school. It seems inconsequential, evidence of compulsiveness, but it is not that at all. When I first saw Awilda Orta, then the principal of a junior high school in New York City, stoop to pick up a scrap of paper from the stairs of her school, I thought it queer behavior, but I have seen Juana Dainis in Spanish Harlem and Nancy Archer in El Paso, Texas, do the same thing. The gesture, and it is a gesture, is a sign to the students of the intentions of the school toward them—its seriousness and its welcome.

Old, overcrowded, in the midst of the tragic social and economic deterioration of Little Havana, populated with many students whose parents have no understanding of the value of education, Coral Way still reflects the meticulous grooming of Mrs. Menendez and the sense of order that may have made the 90-mile voyage from the university at Villanueva. The rules of Coral Way are posted everywhere, and everywhere they are clear, even in a first grade classroom:

Rules

We will walk to and from class quietly.
We will raise our hands before speaking.
We will work quietly.
We will stay in our seats.
We will pay attention always.

Consequences

[one check]	No play time
[two checks]	Detention
[three checks]	Call home
[four checks]	Go to office

Rewards

| Daily rewards and weekly rewards | Stickers, cookies, cereal, candy |

They call it assertive discipline. Much of it is based on peer pressure: "Leonardo can't read until everyone's ready to listen to him. Leonardo, look around and make sure everyone's ready."

And some of it is based simply on kindness and interest. Lourdes Robida, an administrative assistant, pointed out a boy whose situation concerned her. The boy's mother had abandoned her family, leaving the father with four children. "The father was close to a breakdown," Robida said. "The grandparents are trying to help, but it's a very difficult situation." The school would help the child and the father with counseling, extra attention, flexibility. It was, as Mrs. Menendez said, a neighborhood school, her synonym for ordinariness.

Not that Coral Way is without problems. Of more than a thousand students, eleven are considered serious discipline problems, and they are taught separately, in a trailer (one of the temporary classrooms) devoted entirely to them. There are also children with learning disabilities and children who must be socialized. The theory of the school is based on the transfer of skills, which the faculty maintains can be acquired in any language, but those children who arrive with less than the most elementary vocabulary, for example, or who cannot construct a sentence in ordinary speech must be given special attention. And those classes are difficult. The teachers struggle; the children do not concentrate. The need to combine socialization and education in children who may be living in a room with fifteen or twenty other people, strains the ability of Mrs. Inclán's followers to create ordinariness.

At its best, Coral Way connects bilingualism with the most ordinary public things of life. Coral Way attaches no shame to Spanish, and therefore no need for it to be private. In the third grade economics and mathematics classes taught by Maria Piñeiro a game serves to make Spanish as ordinary as laughter. The children play Matemática Gigante, a learning game based on the quiz show section of the popular network television program, *Sábado Gigante*. Four students sit at a table at the front of the room, showing problems to the class, calling on various people to answer them. When a question is answered correctly, the students on the panel nod agreement, and when a student gives an incorrect answer, Mrs. Piñeiro rings a tiny ceramic bell.

She also teaches economics, standing at the side of the class, slim, blonde, dressed not as a teacher, in some basic garments, but in high style, like one of the rich matrons who live in Coral Gables. She speaks effervescent Spanish, greeting correct answers with *Fantástico! Tremendo! Perfecto! Interesante!* Her classroom embodies the two secrets of Coral Way Elementary: worldly ordinariness and the wild optimism the Cuban bourgeoisie cultivated in Miami. If equality was the key ingredient in the success of the American experiment, then Coral Way, a neighborhood school as ordinary as home, a place in which Spanish and English are equally public and private, should continue to be effective.

There are some problems at Coral Way, overcrowding and the inadequate early education with which many of the students enter school, but there is only one real danger: the sense among a few teachers and administrators now that some cultures should be valued less highly than others—*racismo*—which is the end of equality, the death of ordinariness.

2.

No one can make you feel inferior without your consent.

Juana Dainis

When Juana Mercedes Noguera Fuentes Dainis came to work for the first time at her new job, replacing a white woman, she was greeted by a crowd who threw eggs and stones at her and told her to go back where she came from. After that, she was driven to and from her job in a police car. But the police couldn't solve her problems inside the building, where several of the people she was going to supervise suggested that she take courses at Berlitz to get rid of her accent.

Juana Dainis and her husband live in Manhasset, a middle-class suburb on Long Island. A Puerto Rican family had lived in the area once before, but they moved out after neighbors burned their house down. To greet Mrs. Dainis some of the same neighbors stopped by and advised her that they didn't throw garbage into the streets in Manhasset.

The daughter of the newspaper publisher of Cayey and the granddaughter of one of the leading Republicans in the town was not deterred by her welcome to the mainland. "In Puerto Rico we were upper middle class," she said. "Then I come here and they're going to treat me as lower class?" She lifts her head and sniffs with contempt for her tormentors.

In 1988, the U.S. Department of Education recognized 287 schools in the United States for excellence in education. Of those, only 42 were in large urban areas. One was P.S. 206 at the eastern edge of the barrio, across from one of the larger housing projects in Manhattan. Ninety-seven per cent of the students at P.S. 206 come from families on public assistance; 58 percent of the children are Latino, the rest—non–Spanish-speaking blacks. In 1974, after the egg and rock throwing sessions had ended and the school had calmed down, the students of 206 were tested by the New York City Board of Education. Of 612 elementary schools in the city, P.S. 206 ranked 556th. After fourteen years of Spanish-accented administration by Juana Dainis, the school had moved up 510 places in the rankings to 46th.

Dainis came to her task prepared to overcome the neighborhood and the abysmal New York City school system. Her theory of education is: "Once they're in school, I can do wonders with them. I don't care whether they're from single parent homes, broken homes. The norm now is divorce, broken homes; if they do badly in school, it's just a matter of excuses, excuses. In many schools they forget the mission, which is teaching and learning. When that is taking place, many other problems fall into place. And why not have high expectations? Just because they're black and Puerto Rican? There are no double standards here; we have a high standard for everyone." It is her version of Mrs. Inclán's notion of ordinariness.

New York City schools, however, do not become ordinary so easily. The bureaucracy was racist, bloated, lazy, and stupid when Dainis took over P.S. 206 in 1974, and it had not improved much by 1988 when her school was named one of the best in the country. One of the problems she had to overcome was the custodian's reporting relationship. The people who clean the schools do not report to the principals who are responsible for the physical plant. As a result of this managerial anomaly, the custodians are the bandits of the New York school system. They routinely hire relatives and friends in no-show jobs and collect overtime for doing nothing, making them among the highest paid people in the school system and leaving the schools among the dirtiest in the country. The situation is a given in the New York City schools, but not in the school run by Juana Dainis.

"When I came here," she said, "I told the custodian, 'You think you got big balls? I'll cut 'em off.' " She mopped floors and painted classrooms herself after school. Then she threatened the custodian, "If you don't keep these floors clean, I'll call Channel 7 and tell them to come over and watch the principal mopping up." Suddenly, P.S. 206, a nice, relatively new building in terrible condition, began to look cleaner. Dainis, who picks up papers, straightens desks, and arranges chalk and erasers wherever she goes in the school, had begun to make her mark.

The next step was with the teachers. "If the teacher is not working well with the kids," she said, "It's not the kids' fault." She took the teachers out of school to restaurants for meetings, made demands on them, increased teacher training, made certain that "teachers know what they have to teach, give weekly tests, work from a written plan." Her goal was to make the school a happy place, and she thought that it had to begin with the teachers: "I work on the teachers to make them feel self-confident. Teachers have a hard time learning to enjoy success."

For Juana Dainis *racismo* is not yet a problem. Her students live in New York City, where racism dogs dark-skinned people all the days of their lives. The children know before they come to school that whites are rich and they are not. In the black and Latino ghetto from which P.S. 206 draws its students no one has a job, hardly anyone has a father, a fourth of the people use drugs, armed adolescents walk the halls of the housing projects, and less than a mile south of the school the home of the richest people on earth, the Upper East Side of Manhattan, begins.

No child who comes to school at P.S. 206 can be fooled about the race problem in America. Only victims arrived at the doorstep of the daughter of the newspaper publisher of Cayey; her problem from the beginning was to raise them to the level of ordinariness. Her method was to oppose the lies of racism with a wildly energetic hyperbole of her own. She has even made a hyperbole of herself. Every morning she drives up to the entrance of P.S. 206 in the biggest car Cadillac makes. She wears mink when it's cold and carries a Burberry umbrella when it rains. And when she goes through the class-rooms of her school, she performs the counterpoint to racism for her stu-dents. "Who's number 1?" she asks, holding up a long, perfectly manicured forefinger. Then she leads them in the answer, "We're number 1!"

And again.

And again.

She tells them until it cannot be otherwise. She demonstrates it for them with her Cadillac and mink, her height and energy. She proves their position in the world with her accent and the color of her skin. She gives them her confidence, demands that they accept it. "I expect the children to be ladies and gentlemen. I tell them the way you dress for church or a party, you must also dress for school. I never had a pregnancy in this school. I never had a problem with drugs."

Juana Dainis revels in the idea of being Puerto Rican. At a luncheon meeting with her teachers she reaches into her purse and takes out a bag of fried plantain chips. "I can't get along without my *tostones,*" she said, offer-ing the chips to the Anglos on her staff, all of whom politely declined.

"I don't understand these Americans," she says. "They talk all day at work and then they go out at night and talk. Not me. When I go out, I like to go dancing. You have to put spice in your life." She laughs. The principal becomes entirely the woman, tall, a dancer more sinuous than salsa, with reddish hair and skin neither black nor white, but tropical, the color of spice. "You see this skin? I think the whites must like this skin; I've had two white husbands." Then, for an instant, she puts the hyperbole into abeyance: "I feel the prejudice. My mother-in-law didn't like the idea of her son marrying a Puerto Rican. She loves me now, but she didn't like the idea then. And my white colleagues are very friendly to me at work, but they don't invite me to their houses."

Nor do the parents and teachers of P.S. 206 favor the culture of Puerto Rico in the classroom. They have consistently opposed bilingual education, forcing Juana Dainis to create an effective school for first- and second-generation Latino children entirely in English. Were it not for the powerful figure of the principal of 206, the program would have been an argument for the efficacy of submersion, but no Latino child could feel he or she was drowning in the presence of the daughter of the newspaper publisher of Cayey.

3.

I don't accept the "dumb Mexican" theory.

Nancy Archer

In a state known for the poor quality of its public schools, in a school district so filled with incompetent teachers and administrators that the average of standardized test scores for all schools in the district does not meet the acceptable minimum for Texas and many schools achieve only half of the minimum, Schuster School was one of the worst. Even the feckless administrators of the El Paso Independent School District could no longer tolerate the level of education provided at Schuster. They fired the principal and brought in Nancy Archer and an almost entirely new staff.

Four years later the U.S. Department of Education cited Schuster Elementary School as one of the best in the country. It ranked sixth of sixty-seven schools in the El Paso Independent School District that year. The next year, 1989, Schuster ranked first in the district based on the results of the Texas Educational Assessment Minimum Skills (TEAMS) test. The Schuster School gets no special help from the city. On the contrary, learning-disabled children are bused in[2] and gifted children are bused out.

Seventy-five per cent of the students at Schuster are minorities, most of them Mexican-American, and although there is not a one-to-one correspondence between racial and ethnic groups and poverty, the proportion of children who come from poor families, making them eligible to receive free lunches, is also 75 percent. Nancy Archer makes a point of the racial, ethnic, and economic background of her students, because she considers her competition the schools on the west side of the city, where most of the students are Anglo and middle or upper middle class. She believes that poor Mexican children can learn as well as anyone else—she does not confuse culture with capability—and she uses the TEAMS test scores to prove her point.

Her methods agree with those of Coral Way and P.S. 206. The Schuster School looks new now, although it is almost thirty years old. The front yard is tidy, with as much green grass and shrubbery as one can hope for in the high desert. In 1984, the yard was overgrown with weeds. That was when Mrs. Archer and her students and teachers attacked the problems of the physical plant. They pulled weeds together, cleared the broken desks and

[2]These children are not required to take the TEAMS test.

chairs and other junk out of the storerooms and classrooms, and started keeping the floors and walls clean. "I've fired four janitors," Archer said, "but I take very good care of those who do well."

The children have become so concerned about the appearance of the school that she and her assistant principal, Helen Tornatta, think they may have gone too far. After a rainstorm they found the children using their handkerchiefs to wipe up the mud they had tracked into the school.

Nancy Archer has a Texas drawl and she wears her hair in light brown beauty-parlor curls, but this fair, fine-featured Southern woman has the intensity and drive and astounding sense of efficiency of the manager of a Japanese automobile plant. For example, children at the Schuster School spend the whole day in the same room, while children in many other schools change classrooms at the end of each period. Nancy Archer reasons, "I save a month of school by not changing rooms. It's fifteen minutes every time they change classes. That's seventy-five minutes times 175 days a year."

Like the Japanese, she has a simple, straightforward approach to every situation, a practical solution to every problem. Success should be ordinary, nothing more, the routine of getting ahead, of getting equal. "Children must read every day after school. Every Monday they must bring in a book slip signed by a parent. For reading six books they get a free hot dog and a coke from the Weiner Schnitzel Company."[3]

She uses bumper stickers to keep parents interested in the school. One bumper sticker reads, "My child is an honor student at Schuster School." And for every six weeks the child spends on the honor roll the principal sends home a star to be added to the bumper sticker. There are also bumper stickers for attendance. And every six weeks Schuster holds honors and attendance parties for the children. The rate of attendance at Schuster is 96 percent for students, 97 percent for teachers.

To get over the doldrums of the last six weeks of school, when the teachers and the students are tired, she introduced the BUG campaign. BUG stands for "brought up grades." A child must bring up two grades during the last six weeks to earn a BUG button, a big badge showing a stylized drawing of a ladybug.

The entire plan of the school is based on rewards. "Catch them being good" is the motto. Teachers must send home three "good" notes per class per week, and the principal must get a copy of every note. There are four hundred children in the school. Nancy Archer knows them all by name.

---

[3]She made a deal with the fast food company to offer this incentive to her students. To help them with preparing for tests, she got her "partner in education," the Coors Breweries, to supply special textbooks for all the children. Where she gets help and how is not important to her; she is utterly ruthless on behalf of the children.

Every day, she seems to find time to touch a large percentage of them. "Ours is a hugging school," she says, "and I have the cleaning bills to prove it. You have no idea how syrup sticks." She says that new children in the school who misbehave are pressured by their peers to be good, for good is the ordinary behavior in Nancy Archer's school.

But there are times when the bumper stickers and honors parties aren't enough, when even a hug won't solve the problem. For those situations the steel will of Mrs. Archer emerges. "We demand that kids come to school," she said. "I had a kid last year who didn't come to school, just wouldn't get out of bed, so I went to his house over in the projects and told him I'd help him get dressed. He was a sixth grader. He didn't miss school again."

The steel will shows more plainly in her willingness to break rules and conventions. At Schuster School, more than a few children flunk kindergarten. She believes, along with many other educators, that the dropout problem starts in kindergarten or first grade. She thinks a major cause of the problem is that children become accustomed to failure in the earliest grades and continue the pattern until they are old enough to drop out of school. "We retain kids in kindergarten or first," she said; "we don't let them go on failing. Some kids just develop faster than others; one year can make an enormous difference. If you push them too fast, they keep failing. So we say that some kids are red-shirted,[4] which the parents understand better than retaining."

A few of the methods at Schuster were learned from the Connecticut Effective Schools program, but most were generated by Mrs. Archer and her teachers. One of the methods at Schuster simply flouted the rules of the Texas system and the El Paso School District plan for bilingual education. Nancy Archer, her teachers, and many of the parents at Schuster opposed the District's new "477" bilingual education program in which first graders spend all but one hour a day learning in Spanish. The Schuster staff preferred a system of split days, with English and Spanish immersion getting equal time.

But in 1990 the 477 program was instituted at Schuster. A few months into the school year, Nancy Archer started to worry. "Bilingual kids are not learning their reading and writing," she said. It was the first sign of regression. As she spoke, a shadow of age passed over her face. Her voice became plaintive. "We don't take their culture away with English immersion. We reinforce their self-concept. I tell them how lucky they are to know two languages, how I wish I did. I favor splitting the day, but one hour of English is not enough. I see my children falling behind in a way that makes it

---

[4]A phrase used to describe a college athlete who does not participate in varsity sports for a year in order to develop his skills and extend the students' four-year period of eligibility.

impossible for them to catch up." In her mind this is extraordinary behavior for Latinos, the kind of externally imposed problem that gives rise to what she calls "the dumb Mexican theory." She refuses to accept the dumb Mexican theory or anything else that makes her kids less than equal, but her battle to maintain the ordinariness of her students is difficult. One has only to look at the recent bureaucratic history of the Schuster School to know how difficult: In 1988 Dr. Patrick Proctor, who taught the Connecticut Effective Schools program to Schuster teachers, said after looking at the school's performance that he could not find an area that needed work. A year later, in 1989, members of the state and local educational bureaucracies also evaluated the school. During that year test scores had risen, teacher training had improved; only the income level of the families who sent their children to Schuster had fallen. In the report of the state evaluators, the Schuster School and its principal, Nancy Archer, were severely criticized and put on notice for failing to carry out the policies prescribed by the state and the district. Following their report, the 477 plan was implemented.

4.

What's good for the rich is good for the poor.

Slogan of 1972 education reform groups in New York York City

During the 1988–89 school year I observed two classes in the Bilingual Bicultural Art School (BBAS) of P.S. 7 in School District 4 in New York City. Until that year, the district had been one of the most famous in America. District 4 had been featured in The Economist, the New York Times, and virtually every magazine devoted to education. The Superintendent had gone to the White House to receive an award from the president of the United States. The mayor of Beijing and the British minister of education had come to visit the district. Its policy of permitting the schools to compete for students had been praised by the American Enterprise Institute as a triumph of economic freedom as applied to education.

Although there had been some spectacular successes in the district—Awilda Orta's turnaround of the junior high school once known as Jailhouse 99, Juana Dainis's work at P.S. 206, and the work of Deborah Meier, the first public school principal to win a MacArthur Foundation "genius" grant—the reading scores for the district as a whole that year were only average for the city and the math scores were just barely out of the bottom third.

District 4 had been a triumph of publicity from the beginning of local control

*of school districts in New York in the early seventies until the 1988–89 school
year. In that year the superintendent and several members of his staff were dismissed and a school board member was removed by the chancellor after charges
of misappropriation of funds were brought by the inspector general. It was also
a terrible year in the neighborhood; crack cocaine had become epidemic in the
streets surrounding P.S. 7 at 119th and Lexington,[5] and its effect on the families
of the children was murderous.*

*In fairness to the teachers and students of BBAS, it was not a good time to be
observed. Had I been in their position, I think I might have barred the doors to
a writer.*

———

P.S. 7 is a squat, "modern," postwar New York building constructed of
steel and concrete, with a skin of glass and painted steel panels. The windows and the painted steel are always dirty, permanently streaked by the
chemical-laden soot of the city air, and the naked metal that holds the windows and panels in place is pitted and discolored. There is no grass in the
school yard, which is enclosed by the building on two sides and by a high
chainlink fence on the others. Heavy trucks and buses rumble by on the
Lexington Avenue side. Across the street, on the corner, under the yellow
bodega sign, the telephones have been torn out of the wall, leaving the
indestructible steel-wrapped cables sticking out like the antennae of some
postapocalyptic beast. Garbage floats everywhere in the puddles of yesterday's rain.

The little girls in the schoolyard wear little-old-lady clothes: clumsy shoes
and long, ill-fitting skirts. The boys look more normal, dressed in the dis-
habille of kids, their shirttails hanging out, their shoes untied, their baseball
caps falling over their ears. They are second and third graders, blacks and
Latinos, poor kids, immigrants, refugees, ghosts stopping by on their way to
or from the island. A teacher speaks to them through a bullhorn. "Don't run!
I told you not to fight! You have to share!"

In the principal's office on the main floor, around the corner from the
table where the guard sits in her semblance of a uniform, Robert Negrón
works at his desk. He is a quick, thin man, balding, neat; he wears blazers,
keeps razor-sharp creases in his trousers. Negrón grew up on the Lower East
Side in a tiny flat with five siblings. He said he never had more than two pairs
of pants, that his mother washed them every night so that her son, all her

---

[5]Wilfredo Laboy, former director of bilingual education in District 4, and I occasionally
have lunch at a restaurant on Third Avenue and 116th Street, then walk back to his office. On
the west side of Second Avenue between 116th and 117th Streets, less than a block from P.S.
155, where the district's offices are housed, crack pushers work out of an abandoned building.

children, would have clean clothes every day. Parents aren't like that any-more, he says. The parents are the problem now. The blame shouldn't be placed on society, but on the parents: They don't keep the children clean; they don't speak to them in good English or good Spanish; they abuse them; they let them go hungry; they make errors in grammar; they use drugs.

He can't make up his mind about bilingual education. All they have at BBAS, which is housed in his school, is a transitional program; he doesn't know what good it does. Bilingual education, he says, leads "to more segre-gation than education."

Negrón judges his school by the exceptions. He points to Yesenia Cha-parro, a P.S. 7 student who won a scholarship to Miss Hewitt's School: "That's worth fifteen thousand dollars a year." Yesenia Chaparro pleases him; she's out of the ordinary. He has others in his school, too: in the math room, where the teacher, a Portuguese woman, also favors extraordinary children and opposes bilingual education.

Upstairs, in the BBAS principal's office, Antonia Rodríguez shifts between social work and education. The families of her students are crumbling; not only must the children be educated, they must be kept alive, clean, fed, whole enough somehow to look up at the blackboard, to hear the teacher's voice through the din of terrors. The principal knows her students as if they were memories of her own childhood; she was raised in the South Bronx, the daughter of a Puerto Rican mother and a father from Jalisco, Mexico. She remembers the slum, not far from Charlotte Street. There were rats in the hallways, roaches, plaster falling from the ceilings and the walls. Like Ne-grón, she thinks of her mother, who cared for her, who urged her to go to school.

At her desk, seen through the open door into the hallway, unprotected as principals usually are by secretaries and anterooms, she smiles, a tiny woman, with a pretty, elfin face. But she smiles too delicately. The enthusi-asm of her voice, her composite New York–Central European, Mexican, Puerto Rican, Nuyorican voice sounds a contradiction of cultures. She sees with blue-green eyes, meant to be beautiful, seductive, a genetic triumph in the Bronx and the barrio, but the glistening of her eyes reveals a cache of tears. The quickness of her, the pace of her heels echoing in the halls of the school, the fit and color of her clothes, the style, the young woman's figure, and the midtown style: All are betrayed by the filigree of sadness over her smile, the pain of broken promises in her blue-green eyes.

It is a difficult morning for her, as every morning is difficult: She has driven in from Nyack, where her husband lies ill, suffering the aftermath of a stroke. She must put aside one set of problems for another: budgets, new definitions of bilingual education, test scores, a child abandoned, a child who begs, a change in the meaning of Limited English Proficiency (LEP) for the purpose of ranking the school's performance, more children entering, more children leaving. Crack, rock cocaine is always with her now. She has seen it destroy the neighborhoods, the young women, the homes of the children. There is no sense of order in the community; the rules of law and culture have been superseded by a kind of capitalism gone wild. She fights it with a new idea: The children will wear uniforms to school, dark skirts and trousers, white shirts or blouses; the uniforms will give them a sense of order, a code in opposition to the code of the streets.

The parents approve of the dress code, but too few have the money to buy uniforms. Children in her school wear hand-me-downs, *segundos* from the Mexican border, homemades brought from the island. The dress code has been most successful in the lower grades. She hopes it will grow up with the children.

Antonia Rodríguez sits at a small, battered wooden desk. She talks to parents, children, and teachers in that room, in that place, where only public embarrassments can be. At the farther end of the oblong room, Nilda Ríos, the assistant principal, sits at a desk facing Mrs. Rodríguez. Two women who do clerical work also sit in the one-room office, which was once a classroom. One is very pregnant; she brings cookies to work and eats.

Nilda Ríos is the sergeant of the school. That is the assistant principal's work and it is also her demeanor. She wears gold-rimmed eyeglasses and chops her hair in straight, stern lines. She will be the one to maintain order in the dining room, the keeper of the bullhorn, calling out the names of the shouters and fighters and runners, the screamers and food throwers and the ones who cut the line; she will call out the names of all the offenders of what little remains of the code of behavior. "Don't run! Don't hit him! Stand here against the wall!" Some of the sixth grade boys will be bigger than Nilda Ríos; she will challenge them with the conviction of her voice, the tensions of her jaw, the sign in her stance that she, too, has come to the edge of decorum, the last civilized moment.

The odor of institutional food is in the halls. Lunch will be served soon. She wears a sterner face.

Of all the staff of BBAS none speaks in a more forceful, more clearly enunciated manner or shows a harder surface than the assistant principal. She is the youngest of seven children, all born in Puerto Rico. The first six did not do well, she said, but her mother cared, she tried, she learned with each one, until the last, Nilda, went to college. And when Nilda graduated, her mother got divorced and looked for a life of her own.

Our people, she says, must be tougher. She admires Juana Dainis, who suffered for her efforts to defend the children, but who succeeded because of her toughness, her demanding, no-nonsense attitude. Be gentle with the children, she thinks, help them, but with the parents, get tough, make demands. Let the day be tough; let the world be tough with our people; let us get nothing we do not earn, no welfare, nothing. We can take care of ourselves. Give us something to do, not just money; give us something to do, demand something of us.

Then there is the boy from the Bronx. "You know that boy, he comes to my office all the time. Every time he walks by, he finds a reason to stick his head in. He's from the Bronx. He comes all the way from the Bronx to school here. Now I have to send him to a school in the Bronx. You know that boy, every day he eats lunch with me in the lunchroom. His mother's a crack addict, she doesn't care nothing for him. She has one other one, a girl, fifteen; she's already out to here pregnant. The mother came here one day, she said to me, 'You want him, take him.' But I can't take him, he has a mother, a home. His mother's a crack addict. Every day he eats lunch with me in the lunchroom. Now I have to send him to a school in the Bronx."

They work together well, the stern one and the elfin one with the filigree of sadness over her smile. But they are not providers of bilingual education; the business of BBAS is triage.

—

On a piece of construction paper tacked to the front of the supply cupboard Edna Montañez has written the names of the children in her first grade class, among them

> *Yadira*
> *Nixzalyz*
> *Yaritza*
> *Ivalisse*
> *Nashlisette*
> *Mari lú.*

They are the names of dreams, appropriate to ghosts.

One of the dreamgirls, a child with streaks of yellow in her hair and eyes more tired than middle age, cannot seem to sit in her chair. She writhes, in pain or boredom, as if she cannot find a comfortable place inside her skin. She puts an arm into the air, a leg behind her, sits up, half-stands to curl her legs under her. Of all the children in the room, she is the prettiest and the least able to speak or understand English. She does not hold a pencil between her thumb and two fingers, but grasps it in her fist as if it were a dagger.

Her father is away again, this time for a construction job in another town. The money he sends home is gone. No more will be coming soon. The mother of the dream girl has spent it all on crack cocaine. And in the excitement of the drug the girl has been replaced by other apparitions. Now the dreamgirl's clothes are filthy. Her hair smells of beer again. Has she been washing in beer? drinking beer? Has the mother of the dreamgirl spilled beer again or thrown it at the yellow streaked hair of her child?

The dreamgirl who cannot sit still does not understand anything in English, not so much as "Thank you" or "Good morning, Miss Montañez." At times, she stands up and wanders through the room or stares at the sky. Something like madness or a failure in the connection of the nerves seems to have ruined her life. She exhibits a kind of wildness, like a child raised in the woods, or the offspring of wolves, unable to survive in captivity. When the teacher calls on her, she does not always choose to answer, responding more to the tone of the teacher's voice than to the content of her commands.

In the middle of the morning, the dreamgirl's writhing begins. It comes with the first odors of food rising from the lunchroom kitchen, the mix of mush and oil, the brown smell of institutional food. Like an animal, the dreamgirl responds to the smell of food. She wakes up to it, she pushes everything else aside for it.

A week ago, the mother of the dreamgirl came to speak to the principal of BBAS. "What do you want me to do," the mother asked, "kill myself? All right, I'll commit suicide, then you can take the child from me." Next week, Antonia Rodríguez will see the mother and father together. She will not let the dreamgirl sink. There will be a contest between the principal and the drug. In this case, the first victory will go to the principal. The dreamgirl will learn to hold a pencil, speak some English, obey the rules of sitting and standing in the classroom. Her hair will be clean and she will wear something other than blue jeans and a dirty sweat shirt. Until late in spring, the principal's ploy will work, and then one morning in the rain the dreamgirl will come to school without a coat, damp and dirty, a creature seated all awry again, wild, as if she were allergic to the inside of her skin.

Edna Montañez passes impatiently between the low tables at which the children sit. She goes to the blackboard, a mountainous woman in blue jeans and a loose overblouse, highlighted by crimson lipstick and long red fingernails at the end of her inflated fingers. She has a New York voice, a response to the competition of jackhammers, subway cars, and crowding. Ms. Montañez is Nuyorican, Loisaida, born to a family of teachers and artists and lost to the culture of the city in which she was raised.

There will be a test today, administered in English to children who speak no English. Ms. Montañez goes to the blackboard and writes out a sample question:

It is Tim's birth _____ *now.*
- *boy*
- *day*
- *time*
- *fast*

"I'm going to read you the sentence," she says in English after explaining to them in Spanish that they will be taking a test.

She asks the class which is the right answer. The children raise their hands anxiously, calling out her name, Miss Montañez, Miss Montañez! She points to a boy.

"Fast!" he answers.

She shakes her head, and points to another child, this time a girl.

"Time."

Finally, she tells them the correct answer is either birthday or birthboy. "Which one is it?"

A boy raises his hand, nearly airborne in his urgency to answer the question. When she calls his name, he looks around the room and smiles, savoring the moment before he answers: "Boy!"

The disappointment on her face sends the child back down in his seat. Everyone in the class knows. When she tells them the correct answer, they do not listen, they have lost interest. Noise takes over the class. The children talk to each other, go to the front of the room to get drinks of water from the fountain. The class is out of control. Miss Montañez shouts at them, whips them with her voice as if they were animals.

She reads a long series of story questions. They understand nothing. She speaks to them in English and they answer in Spanish. It is a strange reversal of the situation at home, where the children answer in English to questions posed in Spanish by their parents. Miss Montañez shouts at them. "Go to your seats. This is a test!" Over and over, she tells them, "Go to the next page, darken in the spaces."

There is no order in the room: Children wander around, draw, talk to each other. The noise is wild, out of control; every child seems to be talking, trying to be heard over the voices of the others. The children ask for water, ask to be allowed to go to the bathroom. They sharpen their pencils, go to the coat room to root around in the backpacks and coats piled on the floor, searching for an eraser, a pencil, something, anything to get through the morning until lunch.

Twenty children have come to school; only a few are absent, and some of them may be lost, gone back to Puerto Rico or the Bronx. The colors of the children range from blonde to black. Some look Spanish, others Indian; most are varying mixtures of Spanish, black, and Indian. Eight of the twenty are wearing the blue and white uniforms suggested by the principal.

After the test and before lunch, they go upstairs to the computer room, where the teacher, a young Latino, instructs them more in discipline than in the use of computers. Before they are permitted to go by pairs to the Apple computers around the perimeter of the room, they must sit quietly in their chairs. He lectures them on behavior, threatening them in English and Spanish. Much of the period, perhaps half, is taken up with trying to establish order.

When they are finally quiet, he chooses pairs and sends them to the computers to work with simple programs. The goal of the class is to make the children "computer-literate," that is, to teach them the functions of the rudimentary devices supplied to the school. All of the computer programs are in English, which leaves some of the children completely baffled. Those who can understand explain to the others. In the computer room, there is an unsubtle hierarchy of children, structured according to their ability to speak English. The teacher would like to have programs in Spanish; he says he has looked for them, but there are none available. It has not occurred to him to investigate computer programs used in Spain or Latin America, or to do the simple translations himself and edit the programs, as if he did not know that apples are *manzanas* and clowns are *payasos*.

In the classroom again Miss Montañez sits at her desk while the children come up to her one at a time so that she can examine their workbooks. During the slow parade, all the other children float, talking, laughing, pinching and kicking each other, waiting, disorderly, a cacophony of children with nothing to do, nowhere to go, waiting. As the books pass before her, there is never a word of praise from Miss Montañez. Whatever positive reinforcement she offers is rote and silent, a star uneasily drawn on a paper, grim assent, nothing more. There are no victories in Miss Montañez's class.

The children have begun to ask about lunch. Miss Montañez, they say, singing out her name, Miss Montañez. Is it time for lunch, Miss Montañez? Every child in the class is entitled to a free lunch; every child in the class comes from a family on some kind of public assistance. The school serves breakfast, too, but many of them come too late for breakfast. Those children spend the morning in hunger, waiting for the food, by eleven in the morning lost to anything but the smell of the brown food coming up from the kitchen. Miss Montañez, when are we going to eat, Miss Montañez?

When they line up for lunch, it is with some excitement, for they have been a long time without food. It is near the end of the month, before the welfare checks come. The children do not have notebooks or other supplies and many are hungry. The class begins to look dirty by the time the checks are due. Even little Carlos, whose quick mind has already raised him to the status of star in the first grade class, has lost his grip by the time the checks are due. He wears the same red shirt every day, with TOUCH written on one sleeve, DOWN on the other, and SCORE across the front.

In the chaos of the lunchroom, Yaritza misbehaves and is sent to stand against the wall. She eases herself across the space slowly to where I stand, careful always to keep her back against the wall, her arms straight at her sides. Day after day she has kept her eye on me, wondering why I sit in the back of the room, watching her. Miss Montañez has never explained my presence in the class.

Yaritza knows everything that happens in the room. She follows the moods of Miss Montañez; it pleases her to taunt the teacher on the teacher's worst days. She understands the fear in the eyes of the dreamgirl. One day she took a pencil from her. Another day she whispered a wrong answer in her ear. Yaritza is the wise woman of the class, dark, with gray tones in her skin, a perfectly formed child, yet clumsy, like an old woman, with an old woman's kinky hair cut close to her head, dark eyes, not black, not startling, but dark brown, with yellow flecks to disturb the color. Her nose is tiny, but straight, in perfect proportion. She wears a dot of gold-colored metal in each ear. Her skirt, which is too long, was black, would be black again if it were washed. She has no blouse, only a purple knit top, too thin to be a sweater. The secret, sorrowful life of Yaritza is spoken by her shoes, which are too big and have no laces, and by the flat pouches under her eyes, the deflated flesh, the lines of tired skin, all the elasticity of youth used up, gone.

She turns her face toward me. I am the only business left to do as she stands in isolation against the wall. She smiles. "You're the one who eats candy in the class. Can I have some candy? Would you give me a quarter for candy?"

The manner of presentation of her case makes me laugh. She has remembered the day I brought a package of Lifesavers to class and she has put us together in isolation against the wall—two who break the rules.

"What about your lunch?"

"I don't like my lunch. Would you give me a quarter for cocoa? Give me some money. I need some money."

"Eat your lunch; it's better for you than candy. I'll bring candy to school for all the children."

"I don't like my lunch. I'll eat the apple, that's all. I throw the rest away."

"You should eat all of your lunch. It's very important for children to eat well."

"I need money. Give me some money. I need money."

The conversation ended when Nilda Ríos signaled to Yaritza that she could leave her place against the wall and go to the end of the cafeteria line. Yaritza slid away from me along the wall for a few feet, then walked to the end of the line, moving slowly and with great dignity, her shoes flapping slightly, her dirty black skirt dancing against her knees.

In a few moments, she came out of the serving area with a paper tray in her hands. It was almost the end of the lunch period. She gulped two or three balls of fried fish, ate her apple (which turned out to be a banana), sipped at her milk, then made eye contact with me. Deliberately, with admirable insouciance, she held her paper napkin between her thumb and forefinger, as if to show it to me, then let the napkin fall to the floor.

After the lunch hour, I found the principal and assistant principal in their office and told them about the incident in the lunchroom. "The child's in trouble," I said. Ríos and Rodríguez gave me the special smile that only teachers can deliver; it is a gift they bestow on students who have somehow rescued themselves from blindness and ignorance. "Yes, we know," the principal said, and then she and the assistant principal told what had happened to the child.

Yaritza's family had been getting along fairly well until the father left home and the mother began using drugs and bringing men home. Then the mother abandoned the children and an aunt came from Puerto Rico to take care of them. Meanwhile, the mother moved in with the family of a cousin, whose children also attended P.S. 7. The mother started bringing men into the cousin's house, causing that family, which had been stable for a long time, to deteriorate. A child, a very good student who lived in the cousin's house, started failing in school. The aunt could not cope with the two women; she decided to take the children back to Puerto Rico.

Rodríguez tried to persuade the aunt to wait until May fifteenth so the child could complete her reading test and take it with her to the school in Puerto Rico. Meanwhile, she was able to get weekly counseling sessions for the cousin, but not yet for Yaritza. She and Ríos shrug about the counseling. "It gives the child an opportunity to vent," she said, "but it doesn't solve the problem at home." After that, they turn to other things. They are not optimistic. Yaritza will have gone to Puerto Rico before May fifteenth. And there she will have no chance at all. For the poor in Puerto Rico the dropout rate is 70 percent. Yaritza is gone. They turn their attention to those who remain. The business of the school is not mourning, but triage.

In the classroom Miss Montañez is teaching phonics. She draws a picture on the blackboard of a shoe and asks the children what it is. The sound of the morning is *sh*.

A boy raises his hand: *"Es un zapato."*

"Sí, es un zapato, but this morning we are speaking English."

Carlos tells her it is a shoe.

"Yes, Carlos, it is a shoe. And class, what is the sound?"

"Ssshhhh," they answer.

She draws a picture of a ship. "What do we call this?"

"Es un barco."

"Sí, es un barco, en Español, but we are speaking English this morning."

She gets the answer, then draws a picture of a shell and asks for the initial sound. After a time, she gets the correct word, then she asks where a shell is found, and a child answers, *"En la playa."*

For a picture of a shirt, she gets *blusa,* then *camisa.* By now, half the children are shouting. "Alexandra," she says, and ten children shout "shirt." She refuses to accept the answer. "The only person I called their name was Alexandra," she says.

The class goes on and on in the same vein, filled with shouting, talking, children wandering around the room. The walls in this bilingual class have no signs in Spanish; the clothes closet is a mess, jackets and backpacks lying in piles on the floor. By the end of the day, the chaos has left the teacher and the class exhausted. As the children get ready to line up to file out at the final bell, one of the little girls begins to pester the teacher. "Miss Montañez, Miss Montañez"—she dances up and down in front of her—*"Mi brazalete."*

"Go to your seat. I didn't tell you to get up from your table," Miss Montañez tells her.

"Mi brazalete, Miss Montañez. Miss Montañez."

Suddenly, Miss Montañez leaves the child standing beside her desk while she goes into the supply room. She returns with something enclosed in the little Botero sausages and red fingernails of her fist. "Miss Montañez," the child calls, "Miss Montañez," repeating the name, singing the name.

The teacher opens her other hand and the little girl drops a quarter into it. Only then does Miss Montañez let the fingers of her fist open to reveal a tiny row of beads on an elastic string. It is the bracelet. The girl grabs it out of her hand and puts it on her wrist.

"The parents don't buy them what they need," Miss Montañez explains, "so I keep pencils, erasers, the things they need, in the closet. I buy them for them." She speaks very quickly, trying to explain, the little red fishmouth in the pock-marked moon of her face pumping out the words.

It is time for the children to put on their coats. They get up in groups. When his turn comes, Carlos, the little boy who gets all the answers right, sees that many of the coats have fallen or been thrown on the floor. He gets his coat, starts to go back to his chair, then changes his mind and begins picking the coats up off the floor and hanging them up, not carefully, not neatly, but hanging them up, putting order into the room. Outside, on 119th Street, his mother, who has come only recently from Ecuador, waits for Carlos and his brother. She wears her hair in bangs cut straight and low over her eyes and has two gold teeth; she stands silently, at ease inside a striped woolen cloak, like the cloaks her ancestors have worn for tens of generations in the mountains of Ecuador.

"Ladies and gentlemen, let's put our butts down on our chairs and sit up straight and get to work."

"C'mon, guys, let's brainstorm this problem. Okay, if you're going to do this contest thing, I'll help you to do it in Spanish. You write it, and I'll do a little spelling for you, okay?"

It is a voice unlike any other in the school, the sound of the teacher of expectations, always a mix of formality and the streets, of teasing and loving, youth and the old rules, Spanish and English, gentrification and reality, energy and order. The speaker is Nuyorican, a young woman as pretty as the sister of the hero in a sentimental movie about New York. She wears no makeup, dresses in light-colored clothes—white suits, pastels, yellows—and speaks softly, almost intimately, so that a whisper or a cough from one of the children will obscure her words. On some days she wears eyeglasses with clear plastic frames, which turn her face pale and stern.

At the beginning of the year, she makes a speech to the new class. She tells them, "Ladies and gentlemen, I want your best, not your worst—not less than your best, your best. I expect it."

In college, one of her teachers told her not to smile in the classroom, because smiling would cause her to lose control of the children. She tried that for a year, but then she realized that school wasn't any fun. The next year she smiled, and drove the class harder, covering more material every day. No one loafs in Mrs. Ojeda's class, and no one talks out of turn or fails to pay attention to the work at hand, but everyone can smile, for the teacher smiles.

Although Mrs. Ojeda is not a reader of the essays of Valéry, she teaches walking to her children, leaving the dancing for special moments. She is the most practical of teachers, a woman who knows the value of prose and the problems of poetry for children who sometimes do not have enough to eat. Bilingual education means practicality to her; it makes education possible for the children who do not speak English.

All day, in the classroom, she reads the faces of the children: Gerson, the slight, quick Mormon boy, with merchant's dreams, who has just come from Bolivia; Yissel,[6] the prissy child newly arrived from the Dominican Republic, dressed always with lace at her throat, like an eighteenth-century Spanish princess; the stocky, silent Mexican girl who sits, stolid as an Olmec idol, next to Francisco, while he whispers translations to her. When their faces are flat and no flicker of comprehension shows in their eyes, she repeats her question or instruction in Spanish. "The temperatures in the mountains are higher or lower than in the lowlands? Las temperaturas en las sierras . . ."

She says the Spanish quickly, as an aside; it is for six of the children, sometimes for eight, depending upon the complexity of the statement. She

[6]Pronounced as if it were spelled Giselle

does not say everything twice; she uses the Spanish as if it were a thin railing, something to hold on to while ascending a very steep set of stairs. In Mrs. Ojeda's class, Spanish comforts the children; it rescues them from danger, finds them when they are lost, teaches them what they cannot otherwise comprehend; it gives them confidence, tells them they are beautiful, lightens and softens the world; Spanish sings to them, loves them, takes away the strangeness, makes them ordinary: it is the mother tongue.

If there is a sadness in the class, it is that the Spanish language is dying there, in the Bilingual Bicultural Art School. Although she speaks easily and with an effort to avoid the extremes of pronunciation of the Nuyorican accent, Spanish is not Mrs. Ojeda's first language. Words often escape her. "Thumb," she asks, "what is the Spanish word for thumb?" One of the newly arrived children chances an answer: *"Dedo gordo?"* And Mrs. Ojeda and the whole class laugh; "fat finger" is a funny way to say thumb.

There is a similar problem with "coordinate." She does not know the Spanish word. No one in the class can help. They turn to the dictionary.

She fights the tendency on the part of the Nuyorican children to speak Spanglish, to say *ponche* for punch and *lonche* for sandwich. But then she cannot recall the word for punch until one of the new arrivals tells her *dar*. The theory that these new arrivals will keep the language alive simply because they are here cannot be proved in Mrs. Ojeda's class; the Nuyoricans have lost too much of the language to learn it again without formal study. Gerson, the boy from Bolivia, has made an arrangement with one of the Puerto Ricans in the class who speaks very little Spanish: Gerson will teach him Spanish and he will teach English to Gerson.

Spanish is too strange to tempt most of them. It is not a common "American" language as they are not common "Americans." These distinctions draw the battle lines for the class. They wish to be American; their parents wish them to be American. The avowed purpose of BBAS is, as Antonia Rodríguez said, "to mainstream them as fast as possible, not to teach them Spanish."

Although she does not use the term, no teacher understands the concept of ordinariness more clearly than Mrs. Ojeda. She comes to school from her home in a middle-class, mostly Jewish section of Queens. There are two salaries and two children in the Ojeda household. Mrs. Ojeda's mother cares for the children during the day. Like many young families, the Ojedas are considering leaving New York, perhaps to move to Florida; they have heard that things are booming in Orlando. Mr. Ojeda is in hotel administration, and there are plenty of hotels around Orlando; the question is whether she could find work as a teacher there, and who would care for the children.

This ordinariness, this equality, this sense of being more like than different, is the underlying message of her class. She teaches reading, mathematics, geography, science, and signals ordinariness. It is not the best class she has taught—some of the children are slow—but she is certain that this class will produce its share of doctors, lawyers, and teachers, like any other class in any other school, like any other group of children of any other racial or ethnic group. "Ladies and gentlemen," she says to them, "Ladies and gentlemen"; it is a phrase she will not permit them to forget. She teaches under a ceiling on which someone has scrawled graffiti in the grime, sits beside a window that has not been washed for a season or more, and speaks over the rumble of trucks and buses on the avenue outside. "Ladies and gentlemen," she says, speaking the magical incantation that cleans the ceiling and windows and makes the room as quiet as a snowy afternoon in New England.

She will not permit them to esteem themselves any less than the whites, the Anglos, the Americans. Following the publicity over the brutal rape of the "Central Park jogger," through which the word "wilding"[7] entered the language, Mrs. Ojeda held a debate in the form of a mock trial in her class. Teams of students argued both sides of the issue of capital punishment. The judges wore paper hats to indicate their authority. Although the children were not aware of what was going on in the class, the teacher had taken them away from identifying with the criminals, the people of color who had attacked a white woman stockbroker, to imitating the roles of those who administer the law. She had made them part of the establishment, peers, equals; she had elevated the poor and the newcomers into citizens who have the power to do the ordinary work of maintaining the society, which is the first task of politics. The debaters were well-prepared, fierce. They made her laugh. At the end, the judges pronounced the debate very close and awarded the victory to the side that opposed capital punishment.

Later, when a spate of violence erupted in the neighborhood, she gave them lessons in conflict resolution. She assigned the problems of drugs and guns as homework, asking them to write out five reasons why they should stay away from guns and drugs. As always, the school was ordinary: Education walked; later, there would be time for dancing.

She holds up the bottom of the class as best she can, but her attention is on the future doctors and lawyers; there are four in the class who are very bright, perhaps five, maybe even a sixth. She makes them gold and silver honor roll students; she pushes them and praises them to ever better work. Joseph, the son of the school nurse, was the brightest boy in the class at the

---

[7]P.S. 7 is not far from the northern end of Central Park, where the woman was accosted, beaten, and raped by young men from East Harlem. One of the boys arrested for the crime had been a teacher's aide at BBAS. Edna Montañez said that when she saw him on television, she wept, for she had known him as one of the most gentle high school students who had ever come to help at BBAS.

beginning of the year, well-dressed and well-spoken, bespectacled, charming to the teacher, but cruel to his classmates, especially the slower ones. Others are catching up: Bianca and Vincent will be joining him on the gold honor role, Marie and Rubie will get on the silver honor role, and by the end of the year Francisco will have roused himself out of his fears and self-doubts to appear suddenly as one of the brightest of them all.

No one works harder than Rubie, the daughter of a computer technician, a pudgy little girl with glasses whose favorite book is the encyclopedia. Rubie is the youngest of seven children, the fifth girl. She has been watching the world very carefully. Her oldest sister is twenty-four, the mother of two children. Her sister-in-law delivered a child at sixteen. "Nobody should be forced into growing up too fast," Rubie thinks. She is taking her time, studying hard, getting A's. "I have fourteen medals at home," she said. "I want to be a doctor. It's not really that I want it for the money, I want to help people. Before my mom passed away, she was really sick."

Her father wants to go back to Puerto Rico, but Rubie begs him to stay. "My classmates are my family," she says; "I really like it here."

Bianca and Rubie are best friends, although Rubie knows that Bianca is quicker, able to get better grades without working so hard. They study together, make plans—ordinary girls with ordinary dreams—in English.

Among those who will be catching up, if not this year, then next year or the year after, are Gerson and Wendy. Within a month after arriving in the United States, Gerson preferred to speak English rather than Spanish. He organized the ESL students in his class into a study group, gathering them at lunch and in free play periods to study basic algebra. His father was a businessman in Bolivia; Gerson will be a businessman in the barrio; he has already found a way to use his lunch hour profitably.

Wendy Saenz started school immediately after arriving from Ecuador in the spring, before she could find out anything about New York except that it is cold and corrupt, an unwelcoming place. Mrs. Ojeda put her at a table in the back of the room along with Joseph, the smart, cruel boy; a very slow, almost retarded boy, who is the butt of many of Joseph's jokes; a streetwise girl who wears dangling earrings and lipstick; and Mary, a burly black girl, whose sweet features and almost permanent smile belie a streak of brutal aggressiveness.

Although she makes no official assignments, Mrs. Ojeda depends on the "buddy system" to bring the ESL students into the mainstream of the class and to help the slower students keep pace; she is also aware that children learn by teaching. As a result, there is often a low current of whispers in the class, a sound that Mrs. Ojeda, with a teacher's instinct, can distinguish from horseplay or gossip. The student more or less assigned to Wendy is Mary, who sits on her right at the very back of the room. Mary wears blue jeans and sweaters to school; she seems always to be prepared for slush or snow, even though the season is over. Wendy comes dressed in pink shoes, pale blue socks, a pastel dress with starched puff sleeves, and carries a tiny folding umbrella in her book bag. Mary has the vigor of a New York street kid in her face and gestures. Wendy has classic Ecuadoran features, the hooked, almost broken nose, and Oriental eyes that resonate of Tibet and ancient Egypt. "Are you from the capital, Quito?" I asked, and she answered that she was from Guayaquil, on the sea. "But how do you know Quito is the capital of Ecuador?" she asked, as if she had come not from South America but from an unknown province of the moon.

She explained that in Guayaquil she was a very good student; they graded on a scale of one to twenty, and she almost always got twenty. But she did not know what would happen to her in the United States. English was very difficult; she had been in New York for almost two weeks and she could not speak English yet. She was worried. When Mrs. Ojeda called on her, in Spanish, to answer a math question, Wendy rose from her chair, stood very straight, with her hands at her sides, repeated the question, then gave the correct answer. The other children at the table mocked her, pretending they were automatons.

Mary nudged her. "Give me a sheet of paper." Wendy reached into her schoolbag, which was not like the knapsacks the other children carried, but a black plastic sack stamped to look like brocade, and took out a sheet of paper. The girl with dangling earrings and lipstick also demanded a sheet of paper. Wendy looked at her dwindling supply. *"Uno,"* she whispered, took out the paper, then pushed the remainder down deep into her plastic sack.

A week later, Wendy still wore pastels and pink shoes, but she no longer stood up to answer a question, and in those times when Mrs. Ojeda gave her attention to another student or to another group within the class, Wendy and Mary exchanged pinches and punches. Sometimes, when the teacher was very busy, Mary and Wendy arm wrestled. They were the same height and weight, and although Mary had bigger hands, they were so well matched that most of the contests ended in draws. Wendy was still ahead of the other children in math, able to transfer her conceptual skills, as the theorists of bilingual education promised, but the battle for her future had been joined. On one side, the fists and smiles of Mary and the long earrings of her pal, and on the other the expectations of Maria Ojeda and the memory of the nuns of Guayaquil.

Not long after Wendy arrived, the students posed for their class picture. In the photograph Mrs. Ojeda stands on the right, dressed in a bright yellow military tunic, with a wide belt. Her long, straight hair is pulled back over her ears, her eyes are open wide as if she were startled by the camera, and she wears a spontaneous smile. Roberto poses in the front row in the same blue warmup suit with the wide white stripe across the chest that he wears almost every day. Sitting next to him, cross-legged, wearing white socks, dark trousers, and a long-sleeved white shirt that gaps just a little at the belly, revealing a triangle of skin above his belt, is Francisco; he smiles, but he is the only one in the class who does not look directly at the camera. Rubie, the most soberly dressed child, in a wool olive drab dress, squints just a little, having taken off her glasses for the picture. Yissel wears a lacy white dress with tiny cap sleeves and a square open neck.

Mary is transformed in the picture. She has come to school in a bright yellow lace dress, so delicately made one can see through the fabric of the sleeves. Strands of pearls are woven through her hair. She wears golden earrings, a beatific smile, and engineer's boots. Vincent stands on the right next to Mrs. Ojeda wearing a loose knit white-and-brown sweater over a white shirt and tie. Joseph stands next to him wearing a plain shirt open at the collar. He too has taken off his glasses for the picture. The class clown comes next, with his bow tie, his half-crazy smile, and his slightly cocked head, as if he had just pulled off a miraculous trick or escaped from an airtight box. On the left end of the back row is one of the slow kids, and next to him another and next to him yet another; they are smiling, more or less, but not wholeheartedly, not with pleasure or pride, not with the proper turns to their mouths or lights in their eyes; once again, they have missed the point, failing to grasp the idea of the picture as it passed them by. In the second row, Bianca, who is the smartest person in the class, smiles in tight-lipped satisfaction, or is she just trying to keep from laughing out loud?

Thirty-nine students are carried as members of Mrs. Ojeda's class. Seven have not come to school for a long time; no one knows whether they are truants or transfers or dropouts. They remain on the books. Of the remaining thirty-two, thirty appear in the photograph. At the end of the year, Mrs. Ojeda will transfer half a dozen of them out of BBAS to a fast track class in the regular school. That will enable the transfers to move on to an academically oriented junior high school. Based on current statistics, more than ten, perhaps as many as thirteen, of the children in Class 5, Room 238, will not complete high school. Projecting forward from the same statistics, Mrs. Ojeda's estimate of doctors and lawyers is wildly optimistic; it is highly unlikely that any of the children will complete a postgraduate degree. According to the laws of probability in the barrio, twelve years after the class picture was taken, more of the children will have died or been killed than graduated from a four-year college.

14

THE WALL

She began in the traditional way, speaking in graceful, Mexican-accented Spanish, with a *testimonio*. Her parents were poor, she said, people from Mexico. Her mother worked as a cleaning woman at Disney Studios, her father was a silversmith. At Immaculate Heart High School in Los Angeles she learned about social justice from the nuns. At Yale University she saw very few people of color, almost no Latinos. She was angry and sad all the time she was there. Her older brother had left Yale after a year, unable to live with the loneliness and strangeness of the situation. "I want more Latinos to go to Yale," she said, "your children."

Standing there at the front of the room, pretty, young, dark-eyed, and delicate, but not demure, not noticeably, debilitatingly demure, María Elena Fernández was an American ideal, the hope of all of the people in the room, more than they might ever have been, what their children might become. She studied her audience: women holding nursing babies in their laps; *abuelas* as dark as wood, wearing their hair in thick braids; middle-aged mothers not yet thirty years old, who looked over into the noisy next room, where their children played with strangers; couples who sat closely together in their old country clothes, men with straw hats, the tassels dangling, and women in wide-necked blouses.

She paused to inventory the progress of her testimony, to ask who had heard of Yale. "Raise your hand, please, if you have heard of Yale University."

Not one hand went up.

"Harvard?"

One hand.

"Stanford University."

No hands were raised, even though the name of the place in which they met was the Stanford School.

For a moment, she did not speak, trying to gather her thoughts. It was not going quite the way she had planned. They did not understand the promise. It was a problem to convince these people of the need to send their children to college, for many of them were barely able to imagine high school. She could comfort herself, however, with the success of the meeting. Thirty had been expected, forty at most, but eighty-one people were gathered there before her. Although no one knew what had drawn them to the school on Illinois Street early on a summer evening, the mere fact of their appearance was a success.

It had come about slowly. The women had been reluctant to work on the meeting. The rules of machismo, imported from the old country, kept almost all of the men from taking part. At first, when the women had been asked to write on big sheets of paper to make posters for the meeting, they had said they couldn't write well enough. Then the organizers asked them to hang up the posters around the neighborhood, and the women said they would rather do the writing. No one had come easily to the meeting or even to the idea of the meeting. It was a gathering of the dissatisfied, and no one in the town of Southgate, which is a flat, hard area of factories and bungalows south of the city of Los Angeles, wanted to appear dissatisfied. Most of them had come to the United States from Mexico, and they were not dissatisfied: They were grateful. They were also vulnerable; that is, they felt vulnerable, which is not the same as being afraid, but similar, and in some ways worse, for those who feel vulnerable cannot change their fate either through courage or cowardice; they can do nothing but keep their heads down and endure —*aguantar*.

María Elena paused to gather her arguments again. If they did not know the names of universities, she would set different goals, another set of dreams. "What do you hope for your children? What is it you would like them to be? What are the best jobs?"

The dreams came slowly: senator, lawyer, engineer. She wrote out the dreams with a marker on a large pad of white paper mounted on an easel. After every occupation, she coaxed out another: judge, doctor, executive, diplomat, community leader.

It was the end of the first act.

She explained then that she was from the Mexican American Legal Defense and Education Fund, saying the proper name in English and then repeating it in Spanish. The people in the audience seemed put off by the name in Spanish; there was a murmur—*defensa legal!* What had they done wrong? The speaker responded with an explanation.

Then, pointing to the dream careers listed on the paper, she asked, "How can you make a difference in your children's future?"

There was no response.

"Your children's future depends on their success in school."

She drew a pie chart of the Los Angeles Unified School District, showing that of the 600,000 students enrolled, 60 percent were Latino. Then she picked up a piece of paper and tore it into smaller and smaller pieces, showing them first the whole of the Latino contingent, then the part who finished grade school, the smaller part who completed high school, the very small part who went on to college, and the shred, pinched between two fingers, who completed four years of college.

"In the Stanford School," she told them, "only 20 percent of the students are reading at grade level." Finally, she unveiled her plan: a source for parents in which they could learn to help their children get good grades, meet other parents, learn to communicate with their children's teachers, and come to understand their rights as parents. To do this, however, was not easy. They would have to attend a class for parents once a week for twelve weeks.

It would be necessary for them to sign a contract, an agreement between the parents and the program, a commitment to the future of their children. Both parents should sign, she said, even though only one may actually attend the classes.

She told them the date of the first class. With that, the meeting was over.

The children flooded into the room—they made a crowd, the little chaos of children—then the doors to the schoolyard were opened and the room emptied out into the evening. The first antagonists approached her. They were the ones who had sat in the last row listening to the whispered translation into English provided by a graduate student from Harvard. They could not understand Spanish, they told her. They were third generation Americans of Mexican descent; the program was not for them; they did not feel comfortable there—they spoke English.

She tried to convince them to stay in the program, but they had not come to argue; this was their declaration against her. The weariness that comes so soon to radicals, painting them with signs of sleeplessness, transformed the face of the girl María Elena; the woman appeared, the history was written on her face, in the faint, fine hair that lay along her cheek. After all the success, she was reminded that the distance between her and these third generation people was even greater than that between Yale and the *abuelas* with their gray braids and dark faces solemn with hope.

Some were lost that evening. There would be more. The next problem would be to overcome the awe the parents felt in the presence of teachers, and there would always be the problem of the men: If the women went to a class between six-thirty and eight-thirty, who would do the women's work? A man who lives in the hills without a house cooks his own food. A man who has a house, furniture, flowers in the front yard, a car in the driveway, does not cook his own food, unless he is a widower with no grown daughters. The director of the parent leadership program was caught in the contradictions of a culture in yet another transition. She had to overcome forms of love and anger, rules of men and women, stratifications of society dating back to the Aztec hegemony—the set of feelings and ideas first confounded by the arrival of the men with spurs,[1] now made grotesque in an advanced industrial society.

This was a pilot program. The goal was to change the relationship between the family, the child, and the school. Something terrible was happening to Latino children, akin to a disease that would haunt them and all the generations that followed. The school dropout rate, publicized as 35 percent, but really closer to 50 or even 70 percent, was destroying her people. María Elena believed that the problem began in the first years of school, on the first day or the day before that. She had discovered the secret, she thought—the answer.

"I am chicana y Católica and I have been to Yale," she said, and took it therefore as her duty to change the world of children.

—

Of all the woes that can befall a family, none gives more pain than the suffering of its children. Yet for generations, centuries, Latinos in North America accepted the idea that their children would fare no better than they, perhaps worse. The parents and then the children suffered and endured. The philosophy of *aguantar* pervaded the Southwest, and the hopelessness of colonialism came to the barrios of the Northeast in the shopping bags and suitcases of the migrants from the Caribbean. On the other hand, Latinos who had come to the United States from middle- and upper middle-class lives in Mexico or Puerto Rico or South America or Spain continued in the old pattern, educating their children in the best schools and universities, maintaining the distinctions of class. Culturally, there was less and less to separate them from rich Anglos; they were also of the world. Their children also went to Harvard, Cambridge, the Sorbonne, or the École Militaire.

No matter what else influences the educational lives of Latino children, class is almost always the determining factor. The success of the children of

---

[1]Mexicans call Spaniards *Gachupines,* from the Náhuatl word meaning "men who wear spurs."

the first wave of Cuban exiles proved that an economic and intellectual class reproduces itself, as if it were carried on a chromosome. Although exiles hold on to their language more than any other group of immigrants and the Cuban exiles make a fetish of maintaining their language, ostensibly for use upon their return, they have obviously not been hindered by their commitment to bilingualism or biculturalism, the very characteristics that many people claim are the cause of the dreadful educational record of Latino children.

The effect of class shows up again at graduation. College entrance rates for blacks and Latinos fell all through the Reagan presidency. By 1988, only 35 percent of low-income Latino high school graduates went on to college, while the number for students from middle-income families was 46 percent. The official high school dropout rate for Latinos was much higher than that for blacks, yet the college entrance rate for Latinos was also higher.[2] The statistics point to the nature of the problem and to the place where the deviation from the path to an ordinary middle-class life appears to take place.

For a poor or working-class or even lower middle-class Latino to be able to finish high school and go on to use all of his or her intellectual potential requires that the child overcome six barriers: money, history, psychology, prophecy, language, and the wall.

Before looking into those categories, it may be useful to know that to drop out of school is not necessarily an evil act or even entirely an act of will. Some dropouts—and I do not pretend to know how many or what part of the whole great cohort of lost children are of this kind—are victims. If the word *victim* has been made unpalatable by Shelby Steele and other apologists for the ruins caused by racism, then it would be fair, at the least, to say that many of the children are innocent. And if innocence is denied them, for their failure is so often a result of sexual activity, then surely they have committed crimes in which there are no victims but themselves—unless the children who are born out of these early liaisons are victims, which brings the argument back to its beginning, before the advent of Steele's apology.

MONEY

At a high school in Houston a boy dropped out because his mother told him she needed money for pretty clothes, perfume, and paint for her cheeks and fingernails. To get the money for her he took a job at the minimum wage. It did not occur to him then that because he dropped out of school he would probably never in all his life earn more than the minimum. His

[2]American Council on Education, reported in the *New York Times,* January 14, 1989.

mother wanted something; the rules of *familia* dictated that he provide it for her.

The reasoning of the boy in Houston is an extreme example, but the demands of *familia* live at the extremes. Greedy parents, hungry siblings, broken homes, mortgages, one economic crisis or another challenges every poor or working-class Latino child. Many survive, perhaps half of those who face the challenge, but the effort exhausts them, all but the extraordinary ones. To have a paper route during grade school, work after school and on weekends during every day of high school, and then try to maintain the momentum for another four years exceeds the reserves of spirit and energy granted to most human beings.

If a Latino faces a choice between family and education, family must come first. To choose otherwise would be unmanly, ungrateful, inhuman, sinful. Even when money problems can be partially overcome by scholarships, the emotional demands of *familia* may draw a child out of school. A young Puerto Rican from New York stayed in school long enough and did well enough to win admission to Harvard College, but when he got there he had to deal with family problems: a sister who was going out with a bad crowd, a mother who needed money. His grades deteriorated, he changed from pre-med to a less rigorous course schedule. He ran up huge telephone bills. Almost every weekend he went home to New York. Eventually, he dropped out.

In the traditional Latino family, the rules follow rural traditions; that is, children are considered an asset, adding to the family's ability to plant and harvest crops or to bring in money. Each person understands himself and his role in terms of the family—the responsibility of the individual is to contribute to the group. Adjustment to urban ways, in which the individual exists for himself and the family is responsible for the individual, the parent for the child, is very difficult. The notion of a mother scrubbing floors to send a child to college makes sense in the urban, individualistic world. In the rural, familial world, it makes sense for the child to scrub floors to help the mother.

—

No one in America, particularly no young person, can live a poor but dignified life, for the wizards of marketing have taught children that what they have determines their value as human beings. In its malignant form, materialism leads to one boy murdering another for a pair of sneakers or a gang jacket. In its quotidian form, the ineluctable desire for material goods leads hundreds of thousands of children to drop out of school.

Fifty years ago, people could allow themselves to become the salesman's victims and still survive. A boy and sometimes a girl who left school at sixteen to become an apprentice to a carpenter or an adjunct of a machine on an assembly line could earn a fair living, especially in a union shop. Two generations ago, entrepreneurs still bragged of having only a grade school education. Current victims of the salesman's seductions enter a classic double bind the moment they succumb. To get the things they come to believe are necessary to be whole—clothing, compact discs, a car—children take minimum wage jobs. Their immediate reward is less than four dollars an hour, take-home pay of a little more than a hundred dollars for a full forty-hour week, enough to buy some of the things dear to high-school students. Very soon, however, they find that a hundred dollars a week won't support a car payment or an apartment, and it will hardly make a dent in the expenses of a family.

Only then do the dropouts realize that they have made a bad bargain: To get $4.25 an hour now, they have entered into a contract to earn $4.25 an hour forever. Less, really, for the minimum wage consistently lags behind the rate of inflation. It is a conundrum: To get more, they must accept less. Economically deceived, destined to be poor forever, dropouts live between regret and despair, with nothing to comfort them but anger and dreaming. The women revert to old agrarian values, raising children for riches; the men have no land, no hope, no self-respect; they settle often into deadly routine punctuated by rage. Alcohol helps—if not alcohol, religion and recollection. Most dropouts who do not have the obligation of children find a way to blur the two kinds of materialism; they buy things for themselves and contribute to the family: "With my first payday I got these L.A. Gear and a gold chain for my mother. *Ahorita* I'm saving up for a car." The pull of *familia* is not merely a rationalization; dreams and responsibilities, both burdens of the economic life of poor and working-class Latino children, militate against staying in school.

HISTORY

Mario García described the policies of the educational system in El Paso, where the dropout rate was close to 100 percent in 1930. Jimmy Vásquez told how few of his classmates graduated from high school in San Antonio, where the dropout rate was nearly 90 percent before World War II. In New York City, the official dropout rate for Puerto Rican children was 57 percent as late as 1971, which means the true rate[3]—that is, the entering first grade

[3]Dropout rates are almost universally below the true figure. In many places the formula counts only those who dropout of grades 9 through 12, even though a significant number of Latino children drop out in junior high school or before.

For example, the following table was produced by the New York City Public Schools. It

class compared to the graduating class twelve years later—was probably 70 percent or more.

Second, third, fourth, and fifth generation Latino children bear this historic burden in two ways: The children and grandchildren of dropouts tend to have less intellectual stimulation at home and no role models upon which to base their attitude toward education. The great respect Mexicans and Mexican-Americans show toward teachers does not manifest itself in success in school, only in deference to teachers. At the same time, the history of failure leads teachers and administrators to expect that Latino children will fail. Almost every successful Latino, in business, the professions, and education, can recall being told by a school counselor or teacher to choose a vocational course. Women had the added problems associated with their gender, making it all but impossible until very recently for even the brightest Latinas, including those from middle-class families, to get through high school and go on to college.

The burden of history has been lightened somewhat by civil rights

---

describes the progress of Limited English Proficiency (LEP) students, but it is useful here to demonstrate the criteria for determining the dropout rate.

Spring 1986 Status of LEP Students in Grades Eight through Twelve Who Were New Entrants to an English-Language School System in Spring 1982

Status	Number	Percent
Still enrolled	1,145	24.6
Graduated	1,386	29.8
Moved out of N.Y.C.	467	10.0
Transferred	330	7.1
Dropped Out	1,111	23.9
Missing Data	215	4.6
TOTAL	4,654	100.0

It might be argued that the dropout rate of 23.9 percent for this cohort is excellent. However, 21.6 percent are either missing, have transferred, or have moved. Eliminating the unknowns raises the rate to 30.5 percent. Applying the dropout rate to those still enrolled reduces that number to 796, raising the dropout rate to 44.3 percent, which is the lowest realistic number for the cohort. The only known fact, the number who actually graduated at the end of twelve years, is 29.8 percent. (The still-enrolled category includes any student attending one or more courses in any institution.) In other words, the success rate for this cohort of Latino students in New York City is the same as the rate for Jefferson High School in Houston, 30 percent. By choosing to speak of a dropout rate instead of a success rate, educators have been able to apply all the cosmetic qualities of statistics to a national tragedy.

groups, which have demanded that Latino children not be funneled into programs that lead to less desirable careers, but schools still view every Latino child as a potential, even a probable, failure. Early on, the children are identified as possible dropouts and put into dropout retention programs, which some educators now argue are self-fulfilling prophecies, almost guaranteeing that the children will think of themselves as failures.

Children in the United States whose parents did not complete high school no longer qualify as ordinary. This difficulty of being different comes to kindergarten with the children and remains, like a birthmark or some other conspicuous failure of the genes, engendering doubt at every test of wit or will.

History weighs most heavily on the children who have come to the United States from another country where parents had little or no education, for their parents may not understand the concept of school beyond the requirement for rudimentary literacy, if that. Some of these children who come from the south of Mexico or the small towns of the mountains and isolated seacoast cities of Central America bring a history not only of illiteracy but of a lack of nouns suitable to the modern urban world.

Roxanne Segura was such a child. History weighed so heavily on her at the age of twelve that school officials at the Intake Center for the San Francisco School District thought it unlikely that she would become fully literate in Spanish or English before she dropped out of school. Roxanne came from Chiquimulilla, a small fishing town on the east coast of Guatemala. Until 1980, people in the village lived a decent, although very simple life. Chiquimulilla had a few stores, an occasional approximation of a school, and no electricity for its population of four hundred. The only regular connection with the outside world other than trade and a few portable radios was the weekly arrival of the man with the movie projector and the generator. He pinned a white sheet to the wall of a house and showed a film. The price of a ticket was very low and the attendance was very good, even when it was the third or fourth showing of the same film.

Chiquimulilla had been a good place for fishing, because it was at the mouth of a river that led to a spawning place. Every year, the fish swam upriver and spawned in the lake. Then some outsiders came and took the fish in the sea on their way to the mouth of the river and it was the end of the prosperity of Chiquimulilla. Roxanne Segura's grandmother told her oldest daughter that she would have to go north and earn money to feed her children. There were six; the oldest was eight.

Mrs. Segura said goodbye to her children and made her way north. It was a difficult time for her and for the children. The parting was painful, although they did not think it would be for long. Instead, Mrs. Segura had to work in the United States for seven years to get enough money to bring two of her children north to San Francisco. Most of the time, she took care of other women's children, while she pined for her own.

For seven years Mrs. Segura had shared an apartment with other women while she sent money home. When the children arrived, she moved to a larger apartment with another family. After Mrs. Segura paid her half of the rent and utilities and sent money home for her remaining children and her mother, there was not enough for her and the two children to buy food and clothing. She didn't know what she would do, she said, but she was happy to have at least two of her children with her.

Roxanne, who was fifteen years old and could not read Spanish at the second grade level, would have to go to work as soon as possible. Her mother was not at all concerned. History, which determined the future of her children, did not exist for Mrs. Segura. She had learned to think in Chiquimulilla: There was now and nothing more; she had surrendered everything before and beyond the moment to fate.

PSYCHOLOGY

Racism and *racismo,* the twin foes of Latino children, put them in the position of a prize in the struggle between love and society. Every educator who works with Latino children speaks of the problem of "self-concept" or self-esteem. Children who do not think well of themselves will fail; it is as simple as that. Seen from a distance, with the humor and seductive vitality pared away, the efforts of Juana Dainis were all aimed at increasing the self-esteem of the children in her school. Her method was to wave a finger and say, "We're number one," but it was also to touch the children, to embrace them when they were hurt or failing. Nancy Archer described her school as a "hugging place," and Awilda Orta dispensed blessings on junior high school students in the form of kisses on the forehead.

Maria Ojeda, seated at a table with six or eight of her best students gathered around her, talking to them in a hushed voice, intimate, close, teaching geography as if it were a delicious secret to be stolen from the world and treasured forever, momentarily raises the state of being of her children to the paradise of the beloved. It is true, as Antonia Rodríguez and Nilda Ríos say, that when the children leave the school they get twenty slaps for every good moment they had in the classroom, but the teacher can help to make it a contest with society for the children's sense of themselves.

A second battle for the child's ego takes place at home, where the contestants are the parents, usually the mother, and the world. The father often plays only a small role in a Latino child's life. In many families the father has more than one job, sometimes as many as three, which leaves him little time to spend at home with the children; he becomes a stranger, a person who appears to be a tyrant whether he is or not. In the failing family, the father lacks the self-esteem to establish a loving relationship with his wife or children. A young Dominican professional man in New York described how this happened to his own father: "In the D.R., he was the boss of the family. We lived on a farm there. It was owned by my grandmother, but my father ran the farm. He hired workers to help bring in the crops, negotiated the prices at the market, everything. Then we came here. He couldn't get a job, but my mother got work cleaning houses. He couldn't stand it. All day, he had nothing to do, so he went to the bars. He became an alcoholic. My mother kept the family together."

In both kinds of immoderate situation the father gets cut out, which may be one of the causes of the new phenomenon of the breakdown of the Latino family. The burden of the battle for the sense of self of the child falls to the mother. Every day, the mother[4] must pit her vision of the child against that of society. If the mother does not succeed, the battle will be left entirely to the school, and if both the mother and the school fail, the child will drown.

The number of victories for mothers and schools, the success rate—that is, the number of children who graduate from high school at the end of twelve or thirteen years—indicates the power of the children's twin enemies. Racism and *racismo* attack the intellectual prowess of victims; if children accept the vision of themselves projected by the antagonistic world, what hope have they of succeeding in school? By taking away the intellectual weapons of the children, racism makes them vulnerable to its thesis. When a writer like Shelby Steele argues that it is not the racism of the majority that leads members of minority groups to think of themselves as victims, he misunderstands the very nature of racism, which is to weaken the victim in his innocence by convincing him that he is a victim not of racism but of fate or nature.

When people are poor or otherwise in a weakened state, the argument of the racist works best. As the Nazis learned in their destruction of the Jews of Europe, each act of racism facilitates the next. The theory holds for the Latino world. Puerto Ricans suffer most because they have endured conquest without respite since the end of the fifteenth century. Mejicanos and Mexican-Americans suffer according to where they came from (class, race, and geography) in Mexico and whether the victories, however hollow, of independence and revolution affected their ancestors. Cubans suffer less or more

---

[4]Or grandmother: In single parent homes or homes in which the father cannot support the family, the mother may work at one or more jobs, leaving the children to the grandmother to raise. Once the grandmother enters the picture, the situation becomes much more complex, for the grandmother may love the child and yet be so far from the child's cultural world and so antagonistic to the mores of current U.S. society that she injures the child's sense of self.

depending on their color and whether they came out as angry exiles or the people Castro rejected.

PROPHECY

The dropout rate predicts the dropout rate. A child who grows up in a housing project is—as the children in the Salazar Project in El Paso and the Aliso Pico area projects in Los Angeles said—stereotyped. A life in the Bronx predicts a death in the Bronx, including all the failures between the first breath and the last. Whoever grows up in the cotton fields and grapefruit orchards of South Texas in spring and the strawberry fields of Michigan in summer is expected to continue that pattern all the rest of his days, without ever learning to write a poem or program a computer or pay off a mortgage.

In a migrant worker's trailer rented for a season in South Florida, a little girl cooked chalupas for her injured father and her younger brothers. She spoke some English, enough to earn Bs in the bilingual classes at the nearby school for children of migrant workers. Although she was only eleven years old, she said she expected to leave school soon to work *en el labor,* which is the phrase the Mexican *Norteños* and most migrants use to mean "in the fields" *(milpas).* Her brother, who was eight years old, agreed. Like his sister, he had already begun picking tomatoes on the weekends. The eight-year-old boy did not think school was for people like him.

Part of the prediction of failure in school comes from the rural background of many Latinos. Although the overwhelming majority of Latinos live in cities in the United States, they carry with them the mores of the farm culture. Formal education was of little use to a person who worked in a cornfield or on a tomato farm, even if it was his own. Other talents were required. A man who could not read could still tell by looking at the ground cover whether the water in the area was sweet or alkaline and if it was alkaline whether it was good enough to grow any kind of crop at all. Similarly, no formal education is required to deliver a calf or breed chickens or cut hay. The prophecy of little or no education for the children of an agrarian culture is not a prophecy of doom or even extraordinary difficulty, unless the children happen to live in Boston or Chicago or Denver or San Diego.

A more dangerous prophecy grows out of the failure of past generations in the United States. Newcomers can often overcome the prophecy of their past by the revolutionary's optimism. Children of first generation parents have the greatest chance of defeating the odds. If they fail, however, a pattern will have been set, and the fate of the parents will almost inevitably be visited upon the children. The child of the newcomer knows that a change has occurred; he or she can be different from the last generation because the circumstances are different, the defeat of the prophecy of the past is logical.

The child of the failed family has no reason to think his situation will be different from that of his parents, for nothing has changed.

LANGUAGE

Children who do not speak English are no longer put into the lowest grade or declared mentally defective, but a child who speaks only Spanish and is not allowed to develop his conceptual abilities in his own language while he learns to speak another will fall behind his peers. After the first failure, the next comes easily; the pattern develops so quickly that a child in the third or second or even the first grade may be lost to despair.

—

Keith Baker, who argues against bilingual education for U.S. English and other interest groups, made the following case about language:

DROPOUT RATES[5]

	1968	1988
Whites	14.6	12.7
Blacks	27.4	14.9
Hispanics	34.3	35.8

[5]National Center for Education Statistics, research reported in the *Washington Post*, September 15, 1989.

"Note the big decline over the last twenty years in the Black dropout rate," he wrote, "while the Hispanic dropout rate did not change. What do we know is different between the education programs of Blacks and Hispanics? Bilingual education programs."

The massive increase in the number of newly arrived Latinos over that twenty year period, the change in the law won by MALDEF in Texas requiring that children be educated without regard to citizenship, the lower educational level of new arrivals compared to those who came earlier, and information about other demographic changes apparently was not available to Baker. If the demographic changes were quantified—for example, the description by the teachers in the Socorro, Texas, schools of the change in the kind of students arriving from Mexico—it might be shown that the dropout rate for Latinos also fell, compared to what it would have been without bilingual education programs.

He might also have noted that schools in Texas, which has a large Latino population, were segregated during the entire twenty-year period according

[5]National Center for Education Statisitics, research reported in the *Washington Post*, September 15, 1989

to the income of the school district, with the poorest districts those in which Latinos lived. The equalization decision in the Texas Supreme Court did not come until later. Latinos went to schools that didn't have enough money to establish dropout retention programs, hire counselors, and so on. The schools may have followed the letter of the law mandating bilingual education, but only to the extent their poverty permitted.

The Bilingual Education Act only guarantees equal education to children who do not speak English; it does not specify how that education will be made equal. Most bilingual education programs have no other goal than to move children as quickly as possible out of the bilingual program.

Finally, the hostility toward the Spanish language expressed in English-only laws and other ethnocentric activities pushes the children into an intellectual netherworld, where music and the clichés of slang supplant the painful clarity of precise expression. For many children the only way to validate themselves in their language is to deny the language of the dominant society and its place of worship—the school. Not only the children of the poor choose to enter the private antiworld of the uncommon language. The lure of a world apart attracts the children of lawyers, nurses, doctors, executives, and entrepreneurs. As dangerous as this intellectual netherworld may be, it is also safe from the gringos. The children slip over into it comfortably *hablando, platicando, conversando, charlando, chiflando, chinchorreando, murmurando, turuquiando,* but not talking.

THE WALL

When my sister, Mary Jean, was the speech therapist in a tiny school in Canutillo, Texas, a child was brought to her office because he did not speak. Apparently, his teacher reported, he could hear, for he never failed to obey commands, but when he was asked to speak, even to say his own name, he remained silent. A physician had examined the boy and pronounced him physically equipped for speech. Was he a neurological mute, the teacher wanted to know, or was he a behavior problem?

In the speech therapist's office the boy was polite and responsive to commands in both English and Spanish, but he did not speak. After several visits, Mary Jean decided to visit the boy's home to find out whether his mother could provide some information that would lead to understanding the boy's behavior.

Canutillo is an agricultural town north of El Paso near the New Mexico line. Many of the people who live there are migrant workers who pick the crops along the Rio Grande in season and travel north in summer to look for work. Some are citizens or residents; many are not.

The boy who would not speak came from a family of migrants who lived in a

one room structure something like a house. There was no electricity or running
water in the structure. The boy lived there with his mother and father and
grandmother, fifteen siblings, a flock of chickens, two pigs, and a goat. He was
not mute, but he had found as the youngest of the children that it was no use to
make sounds, for there was so much noise in the room that no one heard him.
Eventually, he became mute, docile on the surface of his life, but underneath
seething in silence.

—

On the first day of the first grade Latino children are presented with a
wall. It is made of culture, and it is very high and thick. To enter the society
of school they must get beyond the wall. If they do not overcome it at the
beginning, the wall will grow higher and thicker with each succeeding day. It
is not the making of a metaphor to say that there are no dropouts, only
children who did not enter the society of school. The wall is as solid as a
word, as enduring as the sting of a slap.

The error of using dropout statistics, however inaccurate, as a measure of
the effectiveness of education is that for Latinos it concentrates attention at
the wrong end of the process. In the struggle between love and the inhospitable world for the life of the child, the moral failures are not grand or
violent; they are the daily business of education and its accomplices in the
streets and houses of the barrios. The result of these failures is that the wall
looms larger every day, and the child beholds it in the silence of awe.

Some children become "the dead," as teachers in the Southwest call them;
in the Northeast, the children create a silence of white noise. The wall they
encounter in school is like the wall encountered on the first day of his life by
the speechless boy of Canutillo. When he found that he could not communicate, he arranged his life around silence, preparing to drop out even when he
was still an infant. The love of his overworked mother or his weary father
would have mitigated the work of the world of the household on their child,
but they chose instead to accept his silence.

The school attempted to breach the wall for him, to pull him through into
society, but by then the wall had been growing and solidifying for nearly
seven years; the work should have begun at the beginning.

—

The struggle to solve the educational problems of Latinos has barely
begun. As more and more Latinos become immigrants and move into the
middle class, the number of children who succeed will increase. At the same
time, more newcomers—with less education in Spanish, with fewer skills to
transfer into English—will transport the woes of the old country to the
United States. The real tragedy, however, is that failure produces failure, and

the multiplier effect of dropouts marrying dropouts and producing children who will drop out promises a twenty-first-century Latino underclass of enormous size; by midcentury there could be twenty-five or thirty million Latinos in the United States without the skills necessary to earn a decent living.

As Cervantes said, the world is divided into two families, the Haves and the Have-nots. Nowhere is that clearer than among Latinos. Even now, the class structure and educational system have produced two distinct classes nationally, like those that have existed for many years in San Antonio. Only the schools can keep the classes from rigid separation: On the one hand a prosperous, literate, largely assimilated group of immigrants and former exiles in control of their own destiny and on the other an underclass of Spanglish-speaking transporters, stranded sojourners, and ghosts more fatalistic than their rural ancestors.

In light of the realities of education for Latinos, many of the arguments over bilingual education appear ridiculous. Children learn in effective schools. When these schools are bilingual and bicultural, the children learn more: another language and another culture. And the more ordinary bilingual education becomes, the better it will succeed.

As a means to move children more comfortably from one language to another, bilingual education is kind and helpful, but ultimately inefficient. The loss of the dominant language of the hemisphere is an intellectual and economic waste. If there is any injustice in bilingual education in the United States, it is that children who speak the majority or dominant language are not often exposed to education in two languages. A solid, hard-headed Yankee approach to the problem would call for the maintenance of language skills in children who already have them and the addition of new skills to those who will be able to use them later.

15
LATINOS FOR SALE

I.

An art director with a literal mind designed the cover of the sales brochure for the *Advertising Age* Marketing to Hispanics symposium: it was the color of money. Inside it said, "Keynote Address—Henry Cisneros, chairman, Cisneros Asset Management, nationally known Hispanic personality, focuses on growing economic and political power of the U.S. Hispanic market, expressed in human terms." In the accompanying photograph the former mayor of San Antonio looked unhappy, sad-eyed, near to weeping. Perhaps he had been thinking of the nature of markets, which do not have power but are a source of power for those who know how to exploit them. Perhaps he really had been thinking of the market "in human terms," how much it would cost Latinos to satisfy the hungers of the marketers who had come to the two-day symposium. There was no indication that he was thinking "in human terms" of the difference between those who consider themselves an economic subject and those who are merely an object for the exploitation of others, a market; the elegantly educated former mayor of San Antonio is not a radical.

The keynote address was the first of many presentations. A woman named Sara Sunshine of Publicidad Siboney was going to speak on Hispanic creativity. A man from the Immigration and Naturalization Service in Washington promised to deliver his thoughts about "The Outlook on Inflow" with its "impact on the content of the Hispanic Market." The most openly exploitive presentation was "Cause Related Marketing . . . The Human Approach to Hispanic Marketing: Jim Estrada, director, Hispanic Marketing, Anheuser-Busch, shares thoughts on contemporary techniques for corporate public relations and new efforts in the area of cause-related marketing."

In the 1960s marketing related to Latino causes meant boycotting grapes or lettuce to help Cesar Chávez and Dolores Huerta establish the United Farm Workers union. Obviously, Mr. Estrada did not have in mind a boycott of his employer's Budweiser Beer. He was teaching something much more complex: the perversion of political and social causes to the end of extracting more money from the very people the causes were intended to help.

The symposium gave evidence that a shift had taken place in the business establishment's view of Latinos, which, in turn, produced a change in the way Latinos viewed themselves. When Latinos were fewer and without much money to spend, major corporations were not interested in them. But with information provided by the 1980 U.S. Census in their briefcases, the sales staffs of the Latino media could argue to corporate marketing directors that there was money to be made: Latinos earned over $50 billion a year. And as if $50 billion were not enough, the salesmen dressed the statistics in the secrets of the community: the uncounted purchasing power of the people who had not responded to the census, the "illegals" and the "illiterates." There was an even richer uncounted group, they whispered: the households in which an Anglo male brought home the money and his Latina spouse spent it.

With a little help from inflation, the value of the market nearly tripled during the 1980s. Latinos could no longer be ignored. They were heading toward 10 percent of the population and more. Whoever locked in brand loyalty among the Latinos now would profit for decades to come: Surveys had shown that Latinos bought high quality, brand name products to a greater extent than any other identifiable group, and their loyalty to brands was phenomenal. They were an ideal target market: susceptible and growing in both size and spending power, but still living so close to the bone that they had to spend what they earned, all of it, everything.

Although more than a fourth of all Latinos were poor and many more had to stretch incomes near the poverty level to support large families, the marketers who went after their money did not appear to have the health and welfare of the people as their first priority. According to *Hispanic Business Magazine,* six of the top ten advertisers to the Latino market in 1990 sold beer, cigarettes, soft drinks, or fast food.

Despite the harm the "human approach" of these marketers did to their people—who suffered from poor nutrition and high death rates from cancer, coronary heart disease, and other illnesses associated with smoking, alcohol, and high fat diets—Latinos celebrated their emergence as a market. The Latino business community saw an opportunity to sell real estate and services to the Anglos who, in turn, sold fast food and alcohol to the Latinos. Through the magic of economics, as explained by the Chamber of Commerce, the process of taking more money out of the community was guaranteed to increase its wealth. Latino political and social scientists, with the exception of a few radicals who just couldn't understand the pleasure of being sought after, agreed. It was as if trade had suddenly been opened with an underdeveloped country. Latino advertising agencies proliferated; an industry was founded on the need for guides to the exotic mind of the Latino consumer. More radio and television stations, more magazines and newspapers spoke to the new market. When people like Rodolfo Acuña pointed out that businesses were entering new markets to exploit them, the pillars of the Latino community recalled the Marxist origins of his ideas.

Awareness of their existence as a market was a sign to many Latinos that they had entered the mainstream: To be a consumer was to be wanted; to be wanted was to be equal; to be equal was to be an American at last.

They had given blood and sweat to their country, and it had given them very little in return. If they had money to give, if they were a market, perhaps they could win the kind of respect accorded the other markets.

Part of that notion was an attempt to break the connection in the national consciousness between Latinos and poverty. Linda Chavez, writing in *Vista*[1] (a free-standing newspaper insert in English), said she ran a computer search and found more than 2,500 stories in a single year "linking Hispanics and poverty." It was a mistake, she argued, to concentrate on the 26 percent of Latinos who are poor rather than the 74 percent who are not. She reiterated her theory that there are only two groups of poor Hispanics: new immigrants and Puerto Ricans.

The problem with her theory is that statistics often do not paint a good picture of reality: A visit to east Los Angeles or the colonias of South Texas or the south side of San Antonio is a reminder of the "fallacy of induction." The official poverty line isn't about having a decent life, an equal life, a hopeful life; it is about hunger, cold, and unsanitary conditions. One percent above the official poverty line isn't good enough. And even if it were, her argument is abhorrent on moral grounds: The 26 percent who are poor, if indeed only 26 percent are poor, are those who need attention; the rich presumably can take care of themselves.

Chavez has a public relations point, however; concentrating on the poverty of many Latinos may harm the prosperity of the majority. As those Latinos who take pride in being an exploitable market know, America doesn't like poor people. In a salesman's society, those who can't afford to buy anything don't merit respect or even interest.

The media and their allies, the advertising agencies, claim that the best

[1]February 18, 1990.

thing they can do to help the Latino community is to deliver it to advertisers (preferably national advertisers, since most media charge these companies higher rates). By selling Latinos to corporate America, say the media, they not only counter the image of the poor victim, they earn money to continue publishing or broadcasting news, entertainment, and information for the community.

If the purpose of Latino media is to raise the estimation of the economic strength of Latinos in the eyes of advertisers, they have had some success: Half a billion dollars was spent on media aimed at Latinos in 1990.[2] But ethnic media may have other uses. At the end of the 1960s Rubén Salazar challenged the market-oriented view. In his mind the press was a political instrument, and it was to be used to bring about a better life for his people. He wrote his columns and made his broadcasts on KMEX-TV in Los Angeles with no other intent. Although he was not the first Latino to challenge the status quo in the media—José Martí and Ricardo Flores Magón and others had written in defense of their people—he was the first to do it in advertiser-supported media.

The moral dilemma of serving two masters did not enter into Salazar's considerations. Like Martí and Flores Magón, he believed the responsibility of the press was to justice and fairness. And he believed there was a special obligation on the part of any medium directed toward Latinos, for so many of them lived like mutes, poor and unable to speak English, segregated, suffering in silence. With no way to express their anger, they had no way to incite their children to hope. For one coruscating moment Rubén Salazar gave political and social purpose to Latino media. Then he was killed, and the darkness of confusion returned. Questions of intent were put aside; the transformation from a people to a market had begun.

2.

There is, in fact, no Latino market. Latinos are so diverse in custom, income, and language that the term comprises several distinct markets and audiences. Moreover, the divisions between the component groups are not

---

[2]Estimates of total advertising expenditures are not reliable, because most advertisers do not divulge their budgets. Advertising research groups attempt to gather the figures by monitoring the media, but since most prices are negotiated (and the smaller the advertising medium the more negotiable its prices) monitoring is not accurate either. Sources in the business say the margin of error for estimates of small components such as a single company's expenditures in ethnic media is at least 50 percent. For example: Castor GS&B, the largest Latino advertising agency, estimates 1990 total expenditures in the market at $500 million; *Hispanic Business Magazine* estimates it at $628 million.

the same for the media and the advertisers. An advertiser trying to sell black beans to Puerto Ricans or chiles serranos to Cubans has a problem, because of the mismatch of products and audiences. But the bigger problem belongs to the media, for they must deal with the division between English and Spanish. Many first generation Latinos do not understand English, while a huge and growing number of the children and grandchildren of immigrants cannot understand enough Spanish to watch Spanish television or read a Spanish newspaper.

The Spanish-language media depend upon an explicit cultural difference between their audience and the rest of the people; their audience has no access to the general media. The existence of English media addressed exclusively to Latinos implies something very different; they must build their aspirations on race, or they will disappear into the melting pot along with German-American, Scottish-American, Italian-American, and other ethnic publications.

Arturo Villar, the charming, sophisticated, and forthright Cuban who was publisher of *Vista*, said that the readers of his publication were the most affluent Latinos, the richest market, and that there were millions of them. Furthermore, he expected continued acculturation for Latinos, which he believed made the growth of *Vista* inevitable.

Villar was undoubtedly right about acculturation and the prospective audience for such a magazine. His problem was that in many cities *Vista* was inserted in newspapers according to zip code. Only those zip codes with large Latino populations got the magazine. Unfortunately, those are the zip codes in which many newcomers live, and newcomers often don't speak English. On the other hand, many of the English-speaking Latinos have moved out to predominantly Anglo suburbs, which don't get the insert. As more newspapers inserted the magazine in their full run, *Vista* covered more of its richer prospects, found a few Anglo readers, and wasted a lot of its circulation. Despite these distribution problems, it had become by far the most important national publication ever addressed to Latinos.

The editorial policy of *Vista* during Villar's tenure was to deliver the good news. Villar argued that it served as a counter to the stereotype of "welfare, gangsters, maids, and prostitutes." Like Linda Chavez, he believes the situation of Puerto Ricans in New York, because it is the media capital, has affected the "image of Hispanics more than anything else."

Although neither Villar nor the former editor of *Vista*, Harry Caicedo,[3] saw the creation of a pan-Latino movement as the purpose of the magazine,

---

[3]Arturo Villar, who was born in Spain and raised in Cuba, identifies himself as a Cuban exile. The editorial offices of the magazine are located in Miami. Harry Caicedo is a Colombian from New York City.

they argued that a Cuban and a Mexican in California have more in common than a Mexican in California and a Mexican in Tamaulipas. Caicedo did a remarkable job of balancing ethnic groups in the magazine; he served his market (or markets) by favoring Mexican-Americans (because there are so many of them) and reporting regularly on the accomplishments of Cubans (because so many of them are doing well), while not neglecting the rest of the Latino world.

Vista looked a little like *Parade,* its general-audience model, and it speaks to a similar audience, although the writing in *Vista* was even more elementary and the stories were more optimistic. The flaw in Villar and Caicedo's editorial policy was its unwillingness to confront many of the problems that beset the Latino community. No magazine could have been more encouraging about higher education, yet *Vista* all but ignored the other side of the educational issue: the dropout problem, declining Latino matriculation in college, the falling number of Latinos who complete four years of college, and the appalling paucity of Latino faculty members in law, education, and other disciplines at the university level. The magazine covered every Latino celebrity, but devoted very little space to health, including the spread of La SIDA (AIDS) among Latinos.

The editorial question Villar and Caicedo faced at *Vista* plagues every Latino or black journalistic venture: Are they writing about the rich or the poor? People who are doing better or suffering more? The answer, of course, is both. The dilemma is that writing about the problems may cause a magazine to lose readers and advertisers, making it impossible to write about anything, including problems.

In 1990, Villar and Caicedo sold part of the magazine to raise capital. Although *Vista* appeared in more and more newspapers, the cost of printing and distributing it demanded more advertising, and the ads weren't coming in. Time-Warner bought part of the magazine, as did the publisher of *Hispanic.* A year later, with advertising revenues down during the recession and the war in the Middle East, the board of directors called Villar and Caicedo to task. They could get pages from Pepsi and Coors and the cigarette companies, the goons of the advertising business, if Villar and Caicedo were willing to play ball by running stories about the companies, their Latino advertising directors, and their causes. The August 1990 issue of *Hispanic* showed the way. It carried a full page editorial in defense of the cigarette industry. On page 25 it published an Apple Computer ad about the company's "commitment to diversity," and on page 40 it carried a story entitled, "Encouraging Diversity," about Santiago Rodriguez, the multicultural program manager at Apple Computer. When Villar insisted to his new bosses from Time-Warner and *Hispanic* that the editorial content of a magazine should serve its readers, not its advertisers, the board of directors threw him out and Caicedo with him.

—

Two magazines aimed at Latinos with money, *Hispanic* and *Hispanic Business,* are also written in English. *Hispanic* appears to have no mission other than selling advertising. *Hispanic Business* is a slick monthly magazine published in English that attempts to do for Latinos what *Business Week, Forbes, Fortune,* and *Advertising Age* do for Anglos. Its editorial policy mixes service articles, boosterism, and lists of the top hundred or fifty or twenty-five in every conceivable category: profits, gross revenues, growth, salary, corporate titles, and so on. As a booster, it substitutes people for place. Rather than St. Louis or the state of Oklahoma, *Hispanic Business* touts the Latino territory. As a service magazine it provides solid information on the names of purchasing agents, uses of labor-saving devices, investments, tax policy, and other business practices.

At its best, *Hispanic Business* serves as an emotional and intellectual support system. It sells the idea of a separate elite, a mirror of Anglo success, sometimes with the tragicomic results that come when minorities dress up in the clothes of the establishment. The list of the largest "Hispanic-owned businesses" contains too many automobile dealerships and laundries and bakeries.[4] The list of highly placed corporate executives falls precipitously from the chairman of the board of Coca-Cola to vice-presidents of small corporations. The cover line of a story in the April 1990 issue read "CEOs CHARGING INTO THE 90s," but then reported that over 36 percent of the five hundred largest Latino-owned corporations were still essentially "Mom and Pop" operations in which both the husband and wife worked.

However foolish the aggrandizement of small accomplishments sometimes seems in *Hispanic Business,* the magazine does offer confidence to the timid and praise to the successful. Once the articles are adjusted for scale, they are no more ridiculous than the profiles of businessmen and women in *Forbes* or *Fortune* and no more parochial than the magnifications of arcane industries in the *Wall Street Journal.* Like every business magazine, *Hispanic Business* is a fancy trade journal, the main difference being that it inflates Latinos instead of tire or toiletries manufacturers.

If Arturo Villar's theory is correct, national magazines in Spanish would seem to face the problem of a decreasing audience of people with money to spend for magazines or the products advertised in them. Univision, a subsid-

---

[4]In 1990, only thirty of the one hundred "fastest growing companies" had one hundred or more employees and only nine had gross sales of more than $25 million.

iary of the Hallmark Company, solved part of the problem by sending its new bimonthly, *Más*, free to over half a million subscribers. Like any controlled circulation magazine, *Más* owes it allegiance to its advertisers.

—

There are no daily newspapers, radio stations, or television networks in English directed to Latinos. The Spanish newspapers, some of which have been published for many years, generally hold to the standards of good tabloid journalism, but a few are much more ambitious. *La Opinión*, founded in 1926 and owned by the Lozano family until it sold a major interest to the Los Angeles *Times* in 1990, sells a hundred thousand copies a day to a critical and attentive audience. Many second- and third-generation Latinos in the United States learned sophisticated Spanish by sitting with their parents and reading *La Opinión*.

Historically, coverage of Latin America and other foreign news was often better in *La Opinión* than in its English-language competitors. It carried the only coverage of the Latino community in Los Angeles for most of its three-quarters of a century, since the *Examiner* and the *Times* generally disregarded Latinos except to report on murders, riots, and so on.

Politically, the newspaper was never radical, always slightly liberal, always in favor of gentle behavior, good manners, good Spanish, niceness. *La Opinión* mixed the notions of *aguantar* and *respeto*, satisfying both by maintaining its standards of good taste and objectivity everywhere but in its designated editorials. It was born gray, and it was conveyed gray into the hands of the *Times*. Few newspapers in the last part of the twentieth century looked more serious than *La Opinión;* none expressed so perfectly the Mexican saying about the ideal character of a man: *feo, fuerte y formal.*[5]

La Opinión succeeded by ignoring television, serving its readers not only with news, but with the sense of dignity of men who read a serious newspaper, a miraculously democratic sense, equally applicable to shoeshine boys and moguls, to anyone who enjoyed the gift of literacy. It separated those who could read from those who could not, it was the champion of literacy and culture, the light opera of literature. Whether its new owners and its new readers from southern Mexico, Guatemala, and points south will change the gray gentleman of Latino journalism is unknown, but it is not unlikely.

Miami has two Spanish dailies: *Diario Las Americas* and *El Nuevo Herald*, which is published by the Miami *Herald*, the surviving English language newspaper.[6] *Diario*, which is owned by Nicaraguan exiles, is more rightist

---

[5]Fierce in appearance, strong, and dignified.
[6]The Miami *News* died slowly in the late 1980s. Many people blamed its demise on the

than *El Nuevo Herald,* which has a conservative editorial policy. The Cuban American National Foundation generally approves of *Diario* and vice versa, but the fanatical anti-Castro groups in Miami often see the mildly conservative views of *El Nuevo Herald* as heretical, verging on unpatriotic.

Editorial matters are taken very seriously in Miami, but not so seriously as the society pages of *Diario:* Only the imminence of the fall of Castro excites more speculation. *Diario* was founded in 1953 but didn't come into its own until the exile and the fantastic adjustment of the Cuban middle class to life in the United States. The writers at *Diario,* although utterly, absolutely, unalterably opposed to the Castro regime and supportive of conservative politics in the United States, are far more sophisticated than the enforcers of the Cuban American National Foundation under Jorge Más Canosa.

Ariel Remos, who writes on economics and international politics in *Diario* prefers talking about Aristotle to discussing the squabbles of Miami politics. Remos, who was an attorney in Cuba and a philosophy student before he turned to the law, has no illusions about Cuba under Batista. "We were democratic," he said, "and not racist. When we went to the baseball, our *chofer* sat with us." He laughed. "The first two blacks who came from Cuba were two brothers who worked in my house. And now every year they send gifts to my mother." He sips at his tiny plastic cup of coffee. "We had a *white* middle class in Cuba."

Remos answers the telephone, speaks brusquely, then returns to his thoughts. His hair has turned the color of ashes and his sportcoat is made of polyester. "The economic aspect is more important than politics. The real import is always economical. Economics determines everything in Cuba now. Yes, of course, man is a political animal, but in Cuba the question is economics. That's why we must isolate the island economically, to force him out."

If his views of the world seem to originate in a Marxist understanding of political economy, it does not disturb him. He also has a capitalist's appreciation of the U.S. economy: "People who want to work here can work. People who want to accept welfare are destroyed." It is as simple as that in the complex mind of the man who covers international politics for the most powerful rightist newspaper in Miami, perhaps in the United States.

El Nuevo Herald attempts a more sociological view of the world, perhaps as a way of avoiding the constant controversy of exile politics.[7] It shows a

---

liberal editorial policy of the paper, arguing that pressures from the Cuban and Nicaraguan exile communities cost it advertisers and readers.

[7] *El Nuevo Herald* claimed daily circulation of 102,000 and Sunday circulation of 119,000 at the beginning of 1991.

more conservative side in the Spanish paper than in its English fraternal twin. And it is very careful not to upset the right-wing exile community in either publication. The political lesson of the demise of the Miami *News* may be apocryphal, but no one in the media in Miami dares to forget it.

Along the border, newspapers printed on the Mexican side, from Matamoros to Tijuana, serve the Latino community, often with outrageously exaggerated tales. Newspapers on the U.S. side carry more news from Mexico now, because of the *maquiladoras* (enterprise zones) and the inescapable export of pollution, crime, hunger, and disease across the river and the desert.[8] News of the Latino community does not get reported adequately on either side in Spanish, which may be one of the causes of its political ineffectiveness.

In New York City *El Diario/La Prensa* sells about sixty thousand copies a day. The masthead claims that it is the "oldest Spanish language newspaper in the U.S.A." founded in 1913. Although it is a tabloid, *Diario/La Prensa* publishes no lurid photographs or bizarre stories. The strengths of the paper are its antiestablishment view of local politics and its heavy coverage of *"nuestros paises,"* four pages or more devoted to major news stories from Latin America and Spain.

The problem with publishing a Spanish-language daily in a city no longer dominated by a single group of Latinos is that every group wants to control the editorial policy of the paper. *Diario/La Prensa* has an Anglo owner and president and strives for balance in its editorial management among Cubans, who have a disproportionate amount of power; Puerto Ricans, who demand more representation and more power; and Dominicans, Mexicans, and Central and South Americans, all of whom want control and, short of control, influence and, short of influence, a job. Every group reads the paper and every group complains about the control of the Cubans, including the Cubans, who say they are barred from good positions on the paper because it doesn't want to hire any more of them.

Neither national nor major local advertisers, such as department stores, understand the importance of Spanish-language newspapers, which derive their style and content from continental Europe and their social import from the cultural gulf between the whites and the preliterate natives of Africa and the Americas. As a result, Latino newspapers, with the exception of the

---

[8]At the end of the 1950s, when I worked as a journalist in El Paso, I covered the Ciudad Juárez beat for the *Herald-Post* and Ramón Villalobos covered it for the *Times*. We were limited mainly to stories about U.S. citizens and tourist attractions. Villalobos and I both wrote about the bullfights and occasionally cleaned up a publicity handout about an entertainer who was appearing in a nightclub, but local Mexican economics and politics, with the exception of a short piece on the election of a new mayor, didn't make the papers. We couldn't even get a murder into the paper, unless the killer or the victim had at least a green card.

Herald twins of Miami, depend on the fringes of the economic world for advertising support. Even before Christmas the newspapers are thin, feeding on a few electronics stores in addition to the usual ads for lawyers, travel agencies, cures for baldness and sexual impotence, and liquor. Some of the papers carry ads from major food chains, but the space is sold at huge discounts. For most newspapers addressed to Latinos the bread and butter must come from classified advertising.

Because of the failure of advertisers to understand the importance of these newspapers, they have suffered less than most from the confusion of intent that plagues the media in the United States; they must serve their readers and only their readers, for no one else pays the bills. The opinion pages of *Diario las Americas, El Nuevo Herald, La Opinión* and *El Diario/La Prensa* are generally sophisticated, closely reasoned, and written with style. Unlike most of the newspapers in the United States, the major Spanish-language dailies have kept their dignity; that is what they sell, for it is widely understood by the older generation of Latinos that people of quality read.

A new generation is coming.

3.

> *. . . con ellos gozamos*
> *el placer de la amistad*
> *y un poco nos olvidamos*
> *de la amarga realidad.*
>
> *"Fransil"*[9]

On Sunday, July 18, 1982, Mr. and Mrs. Television celebrated their golden anniversary in show business. It was an afternoon of nostalgia, for they had not been home in more than twenty years. The men and women, *los viejos, las abuelas,* the memorialists and the weary warriors who gathered in the Dade County Auditorium had also been abroad for a long time, but they had not forgotten "Casino de la Alegría" and the most popular weekly program on television, "Cabaret Regalías." The old, the doddering ones, and those who remembered everything could still recall "El Show del Viernes"

[9]. . . with them we enjoy
the pleasure of friendship
and forget a little
of the bitter reality.
              Francisco Silva Trujillo, 1966

on radio. There were others who had seen the grand performances at Teatro Martí, who had been present at the entertainment of the Americans in the night clubs. And who could ever forget "La dulce y buena madre de la familia Pilón" on CMQ-TV?

It was a touching and terrible moment in the exile, for Pepa Berrio and Rolando Ochoa had been the soul of popular culture in Cuba. But that had been so long ago. Would they ever return? And if they went home again, could it ever be the same? Would Rolando still do his half-man/half-woman act? How could his son, Rolandito, do his comic imitation of Pedro Infante now that the boy was grown up, more than grown up, middle-aged?

Their old friend Ariel Remos had written a tribute to them in *Diario Las Américas*. He had spoken of their wildly successful years in broadcasting, Mr. and Mrs. Television, until 1961 when they, like a million others, fled into exile.

What the tributes did not say, what they did not even dare to intimate was that the nighttime, show business, café society spirit of La Habana had not been carried into exile. Cuba could be remembered, but it was not portable. The view from Hialeah was of a different world. "Work, work, and work," said Cecilia, the first daughter of Pepa and Rolando, "that's all we do in Miami. At the end of the day, we're so tired. But in Havana there was excitement; we were out all night in the cafés, in the nightclubs. And then we would go to work in the morning. We always had someone at home to do the cooking and cleaning. You didn't have to do that. You could feel the excitement in Havana. It was like no other city in the world.

"Now, we work all day, and when we come home, there is also work to do. Fortunately, there's a service here in Hialeah that brings meals to your house every night. You make the order for the week, and every night when you come home, they bring the meals for you and your husband and children. But it's not like Cuba. Here, we only go out on the weekends."

She looked over at her parents. They were tired, retired, living in a small cooperative apartment they had received in payment for doing a series of television commercials. Pepa had difficulty getting around. The sweet and good mother of television soap operas had become the sweet and good grandmother of life, cooking, cleaning, thinking back on CMQ and Teatro Martí, remembering the first tour of Latin America by the dance team of Pepa and Rolando. The man of many faces—actor, dancer, nightclub master of ceremonies, television host, comedian—recited patriotic poems and made ever more infrequent public appearances. Although Miami had become the place of origin for much of the Spanish-language television broadcast in the United States and the Cuban exiles and their children had begun to exert a powerful, almost controlling interest over Spanish-language media in every city, Pepa and Rolando did not like what they saw and heard. Neither the music nor the morals appealed to them, and they saw very little on television that was mindful of the fact of exile. Rolando Ochoa had been the star the *guajiros* loved, the show business personality with the country boy's charm; in the new time, in the new place, he was Old Havana, homesickness, history.

Spanish-language television in the United States never had a golden age. It came north from Mexico burdened with boxing and *churros,* the third rate movies ground out in the studios of Churubusco, but in a pun, more aptly named for the Mexican sugar-coated fried pastries sold in the streets. Its parent was Spanish-language radio, which is essentially a jukebox, except in Miami, where some stations provide round-the-clock arguments over Cuban politics.

There was only Mexico in the beginning, then Puerto Rico, Cuba, and Argentina. One network, then two, and when there were enough local stations and enough viewers, the networks built studios in Miami to produce soap operas, quiz programs, and variety shows for the U.S. audience. Nothing ever got better on Spanish language television but the technology. World and national news from Mexico City[10] was replaced by more local news, but local news programming of far better quality than that offered by local English-language stations, particularly in New York City: The Spanish local news is dignified, if hurried, and makes the effort to supplement its local news, sports, and weather with stories and videos from Latin America and the rest of the world. Soap operas without sex were replaced by soap operas with sex.

Other than occasional Cantinflas films or a lively variety show, the programming was as artless and crude as that of the Fox Network, and worse. It offered nothing to its viewers but news from home in a language similar to the language of home. And music: The real language of Spanish television is salsa, cumbia, merengue, polka;

three men in ruffled shirts and shiny shoes dancing in place;

a woman in a jeweled sombrero drawling a story of love and revenge;

a band of men standing in the plaza of a tiny town in Colombia or Ecuador singing songs woven together out of music for the flutes and drums of Indians, court dances of sixteenth-century Europe, and the electronic feedback amplifier;

a girl with sturdy legs, dressed in a tight black leather skirt, wailing to a hundred thousand people gathered in front of a stage on Calle Ocho;

---

[10]"24 Horas," the network news from Mexico, now appears on Galavision, a premium-priced cable channel. When I appeared on the program a few years ago I found the staff crisp and professional. Jacobo Zabludovsky, the anchor man, a political conservative, is extremely popular in Mexico.

and Julio Iglesias, under a hundred names, a hundred faces, a grown man singing with an adolescent bleat, Julio Iglesias, always Julio Iglesias, always.

Rubén Salazar's Lincolnesque vision of television by the people and for the people died with him. The two Spanish networks are owned by Anglo companies. Hallmark, the greeting card company, owns Univision (formerly Spanish International Network, SIN) and a company controlled by a Wall Street investor, Saul Steinberg, owns Telemundo. Both networks were purchased in the 1980s with junk bonds, and both have lost money since Hallmark and Steinberg took control. They bought the networks because they believed they could deliver the audience to the marketers. If they suffered any confusion of intent, the financial pressure cleared their minds. By the beginning of the second quarter of 1992, Hallmark had all but completed a deal to sell Univision to a syndicate headed by A. Jerrold Perenchio, and the owners of Telemundo were negotiating to restructure their debt.

The management of the networks and the local stations is largely Cuban and South American, with Mexicans and Puerto Ricans, who together represent 75 percent of all Latinos, almost completely excluded. Only Galavision, the cable network, is Mexican owned and managed. The color of the networks and the local stations is white; except for a few athletes and musicians, Spanish television looks like television from Spain. Zabludovsky is a European; so is Mario Kreutzberger, the Chilean host of "Sábado Gigante," probably the most popular program on Spanish television.

The networks have promised to build studios in Los Angeles to balance the production of programs in Miami, but the financial problems and competition from Galavision, make that unlikely. "Cubanization" provides a convenient focus for the deeper concern Latinos feel about Spanish-language television: the homogenization of cultures, an electronic melting pot in which words, customs, gestures, histories disappear. With the Anglos on one side and the television networks on the other, what hope have Latinos to retain anything of the past, any memory, any sense of self? The naked, textbook language is not enough; Spanish is not a schoolboy's idiom; it is made of *gua guas* and *chingazos, patojos, traidas, fachas, papas* and *patatas, colibrís* and *chuparosas.*[11] It sings, drawls, lolls on the tongue, or goes at machine gun pace; swallows, speaks, or whistles its sibilants; clears its throat when it should be rolling its *r*s. Every Spanish-speakers' town in every time in every country has a word, a sound, a name that is its own and cannot be properly spoken on the tongue of a native of any other town on earth. No people is more rooted, more loyal to the particularity of a place than the

---

[11]Busses in Cuba, fistfights in Mexico, babies in El Salvador, girlfriends in Guatemala, baby bottles in parts of Guatemala, Popes in Spain and potatoes in Mexico, potatoes in Spain, hummingbirds in Spain and hummingbirds on the U.S./Mexican border

Puerto Ricans, unless it is the Mexicans, who can never escape the light and the smell of the earth of their *patria chica*.

There is no little country, no home town in the United States; Cubans have claimed Miami, Los Angeles belongs to the Mexicans and Mexican-Americans, but all Latinos live under the democratic pressure to conform. The very fact of being different offends the inhospitable majority, which responds with murderous alternatives: absorption or destruction. Racism destroys by reducing a people to generalities; culture nurtures a people by celebrating its particulars.

A television network can have no particulars: It is national, international. On the screen particulars become the stuff of comedy: tasseled hats, shoes made of old truck tires, one-string violins, tiny drums, piglets, derby hats, and tiny metal eyes, arms, legs, hearts, babies tacked to the thighs of a wooden saint. Network television is the killing of culture by displacement. It pretends to particulars—"Here is your program from Colombia; listen to these singers from la Republica Dominicana; tonight we shall broadcast from the jungles of Chiapas, the mountains of Guatemala, the shores of Nicaragua . . ."—but only for a moment. Then all the men will look like Julio Iglesias again and all the women will belong to the Miami Sound Machine.

When the work of the networks is done, and Latino groups, like the Anglos before them, have lost their uniqueness, when all the fragments have been compressed into a soft gray stone, they will be much easier to deliver to the advertisers, for all the life of them will be gone and there will be nothing left but a market.

16

SHOEBOX BUSINESS

What have we got here in the Mission? The Chinese buying out the Latinos, a lot of stores where people keep their money in a shoebox. They have no records, no bank account, no way to get credit. Shoebox business, I call it.　　　Margaret Cruz, San Francisco attorney

I.

At the beginning of the nineteenth century all the businesses in the Southwest belonged to Mexicans, for all the land from Louisiana to California, from the Río Bravo to the mountains of Colorado, was Mexico. Then the gringos came and took the big business, which was the land, and all the little businesses that served the people who worked the farms and drove the cattle. In South Texas, the King Ranch was pieced together out of the bad luck and lack of capital of many Mejicanos. The names and numbers of the land sales, reported by David Montejano in his history of *Anglos and Mexicans in the Making of Texas,* describe in measured columns, without embroidery, the tragedy of country, class, and culture lost. It was the same in West Texas and California. After the war with Mexico, men like Frémont went west from Texas to New Mexico to California, overturning the Mejicano world and its poorly capitalized economy as they went.

When the taking of what had been the north of Mexico was complete and the borders were firmly established, the economic disenfranchisement of the Mejicanos went ahead rapidly. The Anglos opened stores and set themselves up in the construction business or the professions, pushing the Mejicanos out and down. The families of former owners of businesses and ranches were lucky to find work as clerks and laborers. By the end of the nineteenth century the wealth of the Southwest had been transferred from the Mexicans to the Anglos. In San Antonio and San Ygnacio, in Los Angeles and the hot

green valleys of California, in the Arizona desert and the New Mexico highlands, the Anglos were the greatest number and the richest race. After the
war and the Treaty of Guadalupe Hidalgo, the Mexicans who came across the
border, which was open through the early years of the twentieth-century,
arrived as poor strangers in what had been their own land.

Unlike the blacks, the Mexicans who came north to Texas could not speak
the language; they did not know the tools, the agricultural methods, nor all
the names and traits of the crops. An Indian who knew seven names for a
stalk of corn had difficulty with the ways of wheat. The farther south they had
lived in Mexico, the more difficult it was for them to comprehend life in the
country to the north. Many came with no more than a blanket and a change
of clothes. They began with nothing; they had no assets; they were raw labor.
The exploitation of them was absolute, for they had no allies, neither in the
unions, nor the churches, nor the government; to the owners of the mines
and factories and railroads they were the surplus labor that keeps wages low.

A harsh pattern of settlement emerged; racism so limited the opportunities for Mejicanos that only the most extraordinary acts of will could break
the bonds of the prescribed life. At the end of the nineteenth and the beginning of the twentieth century, most Mejicanos lived in ghettos in adobe
tenements without running water or toilets. There was no place to bathe, no
privacy, no quiet, no room to lie down alone, to be free of the molestations of
chickens and children. The Anglos said the people who lived in these conditions were not clean, and it was true; there was no way to keep clean in the
mud huts and shacks of the "Mexicantowns" of the Southwest. But the
sorrows of squalor were not known to the Anglos, only to the women who
had once washed their hair in streams and laid their freshly scrubbed clothing out to dry in the bleaching sun.

The soggy stench of overcrowded urban housing upset the campesinos,
who had come from poverty, but not from filth. The Anglos could not
understand them or the way they lived; only someone who has lived with a
floor that can be swept away understands the hygienic properties of dirt. The
burden of the new country was on the women, who had not expected filth in
paradise. They washed: They washed every day; they washed their children
and their clothing; they washed and braided their long, straight Indian hair,
uncut for Saint Anthony's sake; they washed until their fingers puckered and
the colors faded from their clothes; they washed to cleanse themselves of the
grime of the cities, of the airless winters and roach ridden summers, of the
sour scent of cities. And they did not succeed. They could not bring back the
old life.

It was common for the men to work two jobs or more to pay the rent and
feed and clothe the family. Rents were high, food was no bargain in paradise;
winter was an enemy season. Wages for Mejicanos were lower than those

paid to any other group in the United States. A man who could find work in the day sought more work in the night. A man who worked day and night looked for a way to earn something extra on Sundays. Only the women had the freedom for entrepreneurial adventures. They were the fortune tellers and herb sellers, the seamstresses and the purveyors of vegetables, lard, corn, beans, candles, needles and thread.

A woman with a baby at her breast or a dress and shawl of widow's black could sit in the street, leaning against a wall, selling tacos fried on a blackened grill. Any flesh, any flavor would do to fill the tortilla, to vary the routine of lard and beans.

Another could cook fresh tortillas, soaking the corn in limewater, grinding the masa, patting out the dough, and cooking it on a grill until the first bubble appeared. It was a business for widows and spinsters, but also for women who sought to augment the family income.

In the tenements, women hung out the dresses, shirts, and trousers they had cut and sewed; they made a bazaar of their little houses, they sold what they could. Weavers and embroiderers also displayed their work. On the streets women made markets of herbs, amulets, potions, and arcane prayers. That the women should have become the first entrepreneurs—economics derives from the Greek word for household—was not extraordinary, for the first things that were sold, the most important things, were those of the home. In simpler places and times, such things were bartered. In the more impersonal economy of the United States, a *cocinera*[1] or *costurera*[2] became a businesswoman.

It was often the woman who kept the household accounts, for she was responsible for buying food and clothing. The man might rule at the dinnertable. He could drink up his paycheck or gamble it away, but if he brought the money home, the wealth belonged to the woman, for she was the keeper of the household. So it was the women who opened the first little stores and two-table restaurants, for they understood business. They were not hired, like the men; they initiated the economics.

In the utterly segregated worlds of the Southwest, the men went outside the *barrio* to work in factories or on farms, as waiters, cooks, cleaners, carpenters, in every low-paying or underpaid job in the community. The women stayed behind and built the tiny economies of the *barrio*. Only the barber and the priest were always male.

Women also hired out as maids, cooks, and laundresses, but the rules of the Mexican family made it preferable for women to work closer to home, where they conducted business in a small way, among neighbors and ac-

[1]Cook
[2]Seamstress

quaintances, putting their meager profits in a knotted cloth or a pocket hidden in the folds of a heavy skirt until they could open a store or buy a stand to sell fruit juices or hand-embroidered blouses.

Among migrant farmworkers the first entrepreneurs after the women were men who owned trucks. A migrant worker from Mexico or South Texas, who put his wife and children to work in the fields alongside him and saved his money, could save enough in a few years to buy a truck. Once he owned the truck, he could offer to bring several families to pick cotton along the Rio Grande or strawberries in Michigan or tomatoes in Illinois. He charged the families for transportation and took a percentage of their pay for arranging the contract with a farmer. Some contractors took only a small amount of money, worked for the same farmers year after year, and were generally decent small businessmen. Others were thieves who stole the wages and used the women of the families who worked for them, taking half, even two-thirds of their earnings.

The agreements between the farmers and the contractors lasted for generations. It made no difference who the contractors brought to the fields, as long as they were not union organizers. An old man or a six-year-old girl received the same pay for a bucket of tomatoes. When the refugees of the 1980s came across the border, the contractors found them and brought them to the fields in place of the Mexicans and Mexican-Americans. The Guatemalans were the most desirable, for no one worked harder or was more docile than the *chapines.*

A Cakchiquel-speaking Mexican-American who worked as a contractor and interpreter for a farmer in Florida shook his head over the *chapines.* "They work like mules *en el labor,* but they don't know nothing. They don't talk Spanish. They don't eat nothing but their own little beans. They're so ignorant they don't even know how to make a *chalupa!*"

2.

Businesses in the barrios of the Southwest could not expand for lack of capital. The Mejicanos who sewed at home or owned tiny stands or stores were confined by the owners of the economy. The Mejicanos sold nothing, even in their stores, but labor. There was no surplus to convert into capital; they were lucky to survive with the help of relatives and children. The economics of the store were like those of the farm—children, widows, and spinsters were assets, paid in home cooking and hand-me-down clothing.

Wholesale businesses belonged to the Anglos, with but a few exceptions, among them the de la Garzas of Brownsville who were able to establish a wholesale produce business. A few hundred miles west, at San Ygnacio, the

Proceso Martínez family, which had opened a general store early in the nineteenth century and expanded timidly over two generations, put its money into land instead of retailing. The business dwindled and disappeared and the land lay fallow for decades until great deposits of natural gas were discovered below the surface.

On the streets of El Paso's Segundo Barrio the little stores, restaurants, and taverns, which had provided a good living to Mexican-Americans for more than a century, are being replaced by discount operations owned by Asian clans. Even Freddie's Restaurant, which had been a Sunday morning meeting place for politically involved Latinos, among them the very people who were trying to rejuvenate Segundo Barrio, closed. The Mission District in San Francisco is undergoing a similar change of ownership. Asian clans, much more sophisticated in the manipulation of capital, buy out the Latinos and earn good profits out of the stores by participating in complex distribution arrangements that begin with low-cost manufacturing in the Far East or in Asian-owned sweatshops employing Latino workers in California and Texas.

Like Latinos and other immigrant groups, Asians employ the entire family in a business. The difference is in the willingness to risk capital. According to Margaret Cruz, the fearless, funny, beloved voice of indignation in San Francisco's Latino community, the problem lies in the unwillingness of Mejicanos to take risks based on a sound understanding of modern business methods. Cruz made her own commitment to risk when she was a child, working beside her mother on a farm. She looked down at her bloody knees, she said, and swore she would live better. She was past sixty when she graduated from law school, a long-time political activist completing the vow made during the Great Depression.

Margaret Cruz's political goals for the community have shifted with time, from civil rights and survival to the taking of political and economic power. She strongly supports the work of the Mission Economic and Cultural Association (MECA), which helps the merchants in the area learn how to write a business plan, sign a lease, get a proper license, do accounts, and apply for low-cost loans for working capital. "The problem," said Robert Hernández, who heads MECA, "is that people come here and try to do business just like they did in the old country."

Efforts to turn barrio business districts into tourist attractions in the Southwest seek to reproduce the enormous success of the Calle Ocho event in Miami and the development of the River Walk in San Antonio, which were inspired by the success of tourism in Mexico and prerevolutionary Cuba. Unfortunately, neither Calle Ocho nor River Walk has produced what the promoters promised. The Calle Ocho festivities attract over 1.5 million people, but the street itself has continued to deteriorate. The wealthy Cubans have moved away. Criminals have moved in, especially at the eastern end of the street. After dark Calle Ocho is almost empty.

River Walk was part of Henry Cisneros's plan to revitalize San Antonio by turning the city into a tourist center. It helped the downtown area for a while, but the northward movement of money continued. River Walk came to belong more and more to the tourists, as giant malls, condominium complexes, and endless rows of shops and restaurants on the north side of the city sapped the downtown area. Tourist attractions, intended to replace the shrinking Department of Defense installations as a source of revenue, brought new jobs with them, but mainly the worst and lowest paying kind of work; tourism is, after all, not a service industry so much as a servant industry. Apparently, the boosters who dream of tourist dollars for Latino business districts do not know that billions of tourist dollars in Mexico have created millions of chambermaids and waiters or that prerevolutionary Cuba was a political, social, and moral cesspool: According to Fidel Castro, there were 267 whorehouses in Havana on the last day of the Batista government.

3.

In earlier immigrant communities capital was amassed by illegal means—drugs, prostitution, gambling—and used to establish informal banks, which loaned money at usurious rates. Latino storeowners, barred from the established banks, must endure the same loan-sharking tactics. The difference is that the Italian, Irish, and Jewish thugs worked their own communities, while the loan sharks who rent money to the Latinos come from outside. In San Francisco, Robert Hernández reported Mission District storeowners paying annual interest rates of 40 percent. In New York, the rates are slightly lower.

The loan shark is not a villain in the barrio. On the contrary, he has assumed the role once accorded to an officer of a small bank, for he is almost the only source of capital available to a person with no collateral other than his willingness to work. The loan shark trusts poor people; he invests in them and in their community, believing that even if the individual fails, the community will prevail, and the value of the business in which the loan shark's money is invested will increase.

His place of prominence is a gift from the establishment; banks just don't like or trust poor people. They show their distaste by redlining (withholding capital from minority communities), and they do it in every city and town in the United States. Government agencies have made feeble attempts to break the practice, but following the bank and savings and loan problems of 1990 and 1991 it is unlikely that there will be any pressure on banks to make risky loans. With a bodega in New York City, which may seem to be a small business, now selling for fifty or a hundred thousand dollars or more, the loan shark will become an even more prominent figure as the banks withdraw further from the barrio.

In the movies loan sharks send goons to break the bones of people who don't pay their debts. In reality, the loan shark's office is generally filled with people, including children of ten or twelve, waiting to hand over cash and get a receipt for the weekly payment on a store or car loan. Every transaction the loan shark makes is carefully scrutinized by his attorney. To avoid the usury laws in the State of New York, for example, some loansharks who work the barrios of New York City have moved to Connecticut.

The loan shark transacts business almost as a bank would, except for the way the down payment is figured. It is made in cash and not recorded. After that, legal procedures are carefully followed, and a loan at the maximum legal rate is made. However, the buyer must repay the entire sales price plus interest on that amount, over and above the down payment of about one-third of the value of the store. Translated into the language of ordinary loans, the interest rate would be 18 percent of 100 percent plus 25 or 35 points. Since the loan shark holds the mortgage, just as a bank would, there is no need for strong-arm tactics. If the borrower can't repay the money, the loan shark institutes legal foreclosure proceedings, takes possession of the property, and sells it again.

To support the exorbitant loan rates, the owner of the bodega must charge high prices and work 125 hours a week (6 A.M. to midnight, seven days a week) until the loan is paid off. After that, the business becomes very profitable. The owner can then sell the store and go into some less demanding business, or retire to Mexico, Puerto Rico, or the Dominican Republic, or become a capitalist himself, hiring others to work in the store while he enjoys the profits.

The owner of a shop or store in the barrio must handle all the normal problems of stocking his business with the right merchandise, keeping the premises clean (especially if it is a food store), paying his creditors, and maintaining good relations with his customers. And he must also offer credit himself—every customer wants to be able to buy what pleases him or her and say to the store clerk, *"Apuntelo!"* To have a charge account in the bodega is not only a sign of one's position in the neighborhood, it is a necessity for people who live from one paycheck to the next. So the shopkeeper in the barrio becomes, in turn, a kind of loan shark, factoring the interest costs into his prices, pushing the burden of the failure of the banks down another step onto the barrio family, who pays the ultimate bill. He almost always augments his income from overcharging by selling numbers, by installing videogames in a corner of the store, and, in New York City, by permitting one of the unethical communications companies to install pay telephones and charge exorbitant rates, as much as ten times those of AT&T or MCI for long distance.

Latino shopkeepers seldom complain of usury, which they understand as the price of opportunity for an immigrant. The real burden of the barrio shopkeeper carries a gun and wears a stocking over his face. From the delivery boy just arrived from Puebla, Mexico, who says, with a fatalistic shrug, "De vez en cuando nos roban,"[3] to the owner of a bodega who takes his own pistol from beneath the counter and fights a pitched battle with an armed robber, every shopkeeper, every clerk, and every deliveryman in the barrio worries constantly about crime. Cashiers in grocery stores, liquor stores, and drugstores work in cages protected by bulletproof glass. But nothing can save them from automatic weapons and the desire for rock cocaine; the bodega owner can expect to be robbed as he closes his store or opens it or walks to the bank with the day's receipts. A cash business is dangerous, and any retail store is a cash business, even if the style of the barrio requires that many of the purchases are simply "noted."

With no insurance to protect him and a loan shark waiting to repossess his store, the barrio shopkeeper cannot afford a robbery. Not just one day's receipts, but years of working day and night can be taken from him in a moment. So he fights. The little fat man who eats to stay awake, whose face turns gray before there is a sign of age in his hair, reaches under the counter and draws a gun against the gun pointed at his history and his future, and sometimes he dies. He has no choice. He does business out of a shoebox. There is not much pleasure in his profits.

4.

Somewhere in Colombia or Singapore or Hong Kong or off the coast of Florida, the drug business operates like a great corporation. Accountants, marketing experts, the geniuses of distribution and sales work in luxurious offices, the palaces of illegality. Perhaps there are also such places in New Jersey or Florida or under the California desert palms, but in the Latino community the drug business belongs to the shoebox. Sometimes it is the richest of shoeboxes—I have heard tales of rooms filled with cash—but it is always a shoebox.

The very bottom of the business has been given over to children. In the densely populated barrios of New York, crack dealers pay schoolchildren twenty-five cents each for empty crack vials picked up on the streets. Compared to grocers who pay only a nickel for an empty soft drink bottle, the

---

[3]"Every now and then they rob us."

crack dealers are the free-spending uncles of the barrio. Their generosity instructs the children in a kind of hero not known to Thomas Carlyle, the hero as criminal, and it enables these "heroes" to use the children as lookouts, runners, and eventually as colleagues and customers.

In Los Angeles children sell small amounts of marijuana and cocaine. They are the last leaves at the end of the smallest branches of a tree that begins in Southeast Asia or South America or Mexico. Cocaine comes to the Latinos through the Crips or Bloods, the gangs of young blacks organized to distribute drugs in cities across the country. Cocaine may also come down through the Mexican Mafia or La Familia. Heroin and large amounts of cocaine are distributed by Asian drug dealers to both blacks and Latinos.

The last leaves of one branch—Pistol, Robot, and Crosseye[4]—sat on the steps of a schoolhouse one afternoon smoking cigarettes and "kicking back," passing time, waiting for something to happen. Crosseye, who had just been released from the juvenile detention center, wore his hat backwards and his pants just below his hips. He was a fat kid, not obese, but sloppy; he had lumpy arms and a mound of belly inside his sweatshirt. He smoked cigarettes and blustered. Crosseye could have been the grandnephew of a James T. Farrell kid or a Nelson Algren creature from Chicago, a Mexican-American descendant of Studs Lonigan or the sad adolescents of *Never Come Morning*. Instead of a Polish or Irish accent, he spoke in the Spanish/western/black English patois of east Los Angeles, but his bumbling, guilt-ridden rebelliousness belonged in the long history of adolescence in America.

As a neighborhood girl passed by in a slow-moving car, he said, "Look at her! Look at her! I like to go up inside her." The girl leaned out the window of the car, and called to him, "Crosseye, I think your pants are falling down. Pull up your pants, Crosseye."

He sucked the stub of his cigarette, then threw it after her car. *"Puta!"*

Crosseye strutted. After coming out of the detention center, he had sworn to the police, his mother, and the priest that he wasn't going to sell drugs or "do dirt" (fight); he was getting out of the gang. He hadn't announced his capitulation to Robot and Pistol, who had known him since they were termites, but were no longer comfortable with him, watching him now without speaking. Crosseye performed a monologue, turning and twisting, pacing, sucking one cigarette after another. He had been arrested, charged, and suddenly released. It was unusual for a gangster to be released so quickly. For similar offenses Robot and Pistol had been sent to work camp. Something was wrong with Crosseye, not enough to hold a court and punish him or even jump him out, but something. They couldn't put their finger on it, not yet. They watched him.

---

[4]Not their real street names.

Robot was very thin, tight-lipped, narrow. He wore a hairnet knotted at the center of his forehead. His teal blue nylon shirt was buttoned only at the collar. Although he was just sixteen years old, he had earned a reputation for wildness; he knew where the gang kept one of its guns, and he was said to have used it; he was a shooter, a real *vato loco.*

A maroon sedan entered the street. Two men in suitcoats sat in the front seat. Crosseye recognized the car. "Oh, oh," he said, "CRASH.[5] Oh, shit! I'm holding." He pulled the peak of his cap around toward the front, turned on his heel, and started walking rapidly away from the stone steps where Robot and Pistol sat. As soon as the CRASH unit had passed, Crosseye came back, strutting again, but sweating. His pants had fallen a little more. The pantlegs pooled around his ankles.

"Let's get some beer," Pistol said.

Robot turned to Crosseye, "Get some money."

"I have to sell this shit," Crosseye answered. "And I have to be careful, because I just got out of detention."

"Let's get some beer," Pistol said.

Crosseye pulled the pockets out of his trousers to show that he had nothing. He wiped his face with his blue bandanna, his rag. "I have to sell this shit. Then we'll get some beer, go in the park, and kick. Oh oh, fucking CRASH." The car came around the corner of the block, and again Crosseye turned his hat around and began walking away.

After the CRASH unit passed, Crosseye, Robot, and Pistol walked around to the far corner of the schoolyard where some workmen were repairing a sewer pipe. They went like dancers, swaying and rolling, leaning back, all in unison; Robot and Pistol both thin and graceful, while Crosseye lumbered beside them, thick in the thighs. They glided, dancers on a waxed floor; Crosseye's sneakers grabbed the concrete.

At the corner, Crosseye went inside the fence of the schoolyard to talk to the workmen. Robot and Pistol strolled on, crossed the street, waited on the corner. Crosseye made the sale. He took off his shoe and fished out a small bag of cocaine. Robot wrinkled his nose at the idea of snorting coke from Crosseye's shoe. Pistol laughed.

When Crosseye came across the street, he had the money wadded up in his hand. "Let's get some beer and go to the park and kick."

Robot's girlfriend came by in a black Mustang convertible. Without a word, he walked over to the car, got in, and drove off with her. Pistol slipped away, down the street, talking of his house, dinner, kicking; the words came out unclearly, as if he hadn't meant for them to be understood.

---

[5]Community Resources Against Street Hoodlums, a special police unit known to use Draconian measures in dealing with gang members.

Crosseye held on to the money. There was sweat on his upper lip. His pants hung very low and he moved in clumsy jumps, like a fat Cantinflas. He called after Pistol, "Let's go to the park and kick. Fuck the Housing. Fuck the police. I'm not afraid of the Housing. Fuck the Housing. Fuck the Housing!"

—

There are two theories about the use of drugs in the barrios; one is based on the user's need and the other on the seller's logic. Poor people use drugs, the gentle theorists say, because of the economics of the ghetto. A person who is really poor learns to think of getting through the day, finding food, a place to sleep; it is a sense of existing in the present as primitive as that of early stone age hunter-gatherer societies. Cocaine fits the sense of present-ness: It gets the user through the hour or the day; it makes him feel good in the moment, like a meal for the hungry or a warm place in the cold. Marijuana is the distracting drug, like sitting in the movies or watching television when there is no heat in winter and nothing to eat. Heroin compresses the day into a painless moment. Alcohol combines some of the properties of all of the other drugs, which makes it the most common drug among Latinos, as it is among all other groups.

Sellers have a different outlook; they understand themselves as capitalists, not unlike Anheuser-Busch or Coors, and they consider the people who use drugs as a market. J, who lives in the Washington Heights section of Manhattan, said, "There used to be gangs, a long time ago. Now, everybody's just for himself; everybody just wants money. That's why you got drugs—for the money.

"You know, the drug dealers, they're not robbing anyone, not selling anyone anything they don't want. They say that if the people don't want to buy, they don't have to. So the drug dealers don't think they're doing anything wrong."

J lives on Audubon Avenue between 177th and 178th Streets, the supermarket of the Dominican-run drug business in New York. He is twenty years old, and like every other young man on the block, he has a tangential relationship with the family that runs the big operation in the apartment building on the east side of the street. J's friend, MX, who lives with his grandmother but stays often with his parents or with a friend in an apartment building on the west side of the street, holds a pistol for one of the younger members of the drug family.

In 1989, there was an argument in the street between a young man and his father, the head of the drug family. It began when the son accused the father of caring more about the drug business than he cared about his own family. All the members of the family, all the nephews and cousins, all the other sons came down to the street to watch the confrontation. The people came out of the bodegas and the laundry; everyone who stood in the court-yards of the weary art deco buildings came to the curb. They sat on the hoods of the cars, peered between the cars into the street, where the father and son stood, facing each other, screaming and threatening. Then the son broke away and ran into the building where MX lived. He did not wait for the elevator. He went up the stairs to the third floor and into the apartment where MX's parents lived, surrounded by empty beer bottles and ruined furniture. MX handed him the pistol.

Downstairs, in the street, the father was laughing, joking with the cousins and nephews and the other sons about the one who had run away. A few cars had begun to make their way down the avenue. When the son appeared, he had the pistol in his hand. The father turned away from the crowd of relatives who stood under the yellow metal awning of the bodega and came out again into the center of the street. The son approached him, with the gun in his hand, like a robber showing his weapon to a victim.

The father and the son faced each other in the middle of the street. They spoke softly, in the privacy of whispers. No one, not even the people who sat on the cars, heard what they said. Suddenly, the father grabbed the pistol. He hit the son once with his fist, perhaps with the pistol. The boy fell down, stunned, like a steer prepared for slaughter. While everyone on the street watched, the father, who was smaller than the son, a dark man, no thicker and no more gentle than a steel cable, a man with African skin and a knife-blade Spanish nose, put his foot on the boy's neck. Then he leaned over and touched the barrel of the pistol to his son's temple. The boy looked away, but as his father spoke, the boy turned his head slowly to look up at him. Then the pistol was pointed at the boy's eyes, so that he looked into the black hole at the end of the barrel.

When the father had finished speaking, he tossed the pistol onto the son's belly, and walked slowly back to the building beside the bodega.

The drug business on Audubon Avenue opens at nine in the morning and goes on through the day into the night, until the last customer has driven over the bridge from New Jersey or up from midtown or the Village. The dealers stand out on the street on the hottest days and the coldest days. When it rains or snows, they gather under the yellow and black awning of the bodega, sneaking moments inside to warm up or buy one of the peeled oranges waiting like white-veined naked breasts on the counter beside the candy.

All day and night the dealers wait for their customers, laughing, talking, whiling away the day between buys. Thieves approach them selling watches, gold, shirts. The dealers watch the street, stepping out, moving back under the metal awning, nervous, watching, walking over to the dry cleaners on the corner, moving, watching, men with big mustaches and skinny men, dark and light, tense, wearing jackets and jeans, waiting for their customers to appear. Every car that passes is scrutinized. A member of the family sits in the battered yellow Ford Pinto parked in front of the bodega. He looks out at the street and watches in the rear view mirror for a sign from one of the dealers standing in front of the bodega. His hand rests on an electronic beeper. If the police come, he will signal the apartment with the metal door upstairs.

A special kind of vision has been developed by the men who stand under the awning. Like the Navahos, who can see the pale brown wool of a sheep against the pale brown desert a thousand yards away, they squint into the light of the afternoon, as if in limited light the familiarity of objects and actions in the distance will be revealed. The men who stood under the awning feared nothing but surprise. They understood the law. Given only a minute or two of warning, they could evade the police; they were safe.

The drug building was filled with "legal" apartments occupied largely by old people whose rent was subsidized by the drug family in return for the occasional emergency use of the "legal" apartment. Of all the apartments in the building, only the whorehouse, where the women smoked crack between customers, and the drug apartment were not legal. To get to the whorehouse or the drug apartment it was necessary to ride up in the slow elevator with the porthole window in the door or climb ten flights of stairs. The drug apartment had a metal door with a small slot in the center, just large enough for a hand to pass through.

One customer at a time was brought upstairs by a dealer, and led to the slotted door. The customer put his or her money into the slot and got cocaine in return. The dealers did not touch either the money or the drugs. If the customer was an undercover narcotics agent, the heavy metal door was protection for the people inside, and the system protected the dealer, who never had the drugs or money in his possession.

If the police learned of the apartment through informants or undercover agents, the "legal" apartments came into use. The lookout in the yellow Pinto beeped the people upstairs, who gathered up the drugs and cash and moved them to one of the legal apartments. Since the search warrant must specify an apartment number, drugs captured from an apartment not shown on the warrant cannot be used as evidence in court, for they would have been found in an illegal search. The rules of the Audubon Avenue family were simple: Employ only family members, bring them from the Dominican Republic to work in the business, keep them undocumented so they don't get interested in leaving the business, maintain iron discipline, and always stay on the best of terms with everyone in the neighborhood.

Early every morning, the members of the drug family came out to begin their work. They swept the streets and sidewalks of Audubon Avenue; they helped old people with their rent; they loaned money to the bodega owners and to the man who wanted to start a dry cleaning business on their block. They were mainly retailers, although they did sometimes sell to other, smaller retailers, people outside the family, but they never allowed them in, never let them become anything more than customers.

To avoid the confiscation provisions in the law, they never bought anything for themselves. They did not own houses or elegant cars or furs or gold. They worked and sent their cash home. In the Dominican Republic they owned fine automobiles and beautiful houses, but in the United States they worked. They did not suffer from false pride: When it rained, they stood in the rain; when the street was not clean, they swept the street; when it was time to go to prison, they took their losses—they put up the money for bail and went home to the Dominican Republic. Somewhere, in Miami or the jungles of Columbia or the hills of Hong Kong, there was a complex corporate structure, but in Washington Heights and East L.A. it was shoebox business.

5.

Elena makes mangoes into flowers, as if it were possible to reverse the order of the world, to force nature to retreat from the business of the seed to the beauty of the bloom. She stands all day in the sun on the street corner across from MacArthur Park. Her method looks like magic. She reaches into her box of fruit, impales the weak spot of the seed on a stick, peels the mango with a dozen deft strokes of a razor, and with a few chops of a huge chef's knife, cuts the orange flesh into a flower. Time is turned around; the fruit becomes the blossom.

For her crime against the order of nature, Elena is hunted by the Los Angeles police. They prowl the streets, slowing as they pass her corner. Sometimes they only confiscate the elements of her magical work. Twice they have taken her to prison. The last time the police captured her, she languished in the city jail for sixty days, an unnaturalist, a practitioner of sunny magic, a lesser felon among drug dealers, shoplifters, assassins, and thieves.

Elena is a thick woman, a sensualist, as befits one who sniffs mangoes and every now and then steals a petal from one of her flowers, dampening it with lemon and dusting it with herbs before she touches it to her tongue. In the market, in the morning, she exposes the fruits in their boxes of twelve, runs her hands over them, studies the underside of their fleshiest places, taking only the best; not the soft ones, not the green, but the succulent ones, the mangoes that turn to juice on the tongue.

All around her, in the park and on the corners, the drug dealers and prostitutes work; the thieves sell the loot cached inside their shirts, up their sleeves, in their hats and deep pockets. There are killers, too, standing back, waiting in the shade.

Elena keeps the mangoes in a paper barrel, which is also the table of her operations and the storehouse of condiments and lemons and plastic bags and pointed sticks. In El Salvador, where her three children wait, she was also a street vendor, but she had a permanent place, a stand, a shaded spot; her skin was not so dark, she said, in El Salvador. She paid the police a bribe in those days, in El Salvador; she did not have to run from them. It surprised her when the army came and killed her husband.

Now she buys five boxes of mangoes for fifty dollars in the morning and turns them into seventy-five dollars by the end of the day, sometimes even before dark. That is the magic, she said; the other part, which seems like a miracle, is no more than sleight of hand, quickness, like a cardsharp's trick. Elena keeps the proceeds of her magic in a wad, tucked in an apron pocket. If business were better, she said, if she had a permanent place, she would lay the bills and coins out in an orderly way, in a box, a nice box, one with a shiny paper exterior that could be wiped clean with a damp cloth, like a shoebox.

17

THE ROUND OF REFUGE

Ningún ser humano es illegal.
(No human being is illegal.)

> Slogan of the campaign to gain
> political asylum for Central
> American refugees.

I. THE BORDER

Border rats, my mother used to call us. She meant it for a joke, but there was some truth in what she said, for our family has lived along the Mexican border, in Arizona and Texas, since the 1940s. I am the only one who went away. And that was a long time ago.

Going home, traveling two thousand miles west from the Gulf, along the river to El Paso, and then through the desert to the Pacific, I expected the remembered place, where the rich country and the poor met in an ironic embrace of hope and commerce. Instead, I came across the dark side of home: a line of violence and needless cruelty, beginning in a cluster of concentration camps and ending in an open sewer.

The border has never been a gentle place. On that history and myth agree. But the nature of its rages has changed. In the past, violence had the good manners to stay off Main Street. Now, there are signs of it everywhere. It is the view from the living room of my sister's house. Between her windows and the nearby canyons of the Sierra Madres a chain-link fence topped with barbed wire has been erected, for when the sun goes down, crowds of desperate people come across the river and through the canyons to rob the houses and steal the cars of the rich.

In the war between the Immigration and Naturalization Service (INS) and the tens of thousands of people without papers who come across the border every day, the old rules of racist civility have been abandoned. It is a brutal business now, done to no one's credit. The Border Patrol is the failed police arm of the INS, a mismanaged collection of 3,800 sour agents who have no effect on the drug trade and whose presence barely slows the rate of illegal crossings into the United States. According to INS publicists, they catch a third of all the people who enter the country illegally; if so, the border must be a busy place, for there are many undocumented people in the United States, perhaps as many as five million or more.

When I was a young man in these border towns, murder was a modest business done between rivals and lovers behind closed doors. Now hundreds of bodies are found along the border every year. The deaths take place in public, as if murder had lost its shame. Most of those who die have no documents. Police and Border Patrol agents kill some of them. Others die trying to cross the freeways under the protection of night. So many have been run down that the State of California now posts signs on the roads near the border advising drivers to watch out for people crossing.

Bandits and *cholos* do most of the killing. That's the rumor, and in this case, I think rumor is a good detective. A high school kid in Chula Vista, California, said that whenever the *cholos* from his school need money, they look for undocumented people, because they are so easy to rob. And sometimes, he said, the *cholos* hunt Mexican Indians who live in the hills east of Oceanside just for fun.

No one knows for certain how many are killed; the unknown dead lie somewhere in the desert. No one counts the useless cruelties, the physical and psychological beatings of the border. I have no numbers to offer. My own history puts me in danger of overstating the case.

—

Brownsville, the Texas Key Shelter: I first saw the Nicaraguan woman coming across the lawn from the south security post. She walked quickly, at a shopkeeper's purposeful pace. Her skirt, which was still wet at the hem from crossing the river, was too long and her low-heeled pumps were stretched out of shape by the journey, gapped at the instep. She was as round as a barrel and as proper as geometry. Her glasses were rimless, fixed to her nose by wire and will. Her hair was light brown and blonde and gray, pulled back tightly, gathered at the neck, trailing halfway down her back.

Without stopping to ask directions, she headed straight for the intake desk. The young man on duty welcomed her and began filling out the usual documents.

She gave her name and date of birth, January 5, 1933.

Although she was no more than four-and-a-half-feet tall, she seemed bigger, for she stood very straight, like a sergeant of the bourgeoisie.

"Su destino?" he asked.

"Miami. My son is in Miami."

"We'll help you to telephone him. Do you know his number?"

"Me robaron en el camino," she said. The Spanish consonants squeezed her face into an infant's grimace. Tears came. "The bandits took everything," she said, weeping, "even the paper that had his number."

Beatriz, the shift supervisor, came out of an inner office. She was a foot taller than the Nicaraguan lady and heavy. With one great arm, Beatriz hugged the little woman. She held her close and stroked her arm; she cradled her. Then she led her down the corridor to the nurse's aide on duty. In the security of white uniforms and the smell of antiseptics, the little lady told of her experience at the border, of the men who had violated her, of how she had wept and bled, and wandered for a month, alone at first, then working here and there while the physical wounds healed and the shame receded and she made herself ready to try again to cross the river.

After the woman left the examining room, the nurse's aide, whose heart knows no limits, but who is as crude as a used truck, made jokes about rape. Then, for no apparent reason, her eyes narrowed and the fat laughters in her face turned cold. She said that there are places in Mexico on the way to the border where every woman who passes through is raped. She shook her head. There was no way to know how many of the refugee women had been raped. Half of them? Three-fourths? The Nicaraguan woman was a city dweller; she could talk about her experience. Modesty makes such frankness impossible for an Indian.

———

Bayview, the INS Processing Center: The camp lies well to the north of the river, covering 317 acres in the flatlands beside the Gulf of Mexico. At the end of a long skein of narrow, unmarked roads it appears abruptly, as if the horizon had parted to reveal the widely separated buildings, partially obliterated by the glare of the sun. Only a small sign identifies the place known as El Corralón, the big corral, the great animal pen, the concentration camp.

Two chain-link fences, topped with barbed wire and separated by a dead corridor of sand and brown grass, surround the camp. Television cameras watch the corridor and the corners, look into the barracks and the exercise yards; the entire camp is under constant electronic surveillance.

Bright orange jumpsuits identify the prisoners: all the prisoners alike, men and women, Guatemalans, Hondurans, Salvadorans, Nicaraguans, young, old, Contras, Sandinistas, Somocistas, criminals, schoolteachers, drug dealers, union organizers, shopkeepers, peasants. The first rule of El Corralón is the rule of we and they—the aliens wear orange. Since they all look alike, they appear to be nobody; yet they glow like traffic signs or ripe fruit among green leaves, so they have no privacy. They are observed but unknown—aliens.

They come by the busload—and wait: in the bus and then in long lines. Each person's name becomes a shout, an electronic rumbling in the public address system, a handle, no longer a name, a thing by which the handler takes hold. They come wearing tennis shoes, tee-shirts, blouses still redolent of cooking fires, blue jeans, embroideries. The camp commander says he can tell a person's country of origin by his clothing. The guards take the clothing away first. Public showers and examinations follow. Each person submits his body for inspection, feels a stranger push and part his hair in the search for lice.

Then nothing: The days are given to waiting. Some prisoners clean the barracks, some do the laundry; they work to get through the days. But the days go on too long. It is a prison without sentences; one can post a bond of fifteen hundred or three thousand dollars and be discharged in two or three days, but a person without money can remain for months and months without end while the courts consider their appeals for political asylum.

Outside their barracks, two women in orange jumpsuits lay in the dust and dead grass, resting their heads on a concrete walkway. They had been in El Corralón for a long time. One spoke lazily to the camp commander as he walked by, asking about her case. He had no news. He smiled politely. His gleaming boots, the knife crease of his trousers passed within inches of her head.

Trouble comes, the camp commander says, when anxiety takes over. In the spring of 1990, the INS threatened to stop releasing people from the camp on bond or on their own recognizance. The population of the camp, which was designed to hold 600 adult males and females would be expanded. The new limit would be 10,500.

Crowding, Primo Levi said, was one of the useless cruelties of the camps he knew.

—

San Benito, the Texas Key Shelter for refugee families: Hundreds of men, women, and their children live together in one great room. No walls, no partitions, not more than a few feet of space separates the families. Each family is a clump on the open floor, and every clump represents an attempt to make a room of cardboard boxes, a footlocker, a basket, any opaque object. All fail—there is no place where a baby can sleep unmolested in the afternoon, nor is there any structure sufficient to contain whispers, dreams, or an act of love.

The human and electronic voices of San Benito rise into the rafters of the barnlike building and roll around there, gaining power; the naked, white wooden walls give back nothing but noise. A public address system squawks above the din. It is the sound of the camps.

After a while the noise and the anonymity of incessant publicity crack the constructs of reason. As the months go by, some people lose the ability to sleep; others complain of bad dreams. Uncontrollable anxiety possesses one member of a family and infects all the rest. Those who break down completely become catatonic.

The Martínez family—six tiny people, like darkly Oriental dolls, the mother with a touch of rouge on her cocoa-colored cheeks—lived in a huddle of boxes on the floor of the shelter. They have no relatives in the United States and no money. The three to five thousand dollar bond is an insurmountable barrier to them; they will have to wait in San Benito until the INS judges their request for political asylum.

On the way north to Brownsville, they were robbed twice. After the first robbery, they got more money from home, but with only a tiny stake, they could not afford a coyote to guide them through the bandits at the border. In the mountains of central Mexico, they were surrounded by men on horseback armed with machetes. One of the men grabbed the youngest Martínez child and raised his machete over her head. He demanded everything, money, rings, earrings, belts, shoes, in exchange for the girl's life. "Hasta sus zapatos," they say about the bandits who work the border; they take everything from the innocents, right down to their shoes.

So Señor Martínez unbuttoned his trousers and reached inside his underwear to the secret pocket his wife had sewn for him there, and gave the bandits everything. He saved only the paper the guerrillas had delivered to him in his village, demanding that he join them, for he knew that the paper—proof of the threat to his life and the lives of his children—was his hope for political asylum, evidence. He was not a communist, he said; he left because of them.

He showed me the paper, he held up the paper and read from it, but he could not concentrate on politics; the robbery occupied his mind, the men on horseback, the machetes. The bandits had made them all lie face down on the ground. Martínez remembered the machetes, his child. "I would die for my children," he said, and said again and again, as if this willingness to die had become his reason for existence.

———

Brownsville, the river: Sergio Ramírez, a man who sits like a hunting animal, looked through the window, cutting signs, searching for footprints, discarded clothing, the plastic bags in which emigrants carry dry clothing while crossing the river.

As the Border Patrol van moved along the levee under the bridge to Matamoros, Ramírez saw two men half-hidden in the brush beneath the steel supports. Frank López, his partner, drove the van a few yards downriver. Ramírez climbed the steep side of the bank, loosening his .357 Magnum in its holster. He put the men up against the side of the embankment, patted them down, found nothing.

"Glue-sniffers," he told his partner. "It was all over their face. If I'd of known, I would have told you to come with me."

"Those bastards are superhuman," López explained to me. "I've seen three, four men beat the shit out of one of them, still couldn't subdue him." I nodded. Kids had been getting high on the fumes of airplane glue since I was a boy, but I remembered them befuddled, not beasts.

They were sure the glue-sniffers had hidden weapons somewhere in the grasses under the bridge. They knew that before the night was over someone crossing the river would be caught and driven up into the shadows where the bandits do their work, but they could not wait.

Further down the river, where many people cross, paying fifty cents to a man who brings them over in a rubber raft, we passed a place where the rocks were still stained with the blood of an emigrant who resisted the bandits. López said he worries about the bandits, especially after dark, when the roaring, rattling van makes a good target. Sometimes the bandits stand on the opposite bank of the river, he said, showing their weapons to La Migra and laughing.

"La Migra," he said, "La Pinche Migra." He paused, as if to turn the insult over in his mind, to examine all the aspects of it, to taste the venom— "Pinche Migra."

Back in the city, they drove through the downtown streets near the river. The fixtureless storefront businesses selling secondhand clothing by the pound, the cheap jewelry and appliance stores had closed. In the dark, the streets belonged to the transvestites, men who cross the river carrying their costumes and makeup in waterproof bags, then dress and go to work in the streets. Ramírez called out the window to them, "Oye, chula, how can somebody so ugly do any business?"

"*Orale,* guy, let's go."

The transvestites have no papers, but no one arrests them, no one touches them: "They're unpredictable," Ramírez said, "they scratch and bite, and they might have AIDS."

The shift was quiet, slow for a weekend night, until someone crossed the river and set off one of the seismic sensors. The dispatcher gave the sector number over the radio. López drove to a building near the highway and parked the van behind it. Ramírez climbed out and walked to the edge of the building, moving carefully, staying in shadows. He stuck his head out quickly to look around the side—nothing. He knew someone was coming: a trembling refugee or a group of drug runners carrying automatic weapons.

The sensor gives no indication. It registers a footfall. Something heavier than a dog. No more information than that. He waited, looked and looked again.

"Arriba las manos! Up against the wall. Shut up! Shut up!"

He screamed at the shapes, kept on screaming, shining his flashlight, pushing them, pushing, screaming. There were three of them, and they were just boys. Ramírez shone his light on the seat of their pants. It showed the outline of their underwear, which was still wet from crossing the river. López arrived in the van and they put the boys inside. There was no conversation. At the bridge to Mexico, Ramírez let them out. He spent a moment with them in front of the truck, making empty threats, then herded them back across.

The operation took less than ten minutes. While it was brutally efficient, it violated the Constitution, a host of rulings by the federal courts, and the administrative procedures of the INS. An older, but informal law was also violated. Ramírez says that when he picks up people he calls "wets," they often appeal to him, one Latino to another, to let them go. He never does. They are not Americans, he says; he has no feeling for them, no connection to them; he particularly despises the refugees from Central America who refuse to fight for their country.

In considering this it is useful to know that Sergio Ramírez is the son of a man who entered the United States illegally.

—

El Paso, the river: In the vans used by the Border Patrol at El Paso, the back seats have been removed. Undocumented people sit or crouch on the floor, sometimes for hours, while La Migra does its work. The people, often as many as ten or twelve crammed into the back of a van, have no seat belts, no seats, nothing to hang onto as the van races through the streets and out along the rough, rutted roads near the river, chasing more Mexicans to pack into the back of the vehicle.

For many years, teams of Border Patrol agents and local police burst into cantinas frequented by Latinos in South El Paso, near the border, lined up the patrons and demanded to see proof of citizenship. Native-born Americans of Mexican descent were often arrested, piled into Border Patrol vans, and held in prison cells until they could prove their citizenship. The practice slowed, but did not stop after civil rights lawyers won an injunction in U.S. District Court.

A report released by the Mexican consul in El Paso claimed over two thousand abuses of human rights in the State of Texas in 1988 alone. All the victims were Mexicans or Mexican-Americans. The majority of the abuses took place along the border.

Border Patrol agents say that the treatment of undocumented people along the Texas/Mexico border is more humane than in California. "Why do people criticize us?" one of them said. "We're just doing our job. We don't bring all these people here. It's a political problem."

—

Vista, California, the canyons southeast of the town: When we broke out of the wooded area and began climbing, there was suddenly the blue-white light of the undiminished moon. We could see everything, the hills, the tomato fields somewhere ahead, and more woods. Sergio Méndez led the way, climbing quickly to the level of the tomato field. We crossed over the low plastic fence that bordered the field and walked across the rows. After the field, which was on one of the few flat places, we came to a steep drop. At first, we tried to climb down, but we quickly realized that it was impassable, a tiny canyon. Méndez turned west, looking for a place to cross or descend. In his fleece-lined denim jacket and workman's pants, he was a cube of a man, thick and strong, an indígeno, he called himself, of the Mixteca. His fingers were short, but his hand was so wide and thick that I could not grasp it properly when we helped each other down the side of the hill.

He moved quickly. He knew the way, although there was no trail or other marking that I could see in the moonlight. Deeper into the trees, he saw a passable place, and we climbed down. Méndez went first, finding the hand and footholds. I came after, trying to pick the same places. There was a little jump at the end into the soft dirt of the woods.

Then we moved through a deeply wooded area, following a clearly de-fined path. I heard voices and smelled a cooking fire somewhere down the hill. Méndez moved faster, certain of his bearings. It was dark in among the trees where the moonlight did not penetrate. The dogs rushed out at us there, snarling and barking. There were three, possibly four dogs. They surrounded Méndez, who hissed at them and called ahead in a soft voice to people he thought might know him.

A man came out of the darkness to silence the dogs. Méndez and I followed him down the hill to the lean-to where the smell of the cooking fires originated. Five men sat inside the lean-to, which was warmed by two fires inside metal drums. There was no light but a candle and the little glow of the fire from inside the metal drums. The men did not sleep in the lean-to. It was a place for cooking and talking. They slept farther out on the hill, in places they had dug into the ground; not in caves, but in burrows, holes dug at the base of a tree.

There were two older men and three young ones. The young ones did not have papers, which made them nervous at first. They stayed back, at the edge of the candlelight. Méndez spoke of his business, of laws and rights, of the need to preserve the Mixteco culture, then the men and I talked.

Tens of thousands of Mixtec Indians have come from the villages of

Oaxaca to work and live in Baja California and in the towns across the border. Méndez said they are despised in Mexico and in the United States because they are small and very dark-skinned. In Mexico, they have become the labor force of the Valle de San Quintín, the gigantic complex of Japanese-owned truck farms, where people live inside barbed-wire enclosed compounds, eighteen to a room, existing in something he describes as slavery or what others have told him is a concentration camp.

On the U.S. side, the Mixtecos live in constant fear of attack from *cholos* or white racists. Not far from where we were sitting, a Mixteco had been found with his throat cut. Down on the main road, behind a grocery store, two Mixtecos were grabbed from behind, blindfolded, robbed, and beaten. Between July 31 and August 14 of 1989, seven murders, shootings, and stabbings of migrant workers were reported to police in the little cluster of farm towns in San Diego County. It is the way of life here, the risk men run to earn enough money to send home to their families in Oaxaca or Baja California. Generally, they suffer in secret, silent except among themselves. If they are sick, the hospitals turn them away. If they are robbed or beaten or shot, the police turn them over to the Border Patrol. None of these men speak English; many are more comfortable in Mixtecan than Spanish. They have no alternative but to endure.

The men inside the lean-to said that when they go out to work during the day, they sometimes come back to find that the *cholos* have been there, and everything of value is gone. Even so, they are glad to be alive and whole. They make the only possible adjustment: If they cannot defend their personal belongings, they will have none. They live for the winter, when they can go home.

I asked them why they did not bring their families across the border. One man answered by describing his village in Oaxaca. Another said he did not want his children to live in the United States, because there was nothing here for them but drugs, violence, and rock and roll.

—

San Ysidro, the U.S. side of the border: A twenty-three-year-old Mexican man was shot by a Border Patrol agent, who said the man had thrown a rock at him. In his defense the man said he had picked up a rock and threatened the agent after the agent grabbed his pregnant wife by the hair, pulled her down to the ground, and stepped on her belly. A jury in U.S. District Court found the wounded man not guilty of throwing rocks.

Fifteen years ago the Border Patrol began hiring Mexican-Americans. Instead of changing the agency's racist attitudes, it added the more brutal racism of the dark-skinned overseer, the one who proves to his white masters that he is loyal and who separates himself from his own people by brutalizing them. One of these overseers is reported to have used the public address system of his Border Patrol vehicle to taunt Mexicans who stood on the other side of the line waiting to cross. He spent a long time telling the Mexicans that their mothers were whores and that the only good Mexicans were Texans.

Two hours later, in the same area, Border Patrol agents shot a boy who they said was throwing rocks at them. Like many of the people shot by the Border Patrol, the bullet entered his body from the back.

Everywhere along the California border the response to violence has been to create more violence. A Border Crime Prevention Unit formed jointly by San Diego police and the Border Patrol shot thirty-one people, all Mexican citizens, in five years. Nineteen of them died. The level of violence connected with the unit is astonishing; in less than six years of operation the entire unit has been suspended twice, both times after a rash of killings.

At the edges of the countries, the border, the social order no longer holds; war has given way to anomie. And yet, the coyotes, the travel agents, of the undocumented, and their flocks of chickens have no fear of the Border Patrol; the universal nightmare is the Mexican police.

—

Tijuana, B.C., El Bordo: A deep ditch, wider than two football fields, separates the United States from Mexico at Tijuana. An open sewer runs down the center of the ditch and a great, wide levee rises up on either side. Near the offices of the ruling party, the PRI, in Tijuana, the boundary between the countries curls like a scorpion's tail, making the levee as well as the ditch U.S. territory from that point west. A chain-link fence, long ago ripped open, marks the place.

Every day, people gather on the Mexican side of the levee at a place known as El Bordo. Dope dealers walk the levee. Glue sniffers sit or stand, half-crazed in the stinking night air. It is difficult to tell who is armed and who is innocent. There is always someone bleeding, half-dead, dying, or asleep. No police, no ambulances, no Red Cross workers come to El Bordo, only La Migra, driving fifty miles an hour down the U.S. side of the levee in a Blazer truck, sending people scrambling, screaming in the night. Some are run over. Some pick up stones to throw in anger and are beaten or shot.

At dusk, the emigrants and their coyotes, the dope dealers and the day trippers, walk through the hole in the fence and move west along the levee to more difficult terrain, where they have a better chance of outwitting and outrunning La Migra. The children are the greatest worry, the coyotes say; they don't know how to hide or get on their bellies and crawl when La Migra is nearby. They don't know how to act like coyotes.

To get to the United States, to run the gauntlet of *cholos* waiting to rob or kill them, to travel in terror through the highway checkpoints and moonlit fields, to cross the freeways in the night, as innocent as deer in the transfixing gleam of headlights, everyone, all the thousands who cross here, will have to walk or run through the stinking black water of the open sewer. Some will tie plastic bags around their feet and ankles, most will simply remove their shoes and socks, roll up their pantlegs or lift their skirts, and immerse their feet in shit.

———

Tijuana, B.C., the Cañón Zapata: A long, deeply rutted road leads down into the canyon. It is strewn with garbage, made almost impassable by stones and sudden breaks in the steep slope. On the left, the houses of the old colonia have been constructed in a style peculiar to Tijuana: The backs rest against the slope of the hill, and the fronts are held level by foundations made of discarded automobile tires.

On the right, as the road falls sharply down through the rounded hills, the shell of an automobile, completely covered with rust, from the roof to the base of the fenders, sits starkly against the north sky, orange and monumental.

No line, no fence, no river marks the boundary between the United States and Mexico here; only a row of small stones halfway down the side of one of the hills. By late afternoon, seventy-five or a hundred people had gathered. More filtered down through the hills and between the houses as the daylight weakened. Tables and cooking fires had been set up in the flat places on the hill. Women dressed in layers of clothing against the cold cooked fried chicken, beans, hot coffee. A peddler wandered among the waiting people selling blankets, scarves, beans, and small bottles of tequila.

Their only customers were the people without papers; they are everybody's customers, everybody's prey; they belong to the coyotes and the glove sellers and the tequila peddlers and the coffee and chicken sellers, even to the waifs who walk the hills selling chiclets. If the emigrants try to cross without a coyote to guide them to the other side[1] or all the way to Los Angeles, and they have bad luck, they will become customers of the *cholos,* who will leave them picked clean, barefoot, beaten, and raped, able only to crawl back into Mexico.

As the sun went down behind the hills, leaving parts of the canyon in

---

[1]Fees are almost standard: $100 to cross the border; $350 to be led across the border and transported through the Border Patrol checkpoints to Los Angeles. Coyotes survive on their reputation for providing safe passage. Much of their business comes from people in the interior of Mexico who have heard from relatives or friends of the prowess of one coyote or another. Prices, dates of passage, and so on are then arranged by telephone, much as one would work with a travel agent.

sudden shadow, people began looking over at the long ridge to the north, to the place called the soccer field, where La Migra waited in a pale green van and a four-wheel-drive truck, watching, waiting for the first of the emigrants to file down the path between the hills into the deep shadows of the floor of the canyon from which they would make their run.

The emigrants stood or sat in small groups, waiting until it was time to go. Although the number of people on the hills increased rapidly with the coming of the dark, there was very little noise. Only those who were not going across spoke. All the rest were quiet, waiting.

The coyotes appeared then, counting their chickens. Somewhere down in the darkness the *cholos* waited. The emigrants knew this was the existential place, without law or family, outside the rules of order, beyond prediction. A young woman made jokes, insouciant in the dangerous moment. She had put on makeup and had her hair done before crossing the line; she wore white tennis shoes. Beside her, three more women huddled inside their blankets. One was terrified. She said she knew no one on the other side, she had no job, no place to go. I wrote out the name of a sanctuary in Los Angeles. "If you get that far," I said, "you can rest there for a few days and get something to eat. This is my name. The priest is my friend." She took the paper and folded it up and reached inside her blanket to hide it in her blouse. She cried a little over the paper. Then she drew the blanket tightly around herself, as if it could shield her from what was to come.

The danger is real. By the time they get across the border into the United States, most of the emigrants will have been robbed, beaten, extorted, or raped by bandits or the Mexican police. The Binational Center for Human Rights in Tijuana puts the number at 65 percent.

At dark a man in a shiny warmup jacket, his wife, and three children started down the narrow path into the deepest part of the canyon. The woman carried a baby slung across her back in a rebozo. All the others carried plastic grocery bags. Up on the hill the coyotes nodded to their little herds of chickens to get ready. Near the stones that mark the boundary, the woman who knew no one on the other side folded up her blanket and prepared to go. The emigrants went quietly, moving like animals through the night, atavistic shapes, bent low to the ground, neolithic runners in postmodern shoes.

2. THE TONKS

In 1989, a massive case against the INS was heard in federal district court in San Jose, California. Three major civil rights organizations—the Poverty Law Center in San Francisco, the Mexican American Legal Defense and

Education Fund, and the American Civil Liberties Union—pooled their resources to seek out witnesses, take depositions, go through a long and difficult discovery process, and conduct the case. Their aim was to get a permanent injunction barring the INS from discriminatory enforcement practices and illegal searches and seizures. On the government side U.S. Attorney Joseph Russoniello, a former FBI agent who had been nominated for the post by S. I. Hayakawa and appointed by Ronald Reagan, personally took on the defense. The presiding U.S. District Court judge was a Carter appointee, Robert Aguilar.

On the surface the case in San Jose, known as *Pearl Meadows Mushroom Farms Inc. v. Alan Nelson, Commissioner, Immigration and Naturalization Service*, was a straightforward battle over violations of the Fourth and Fifth Amendments by a rogue agency of the federal government. Suit was first brought in 1982 after the INS carried out a series of workplace raids under Project Jobs, part of the Reagan administration's effort to blame undocumented workers for high unemployment, especially in the Southwest. The INS was accused of a pattern of discrimination and racial harassment, physical and verbal abuse of workers, entering workplaces without proper warrants, and seizing people without reasonable cause for suspicion.

Such cases are difficult to prove, because the courts, following the Rehnquist lead, typically require that an institutional pattern be shown, and the U.S. Attorney argued that every violation of the law by the INS was merely a matter of "deviant behavior." The lawyers countered with the testimony of a hundred witnesses and with the startling information that no INS agent had every been formally disciplined for abusing or violating the rights of a person in a workplace.

Although there were many witnesses, and according to an early ruling by Judge Aguilar it was not necessary for them to say whether they had come to the United States with or without working papers, each person came to the stand knowing that the interrogation could be difficult, fearing that La Migra would be waiting outside the courtroom. Some traveled a long way to testify; none were paid anything other than the thirty-five dollar witness fee.

A fifty-seven-year-old farm laborer, a timid man who cried on the witness stand, spoke to one of the most serious issues in the case. Testifying through an interpreter, he described how INS agents beat his head against the side of a car and told him that he had no rights, no rights at all, in this country. "The one that was mistreating me," he said, "his parents were also foreigners here. I believe that in this land we have all arrived here as adventurers and trying to make a life for our children. I believe that it is not a crime to be a worker. Being a worker is one of the most beautiful things, because he is doing no wrong to anyone. To the contrary, he is giving life to all of humanity."

The U.S. Attorney made a sophisticated version of the INS agent's argument against the rights of the undocumented. Early on in the trial he submitted a strange brief saying in effect that constitutional guarantees do not apply to undocumented workers in the United States. In opposition to a motion to exclude evidence of unlawful immigration status Russoniello wrote:

> The unclean hands doctrine "closes the doors of a court of equity to one tainted with inequitableness or bad faith relative to the matter in which he seeks relief, however improper may have been the behavior of the defendant." *Precision Instrument Mfg. Co. v. Automotive Maintenance Machinery Co., 324 U.S. 806, 814 (1945)*. . . . Persons . . . who were illegally in the United States and working brought about the INS actions plaintiffs now challenge. Such persons' hands are "unclean," and they can receive no equitable relief.

The judge ruled in favor of the plaintiffs without commenting on the unclean hands argument.

There were other, more subtle arguments. "Employers hire illegals," the U.S. Attorney said, following the line taken by the Reagan administration's Project Jobs, "because they're docile, they don't complain, they're easily exploitable, almost all are non-organized. The work is hard. It offers little in the way of advancement and certainly no security.

"The noncooperating employer is the villain of the piece. They use illegals to meet their affirmative action quotas. It gives employers an excuse not to hire other minorities, blacks and the inner-city poor."

When the people who took the witness stand told of working in the dark, in damp caves where mushrooms are grown or of standing beside a conveyor belt, pulling the guts out of freshly slaughtered chickens, it seemed less likely that they were taking the jobs that citizens desired. In fact, they worked as immigrants always have: They took the worst of jobs, the ugly work, the dangerous work, the backbreaking, debilitating work, the jobs that even the jobless reject.

The Immigration and Reform Act of 1986 (IRCA), which was to prevent undocumented people from working at any kinds of jobs in the United States by applying sanctions including heavy fines against employers who hired them, had instead caused a sudden rise in discrimination against foreign-looking or foreign-sounding job applicants. By 1988, a General Accounting Office survey found 528,000 instances of job discrimination related to IRCA.

John True, the lead attorney for the consortium of civil rights lawyers, spoke to the issue of discrimination as it affected the arrest and detention of people suspected of working without papers. Just as employers needed cause for failing to hire someone, the INS needed cause for stopping a person on the street or in a factory. "What does a Mexican look like?" True asked. "Is he a person with brown skin? Is he a person with brown skin and dirty clothes? Is he a person with brown skin and dirty clothes who won't look you in the eye?"

Francisco García-Rodríguez, a MALDEF attorney, carried on True's argument about INS practices: "In legal terms our claim is that they target Latino workers; they don't target white workers. It is clear that these people tailor their enforcement policy along racist lines. They use the word 'wets.' They beat witnesses. They insult them. It's in their own documents. You cannot question someone on the basis of ethnic appearance. You cannot use a racist factor. If I were in the work force, they would question me and not John True. And John's a friend of mine, but that's the way it is."

García-Rodríguez, who was born in Mexico, raised in Los Angeles, and educated at Harvard College and Boalt Law School, has a geopolitical view of the problem. "The root causes are of international concern," he said. "It requires a State Department and not an Immigration solution. The solution is not building walls or digging ditches." Nor does he see the new immigration law as a solution. "IRCA makes employers de facto immigration agents," he said. "Ultimately, IRCA could come down to a license to raid workplaces everywhere in the United States."

The legal arguments filled days in the courtroom and stacks of briefs, but it was the testimony of the witnesses and the tactics of the U.S. Attorney that made the situation clear. One witness, crying on the stand, described how INS agents sat him in a chair, handcuffed him from behind and pushed his face down toward some dogshit on the floor, saying, "That's what you are."

Another witness, also speaking through an interpreter, reported a conversation between two INS agents: "The one who grabbed me by the waist said to another short, black man that I had my papers in my house." The witness told the second agent's response in English: " 'Fucking Mexicans lie every time.' "

One of the government attorneys objected: "That statement should be stricken. There's no indication of how the agent responded, in English or Spanish. This person here is testifying with an interpreter. There's no basis what his understanding of English was back six years ago and by the fact that he's testifying here with an interpreter makes his understanding of English, if indeed it was in English, what that statement was—"

He was overruled before he could finish the argument.

The presentation of evidence went on for months. Russoniello knew it would be a difficult case to win, for there were so many witnesses against the INS. There was also a curious bit of evidence found by a paralegal in the San Francisco office of MALDEF, which would hang over every argument the U.S. Attorney made in defense of La Migra. In going through INS memorandums, the paralegal had noticed several in which agents described people as "tonks." The attorneys asked one agent after another what the word meant, but no one would answer. Finally, Agent Larry Moy, after testifying that it was a derogatory term used by some INS agents for "illegal aliens," said, "I don't know the origin of it. I've asked other people how that term came about, so I can only repeat what other people have said to me. That's why I said I don't know the origin of it." Pressed by the lawyer who was taking his deposition, Moy said, "They told me that it's the sound of a flashlight hitting somebody's head: tonk."

At the conclusion of the case against the INS, Judge Aguilar issued his findings in fact and law. There was little doubt in his mind that the plaintiffs had proved their case; he believed the testimony of the hundred witnesses. But the judge's findings were overshadowed by the judge himself. During the entire trial there had been rumors about an investigation of Judge Aguilar. He had been a criminal defense lawyer before being appointed to the federal bench. He knew unsavory people. There were rumors that he had made phone calls to help old friends, former clients; perhaps he had even tipped one of them about a wiretap. Just as his findings in the *Pearl Meadows* case were presented, Judge Robert Aguilar became the first U.S. District Court judge ever to be indicted under the federal racketeering statute, the RICO law.

The case was thrown into limbo. There was no precedent to follow; few federal judges have been indicted, and never had there been a judge indicted after hearing a year of testimony in a case to be decided by the judge alone. If the case had to begin again before another judge, it would be difficult for the civil rights groups to find the human and financial resources to present it again. It would be even more difficult to overcome the wounds of irony.

4. THE ROUND

In San Francisco, there is a round of refuge. A person may enter at any place and be connected through a network of refugees to all the rest. The round includes social workers, psychologists, lawyers, teachers, a job cooperative, and a food cooperative. Most of the refugees in the round are well-educated, young, displaced members of the middle and upper middle classes, intellectuals, the wealth of their countries now committed to helping the poor who have followed them on the road north. All of them know the terror of repression. One still uses a pseudonym because he is afraid that the Guatemalan government will take reprisals against his family. He calls himself Ernesto Segura now.

In Guatemala, he was a professor of sociology and social economy in the law school of the University of San Carlos. There were ten members of his section of the faculty. Seven were killed; two escaped to Costa Rica; Segura lives in the United States. When the government decided to kill Segura, they telephoned his house to tell him so. The little professor—slim and as sweet of face as any grown man could possibly be, just thirty years old, a social democrat—hung up the telephone and ran out into the street. The secret police were waiting for him in a white Ford Bronco.

Segura ran, and the Bronco followed, chasing him through the streets, trying to run him down. He turned down alleyways, ran between cars, but the Bronco was always there, just behind him, roaring down the streets, up on the sidewalks, trying to kill him. He kept running, turning this way and that, as if in a nightmare, through the narrowest streets, the most heavily traveled streets, until finally, in a maze of alleyways and narrow passages in an old section of the capital, he lost them. For two months he hid out, waiting for his chance to escape. He slipped into the U.S. embassy, applied for a student visa, saying that he wanted to take some courses in the United States, and went north. He carried seven suits, a book of poems, a dictionary, and a Bible that his mother pressed on him before he left.

Without a green card,[2] finding work was difficult. After nine months in the United States, he was able to write to his wife, "I am working again in a university, except before I was a professor in the law school, and now I am a janitor in the University of California."

Eventually, he was granted political asylum and working papers, which meant he could get a decent job and bring his family up from Guatemala. He became a placement counselor at the Intake Center for the San Francisco public schools, working with children who had recently arrived from Latin America, many of them refugees from El Salvador, Nicaragua, and Guatemala. Segura is the first person they meet in the system. Although he is required only to guide them into the schools, he has made himself into a referral center, an entry into the round of refuge. If they are Central Americans, he may send them to CRECE or CARECEN,[3] where they can get legal help, food, or even temporary work.

He sends some of the preschool children to the CYO (Catholic Youth Organization) in the Mission District, where they can get counseling as well as early education in a sympathetic setting. Older children are often sent to the Newcomer High School.

The experience of civil war and death squads has produced a generation of refugee children whose emotional problems cannot be fitted into the routine of education. When Raymond del Portillo founded Newcomer High

[2]Residence papers, no longer green, which permit the holder to work in the United States.
[3]Central American Refugee Committee and Central American Refugee Center

School in 1979, it was to solve cultural problems. Paul Cheng, the new principal, faces different issues. He told of a girl from a village outside San Salvador who suddenly began to hyperventilate. A teacher had brought on the attack, Cheng said, by raising his voice; it reminded the girl of the killing of her mother and her brothers and sisters.

Lilliana Rossi, who directs the CYO school, does not look like most of the other refugees. In the sunlight, her sleekly combed hair, blonde with streaks of light brown, is glamorous, a rich woman's crown. In the schoolroom office, seated across a table, she is earnest, the intellectual, the teacher of teachers; her hair is more brown than blonde; it belongs to a woman of substance. It was not always so for Lilliana Rossi in North America. She cleaned houses for three years while she tried to get residence papers.

Rossi had come from Buenos Aires, where she and her husband were university students. He had belonged to a student organization that displeased the military. She was a psychologist. "The military didn't like psychology or sociology," she said; "they associated psychology with Jewish people and the military was very anti-Jewish. Psychology to them was the work of the big Jew." They left Argentina in 1976. It took them ten years to become legal residents of the United States. "First, I got my American Express card," she said, "then I got my other green card." Although the CYO school accepts children from all backgrounds for its preschool and after-school classes, Rossi is especially interested in the refugee children from Central America, those who have been in jail or who have seen the war and the death squads. The children tell her through the paintings they make in art class what went before; they reproduce the mutilations, they draw the blood. Either completely passive or filled with high tension, they are always a problem, always different, always difficult. They fight, they hide under desks, or they may simply not be there in the room. "The children feel no relief when they arrive here," she said. "They distrust people, any figure of authority, a policeman, for example. Most immigrants are very possessive of things, pencils, jackets. Refugee children don't care. Sometimes, in winter, they come without coats or sweaters. Something has gone wrong at the level of their skin. They are dispossessed of many things, of time, of geography."

They come to her through Segura or she sends them to him. When they are in legal trouble, she and Segura send them to the lawyers of CARECEN. When they have lost their equilibrium in the world, she sends them to the Family Clinic of San Francisco General Hospital or to the Mission Therapy Clinic. When they have nothing, no food, no work, no place to stay, the entire circle of assistance turns to CRECE.

CRECE is the heart of the Central American refugee network. Its offices are housed in space rented from St. John's Lutheran School; the men's shelter is in the basement of a church; three houses are available for families. In the shelter the men sleep on mattresses laid out on the floor; when the night is over, the mattresses are piled up in a corner of the room and it becomes the food distribution center. The basement rooms smell of sweat and vegetables, onions, overripe tomatoes.

A theater of dignity takes place in the rooms. Those who come for food determine how it will be apportioned. Those who use the church decide who will clean it, when the meetings should be held, how they can appease the neighbors who complain of littered streets around the church. These are the lessons in democracy CRECE gives to people who have never known anything but oppression.

CRECE asks the women who come to the free goods distribution to contribute to the cost of running the food cooperative. They give fifty cents, a dollar, never more. What might have been charity becomes a communal effort. The women become shoppers rather than petitioners. "The milk is too warm. The tomatoes are too ripe, but I can cook them up for something."

The food has been donated, bought at wholesale, picked from the piles of rejected fruits and vegetables at the wholesale market. There are bags of rice, loaves of stale bread, bricks of lard, cartons of milk, crates of eggs, bushels of weary vegetables, sacks of beans, and orange juice. It is enough: A family can live, the children can eat. The women take the food in grocery carts, buggies, boxes, baskets. Some walk home, those who live far from the church wait for someone to drive them. It takes a long time to distribute the food, to wait for a ride. No one is pleased with the wait; no one is grateful for the gifts. Dignity requires that it be a cooperative; dignity requires complaints. A three- or four-year-old girl, in the company of her mother and grandmother, sits down with a loud sigh, "Mama, me duellen mis patas, Mama." It is the Salvadoran version of "my dogs are killing me."

CRECE serves Salvadorans and Guatemalans, a few Hondurans and Nicaraguans, but no Mexicans. The experience of Mexicans is different. Some people have been disappeared, and the Indians of the south, the Zapotecos, Mixtecos, Triquis, Chamulas, and others suffer discrimination and exploitation reminiscent of prerevolutionary Mexico, but there has been no large scale war or systematic killing in Mexico. The Mexicans are not refugees; there is a difference between fear and panic.

Years of terror have blurred many of the distinctions between the Salvadorans and the Guatemalans, even though the Guatemalans are mainly of Mayan descent and the Salvadorans are Náhuas. There are linguistic differences: *facha* instead of *biberón* for a "baby bottle," *largos* instead of *ladrones* for "thieves," *bichos* (bugs) instead of *patojos* for "children." One refugee, coming north from El Salvador with forged Guatemalan papers sold out of the Atescatempa (Guat.) city hall, had to learn to speak like a Guatemalan to appear to be in concert with his forged papers. In the meetings of EMPLEOS (jobs), the labor cooperative in San Francisco, such distinctions have faded.

Once a week the cooperative meets in the late afternoon in the beige stucco building that houses the Lutheran school and the offices of CRECE. The people gather around a long row of tables. The women sit in chairs; the men lounge on the floor around the table, leaning against the wall. The organizer of the cooperative sits at the head of the table, an Anglo volunteer sits beside him. The volunteer keeps the records and accepts the checks. The two major functions of the cooperative are to find work for the members and to cash their paychecks. Without the cooperative, the refugees cannot cash their checks, for they have no identification papers, no bank accounts. They float on the economy of the city, helpless, unable to take root; they have nothing to hold on to, no connection but the cooperative.

Children run around the room, little girls in dresses too pretty for Friday afternoon, boys in short pants and sneakers. There is no discipline; the boys shout, the little girls emit squeaks and screams. The mothers, who have worked all day at caring for other people's children, have no rules left to tell to their own; they speak with hugs and smiles, not with reprimands.

"María Esperanza, Hector Castro, Rosa María Palacios," the organizer calls the names of the members.

"Presente."

"Aquí está."

Laughter and greetings surround the table. Women embrace. Each person pays five dollars to the cooperative. Those who have not worked a full week pay less, whatever they can afford. The organizer speaks haltingly, softly. He is fat and bespectacled, and he wears a straw cowboy hat. His shirt buttons are ready to pop; rhomboid figures of brown flesh appear on the centerline over his mountainous belly. He introduces five new members, calling out their names.

In the background, two women hover over a stove, cooking tamales in a gigantic metal pot. They lift them out with a slotted spoon and serve them in red and white checked cardboard baskets. The members of the cooperative eat the tamales with plastic forks. While they eat, the organizer presents a set of rules, speaking slowly, waiting a long time between sentences. After he presents the points, there is a long silence, then the people begin to discuss their jobs, the problems of long hours, lack of transportation, children who misbehave, women who expect too much, hills, rocks, foremen, tools, the cold in the morning and the cold in the evening, the fog, the poor pay. After each speaker there is a silence, no sound but the children babbling, the little voices like water flowing over stones. The meeting proceeds in acts, an opera or a dance; the excitement and the pose. The posing is Spanish, the long silences are Indian. Although the rooms in evening grow dank and the steam of the tamales dies quickly in the chill, the order of the meeting belongs to other times, other places, tropical, ancient, memorious.

Even as the round of refuge did its work, it also failed. New kinds of problems came with the lack of employment, the uncertainty of their legal status, and the curious corruption of life in the United States. The political refugees learned an appetite for things. They studied night and pleasure; they killed their fears. In the new country, in the safe place, where they could not imagine the next moment, where the very fact of being illegal made their world-view more primitive than it had ever been in the highland villages and savannah towns, they were beset by prostitution, drugs, alcoholism, and AIDS. The peasants had become the poor.

18
THE WAR OF THE ORPHANS

Each one of you, when he goes to war to fight,
must think that he has journeyed to a marketplace
where he will find precious stones. He who does not dare go to war,
even though he be the king's son, from now on will be deprived
of all these things. He will have to wear the clothing
of the common man. And in this way his cowardice, his weak heart,
will be known by all. He will not wear cotton garments,
he will not wear feathers, he will not receive flowers,
like the great lords.

From a speech by Tlacaélel, inventor of the guerra florida, in Fray Diego Durán's
History of the Indies, Chapter XXIX, "Which treats of how the king and the nobility
decided to wage a perpetual war. . . ."

I.

After the meeting of the *communidad de base,* the young priest said, "Let's take the long way home." It was early evening. There were children in the streets of the parish. The priest greeted them with a smile or a pat on the head, *"Hola, mihijo."* Then in the black sky above us we saw the helicopter. The white light of its hunting eye appeared. A beam so powerful it seemed palpable, like a pole, played in the spaces between the adobe and stucco houses east of the dead dry riverbed. Our voices were obliterated by the stuttering bark of the engine.

We continued on through the parish. The helicopter moved away. We heard music, someone singing, perhaps over a radio. As we passed a one-room store, a man came hurrying toward us. The man and the priest greeted each other. We all stood in the light that came through the screened entrance to the store. "There are police at the church," the man said.

"How many?"

"Two cars, Father, maybe more."

"Are they going on the property?"

"I think so."

"We'd better hurry," the priest said. "Somehow they seem to know when I'm not there."

By the time we got back to the Dolores Mission the police had gone, but the gang members in the yard behind the chain-link fence were still agitated. "They were here, they came inside the fence," the gangsters said.

"Police said, 'Fuck TMC [The Mob Crowd],' and we said, 'Fuck the po-lice.'"

"They said, 'All your homeboys from TMC nothing but pussies.' We say, 'Beat us down, go ahead; we got a lot of witnesses.' That one with the mustache, he say, 'We'll get you later, we'll fuck you up.'"

All evening the police cars prowled the street in front of the mission. It was part of "strict, high profile enforcement," the policy known officially as Operation Hammer. The gangsters were nervous, worried, for they knew that sooner or later they would have to leave the church property and walk down the contorted streets past the barrackslike buildings of the projects to go home. Then, they said, the police would pick them up, take them to a nearby factory area, which was deserted at night, and "beat them down."

They had reason to be afraid, they were little more than children, but each of them had a history in the dark or in the privacy of the station house. I had heard of their problems with the police first from the young Jesuit priest, Gregory J. Boyle, who ran the .mission. We had been talking about the *comunidades de base,* his use of organizing techniques he had learned in Bolivia, when he said that one of the aims of the *comunidades* was to stop the murderous gang wars that made Aliso-Pico, the poorest parish in Los Angeles, one of the most dangerous. All that evening he had been talking to the women of the *communidad de base* and three young men from the neighborhood, among them the leaders of the East L. A. Dukes. The subject of the meeting had been the impending war between the Dukes and TMC and the constant harassment of the gang members by various police organizations.

The priest's chosen method was not to go along with the general consensus, which was to "squash" the gangsters, but to reach out to them.[1] He had started an alternative school for dropouts, virtually all of whom were gangsters. But the school was a problem because it was located on the top floor of the Mission Dolores Catholic Elementary School; the idea of boys with gang caps, tattoos, and big rags hanging out of their pockets in the school upset the parents.

---

[1] In the late 1950s, in El Paso, Texas, the Reverend Harold J. Rahm, S.J., founded Our Lady of Guadalupe Youth Center to serve the children who lived in the slums along the border.

Harold Rahm was as dedicated and even more beleaguered than Gregory Boyle. Diocesan priests appeared on television to attack Rahm's work with the pachucos. Rahm's goodwill was no match for their skill at church politics. They exerted enormous pressure on the Jesuits, who supported Rahm as long as they could, then moved him to South America. The Jesuit hierarchy has, so far, supported Boyle.

He had made the old white stucco buildings of the mission, which he had declared sanctuary[2] for undocumented workers and their families, into a place where gangsters could gather to watch television or lift weights or just "kick back." He gave them summer jobs at minimum wage, so they could learn an alternative to getting money by selling rock cocaine to wealthy Anglos who came from Beverly Hills and Westwood in their BMWs and Mercedes Benz sedans to do business with the adolescent gangsters of Aliso-Pico. In return, he insisted that they live by his rules when they were on church property: no weapons, no drugs, no alcohol. Slowly, they came to trust him, so that when he demanded an end to the use of Molotov cocktails by the gangs, they changed the rules of war.

They come to him for help in finding jobs, and he, not a lawyer, is the one they telephone when the police allow them their one call after they have been arrested. He is the only real parent most of them have, for they are the children of drug addicts, destroyed homes, single mothers who cannot manage the world around them: orphans. He speaks their language, whether it's Spanish or the argot of the gang. He knows what it means to "diss the hood" or "tag" a place or "cross out." He knows the meaning of "pleito" (problem or fight) and "placa" (name or insignia), and he understands what can happen when a boy has been taunted by the police to the point where he ties the blue war rag on his head and gets drunk and begins to dance with rage.

The gangsters call him G-Dog, a gang name; they have even awarded him the honorific, Loc (from loco, crazy). But the use of the church by the gangsters and the willingness of the priest to consider them human, to say that he loves them, has caused problems in the community: "I get this all the time," he said, "Uno de tus hijos, your kids, and then fill in the blank, spray-painted my door, stole a bike from my kid, stole all my four tires of my car, uno de tus hijos." One of his kids, they say, for they know that the gangsters belong only to each other and to the priest.

The use of the mission by the members of various allied gangs and the priest's attempts to help those gangs and others, some of whom are sworn enemies of the gangsters who use the mission, has caused a serious conflict between the police and the church. "There are," the priest said, "people who want to kick me out of this parish."

The methods of the police are calumny and harassment. If there is a dance at the mission, the police will suddenly invade the property, putting all the dancers up against the wall. If the police see a gangster in a car, they will stop the car, tear it apart looking for dope, and when they find nothing, ticket the gangster for having a broken headlight. In community meetings and casual contacts with members of the parish, the police speak against the priest. It is

---

[2]Local, state, and federal police organizations have generally accepted such declarations of sanctuary by churches in the United States.

not respectable to consider the gangsters human; that is not what the movies show, not what NBC or the *New York Times* or the Los Angeles *Times* says.

When I asked him if what he told me was really policy, a pattern of brutality and harassment or merely isolated instances, he said, "Talk to the gangsters yourself."

—

Ten gangs operate in the barrackslike buildings and contorted streets of Aliso-Pico: TMC, the East L.A. Dukes, East Coast Crips (the one black gang), Al Capone, and Clarence Street are the largest. G-Dog arranged a meeting with members of several of the gangs in a small room in the mission. I sat in a straight chair, the gangsters lounged on broken-down couches or sat on the floor. It was a curious meeting, an extraordinary display of manners by a group of adolescents. They spoke in turn, softly, explaining the language of the gang whenever they sensed that I might be lost. All were chicano but one, a well-spoken black, handsome enough to be an actor and as self-possessed as a member of Skull and Bones at Yale, who said after the meeting that he was from East Coast Crips, a branch of the countywide gang, which is allied with TMC.

This is what he and the others said. They asked that neither their names nor their gang names be used for fear of retaliation by the police.

A: They stopped us at the park, CRASH. I was walking away. He seen me; he was passing by. He jumped over the fence. He hit me here in my face. He picked me up. He grabbed my chains, threw them in the trash. He got me by my balls, started squeezing my balls, and threw me on the ground. He put me in the car, took me to the police station. The cop's name is Shepherd. It happened in April of this year. I'm sixteen. It was at night, about eight-thirty or nine. We were in the park kicking back. They took me to the Glass House [Parker Center County Jail]. They took pictures of what they did to me, then they sent me a letter saying they can't do nothing.

B: We were in the store. A cop came in and hit us, hit him [another boy sitting across the room] in the face. He hit me with the billy club under my arm. He knocked out all the [potato] chips. He bombed on him, made him fly through all the chips. Pah! he hit him like that, and I laughed, and he said, "Put your stuff down." I put it down, slow. Bah! He hit me in my jaw. I said, "Oh, man!" I stepped back. He got me from my back, put me down on the floor.

C: Once I was coming out of my house. There's an archway. We were hanging there. I came out of the house. I stopped to talk to my friend. We were riding off. They were just picking up anybody, anybody they see, beating them up and taking them to the police station. They stopped, just like that, and started beating us up. They hit my homeboy[3] in the head. Cut him up, about six stitches in his head. Came after me, Boom! hit me in my stomach. I fell. Then two other cops come, and one cop started hitting me in the head, bah! about three times. They took us to the station, checked us out. We don't have nothing. They let us go. It was last year; I was fifteen.

D: I was in the station all day, until the night [brought in as a murder suspect; someone else was later arrested and charged with the crime.] They were saying, "We got people saying it was you." And I was like, "If you got so much proof, just take me in." They started beating me up when I said that. They say, "You can't tell me what my job is." You know, socking me, slapping me in the face. This one, he said, "I'm crazy," and he jump up on the table, and he start kicking me in my face. They beat me up, then the sergeant came in. They made me sit on my hands while they asked me a question, because, you know, I was blocking them every time they hit me. They made me sit on my hands, and they started slapping me in the head. I was fifteen.

E: The guy who just left here, they took him to his house, and they told his Mom, "You let your son do this and that." And she say, "No, no," you know. White light! They socked her, and he went crazy, you know. "What did you do that to my mom?" And then they started beating him down, and his mom was like, "No, no." And they socked her again and they handcuffed her to the staircase. And then they were beating him up, and they took his mom too for interfering.

F: Once, we were coming back from the store. It was closed. And this cop and a lady cop stopped us. They hit my homeboy, they were beating him down. He had a beanie. This cop took out his gum from his mouth and picked up the beanie and put the gum on my homeboy's head, and smashed it down with the beanie.[4]

G: It's like another gang beating up our friends. One time, we were in the park, they hurt our friend bad. They like almost broke his ribs. They chased us out of the park, and they catch our friend—he's in jail right

[3]Originally a member of the same gang, now the term is more loosely used for any friend or ally.

[4]The boy with the beanie was later arrested for shooting at police cars from a rooftop. During his interrogation, the police told him G-Dog was no damn good. When the boy defended the priest, saying, "He's the only one who cares about me," the police beat him. According to the priest, they beat the boy for two hours until he confessed to the shooting. Then they read him his Miranda rights.

now—and they have him in the alley where no one can see them, and they beat him down. They beat him *down*. He couldn't even walk. We had to carry him out. They shocked him in the ear with the shocker. You know how many volts that got? We took him to his house and call the ambulance. We told them our friend got beat up, you know. They called the cops, who told us, "You guys get out of here, before we beat you up." We left, and they let him sit right there.

H: Some of the cops are prejudiced. A black get along with a black gang and a *esse*[5] get along with a *esse*, but a *esse* see a black they'll sweat him for that. A black see a *esse*, they'll sweat him. Prejudice. You know some of the cops don't like East Coast, because they like East L.A., because they're *esses*.

I: If you say you want a lawyer, they'll kick ass.

"What did you say? You want to press charges against me?" They'll take you somewhere, they'll take you to the factories and beat the shit out of you. Everybody's scared of the factories. Once they see the factories, they know what's gonna happen.

2.

The gangs are made of fraternity and ethics, not the sort of ethics that make sense to middle-class Latinos or Anglos, but ethics nevertheless. G-Dog has learned the code, and he finds much in it to admire: courage, loyalty, fraternity, dignity, democracy, devotion to home and mother, a sense of justice and fairness, and in many gangs strict rules forbidding the use of hard drugs. Seen in that light, the gangs are admirable, for they adhere to their code, but according to the rules of the middle-class Judeo-Christian world, they are criminals, worse than criminals, sociopaths.

While Latino gangs share a code of ethics, there are great variations in other aspects of culture. Some, like TMC, use black English and have alliances with national black gangs. Others, like the East L.A. Dukes and all the pachuco gangs of El Paso, speak Spanish and Caló, and say that the English-speaking gangs are nothing but *mayate*[6] lovers. Young gangsters, like those who spend time at the Dolores Mission, are very different from those who wear the tattoos of thirteen, which stands for Mexican Mafia, or fourteen, which stands for La Familia[7], the two major Latino criminal organizations in

---

[5]Any person of Mexican descent
[6]Nigger
[7]Thirteen is written as an M with a line under it turned sideways. Fourteen is more abstract,

the Southwest. Even the veterans of the Los Angeles gangs do not display the sudden, cold rages so common among gang members from El Chuco (El Paso). There is a city softness about the L.A. gangsters, a boyishness that has no place in the high desert. The Los Angeles gangsters have cultural connections to the mobsters of New York and Chicago, to the warmth of Italians and Jews, and the disorder of democracy. The pachucos hide their hierarchy in shadows; they turn cold with age.

—

Like all people at the edge of the established world, the gangsters of East L.A. and El Chuco live abruptly; they decide with a glance who is a friend and who intends to kill them; there is no time for contemplation. If they guess wrong, there will always be someone to avenge a betrayal; that is the code and the comfort of the gang. It enables them to adopt new members of the family quickly and completely; people come into the gang like newborn siblings come into the household. There is no vagueness about the relationship; it operates with binary precision—go/no go.

The tragedy of the gangster is in time. Their fate is age. The hubris of the gangster is his insistence upon the timelessness of the moment, eternal youth. Like the eagle and the serpent, the gangsters are immortal ferocities, for they do not believe in age, cannot imagine death. Theirs is still the hero's fatalism; tomorrow, next year, the year after, it will be the fatalism *abuela* put on with her widow's weeds and never put away. The tragedy is not that they will die young, but that they will not; their arms will grow thick, and their bellies will bear the burden of beer; they will live in the projects and cheer for Fernando Valenzuela and Vikki Carr. And they will have nothing to remind them of their immortal moments but a few scars and fading tattoos. If they live, and only if they live, will the war of the orphans have been in vain.

In the glow of this hubris, the victims of a failed immigration spoke of life in East L.A. It was late afternoon. The undocumented men were coming in after their day of labor, showering, playing cards, waiting for their simple meal of tortillas, cheese, and beans. A man recently released from prison tried to stop the fluid from leaking out of the transmission of his car. The police came by to taunt the gangsters, threatening them with the beatings they would administer in the dark. A girl who had recently been "jumped into" a gang walked around the churchyard showing off the bruises of the initiation. Someone was drunk; someone was stoned on marijuana. Every-

---

but one can still see the initials of La Familia in it. Latino gangs, like primitive sodalities, invent arcane signs and adopt totems. In the case of the Aliso-Pico gangs, the totems show a curious progression from the owls, wolves, and jaguars of neolithic tribes: Al Capone and the Mob have more magic than four-legged predators.

one was talking and talking, kicking, proud to be gangsters, expecting some flare of life, a starburst. This is what they said:

J: No *veteranos* in our hood. All dead or in prison.

K: I'm in charge of the guns, and I have it right here. When everybody leaves, we take those guns, we hide 'em somewhere, only we know where it's at. We don't tell everybody, because then word gets out and somebody else might just come and get it and it'll be gone.

   All the gangs are armed. Maybe they won't have a lot of them, but at least they'll have one. Some gangs have a lot of guns, some a little bit.

   Maybe they have more weapons, but we'll have more people shooting. See, like if we had ten guns and you have a war right here, everybody's gonna get a gun and shoot, but if we only have three or four, we'll just get them and shoot. Those guns, like the Uzzis, those we have for fighting. We don't have 'em for like around here.

J: We get the money for the Uzzis selling dope, selling drugs, thieving, people that work.

K: Like, whatever goods there is, it belongs to the neighborhood. Like, if I have a gun, I can't just use it and gang bang. You can't do that. The gun's for the neighborhood.

L: To tell you the truth, we don't know how to shoot. What we do is just point the gun and pull the trigger, that's it. We don't know how to shoot from far and aim at his head and hit him. We just point the gun and shoot. If we hit 'em, we hit 'em; if we don't, we don't.

   We don't practice.

K: I practiced with my cousin. We go way up there in the mountains. My cousin, he has rifles and pistols and everything. He has a 12 gauge, a 14, a 9 millimeter Uzzi, AK47, three .22 rifles, and a 9 millimeter pistol. And if I really need a pistol, I could go to my cousin and he would lend me it, but I have to give it back. But if I lend it to [N] and he gets caught, when he gets caught, you know, it's the loss of a gun, and the gun's registered to my cousin, so only the stolen guns, he'll probably lend it to me, but not the ones that are registered.

L: I could use a gun that belongs to the neighborhood. Anybody could use it. We've been using their pistols, TMC and Clarence, because we're together. If I want to borrow his pistol, I say, "Hey man, lend me your pistol. Lend it to me, I'm gonna do my work. I'm under cover."

   We know where to hide the guns; we know who to trust. We know who to talk to.

J: We don't make peace because there's one gang that's always gonna say, "Well, like if there's gonna be one gang, it's gonna be our gang."

It's like us, see, us, TMC, and like other gangs. TMC say, "Let's make one gang, but let's call it TMC." I ain't gonna want to do that because I'm from one gang, and I'm gonna say, "Why don't we make the whole gang and put it under my name." And you're gonna say, "No," and then we'll just start arguing and start a war right there.

M: When you grow up with a name, you stick with it. You know, I been in my neighborhood for like two, three years, and I ain't gonna say just like that, "All right, I'm gonna be a TMC now." I ain't gonna do that. They ain't gonna do that. Some people been in five, four, three years, whatever. They ain't gonna say, "Let's make it Clarence," because they have pride.

J: We had a shootout right here at the park where we had like seven guns. We had another shootout over here. The East L.A.s [Dukes], they tried to roll up on us. I mean, we can't let nobody else come in a car and come walking, you know, like give us their neighborhood. This our neighborhood, we got to back it up. We shot at them.

Nobody got killed. A couple people got hit. Somebody got hit in the leg. My homeboy Ozzie, you didn't see him sitting down like that. He got shot about two weeks ago. They shot him right here [abdomen right] and it ended right here [abdomen left]. They opened him up and took the bullet out. He's all stitched up.

K: West Side, it's not that they're afraid. It's just that . . . they do a lot of drugs and when they're on into drugs, say my homeboy here jump your car and they're onto drugs, they'll be all drugged out, and say, "We'll go tomorrow or later on." Then tomorrow comes and they say, "Well, we'll go some other day." You know, they'll never come back.

Like us, none of us do drugs, you know. We smoke weed, that ain't really nothin', but you know we smoke dope and we get our ass whipped by all the homeboys. All the homeboys get together. We call that court.

You go to court because you're fucked up.

Everybody is the judge, the whole gang. Like, if he was from my neighborhood and now, my neighborhood say they don't want him, we'll get him out. We'll beat him up, what everybody says. What everybody says, "We're gonna fuck him up. We're gonna fuck him up." You know, it's just what everybody says. What the majority says.

L: We make up meetings and we're all together and, you know, one of the main heads, any of them could say, "All right, the meeting is for this and that. You have to pitch in money to buy some pistols and this and that, and do you think we should kick him out of the neighborhood, yes or no? Should we jump him out? What do you guys think of that?" And they say,

"Aw, he's a punk, he's a punk. Naw, kick him out." If everybody says that, we beat his ass and get on home.

M[8]:If I went to jail and the police has contact with people in the jail, he'll give more privileges to the guys in there for them just to fuck me up. He'll have people sent after me in jail. If I make jail and you have contact with a lot of people in there, you tell them, "I'll give you money, I'll give you what you want, go fuck 'im up."

I have a lot of homeboys that happened to.

They have informants in jail.

If the police wanted to fuck you up in jail, they'll start spreading rumors about you, that you're a snitch and things like that. You're a rapist. You're a child molester. Those guys never make it in jail.

Guys inside, like if you're a molester, they imagine what if he fuck with my little kid or something. That's the way they see it, so they stick you. There's rumors all inside, rumors. They'll just put out a rumor about you. That's all it takes, one little rumor. Whatever row you're on, whatever tier you're on, it'll get to that row, and when you come out for a job, they'll get you right there.

They'll stick you with homemade shanks.[9] In there, you learn: It's like in military; you try to do knives out of scrap. That's how it is in there. You learn to make it out of anything, out of a fork. In your cell you got your bunks and they're like sheet metal, little by little they start getting it loose. They tear it off. Then they sharpen it up real good. They build shanks like that. There's a lot of ways like that.

When you're under eighteen, jail's a big kick back. I'd rather be in juvenile hall than Downey. Juvenile hall's not so bad. They just got some messed up food.

[If] A Mexican's running with a nigger gang, all the Mexicans will jump on you. But other than that, I don't think nothing will happen in juvenile hall.

Then there's firefighter's camp. You go out and fight fires. It's more like an open camp. You got a lot of privileges. You got to be minimum custody to go to those kind of places. They have trust in you, you're not in for something major. You're in for a felony, but not something big. You're not doing a lot of time. No more than three years.

The conversation went on until long after dark. Time and again, it returned to the police and beatings and prison. Everyone had been to prison, and everyone expected to go back. There was talk about money, too, but it

[8]M had just been released from more than two years in prison. He was a short, muscular man, older than the others, heavily tattooed.

[9]Knives

was not the kind of money drug dealers claim to have; instead, the gangsters were trying to borrow a dollar for a hamburger, wondering where it was possible to get enough money to buy a six-pack of beer, a bottle of beer, anything.

One of the gangsters went out and came back drunk. He didn't say where he had found the liquor, nor did he offer to share it. He wandered in and out of the conversation, he blustered, he tied his blue rag on his head, and said he was going out to fight the police. After a long time, he sat down on a bench and was quiet.

At the end of the night, when G-Dog was closing down the mission and the homeless, undocumented men and families who also found sanctuary there were going to bed, the gangsters lost their savagery. Instead of tales of war, they talked about going home. They asked the priest or me to give them a ride, to spare them the beating the police had promised that night. It was not easy for them to be open about their fears. They were children trapped in trenches, with the police behind and the opposing army before them; nothing frightened them more than being afraid. And yet they trembled. I understood then what Gregory Boyle meant when he said he loved them, because he had seen them when they were most vulnerable; he knew them as children.

When it was dark, they could no longer hide their fear. I agreed to drive two of the gangsters home. One, whose street name was Trigger, changed his mind. The other, his good friend, lived far from the mission now, and he was very nervous about both the police and the gangs that occupied the neighborhoods between his house and Aliso-Pico. On the way we talked about school and drugs and G-Dog. There was no adult, other than G-Dog and his own mother, whom he trusted.

He talked easily; his grammar was suddenly better than it had been in the churchyard, and he did not use so much slang. He was quick and his manners were good—more than good, they had become criollo, aristocratic. But he was still a gangster; it was his only point of reference. We talked of many things, but every topic led him back to G-Dog. The priest was hero and confessor, the only leader in the revolution of the gangsters against the life of the ghetto. Gregory Boyle, the big, burly Jesuit, with tiny eyeglasses and a full beard and his sweet Jesus smile, was all that stood between the boy and savagery.

When we arrived at his parents' house, a bungalow on a decent street, far from the projects, the gangster thanked me for the ride, and put out his hand in the most manly way. "My name is Fernando," he said, with great formality, and paused, "but they call me Gumby."

3.

In the meeting of the *communidad de base*, G-Dog had spent part of the time in the kitchen of the little project apartment talking to Smiley, one of the East L.A. Dukes. He was a big, handsome kid in his early twenties, as big as the priest, but slimmer, athletic. When he talked to the priest, he stood very straight, as if he were in church or in the principal's office. He asked for help; he needed a job. G-Dog said he would find him a job somewhere, doing something, he did not know what. In return, he asked for peace in the parish; if not peace, a truce, no more shootings, no more wars. It had taken a long time for the priest and the women of the *communidad* to bring the process this far: The leader of the East L.A. Dukes and two of his lieutenants had agreed to come to the meeting. The gangsters sat together, all three of them on one overstuffed armchair, posing for the women who sat in a circle around the room, the young women and the mothers and grandmothers, the brave ones of the parish.

The evening had been warm. Attendance at the meeting was good; for once, the issue seemed more important than the *telenovelas*, which G-Dog said made forming *communidades* so much more difficult in the United States than in Bolivia. The women passed out sponge cake and cold milk before the priest asked one of them to begin with a prayer. Then we all held hands and were good together, and brave, even the Hang Out Girls and the East L.A. Dukes. Flaco, who sat on the arm of the overstuffed chair, was the least comfortable. He turned his baseball cap around and around again and again. He said nothing. His leader said nothing. Only the women spoke. And now and then the priest.

Many wars were discussed: the war between the Dukes and TMC/Clarence/East Coast, the war between the Housing Authority and the gangsters, and the war between the gangsters and the residents of the parish. The purpose of the meeting in Aliso-Pico was not so different from the meetings Gregory Boyle had organized in Bolivia: The people sought peace, a little security, education for their children, a reason to be hopeful, and at the very least, enough to eat. The real difference was that men did not come to the meetings in Aliso-Pico. The women said it was because the men were cowards; they did not admit that in many families there were no men, which is the sadness of the barrio, the secret shame.

In the meeting no one spoke out of turn, not even the Hang Out Girls in their theatrical eyemakeup and tight pants, not even the woman with curlers and a croaking voice or the woman with the pinched face and rimless eyeglasses or the gently insistent hostess. It was a mannerly meeting, a gathering of diplomats. Perhaps it was the gravity of the issue that calmed and ordered the meeting; the subject after all was war, and in war people are killed.

Throughout the whole of the meeting, the Dukes lounged on the chair. They did not speak. Their pose was almost comic; they were crowded together, so much like schoolboys. Smiley wore pants that ended at midcalf, but without the high stockings that complete the baseball player's uniform. Flaco turned his hat round and round. All of the women stared at the young men on the overstuffed chair; they admired them, they adored them, they feared them, and they feared for them. It was an ancient assignation, the women and the warriors, perpetual accomplices; it was a room of love and mourning; the future had been divined.

———

A truce, if it can be made, cannot last long in East L.A. With no change in the social or economic situation in the ghetto and increasing pressure from the police, the gangsters tear each other apart, like soldiers fighting in their bloody trenches. They cannot run; they cannot win. The gangsters are a metaphor, the work of race and poverty turned quick and clear. It is a valiant life, with flashes of glory, like the life of the bull bred for the spectacle of the ring. The gangsters know the grind of ghetto life, the slow death every Latino fears. They prefer the suddenness, death before the beer belly or the junkie's collapsing veins. They make a deal with death; it is better than loneliness, food stamps, or the scorn of the gringos. A gangster can be feared, hated, but not despised. Killers do not take welfare; they are somebody, if only for a moment; homeboys, shooting stars, and then the dark.

One evening in autumn, the boy who had come to our meeting to complain about the police, a thin boy with the implication of a mustache, the boy who had stayed late in the churchyard to talk about guns, who knew all about guns, who said he rode in the front passenger's seat when a drive-by shooting was done, had a premonition. Trigger told his homeboys that he knew he was going to die. Before the night was over, he was murdered.

In response to the killing, police picked up members of the gang Trigger had belonged to, handcuffed them, and told them to say, "Fuck Trigger." It was all Captain Medina's police knew how to do, beat somebody, humiliate somebody. No one was ever charged with the murder.

It was no secret, not from anyone but the police: The East L.A. Dukes had done it. TMC and Clarence Street claimed they knew who had used the gun. They promised revenge.

As G-Dog said, with the resignation of a man used to comforting the widows of this war of the orphans, "It was *on.*" The killing of Trigger was to lead to many shootings the following year. In 1990, Greg Boyle buried ten gangsters, all children from his parish. Another was paralyzed, and the beatings by the police, mostly from Hollenbeck Station, which had become more brutal under the administration of Captain Bob Medina, increased. Of the ten boys at our original meeting, Trigger had been killed and two others had been severely beaten by the police, dragged from an alleyway to the deserted factory area to Hollenbeck Station, punched and kicked at every stop along the way until their faces were bruised and their teeth were broken.

Five hundred people from the community, both children and their parents, had gathered in the mission to protest the brutality of Medina's police, not only to gangsters, but to any Latino teenager they chose to humiliate: college kids, working people, visitors from outside the projects. Members of Neighborhood Watch told of metro police stopping high-school students, ordinary students, not gangsters, and forcing them to kneel in the street with their hands behind them, while the police shamed and taunted them. And Medina, who said he had once been a member of the Department of Internal Affairs, made only one effort to deal with the problem of police brutality in his jurisdiction: He went to Reverend Boyle's Provincial and tried to get him to remove G-Dog from his post.

In March of 1990, TMC and its allies took revenge for the killing of Trigger: a shooter, working alone, put a bullet through Flaco's head. The rumor was that Tiny, the young black who was liaison between the Crips and TMC, had done it; the police were hunting him. If anyone in East L.A. could elude the police and the Dukes, it was Tiny, the one who was always described by adults as "that good-looking boy." G-Dog said he came in and out of the mission in an almost ghostly way. He might be talking to you one moment, and when you looked around, suddenly, he was gone.

There was something of the romantic about Tiny, who spoke with such pride of being a member of the Crips. And there was also a stronger sense of homelessness about him than any of the others. He had a sister, but no one else. He was black, but he lived among Latinos. He described himself as a go-between, a salesman of sorts, a nowhere man. When he telephoned the priest, he said he knew they were looking for him. G-Dog asked him to give himself up. Tiny said he would think about it. Before the year was out, he would give himself up, wait a long time in prison, and then get off, only to be picked up by Captain Medina's police and dragged from place to place in the ghetto night, beaten in every darkness, "that good-looking boy" beaten but not charged, just beaten.

It was not such a good year for Smiley, the big kid who liked to wear baseball pants; he was shot, hit with so many bullets they did not think he would survive. He was left paralyzed. Chopper and his lady Bambi were killed. And others: Following the killing of Trigger one of the Hang Out Girls made a nasty remark about him in the churchyard after his funeral. A dozen girls attacked her. Even Gumby, the dead boy's close friend, threw a punch.

The girl pointed him out to the police, and Gumby went to jail. One after another, the gangsters went down, killed, beaten, or imprisoned. TMC thought it would be best for the priest if they severed their connection with him; Medina had warned them that he would have the priest removed if he continued to work with the gangsters. After the gang moved away from the mission, they went back to slanging.[10] It was his worst year, G-Dog said: He had never buried so many in all his five years in the mission; he had never seen so many shootings or so many beatings by the police.

On the afternoon of the mass for Flaco, the Reverend Gregory Boyle, S.J., sent word out into the community that members of the gangs opposed to the East L.A. Dukes, mainly TMC and Clarence, were not to show themselves in the area around the mission during the mass, which was scheduled for seven-thirty. It was certain that the East L.A. Dukes would come to the mass heavily armed, prepared for an attack by TMC or Clarence, ready to carry the war into the next phase. G-Dog was worried; the mass could erupt into a pitched battle. He went through the neighborhood on his bicycle, warning the gangsters to be out of the projects before seven o'clock, telling them not to "diss"[11] Flaco now that he was dead.

In the early afternoon, a curious scene took place on the steps of the church. Three of the gangsters discussed the death of Flaco. One proposed disrupting the mass. He said of Flaco, "May he rest in pain." Another argued that the East L.A. Dukes hadn't "dissed" Trigger, so they should not "diss" Flaco. The conversation drifted to the theory of gang banging. The war will go on forever, they agreed, "until all of us are killed or all of them, but it will be all of them.

"East L.A. can't shoot. They put the gun right to your head, like this [he made his finger into a gun and pointed it at my head], and the bullet goes over here [he looked away]. The war is to the death. It never stops. Right now, up there [he pointed heavenward] Trigger is beating up Flaco, beating the shit out of him."

—

The people began to gather around the church a few minutes after seven. They stood on the steps; they gathered on the sidewalk. CRASH cars arrived and cars filled with social workers and parole officers and gang intervention workers, the brutal and the bumbling, the whole bureaucracy, everyone who had failed to prevent the killings. Then the members of the parish arrived. The older ones came first, poor people dressed in their best clothing, which was not much better than housedresses, an occasional skirt and blouse, only

[10]Selling cocaine
[11]Show disrespect, insult

one or two women in real dresses, and all the men in jackets and polyester pants, a few with neckties, not many. Not many men came to the mass, mostly women, some of them crying, heavy women, older women, with great arms and full faces, eyes that could not bear the darkness of another son of the neighborhood buried.

The gangsters came later, the little ones, the termites, the *vatos locos,* and even the *veteranos,* many of them with wives and children, grown men, the few who had escaped death or prison, citizens now, but gangsters still. If they were needed, they seemed to say, if the young ones needed them, they were not afraid; they were the real toughs, the survivors, the beer bellies, the uncles of war.

The Hang Out Girls arrived after the families. Each of them wearing tight pants or jeans, high heels, and a black sweat shirt with the words

In Memory of
Hector
Rest in Peace

embroidered on the back in white Old English letters.

The girls wore heavy makeup, perfume, and the hairdo of the moment, the thick, rich, jet black hair teased into a kind of pompadour in the front. The Hang Out Girls distributed blue and white and yellow papers on which they had written poems and prayers and sentiments about the dead boy. One had an angelic floral arrangement drawn on it dominated by a strangely feminine angel emerging from a chrysalis. It said:

Always
'n'
Forever

In memory of the
  homeboy
Hector (Flaco)
R.I.P.

> To the lord
> up above we send
> you these prayers for
> Hector
>
> Homeboy, they took you away
> Each morning we hope to see u
> Coming down the neighborhood
> Talking with our friends. Until

> One day we all knew you
> Returned to God's world . . .
>
> Love eternally . . .
>
> Hang Out Girls
> Droopy & Traviesa

Another had a reproduction of a drawing of Flaco and a prayer reminiscent of a poem written in Náhuatl by Nezahualcóyotl, the king of Texcoco:

> *Let me do good now.*
>
> *I shall pass through this world but once.*
> *Any good that I can do, or any kindness that*
> *I can show to any human being, let me not*
> *Defer or neglect it, for I shall not pass*
> *This way again.*
> *Let me rest in peace.*

A third contained a letter, which Hector's girlfriend had intended to read, but when she took her place at the pulpit, she broke down and no words came out.

The gangsters were all there now. Termites strutting, moving in a well-defined, almost military line into their pews. *Vatos locos* in hairnets and shirts buttoned only at the collar, their pants hanging low, gangsters in full regalia. A boy on crutches, struggling for every step, but still a gangster, with a gangster's shirt and net over his hair, pulled himself into a pew. One boy in the last pew had difficulty sitting comfortably because the gun tucked into the front of his pants dug into his gut and his groin. He was relieved whenever he had either to stand or kneel.

There was a hair show: Some left their nets on, adjusting them carefully over their ears, fidgeting with them during the service; others whipped off the nets just before the mass began, as if they were removing a hat in respect to the deity. There were fat gangsters with shaved heads. There were rock and roll haircuts, long in the back and crewcut on top. Everywhere there was hair; the church reeked of hair oil.

Father Boyle appeared, wearing huaraches, his white cassock covered with a brilliantly colored poncho, long, like a jorongo, and hooded. He spoke but briefly in his eulogy of Flaco, who he said often made him laugh, a boy he had liked. The priest did not say that Hector was married to a drug addict or that his widow wanted him buried far from the projects, in a secret place, where his homeboys would not find him. Nor did he say that this death was the work of poverty; everyone knew. He said that if the gangsters in attendance were really down for Flaco they would not further the war, for he knew that war was on the mind of every gangster in the church.

Yet, as if to goad the gangsters to killing, to remind them of their duty to vengeance, the girls wore their highest heels and tightest pants and their new black sweatshirts with the words, In Memory of Hector, R.I.P. embroidered on the back.

The priest spoke of peace, but he might as well have spoken of war, for the service he delivered was not the service they heard; this was instead an exhortation in the minds of the attending children, this was instead a ritual of death and vengeance. No one in the room was satisfied. The gangsters stood in the back of the church while the mother of their slain companion, their homeboy, screamed in the hoarse tones of grief. And everywhere the signs on the backs of the girls, taunting, and every girl wearing on the front of her sweatshirt her name and the name of the slain boy, the dead lover, the dream lover, the one so down for them he gave his life.

In the back of the church, halfway out the door, holding the hands of their children, momentarily uxorious, the old men stood, the *veteranos,* the aged knights once again in armor, the defenders of the people, the roaring old men of the tribe, the seasoned warriors, the survivors come to defend the children and the women who were all betrothed now to Hector, the martyred knight of First Street.

There was, in the silence, a sound of trumpets and drums; and everywhere, in all of Aliso-Pico, people noticed the ancient odor of the flowers of war.

19

THE COUNTRY MOUSE AND THE CITY MOUSE

We're not undocumented people; we're from here. We have no work, 60 percent of the people are unemployed. Why is the government spending money to discover the moon, which is a piece of stone in the sky?
                                                                    Carmen Anaya

I. COLONIAS

LAS MILPAS

Perhaps the most eminent person who lives in the colonias[1] on the U.S. side along the Mexican border, surely the most dramatic, is a seventy-year-old woman, who was a schoolteacher in Mexico some generations ago, Carmen Anaya. She is an accomplished orator, a woman whose voice modulates from a whisper to a rage of indignation in the space of a sentence. Mrs. Anaya, who runs the grocery store in Colonia Las Milpas on the main road south toward the border from Pharr, Texas, does not offer many theories; she has a narrator's sense of history. Sitting in the comfortable house she and her husband have built at the side of the grocery store, surrounded by photographs that tell the successes of her children, speaking simply, with a schoolteacher's diction, she tells everything about the tragedy of the Colonia Las Milpas in a single story:

"There was a heavy rain. Because we have no drainage and no sewers, there was no place for the water to go. It came up to the houses, which were level with the street. The casitas (outhouses) were flooded. The worms and the black water came out. The worms crawled up the walls of the houses to the windows.

[1]Unincorporated settlements, usually with no formal government and no services

298

"The children walked and played in the black water. The filth caused them to get sick, rashes broke out on their skin.

"When I saw this, I went to Pharr and told the people who are responsible for sewers and drains to come and see what had happened. When they arrived, I said to them, 'Get into it. Get out of your cars and put yourself in it.'

"One showed me his boots, his fine new boots. He said that he did not want to walk in the filth with his fine new boots. He cared more for his boots than for the children."

SAN YSIDRO

At the far end of the colonia, which still has no drainage system or running water more than ten years after the developer sold the first lots there, a group of abandoned U.S. Army supply shacks rots. The insects of the high desert invaded them decades ago, eating the wood, laying eggs, multiplying over hundreds of generations.

The developer of the colonia, near Socorro, Texas, in the valley east of El Paso, uses the wooden structures to build cheap housing. He moves one of the shacks onto a lot in his development, covers the outside with brick, installs wiring for electricity and plumbing for the water that has not yet arrived, covers the walls with sheetrock, paints the insides, and sells the finished product for $32,000.

When the new owners move in, they find themselves living in a nightmare. The insect eggs, coddled between the brick and sheetrock, hatch, and the termites, spiders, roaches, silverfish, and centipedes, attracted by the scent of food, pass through the seams and outlets in the walls into the houses. No exterminator, no amount of insecticide can stem the invasion.

San Ysidro is one of hundreds of colonias that were established along the Mexican border during the 1980s. Nearly two hundred thousand people live in them, almost always without drainage systems, sewers, or running water. Few people outside the Third World live in such conditions; were the colonias not in the United States, the sanitary conditions would make them eligible for aid from the World Health Organization.

The colonia is a peasant's dream gone wrong, an expression of the will of landless people to have some piece of the earth to call their own. It was this hunger for land that gave rise to the Mexican Revolution of 1910, with its promise of "land and liberty." During his presidency (1934–1940) Lázaro Cárdenas actually distributed huge amounts of land to Mexican peasants, who were then organized into *ejidos* or cooperatives. Twenty years later, most of the land had reverted back to large landowners, and Mexicans again tried to take it back. This time, there was no revolution, but people known as *paracaidistas*[2] established small communities which they formed into colonias or new developments all over Mexico. Some of the colonias were extraordinarily poor even by Third World standards. People built dwellings of corrugated metal, tin cans, or cardboard, sometimes called *jacales,*[3] but rarely even of that quality. They had no sanitation, no running water, and no electricity.

The same urge can be seen in New York City, where Puerto Ricans have taken over the empty lots set aside by the city for growing flowers or vegetables. They construct small shacks, which they call *casitas,*[4] and turn them into kitchens, clubhouses, and even living quarters. Some are rudimentary, made of pieces of wood, metal, and brick found at construction or demolition sites; others are finely fitted out, with pits for roasting suckling pigs, pens for rabbits, chicken houses, picnic tables, refrigerators, everything necessary to a comfortable social club. The one thing common to all of the *casitas* is the existence of farm animals (every one has a rooster that disturbs the neighbors), for the purpose of the *casita* is to recreate the life of one small town or village; it embodies that sense of place, of rootedness, which a tenement apartment can never have.

Latinos are not like immigrants from Germany or Northern Italy or the great cities of Asia. They are mainly country people. Some may have stopped over for a decade or a generation in a Latin American city, but many saw their first airplanes and tall buildings on their way to the United States. At the bus stations in Ciudad Juárez and Tijuana the people coming north still step off the second-class buses carrying their blankets and wearing huaraches and straw hats. They go directly to big cities, where the security and stability of owning land is beyond their dreams, until a developer offers them a piece of land or an unfinished house, some place that a man who is good with his hands can turn into a home. If they owned such a place, the revolution in their lives would be complete; they would have accomplished the full turn of immigration. Thus, the lambs of hope are delivered into the hands of the swindlers.

Most of those who live in the colonias are U.S. citizens or legal residents, landowners now, people who saved their money, made down payments, and built houses, believing that the improvements promised by the developers would be installed soon. But no drains were built, no sewers installed; the cesspools contaminated the ground water, making the wells useless. Potable

---

[2]Literally, parachutists, a colorful description of the squatters who seemed to drop down out of the sky onto the land

[3]An adobe shack, usually with a roof made of branches or thatch

[4]Not to be confused with the Mexican use of the word *casita,* which means outhouse, or *casa chica,* which means the house in which a kept woman lives.

water had to be trucked in. People who had struggled to join the working class, immigrants, sank. The world they had left when they came to the United States was thrust upon them again; the contract they had negotiated with the new country had been breached.

Like most colonias, San Ysidro was once farmland, but as the nearby city grew, the owners of the land decided they could make more money by selling it. A speculator bought them out for very little money, subdivided the land, and began selling it to renters, people who dreamed of one day owning a "home" and were willing to build it themselves. They were promised that the land would be improved within a short time, but no exact date was given, at least not in writing. Ten years later, no one can find any clear evidence of how much time was to have elapsed, although six months seems to have been implied. Since government at all levels in Texas, especially along the border, was generally incompetent, often corrupt,[5] and unfailingly racist, the speculators swindled their Mexican-American customers with impunity. No one monitored the subdivisions, no one enforced the promises of water, drainage, and sewerage; the operating rule of the local and state officials was, as it had always been, caveat chicano. It is said in El Paso County that the county judge didn't learn about conditions in the colonias until he read about them in *Life* magazine.

For most of the people in El Paso the price of the land was several thousand dollars, usually all the money they had in the bank, and a monthly payment to boot. They couldn't afford to wait until the land was improved. Some had been forced out of their homes through a helter-skelter rehabilitation program in the tenement area along the border. Others could not afford to rent a place in town and make payments on their land in the colonia. They bought or rented old trailers or put up makeshift houses of one kind or another and moved in.

Since sewerage, drainage, and electricity were expected soon, many people dug wells for water, but did not spend $1,000 or $1,500 to install a proper septic tank; they merely built *casitas* (outhouses) and dug cesspools. Chemicals and waste materials began leaching into the water supply under the clay. Well water was quickly contaminated. Worse, the children began playing in the waste water in open ditches near the river. Some came down with diphtheria. The most common problems were skin rashes, but the fear of every person who studies the sanitary conditions in the colonias is cholera. The conditions are right. Only luck has spared them so far.

---

[5]For example, Woodrow Bean, former El Paso County judge and chief executive, who once told me, "Son, in El Paso County I am the Democratic party," was convicted of evading state and federal income taxes over many years. Woody, as he was known, was a direct descendant of the Judge Roy Bean who was the "only law west of the Pecos."

If everything had gone wrong, people wouldn't have stayed, but a few surface aspects of modern civilization came about almost immediately. There was electricity in San Ysidro a few months after the first plots of land were sold, but there are still no street lights ten years later. Something like roads and streets were marked off with bulldozers, but after ten years there are no paved roads. In the spring, when the winds blow hard, tumbleweed as big as sheep roll down the streets, the grit strips the paint off cars, and the dust is so thick that it is dangerous to drive there, because another car, especially a white or tan one, can't be seen until it's only twenty feet away.

The astonishing thing about the colonias is that many of the houses no longer look crude or poor. The owners have worked on them, living in trailers or shacks while they built a more substantial house, usually of brick or cement block, sometimes of adobe.

In San Ysidro, one of the nicest houses—even though it is still under construction—belongs to Amadeo and Lorenza Contreras, who began working on it shortly after they bought their land in 1983. At first they put up a very simple structure: one room, with cooking and toilet facilities and a place to eat and sleep.

While they lived in the one-room structure, Amadeo Contreras worked on the house. Before he laid the foundation, he brought in sand and dirt to raise the level of the ground above the road in the event of heavy rains. His wife, a lively, plump woman, with a firm voice, an iron will, and a wardrobe chosen from the stocks of her employer, J.C. Penney, directed the size and shape of the rooms.

Contreras, who had retired from the trailer fabricating plant down the road after seventeen years as a maintenance man, was sixty-three years old when they started the work, or rather when he started the work and she started giving directions. The house he has been building for more than half a decade now has an entry hall, with a laundry room off to the right, a full bath to the left and a living room and large picture window dead ahead. The living room is small and cozy and thoroughly furnished. There are two huge bedrooms—one for Lorenza and Amadeo and one for their son who is a student at MIT—each with a full bath, in one wing of the house. The kitchen, which will occupy most of the other wing, is not yet begun; Lorenza Contreras still cooks in the one-room house out in the back.

With all the careful work in the house, which has the look and feel of a Sunday real estate section publicity story, there is still no water. They buy drinking water in plastic bottles; for bathing they use well water, which is polluted, and then rinse themselves in water they bring in by truck and keep in large drums.

Mary Lou "Mura" Perrez, who lives with her three children in a trailer in San Ysidro, has done less well than the Contreras family. She earns only $95 a week for straightening up the chairs and mopping the floors in three bingo halls, two restaurants, and several offices every night. During the day, she sells Tupperware, but it is not easy for her, because the two old cars that sit in front of her trailer often break down. In the afternoon, she takes care of her children, all of whom have suffered severe skin problems because of the contaminated water. By the end of the week she is too tired to do anything in her house.

She has three dogs, a cat, and a goose. Geese are a very good alarm system, honking whenever a stranger comes by and biting whoever gets too close, but they are vulnerable to dogs. At one time Mary Lou had many geese, but the neighborhood dogs got to all but the lone honker.

Mary Lou was one of the first people in the colonia to get involved with EPISO (El Paso Interreligious Sponsoring Organization), one of the Industrial Areas Foundation (IAF)[6] groups operating in Texas. A street in the colonia, Mura, is named after Mary Lou. Another is named for a priest who worked with the organization, and one is simply called EPISO.

The colonias along the border have had no champion but IAF. In Pharr, where Carmen Anaya lives, Valley Interfaith, organized by a nun, fights for water, drainage, and sewerage in the colonias. EPISO, where Sister Mary Beth Larkin is the organizer, makes the same demands. After nearly ten years, they have had some success. Government money has been allocated to provide services to the colonias, but it has been caught in bureaucratic bungling at the state and county levels. A year after the money was allocated, no work had begun. Sooner or later, there will be heavy rain in the desert, and the water will run through Colonia San Ysidro in a flood. Then the adobe bricks at the base of many of the houses will turn to mud again, and some of the walls will collapse. The cesspools will overflow, and the horrors of Las Milpas will be repeated in San Ysidro.

[6]A community organizing group founded in Chicago by Saul Alinsky, the IAF sponsors groups in twenty cities, from New York to Los Angeles. Ernesto Cortés, Jr., who works out of Austin, supervises organizations in San Antonio, Houston, El Paso, and the Valley. Every IAF organization has a different name and a different agenda. IAF provides each community with an organizer who has no executive or legislative power in the organization. The Metropolitan Organization (TMO) in Houston, Communities Organized to Provide Services (COPS) in San Antonio, and the other IAF groups in Texas are all connected with, organized through, and dependent upon the emotional and institutional support of the Roman Catholic Church, with the exception of TMO, which works through black Protestant churches in the huge Houston black community.

2. EL LABOR

FLORIDA CITY, THE MIGRANT CAMP

A man in his early fifties lies on a brown couch. His leg is encased in a temporary cast, and he has a set of aluminum crutches beside him.

The man's face is thin, pinched. He wears eyeglasses. His mouth expresses the soured delicacy of an aging clerk.

His daughter stands in the kitchen corner of the trailer between the table and the sink. Her name is Laura, and she laughs in modesty. She makes *chalupas,* which she sets out on the round table.

Outside the trailer dogs bark in the darkness.

The trailer has green carpeting on the outdoor steps. Inside it is plain, linoleum and imitation pine.

The girl takes a gallon of milk from the refrigerator and pours a glassful for her youngest brother.

THE VALLEY, TEXAS

On the first day that the woman and her daughter work together *en el labor* there is no shade.

The sandy soil sucks at their feet. They walk like insects wearing dresses, bent over, lifting their legs high to free their feet from the sand.

In the distance there is a tree. The girl tells her mother she is having a dream of sitting under the tree.

THE VALLEY, CALIFORNIA

In *el labor* a man is dreaming:
The *sancho*[7] enters her bedroom.
He has the contractor's face.
A head of lettuce.

[7]The lover of an adulterous woman

The three incidents: The man in Florida City had been run over by a farm machine while picking tomatoes. He told me he had little money and was paid no workmen's compensation. He and his children were living on a few dollars he had saved and some help they received through the Centro Campesino.

A woman in South Texas told me of the first day her daughter worked with her in the fields. Tears came into her eyes as she remembered.

Several men have told me about thinking of the sancho while working in the fields. The

In the 1930s John Steinbeck made heroes of the white Protestants who lost their lands in Oklahoma and Kansas and came through the dust to work the farms of California. He wrote of how they tried to form a union and were beaten down; Woody Guthrie sang of how they tried and were beaten down. Steinbeck's heroes could not win out over the power of the big farm owners; they could not organize in the rich, brutal fields of the San Joaquin Valley. That task waited for César Chávez, a man who knew the dust bowl and the hard life of a farmworker during the Depression, to join the Community Service Organization and learn the organizing ideas of Saul Alinsky.[8] In 1962, ten years after he had started working with the CSO, Chávez left to start the National Farm Workers Association, *La Causa*, which became the United Farm Workers Union.

The hunger strikes of César Chávez made him an American Ghandi. Nothing Steinbeck wrote, nothing Woody Guthrie sang prepared the world for the unbreakable will, the brown skin, and the beautiful, suffered face of César Chávez.

But Chávez could not teach the world outside the vineyards and fields of agrarian America how it was to pick lettuce in California or strawberries in Michigan or tomatoes in Florida. Even he could not convey the life of children on the road and in the migrant camps, for farmwork happens over time; nothing but the days can explain the burden of the days as nothing but the sun can explain its heat. In the mythology of America there is no freer, happier place than the open road, no more romantic moment than the first touch of a human hand to a strawberry weighted with sweetness.

In the real world there is nothing romantic about the place known as *el labor*. The work is so hard, the pay so poor, and the conditions so abominable that the fathers of Mexican-American children in the valley towns of California and Texas often urge their sons or daughters to work for a day, a week, even a summer in the fields so that they will know the alternative to education.

---

myth of the labor contractor as sancho is that he tells the wife her husband will get no more work if she refuses to sleep with him. The man who told me about cutting off the heads of lettuce while thinking of the sancho giggled when he remembered the incident.

[8]Alinsky's ideas and the Industrial Areas Foundation he began figure in many of the cooperative efforts of Mexican-Americans to take control of their lives.

The chain of effects following on Alinsky's work is astonishing: From Alinsky to Fred Ross and the CSO, then to Chávez and the UFW, for whom Joaquín Avila, a student at Yale, organized boycotts. Avila became the president of MALDEF and later was instrumental in achieving redistricting rules that permitted Latinos to be elected to such offices as the Los Angeles County Board of Supervisors. Thus, the election of the first Mexican-American to the county board in more than a hundred years can be credited as much to the organizing ideas of Saul Alinsky as to the character and ambition of the candidate.

If a man or a woman or a child is injured in the fields, there is no help beyond emergency treatment. Unless the farmworker belongs to the union, there is usually no hospitalization insurance,[9] no workmen's compensation, nothing. And there will be no pay for the days of work lost; fieldwork is piecework—counted by the bucket or the bale.

There is decent housing for farmworkers in a few places, built by the Department of Housing and Urban Development (HUD) or by the state in California, but most housing is wretched—shacks, trailers, people living in their trucks and cars. Even in places where the housing is decent, the management is often corrupt; they say it takes a bribe of about five hundred dollars to get one of the good, permanent HUD houses near the fields south of Homestead, Florida.

In the town of Homestead itself, the establishment does not recognize the existence of the migrants; they keep to their own places, out of sight of the main shopping area. The local newspaper, the *South Dade News Leader,* is so racist that it doesn't even report athletic successes by hometown Latinos. There were no Latino reporters on the paper in 1989, even though 60 percent of the town and 30 percent of its readership is Latino. According to Arturo López, who works for a farm worker coalition in South Dade County, when a float built by Mexican-Americans won first prize in a parade held in Homestead in 1987, the next day the *News Leader* published photographs of only the second, third, and fourth prize winners.

The camps themselves are wild places, home to children in the afternoon, lovers in the early evening, gamblers in the night. No police patrol the camps; the law is what a man can do for himself. It is a good idea to have friends.

At the entrance to the Florida City camp, George Garza of the Centro Campesino and I stopped to buy a taco from the little trailer set up there. Four men sat on folding chairs around a card table in front of the stand. They ate what looked like chile verde or some other Tex-Mex stew, picking up the food with tortillas de maize, Indian style, and washing it down with beer. Three were very dark and thick, crude men with sweat-shined cheeks; they deferred to the fourth man, whose front teeth were missing. Garza, who has the manners of a rich man or an Indian, introduced us. The men around the card table smiled like sharks.

Garza is a big man, a square-jawed Mejicano in cowboy boots, a sheriff's hat, and dark glasses that he wears day and night. He looks like the hero of a

---

[9]Even people who work on land in Florida owned by large U.S. insurance companies have no accident insurance. I telephoned the Metropolitan Life Insurance Company four times, asking them to confirm or deny information that the company owned farmland worked by migrants in Florida, but got no answer.

Mexican cowboy movie until he smiles, showing a confusion of teeth. Garza said his parents sent him to work in the fields when he dropped out of college, a punishment of sorts, perhaps a lesson in the value of education. He worked in the fields off and on for the next eleven years, until he got married and stopped drinking. Along the way, he had met the men who sat at the table.

We got some tacos from the trailer-restaurant and ate them standing up. The men at the table asked where I was from and what I was doing in the camp. They did not speak to Garza and he did not speak to them.

"You're from El Paso," the toothless one said; "you must be a pachuco." He used the familiar, which is an insult when a Mexican addresses a stranger.

"*No. Soy escritor,*" I answered. *Y tú?*"

The one next to him was fat. He wore a white shirt open almost to the waist. A crucifix hung between his breasts, which were dark and sweaty; he had cleavage, like a woman. He curled his fingers into fists. He showed the heavy rings, the scarred knuckles.

I looked back at Garza. He had stepped away, out of the circle of hard light around the trailer, into the beginning of the night. It was time to go.

As we drove the narrow farm roads north, Garza talked about the men around the card table. The toothless one was a Martínez, one of the sons of the most notorious labor contractor in South Florida. The father prides himself on being a tough guy, a pitiless enforcer. His three sons, each with an entourage of thugs, do his work. One of the sons is also a pimp, who keeps a stable of three girls: a Mexican, an Indian, and an Anglo. When Garza was still drinking and working in the fields, one of the girls, the Indian, took a shine to him. "She liked me because I was polite to her," he said. "She wanted to go and live with me. When the Martínez brothers saw this, the three of them confronted me and threatened to beat me to death. We were in a bar and the owner stopped the fight, or they would have done it."

He and the Martínez family had been enemies since then. But Garza hates all contractors. "They're thieves," he said; "they get a dollar five a bucket for tomatoes, and they pay the farmworkers forty cents. The contractors say it's for bookkeeping, taxes, social security, workmen's comp., health insurance, but they don't pay anything; they're just thieves." The problem for the workers is that the owners of the farms prefer using the contractors to dealing directly with the farmworkers, because it absolves the owners of any legal responsibility as employers.

The contractor system functions as yet another impediment to organizing farmworkers. The big contractors are brutal defenders of the system that has made them rich. They foment tensions among the various ethnic groups—Puerto Ricans, Nicaraguans, Haitians, not just Mexicans—who work in the fields, making it impossible for a union organizer to pull the workers together. And if the organizer should begin to have some success, the contractors can take care of that too, with fists and knives.

When the contractor system began, the people who have now become the villains of the system were often its heroes. The first contractors were people who saved enough money to buy a truck, then used it to help their friends and neighbors to travel to places where work was available. Being a contractor was a way of rising up out of abject poverty. The first contractors produced a generation of upwardly mobile children. The sheriff of San Ygnacio, Texas, is the son of a man who bought a truck, contracted for farmworkers, then bought another truck and another, until he was able to move from labor contracting to trucking.

The early contractors were stern men, old-fashioned, as hard as the desert. They endured indignities by increasing the severity of their own dignity. One afternoon, in the offices of Centro Campesino, Juanita Mainster talked about growing up in the fields, the daughter of a contractor who traveled to Michigan to work. Mainster, who has a great, winning laugh that includes everyone around her in the good feeling, a moon goddess face, and skin that looks like brown silk, started picking tomatoes when she was six years old.

"In the field that my father contracted, the family Alvarez [her maiden name] always had to be ahead, the best." At home, he was even more demanding. The Alvarez family lived by the old rules. Juanita had to kiss her father's hand whenever he entered the room. When adult guests came to the house, the children were made to sit on the couch in silence. They were not permitted to laugh or talk, and they had to keep their eyes averted from the faces of the guests. The Alvarez children were not allowed to have playmates outside the family; it was not necessary.

By the time Juanita was eleven years old, she negotiated the labor contract for the family, did the taxes, and conducted any family business, such as buying a car or a washing machine, for she spoke English and understood the system. Yet she was not allowed to have friends come to her house nor to look into her father's face.

Susie de la Riva, who is from the Valley in Texas, described a similar life. De la Riva is all East Texas hustle and bustle, smoking, talking, drinking Diet Coke, dressed in brilliant colors made to seem even brighter by the cool, beige formality of Mainster's dress. She said that her father bought his children transistor radios to listen to while they worked, so they wouldn't talk to other children. He believed children had nothing to say. "If he caught us talking among ourselves," she said, "he'd accuse us of being *viejas de ochenta años.*"[10]

De la Riva raised the problem of the stern upbringing: "How can you be self-confident, if you are raised alone, with no friends. It's very difficult for us

[10]Old women of eighty years.

to talk to anybody. I don't know why we're all talking this afternoon. We don't talk to each other about these things."

"I thought I would get married at fifteen," Mainster said, "have a child at sixteen, like my mom. How can you develop self-confidence when you can't even express yourself to your parents? I married a macho who wanted me to work, cook, raise the kids, and go to school on my own time."

De la Riva said, "You couldn't be outgoing, have friends. If you smiled at a boy, they said you were a whore. By the time I was nineteen, I had two kids." Both women are divorced.

They have teenage children now. "I never wanted to raise my children the way I was raised," de la Riva said. She and Mainster are opposed to bilingual education, to the use of Spanish given names, to any kind of separation of Latinos from Anglos; they want somehow to separate the children from their Latino migrant experience. "You grow up fast," Mainster said. "You don't play with dolls. You work. You live in a camp. Migrant kids don't have a dream." She paused, summing up, and then she said, more in anger than satisfaction, "My children have seen another life. They don't live in a camp."

Few Latinos live in rural areas now, only 5 percent of those who are citizens or have residence papers. Perhaps there are 200,000 to 500,000 more who are not counted, not known, phantom people, hands, backs, flesh contaminated by pesticides and stained by earth.

The high-school dropout rate for migrant children is 80 percent, the health and safety conditions for farm workers are abominable, and the work is so debilitating that few people can continue to do it for a lifetime. A migrant worker who earns five thousand dollars a year is doing well. The only way for a family to survive is to have more than two or three people working, an economic situation as ancient as the digging stick and the stone ax. It creates a Third World existence for the children: They cannot be sent to school, because they are needed to contribute to the family income. In a farm worker's family love and hunger meet, like curves on an economist's chart. Generations are sacrificed to the price of strawberries.

3. SWEATSHOPS

A generation or two ago Mejicanos in Los Angeles and Puerto Ricans, Cubans, and Spanish Jews in New York were still able, with luck, to find work at halfway decent wages in poor but not intolerable conditions. Skilled seamstresses could earn a respectable living. Margarita Avila worked in a lingerie factory in Los Angeles; my wife's aunt did similar work in Brooklyn. They worked steadily and became valued employees.

Now the factories open and close. Some cut-make-and-trim shops in Los

Angeles will not hire anyone for more than three days. Now, La Migra comes in its green vans, sometimes with drawn guns, to find the people without papers and deport them. There is a battle between the sweatshop owners and the International Ladies Garment Workers Union that is less fierce than the organizing battles of the 1920s and 1930s, but much more difficult for the unions. The sweatshops compete not with each other now, but with similar shops in Korea, Hong Kong, Singapore, India, China, Mexico, and Indonesia.

In Los Angeles, many of the factory owners are Asians, often Koreans, who apply the rules reserved for dealing with foreign workers in Asia to the Latinos.[11] The workers in their sweatshops have no names, only numbers. When they do not work at the speed the contractors require or when the quality of their work is deemed unacceptable, the sweatshop owners have no way to communicate but to abuse the workers physically. They slap and poke and punch the men and women who sit at the long lines of machines.

Wages in the sweatshops range from eighteen or twenty cents an hour[12] for pieceworkers who haven't learned to sew quickly all the way up to the minimum wage. Most jobs seem to pay about half the minimum wage—a hundred dollars for a fifty or sixty hour week.

Home workers are the most severely exploited. Piecework rates for sewing are so low that many men and women have to work almost around the clock, employing their children and relatives, just to get enough money to buy food and pay the rent. Often two or three or even four single parents and their children will band together in a small apartment, with people sleeping in shifts, sewing all day and all night. Children who have been raised in these home worker cooperatives describe a nightmarish life. They all talk about the dust, which makes it difficult to breathe; the dust is worse than the noise of the machines in the middle of the night or the crowding.

No one can help the Latinos who work in the sweatshops. If sweatshops are forced to raise wages or improve working conditions, they will contract for the work to be done more cheaply overseas. The effect is to make the

[11]Maria Soldatenko, a Mexican-born sociologist working on her doctoral dissertation at UCLA, enrolled in La Escuela Costura Mercedes to learn to sew, then worked for several days in sweatshops in Los Angeles. She reported that half of the people in the sewing school were men. According to Soldatenko, the various nationalities working in the factories did not get on well: "Central Americans say Mexicans are lazy, machos who steal. Chicanos tease people for not knowing English or American culture. People just don't know each other. They say, for example, that Nicaraguans are evil."

[12]Clothing-factory owners in Texas cheat workers by refusing to pay them, claiming they have no money, but that they will have money soon if the workers will just stay on for another week. La Mujer Obrera, a workers' rights organization, has documented hundreds of instances of the swindle. State and local governments have made no effort to protect the workers, almost all of whom are legal residents or citizens of the United States. It is another example of the mixture of racism, arrogance, and incompetence peculiar to all levels of government in Texas.

Latinos who work in the sweatshops the equals not of the U.S. working class, but of the poor of Seoul or Singapore. Newcomers to the United States in the last quarter of a century cannot repeat the experience of their predecessors; a world economy and the Draconian aspects of IRCA bar any possibility of negotiating a new social contract, forcing these Central Americans, Puerto Ricans, Dominicans, Mexicans, Colombians to live as transporters of their old lives or as sojourners, determined to return home.

4. THE CHATTERBOX QUEEN

The great truism of emigration, that the strong and the ambitious, the best people in a bad situation, left the old country, proved to be only partly true in Segundo Barrio. With but a brief journey to make and a border that was never difficult to cross, malcontents and incompetents, people who just didn't have the physical or emotional strength to get along in the old country, also came north, dreaming of Cibola, swept along in the tide of emigration. When these people, who had already been sorted and found wanting in the old country, came to the United States, they were anchored in the barrio. Of those who moved out, some became the landlords and employers of those who remained. Others returned to the barrio to serve as social workers, psychologists, teachers, doctors, nurses, and lawyers for those who were left behind.

Mary Fernández is one of those who came back to work, but not to live. She is a social worker at Proyecto Bravo, a federally funded project attached to a Catholic Church in the barrio. For much of the day Fernández sits at a desk accepting applications for help with electric bills or the rent from women who come surrounded by their children, almost always with the same words in the beginning of their explanation, *"Me descansaron."*[13] (They laid me off).

In the afternoon, Mary Fernández organizes groups of people from the neighborhood. Her purpose is to convince them that they are human beings who have value, to raise their self-esteem, to help them begin to overcome their history and their lives. It is an almost impossible task, for the people in Segundo Barrio are often old, tired, without the capacity for dreaming required to redefine themselves in the world. "We just don't fight discrimination," Fernández said; "we accept our situation." Those who remain in Segundo Barrio evince the passive side of *aguantar*. They do not struggle. Mary Fernández will have to teach them to complain.

[13]*Descansar* means, literally, to rest, to lie fallow, a word imported to the industrial world and applied to a person.

After the 1990 Sun Bowl Parade, Mary Fernández had an idea about self-esteem for the women of South Oregon Street, people who were being relocated while their miserable housing was refurbished to meet minimal standards. To bring spirit to the people, to raise their self-esteem, she would make royalty of the laundresses, great-grandmothers and single parents of South Oregon Street. They would be like the Queen and her court of the Sun Bowl Parade. But instead of choosing the daughter of a wealthy businessman who could afford the cost of ballgowns and great parties, the South Oregon Street relocatees would choose one of their own. And they would crown her at the Armijo Center on South Ochoa Street, a few blocks from the river, on the last Sunday afternoon in February.

Planning for the coronation was done in the small, utterly barren meeting room across the hall from the main office of Proyecto Bravo in South El Paso. There was an election. On Valentine's Day 1990 the name of the queen was revealed to the members of the committee. It was Señora Vásquez, an eighty-five year old woman who came to the meeting dressed in a shiny black warmup jacket with a dragon embroidered on the back. She accepted the applause of her peers in queenly fashion, nodding this way and that, to the laundress with hennaed hair who was the head of the committee, to the social worker and the man and woman from the Housing Department, to the woman with two babies who brought a milky smell into the meeting room, to all those who voted for her and all those who would become members of her court.

She made no speech other than the speech she always made, for no one talked as much as she. Señora Vásquez talked in all the silences and over all the conversations, announcements, explanations, votes and discussions. She was *La Platicona* (The Chatterbox), a name she accepted with garrulous grace.

The head of the committee announced the names of the princesses, asking each of them if she would be able to bring an escort. "Yes, but he's only twelve years old," said one woman. "I'm on the lookout," said another. Every woman answered with a joke, for they were all alone, even the woman who smelled of milk, but they were all in the best of spirits, with the mettle of princesses. They bought many tickets to the coronation, handing the bills to the head of the committee, who tore the tickets off a roll. At the end of the meeting, each of the women presented a valentine to her social worker, and Mary Fernández, a quick, pretty woman with a voice like a tiny bell, made a brief speech to thank them.

—

The day room of the Armijo Center is as big as a basketball court, and sometimes it is that, but on Sunday afternoon there were tables around the perimeter of the floor and at one end a four-piece *conjunto*—Fender bass, electric guitar, electric piano, and saxophone—playing cumbias and polkas. At the other end a group of grandmothers manned two tables selling nachos and burritos. It was the worst of food. The nachos were made of storebought "cheeps" covered with Velveeta cheese and topped with a few little rings of jalapeño chiles. The burritos were wrapped in waxed paper which somehow had become fixed to the big flour tortillas so that everyone who ate a burrito had either to eat the waxed paper or open the burrito and try to eat the filling without a fork. As a result, there were not many customers at the food table, and the women stood together in their aprons, gossiping and giggling while the "cheeps" turned soggy under the cheese and the burritos became fixed more permanently to the paper.

Mary Fernández, dressed in a shiny blue cocktail dress that was only a little bit too tight, went to the microphone, the band played an electric fanfare, and she announced, La Coronacíon de la Reina del Año Mil Novecientos Noventa. "Presenting María González of the House of González and her escort." A woman in a white dress as shapeless as a sheet stepped forward. At the bosom of her dress a single red rose stunned the eye, a ruby in a field of snow. And beside her walked a bearded young man in a pachuco style shirt, white jeans, and snakeskin cowboy boots.

The second princess was a woman in her sixties in a long blue dress. She stood straight and in seemly stance, although the cerulean shimmer of her dress was too bright to live comfortably with her soft brown skin. Her salt and pepper hair was very long, gathered only once at the shoulder with a wide barrette. There was no sign of rouge or lipstick or any coarse cosmetic on her face; she had all the dignity of austerity. A very old man, who may have been her father, walked beside her.

Next came a huge woman in a tight lavender dress. She was as solid as the great statue of Coatlicue, but with tightly curled red hair and square plastic eyeglasses. Her escort, a boy of eleven years, wore white jeans and a white suitcoat that could not have fit him that year or the year before.

Finally, to the martial whoop of the saxophone playing "Pomp and Circumstance," the queen, La Platicona, Señora Vásquez of the House of Vásquez! She wore a purple dress topped by a homesewn crimson sateen cape. A man in a blue suit, perhaps a grandson, stood beside her. As she walked forward into the hall she was preceded by a tiny flowergirl in a white dress. La Platicona carried not just a single rose, but a bouquet of flowers. She was crowned by the deputy assistant director of the housing office. Then Mary Fernández, speaking in her high, thin voice, announced that the queen and her court of honor would dance a waltz.

The band played and the court danced, then all the men and women who sat at the tables at the edge of the floor began to dance, and it was clear that the poorest were the least able to dance in their old age, the most gnarled, the fattest, and the stiffest. Those who seemed to have fared better in the world, who wore suits and more stylish dresses and kept their figures, who could afford vanity, had also been best able to keep their health.

But the band played and they all danced. The queen removed her cape and waltzed with another woman almost her age. A tiny woman with a long braid down her back danced with a tall, heavy man. When they held each other closely, his belly touched her breast. They did not speak or smile, they danced, and all the while he wore a baseball cap with a white triangle in the front and a blue peak.

One couple hunched over toward each other. A dark blue shirt like a guayabera hung outside his brown trousers. She wore a purple dress and t-strap dancing pumps. His face was a wooden mask, carved without detail. She had a tiny head, like an Amazon River trophy. Their shoulders were out of place, their necks were too short. He leaned to one side, she leaned to the other, but they danced and danced and danced. His every step seemed painful; his knees did not quite work. Yet she followed him somehow, running, rhythmless, imitating dance steps they had done forty years ago, imitating steps they never knew. They danced and the band played polkas, norteño music, cumbias, waltzes.

All the old ones danced, the women with their husbands, fathers, sons, neighbors, while the electric instruments twanged and boomed and the saxophone honked out the music. Then the band played the Mexican Hat Dance and the queen and her court and all the courtiers were like children again, their hands clasped behind their backs, tapping their feet, skipping, joining arms at the elbow for a turn while the music grew louder and more rhythmic and the "cheeps" became crisp again and the tortillas separated from the gluey wax paper and the dust outside cleared from the air so that the sun streaming into the windows of the Armijo Center was brilliant, reddening in the late afternoon as if the heavens had been rouged in preparation for the coronation of the estimable queen of the dispossessed of the south side of El Paso del Norte.

20

THE CORPORATE FOX AND THE ENTREPRENEURIAL FOX

I tell my students that these "illegal" immigrants are foreign aid from Mexico.   Sergio Elizondo

We stood in the front garden looking out over the houses nestled in the mountain below. The sun had nearly disappeared into the tall shadows of the mountains that lay beyond the river in New Mexico. Houselights had come on all through the north entrance to the pass: squares of window in the foreground, losing their shape in the distance, down the slope, past the country club, becoming no more than points of light, like stars. The mountain also rose behind us, but there were few houses there, for we were very near the summit.

A chill had come into the air with the end of the sunlight. The others had gone inside; we heard their laughter. The conversation was about our children: Who was married and who was not, and if your youngest daughter and our youngest son . . . He's so handsome! She's just beautiful! Sighs and little shrieks of laughter.

It had been so long since the Morehead School, more than forty years. "Did you know that so-and-so was teaching over at the college?" "And I saw so-and-so in Los Angeles—divorced again." We spoke in English. It would not have occurred to either of us to speak Spanish unless we were ordering food in a Mexican restaurant or doing business with someone who spoke no English. Even then, we would not speak Spanish unless it was unavoidable; this was not the schoolyard of the Morehead School, not anymore—we had escaped.

For some reason, perhaps the chill of the night air, he began to talk about winter mornings in the old neighborhood, how difficult it was to get out of bed in an unheated room. We compared notes about the little gas heaters in the bedrooms of the old adobe and stucco houses. The heaters had no pilot lights; they weren't safe. Every night, at bedtime, we turned them off. When the temperature dropped below freezing and the wind blew hard, ice would form in a glass of water left beside the bed.

He changed the subject. "You saw the girls in San Antonio," he said.

"They asked me about you. They wanted to know what you and Merle were like when you were young. I told them how funny she was, how she used to make us all laugh, but I think they knew that about her. They wanted to know about you."

"I hope you didn't tell them the truth."

"They didn't know about the high school football hero or how serious you were."

"Remember that desk you left when you and Rudy Tellez went to San Francisco to get rich?"

"*He* did."

We laughed.

"The girls said that before they went off to school you lectured them about being Mexican. You told them that because they were brown they would have to be better to be as good."

He nodded. It had been his view of life; he had driven himself furiously, relentlessly from the time he was a boy.

A silence came over us. It was a long climb up the mountain to this place. He was now a well-known man in his profession. Many people said that Robert Navarro was the best civil engineer in West Texas, perhaps the best in the state. He was both imaginative and conservative, they said, precise; it was proper for him to be on the state licensing board.

By every measure he was a success—a very private man, close to his family, not political, a Republican if he had to make a choice. He played tennis now instead of football, and he worked hard, as he always had. Although I knew the small difficulties of his personal world, as he knew mine, the thought of his good fortune, the plain justice of it, delighted me.

—

There have been many such victories in the Latino struggle for a place in America, and it pleases the morale so to bask in the aura of victors that one is tempted simply to say that the war is over and only the mopping up of a few unhappy situations is left to be done. It would be easy and comfortable to write only about successful Latinos and to pretend that the others are mere aberrations, but that would not, of course, be true, nor would it be true to say that success comes easily to Latinos or on the same schedule that brought the Europeans of another time into the economic mainstream of the country. The United States drives a harder bargain now, and it is not color blind.

I. PORTS OF ENTRY

Patterns of upward mobility and social integration for immigrants to the United States were set by Europeans in New York City in the late nineteenth and early twentieth centuries. The paradigm was so clear that shortly after the middle of the century sociologists began to describe the rules of immigration, integration, and assimilation. All of the rules and none of the rules apply to Latinos. Two cultures and a technological revolution distort the paradigm in every case: The revolution, of course, is the decline of manufacturing and the rise of service and information work; one of the distorting cultures is that of the United States and the other is the culture of each particular group of Latinos.

Most of midcentury sociology, which so thoroughly misunderstood Latinos and blacks, overlooked the existence and endurance of culture while vastly underestimating the importance of race in the Americas. From the vantage of an aerie at Columbia or Harvard the prognosis of one immigrant group looked a lot like that of another. The professors, influenced even in revolt by Marxist notions of the way the world worked, sought and found patterns that cut across culture and race. They believed that there was an American paradigm and that it was most evident in New York City.

The South was far away and the West was largely beyond the imagination of most of the people who described the patterns of immigration. There were some notable exceptions to this kind of thinking, chiefly Oscar Handlin, but most scholarly works did not consider the history of Latinos in New Mexico, Texas, Arizona, or California, and people like Martí and Hostos do not appear in the indexes of the books of the time. In defense of the sociologists of the period, secondary source material about Latinos was very thin, so thin, in fact, that it would not have served even to point scholars in the direction of the primary sources.

Nathan Glazer and Daniel Patrick Moynihan were among the first sociologists to write about the Puerto Rican community in New York, basing much of their work on Joseph Fitzpatrick's observations. They conflated Latino and European patterns of immigration, a monumental error that was not a result of foolishness on the part of Glazer and Moynihan but of ethnocentrism in the U.S. intellectual establishment. What Latino radicals call a "Euro-American" bias determined their application of the American paradigm. By the time they reversed their views of the community in the second edition of *Beyond the Melting Pot,* Oscar Lewis had published *La Vida,* which they described as a "powerful but limited" work. "One must record with a sense of shock," they said, summing up in 1970, "the lack of a broad survey of Puerto Ricans in New York."

In itself, a paradigm that ignored the Latino experience could not prevent Latinos from entering the mainstream of business and social life, but it did make finding the means of entry more difficult: The doors were not marked in Spanish. Nevertheless, many Latinos adjusted to the vagaries of life in the United States and found their way into civil service, business, education, and the professions. What they did and how well they did it depended largely upon where they came from and how they were prepared for urban life. No purely economic or psychological or developmental explanations account for what happened; culture made the difference.

INVESTORS

A large and growing number of Latinos have come to the United States in search of a safe haven for their economic or intellectual capital. For these immigrants the new social contract they negotiate is based upon stability. They are quite willing to exchange a sumptuous life in Cali or Managua or Buenos Aires for an upper middle-class existence they can depend on in the United States.

When they wait too long before leaving and must come to the United States without real capital, the investors use the equally valuable capital of education. Physicians, bankers, engineers, chemists find relatively little difficulty rebuilding their lives in the United States. There is sometimes a waiting period for these investors of intellectual capital during which they must endure some privations, but it does not usually last more than five years. The United States, as the new immigration laws demonstrate, wants skilled people, immigrants of immediate utility.

The Latino "investors" hold themselves separate from other immigrants in every city. Wealthy Spaniards in San Francisco have formed a club that has little use for Latinos from this hemisphere, with the exception of a few fair-skinned Cubans. A Spanish club based on nationality and dedicated to the promotion of Spanish culture in Queens (New York) is less exclusive, but the only outsiders it accepts are the spouses of Spaniards.

As refugees from anxiety, the investors make a unique bargain with the new society; what they seek is not the revolution of the immigrant, but the retention of the old ways of life. In pursuit of the reassurance of repetition some Nicaraguan supporters of the Somoza regime, who were able to bring money out of the country before the Sandinista revolution or who have made money in the United States, have begun sending to Nicaragua for their former servants, arranging with the INS to sponsor them. Upper middle-class Colombians have made the same arrangement.

Of all the Latinos who have come to the United States the investors have the least incentive to assimilate or even to integrate. Many of them travel frequently to their home countries. More than a few have reestablished old connections with Spain, buying houses, visiting distant relatives, acting out an ironic conquest of the mother country with New World wealth.

Although the investors are of necessity few, the distribution of wealth being even more unequal in Spain and Latin America than in the United States, they are influential, setting the tone for all high culture of Spanish derivation in the United States and almost universally disparaging U.S. Latino culture.

Nor has there been much effort by the investors to lift their countrymen up along with them. They have generally sought to enter U.S. society at the highest possible level by separating themselves from Latino hoi polloi. Where the investors from Latin America or Spain have chosen to aid the larger Latino community, their help has been invaluable, but such investments are uncommon in a culture that is so unused to private philanthropy that there is not even a word for "fund-raising" in the language.

CIVIL SERVANTS

Great numbers of European immigrants moved into the middle class through government service. At first, they entered through patronage, using their votes to buy jobs. In New York City, the old paradigm of immigration, the Irish, Italians, and Jews split up the uniformed services, the garbage collection, and the schools. They took the jobs the WASPs didn't want and kept them from the blacks and later from the Latinos. In Chicago, which had a huge Slavic population, the Irish and the Jews split up the patronage jobs, keeping out the Poles, until the great influx of blacks from the South following World War II caused a new alliance of all the white ethnics against the blacks, and later, against the Latinos. In Texas and California, Latinos were simply excluded. The only state that allowed significant numbers of Latinos into government service prior to the civil rights decisions of the courts in the 1960s and 1970s was New Mexico, where the Latinos, many of whom practiced a form of magical racism by calling themselves Hispanos, dominated.

When Latinos were employed in government service prior to the civil rights decisions, it was to serve other Latinos or to do those jobs so dirty or dangerous that no one else wanted them. Racism functioned exactly as it was intended; Latinos were discouraged from voting,[1] which kept them from enjoying the fruits of a fair distribution of public sector jobs.

Until World War II the military was not an option, either. Life was hard, pay was low; the cadre was not an enviable place for an enlisted man. And it

---

[1]Texas did not abolish the poll tax until after the 1960 presidential election.

was highly unlikely that a Latino would become an officer. The brilliant service of Latinos during the war opened the military to them as a career, even as it taught them they could serve with Anglos as equals or even superiors. Then the Vietnam War in which the lives and limbs of minority troops were sacrificed in unconscionable proportion closed the military option for many.

Only in the last twenty years have Latinos begun to teach, fight fires, pick up garbage, and shuffle papers in the great government bureaucracies. Nevertheless, the consistently low registration of Latino voters and the low turnout of those who are registered has forced them to depend upon equal opportunity laws and civil service exams when the best jobs are often reserved for patronage.

San Antonio, Texas, indicates what might have happened had racism not prevented Latinos from following the European model earlier on. The Department of Defense, which has been the largest employer in the area for many years, established equitable policies for civilian employees long before many states and municipalities. Although Latinos were prevented from taking full advantage of the federal policies by the blatantly discriminatory policies of the local school system, which did not prepare them as well as Anglos for civil service examinations, they were able to find work on the nearby army and air force bases at fair wages.

A middle class grew up around government employment in San Antonio. The federal employees, military and civilian, did not have the cachet of the old families who brought their money and education north during the Mexican Revolution of 1910, but they had money and stability. They sent their children to parochial schools and good colleges. Former Mayor Henry Cisneros, City Councilman Frank Wing, and hundreds, perhaps thousands, of middle-class Latinos in San Antonio can trace their ascent directly to federal employment.[2] Although the opportunities were late in coming by historical standards, civil service in Texas created a cadre that moved into politics and commerce long before Latinos in California, Illinois, New York, or Florida were able to establish the traditional beachhead in the United States.

The national policies of the Republican party, which decided in the 1970s to begin recruiting members of minority groups on the basis of class and single issue politics (abortion rights, capital punishment), led to the appointment of Latinos to cabinet posts[3] and other high offices. After more

[2]Henry B. González, the legendary chairman of the House Banking Committee, who was one of the first Latinos to achieve political prominence in Texas, came from the other direction. His family came to San Antonio in 1911. His father had been the mayor of a town in Mexico before the revolution.

[3]Lauro Cavazos was a disaster as Secretary of Education, but Joseph Fernández, former head of the Miami school system and now chancellor of the New York City public schools, has

than two hundred years, Latinos and their government had begun to learn how to use each other.

ENTREPRENEURS

According to the Census Bureau's 1987 economic survey, there were 422,-373 Latino-owned businesses in the United States, an increase of 81 percent over 1982. Most were still shoebox businesses; only 20 percent had any paid employees and only 129 had a hundred employees or more. All the businesses together had sales of $24.7 billion, but the average business had receipts of only $59,000. The 1990 Census put the Latino population at close to 10 percent, but Latinos owned only 3 percent of the businesses in the United States. On a comparative basis, only a third as many Latinos as others owned businesses, and based on receipts their businesses were only a third the average size. A third of a third is a long way from parity.

—

The rules of entrepreneurial activity in the economic life of minority enclaves have prevailed since the establishment of the Jewish ghetto of Rome in 1556. Ghetto life leads to two distinct kinds of entrepreneurs, those who do business with insiders and those who deal with outsiders. Since an urban ghetto cannot be self-sustaining, the residents must export either goods or labor to outsiders and import food and raw materials; commerce is inevitable. Racism has always been about who gets the best of the deal.

Inside the ghetto shoebox businesses arise: barbershops, groceries, restaurants, laundries, taverns, and in recent years drugs. A division of labor occurs in some families to accommodate the ghetto situation: The husband goes out of the ghetto to sell his labor while the wife, who according to the ancient rules must stay at home and raise the children, becomes the entrepreneur, selling groceries, restaurant meals, doing her neighbors' hair. When there is no work for the husband outside the ghetto and the woman must become the seller of her labor to the outsiders, the social and psychological rules of the Latino family are broken and problems arise within the family.

European immigrants opened shoebox businesses in their ghettos, but also quickly moved outside: The Jew behind the pushcart sold shoelaces to outsiders, the Italian sold fruits and vegetables. The clichés served as adver-

---

indicated that he would like the job someday. Fernández, who combines Puerto Rican charm with big city toughness, is one of the most interesting figures in education today. He would be an imaginative but not unlikely choice for the job.

tisements. More than that, they staked a claim to an activity: For good fruits and vegetables, for very fine hand tailoring, see the Italian; for a bargain on a suit, to buy a diamond, see the Jew. Latinos, like blacks, have not been able to lay claim to an economic area, and this prevented them from establishing entrepreneurial activities outside the ghetto early on.

Latino entrepreneurs who wanted to go beyond the shoebox stage worked mainly inside the ghetto, selling food, automobiles, and real estate. According to *Hispanic Business Magazine,* in 1988 four of the top ten Latino-owned businesses were involved in food or liquor, three were car dealerships, two were real estate agencies, and one was a bank. Five of the ten largest businesses were headquartered in Dade County, Florida. The eighteenth, twentieth, and twenty-sixth ranked businesses, which were respectively a glass container distributor, an asphalt manufacturer, and an aircraft/auto parts manufacturer, were the largest operating outside the ghetto. The twenty-seventh and twenty-eighth sold Mexican food and imported bananas.

Breaking out of the ghetto is not easy. Goya Foods, Inc., of Secaucus, New Jersey, and Puerto Rico, one of the largest Latino-owned businesses, has attempted to sell its products to Anglos with very little success. It has also failed in attempts to break into the Mexican-American market in the Southwest. But now Goya will also have to defend itself against Campbell Soups and CPC International, which makes the Knorr brand soups. Under the name Casera, Campbell already outsells Goya in Puerto Rico. It will be interesting to see how long Goya can maintain its franchise in the Northeast. In the Miami area Cubans have held on to their markets against all competitors; perhaps Goya will find a way to emulate their success.

Although Cubans account for only a small part of the Latino population in the United States, they dominate the economic realm; they are the investors of real and intellectual capital, and they have chosen to build an economic fortress in Miami, which they use as a base, spreading north and west. Other Latinos speak longingly of the "Cuban paradigm," not realizing that it is an investor's paradigm, with the added advantage of being concentrated in a small area.

Mexican-Americans have also begun to feel the entrepreneurial urge, but not so far with great success. With a community of millions, concentrated in the Southwest as the Cubans are concentrated in Miami, Mexican-Americans have been unable to develop the ghetto as an economic stepping stone into the outside world. There are a few food processors, auto dealers, fast-food chain operators, and grocery chain owners who have built a base in the ghetto, but more successful Mexican-American owned businesses have begun in the general community, often in high technology, construction, and engineering.

Other than shoebox businesses, the Mexican-American ghettos across the Southwest have generally sent their people outside to sell their labor, with the workers returning to the ghetto to spend their money on food, clothing, furniture, and transportation sold in stores owned by Anglos. Self-deprecating Mexican-Americans attribute this failure to docility, lack of nerve, energy, and so on, but it relates much more directly to lack of capital and familiarity with the manipulation of capital. Mexican-Americans, Mejicanos, and Puerto Ricans cannot get beyond the loan-sharking that has drained their ghettos almost from the beginning.

Redlining by the banks has taken the economic heart out of the Latinos, as it did the blacks. The economic subjugation of people of color has been given into the care of the banks, and they have done their work with almost perfect efficiency. By redlining they have made the ghettos into pastures in which their Anglo customers may safely graze. The old complaint of ghetto-dwellers, which is that white landlords and shopowners in the ghetto drain the money out of the area, remains true. Recognizing the problem, the federal government and some corporations, ranging from General Motors on down, have tried to encourage minority businesses by offering a small amount of capital at reasonable rates, but their good works, while helpful, have not broken the pattern set by the banks.

Only the investors have been able to defeat the bankers. It did not take the Cubans and wealthy Central Americans long to realize that one of their first economic activities would have to be the establishment of banks. Otherwise, the Anglo bankers would have imprisoned them just as they have the Mexican-Americans and Puerto Ricans.[4]

To do business outside the ghetto, Latinos have sought government contracts. One obvious reason is the willingness of government at all levels to award contracts to the low bidder rather than the Anglo bidder. Latino businessmen, however, offer a second, even more compelling reason, for seeking government contracts: government, especially the federal government, pays on time. Since Anglo banks redline Latino businessmen even when they do business outside the ghetto, cash flow is always a problem; a business without credit at the bank can't work with customers who pay slowly. By refusing credit to Latino entrepreneurs when they are in the difficult start-up phase, the banks effectively bar them from competing for civilian contracts.

[4]Puerto Rican–based banks, with offices in New York, have not been a source of capital in the barrio.

EXPLOITERS

When Mexicans shout "¡Viva Mexico, hijos de la chingada!" they are describing themselves as the children of the violated one, which refers generally to the conquest and specifically to La Malinche, the native woman who served as mistress and translator to Cortés. Without La Malinche, the Spaniards could not have conquered the Aztecs; she betrayed an entire race. The translators do business differently now. They run advertising agencies, serve as corporate directors for minority affairs, and work for the Anglo political and financial establishment against the interests of Latinos in cities and states across the country. The work pays well. Half a dozen of the largest Latino-owned businesses are advertising agencies whose primary business is delivering Latino dollars to their Anglo clients.

Directors of minority affairs in large corporations get paid well, too. They may work within the company, with its suppliers, with the minority public or publics, or all three depending upon the structure of the corporation. If the corporation perceives its problems or opportunities as sufficiently important, the director of minority affairs may become a vice-president.

Neither the Latinos who advertise to their own people nor the directors of minority affairs necessarily do anything illegal or immoral; a classic avenue into the establishment is to help those in power to deal with one's own minority group. La Malinche was an extreme case. To do the same work in a company like AT&T seems benign, perhaps even helpful to the community. On the other end of the spectrum, however, a Latino who helps to increase the consumption of Budweiser[5] among his own people, knowing full well that alcoholism is a terrible problem among Latinos, is repeating the role of La Malinche.

The use of advertising and various kinds of public affairs efforts by large corporations, such as food processors, to secure their markets in the Latino

[5]Anheuser-Busch is one of the most aggressive and successful marketers to the Mexican-American community. The company has made an expensive and utterly cynical effort to increase the consumption of its products by Latinos. In an industry known for its hamfisted techniques at the wholesale level, Anheuser-Busch has been able to put many of its competitors out of business. Having achieved such dominance, its best opportunity for growth is to increase general consumption. It has targeted the Latino market, particularly Mejicanos and Mexican-Americans, and it employs Latinos at all levels, from the board room to the marketing department to the distributor's trucks, to sell them on the idea of drinking more Budweiser Beer.

They and their colleagues, like Phillip Morris (Miller) and Coors, have been extraordinarily successful. By any measure Latinos consume a lot of beer per capita. The effects of this consumption are apparent in the relative health of the ghetto population: A study of adjacent Anglo and Latino neighborhoods in New York City showed diseases and early deaths associated with alcoholism far more prevalent among Latinos.

community makes it more difficult for Latinos to start their own businesses, even within the ghetto community; a small entrepreneur does not have the capital, the marketing expertise or the use of the media to compete with outsiders who have targeted his people. Puerto Ricans, Cubans, and Mexican-Americans now run the operations that keep Latinos from doing business with Latinos.

At first glance it seems a sign of progress for Latinos to own advertising agencies and to be prominent in the Spanish divisions of Anglo advertising firms and so on, but their function is to exploit their own community to make money for Anglos. The distinction between Latinos (with the exception of Cubans) and other minority groups, particularly Jews, in the way they understand who is selling to whom is not insignificant.

A joke told by Jews has a man from Boston asking one from Chicago how many gentiles there are in his home town. When the Chicagoan says that there are four million gentiles in the city, the man from Boston asks, "Do you need so many?" The story would work as well if Cubans were substituted for Jews, but it would not work for Puerto Ricans or Mexican-Americans, who have yet to understand that the role of La Malinche can be repeated indefinitely and that she is always comfortable in the arms and the employ of Cortés while the rest of the Mexicans bleed. The need to understand others as a market and not to be content as nothing more than a market oneself, to be an economic subject as well as an object, was part of the argument that Rubén Salazar sought to make and much of the reason why the Los Angeles Sheriff's Department found him so dangerous.

PROFESSIONALS

If there is a single universal truth about newcomers to the United States, it is that all immigrant parents want their children to become doctors, lawyers, dentists, engineers, priests, architects, professionals of some kind. This desire cuts across all cultures and economic classes. The only exceptions are those people who come from extremely primitive areas of the world, where they have had only infrequent contact with professionals; sometimes it takes months, even a year or two before these people come to the conclusion that their sons and daughters should be doctors and lawyers. People who cannot read, who cannot understand what is meant by the terms "college" or "university," who would not send their children, especially their daughters, far from home to study, even people who condemn modern civilization and wish to return to the cultures of their parents and grandparents, every rational resident of the United States wants his or her child to be a doctor.

The reason, of course, is that professional status is the quickest way into the stability and respectability of establishment life. The greatest help toward achieving professional status was and continues to be the federal and state laws that require colleges and universities to admit students in some relation to the distribution of racial groups in the general society. The greatest hindrance was and continues to be money, although the social problems of Latinos in elegant prep schools and universities can be almost as daunting.

A fourteen-year-old girl, winner of a full scholarship to one of the most exclusive prep schools in the East, said she preferred studying to spending time with her classmates. "All they like to talk about is their hair," she said.

Her skin was dark, her hair spoke of African origins; she raised her eyes, as if to point at her own hair when she commented on the interests of her classmates. Otherwise, she was the most perfectly self-assured child I have ever met, pretty, the winner of prizes in mathematics, science, and English, beloved of her mother, who had devoted a room in their apartment to the girl's studies. Teachers fawned over her, bought her clothes, took her to the theater and the ballet. She was presented as a heroine, a shining star from the shining star of the Caribbean, a centerpiece at school assemblies.

When we met, it was I who was introduced to her. She smiled indulgently. Many people had been brought to meet her that afternoon, for it was one of the rare times when she returned to the public school where she had first made her reputation. She bestowed her time and her smiles. Her eyes were both innocent and comprehending, advertisements for her mind. She manipulated the conversation as celebrities can, she focused our thoughts upon her accomplishments.

A year later, her grades had fallen from B to C. She was having trouble with trigonometry. I thought about the girls who liked to talk about their hair. What did the shining star of the Caribbean have to say to the girls with straight blonde hair?

Lina Frescas Dobbs, who did well at Harvard, where she earned her undergraduate degree, had several siblings who also matriculated at fine private universities, Yale and Notre Dame among them. But only Lina, the oldest of the Frescas children, who lived in one of the most stylish undergraduate houses at Harvard, a Mexican-American scholarship student among America's most pampered children, stayed on to graduate. A few years later, at Notre Dame, her sister said she was unable to endure being without enough money to buy a candy bar and dropped out of school.

Entry into the economic mainstream through becoming a professional isn't easy. The society sorts for intelligence, emotional stability, and financial stamina. Latino culture militates against children traveling to distant schools (until recently, most girls were simply forbidden to leave town). Only a few years ago Latino students at Ivy League schools encountered the same cultural problems that make life complicated for foreign students: Francisco

García-Rodríguez, once a low rider[6] in Los Angeles, said that while attending Harvard he and the few other chicanos on campus traveled great distances to find palatable Mexican food. Joaquín Avila said his mother used to send care packages to him at Yale. Both men went on to become successful professionals, but neither can forget the loneliness of undergraduate school.

Once a person holds a professional degree and license the entrepreneurial problems arise: A lawyer can work for civil rights organizations, the government, a law firm, a corporation, or hang out a shingle. Heriberto Cabrera, a young Dominican who got part of his education in a seminary before attending Boston College, chose to work in the Manhattan district attorney's office when he got out of law school. It is one of the most stylish places for a young litigator to begin a career; important cases are reported in the *New York Times* and the bureaus often include the children of famous political figures—Cuomo, Kennedy, and so on. As a prosecutor, Cabrera earned a curious reputation. He was well-spoken, hard working, and he knew the law, but he was gullible; he believed the touching, often preposterous tales told by the people who were dragged up out of the holding pens to stand before the court.

Perhaps Cabrera merely illustrates a new rule of Catholic social philosophy: The Inquisition is long over; boys educated in seminaries no longer make good prosecutors. But he is a complex man; on the surface a New York kind of guy, a tenor talking stickball, street talk, coaxing everyone, even the Puerto Rican counterman in the coffee shop—in English or Spanish: "Hey, *jíbaro!*" to get the counterman's attention, or "C'mon. Hey, you're a kidder. Tell me about it, turkey," coaxing, knowing, the New York style of dealing with the world as if you had a tap on everyone's telephone and knew all their secrets.

The other man who goes by the name of Heriberto Cabrera is full of dreams, a collection of Brooklyn and Dominican memories warring just below the surface of his days. "My sister was two years older than I was and my brother was two years younger, and we used to imitate the English-speakers. We used to go, 'Shabballi, shabballishabballishabballi.'[7] I remember in the third grade I got left back. There was a kid, George, a big red-faced kid, who pushed me, and I didn't fight back. The teacher wrote on the blackboard, 'Herb is a hero' or something. Everyone laughed. I couldn't read what she wrote. I think I laughed, too. I didn't know how to behave."

---

[6]So named for the low slung cars driven by rebellious Mexican-American teenagers in the 1950s and 1960s

[7]This practice is not confined to Latinos. A French woman, newly arrived in the United States, was surprised to find her three-year-old daughter standing in front of the mirror, saying, "Blahblahblahblah." When the woman asked the girl what she was doing, the child answered, in French, that she was speaking English.

If his gullibility had a single, discernible cause, the moment and the place Cabrera recalls was the family farm in the Dominican Republic when his grandmother invited the poor workers to eat with them and he wondered why his grandmother didn't keep the food for the family. He said he felt bad about the thought the moment he had it, and he has felt bad about it ever since.

Now when he gets the case of a poor Dominican woman who arrived in the U.S. with plastic sacks of cocaine taped to her body, he asks whether she knew what she was doing, whether she understood the penalty. When a poor kid from Washington Heights is arrested for being a passenger in a stolen car, Cabrera assumes that the boy is an innocent, as he claims, and when he finds out later that his client has been identified by a host of people as an armed robber, he feels betrayed.

His father was an alcoholic, but Cabrera finds cause, if not an excuse, for the failing: mainly in the problems of a man who came to a new country and could not find work. He understands the injury to the pride of a man who must stay home while his wife goes out to work. It was not that way in the Dominican Republic; the man farmed, took the crops to market, built houses, disciplined the children—he was the provider. In New York, Cabrera remembers how the stigma of poverty was on his household—they did not have a telephone. He finds reasons, too, in the Dominican immigration itself: "We're the last ones in, the campesinos, the hillbillies; everyone needs someone to laugh at. There's prejudice against Dominicans—we own bodegas, that's all we know how to do. In law school there was a Hispanic students' association, but the Mexicans stayed in one group and the Cubans stayed in their group and then there were all the rest of us. I don't like Colombians because of that; in law school the Colombians said the Dominicans were only interested in partying and drinking."

He left the district attorney's office to open his own practice, doing everything from real estate transactions to defending drug dealers and petty crooks. He works out of a small suite of offices in a rundown building at 401 Broadway filled with lawyers who live on small fees from court-appointed cases. After a few years on his own, he has put on weight, his curly hair is going gray, his mustache is fuller, neater; he wears a dark blue cashmere coat as he rushes into the courtroom, looking like an old choir boy who struck it rich.

Soon the big cases will be coming to Cabrera. He almost had one: a drug dealer who killed a cop. He did the arraignment, then the case was taken away from him and given to an older, better-known lawyer. For a moment, Cabrera and his wife thought they had the big case, the $100,000 defense.

They worry. There are two children in the family now. At night, Cabrera wakes up covered with sweat. He remembers himself holding on, knowing that if he let go, he'd die. It is a recurring dream.

Large law firms have not been anxious to hire Latinos, unless they are fair-haired or can be useful in international business. Some of the best young lawyers have chosen civil rights work, which does not translate easily into corporate law. Vilma Martínez, who moved from the presidency of MALDEF to a large Los Angeles law firm, became a public figure before going to the private sector.

The problem for Latino lawyers lies in the lack of wealthy Latino corporate clients. The lawyer who doesn't have a list of clients of his own has less and less value to large firms as the glut of lawyers grows and the field becomes more competitive, and since lawyer/client relationships are often very personal, "old school ties" count. Latinos can become lawyers, but the legal establishment, while hiding behind mumblings about law and language, has used economic considerations to keep Latinos out of the lucrative part of the profession, limiting them largely to the threadbare business of civil rights and the tawdry life of criminal law. Excuses by university law schools have been even more eloquent. The Hispanic National Bar Association lists the "dirty dozen" law schools, which have a significant number of Latino students but no Latino faculty members: Harvard, Columbia, Georgetown, Texas, Florida, Florida State, Miami, Rutgers, Brooklyn, South Texas, Southern California Law Center, and the Southwestern School of Law.

The American Bar Association keeps no statistics on the numbers of Latino lawyers or their firm affiliations. Neither does Martindale-Hubbell, which publishes an annual list of law firms and their employees. The view of individual firms toward the question was expressed by Kenneth Reichley, communications coordinator of Davis Polk, one of the nation's largest and most prestigious law firms. He said he had no statistics, that his firm was a partnership, not a corporation, and that they were not government contractors. As far as he knew, Equal Employment Opportunity Commission rules did not apply to the firm. He went on to talk about the "privatist" character of law firms. Young Latino lawyers, knowing that less than one-half of 1 percent of all the partners in large law firms are Latinos, say they do not even bother to apply to Davis Polk and many of the other prestigious firms. The notion that bright, well-educated young Latinos can write their own ticket in the business world is a myth, especially in the legal profession, where the rules of racism are applied with the kind of precision characteristic of the best legal minds.

—

Cubans and other refugees with medical degrees have swelled the ranks of Latino doctors in the United States, but the cost of getting through college and medical school and setting up a practice makes it extremely difficult for a Latino born here. In Houston, for example, almost all of the Latino doctors are refugees, most of them Cubans. The number of Latino dentists in New

York City is so small it would seem that Puerto Ricans and Dominicans must be toothless.

The skylines of Latin America would lead one to expect a major Latino presence in architecture, but other than the Cubans, who brought their profession with them and then taught it to their children, the talent that is so apparent in the rest of the hemisphere has not surfaced in the United States. Architecture at the level of individual houses and small buildings depends upon connections to wealth, effectively barring newcomers from the day to 'day practice of the profession. The successful Latino firms have mixed construction and architecture, designing and building a house, selling it at a profit, designing and building two more houses, selling those, and so on. It is a slow process in which they must create wealth before they can use their own talents to serve it.

Some people seek to explain the low number of Latino professionals by arguing that the situation begins with the dropout rate, which has cultural, economic, and psychological roots. The argument may have some validity, but it cannot account completely for the paucity of Latino professionals or the inability of those few to penetrate the profitable spheres of their professions. The nature of the real barrier—Anglos for Anglos—cannot be kept from the children. Latino parents dream of the professional life for their sons and sometimes for their daughters, and the ambitions of the children drown in reality.

2. RULES OF THE GAME

Now that national chains and immigrant Asian owners have begun penetrating the business districts in the barrios of the Southwest, some Latino political activists blame themselves for losing the "shoebox" franchise. "We just want the security of the corporation," they say. "You know how Mexicans are; we're very conservative. We don't like to take risks." Puerto Ricans can explain the problem by their wish to have a good time, Dominicans through their inability to understand any business but the bodega, with its implied connection to the simple economy of a rural population. "We just want to be on welfare," Puerto Ricans say. "All we want is a job in a corporation, where we can depend on someone else to take care of us and tell us what to do; we need a *patrón*," the Mexicans say. "That's what we're used to."

Latinos who understand the problems of the small business in a redlined area have a different view. Interest rates of 40 percent combined with competition from national supermarket chains and franchises present the owner of a small business with nearly insurmountable problems. Only the poverty of his or her customers who need credit and the insularity of culture permit the Latino shopkeeper to stay in business. And if the Von's supermarket chain in Los Angeles has guessed right with its Tanguis supermarkets devoted to Latino customers, the shield of insularity may soon be taken away from the corner grocery-store owner in the barrio.

Perhaps the best opportunity for Latinos is in corporations, and the choice of corporate life is a matter of adaptability rather than weakness. In 1990 there were about a hundred Latinos in executive positions in U.S. corporations. As a percentage of all the executives in those corporations, the number is infinitesimal, probably less than one-tenth of 1 percent of the officers of the 1,000 largest corporations. But the kind of executive positions held by Latinos offers some clues to the most likely points of entry into the executive ranks. One of them is the place the advocates of bilingual education point to: international business, often but not always related to Latin America. Being fluent in Spanish helps, but the greater fluency, the sophistication of bicultural people, appears to be even more important. In a perilously small sample, Latinos appear to be able to use biculturalism as a tool in managing international divisions of large corporations.

Latinos also rise to management positions in companies interested in exploiting the Latino market. Unfortunately, the corporate executive extracts wealth from the community rather than building it—La Malinche again. Unless Latinos find a way to demand some return of wealth to the community through employment or letting contracts to Latino suppliers, the transaction will continue to be lopsided in favor of the seller, exploitation rather than exchange.

Business, however, has learned the value of Latinos as employees. Although corporate personnel directors do not discuss the virtues of racial or ethnic groups as a labor source, they indicate that the stereotype of docility is not what attracts them. In fact, Latinos have shown a more than average interest in joining unions, with Dennis Rivera and his New York hospital workers and the largely Latino UAW local at the General Motors Van Nuys plant demonstrating an almost anachronistic militancy and effectiveness. The cultural characteristic employers have begun to recognize and value is loyalty.

This sense of loyalty in Latinos grows out of a connection to land, family, and church. It is strongest in Puerto Ricans, Mexicans, and Central Americans, all of whom have ties to their home towns or districts. Salvadorans do not speak of San Salvador as a place of origin, but of a district within the city. Puerto Ricans from San Juan name the district from which they came. The sense of loyalty to place devolves from the earlier rural life in which place and family were synonymous. Without committing an anthropological dissection, Edward Rivera's memoir *Family Installments* shows very clearly the connection between a Puerto Rican family and place.

In their devotion to the New York Yankees, Puerto Ricans in New York and on the island demonstrate a sense of loyalty beyond that of ordinary fans. When many of them were children on the island, they heard only Yankees, Giants, and Dodgers games on radio broadcasts. The Giants and the Dodgers betrayed them, moving to California, but the Yankees stayed in New York. Loyalty begets loyalty in the Puerto Rican view; the New York Mets—underdogs, newcomers, metaphors who should appeal to the underdogs and newcomers in the city—cannot break the bond between the team that carries the name of the conquerors of the island and its most loyal fans.

Latinos learn their place in a large hierarchy from the Catholic Church, which gives lessons in loyalty and obedience, and imparts to all its followers the sense of a structured world in which each person plays an unquestioning role. Those who stray from the Church and its teachings endure eternal punishment, while those who remain loyal may be forgiven any transgression. The relation of religion to economics has been diagnosed by Weber, Tawney, and others; in the modern world the relationship seems clearest in the Latino community, where those who accept the hierarchy may become saints and Martin Luther remains the exemplary entrepreneur.

Even before the Church family ties teach enduring lessons of loyalty, creating the structure that the other aspects reinforce by repetition. The Latino world builds outward from the life-giving center of home, church, and town. The person belongs to the group, relies on the group, is a person by virtue of belonging. A Latino carries his mother's as well as his father's name. A whole person has parents, family, and is so defined. Individualism, which defines the world according to the person, creates different structures in the mind, looser, more free flowing, not necessarily less loyal, but less bound to loyalty; no one could ever mistake Ralph Waldo Emerson or Henry David Thoreau for a Latino. Not that Latinos are incapable of self-reliance or passive resistance to government, but self-reliance would be considered loneliness, the way of an outcast, and a Latino who resisted his government would not be likely to do so alone. Again, the reason would not be cowardice, but culture.

The tragedy of loyalty lies in disappointment, which comes so often for Latinos that it seems like the motif of their business lives. After twenty or thirty years on the job, a man or woman is suddenly fired, told that the company is closing or the job has been eliminated. Only then does he find out that he has no pension, his medical insurance terminates on the last day of employment, and he will get only two weeks or a month's severance pay. Innocently, confusing the structures of public and private life, the Latino employee fails to ask for guarantees, a contract; he expects that his loyalty will be returned. When the end comes, he retreats to the loyal core of his life, family and church, and if he has luck, to the town or neighborhood he once called home.

The irony of loyalty is that it both serves and deceives him. In the beginning, it makes the Latino a desireable employee, the one who gets the job, and in the end it leaves him old and abandoned, love's labors lost.

3. THE CUBAN PARADIGM

All other Latinos now study the economic history of Cubans in the United States, hoping to learn how to emulate their success. In the case of the Cubans, history and culture determined success; for other Latinos to copy the Cuban paradigm would require the defeat of history and the dismantling of culture.

Cubans identify with the conquerors, not the conquered, the subject, not the object. As exiles rather than immigrants or sojourners, they think of the United States as a useful place, more like a rental than a home. The fact that most Cubans would not move back to the island under any conditions makes no difference; the Cuban has located the center of the world, and he is standing there. By contrast, the Mejicano professor who says, "We are Mexico's foreign aid to the United States," describes a world-view so different that it eliminates the possibility of a Mexican-American repetition of the Cuban experience.

The Cuban economic paradigm, so devoutly wished for by other Latinos, particularly from the Caribbean, was not a Cuban invention. Spain invented the Cuban success in the United States at the end of the fifteenth century when it chose Cuba rather than Hispañola or Puerto Rico as its transfer point in the Americas. After that decision was made, the Cubans became part of the conquest. The connection of the island to Spain was never broken. At the beginning of the exile, many families went to Spain from Cuba, because they had relatives who were glad to help them. It is not uncommon for Cubans in Miami to send their children to Spain to visit relatives and learn the fine points of the language and the culture. In the bilingual schools of Miami, the textbooks in Spanish come from Spain rather than Latin America. And the meticulous racism of the white Cubans springs unalloyed from the Spanish Inquisition of the fifteenth century.

Cubans, who have the highest percentage of practicing Catholics of the three largest groups of Latinos, are generally pleased to hear themselves described as the Jews of the Caribbean, for the Cuban economic pattern has been a foreshortened version of the Jewish experience in the United States. Literacy, close family relationships, a sense of chosenness, ties to commerce rather than agriculture, all propelled both groups forward economically. The Cubans had the additional impetus of the Cuban loan, one of many programs that provided direct assistance for medical care, education of Cuban children, social security for the elderly, and so on between 1962 and 1976.[8] No other group of immigrants or exiles in the United States has ever been treated so generously.

Combining the huge welcoming gift from the United States with their own vast intellectual capital, the exiles set out to reproduce a Cuba-without-the-lower-classes (white Cuba) in Dade County. It became home, the place where the Cuban economic miracle began. Instead of hiring out to corporations or even to each other, the Cubans went into business for themselves. After nearly twenty years of exile, the average Cuban-owned business had only a few employees. It was a mom-and-pop economy for the most part. Even the largest Cuban-owned businesses by dollar volume—banks, import-export companies, wholesalers, publishers—were of the kind that required few employees. Many of them were rooted in the Latino community, from Arturo Villar's national newspaper insert to his friend and former business partner Ramón Cernuda's company, which published English lessons. On a local level the Cubans bought and sold within the Cuban city, and as they expanded, they stayed as much as possible within the Spanish-speaking universe, dealing with Latinos in the United States and doing import/export business with Latin America. Thus, the Cubans were both adventurous and cautious, entrepreneurs who did business in familiar territory.

4. LIFE AMONG THE GOOD OLE BOYS

All the major automobile dealerships in El Paso, Texas, still belong to Anglos, the banks remain an Anglo stronghold, the Chamber of Commerce belongs to the Anglos, the local branch of the University of Texas has a Latino front and an Anglo superstructure, and all the maquilas across the river in Ciudad Juárez belong to Anglo corporations and have Anglo managers, but 400 years after founding the town, Latinos are starting to take a share of the profits.

Nothing much in the way of economics went on in El Paso del Norte between the Oñate expedition at the end of the fifteenth century and the

---

[8]In *Miami: City of the Future,* T. D. Allman estimates that the total amount of aid to Cubans from all sources during that period came to $4 billion. To put that number in some perspective, Allman wrote: "But even if only direct federal expenditures are counted, the $2.1 billion in aid for the Cubans was greater than the entire budget for the Alliance for Progress—designed to finance what President Kennedy called "a true revolution of progress and freedom" throughout the whole of Latin America.

defeat of Santa Anna in the middle of the nineteenth century. Its Spanish-speaking conquerors considered El Paso del Norte nothing more than an outpost in the wilderness, a mission to the natives, and wasted no capital in the development of it. Cattle, mining, and smelting, a steady import/export business, the railroad, and Fort Bliss kept the town growing slowly through the first half of the twentieth century. Although the population was over-whelmingly Mejicano and Mexican-American and the language was mainly Spanish, the Anglos had all the money and the Latinos provided the labor. After World War II, Mexican-Americans appeared briefly in local politics, then fell back. The Anglo business community brooked no intruders. Anglos were willing to hire educated Latinos, but through a combination of banking, land interests, and control of the utilities Anglos were able to keep them from gaining control of any but the smallest economic entities in the town.

Only now, more than twenty years after the civil rights movement, after the Chicano Movement and the Brown Berets, after the acronyms and the marches and the education and the anger of a second generation of war veterans, have Latinos in El Paso begun a serious assault on the fortress of Anglo economic power. A similar assault is taking place in Laredo, where Latinos control a major bank, oil and gas interests, and some retail business. In Dallas, a Hispanic Chamber of Commerce has helped Latinos to develop the kind of networking and the systems of exclusion that the Anglos used against them in the past. A Mexican-American version of the Cuban system of *socios* has not yet developed, but the establishment of Latino business organizations may be a step in that direction. The difficulties for Latinos, other than the investors, are the lack of capital and a business history—they do not inherit money, mentors, or models; they start from scratch.

Two businessmen in El Paso, Robert Ortega, whose CMA construction company appears on most lists of the largest Latino-owned businesses, and Pablo Salcido, a young entrepreneur, undaunted by a couple of difficult experiences, still looking for his first real success, may be the harbingers of the economic future of Latinos in the Southwest. Between them they have encountered most of the problems Latinos will face in the business commu-nity. Ortega is tough-minded, solid, a fortress of a man. Salcido is boyish, expectant, resilient, an unstoppable talker who cannot resist doing at least three things at once; he owns a small wholesale office supply company, and he is already a conglomerate. Both men made their way in the world from humble beginnings. One understands political power as an outgrowth of economic power; the other wants to use politics to help his business.

"At the age of sixteen I was supporting the family," Ortega said. "My mother couldn't get a job. We did go on welfare once, but we got out of it. That didn't phase me. It's very easy to give up, but my mother was very much for us staying in school. Back in the sixties parental pressure had a lot to do with people growing up. Hers was 'Get down and study and do your homework.' If you don't bring home A's, then she's gonna be all over you. It was that pressure right along that allowed most of us to be able to succeed."

The offices of his company, in Dallas and El Paso, have the same stern, driving atmosphere. Everyone must wear a badge, as if the office were a construction site. Intercom systems, portable computers, laser printers, drafting tools, complex telephones set the tone of the offices. Everything has a place and a purpose. Ortega works a five-and-a-half day week. On Saturday afternoon someone has a party. But the party doesn't start until Bob Ortega gets there, and he doesn't leave the office until all the work is done.

Ortega's mother grew up in south El Paso, married at fifteen, and dropped out of school. "She was very intelligent," he said. He thinks her own disappointment may have been what caused her to press the children to stay on, get "over that hill." Only one succeeded. And it was not easy. He married early, got through college with the help of his wife and a fifty dollar scholarship from the Optimist Club. It took him five years, working all the way, but he got through and got a job with the U. S. Public Health Service as an officer in charge of building water and sewer systems on Indian reservations.

"My high school counselor advised that I was not college material, that I should do what my father did; that is, be a truck driver. What she meant was, 'Stay where you're supposed to stay.' She was Anglo. I was taught not to buck the system. It was a 'yes, ma'am, yes, sir,' type of situation. What I did was go in and apply for the Naval Academy. And that was her response, 'Why are you trying to leave here? Aren't you satisfied with your own life?'

"It was kind of sweet justice later on in life: her husband was working indirectly under me. Things always come around."

Ortega, who says he is a Republican, has quietly supported EPISO since the group began helping the people in the colonias outside El Paso. It seems incongruous for a prominent member of the Republican party to have deep ties to an Industrial Areas Foundation group, but Ortega is not a simple man. He is burly, neat, a man with a black beard that belongs on a bedouin prince or a conquistador, and his aggressiveness, his sense of revenge, of the rightness of retribution lurks in everything he does and says.

"I wasn't raised in the right circles with the right people and therefore I don't have the opportunity to do business with those people. You have a lot of people who were born into the money. And when you're born of a laborer . . . The thing is those doctors know each other, likewise attorneys and so forth. Here I come out of nowhere and I want to do business with them: 'Well, who are you? What's your blood line? What's your pedigree?'

"I am very much a worker in this company. I am not by any means an extra person. I roll up my sleeves and get in there with everybody, so I don't have the luxury of time to be in the Rotary. I'm not used to it. I don't have time for it. It translates to arrogance the way it comes back to me. 'Why don't you have time for us? Why don't you go to the symphony and this and that?'

"I get lots of invitations as the bankers and accountants and attorneys see the company start growing. I say, 'I can't.' My life is full of working, my civic organizations, my church, and my kids, and I want to fill it that way. But it looks like I'm snubbing people because I'm not belonging to the right things.

"Once anybody reaches a level of significance measured by finances, then the doors are open. The doors are not open unless you reach that. When I started my company, a banker said to me, 'Why don't you come back when you have money and I'll lend you some.' I don't mind saying that to people when they now are in my office looking for us to move accounts. While I like to be the one to say that I don't harbor ill feelings of the past, those things, like that banker and that counselor, those are feelings that you carry for life. And also they're good launching points. Those things drive you to succeed.

"Right now, we use the banks very little. We sell finance. We roll our money. So when we establish accounts at banks, we don't borrow, so we don't get brownie points for doing business the right way and aren't being accepted into the right circles.

"In construction, if you're low bid, you get the job. But the architects in town will invite their buddies. I can always write and say, 'If you want a low bid, I can do it,' because I've got a good track record. I'm not the first five they call, but I've not been refused when I write. So I'm not blocked. In construction, it's the dollar that talks. If you're low bidder, they'll take anybody.

"The bankers all talk to each other. They see your financial statements; that would be the first ticket into the establishment that they would start seeing. I have to feel that there's no sacredness to someone's financial statements.

"If you have a sustained growth, perhaps when you start flirting with a million dollar net worth, that's when they start paying attention to you. And it doesn't do any good unless you start spending it around town. You have to give to the symphony, the right places. It doesn't do any good to give to the church and the social causes."

He sees Latino businessmen getting respect from politicians and other business people in Dallas, where there are a few successful Latinos, but not in El Paso, where there are many more. Latinos in El Paso are still timid. He points to a successful computer software manufacturer who "did well with the Anglo community by hiding his color, not being an advocate of his color. I respect him very much, and I would never say anything derogatory about him, but what he did, he never stood up for Hispanic causes. He stayed very clear of those issues." There are no powerful Latino business organizations, not even a Latino Chamber of Commerce in El Paso, he says, "because when the Anglos hear power, they run and get the cannons."

The failure of Latinos to hold their fair share of power in the town grows out of economics "and our upbringing," he said. "We're brought up Yowser. I think that's gonna carry with you. To a certain degree we're humble, more humble than the Anglo population: 'Yes, sir, go ahead and take it.' While the Anglo is more aggressive; they've been brought up in the business circle. I think it's the cultural upbringing, the respect for elders, don't speak unless you're spoken to, all of those little things. An Hispanic is not brought up aggressive: Give up your seat, do this and that. And the Anglo has the better words. They can always speak better, traditionally. The Hispanic is just not brought up aggressive enough to deal in this world."

He had just won the contract to build the new U.S. Embassy in Bolivia. Alicia Chacón, the candidate he was backing in a clear brown/white contest for the most powerful job in the county, was almost certain to become the first Mexican-American ever to be elected to that office. A group of young El Paso businessmen was trying to start a separate Latino Chamber of Commerce. Latino voter registration in El Paso had reached 50 percent. Networking among Latino businessmen had begun. Ortega smiled; he had caught himself thinking about the past. He leaned back in his chair to do a new calculation, then came forward again with his bid. "I think El Paso will start changing radically," he said. "I hope that when the Hispanics see they can have power, we don't screw things up, but run the city properly for everybody's benefit." He shook his head, "The utopian dream."

——

Pablo Salcido, who was born in El Paso almost a generation after Robert Ortega, earned a masters degree in Public Administration from the LBJ School of the University of Texas at Austin in 1983 and moved a few miles south to San Antonio to become part of the Henry Cisneros administration. For a young man with roots in Smeltertown, the son of a man who raised eleven children without ever earning more than $14,000 in a year, it must have been a heady time. Cisneros was the first glamorous Latino in U.S. politics, and he had glamorous ideas: high tech, a stadium for a professional football team, a plan for a Sea World amusement park in San Antonio, where the deepest water anybody had seen up until then had been the annual flooding caused by the lack of drainage in the Mexican section of town.

A year and a half after coming out of graduate school, Pablo Salcido moved from his job in the city manager's office to take a role in putting together the Sea World Project. In 1984 and 1985 he was named in one of the lists of outstanding young men in America. He caught the attention of the mayor of El Paso who brought him home to direct the city's Department of Economic Development.

The El Paso city council was split into factions. "Any time I got a council member's support for a project," Salcido said, "those council members who didn't like that one would vote it down. It got to the point where they were trying to make an ass of me. I was getting offers up the kazoo. I looked at all of them, but I really wanted to stay in El Paso. I went to KINT (one of the Spanish-language television stations in the area). Ten months later, my whole dream fell apart. I didn't ask the right questions when I started. After eighteen months, they sued me for breach of contract. We negotiated a one year salary."

By then Pablo Salcido had been featured in *Texas Monthly* magazine, named as a "rising star" in *Texas Business* magazine and honored as graduate of the decade by Austin College, where he did his undergraduate work. In El Paso, he was a member of the board of directors of the Chamber of Commerce. He was also married, unemployed, and beginning to learn that where money and power were concerned the "good ole boys" play to win. In San Antonio Henry Cisneros had made a deal with the Anglo power structure; in El Paso Pablo Salcido was on his own.

With the money from the KINT settlement, he started Salcido Enterprises. The first acquisition was a small office supply company, Business Products Unlimited (BPU). "I think at the end of this year we'll be able to live very comfortably off this business. We still have to get to the point where we're doing forty-five thou[sand] a month. At forty-five thou a month, it pays me the salary I want, gives us three or four grand at the end of every month to add to our working capital, so by December of this year, we can start thinking about hiring somebody to manage this operation for us. Then we can go on and start another one, or, with my family, invest in another business and also play with the community."

He does business only partly by following the Cuban paradigm: "I'm networking. I'm going after all those Hispanic purchasing agents, all those Hispanic lawyers. I call up and they say, 'Call my purchasing agent.' On the basis of that, I've been able to go from a little mom-and-pop organization to five-and-a-half employees in less than two years and do over half a million dollars our second full year in business."

But the system of *socios* doesn't work as well in Texas. Salcido wants government business, he needs it. "Last year, I did fifty-five grand worth of business with the county," he said. "I did two grand with the city. Why? If the city has a bona fide minority purchasing director and the county doesn't, it doesn't make any sense. I bid and I bid and I bid, and I never get anything. I ask if he [the city minority purchasing director] has set asides, if he buys 30 percent or 40 percent from minorities, and he says, 'I just go by the lowest bid.' Then I ask why do we have a minority purchasing director? So, I said, 'Gene [Fink, a liberal member of the city council], it doesn't make sense, that guy is just going by the lowest bid. The big boys'll always give the lowest bid.' So I'm going to City Hall and I'm going to change that policy. It's not for me, it's for attorneys who are Hispanic, for accountants who are Hispanic, it's for contractors who are Hispanic.

"We [the City of El Paso] buy great [from] a company out of Los Angeles. And all those millions go to Los Angeles. Where are the El Paso jobs? Where's the sales tax generation? Where's the property tax generation? Where are the jobs created? You know what they say? 'We are encouraged to [buy from the lowest bidder] because we get federal grants.'

"Well, by God, you're gonna be more than encouraged, you're gonna set it aside. By God, I'm gonna show you that I can provide you with quality product and prices just like the good ole boys do. If you give me [the opportunity to bid on] 10 percent [of the entire purchase], I will lower my prices to match the good ole boys'. I never had 10 percent of a bid. I may have had a .0002 of a bid."

He works out of a small room in the back of his store. His wife, Cheryl, blonde and pretty, with their first child in a tiny crib beside her, makes telephone calls from numbers on a big Rolodex wheel. A small room beyond her appears to be a place where someone sleeps. The office has the feeling of the mom-and-pop business BPU had been until the day before yesterday: metal shelving, a couch, a television set, a place to eat lunch or dinner. A small radio plays bland music and news headlines from the town's only classical station. Pablo Salcido leans into his conversation. He is pale and freckled, an intense, bleached man. "The power structure here has never been so embattled, so disorganized," he says. "These are good ole boys, some of them who are on the conservative end and some of them who are literally under the shirt redneck bigots. They're all at each other's throats right now. They really don't have a power source. The existing power structure is on its knees. They don't know the beat of the community. They gather together up at M Bank or TCB International Club to protect each other. They're twenty; they call themselves The Twenty. They're good ole boys. These are the CEOs of the largest employers and that's their little CEO club.

"No, the power structure hasn't changed. I'm sorry they didn't make the transition easy, because it could be volatile, it could be ugly; there could be some nasty name calling, major problems with some companies, with business relationships.

"We're law abiding. We put up with discrimination. 'Hey, Mihijo, maybe I'll get another promotion some time.' That's my father. He would never fight the system. 'The Lord has blessed my life,' he says, 'I have a job.'

"Things have changed. There are a lot of Pablo Salcidos here. We're about to emerge."

21

CORRIDOS

Corrido. *Romance popular que contiene alguna his-*
toria o aventura, se canta o se recita. . . .[1]   *F. J. Santamaría*

Not a hero only is needed, but a world fit for him. . . .
      Thomas Carlyle On Heroes and Hero Worship

I. THE ELECTION OF CRUZ GÓMEZ

A long time ago, before World War II, only a few Mexicans lived in
Watsonville, California. The canneries were small; the migrants who worked
the farms picking strawberries and artichokes didn't stay long; much of the
land in the interior still lay fallow. Fishermen worked out of the little beach
towns nearby, but they did not hire many people: The law did not allow
them to use braceros. San Jose was just a hot, dry agricultural town, Santa
Cruz didn't have a college campus, Teatro Campesino had not yet made San
Juan Bautista famous, and the parents of the people who would make the city
of Watsonville into the defendant in a federal voting rights case still lived in
Michoacán, Mexico. Everything was quiet in Watsonville before the war and
even for many years afterward. The Mexicans did not complain about the
backbreaking short hoe; they worked hard, kept to themselves, and took
what little money they had left at the end of a season home to Mexico.

After the war, more Mexican families stayed in town to work in the
canneries and to care for the fields during the growing season. They lived
mostly in substandard housing, with few amenities. The schools mistreated
their children, segregating them, putting those who could not speak English
into classes for the feeble-minded. Watsonville was two towns: American
and Mexican or *gabacho y Mejicano*. They met in labor and commerce, but

---

[1]"***Corrido***   Popular ballad, sung or recited, containing some story or adventure. . . ."

rarely in friendship. In the sixties some new Latinos came to town, mainly to teach in the schools or to work in federal programs. Some were from Texas and some were from other parts of California, but very few were natives of Watsonville or Michoacán. These new Latinos, about a hundred families, did not live with the old farmworkers and cannery workers. They moved into the new subdivisions out at the edge of town where the Anglos lived. They made their lives partly with the Anglos, partly with each other, but mainly with television: They were the TV Americans; they learned how to live from "Leave It to Beaver." They did not spend their time with radicals, hippies, or cannery workers; they found the Republican party appealing.

When the strike came at the cannery, the hundred middle-class families did not publicly support the strikers. Radicals were involved; higher wages could drive the canners out of town;[2] there had already been the problem of moving from cans to frozen foods; how much could the packers take? Did a strike have to last for nineteen months?

Among those who supported the strikers, was arrested with them, and yet had contact with the middle-class chicanos was a woman who had first come to town as part of a nutrition education project, Cruz Gómez. She didn't look like a troublemaker. She was so light-skinned and her hair was soft and brown, like an Irish woman's skin, like a European woman's hair, not a Spanish woman, but a European, French or German. She was pretty; her face was softening, sweetening in middle age; her eyes did not know malice; to look at her was to like her.

When she came to town she was not comfortable in Spanish; she spoke only a little and with a very strong English accent. Yet she believed in La Llorona,[3] was afraid of the dark. She knew enough not to hurt *los niños de la tierra*, the potato beetles with tiny human faces. And if you asked this woman, so *güera*, so gringa, "What does it mean to see a black moth in the house?" she could tell you that it was a sign: A letter was coming and it would bring bad news. She knew, she knew that a woman should not eat oranges or lemons when she had her period; she knew not to cut a child's hair when his stomach is full; she knew that certain spirits stay around money and that other spirits are interested in unfinished business. She thought like a woman who could go to jail with the strikers, but she looked and talked like one of the middle class, a Republican.

She was two women, *gringa y chicana*. How could anyone trust her? But

[2]Their fears were not entirely unjustified. Rather than give the work to union members in California, the canners have shipped much of it across the border to Mexico to take advantage of the wage differential.

[3]Literally, "The Weeper": The ghost of a woman who killed her children and threw them into a river, and now walks the streets at night mourning them; she is the Mexican version of the bogeyman.

everyone did. As she went through the migrant workers' camps, talking to the women, teaching them to balance the diets of their families, to cook more vegetables, to use less lard, to eat more fresh fruit, she learned from them. Women who did not know their birthdays, Michi Indians from Mexico, reinvented the woman who had come down from Oregon with no sense of community, with nothing but a vague memory of Spanish.

So Cruz Gómez came to be chicana in Watsonville. She had been born near the coast, in Goleta, near Santa Barbara, adopted by an older couple with eight grown children, people from Guadalajara who had been in the United States for only a few years. They were very Mexican and very proper. But they did not enjoy an easy existence. They lived on a farm, where water was in short supply and where there were no rules of etiquette or behavior other than those that had been brought north from rural Mexico. Only later, in the town, did the girl learn to flush the toilet every time it was used instead of when it was necessary. Only later, did she learn to eat with a fork instead of a tortilla.

She lived the formal, humble life of a Mexican girl. She did not speak to adults unless they spoke first to her; she kept her eyes lowered in the presence of adults and strangers: If she spoke in a familiar way to an adult, she would be punished for the infraction of the rules. And she learned other social rules, too: Not to visit someone unless you telephoned first to make an appointment, and then never to be late.

Because she lived with adoptive parents, she had two lives early on, even two birth certificates: Dolores Marcia Gómez and Marcia Cruz Vásquez. When it came time for her to attend school, the adopted girl was sent to the school her natural mother had attended. Discrimination was more subtle than it had been when her mother was made to use only the back door of the school. The message, Cruz Gómez said, was "Learn English!" By junior high school discrimination was less subtle: The Mexican children were bused to their own school.

Her adoptive mother died when the girl was still in school. After that, she lived with friends, in a foster home, with teachers, a man and a woman who said, "Go to college." Her life changed. She was fair-skinned enough to slip across the line into the Anglo world. She learned not to spend time with "those kids," who were better coordinated and always trounced the Anglos, her new kind, in athletics, but that was unimportant now; she was in the college tracking program, heading for Santa Barbara College. She married after college and moved to Oregon. Nothing Latina was left in her life. She was like "most chicano professionals . . . estranged from the culture."

The cultural differences are apparent to her now. "Twenty years ago, if someone in my family was sick, I wouldn't drop everything and go to their bedside; twenty years ago I was Anglo. The Anglo world thinks of what is practical. In the Mexican world, you do something because the other person wants you to. Immigration officials wonder why people go back to Mexico because of so many emergencies."

When Cruz Gómez, *agringada,* arrived in Watsonville and began working with the migrant women, her education told her that they were ignorant. "Slowly," she said, "the association of people and my politics told me what makes you a valuable entity. As I learned the language, I learned that *we* understand everything. There is respect and dignity. We believe everyone is worth something."

She muses on herself, her life: "When I was growing up (in a Mexican family), I was much more generous than I am now. When I was Anglo, in Oregon, I remember berating a family for helping a sister when they could hardly feed themselves. Now, I'm more the way I was [as a child], but I still look out for me first. I want my privacy."

After she settled down in Watsonville, Cruz Gómez bought a house. She made the payments for a long time, then lost the house when she could not make the balloon payment at the end. She rents a place now at the end of the block that houses her headquarters: the Migrant Media Education Project. She was doing her business in the project when Joaquín Avila came to town.

He was a famous man in Latino circles in the Southwest: He had been the head of the Mexican American Legal Defense and Education Fund. Everyone knew MALDEF; everyone knew him. He had something on his mind, voting rights. Joaquín Avila believed that the at-large voting laws in the Southwest kept Mexican-Americans from electing their own candidates to school boards and city councils in hundreds of towns like Watsonville. With at-large rules, a town that was 49 percent Latino, like Watsonville, wound up having no Latino representation on the city council, instead of the four or five out of ten that would reflect the town's population. Until representation by geographic district could be made the law, Mexican-Americans were effectively excluded from government. The concept was clear, the Voting Rights Act of 1965 was a solid legal foundation, but Avila needed a test case. Who would dare to lead the plaintiffs in a suit against the very town in which they lived? After Cruz Gómez had run for office under the at-large system and been thrashed, she realized that the system needed changing. Avila had come to the right person. She agreed to fight city hall.

The case was brought in 1985. The city of Watsonville fought it all the way up to the U.S. Supreme Court, which said in March 1989 that it would let stand an order for redistricting by the federal circuit court in San Francisco in 1988. In the first election to be held under the law, one Latina ran for office from the heavily Mexican-American first district, Cruz Gómez.

She did not think it would be an easy contest. She knew the district well and she knew the power of the councilman who represented it. Standing in front of a map pinned to a wall outside her office, she pointed to the factories and the railroad tracks and the problems of registration in her district near the downtown area. Eighty per cent of her district was Mexican, but only a hundred of the Mexican-Americans were registered to vote; 20 percent of the district, mainly a new development of townhouses, was Anglo, but four hundred Anglos were registered. It would be difficult, but there were people who would help her. They had to. After winning a landmark decision in court, winning the election was vital.

The earthquake that struck California in 1989 was centered in the mountains east of Watsonville. No town was hit harder. The downtown area and the poorest neighborhoods were almost totally destroyed. People were left without food, water, clothing, or sanitation. Some were hurt, some died. Hundreds had no shelter but tents set up in parks and open spaces cleared of rubble. And with every terrifying aftershock conditions got worse. Even those whose houses were left standing were afraid to go home. What if the next aftershock brought the house down on them? What if their children were killed? Better to stay in the tents.

In the cold and frightening days that followed the earthquake, Cruz Gómez worked constantly among the people who had lost their homes. She comforted them when they were afraid, found food and water for them when they were in need. She went to the Red Cross and the state of California to get help for them. Unlike the Anglos who could go to the bank or to relatives for help, her people had no resources. They looked to her. She never turned them away.

A month later, the election in the first district was won by an Anglo who had served for many years on the City Council. It was not a close contest. The Mexican-American candidate had failed to register many new voters. She had been with them every day, in the tents, in their half-destroyed houses, but there had been no voter registration cards in her pocket; she had let the election get away.

In the post-mortems that followed her loss the sophisticated political point of view was that Cruz Gómez had sacrificed the larger, long-term good of the entire Latino community of Watsonville to the immediate needs of relatively few people. She did not disagree; she said only that the people had needed food and water. But she did not say "water" in the old way, the way she had said it in Oregon; the word that came out had a long, lyrical *a*, "waader." In the loss there had also been a victory: the gringa had been defeated, Cruz Gómez was complete.

2. JORGE VALLS IS BURNING

A man walks at night in Miami. He is tall and too thin. Judging by the length of his white hair and the Italian shoulder bag he carries, the man might be an actor or an impresario, a European passing through the city. Surely, he must be a stranger: No one walks in Miami, and a bus is not due soon. Perhaps he is an actor, for his features are fine, aristocratic; if he is European, there are titles in his background—one can see the history in the bones. But there is something not quite correct about the man; his face is scarred, there is a redness, a thickening across the delicate bones of the nose. An accident, perhaps, something untoward.

Cars pass. They seem to come from great distances, as if the Miami street were a tube. At an intersection a truck stops. Two men in the cab look over at the walker; they study him. The men are *guajiros,* country people, perhaps they were in the boats that left from Mariel. The light changes, but the truck does not move. The man on the passenger side lowers his window. "Jorge Valls," he says, putting the names together as if they were one, "where are you going?"

The men offer to drive Jorge Valls wherever he wants to go, and he accepts their offer, for he is not an arrogant man nor is he a stranger; he knows that no one walks in Miami. Moreover, he is a bit tired and he has already spent too much time in darkness. He enters the truck, and they drive off together, chatting easily. It is not an uncommon occurrence, for every Cuban in America knows Jorge Valls.

"He was my teacher when I lived in La Habana," one man says. "I knew him in school," says another. "He was my father's classmate," a young woman explains. Someone else met Jorge Valls in New York. Or Paris. Others were in the Directorio Revolucionario with him. And now and then a man will say that they were in La Cabaña or the Isle of Pines or the Combinado del Este together, one of the places in which Valls was imprisoned for twenty years and forty days[4] by the Castro government.

In La Cabaña he wrote the poem that gave title to his first book: *Where I Am There Is No Light.*

> *Where I am, inside the grating,*
> *there is no light.*
> *But next door*
> *the space is illuminated,*

[4]*Twenty Years and Forty Days* is the title of his prison memoir.

so light must exist.
Yet further on
is a darkness even more obscure. . . .

We have no hanged ones here:
everyone is burning.
(Could they be filled with kerosene?)

And they go on chatting,
pacing from here to there,
up and back,
endlessly.
Some few sleep.
Someone is outside.
Somewhere there is sunlight.
Surely, sunlight exists.

I cannot go out now:
I will go to sleep.
Inevitably I will awaken.
And so on and on.
The inexhaustible kerosene burns.

It was easy to publish when he was in prison, Jorge Valls said. His work won five prizes, including the Grand Prix at the International Poetry Festival in Rotterdam. His play was performed in New York. Translations were made. Americas Watch published a crude version of his prison memoirs. There was a moment, in Rome, Argentina, Paris, Miami, New York . . . He was the one who had been a poet before he went to prison. He was the one who had taught philosophy. Of all the prisoners of conscience only Jorge Valls had been jailed by Batista and then by Castro. Some say that he could have been the one, the famous one, if he had permitted himself to be useful.

Was it so, I asked him, had there been such a moment?

"Yes, yes, I could have had a Mercedes in the garage," he said, then he smiled. It was night, and I was driving, so there was no time to read the smile for irony. "But would you talk to me then?" he asked and looked away, out the window at the lights of the houses of Miami passing in a blur. He did not want an answer. It is his way to make the less of himself—the foreword to his second book of poems concludes by begging a thousand pardons. Even so, he is not modest; poetry precludes that response to the world. Then what does he wish of these modest words?

We had talked many times: in restaurants, by telephone, over coffee, across the dinner table in my house. We had attempted to write an article together, but one evening, in the small apartment my wife and I had rented in Miami, Jorge Valls and I had spoken in a formal way, for the words were being recorded. The man of whispers declaimed, he spoke in paragraphs, in pages. While he spoke, I thought of how he must have been in earlier times: in the meetings of the directorio, in the offices of his accusers, in the apartment of Fidel before the trial, and in jail, where in cells without windows, he taught philosophy to the ordinary prisoners, lecturing in whispers while they made notes in microscopic script on smuggled scraps of paper.

"Prisoner of conscience" is the phrase applied to men like Jorge Valls. The wish of his words is that the listener have the courage to be as free as a prisoner, to burn inexhaustibly, to be the sunlight in his own cell, political.

It is not a popular argument in Miami; it is not useful in a city where men trade in cocaine and profits are generated by the little wars in Central America. The rich businessmen of the Cuban American National Foundation sneer and say that Jorge Valls is a *liberal*. It does not matter to them, these millionaires of the counterrevolution, that while they fattened themselves in Miami and complained about Castro in Washington, Jorge Valls lived for twenty years and forty days in Cuban prisons.

Miami is a city in which morality died; therefore, it is rich in ironies. And Jorge Valls, because he will not have a Mercedes in his garage, figures in several of them. An old irony in the Cuban city of Miami involves the president of the Republic Bank, Luis Botifoll, a belligerent patriot and hater of tyranny. The armed security guards who protect Botifoll's bank are employed by another patriot, Esteban Ventura, a man who is well known to Cuban exiles, for Colonel Ventura was the chief of Fulgencio Batista's political police.

Jorge Valls has also had business with Ventura; they met in Havana before the revolution. "I was in Colonel Ventura's 'office,'" he said, "the place where they gave the beatings. I was sitting on the floor waiting, and I took out a volume of Plato that my father had given me. And when they saw that, they beat me."

Why beat a man for reading Plato? Jorge Valls was, as Hugh Thomas wrote in his history of Cuba, the intellectual leader of the Directorio Revolucionario, but the Colonel in charge of the political police would have known that anyway. Why beat him then for reading Plato, for merely opening a book of dialogues? I had heard Jorge speak often of Plato, which he pronounces with a soft Spanish *a*, but I had not understood the significance of what he had said until one night after I left Miami, when the idea awakened me from my sleep, as if philosophy could be done in dreams.

I know now that there is a moral dance in progress in Cuban Miami, a figure in which the unwilling partners are Valls and Ventura, the pacifist and the butcher, the philosopher and the pragmatist. They are both wise men in their ways: One reads Plato and the other knows the meaning of that act. All the city around them may be described as a chorus mirroring the ballet of the servant and the one who will not serve.

The powerful, the rich anticommunists like Botifoll, have chosen Ventura. He makes them safe so that their businesses can prosper and their social lives can appear in the pages of *Diario Las Americas;* he opens doors for them in Washington; he hates. Therefore they put the gun in his hands.

Who chooses Valls? The nature of the man is to be difficult. He has no money and no car; he does not, as he said one day, even have an address. And he speaks of the violence in Miami, of the poverty of the people in Overtown and Liberty City. The man has been out of prison for only a few years and already the title poem of his new book, *Quicksilver Conversations,* speaks of gray seas filled with dead fish and a plastic roof in place of the sky, of a man who has lost the ability to remain quiet until hope comes.

After so many years in a communist prison, he comes to America, where he is free, and he says, "I believe in a doctrine which is key to my philosophical development: Man is unique and unsubstitutable; even a man who is an idiot or who is a fool or who is mad is for me so important that he is sacred. He has to be what he is and not any other thing. It is this authenticity of men that has to be saved, and it is being destroyed in the world. If I am against totalitarianism in Cuba and I am against the merchant or the markets type that I find in many other places in the world, it's because you destroyed the possibility of the man. The real man doesn't need shoes: He knows how to walk. And he walks and knows how to choose his destiny."

If Cubans were uncomplicated people, Jorge Valls would have but few allies and he would find them among the liberal intellectuals in the universities and the professions. But Cuba is a crossroads, a vantage point from which to survey the hemisphere, a tiny place forever seeking to be something other than a colony, producing a little sugar, a little tobacco, and a crop of ideas out of all proportion to the size of the nation. Pacifists and socialists abound, the population is aging, and the people wish to be whole. Among Cubans, even in Miami, a philosopher can find a following.

Yet, if they would admire him for his courage, he answers, "One is neither brave nor cowardly, one simply tries to live through life."

If they charge him with optimism, he will tell them of the young Marielito dying of AIDS, who said, "I come from the future."

If they would admire him for his religious poetry, he will tell them a poem about dogshit, skyscrapers, and the unnoticed vomit of a wanderer on the streets of Miami.

To those who wish war he is a pacifist; to the pacifists he says, "I don't know if I am violent or nonviolent, but I don't believe in violence as a way to obtain justice."

And to anyone who thinks that after twenty years in prison Jorge Valls regrets the overthrow of the government, he answers, "I am a revolutionist. I believe in the redemption of man; that is, that a bad law can be changed into a better law, a bad habit can be changed into a good habit, that the poor ideal can be changed into a worthy ideal."

Then who chooses Jorge Valls, this man who sees civil war where others see revolution, who understands Cuba in terms of the war between the father and the son as told in the ancient flood myth of the creation of the Antilles?

He speaks of Babylon, like so many Cubans who compare their plight to the Diaspora of the Jews. "Exile is when you develop the consciousness of your being and your possibilities of being. You see, when you are inside the country, the island, it becomes fighting for power, a political party and other things. Now, when you come out of the country, power is not important. Music is much more important."

For almost five years after the revolution Jorge Valls, the Cuban, remained in his country, more or less free, apparently unafraid, one of the few critics tolerated by the Castro government. In 1964 he was arrested and sentenced to twenty years in prison. When I asked him why he continued his criticism, why he hadn't permitted himself to be used, he began his answer with a sigh.

"I fought against Batista. I . . . let's not use I, let's use we . . . we defined the categories of the revolution. Then, after 1959, many of the things we thought should be done, had a chance of being done, and were being done. Now, why didn't I back the Cuban government, why didn't I accept that?

"The way it was being done was in contradiction with what I consider a universal value, and I had to assume the opposite position. Then I was in the opposition, but in the opposition were also those who didn't want the revolution, who didn't want Cuban independence—reactionaries. Perhaps this was the anguish of the beginning.

"Between nationalism and universalism I believe that the nation, the *patria,* has a meaning, but not the highest meaning. Something must be above that. That is just an intermediary, because a fatherland or a nation is just a part; humanity is greater than a people. So in 1959 there was the option: Either I defend the Republic of Cuba, the nation of Cuba, the land of Cuba, the power of Cuba, or I defend a principle that is useful for all men."

So his crime is that he does not believe in the gods of the State, but has divinities of his own. That is the revelation of the middle of the night: The charge against a prisoner of conscience is still the ancient accusation, as old as Socrates at seventy. Jorge Valls reads the *Apology* as if it were a book of instruction. He does not merely do philosophy: He is a philosopher.

3. JUANA BEATRIZ GUTIÉRREZ,
MOTHER CORAJE

Los Angeles is the most permanently, brutally segregated city in the United States. No other city has built walls around its ghettos; no other city has so deliberately isolated a single group of its residents and then burdened them with the mistakes of civilization: prisons, waste disposal plants, land-fills, freeways, and pollution.

With each new freeway, prison, or incinerator, conditions in east Los Angeles deteriorated. The new Pomona Freeway tore the barrio apart, dividing church parishes, community organizations, neighborhoods, friendships, even gangs. Children who lived beside the busiest freeways in the world suffered lead poisoning and the more insidious problems of noise pollution. An escapee from one of the prisons killed an entire family. Incinerators fouled the air and landfills ruined the earth.

Latinos had no connections to power. Each new affront to the body and soul of the community appeared suddenly, without warning. No one asked them about locating another freeway in east Los Angeles, no one told them; they found out they were in trouble when the bulldozers arrived.

Considering the history of the barrio and the tenor of the decade—the middle of the Reagan presidency and the great boom in California—Governor George Deukmejian expected no problems when he decided to build yet another prison, the sixth, in east Los Angeles. What actually happened, how the Latinos found out about the proposed location of the prison, what the priest said and how the woman from Zacatecas got involved is not exactly clear.

Frank Villalobos, a landscape architect, may have been the first one in the community to hear about the prison. "The Senate, including all of our elected officials, passed a bill siting the prison on December 3, 1985," he said. Villalobos had been in Sacramento often during the period, lobbying to get an enterprise zone for Los Angeles's east side.

After news about the prison got back to the east Los Angeles community, leaders demanded a meeting with the Bureau of Prisons. It was too late, however; the bill had been passed. Nothing could be done. Or so it must have seemed to Governor Deukmejian and the California State Senate, who did not know of Ricardo and Juana Beatriz Gutiérrez.

Ricardo and Juana are in their fifties. Her eyebrows still arch high over cat's eyes, and her round nose still belongs to a little girl, but her face has set, squared, become a stonecutter's work, with two deep vertical lines in her forehead, so that she seems stern even when she laughs. He looks like

Pancho Villa, not the movie version, but the real Pancho Villa, the retired general, full-faced, with curly Frenchman's hair and a quick-tempered twinkle in his eyes. He manages a shoestore; she runs a household that has been home to their nine children and to a hundred others, all the hopefuls, radicals, politicals, intellectuals, and insatiables of the neighborhood. She was Mother Coraje, the teacher of righteous anger; her front door, her refrigerator were always open to any boy or girl in that part of east Los Angeles who refused to submit to the life plan laid out by the circumstances of birth.

She is also the investiture of *respeto*. The neighborhood boys who have known her since they were small children show respect for her: She is not afraid of the gangsters; they are afraid of her. She started taking the neighborhood back from them when she joined the PTA. "I started telling people that we shouldn't be afraid," she said. "This was our neighborhood and we shouldn't have to go anywhere else. We wrote a letter in English and Spanish to the chief of police. I went door to door with the letter.

"At first, the neighbors were afraid. After we started, more and more people came. Then the police got interested in taking care of the neighborhood." It was the beginning, the development of a method of organizing by example. She learned to expect the hesitation that followed the first step, to overcome it, to lead. She would not accept the destiny assigned to people in east Los Angeles, not for this generation or the next.

Her own children went to college, eight out of nine, and the ninth, who wanted to get married and have children, plans to go back soon. Ricardo makes jokes now about having so many children in college at once. When he had one at Princeton, it was expensive, he said, but by the time two of his children were going to school there, it cost less, and when he had four in college at once, it cost nothing at all. "So you see," he said, laughing as he described the magic of scholarships, "the more you have in college, the less it costs."

He was born in Mexico and came to El Paso, Texas, when he was nine years old. He said he spoke no English, so they put him in kindergarten. Ricardo Gutiérrez believes that because he was educated in Mexico until he was nine, he learned the fundamentals of reading, writing, and arithmetic, enabling him to get double-promoted rapidly through the lower grades in El Paso as he learned English. By the time he was in high school, he was bored with the curriculum, so he dropped out.

Like hundreds of thousands of Mejicanos before them, the Gutiérrezes gathered everything they had in the world into a weary automobile and made the trip west from El Paso to opportunity. They liked Los Angeles. Their house was very large, with many bedrooms.

The problem with living in east Los Angeles and restoring the community, however, was that it had become a dumping ground for everything the rest of California didn't want. When Mrs. Gutiérrez heard about the new prison, she said it was wrong. Her friends on the block and in Neighborhood Watch and in her church agreed that it was wrong. They felt angry, deceived; once again "they had put one over on us." Mr. and Mrs. Gutiérrez called a meeting. Luis Garbo, a priest, was with them. Lucy Ramos and Aurora Castillo, Herlinda Robles, Josefina del Pozo and María Roybal were also there at the beginning, but the force, the strength was Juana Gutiérrez. She and her husband once gathered nine hundred signatures on a petition in a single day. They were always ready to work, never afraid.

John Moretta, another priest, named the group who opposed the prison Mothers of East L.A., but before the women accepted the name they went to Luis Garbo, the Latino priest, to make certain that MELA, the acronym, did not mean anything bad.[5] Then the protests began. The Mothers of East L.A. appeared at meetings, at banquets, in the state capitol. They demonstrated every Monday afternoon. At one demonstration they gathered 1,000 people, at another they crowded 7,500 people, almost all of them women, onto a bridge. More were coming, but the leaders of the protest had to stop them before the steel and concrete structure collapsed under the weight of the Mothers of East L.A.

Students came from San Diego and San Francisco to march with them; movie stars came from the west side to march with them; César Chávez and the UFW came from Delano to march with them. And with MELA always were Lucille Roybal-Allard and Gloria Molina, the official voices, the elected, established voices. But the power came from Juana Beatriz, as it always had, in the PTA, in Neighborhood Watch, in church, and now in the streets.

No new prison was built in east Los Angeles, nor was the incinerator for toxic waste material built upwind of their neighborhood. The landfill was put somewhere else, and the pipeline was rerouted. It is not as if the meek had suddenly inherited the earth, however; the truth is that the meek had been supplanted. "We are different from the people who came before," Ricardo Gutiérrez said. "We are urban. When people ask why my family is outstanding, why my children all went to college, I explain to them that the people who came before were afraid to let their children go away to school. They were country people; we are not."

The difference he points out between the kinds of immigrants is based perhaps as much on class as on the degree to which people have been urbanized. But it cannot be disputed that the sense of *aguantar,* which grew out of timidity, belonged to a world of peasants, people who had known nothing but exploitation from the time of the Spanish conquest, perhaps even before, during the Toltec and Aztec hegemonies. The Gutiérrez family

---

[5]*Mela* has no meaning in standard Spanish. In Caló it means the head of a person.

had no fear; for them *aguantar* denoted an ancient virtue—the sense of place that fosters community. "We could sell our property now," Juana Beatriz Gutiérrez said, "and get a lot of money for it. Then we could move to a much better neighborhood. But our roots and our destiny are here. How can I go to another part of the city and get to know different people? And maybe they won't be of my race; I want to live with my own people."

As El Paso was the gateway to the United States for millions of Mexicans, east Los Angeles was the beachhead just beyond the gate. For most of the history of the twentieth century, immigrants in every city have gained a foothold on the beach and then moved on, but something new was happening in east Los Angeles. The Mothers of East L.A. had decided to stay on the beach, to resurrect it and complete the immigrant's revolution there. If they did indeed stay and if young Martín Gutiérrez and his friend and colleague Miguel Mendívil also stayed, and if Frank Villalobos did not move out and Lucy Ramos did not find the suburbs more appealing, it was possible that a tide of self-respect would come to the barrio and lift up all the residents, even the beleaguered children and fatalistic grandchildren and great-grandchildren of timid country people.

4. JAIME INCLÁN'S LOISAIDA CLINIC

The Puerto Rican immigration has been a difficult one, a step forward and a step back, a step north and a step south, formal and directionless, not a progression, but a dance. Nostalgia grips the Puerto Ricans; like Odysseus, they have been to war in a foreign place, and they are now drawn and driven by homesickness. For many of them the pain of life in New York has been unbearable; the family, the traditional strength of Latino life, has not been able to withstand the stresses of a foreign language, unemployment, racism, poverty, welfare, and the liberation of women and children from their historic roles.

Few people have tried to alleviate the suffering of their bodies, and fewer have been concerned about the mental pain of these ghosts in New York. Only their souls have been of interest; they have been a market to the minions of the Lord: Catholic, Protestant, Evangelical, Spiritist, and Santero. As the families disintegrated in the maw of New York City, no one else spoke to them in their own language, especially to the *jíbaros*, who said *belleza* (which means beauty) for *dinero* (which means money). Who knew what they meant by *fula* (excrement)? Would a Mexican connect it to *fuchi*? How would a therapist who learned Spanish in school discover the meaning of a common word in the vocabulary of a family newly arrived from the mountains when the word did not appear in any dictionary? And if a woman from San Juan were to describe her husband as a *cacatúa*, would he be a cockatoo?

a dandy? a useless person? a person with bowel problems? a nasty person? a loafer?[6]

Since people speak intimate thoughts in their first language, not academic Spanish or English but the slang of the household, how would the therapist ever know what they were saying? Caribbean slang is filled with Africanisms; Cuban street talk has a number of seaman's terms because of its geographic and economic history; Mexican Spanish is heavily laden with Náhuatl terms; Guatemalans use words borrowed from Quiché. The situation for a monolingual therapist would be all but hopeless. Latinos in New York City, deprived of medical care at every level, were almost entirely cut off from psychological help. Furthermore, there was no tradition of seeking professional counseling: Rolando Fernández, a Cuban psychiatrist trained in New York, went home to Miami, because he could not find enough patients to keep him in private practice in New York.

The need for counseling in the language of Puerto Rico, available in the neighborhood, where it was not threatening to people who are strangers in the city, had been obvious for at least two generations when Jaime Inclán decided that he would open the Family Guidance Center. From the first, Inclán had a radical view of the role of the center. He wanted to call it the Loisaida Family Guidance Center. To do so would have been to steal the history of the area from the other groups that had passed through, to make it Puerto Rican, named for a Taino princess as much as for a part of the city. Politically, it was impossible. Inclán needed city funds to start the clinic and to operate it. He changed the name to the Roberto Clemente Family Guidance Center, honoring the great, good-hearted baseball star from Puerto Rico, got a demonstration grant from the New York State Office of Mental Health, and went into business.

No man was less likely at birth to be the founder of a family therapy clinic on the Loisaida of New York. Jaime E. Inclán is Spanish on one side and Scottish and Swiss on the other. He is a stocky man whose ruddy face and generous eyes promote healing in whoever stands in his presence. Inclán contains the complete Spanish character: shrewd, earthy, and realistic, like Sancho Panza, and with the proper breadbasket; dreamy and unconsciously critical, as madly imaginative as Don Quixote. He climbs aboard his bicycle and pedals furiously across the Loisaida to his Greenwich Village office where he sees private patients every evening. He runs a large clinic, arranges for interns from every Spanish-speaking country (including the United States) to work there, and owns a part of an ancient convent on the Spanish Costa Brava, "something from the heart more than a practical thing," he said.

Dr. Jaime E. Inclán publishes often in his field, and usually in the proper

---

[6]A *cacatúa* or cockatoo is a useless person, inefficient and lazy.

academic manner, but his most fascinating paper has a Quixotic touch. He titled it, "Interpersonal Relations Among Puerto Rican Men or Why So Much Dominoes?" The subject of the paper, systems thinking, appears in most of his other work, for he advocates a systems view of the family in society. Whether his systems view of society preceded his systems view of dominoes is not so interesting as his isomorphic imagining of the order of large and small worlds. In other words, the doctor is capable of dreaming, that other side of the Spanish, Puerto Rican, Nuyorican mind.

The sixties formed Inclán as much as Switzerland, Spain, Portsmouth Abbey School, or Puerto Rico did. He remembers taking pictures of a friend of his and Abbie Hoffman together, one with a Puerto Rican flag draped around him and the other with his yippie flag. But it was not easy for a rich island boy to enter the Nuyorican world. "In Puerto Rico, where you stand on *independentista* defines you," he said. "When I came here that political stand didn't define you. My friends here were more interested in were you white or were you black? We weren't getting anywhere for more than a year; we were in bitter disputes and fights. They were very distrustful of someone like me whose class, social position, and racial features were different from and alien to their reality. And I was equally opinionated about my judgments about them. It took us a while to understand enough to agree to disagree."

Dealing with the lot of Puerto Ricans in New York radicalized Inclán, not that he is a bomb thrower or a fringe man; he is intellectually restless, as the best radicals must be. He remains a believer in his systems view, which might be better described as a syncretic view (he blames both society and the victim for the failures of poor people and minorities), but his concerns have shifted from systems to history and culture to the developmental problems of immigrants in the United States.

The real radicalism of Jaime Inclán, however, is that he cannot or will not separate himself from the world in which he lives. "In the Puerto Rican case, what we have is that first generation guided by the dream. Everybody likes to work with them because their values are good values: They believe in the family, in discipline, in schooling. They believe in hard work. They have that Catholic mentality that if you're good now, you will be rewarded hereafter. I think that the children of them [are] a totally antithesis generation. It is a generation that is very difficult, is lost, especially the men. It is a generation that has seen that the promise was a false promise, that the results that were expected were not forthcoming, that the sacrifices were not rewarded.

"Ideologically, what we see and what we experience is more the infrastructure than the family. I think that what we found was the typical first generation man was out working two jobs, eight to four and then a service job afterwards, working in a hotel or in a building or running an elevator or what have you. What happens to the family in the meantime is it develops and it grows to be mother centered, with a peripheral father. But the father is not peripheral out of straight family pathology. He was out working two jobs. As a result the family grew as a structure that was monoparental, headed by a woman. My sense is that in that process, particularly the men, the men in the second generation are disasters. They're nowhere to be found. They're failures. There are some outstanding women, but it would be a marvelous study to make, the comparison of the men and the women, that second generation and what's going on."

He sees the problem clearly and it pains him, the alcoholism, fighting, crime, abuse of women, all the efforts the broken men make to hold on to some semblance of dignity. They were farmers, many of them, and they have come to what he calls "the belly of the monster" instead of going to rural Arkansas, where they could have made a life.

In his systems view of the world, the clinic is but a small part of what must be done. He deals in politics (Latino candidates for jobs come to New York and sleep in Jaime Inclán's house). He wheels and deals and worries about Latino leadership in New York and the lack of a cultural center, the failure of Puerto Ricans to emulate the Mexicans in their interest in indigenous cultures. His phone rings—favors, requests; his interns are waiting for him to lecture on the family on the Loisaida; he will have to be on time for his private patients; he makes a note, he hurries, he laughs, stirs up an argument, calms another—pepper and oil.

There is a mural outside his clinic. It tells the history of Puerto Rico through pictures of heroes, including Roberto Clemente. The mural faces an abandoned building, a place in which squatters and crackheads battle with the police. At one time, the Roberto Clemente Family Guidance Center was used almost entirely by Puerto Ricans; now the people come from Mexico, Ecuador, the Dominican Republic, Colombia, El Salvador, Guatemala. The families seem to be falling apart all over the world, an unending, constantly increasing stream. Jaime Inclán stands in the middle of them—the monoparental, jaggedly acculturating stream of fragments. He reaches out for them, pulling them together—the excluded fathers, the failed fathers, the children who never learned respect, the burdened mothers, blacks and whites, everyone, the leaderless, atomized, dreamless thousands. It is his work; it is, he said, the flag he carries.

5. DR. PELLY'S MUSTACHE

Dr. Pelly was eating a candy bar and chuckling at what he had just done to one of his colleagues. "I got the tube down the patient's throat," he said, speaking softly in English, with a distinctly Cuban accent. "There is no need to operate. When his surgeon comes tomorrow, he will see that Pelly cost him a fee."

He laughed almost inaudibly, as if a separate life, a different man, lived under the doctor's breath. It was his night to talk, his long night, like so many nights when he read medical journals until three in the morning, then watched CNN to connect with the world for half an hour before he slept, awakening again at six. Intern's hours: he was more than fifty years old and still living intern's hours, thinking, examining the bodies and the souls of people and nations from his vantage point at the fetid end of the United States.

Dr. Pelly looks his part; a tall man, slim, with the careless beginning of a pot belly, the physique proper for a gentleman in the tropics. His hair is going gray, becoming thin, straight, and fine. He has a little mustache, very British. "Pelly, Pelly," he thinks aloud of himself. "You think I'm Cuban, because I was born there, but this is not a Cuban face. Pelly is not a Cuban name. The Pelly family came to Cuba from England. My English father married my Spanish mother. I had thought Pelly was English, but that is not the case. I studied it. Pelly is "Pele," a Scandinavian name. Pele came down to Normandy and across to Britain. So you may think I'm English, this face, this coloring in the cheeks and the eyes, but the ancestry is Scandinavian, Pele." He speaks urgently, as if to explain himself, like a man who is guilty about his very being in the world. It is survivor's speech.

He moved slowly, remembering that a colleague had died of a heart attack only a week before. Dr. Pelly did not want to die. He had work to do. At the end of a Sunday he wore a muted plaid shirt, khaki trousers, and a jacket of fine summer cloth, the palest tan, almost white, a memory of La Habana.

The beeper on his belt called him to the telephone. It was Sister Norma at Casa Romero. Something dreadful had happened to one of the refugees. He had frothed at the mouth and fallen into a coma. An ambulance was coming to take him to the hospital. Of course, Dr. Pelly would see him. He spoke to her in English about the sick man, then he switched to Spanish to discuss the very old Sister who had been in the hospital for a long time. He advised Sister Norma that he had done what he could, that it was not in his hands anymore. He said it would be wise for them to begin preparing to say goodbye to her.

Dr. Pelly does not know how to behave like a contemporary physician. He said he makes house calls, because that is the only place in which a doctor can treat the whole patient. He spoke of a woman who had asthma that he couldn't treat. No matter what he prescribed, the asthma returned. Then he went to her house and saw that the walls were filled with holes, that she lived in dust and stress, and then he knew why she had such severe attacks and that he could not cure them.

In the emergency room of the hospital the man from Casa Romero lay on an examining table. He was dark, very small, probably Guatemalan, with a little mustache, not a British mustache, like Dr. Pelly's, but a timid mustache, black on dark brown skin. Dr. Pelly talked to the man who lay on the table, stripped to the waist. He asked someone to take the man's blood pressure. Dr. Pelly kept talking to the man, softly, then more loudly. "Viejo. Viejo! VIEJO!" The man did not respond. His eyes rolled wildly in his head, like dice in a cup. Dr. Pelly had trouble with the ophthalmoscope; he could not get the man to hold still while he looked into his eyes.

After a while, the man seemed to become calmer. It was still not clear whether he was epileptic or suffering from an anxiety reaction, which is not uncommon among refugees who are held in one place or another for a long time. Then the man came around a little and Pelly was able to speak to him. The man said he had had epilepsy for eight years. He had a wife and children in Guatemala. He had been robbed on the way north and had no money or papers other than his release form from the Bayview Detention Center.

When the clerk in the emergency room came in to fill out the required forms, he asked if the patient was from Casa Romero. "No," Dr. Pelly said, "he was just visiting there." It was a small lie, but good enough to keep the hospital from sending a bill to Casa Romero.

The doctor knew something about refugees and prisons, for he had been a political prisoner in Cuba before he came to the United States, and when he arrived here at the age of nineteen, he was sent to the Federal Detention Center at Opa-Locka, Florida. He didn't mind Opa-Locka, he said, for he was glad to be in the United States. When they let him out, he moved around, became interested in chemistry, attended St. Louis University, and then went to medical school in Mexico.

If he was not aware of class or of the ironies of Latin American life in Cuba or in prison, he learned in Mexico, for he lived in a small town, where there was water for only one hour a day, and on weekends he went to Mexico City and mixed with the most elegant people.

He lives in these contrasts: He understands the border not as a line but as an irony, an engine of irony. Dr. Pelly has a son and an adopted daughter. The girl has a sister who lives in Mexico. "One is barefoot and hungry," he says, "and one lives comfortably in my house. They are sisters, both of the same mother. What is the moral of that?"

The border intrigues him, haunts him; he came to Brownsville because it was the border. "Look! There is one of my patients," he said, pointing to a middle-aged customer in a restaurant. "They brought him across the border to me. If he had remained in Mexico, he would have died. It is only a line. On one side the medical care is such that the man would have died; on the other side, he was saved."

Death and the border, the irony of a line that seems to him absurd. He does not say inhumane. Dr. Pelly never uses sentimental words. He is board certified in internal medicine, a physician, a man of science and a collector of Mexican folk art, a student of death's courtiers. "There is a writer in Peru," he said, "who wrote a book about the dead speaking to the dead. There is also such an idea in the New Testament. The dead speak to those who are going to die."

Nothing disconnected comes from him. He speaks of borders, the irony of lines. Of the vast immigration from Latin America across the line he says with a physician's calm: "When there are too many Latinos in the United States, they will tilt the character of the country. Latinos cannot govern themselves; they are ungovernable, because of their culture. To save the country, the government will have to let in more disciplined Germans and intelligent Orientals; there will have to be enough diversity to keep this one group from shifting the character of the country."

When I pointed out to him that this sounded as if culture were defined by race, he thought about it for a moment, then agreed, but he did not revise his theory. That he knew something about politics was revealed later.

We were having dinner at a restaurant across the border in Matamoros. Dr. Pelly was eating Châteaubriand and drinking *agua mineral;* a band was playing old Mexican songs. The doctor, who had not remembered to remove the stethoscope from around his neck until after we had entered the restaurant, dropped out of the conversation for a moment to listen to the music, an Agustín Lara melody played softly, with loving imperfection, or a mambo, some aged Pérez Prado tune revived from La Habana of memory.

Pelly spoke of La Cabaña, the prison where he was held for three months. He remembered how the prisoners had to sleep head to foot, like pieces of a puzzle, to fit onto the floor of the cell. He recalled the watered milk, the thin soup, the days of rice and beans. At one time he was in the *galleria* near the wall where men were shot to death at night. He said he heard the shots and the sound of the bodies falling. He does not recall anyone shouting, "Viva Cristo Rey!" He knows who men ask for in prison.

"One day I remember," he said, "it was Mother's Day. The guard came by, rapping his stick on the bars to see if any of them had been cut, when a man began singing the Mother's Day song. Then all of us, all the political prisoners in the *galleria* began singing." Lorenzo Pelly, M.D., put down his knife and fork and sang softly. His voice was sweet, manly, loving; tears came into the eyes of the physician with the small, very British mustache. He was gone from the room, back in La Cabaña again, and before that, a boy, the son of an English father and a Spanish mother.

> *Madrecita del alma querida,*
> *en mi pecho yo llevo una flor.*

No importe el color que ya tenga,
porque al fin tú eres madre, una flor. [7]

When he returned to the moment, he said, "Sometimes I think of retiring to an HMO in Miami and working nine to five. And sometimes I think of going to work in the jungles of Brazil."

[7]Dear Mother, beloved soul,
in my heart I carry a flower.
The color does not matter,
for you are always Mother, a flower.

In Cuba and Mexico, a red rose signifies one's love for a mother who is alive and a white rose for a mother who has passed on.

22

CHRIST, QUETZALCÓATL, SANTA BARBARA, AND THAT OLD TIME RELIGION

I am a practicing Catholic, but in the Church of God, not in the Church of Rome.   *Penny Lernoux[1]*

They tell us we Mexicans are worthless. I thought I was worthless. I was alcoholic. Until I came to God. Preacher, Christian Evangelical Church

Everyone in South San Antonio knows the old man who walks the streets with his head thrown back, looking straight into the sun. His hair is white, uncombed, a thatch to cover his dark brown, deeply grained face. He pushes a supermarket basket before him. It holds the luck of his day, a few bottles, a pile of empty cans, a good stick, one shoe.

As the old man passed by the house of Mrs. Inés Ramírez, she pointed him out to her daughter and granddaughter, and said, "See how he looks up into the sun!"

She watched the old man, following his progress down the street. If he was blind, how did he locate the bottles and cans? If he was not blind, how did he stare into the sun? Whether he was blind or not, how was it that he did not trip and fall on the broken, rock strewn road?

West of Somerset, on Golden Street and LaVioleta too, people ask metaphysical questions. The sadness in the face of Mrs. Ramírez tells the luck of the neighborhood: A year ago, her youngest son, her "baby," and his fiancée were sitting in his car in the park, when they were attacked by a band of *cholos*. The thugs made her baby watch while they raped the girl, then they shot him to death.

---

[1] Taken from a conversation with the author about *People of God*, Penny Lernoux's book on the worldwide struggle between "the church of Caesar, powerful and rich, and the church of Christ—loving, poor and spiritually rich"

Mrs. Ramírez watched the old man, noting the angle of his head, the way it exposed his throat. "St. Agnes," she said. Her daughter nodded; God has many lambs.

—

All Latinos are metaphysicians; no other historical, cultural, economic, or racial difference so clearly separates them from the worldly Anglos of North America. No businesslike British philosophies, no pragmatic Yankee views, no grumpy German upstart notions divert the Latino mind from the contemplation of unseen yet obvious forces. The three golden ages in the Latino history of origins—Native American, African, and Spanish—have little in common other than metaphysics, which allowed the shrewd Spanish priests to convert conquered nations to Catholicism without changing their fundamental orientation. One man's metaphysics, of course, is another man's superstition; the Spaniards drew the distinction with the sword, then with the missal; finally they blurred it with syncretism. The replacement of the Aztec Tonantzin with *la Virgen de Guadalupe* helped the Náhuas to translate their pagan beliefs into a new language of symbols, without altering the essence of their philosophy. Santería, the Afro-Catholic religion of the Caribbean, identified its entire pantheon with Catholic saints.

The ferocity of the Spanish character matched that of the domineering Caribs and Aztecs almost exactly, and both the invaders and their opponents were armed with metaphysical rationalizations produced by St. Augustine or the Náhua authors of the *Cantares Mexicanos*. The Spaniards conducted the Inquisition to please their God, and the Aztecs sacrificed captives to provide the fluid of movement that fed the gods and enabled the sun to continue its rounds. The Fulani carried the banner of Islam into their wars against the Yoruba, whom they sold as slaves to work the plantations of the Caribbean. And the Caribs ate the Tainos. For both the Aztec Blue Hummingbird of the South and the Yoruba Owner of All Destinies, the sixteenth century marked the beginning of their defeat by the Father, the Son, and the Holy Ghost.

Until recently, however, the notion that only Judeo-Christian religions had any sense of a nonanthropomorphic god led to the popular misconception of African and Native American religions as somehow crude, lacking a true sense of the divine. In 1956, Miguel León-Portilla described the metaphysics of the Náhuas through his analysis of Ometéotl, the Lord and Lady of Duality: "Recognizing that he had his roots in the mysterious duality of the Divine, Náhuatl man acknowledged Ometéotl's transcendency by declaring that he was invisible like the night and intangible like the wind. Feeling all this, the pre-Columbian thinker asked himself if he would someday live in the presence of the Giver of Life, in his dwelling place, from which the 'flowers and songs' came."

By the 1980s a sophisticated interpretation of Yoruba or Lucumí metaphysics had taken the place of mumbo jumbo. Joseph M. Murphy said the Yoruba god, Olodumare, "is the ultimate destiny of all creation; from him all existence comes forth, and to him it all returns. His breath is this force, this pulse of life and death." John Mason of the Yoruba Theological Archministry wrote, "The Yoruba believe that God is too vast an idea to comprehend. So he picks a portion of God—an Orisha—and tries, through comprehension of the part, to gain knowledge of the whole." Nearly five hundred years after the arrival of Columbus in the Western Hemisphere, some idea of what he encountered and what subsequent people brought from Africa made it possible to grasp two of the three sources of the Latino world-view.

Little more need be said of Roman Catholic metaphysics. It is interesting, however, to note how often Latinos, in conversation and in published works, speak of the taking of the Host at Communion. Edward Rivera makes a sweetly comic set piece of a Puerto Rican boy taking his First Communion from an Irish priest in *Family Installments,* but within the comedy he reveals the concern of the boy with the notion of transubstantiation. It is, after all, the instant in which the material world becomes the spiritual; It offers an entrance to the mysteries of metaphysics, signifies a crisis of belief. Later in life, the virgin birth comes to symbolize even more the mystery of faith, the victory of the metaphysical over the material world, a concept to which Latinos cling like no other people on earth. Looking back on the conquest, it seems unlikely that any religion but Catholicism could have melded so easily with the American and African religions, expressing mystical notions through symbols even more realistic and concrete than the phantasmagoric figures of the Aztecs or the Yorubas.

The Náhuas used the figure called *difrasismo,* two concrete objects conjoined to express an abstraction: flowers and song for beauty, night and wind for invisibility, and so on. The Spanish priests translated the *difrasismos* into the abstractions the Náhuas could imagine but could not say. They found the linguistic meeting place of the cultures. A mystical common ground was not far off. The Spaniards did not convert the Americans and Africans; they translated them, producing variant religions more mystical and fatalistic than anything known in Europe for many centuries.

The most useful part of metaphysics for the metaphysician, of course, is that it explains the world. Claude Lévi-Strauss contrasted modern and neolithic (primitive) societies by showing how the neolithic circle permitted everything to be explained, while the straight line of modern society left the world open ended, inexplicable. Catholicism, which explained the inexplicable through faith and mystery, bridged the two worlds; it could produce a Galileo, but it could not countenance him.

With its promise of a reward in the afterlife, Catholicism, like its predecessor religions, enabled the people to endure their lives; it made good workers of the peasants and allowed the rich to pleasure themselves in the certainty of forgiveness. The only flaw in an otherwise perfect system for those in power lay in the ethical teachings of the Bible and its commentators; the hierarchy of the Church in Latin America was never able to control the clergy completely. Intellectually, Latinos were not docile.

In what can best be characterized as a seesaw battle, the metaphysical aspect of Roman Catholicism, the power base of the hierarchy, fought to obliterate the ethical aspect, but it was impossible; trouble began in the Americas with the Indianist arguments of Las Casas in the sixteenth century and never ended. Hidalgo, the village priest who started the independence movement in Mexico, was a terrible problem for both the Church and the Spanish government, which finally executed him and mounted his head on the wall of a granary in Guanajuato. So too, in her way, was the feminist Sor Juana[2] a problem. After Vatican II and the meetings of the Latin American bishops at Medellín in 1968 and Puebla in 1979, with their pronouncements of a "preference for the poor," the hierarchy in Rome was in for a fierce challenge, one that might well decide the future of the Church. The meek had embraced the new dogma of John XXIII. They were wed to the notion that they would inherit the earth and to the "people of God" concept which told them they deserved it.

Mrs. Ramírez, who knew things like the details of the martyrdom of St. Agnes (she was stabbed in the throat), belonged to St. Clare's. Through St. Clare's, she had become one of the first members of Communities Organized for Public Service (COPS).[3] The Church was not only her spiritual home, it was her social and political home as well. Bishop Patricio Flores and Ernesto Cortés, Jr., of IAF had brought together the metaphysical and ethical aspects of the Church: If a wafer could actually be the body of Christ, God could actually be sidewalks, drainage, and paved streets for South San Antonio. But down the street from St. Clare's another ethics and another metaphysics, warmer, closer, smaller, and far less complex, had gained a foothold. The Roman Catholic Church, for so long the only religious force among Latinos, encountered a new problem in the twentieth century: evangelical Protestantism. The new church in the neighborhood was housed in a tiny building no bigger than a grocery store. It had no gymnasium, no school, no community center; its members sat on folding chairs. Still, whole families came to the little church—women, children, and (unlike St. Clare's) men.

Of all the many differences between the two religions, the involvement of

[2]Sor Juana Inés de la Cruz (1651–1695), Mexican poet, feminist, censured by the Church
[3]COPS is the powerful Industrial Areas Foundation group in San Antonio, whose executive director (in 1990), Tom Holler, had studied for the priesthood.

men in the evangelical churches was the most pronounced. Maria Elisa Aguilar, a Mexican-American who attended Roman Catholic schools in Chicago, said, "In Catholic Church, the priest is in charge, and he's a man, so there seem to be few men who come to church and get involved. In the evangelical church, the men can be in charge. They can't find a place in the Catholic Church." She has remained in the Church, but her parish is a world of women, many of whom cannot talk to the priest, a Pole from the Midwest who speaks no Spanish.

The Native American and African religions made a peaceful marriage with Roman Catholicism, but the evangelicals present a different problem, much more like the Reformation than the Conquest; the Protestants are bold attackers rather than frightened defenders of the faith. The evangelicals show only a minimal concern for the otherworldly aspects of religion. The symbolism of the Catholic Church is odious to them; they attack the Mexican belief in *la Virgen de Guadalupe* as idolatry. Read the Bible, they say, not your missal. Their arguments are simple, blunt, often formulated for untutored parishioners by equally untutored preachers. The great ontological and epistemological issues of metaphysics do not have an important place in the informal liturgy of the little churches that grow up in storefronts and basements. The evangelicals are neither Roman nor European nor Latin American. They are the church of the United States of America, the apotheosis of American values: generous, warm, informal, egalitarian, and utterly devoted to the principle of self-improvement.

I. SANTERÍA, ESPIRITISMO Y MEDIOS

Carlota del Portillo, Ph. D., relative of a Nobel prize–winner, the niece of a bishop, a woman of such tremendous energy she cannot talk fast enough to keep up with the stream of thoughts, opinions, stories, pronouncements, jokes, and *dichos* that come roaring into her consciousness, leaned across the corner of the table in one of San Francisco's more stylish restaurants and whispered, "Of course, I see a *medio* (medium). Every Puerto Rican sees one; we all have a sense of the spiritual world. My aunt in Brooklyn knows a woman who is absolutely fantastic. She helped my cousin to marry a nice Italian boy. Whenever I'm in New York . . ." A moment later, she was discussing the politics of education, asking from her feminist perspective whether Latinas were unwilling, unprepared, or prevented from taking full advantage, and whether her daughter from her first marriage, who has recently completed law school, is being held back because she is dark-skinned. One must listen carefully to the conversation of Dr. del Portillo, pick a thread and stay with it. In this case, the thread was *medios*.

No person could be more worldly, yet she would not be dissuaded from her credulousness. Does Dr. del Portillo really run her life according to the divinations of a medium? This seems unlikely. In the living room of the del Portillo's two-story house at the top of one of San Francisco's hills, with the lights of the city and the Bay Bridge below, this seems impossible. Carlota del Portillo is a driven careerist, gracious, generous, but driven. If she has occasion to meet spirits from another world, it must be to debate them.

And yet, like many Puerto Ricans, she lacks guile; if she says she goes credulously to a medium in Brooklyn, it must be so. Her purpose is not to find out how to run the San Francisco school district, but to enjoy the warmth of an ancient form of psychotherapy, the healing of community. Unlike Western medicine, Santería, spiritism, and the folk medicine of Mexico practiced by *curanderos* and a few *brujos*[4] on both sides of the border are not cold and lonely acts. The healer or shaman, who may be called a *medio* or *babalawo* or the *curandero* of this or that, is often a person who has learned through some personal disability (blindness, obesity, dwarfism, disfigurement) of the cruelties of fate and life and how to cope with them.

The shaman, unlike the medical doctor or Western psychotherapist, has no professional organizations or diplomas to bolster his credibility; he must always begin by demonstrating that he knows something, then he can multiply the power of his knowledge by the history of his successes. Compared to the shaman, Western doctors and psychotherapists are as vulgar as butchers. Physicians resort to the knife when the word will do, and psychotherapists have no talent but tenacity in the talking cure, which they carry on for years without ever achieving the kind of results a shaman delivers in an afternoon.[5]

What appears, at first, to be occult or bizarre in Native American medicine is, I think, more often connected to the concept of knowing something: The healer has access to knowledge, which the patient recognizes as power. Carlos Castaneda's books about Don Juan, a *brujo,* and the fantastic alter ego known to Mexicans as a *náhual,* are based on the idea of knowledge as power: The *brujo* makes contact with his *náhual,* who becomes his guide to knowledge. Since the books were published in the 1960s, the use of drugs as an aid to gaining knowledge became more widely known than the more intellectually interesting aspects of *brujería.*

Every *brujo* and every *curandero* must demonstrate some special knowledge. The *curandero de Pancho Villa* claims to gain his power through intimate knowledge of the Mexican revolutionary. Some years ago, when I was

---

[4]Healers and witches

[5]In *The Death of the Great Spirit* (Simon & Schuster, 1971), I described a cure of Bell's palsy, partial paralysis of the face, by Navajo medicine.

thinking through a novel about Villa, I visited with the *curandero* at his house in Los Charcos, a tiny village in northern Mexico. I could see immediately that business had been bad of late. He was disturbed by the building of a house of cement block nearby, and he had not been well: For several days he had been bedridden, feverish, and without sensation in his legs. A white stubble had grown on his face, his undershirt was stained, and he said the sun caused him to feel chilled. These were natural things, he said, incurable signs of old age, like the loss of his teeth and the failing tone of the muscles in his upper arms. He sighed and smoked, leaning on the adobe fence in front of his house. His right eye was sightless, turned off to one side, partially covered by a thick yellow cataract; he squinted the other eye in the sun. A pig, docile as a pet, stood beside him.

Inside his house it was cool and dark. A pair of sunglasses, a safety razor, and a bar of soap lay on the gray blanket that covered his narrow bed. He sat on the bed, put on his sunglasses, and invited his guest to sit in the chair beside him. He spoke in a hoarse voice: The slow singing of the border was not in his voice; he drove his words. The man was like the room of his house: The adobe walls were bare; the floor was hard dirt; the door was raised a foot above the level of the ground, distrustful of the rains.

The *curandero* led me to a small room attached to the back of the house. It was an airless box, four feet wide, eight feet long, and five feet high. There were no windows. The only source of light was a bulb fixed to the wall above the chair in which he sat.

The altar beside him, made of stucco, pale green, like the walls and the ceiling, was decorated with framed pictures in a photographically unreal style. A benign, pastel Jesus looked out at the patient. Crucifixes and deer-skin pouches were affixed to the wall above the altar. On the wall to the left of the *curandero* was a photograph of Pancho Villa leading a troop of cavalry. Behind the chair in which the patient sits a portrait of Villa was hung beside a small Mexican flag.

The *curandero* and his patient faced each other across the narrowness of the room, each in his wooden chair with a caved-in upholstered seat. The lower part of the *curandero*'s chair was draped with unbleached cotton cloth that reached to the floor. The patient's chair was unsteady; the rungs had lost their paint; the wood was gray.

We smoked, filling the room with the palest blue. He wore sunglasses, he smiled; his undershirt shifted, revealing the fragility of his yellowing old man's skin; his teeth were staggers of brown and yellow, his hands were thick and bent, the fingernails were funereal. The smoke stung our eyes.

The *curandero* began a litany of the life of Pancho Villa with the birth of Doroteo Arango at La Coyotada. An ordered, accurate history emerged, neither said nor sung, but recited, as all long-known truths are told, formally, in rhythms of certainty and sanctification. But the proof of the powers of Pancho Villa was not for me. I had come for information: What kind of man was he? Did you know him? I know his history, I am seeking to understand his character.

A moment cracked, a system trembled, he breathed and rubbed his dying thigh. "Pancho Villa was a very serious man. He did not drink or smoke or use bad language. He used the root to learn that his spirit was a small bird."

"What root? Peyote?"

"Peyote is not a root. He used the root of gold [*raíz de oro*] to see [*ver*]."

"To see what? Visions? To see as in dreams?"

"No. To see. When a man uses this *raíz de oro,* he sleeps for two or three minutes. Then he wakes up, and he sees clearly."

We looked at each other blankly. There is no Spanish word for insight. "How do you know he used this root?"

"Because of the spirit of the small bird," he said, and then he began again to tell the history of Villa. While he spoke, I concentrated on his face and his words. In the periphery of the field of vision of my right eye a small black bird appeared. The *curandero* seemed to know, for he changed the direction of his speech; the history eased over into the mystical experience. "You can speak to Pancho Villa. His is the greatest power. Well, the greatest power after the power of Our Lord. He will speak through you, the power of him will be in you."

The bird was there, as real as the room, still, black, larger than a crow. I saw its head, its eye, the gleam and the crackling mechanical moves of it. The sealed green room had been entered by the spirit of Pancho Villa; there could be no doubt about it. The picture over my head was a symbol of the position of Villa; he would speak through me.

The old man spoke, too. His blind, crooked eye was turned up in my direction, raised above the cataract, looking at me. "Villa's spirit will come through you. He will speak from your mouth. It will be expensive. The spirit of Pancho Villa must be paid. Do you have money?"

"Yes, yes, how much?"

"He will tell you."

Everything I saw was true, yet I could not believe it, as I do not truly believe that airplanes fly above the clouds or that men have walked on the moon.

We negotiated. We talked of art and insight and the spirit of Pancho Villa. I insisted upon consciousness; he spoke of the world beyond knowing. I watched his crooked eye and his brown teeth. The painting of Christ glowed; the deerskin bags hung heavy with secrets; the pastel-colored photograph of Villa on Siete Leguas, his favorite horse, achieved dimension. The bird was gone.

The opportunity had disappeared. How had I allowed it to escape me? The eye stared, the man spoke, but I thought only of the spirit of Pancho Villa. Significant men do not have such failures. Literature belongs to the quick. Other failures passed between my eyes and the eye of the *curandero*: novels written too soon, essays written too late, summer girls of adolescence lost in a phrase. The blind eye was now unbearable; I could sense the texture of the cataract, the inevitability with which it crawled across his eye. And what was his illness? He coughed, his face was damp: Typhoid had been reported in northern Mexico.

"We are good Catholics," he said. "We believe in God. God permits man to eat whatever is on this earth. It is not a sin to use peyote or *raiz de oro.*" On and on went the argument, the same one I had heard from peyotists in South Dakota, Montana, California, and Arizona. I was the bored victim of my own skepticism, having learned too late that credulity is a virtue of heroes. Villa, Villa, Villa, what he might have said; the photograph was smiling as if the bird was now saved from revealing its secrets to me.

Stingy fool! If only I had immediately agreed to pay. The gods of Mexico are insatiable. This one wanted only money; Huitzilopochtli would have asked for the flesh of my heart. My eyes fell; I could not hear. I watched the feet of the *curandero,* the toes as tough as hooves, the skin the color of the servant of the sun. Behind the feet the cloth moved. And there was the bird, the spirit of Pancho Villa, caged in cloth beneath an old man's chair. I gave the *curandero* a handful of pesos and went away laughing, for he had taught me the rule of magic, which is that it is either there or it is not; as in logic, there is no middle ground. Those who abandon magic to live completely in the modern world cannot ever hope to know what the *curandero* knows. The *mestizaje* of minds goes only forward in time, trudging into the modern, unknowing world.

The methods of the *curandero de Pancho Villa* apply across the many worlds of Latino culture, even to the use of physical deformity. It may be coincidence, but the *babalawo* of Brooklyn has only a blank white cornea where his left eye should be. He is an enormous man, as big as a taxicab, outsized except for his head, which he sometimes holds in his giant hand as if it were a coconut. When he speaks of the head, he puts his hand on the top of his skull and grasps it down to the temples, to the ears, as if he were about to pick it off the stem of his neck and toss the talking, white-eyed thing into a corner.

He has no shyness, no modesty. What would be the use? He speaks of Shango/Santa Barbara, then of Ogun/Santiago, the Yoruba god of energy— war, inheritance, medicine, and perspiration—and it may be that when his conversation turns to rape and martial arts, to bashing in a man's head with a brick or raping one's mother, it is not the *babalawo,* but Ogun who is speaking. The *babalawo* is a diviner, a reader of seashells and pieces of coconut. He knows something, speaks often of himself and what he knows: "I studied martial arts. My father told me . . . When I was in college . . . At the age of thirty-four I owned all these buildings . . . They call me to strange places to do divinations. In my garden of herbs . . . I had to take out the tree, to remove it by the roots, to rape the land. When I was the curator . . . In Cuba . . . The word in Spanish, *vega,* it means farmer. My son . . . My house . . . In Yoruba, we say . . ." He is a laughing god, a good-time medicine man, with a blind, omniscient eye and a Churchillian cigar in the breast pocket of his black and white checked shirt.

In Santería, every *babalawo* knows something more than his patients about the *orishas,* and so does every *santero* who has been initiated, that is, possessed by an *orisha* or god in a trance. Advice on everything from love to picking a winning number in the lottery to making good business deals can be gained from a medium (a *babalawo* or a person who has been initiated) or direct from an *orisha* during a trance. In fact, the *babalawo* practices herbal medicine and effective short-term psychotherapy. His magic may be either contagious or sympathetic, but it is always supportive.

Santería, like the religion of the Aztecs and Christianity,[6] holds that there is an interdependent relation between the secular and divine worlds. The putative effect of the gods upon humans in African and Native American religions is widely known, but the effect of humans upon the gods is seldom discussed. Joseph Murphy quotes a Yoruba proverb which says that without human beings there would be no *orishas.* The Aztecs fed human blood to their gods to maintain the motion of the sun. Christians say that sin causes pain to Christ and that there is a divine spark in every person. In all three cases the interrelationship between man and his gods gives dignity to man by making him more than a powerless object. Although there is no hint in Native American religion, as far as I know, of the Freudian notion of man creating god, the value of man in relation to his gods is greater in Native American belief than in Christianity.

These syncretic religions of the Americas, which appear strange, primitive to the Anglo observer, bring humanity into a different, more personal, and more egalitarian relationship with its gods. To the degree that these religions are arcane, they are powerful, for the value of knowledge in the spiritual world decreases in direct relation to the number of people who possess it. But the point that cannot be overlooked is that these religions are powerful, if by powerful we mean efficacious. Santería, Espiritismo, and Brujería make sick people whole, whether the sickness is of the mind or the body.

---

[6] With the exception, of course, of Christian existentialists

Unfortunately, these religions also contribute to making people sick, for they are a part of the culture that causes Latinos to be rejected by Anglo society, a contribution to the rationale for discrimination. The tension between the practitioners of Santería and modern medicine is so great that some *babalawos* promise serious harm to people who go to medical doctors or hospitals for treatment. And no medical doctor would ever consult with a *curandero*. Both sides draw a line at the stethoscope. If some people suffer or die because the line cannot be crossed, it is of little importance to the practitioners: The line is more important than the life. If Latinos wish to succeed in the United States, the medical doctors and the psychologists say, they must learn to respect the preeminence of the material world; the *brujos* and the *babalawos* claim a different truth.

2. CATHOLICISM

Penny Lernoux's distinction between "the Church of Rome" and "the Church of God" limns the schism in the Roman Catholic Church in the United States. On the one hand, the Church defends the poor in sanctuaries for undocumented immigrants, fights for water in the colonias along the border, and is home to almost all of the social action groups working in the Latino community; on the other hand, the U.S. clergy is overwhelmingly Anglo, Irish, or German, and many of the priests have the same view of Latinos that Bishop Lamy brought to New Mexico in the middle of the nineteenth century. The conflict between the reactionary Frenchman and the people's priest of Chimayó is repeated in parishes in New York, in Chicago, and across the Southwest. Sister Mary Beth Larkin in El Paso uses the word "racist" to describe the clergy.

She refers to people like James Steffens, the priest at Our Lady of Guadalupe Church in Houston, the first church in that city to hold Mass in Spanish, who speaks of his parishioners, all of whom are Latinos, as if he were a missionary among savages. Latinos return the favor: At a church on the west side of San Antonio, some of the parishioners refer to their Anglo priest as "a dope."

Even when the Church tries to overcome its racial and ethnic problems, it often fails. To reach out to the Latino community of Houston the church sends an icy Cuban priest to be its auxiliary bishop, a man more interested in the rightist politics of Armando Valladares than the liberal political views of his flock, many of whom are poor, including the refugees who have fled from the right-wing death squads in El Salvador.

About a third of the Catholics in the United States are Latinos. A tiny fraction, perhaps one in a hundred, of the priests who minister to them are

U.S. born Latinos. Even though priests like Gregory Boyle and nuns like Mary Beth Larkin work in the United States, the general character of the Catholic Church remains colonial, cold, with perfunctory ritual taking the place of prayer. Roberto Piña, a bold layman in San Antonio, described the situation in an article in *New Catholic World*:

Earlier this year, Rosie [Mrs. Piña] and I attended a Rosary for Rosie's aunt. We experienced the utter frustration and painful vacuum that we have experienced so often before when the priest walked up to the kneeler and without so much as a word of greeting or explanation started the monotone utterances which fell so short of what a prayer to our Blessed Mother should be. He finished in the same tone as he started and departed. Rosie and I were exchanging comments on our disappointment and wondering why—why especially since at least half of the family there were Protestants who had once been Catholics. (Of course the priest had no way of knowing that, unless he had made some effort to find out something about the family beforehand.) While we were still in this state of questioning and thirsting, one of the Protestant members of the family went to the front and spoke as a Christian thanking and welcoming other Christians for coming together to accompany the family in their moment of sorrow. He gave witness to the faith he represented and used those moments to call us all to get in touch with ourselves and the present state of our relationship with God and our fellow men. I'm sure he reached the hearts of many and possibly had many thinking, *I wish I belonged to his church.*

Piña was not proselytizing for Protestantism; he is a full-time lay employee of the Catholic Church. His office is in the Mexican American Cultural Center (MACC), which was founded in 1972 as a bridge between what its literature euphemistically calls "the Hispanic and the North American way of life." The center trains the Catholic clergy, members of various religious orders, and some laymen in the language and culture of Latinos, primarily Mexican-Americans. Courses include *Musica hispana en la liturgia,* Religious Celebrations with Hispanic Youth, *La conciencia religiosa del mexicoamericano,* Counseling with Hispanic Families, *La Mujer Hispana: Desafios y aspiraciones.*[7]

The MACC campus feels like that of an old, very small, and poorly endowed midwestern college. A few people in clerical garb walk around the campus, but it is largely a lay institution, Mexican Catholic more than Roman

[7]The titles in Spanish above are: Spanish Music in the Liturgy, The Religious Conscience of the Mexican American, The Spanish Woman: Challenges and Hopes.

Catholic. The members of the faculty remember Chicanismo; they compare themselves to Juan Diego[8] rather than to the Spanish priests who converted him. MACC has chosen the people; it recognizes that its mission is to make a different, more personal connection between the Catholic Church and its Latino parishioners.

Leonard Anguiano, a faculty member who edited a book of chicano writing, works with Salvadoran refugees now. Some of them stay in his house, while they look for work or try to make connections to go northeast to Washington, D.C. or west to California. Anguiano, Piña, and others on the MACC faculty recognize the problem of the Church as distance from its parishioners. They remark on the size of some of the parishes, 80,000 to 100,000 in Mexico City. How can a priest be close to 100,000 people? The minister of a Protestant evangelical church, one who participates in healing, they say, is much closer to a *curandero* than to a priest; he works in a small group, knows everyone, is familiar with them, is one of them. But then Anguiano points out a major social difference between the Catholic Church and the little Protestant evangelical churches. "They collect money only to help each other. We collect to help everyone." It does not occur to him that what he sees as a moral strength is an organizational weakness.

A few miles away at St. Alphonsus Roman Catholic Church, the Anglo priest, known to his Latino parishioners as Father Norm, speaks of the Church losing hundreds of members every month. When he walks through the dayroom after Mass on Sunday morning, he sees his parishioners eating breakfast tacos of fried potatoes and chiles or sausages and eggs, and they are all grandmothers, rows and rows of grandmothers, cooking and gossiping, with only a few old men sitting by themselves gumming soft tacos and drinking coffee out of paper cups. Men like Father Norm, although they have the best intentions, may be at the heart of the Church's problem, for they are strangers to the culture, too human and not human enough.

A couple in south central Los Angeles, retired, the grandparents of teenagers, with a strong sense of having made a success of their lives, of having raised strong generations to follow, have left the Church. Both were born in Mexico, raised in the Church, and still consider themselves Catholic, but the husband said, "I only go to Church for weddings and funerals. That's all. I don't go to Mass. I don't give them anything."

The wife said, "I'm not afraid of dying, so I don't go anymore. I don't believe in confessing to a man. Sometimes, when I lie in bed at night, I talk to God."

He is the realist and she is the metaphysician. The Church has lost them both. It has also lost their children and their children's children, generations, an entire extended family.

---

[8]The Mexican Indian to whom la Virgen de Guadalupe appeared

There are other reasons for the weakening of the Church, and they are not so esoteric. Father Jesse Montes, a big, burly, balding, bespectacled, delicate, courageous, timid, outspoken priest who teaches at the Don Bosco Technical Institute in Los Angeles, knows exactly what is wrong. He worked in a parish in east Los Angeles until the church had to be closed after the earthquake. He still goes back there often in his sputtering old car to visit *las viejas* or to talk to the children.

Jesse Montes was born in east Los Angeles to a mother he describes as paranoid and a father who never worked steadily because of a broken leg. The father was a tyrant who did odd jobs and lied to the welfare worker about them. Jesse was close to his mother, who was frightened of the world, including the caseworkers from the welfare department, gringos who burst in on them without warning at any hour of the day or night to inspect the way they lived.

"We were desperately poor," Montes said. "Everything came from the government: food, housing, even our clothing."

The relation of people to institutions is constantly in his conversation. "The social workers then were gringos who demeaned people. Now, they're chicanos who can't speak Spanish. This one chicano social worker was addressing an old Mexican woman as *tú*. Finally, he said to her '*Vete, vete,*' just as you would to a child or an animal. My mother was there and she saw everything. It made her more paranoid than ever."

Anglos dominated every aspect of life in east Los Angeles when he was a child, even the naming of children. His mother called him Jesús, but the Anglo nuns at school told him no one should be named Jesus, so they changed his name to Jesse.

In the parish Father Jesse was known for his attentiveness and his Mejicanismo. He was always there when he was needed—he would leave his dinner half-eaten or go out in the middle of the night—to give the last rites or comfort the sick or break up a gang fight in the street. Not so the Spanish priests, he said. "They don't understand the needs of Mexicans to do something at the moment. When their parishioners call for a priest, the Spaniards put them off. They're like the Church, too structured. Mexican life is not so structured."

He shakes his head when comparing evangelicals to Catholics: "With us, so many are trying to make money. For a *quinceañera* they charge twenty-five dollars for a little one, but if it's big, with a lot of relatives, they charge a hundred dollars. These Spanish priests say the family is spending so much money. They don't know the man saved for years; it's everything he has."

Father Jesse has no solution for the problems of the Church. Life has not been easy for him. Ever since he was hit in the head with a broken bottle while trying to break up a fight he has been very afraid of gangs. There are too many demands on him; he tries to please everyone: his fellow priest who wants to go to the ballet, his mother, his students, a young Mexican-American social worker in east Los Angeles. Drugs frighten him; he is hungry for a good steak dinner instead of the food at the Don Bosco Institute. At the end of a two-day retreat of Carisima en Misiones at the Sociedad Misionera de Evangelización Católica Father Jesse stands in the back of the hall, listening to a young lay preacher from Mexico discuss the relation of lay people to the Catholic Church in terms of the parts of the body; the lay people are at the extremes of the limbs.

Nothing arcane enters the young Mexican's sermon. He speaks of pornography, Satanism, *Brujería, porquería.*[9] Behind him a small band of musicians waits its turn to play electronic instruments. Only one man works during the sermon, playing softly on an acoustic guitar. No priests come to speak.

Many of the people in the audience still have the look of the old country, the young women with long hair, John the Baptist hair, the young men trying harder to abandon *el otro lado,*[10] seeking to look more like the *cholos* and pachucos of East L.A. All the people in the room have paid twelve dollars for the retreat, including meals; there will be one more meal. It is hot; the air is polluted at the end of another dry summer. Huge fans roil the air; a great lamp hung from the ceiling swings easily in the breeze. The preacher holds a microphone in his hand, now whispering, now shouting. Lunch will be late. There is a flea market outside.

"The Protestants have rock stars," Father Jesse said.

—

In *Occupied America,* Rodolfo Acuña spoke of the reasons for the increasing weakness of the Church among Mexican-Americans, then turned to some of the changes that may eventually bring them together again. He concentrated on Los Angeles, where the attitude of the Church toward Latinos and their problems improved immediately after Archbishop John Francis McIntyre was replaced. The other accommodation Acuña saw was the involvement of the Church in various IAF organizations in Texas and California. With his focus on Los Angeles, where he lives, Acuña was acutely aware of the problems IAF had in its local organization, UNO. The east Los Angeles area, as he noted, is made up largely of poor people, mainly from rural Mexico, many of them undocumented. In his view, UNO was less successful than other IAF organizations because of its constituency.

He may be correct, but other factors are also important. The history of the Catholic Church in Los Angeles, dominated for so many years by McIntyre's reactionary politics, may have made it a less useful ally. The presence of

---

[9]Rubbish, filth
[10]The other side (of the Rio Grande)

Ernesto Cortés, Jr., who brought the Alinsky methods to Texas in 1973 and still manages IAF in the state, could be the reason for its success there. The few, but courageous, Latinos in the Catholic hierarchy in Texas could also account for the difference. Certainly, Bishop Flores made EPISO possible in El Paso.

But more than anything else, the IAF in Texas, like the Mothers of East L.A., has caught the Mexican-American community where it dreams, not in the middle class, but at the entrance to the middle class. In Houston, El Paso, San Antonio, Pharr, and Los Angeles, the people who provide the impetus to IAF and similar organizations come almost entirely from an emerging middle class. They are intelligent, unafraid, homeowners who have little or no other capital, practicing Catholics and frequently the parents of successful children—immigrants.

IAF or MELA is the instrument they use to bargain for the new social contract that distinguishes immigrants from transporters, sojourners, and ghosts. The Catholic Church, which for centuries advised the transporters and sojourners not to worry about their contract with this world, but to endure suffering (*aguantar*) in preparation for the next world, has increasingly become a supporter of the struggle to immigrate. It has joined in that true political and economic revolution, but not in the social revolution that accompanies it.

The flaw in the dependence of IAF on the institution of the Catholic Church, according to its critics on the left, is that IAF teaches the form of change, but not the content. IAF groups are politically liberal, the critics say, but socially reactionary. The Church aids IAF with money, meeting places, and its blessing, but in return the Church gains great numbers of political activists who support its social agenda: opposition to abortion, condemnation of homosexuality, and so on. What would happen, the liberals ask, if the Church were to turn to IAF for help in implementing its social programs? What if Rome should demand . . .

For many Latinos a Church that feels "a preferential option for the poor"[11] can also oppose abortion and divorce, demand celibacy from its clergy, refuse heaven to an infant that dies without the last rites, and show no mercy in its war against homosexuals; they see no conflict. At some level far beyond a layman's ability to comprehend, everything is of a piece, unified by faith. Meanwhile, there are births and First Communions and *quinceañeras* and weddings and last rites and Masses for the dead. The priest must come soon; there is no time to waste. No one knows death so well as the priest; no one is so versed in the symbols and rituals that connect this world to the other, to the City of God, Mictlán, Paradise.

Metaphysics.

---

[11]Expressed by John XXIII, the Medellín Conference, and John Paul during his U.S. tours

3. OLD TIME RELIGION

At dark the music begins. From a distance, across the parking lot of the shopping center or on the road that leads out of Chula Vista to the main highway south to Tijuana, it sounds like a recording—hands clapping, tambourines and drummers keeping time. It sounds like that old time religion.

"Yes, sir!"

"Come on!"

"That's right!"

"Come on, brother! Come on!"

"Orale!"

"Come on!"

In a storefront, long and narrow, sixty chairs, a raised platform, and a podium constitute a church. Beside the platform an electric piano, bass, guitar, and drums face a quartet of music stands. Because of the narrowness of the room, there are only three rows of chairs, twenty in each row, with an aisle in the center—a church of sixty, never more.

The preacher's son, a fat-faced high-school boy, plays guitar. A boy too handsome for the movies, dressed in a maroon turtleneck sweater and wearing his hair in a pompadour, plays the drums. The boy who sits at the electric piano is very thin and has a painful case of acne. They play Christian rock music. The congregation of twenty-three sings loudly.

When he thinks no more people will come, the preacher gets up out of his chair and stands beside the podium. He is a short, muscular man who combs his hair straight back and looks at his congregation out of Oriental eyes, but the sinister aspect of his face is relieved as soon as he smiles, showing deep dimples in both cheeks. He was a gangster as a boy, and he still exhibits some of the cockiness, the swagger of youth. Although he has put on a white shirt, a tie, and a sportcoat for the meeting, the tattoos are somehow visible under his coat, and the pachuco cross on his hand is real.

The reformed gangster will be followed to the pulpit by a visiting preacher who is a reformed alcoholic. It is a scene from St. Augustine: The audience will be bathed in confessions. The aim of the evening is nothing less than to repeat the fall of Rome, for a humble church of God to topple Caesar once again.

It begins with morality plays presented by the members of the congregation. They come out of a small room at the back of store/church and mount the platform to act out for the audience, greatly diminished in size by the number of people involved in the drama, a play they have themselves conceived. In the play a judge hears two women give witness to how they sought out Satan. One of the women calls herself Tiny Loca, explaining that she is the female version of a *vato loco* and that she uses drugs; the other is Madonna Marrana, who says she calls herself a virgin, but she was never really a virgin. Satan then attempts to defend what he has done to these women, but the judge finds him evil and sends him to Hell.

After the drama, a woman stands up and sings in Spanish about *Una Christiana Evangelica*. She sings sweetly, beautifully, accompanied by an acoustic guitar. The performance is very moving and there is a little silence after she finishes singing, as if she were truly to be praised before the applause begins.

Many of the people in the congregation are related. Of the forty or more people who come to the service only five different families are represented; the church is, in fact, little more than an extended family praying together. This one, however, is in trouble. The preacher explains that he has been laid off from his job and has not received a paycheck for two weeks; the church owes $700 rent for the store. Several times during the meeting he appeals for money.

When several dramas have been presented and more songs have been sung, the guest preacher is introduced. He calls his wife up to testify. She speaks for a moment or two about the spirit of God being in the room, then she starts to cry and has to sit down. He thanks her, "My little red jalapeño pepper." She is a fat lady with very white skin.

The guest preacher, a tall, ungainly man with a deeply pocked face, begins by suggesting that people read several passages from scripture. The people open their Bibles, which are well-used, many of them in zippered leather bindings, some underlined, some marked with yellow highlighter.

He speaks of Moses and Aaron, the voodoo churches in Tijuana, the way the devil seems to be over this church. At one point he sits down in a folding chair and reads, with flourishes, from a book of children's stories, the tale "The Emperor's New Clothes." Everyone is intrigued by the story; they laugh loudly at the end.

Half of his stories are pointless. Sometimes he forgets the punchlines. "There was a woman whose tongue was so long," he said, speaking of gossip, "that she could . . ."—then he got lost, wandered around the platform for a moment, and finally said—". . . lick the pot in the kitchen."

He spoke of illusion, how people got nicknames put on them, how he, for instance was called Flojo (lazy), because he spoke slowly. Then he spoke of alcoholism. He told of the death of his grandmother, how she left his grandfather with seven children, a life that soon sent his grandfather to drink, which caused him to die of liver disease, leaving the children to raise each other. "All seven children," he said, "including the mother of your preacher this evening, became alcoholics. I was an alcoholic too, until Jesus saved me."

Only then does he begin the part of the service the people have come for.

He asks them to come forward, to come to Jesus. Everyone but his wife and the wife of the preacher whose church it is rises and walks toward the platform, gathering around him, crowding close to him, so that he can lean over them from the height of his platform and lay hands on them. They speak in tongues, he speaks in tongues. The other preacher stands behind laying on hands, speaking in tongues. The woman who played Tiny Loca speaks loudest in tongues, weeping through the sounds. There is a great babble—Hebrew, African, Arabic—the sound of the tongue gone wild in the mouth, uncontrollable. It is an ironic version of YHWH, the ancient Hebrew notion of the ineffability of the name of God, and it is everyone's, this wordless, dreamed, felt, metaphysical creator to whom they are all speaking, saying what words cannot tell, while the preachers shout Hallelujahs, Amens, Hosannahs. Come on! Orale! Hallelujah! Come on to Jesus! Come on!

4. UPON THIS ROCK I BUILD MY CHURCH

The ex-Pinto took off his dark glasses and looked me cold in the face. He had a deadly stare, narrow eyes and dark, tight skin stretched over high cheekbones, like a killing snake. If I had not known him, I would have thought he was preparing his soul for murder.

We drank iced tea and ate a *caldillo* of ground meat and red chiles. It was early afternoon. A few people sat at the bar of the cantina, which was south of the freeway, near the line between El Chuco and Juaritas. A neighborhood whore and a man in a black shirt with a white vest printed on the front drank beer. No one used the pool table. The jukebox was quiet. The high desert sun made a blinding rectangle of the doorway.

He had been to prison three times: twice in California, once in Texas; once as a juvenile, twice as an adult; always for armed robbery, always because he needed money to buy heroin. He was not an ordinary man anymore; he spoke by hand signs, tattoos, in English, Spanish, Caló; he preferred not to speak at all.

"I saw this guy on the street," he said. "I was going to rob him. Then I saw these two brothers from Victory House.[12] I had to choose—rob the man or join the church. I saw in their eyes that God was watching me. I made the decision for God. I'm still clean since then."

He put his dark glasses on, completely cool; he was St. Peter of the Christian Evangelical Church of El Chuco.

---

[12]A rehabilitation program for drug addicts and criminals run by Protestant evangelicals

23
NEITHER HERE NOR THERE

When the theory of the melting pot still operated in the United States, artists said, in a flat-footed way, I am an American writer or painter or composer. They did not want to be Italian-American or Irish-American or Jewish-American, for the hyphen, that lonely segment of the great line of human society, separated them from the rest of the Americans; it cast them back into the inhospitable world from which they had so recently escaped.

Even so, some of the writers who came in the great waves of immigration of the late nineteenth and early twentieth centuries wrote of the old country, for memory was all they knew, and if it was good writing, like that of Isaac Bashevis Singer, the literature of some universal country located in Poland or Germany or Italy, their work was widely read first by their fellow immigrants and later translated into other languages. For the most part, however, the literature of the European immigrants was neither about Europe nor America; it was about becoming American. The accompanying music went beyond being American, it was downright chauvinistic: George M. Cohan was not an Irish-American dandy, he was a "Yankee Doodle dandy, . . . born on the Fourth of July."

The wish for assimilation overwhelmed the connection to the old world; the artists of those generations had either to paint, write, dance, and make music for an audience bent upon assimilation or be content to keep their work within a narrowing world. The purpose of the famous "Bintel Brief," a column in the *Jewish Daily Forward,* was to help the immigrant population of the Lower East Side of New York understand their new country and become a part of it. Detailed news of an immigrant's homeland was not likely to be found in the *Forward*. The paper was true to its name; it did not look back.

Black writers, known then as Negroes, but not hyphenated, dealt with their problems as Americans, grievously wronged Americans, but Americans nevertheless. The genius of Richard Wright, Ralph Ellison, and James Baldwin grew out of their *American* anger, not their African ancestry. Alex Haley, a black writer, did finally produce a book about his African heritage, but it was not art; *Roots* had the labored grace of good intentions.

During the 1950s, when the drive for assimilation was at its peak, the "happens to be" artists appeared: "I am an American writer who happens to be black" or "I am an American violinist who happens to be Jewish." In other words, ethnicity was an accident; one was American by choice, and in a time dominated by a vague conception of the existential burden of freedom, choice was all that mattered. Twenty years later, it was too late for white artists to be anything but Americans. It was time for black artists to take their turn at struggling with the hyphen, but black culture was so woven into the general American culture that separating out antecedents was impossible; the language of American music and literature could not be described as black or white. And Wright, Baldwin, and Ellison knew little, if anything, about African literature and certainly could not read, write, or even speak an African language. Racism—not the hyphen of language, story, or song— separated blacks from other American artists.

For one group of American artists, however, the hyphen had a different meaning; Latinos could not abandon the old country or its culture, for they were too close to home. Martí did not write about American issues while he lived in New York; he wrote about Cuba. Nor did Hostos or Ricardo Flores Magón concern himself with life in the States. They were sojourners; they all expected to go back. Others came to the United States as transporters, people who never left their home. The first Latin-American poet to win a Nobel Prize was a teacher who lived on Long Island, New York, but Gabriela Mistral did not write American poetry; her work belonged to Chile.

Contemporary Latino artists have been to the old country, even if the old country is Miami rather than La Habana. Many, perhaps most, have lost their fluency in Spanish, but few have lost their grandmothers. And even if they had, the constant flow of newcomers from Latin America and the contact between native born U.S. citizens and newcomers makes it all but impossible for Latino artists to avoid the hyphen; they are a discrete segment in the long line of culture. They live in a situation which removes the power of choice from their artistic lives, no matter how much they wish it were otherwise. The memoirist Richard Rodriguez argues, in finely crafted English prose, that he is a happens-to-be, but he isn't, he cannot be. To change his situation he would have to be able to "pass" for Anglo; only then would he have the option of inviting the problems of inauthenticity upon himself.

The real issue for Latino artists, the one that can be chosen, involves artistic antecedents. When Yreina Cervantez stands on a scaffold under a freeway in Los Angeles painting a mural of chicano history, she is perfectly aware of her antecedents among the Mexican muralists; she welcomes them; they are her muses. David Hayes-Bautista, who oversees the Chicano Studies Library at UCLA, includes all of Mexican and Spanish literature in the category; he is a collector of antecedents, a man with a view of chicano culture so generously inclusive it verges on universality, which would be logical non-sense (a set cannot be a member of itself). Latino musicians and composers stand gladly on the shoulders of the giants of the old country, although both Latin jazz and conjunto music have a mixed and very complicated ancestry.

The connection of Latino art to its old-country roots would seem incontestable, as the critic Luis Leal, among others, has said, but Héctor Calderón, reviewing Leal's book on Aztlán, claimed that Latino literature has no past, only a future. In support of his argument he quoted the critic and author of a book of interviews with chicano writers, Juan Bruce-Novoa, who says that these writers could not be influenced by Mexican literature, since most of them have not read the work of Mexican writers.[1] Bruce-Novoa wishes to make of chicano literature a new version of the *Jewish Daily Forward;* he wants it to be a literature that does not look back, an immigrant literature, not a literature of sojourners or, worse, transporters. He is the radical intellectual cousin of Richard Rodriguez, a happens-to-be on the most profound level.

There is also something tragic about Bruce-Novoa's position, for in his desire to paint chicanos free of Mexican influence, he perforce paints them ignorant, primitive, or at the very least innocent, much as critics of an earlier period wanted to find Nelson Algren a genuine American primitive and were dismayed to discover he was a well-educated, extremely widely read man who had spent years in the company of Simone de Beauvoir.

Calderón and Bruce-Novoa may be correct about some chicano artists, a few natural writers or born painters, but in the main chicanos and other Latinos in the arts now hold advanced academic degrees in art, music, literature, or creative writing. To suggest that Mexican literature does not influence chicano artists because they have not read it no longer agrees with reality. Elba Sánchez, who writes deliciously sensual, rhythmic poems, teaches literature to Spanish-language students at the University of California at Santa Cruz. Barbara Carrasco holds an M.F.A. from UCLA. Rubén Blades and Martín Espada are attorneys. Sandra Cisneros attended the Iowa Writers' Workshop. The painters César Martínez and Arturo Rodríguez are familiar not only with Mexican, Cuban, and Spanish painting; they are both

---

[1]It is difficult to understand how Bruce-Novoa arrived at his theory, given that the single most important and influential chicano writer, Tomás Rivera, had a Ph.D. in Spanish literature from the University of Oklahoma, a center of Mexican studies.

deeply interested in Latin-American and world literature. The novelist and journalist Ron Arias has a passionate interest in Juan Rulfo; he and I have spent hours discussing the work of the great Mexican novelist. Chicano writers not only know the work of the Mexicans, they also know some of the writers personally, well enough to admire and like Carlos Fuentes and to detest Octavio Paz.

It is too late for Bruce-Novoa's thesis; the development of Latino culture within U.S. culture has proceeded in two directions at once—it has become sophisticated in both English and Spanish; the painters know Siquieros, Goya, and Warhol; the writers have studied Hemingway, Faulkner, Fuentes, Paz, Rulfo, Poniatowska, García Márquez, the streets and the movies; the musicians know polkas, paso dobles, merengues, cumbias, salsa, and the blues. It is too late for Latino art to choose one direction or the other; unlike earlier immigrant cultures, it is destined to have a long, ironic life in both the old country and the new, to be a culture neither here nor there—not pocho, meaning the degradation of two cultures, but Latino.

I.

At the end of the sixteenth century, near the pass between the Rockies and the Sierra Madres, Gaspar Pérez de Villagrá, an officer serving under the command of the explorer Juan de Oñate, took time out from the colonization of what is now New Mexico to write an epic poem. By the time his work was published, in 1610, the British had landed, and Pérez de Villagrá was out of the mainstream. So begins the ironic history of Latino literature in the United States.

Despite the arrival in the hemisphere of a powerful, (although unromantic) language, the Latinos were undaunted. Three hundred twenty years after the rout of Pérez de Villagrá by the Puritans, there was a thriving Spanish-language press in New York, Florida, California, and the Southwest. It had a political as well as a literary history, for it was the Spanish-language press in the United States that published the radical ideas that led to the Cuban and Mexican revolutions. Then the Great Depression arrived and with it a massive deportation of Mexicans and Mexican-Americans. Many of the Spanish-language newspapers and virtually all of the publishing houses in Texas and California and even in the East were forced to close. Darkness descended on the Latino theater.

When the war came, the Latinos went. Statistically, they were braver than most; an extraordinary number died. Some of those who survived went to college, and a few of them chose to write. But it was not until the sixties, when some Latinos decided it was also brave not to die in a war, that the

Latino resistance was born, and the current revival began with the founding of Quinto Sol, the first chicano publishing house.

A revival, however, is not a ticket to the mainstream. Not until 1986 were Latino writers finally recognized by the P.E.N. American Center by being invited to midtown Manhattan to speak at the forty-eighth International P.E.N. Congress. They came from California, Florida, Texas, and the Bronx. Unfortunately, they arrived just after Norman Mailer arranged for a consortium led by Gayfryd Steinberg to make a leveraged buyout of American P.E.N., and there were many great parties and important speeches. So it was that when the Latinos took their places on the dais in a small meeting room not far from the kitchen on a middling floor of the headquarters hotel on Central Park South, they waited and waited for the audience to appear, but no one came.

In that meeting room charged with irony and emptiness, the chairman of the Latino panel, Nicolás Kanellos, drama critic and publisher of Arte Publico Press, rose to speak. He insisted upon using a microphone, as if electronic amplification would create a respectable distance between the speakers and all the eight or twelve listeners, who sat curled in embarrassment or sprawled like laughter across half a row of chairs.

Between interruptions by waiters passing through, pushing carts of empty dishes or uneaten pastries, Kanellos spoke of the repression of Latino writers by the U.S. literary establishment. He did not assign evil motives, arguing instead that the repression was based upon certain erroneous assumptions, which he enumerated:

"Hispanics don't read and can't write, so why publish them?

"No one wants to read about U.S. Hispanics; they are marginal, if anything at all, not even distantly related to the literary boom taking place in Latin America.

"Liberals may be allowed to embrace the great national revolutions in Latin America and their eloquent writers, but similar U.S. Hispanic writers should be deemed 'ethnics,' 'sociological,' 'regional.'

"The political nature of Latin American literature is to be applauded, that of U.S. Hispanic literature is to be censured as not universal, not marketable."[2]

He did not argue the merits of the work; that afternoon, only the politics, sociology, and selling of Latino literature interested him and the novelists and poets whose presentations followed: Gary Soto, the chicano who makes

---

[2]Since that meeting, the *New York Times Book Review* has published a brief version of this chapter and given more review space to the work of Latinos. In the book business such an expression of interest by the editor of the *Book Review* is, in itself, sufficient to change the situation of Latino writers in the United States.

poems of ordinary life; Nicholasa Mohr, the novelist whose straightforward narrations of gentle Puerto Rican life in New York are published against her wishes as books for young adults; and Rolando Hinojosa, who is making of his Klail City novels a kind of Yoknapatawpha County in East Texas. There were others, almost as many speakers as listeners. There was little laughter and no joy. The writers spoke asides in Spanish to the passing waiters, who presented them with an homage of spurned pastries.

Had the meeting been held uptown, in Washington Heights or the Bronx or only as far north as Hunter College, and had the Latino students at those institutions been permitted to attend, the room would have been filled, overflowing. They and students like them in every part of the country, especially in the Southwest, provide an audience for Latino writers—young, parochial, narrowly ethnic readers interested mainly in literature produced by people from the same background. Like all emerging literatures, the work of the Latinos is a neighborhood conversation, people talking to each other of shared experience. A young Cuban writer, Roberto Fernández, used the names of many of his friends and family members in *Raining Backwards,* which makes parts of the novel amusing for someone who knows Rolando and Loly and company, but impossibly arcane for anyone else. Fernández, a literate and talented man, must have assumed that his work would not get beyond the borders of the neighborhood.

According to Fernández, he and the other writers published by Arte Publico have been left to fend for themselves, with no editorial advice, nothing but a small advance against royalties and sales to anthologies. He complains about Kanellos and at the same time appreciates what he has done for Latino writers; without Arte Publico and Bilingual Review Press, Latino writers would not have had the opportunity to see their work in print, to gain the confidence and professionalism that come of publication. Kanellos and Gary Keller, the critic who runs Bilingual Review Press, have been the cranky but consistent midwives to the output of an entire ethnic group. Kanellos and one of his authors, Sandra Cisneros, had a nasty battle over the rights to her work, which may be a good sign for Latino literature, proof that there is something worth fighting over and that a Latina is willing to fight.

Of the Latino writers who have achieved a place in American letters so far, however, not one has been concerned with ethnicity. They may not even have been Latinos. Were John Dos Passos and George Santayana Latino or merely American writers with Spanish surnames? How shall the category be defined? by ancestry? surname? language? subject matter? or geography? What about John Rechy, a chicano from El Paso, Texas? William Carlos Williams, whose mother was Puerto Rican? Thomas Sanchez? or the boxer Floyd Salas? Can Isaac Goldemberg, a novelist who lives in New York and writes in Spanish of his native Peru, be considered a Latino? When Anthony

Shorris publishes a piece on the Op-Ed page of the *New York Times*, should it be considered another step into the mainstream for Latinos? Silvio Martínez Palau, who was born in Colombia, also lives in New York and writes in Spanish, but the ironic punches of his stories are directed at U.S. culture; does that qualify him as a Latino or a visiting Colombian? Is Carlos Fuentes, who was raised in Washington, D.C., culturally a Mexican or a Latino? Which generations of the writing Yglesias family qualify as Latinos? Gary Keller writes serious, important criticism under his own name, but publishes fiction under the pseudonym El Huitlacoche. Why? What's in a name?

Then, as the astonishingly bold young poet Martín Espada writes, there is the question of race:

> *Thirty years ago,*
> *your linen-gowned father stood*
> *in the dayroom of the VA hospital*
> *grabbing at the plastic*
> *identification bracelet*
> *marked Negro,*
> *shouting, "I'm not!*
> *Take it off!*
> *I'm Other!"*

However ill-defined, Latino literature exists, sometimes eloquent, often crude, now and then with more vitality than almost anything else being written in America. Yet it remains secret, available mostly in ghetto bookstores and arcane corners of college campuses, switching codes from English to Spanish or Spanglish or Caló, an original voice in four languages.

Like any literature, the works of Latinos comprise a history and a sensibility; they describe the outer and inner lives of a certain segment of the great ethnic stewpot of America. Because so many Latinos suddenly went to college after World War II, the literature had a curious development: The graduate schools produced literary critics before there was a host literature for them to feed on. Novels and collections of poems were published with critical essays fore and aft, as if to make work for the critics.

The procedure can be numbing, as in one edition of *The Road to Tamazunchale* by Ron Arias. The novel, which went to the school of magic realism, tells the story of a quixotic old man in Los Angeles, entering his dreamy confusion of reality, truth, and fantasy, using the most preposterous situations to convey precisely how people think and live in the Los Angeles barrio. Unfortunately, the hundred pages of the novel are buried between an introduction, complete with two pages of footnotes, a foreword, and a by-lined bibliography so detailed it even lists Arias's listing in another list. *The*

Road to Tamazunchale, for all its vigorous invention and narrative sinew, staggers under the weight of thirty-five critical pages. Only the pompous and the dead have the strength to bear such a burden: Ron Arias is neither. According to the critical introduction, Arias has broken the pattern of chicano literature by writing inventively and with reference to culture outside the barrio. One of the misconceptions about Latino literature is that it is painfully realistic, autobiographical, in the pattern common to other immigrant literatures in the United States. It simply isn't so. Rudolfo Anaya, author of *Bless Me, Ultima,* the major expression of the New Mexico school centered around Albuquerque, uses folk tales and myth in his work. In fact, one of the distinguishing characteristics of Latino literature has been its understanding of an ironic or invented world; a literature descended from Cervantes could not be otherwise.

One of the first major novels of the revival, perhaps the classic Mexican-American novel, Tomás Rivera's *And the Earth Did Not Devour Him,* appears on the surface to be a more or less connected collection of stories about simple people, mainly agricultural workers. The prose seems utterly without artifice, the people exhibit the most elemental feelings, but it soon becomes clear that the book deals with the reality that lies below the surface of the world.

Tomás Rivera, who died in 1984, wrote in Spanish. A bilingual edition of his novel, with a translation by the poet Evangelina Vigil-Piñon, was published in 1987. The ending of the novel gives some indication of its distance from reportorial reality:

> . . . He realized that in reality he hadn't lost anything. He had made a discovery. To discover and rediscover and piece things together. This to this, that to that, all with all. That was it. That was everything. He was thrilled. When he got home he went straight to the tree that was in the yard. He climbed it. He saw a palm tree on the horizon. He imagined someone perched on top, gazing across at him. He even raised one arm and waved it back and forth so that the other could see that he knew he was there.

Although the translation is adequate, a few of the Spanish sentences show the dancelike rhythms the writer achieved:

> Encontrar y reencontrar y juntar. Relacionar esto con esto, eso con aquello, todo con todo. Eso era. Eso era todo. Y le dio más gusto. Luego cuando llegó a la casa se fue al árbol que estaba en el solar. Se subió.

The standard criticism of Santayana's poetry is that he did not ever fully overcome the problem of writing in his second language. Would Rivera have written as well in English or would the sophistication and the natural rhythms have been lost? For many Latinos code-switching may be the natural language, as in *Dalé* gas![3] Others can write only in English.

A cross-cultural literature interested T. S. Eliot and resulted in some of the most astonishing and sophisticated effects in his poetry. Eliot knew as well as any man who ever lived that literature is made of words. When he chose Sanskrit rather than English for the echoing end of *The Waste Land*, he did so with perfect understanding of the meaning and the effect. Sanskrit was not a limit of language for him, but an expansion of culture, a marriage of East and West so stunning in its effect that a first time reader of the poem comes away astonished, changed by the last three Sanskrit words.

Code-switching in Latino poetry and prose has not, so far, had the same effect and certainly does not have the same genesis. When code-switching does not add overtones to the work, but merely serves to fill in the gaps in the writer's fluency, it is not a sign of sophistication, not poetry, but a step back toward folk art. The reader of Latino poetry that uses code-switching, often to reproduce street language, must always be on guard against attributing the complexity and beauty of poetry to work scribbled on a wall. The Latino poet who switches codes always risks the descent of language from the tropes and songs of poetry to the rough hammer of street talk.[4]

Sophistication itself is always at issue in Latino literature. The approach to the craft and to the characters reveals the writer's relation to the ongoing war between the two realities in which Latinos exist: their own complexity and the simpleton's world invented for them by their Anglo observers. In a retreat from the sophistication of Rivera, the chicana from Chicago, Sandra Cisneros, put together a collection of sketches, *The House on Mango Street*, and called it a novel. Juan Rodríguez, the editor of *Carta Abierta*, a newsletter about chicano writing, called Cisneros a throwback to prewar women writers: "Those writers, as popular then among the Euroamerican audience as Cisneros is becoming today among the same group, attempted to appease and appeal to the mainstream even as a defense of La Raza was imbedded in their apologia. The quaint voice of the earlier writers is now delivered in childlike speech."

His attack may have been overly harsh, but the criticism does point to one of the continuing problems of Latino writing, especially in chicano or Mexican-American works: the stereotype of the simple peasant. The book business all too frequently seeks to emulate the movies, and Hollywood has found two images of Latinos that sell: the criminal and the childlike peasant.

---

[3]"Step on it!" Literally, "Give it gas!"

[4]Gary Keller has written an interesting essay on code-switching, "The Literary Stratagems Available to the Bilingual Chicano Writer, which appeared in *The Identification and Analysis of Chicano Literature*.

To make simple a people whose cultural heritage is Spanish, Native American, and sometimes African, crossed with the complex culture of the United States, requires a Latino to have internalized racism and an Anglo to have embraced it. With the collection of sketches, Cisneros found an audience by writing in a childlike voice about a child. She confirmed what the gringos have said about Mexicans since the defeat of Santa Anna.

Her second book, *Woman Hollering Creek,* was published in 1991 by Random House. Cisneros had put the work into the hands of Joni Evans, an editor known for her talents as a marketer. It was a careerist move, but a change had taken place in the quality of the work: Most of the MGM Mexicans had disappeared from her stories. Cisneros still suffered dreadful lapses of taste, and the style and tone often wobbled, but the book contained some beautifully realized stories, characters that the reader married and remarried at the end of every paragraph. When Cisneros was selling herself, saying ". . . I needed to be writer," the book was a disaster, and when she was blathering a confused vision of the Aztec pantheon, it was an embarrassment, but when she was a writer instead of "being writer," it was superb. She had inherited the mantle of Tomás Rivera. She did not speak in Spanish, however; she was the next generation; she had an authentic Mexican-American voice. This second incarnation of Sandra Cisneros is an observant imitator of streetsong and intimacy and an inventor of images that illuminate the reader's world. She is an artist, at least the beginning of an artist, the possibility of an artist, but she is in a dangerous time in literature and in an artist's life; to reach her potential, Cisneros will have to be ambitious enough to overcome her own ambition.

Another Latino writer, Oscar Hijuelos, was a full step ahead of Cisneros in the literary world; his second novel, *The Mambo Kings Play Songs of Love* was a commercial as well as a critical success. It brought him the Pulitzer Prize for fiction in 1990. Hijuelos also drew characters dangerously close to stereotypes, but he is a highly disciplined, very talented writer. His Cuban-American musicians have complex relationships with music, women, popularity, and age—the only adolescent quality in their character is machismo. Using an adult, sophisticated voice, Hijuelos writes with an intensity and sensuality that is missing from much contemporary literature, whether it is produced by Anglos or Latinos. Although his novel is about death, he writes so much and so well of the heat of life that the reader feels death not as an abstraction but as yet another force, albeit a chilling one, in the process of life.

Of all the Latino novelists publishing today in English, Hijuelos demonstrates the greatest professionalism, which may be more a matter of geography than craft. His work differs from that of Rudolfo Anaya, the novelist most widely known and read in the Latino community, in that the Cubans in Hijuelos's novels are urban immigrants and Anaya's Nuevo Mexicanos are rural, connected to folk culture, rooted in the land they have occupied for centuries. The author of *The Mambo Kings Play Songs of Love* can use a device with a history in both art and commerce: His characters include Lucille Ball and Desi Arnaz. By contrast, Anaya writes about witches who work in country towns. In *Bless Me, Ultima* he must overcome not only the cultural difference between his characters and the willing reader in Manhattan; he must cross the continent, push his way through crowded streets, and scale the walls of skyscrapers.

In this wider world two relatively recent memoirs by young men have been favorably received. Although some Latino critics dismissed these books as the commonplace of immigrant writing dominated by autobiography, both are worth reading. Richard Rodriguez writes in a curiously British tone of the tiny agoraphobic world of a child/man determined to revise the history of himself. *Hunger of Memory* is the work of a person who intends to obliterate the influence of his parents by denying the validity of their culture. "It is to those whom my mother refers to as the *gringos* that I write," he says. And in his opposition to affirmative action and bilingual education, he not only addresses his work to the gringos, he aims to please the most ethnocentric of them. As a result, the gifted young writer from Sacramento, California, has become a pariah in the community of his past.

Family Installments, Edward Rivera's frankly autobiographical fiction, bears the subtitle *Memories of Growing Up Hispanic.* It has the sense of place and play, the certainty about who is a man and who is a child, and the unsentimental appreciation of family that inform the American bildungsroman at its best. Rodriguez and Rivera have both read their British literary forefathers, but only Rivera seems to have read Mark Twain—and Piri Thomas. Rivera's work leaps forward in style and sophistication from Thomas's *Down These Mean Streets,* but it could not have been written without it. Rivera is the next generation in immigrant literature—the craftsman, the writer who makes no excuses in either language. Perhaps Rivera's beginnings in rural Puerto Rico give his book life and direction; perhaps he is simply a very good writer. He constructs each paragraph so well that he can use Spanish words or phrases without having to explain them; the context leaves no room for misunderstanding.[5]

The measure of this accomplishment may be the trouble other Latino writers have with language or code-switching. Unlike writers who use an arrogant sprinkling of French, Greek, or Latin, most Latinos solve the problem of Spanish in English-language texts by repeating the Spanish word or phrase in English, which has the effect of comic redundancy, as in " 'Adios,' he said. Goodbye."

---

[5] A Hollywood writer and director, John Sayles, attempted to use Spanish to a great extent in a novel, *Los Gusanos.* It didn't work. Switching codes makes for interesting writing; stealing codes does not.

When Latino writers overcome the need to explain themselves to people who do not understand Spanish and use code-switching to energize and enrich their work, the result can be electrifying. José Montoya or Cecilio García-Camarillo or Jimmy Santiago Baca can write in a voice so authentic that it sounds to me like remembered music, the speech of old friends, one of whom might be the narrator of García-Camarillo's poem about a cool ex-Pinto (ex-con):

> *wáchalo*
> *con su chuco walk*
> *los brazos swinging in rhythm*
> *to a subconscious polka*
>
> *here he comes*
> *wáchalo*
> *por la isleta en el southwest valley*
> *en su barrio*
> *vacilando in his cosmology*
> *y tirándole good vibes*
> *a las barrio queens*
> *with indian faces*
> *and tight jeans*
> *that cruise by*

José Montoya and Tato Laviera have both written of mothers, Montoya from California and Laviera from New York.

> *When I remember the campos*
>   *Y las noches and the sounds*
> *Of those nights en carpas o*
> *Bagones I remember my jefita's*
>   *Palote*[6]
>   *Clik-Clok; clik-clak-clok*
>   *Y su tocesita.*
>
> *(I swear she never slept!)*
>
> *Reluctant awakenings a la media*
> *Noche y la luz predida.*
>
>   *PRRRRRRRRINNNNGGGGGG!*
>
> *A noisy chorro missing the*
> *Basin.*

[6]Rolling pin

The title "La Jefita," means the Little Woman Chief, but the real tenderness in the poem comes in the word tocesita, the diminutive for cough; only in Mexican Spanish could a writer make such a sign of love out of such a noun. On the other hand, the poem is not entirely sentimental: The *chorro* that misses the basin is a stream of urine.

Tato Laviera's poem to his mother, *the song of an oppressor,* repeats the phrase *simplemente* maria (simply, maria), which breaks down into simple and *mente* (mind).

> *They took advantage*
> > *simple*
> *english was foreign to you*
> > *mente*
> *era el goofer del landlord de nuestras vidas*
> > *maria*

> > > > *The tv tube*
> > > > > *simple*
> > > > *whose jeringuillas[7]*
> > > > > *mente*
> > > > *made us addicted de la mente*
> > > > > *maria*

> *how was it done?*   *simplemente maria*

The poets writing in English with little or no code-switching have a different kind of sophistication. Naomi Quiñónes entitles a poem about a young prostitute, "Ultima II True Blue Eye Shadows of the Past and writes about a "max-matter-of-factor-face." The most powerful of the young women poets working mainly in English, Lorna Dee Cervantes, can write of scenes as bleak as a Raymond Carver story, of the rage of the poor who harbor wishes and loves they cannot even speak. Perhaps better than anyone she writes of the cultural ambivalence of the California chicana.

> *Like wet cornstarch, I slide*
> *past my grandmother's eyes. Bible*
> *at her side, she removes her glasses.*
> *The pudding thickens.*
>
> *Mama raised me without language.*
> *I am orphaned from my Spanish name.*
> *The words are foreign, stumbling*
> *on my tongue. I see in the mirror*
> *my reflection: bronzed skin, black hair.*

[7]Syringes

> *I feel I am a captive*
> *aboard the refugee ship.*
> *The ship that will never dock.*
> *El barco que nunca atraca.*

In Boston, Martín Espada has published three volumes of poetry. He writes in English,[8] but his poems have the wit and vigor of the best of the bilingual works, and added to those qualities the dignity of an educated gentleperson from the island. The title of his second book comes from these lines:

> *At the bar two blocks away,*
> *immigrants with Spanish mouths*
> *hear trumpets*
> *from the islands of their eviction.*

Although he is Puerto Rican, born in Brooklyn, Espada's work leaps over the borders of nationality to speak of Mexicans, Nicaraguans, Guatemalans, Chileans. He is a Latino poet, well on his way to becoming *the* Latino poet of his generation. For all his anger, Espada is a gentle man, and he can laugh till the souls of slumlords tremble:

CONFESSIONS OF THE TENANT IN APARTMENT #2

> *The landlord's*
> *beige Fleetwood Cadillac*
> *died in front of the building.*
>
> *and I was secretly happy*
> *that my jumper cables*
> *didn't work*

In his poems Espada describes the lives of poor people; that is the political nature of him. His life involves poor people, whom he counsels in his work as an attorney, but he is not poor, not working class. For all his starburst sense of outrage, Espada must write from memory and observation: He is not the autobiographer of pennilessness; he is a poet. Nor was Tomás Rivera a chronicler of his own poverty; when he died, the son of migrant workers from Crystal City, Texas, he was socially and perhaps economically upper middle-class, chancellor of the University of California, Riverside. Ron Arias, who wrote of a poor Mexican in Los Angeles, is a

---

[8]The third volume was written in English but published in a bilingual edition.

senior writer at Time-Warner and lives beside a small lake in Connecticut. Francisco Alarcón, Edward Rivera, Naomi Quiñónes, Nicholasa Mohr, Denise Chávez, the late Arturo Islas, Jr., and dozens of other novelists and poets have tenure or hold tenure-track jobs at colleges and universities. Rudolfo Anaya is an institution in the University of New Mexico system. The critic Luis Leal retired from the University of Illinois as a professor emeritus.

No group better fits the Marxist complaint about intellectuals not belonging to a class, for these artists have the education or at least the sheepskin to qualify as intellectuals, and they have no loyalty to their economic class, the bourgeoisie, which they generally despise, while they have too much money to be true to the suffering class they embrace. The issues that occupy them personally have more to do with culture, gender, race, and racism than with class; yet their work, almost without exception, deals with poor people. In that respect, they follow exactly the established pattern of American immigrant literature. They deviate from it only by their connection to the culture of their national past, which has been the barrier between them and the mainstream of American culture.

While the literary descendants of the hapless Pérez de Villagrá have kept out of sight of the Anglo mainstream, they have been working hard during the last four centuries. Latinos now have a body of work, a literary mirror in which to see themselves, and the images in the mirror grow more interesting to the rest of the society as they represent an increasingly large segment of the population.

Publishers pay attention; agents consider the possibilities; tomorrow the reviewers may notice. The problem of languages has answers in construction as well as translation. The battle would seem to be won, yet the pattern of ironies established at the beginning of the seventeenth century remains: *The Milagro Beanfield War,* in recent years the most widely read work of fiction about Latinos, was written by John Nichols, and after Danny Santiago won a prize for fiction in 1984, the new Latino literary phenomenon turned out to be the pseudonym of Daniel Lewis James, a blacklisted *gringo* screenwriter.

2.

The East L.A. blowouts of 1968 were exactly the kind of political action that Harry Gamboa, Jr., could understand: 10,000 students refusing to attend high school classes to protest their own failure, a failure that had not yet occurred. Harry was only a junior that year, but he was a born leader, with a 1.1 grade point average and a second-generation Dadaist understanding of the world. When Harry's father, Enrique, who was born in Mexico, enrolled in school in the United States, the Anglo teachers changed his name to Henry, which they said was the correct way to say "Enrique" in America. The former Enrique brought his new name home to his mother, who pronounced it Herry, which sounded a lot like Harry, so that Enrique, Henry, Herry became the boy his mother mispronounced, Harry. Of course, he named his son Harry, Jr.; it was only right.

In a Dada world a boy could not be an ordinary low rider or join a gang; Harry, Jr., became a Jetter,[9] one of the East L.A. teenagers who used exaggerated fashions to parody the styles of both the ghetto and the Anglo city to the west. The Dada dandy led his classmates out of Garfield High School on March 6, the first day of the blowouts, engaging in a different form of protest. It was the first time Mexican-Americans in east Los Angeles had made a powerful expression of their discontent, an alternative to *aguantar*. Gamboa was fascinated. As a leader of the student protesters, he came into the aura of the radical thinkers and organizers of the Mexican-American community: Sal Castro, who had organized the walkout, impressed him, but in Bert Corona, who had learned organizing tactics and politics in the International Longshoremen's and Warehousemen's Union, he found "a great orator, a leader who had a performance element, a role model." At meetings, in conversations, he heard people speak of Marx and Freud. The ideas, the oratory, the performances combined to recreate him as the person who would found a new Mexican-American art movement in Los Angeles.

Gamboa and three pals, Patssi Valdez, Gronk, and Willie Herron, first appeared together on the streets of Los Angeles as murals. Sometimes they were walking murals, as in their version of *The Stations of the Cross* in which Pontius Pilate tossed popcorn to people on the street. At other times they became instant murals, characters suddenly taped to a wall in downtown Los Angeles. In 1972, they went on a visit to the Los Angeles County Museum of Art to see the chicano paintings. When they were told there were none, they became the first chicano painters to show at the Museum by spray-painting their names on a corner of the building.

According to Gamboa, their works were usually greeted with the Spanish expression, *Me da asco,* which means, "You disgust me" or, literally, "You give me nausea." Nothing could have pleased a quartet of young nihilists more; they took the offending word, asco, for their name. Asco prowled the streets of Los Angeles, nauseated by what they saw in a racist, materialist, warring world, doing their best to instill the same disgust in their often unwitting audiences.

---

[9]In The Los Angeles *Times,* October 5, 1985, Kirk Ellis reviewed Gamboa's play, *Jetter's Jinx.* During the late sixties, Ellis wrote, "extravagances of dress and manner served as a placebo for social impotence." No Dadaist now alive could have said it better.

Meanwhile, Gronk, Willie Herron, and Patssi Valdez began to make a reputation for themselves as painters, and Gamboa established himself as a photographer and writer. In 1973, Gronk and Herron painted the mural *Black and White Moratorium* on a wall at Lorena Avenue and Olympic Boulevard in Los Angeles. Their hard-edged black and white celebration or memorial for the 1970 chicano moratorium broke completely with the old Mexican traditions. No Aztec gods or coyotes or sombreros appeared in the comic book (novela) style panels of their work. Mexicans and Mejicanos did not belong in Asco; their intellectual leader, Harry Gamboa, Jr., didn't speak Spanish, and Gronk told people his youth was spent watching cartoons while carrying a book by Camus in his back pocket; they were creating something new politically, culturally, and graphically—Mexican-*American* public art.

A year later, four brilliant young painters, Carlos Almaraz, Gilbert Luján, Beto de la Rocha, and Frank Romero exhibited their work in a show known as Los Four at the University of California, Irvine. Ten years older than the members of Asco, far beyond them as artists and draftsmen, Los Four were the first chicano painters whose work was shown inside the Los Angeles County Museum of Art.

By then Self-Help Graphics, founded by Sister Karen Boccalero, was in its second year of operation on Brooklyn Avenue in the heart of East L.A. Its studios were instrumental in giving space in which to work and exhibit to an entire generation of chicano painters: Gronk, Willie Herron, Diane Gamboa (Harry's sister), Leo Limón, Yreina Cervantez, Margaret García, Frank Romero, Patssi Valdez, Linda Vallejo, Arturo Urista, and others. Their work was interesting, exciting, but it didn't please everyone. When Bill Melendez, one of the leading animators in Hollywood, was asked for his opinion of the work of the new East L.A. artists, he said through his great mustache, "I don't want anyone to show paternalism toward our painters. We shouldn't praise people who can't draw."

Melendez, who owns an animation company, with studios in Hollywood and London, had been visiting east Los Angeles schools for years. As the animator of the *Peanuts* programs on television, he had an immediate connection with the children, and as a role model he was incomparable. Tall, with crewcut hair the color and character of iron, a fin-de-siècle Mexican mustache, a voice that rumbled through rooms and rooms like an earthquake, and a sense of pride in being that gave the lie to the stereotype of the humble Mexican peon—he was the epitome of man redeemed by art. But he gave no quarter when it came to the artist's craft. Work! he said, Learn to draw!

In a housing project in Culver City there was a girl who would eventually challenge Melendez in a contest to see who had learned best how to draw.

Barbara Carrasco was a pretty girl, but troublesome. Like Los Four and Asco, she was nurtured on the politics of resistance, chicanismo, the ideas of Bert Corona, Corky Gonzáles, Rubén Salazar, César Chávez, and Dolores Huerta. She dressed in U.S. Army surplus field jackets and boots and became so involved with the United Farm Workers that her mother once complained, "You are closer to Dolores Huerta than to your own mother." She studied art at UCLA and learned technique by apprenticing herself to Los Four, helping to paint the famous mural *Zoot Suit.*

The Los Angeles Community Redevelopment Agency commissioned Barbara Carrasco to paint a mural in downtown Los Angeles in 1981. The designer, the social activist, the girl who liked to draw produced a 16-by-80 foot portable history of Los Angeles from a Mexican perspective. Fifty-one scenes of the history of the city were braided into the flowing hair of the mythical Queen of the Angels. Included among the scenes were the internment of the Japanese-Americans during World War II, the mass lynching of Chinese at the turn of the century, and the poverty and racism that had been endemic in California since the arrival of Junipero Serra. She was asked to rework the mural to eliminate the vignettes that the Redevelopment Agency thought sure to offend Asian visitors during the Olympics. Carrasco refused.

Her struggle with the city agency was compared to the whitewashing of a mural painted on the side of a building in Los Angeles by David Alfaro Siquieros in 1932, another Olympian year. Carrasco's mural, now stored in a building owned by the United Farm Workers union, and the struggle over it made her famous. Commissions came at her from every direction. A group in Boston, Children Are Our Future, sent her to Soviet Armenia to paint a mural with children from Yerevan. She designed the flag of the UFW and produced a series of drawings about farmworkers and pesticides that were shown on an electronic billboard in Times Square.

But it is her talent for drawing that led to a show of her own at the B-1 Gallery. She draws moral portraits, including a devastating series of people in coffins: twelve tiny drawings on paper done with tools as ordinary as Bic pens. They are entitled *Rest in Poverty, Rest in Plenty, Rest in Politics,* and so on. *Politics* presents the skull of Ronald Reagan atop a body buried in pinstripes, surrounded by microphones. The work has the Day-of-the-Dead satirical madness of the Mexican caricaturist José Guadalupe Posada and an acute sense of moral outrage in the line that resembles the work of Hieronymous Bosch.

For the last few years her explainer, collaborator, publicist, and constant companion has been Harry Gamboa, Jr. Together they are the sweetest of satirists. At forty, Harry Gamboa's eyes still have the piercing innocence of art. Barbara Carrasco has put away her field jacket and boots and let herself be. Anger's little scars lie in the shadows under her eyes, and the struggle against the city bureaucracy has made a darkness at once sad and lovely on her cheeks. In the contest to find out which of the chicano artists was the best draftsman, the old lion with the great mustache finished second behind the acid and ethics of Barbara Carrasco. The victory is in her portfolio. Nihilism has never been so eager.

—

At the end of the 1980s two major shows and a huge increase in prices marked the boom in the Latino art market. Both shows were controversial, and the prices reported in the press differed by at least one order of magnitude from what the painters said they were splitting with their galleries. But they were big shows. They made the papers.

Luis Cancel, the director of the Bronx Museum of the Arts put together an historically based show: "The Latin American Spirit: Art and Artists in the United States, 1920–1970." Some of the work was by U.S. Latinos, but much of it came from overseas: the Cuban Wilfredo Lam; Kahlo, Siquieros, Tamayo, and other Mexicans; and South Americans, including Fernando Botero.

It was a carefully chosen show, a safe show. Cancel told Grace Glueck of the *New York Times* of his iconoclastic aims: "Bright, hot colors, exuberant brushstrokes, lots of folksy storytelling and maybe a little graffiti—that's the cliché Anglo view of Latin American art. But the so-called Latino style is a myth, a phantom. Twentieth-century Latin American artists have worked in every mode, from Surrealism to geometric abstractions to Conceptualism to Expressionist figuration, just as Europeans and North Americans have done. The trouble is that curators in this country have had their own ideas of what constitutes Latin American art, and those who don't conform to it were largely ignored."

The other major show, "Hispanic Art in the United States: Thirty Contemporary Painters and Sculptors" was produced by the Corcoran Gallery in Washington, D.C., and the Houston Museum of Fine Arts. The catalogue carried an essay by the Nobel Prize winner, Octavio Paz.[10] He reminded the reader that psychologists consider birth traumatic, the United States was a state before it was a nation, its population is heterogeneous, and so on before getting down to the real work of the piece, which was to patronize the pochos, the poor half-mute sons of bitches who had moved north of the

---

[10]Unfortunately, it was the brilliant poet, essayist, and critic at less than his best. Something about Latinos turns the author of the most penetrating analysis of Mexican culture, *The Labyrinth of Solitude,* into a cranky and arrogant old man. Could it be that the grand old voice of Mexican letters falls to commonness when he encounters pochos? Could it be that he despises them a little? It is not an unprecedented response among Mexican intellectuals.

border or west of the islands. The one part of the show that interested Paz, who did not deign to comment specifically on any of the other work in it, was a series of pencil and crayon drawings on brown paper by Martín Ramírez, an autistic Mejicano who fled the Revolution of 1910, worked for a while on the railroad, then became mute in 1915. He was placed in a California mental institution in 1935, where he remained until his death in 1960.

Neither Paz nor the curators of the show, Jane Livingston and John Beardsley, could resist the symbolism of a Mejicano mute artist and a certified madman at that. Paz used it to dismiss all other Latino culture, especially literary works, which he knew a priori could not be of any value because of the language problem. The subtle argument of his essay, which finally becomes clear at the end, is that Latino culture does not exist, not even in painting. The work he saw in the show harkened back to Rufino Tamayo, Wilfredo Lam, and Roberto Matta. He delighted in his view that none of the work had deep affinities with forms developed in the United States during the preceding twenty years. Paz saw only diluted Mexicans and Cubans, not aesthetic immigrants creating new forms in a new country, but transporters, the disasters of migration, the failures of time and place. The man who found meaning in the most subtle nuance of language, the barely perceptible change in hue rendered by layers of underpainting, the contents of the meals served in the house in which Sor Juana lived, found nothing to excite his imagination in all the rooms of Latino art but the drawings on brown paper of a long dead autistic patient in a mental hospital.

The error of the curators in choosing Paz to write the essay repeats the fundamental error of the show, the one Luis Cancel sought to avoid: The Corcoran show was a cliché, but not merely an Anglo cliché. To buttress its patronizing view of Latino art it sought out the one Mexican critic who could, with world-renowned subtlety, put the Latinos in their place.

Had they chosen an Anglo critic, like Arthur Danto or even someone with a more superficial approach like Hilton Kramer, the tone of the catalogue would have been different; the essay would not have been a punishment for renegades but an assessment of an ill-conceived show. Even if they had limited their choice to famous Mexicans, they could have called upon Carlos Fuentes, whose understanding of the border and its influences comes from a different experience, one which has produced a courageous tenderness in him, a feeling he has not hesitated to manifest in his dealing with Latino students and artists.

The Anglo curators visited another kind of abuse on the Latinos—ignorance—which in this situation results from the same kind of cultural arrogance the painters and sculptors might encounter in the street. On page 169 of the catalogue, the article on Carmen Lomas Garza begins, "Garza's mother's family. . . ." Wouldn't the curators be surprised to find that Lomas

Garza's mother's name was Garza? They carry the error throughout the catalogue. Luis Cruz Azaceta precedes Rolando Briseño in the alphabetical listings, and the curators refer to him as Azaceta. John Beardsley writes knowingly of the formation of La Raza Unida in Crystal City, Texas, and of the early chicano cultural groups Con Safos and The Royal Chicano Air Force but cannot distinguish between a painter's mother's and father's names.

Much of the work in the Corcoran show displayed the angry beauty one has come to expect of Latino art: brilliant colors, bold brushstrokes, the ironic punch-in-the-nose style of César Martínez or Gronk, the less figurative brilliant bursts of Carlos Almaraz. They are the chicanos. Their work bears no resemblance to the painful longing in the European-influenced paintings of Cruz Azaceta or the dark dreams of Paul Sierra, whose work is Latino in content but stylistically descended from Francis Bacon and Willem de Kooning rather than the Latin Americans. This is not to say that Martínez or Almaraz make folk art. They have progressed to a more personal, formally interesting style than the wood carvings of the santeros of New Mexico or the *ofrenda* (offering) of Lomas Garza or the animal sculptures of Felipe Archuleta.

Latino art has arrived at a moment of choice. It can go forward from the barrio and the isolated New Mexico village to a new stage in which Latinos bring their culture in all its particularity into the main currents of American art, or it can return to the social art forms of the sixties, the mural made small, and the quaint craftsmanship of the village. Although the curators of the Corcoran show have not made up their minds and Octavio Paz thinks the pochos have no possibilities, Latino art seems to be emerging from the folk art tradition, reinterpreting the visual and emotional world of the artist in terms more concerned with art than politics or history; not forgetting its aches or its origins, but including the past in the interpretation of the present.

Three main currents in Latino art at present have geographical and cultural as well as stylistic roots, but the social component has declined; the ethical component of Barbara Carrasco's drawings has been superseded by a desire to explore the forms of art and their relation to the nature of existence; in other words, the content of Latino art has become less European, less nineteenth century in its preoccupations and more Latino.

The Cubans of the East have allied themselves historically with Europe and with the North Americans. Curiously, their connection to Wilfredo Lam and the other twentieth-century Cuban painters is not important. Painters like Arturo Rodríguez, a young Cuban living and working in a small house only two blocks from Calle Ocho, learned their craft in Spain and the United States rather than Latin America. One can see Goya's influence in Rodríguez's madhouse scenes and Gericault in the size and painterliness of some of the work, but nothing of the Cubans. Rodríguez reads Kafka, listens to jazz, stands before his canvas with ontological questions squirming in his head. Like his fellow Cubans, Sierra and Cruz Azaceta, and the Puerto Rican Arnaldo Roche, Arturo Rodríguez is examining himself in the world through his work; he is an exile from Cuba, but a citizen of art.

In San Antonio, working in a converted garage behind his house, still supporting himself by taking photographs for real-estate agents, César Martínez is tied more deeply than ever to his roots in the Southwest. Although his *Hombre que le gustan las mujeres,* a painting of a porky chicano with his shirt open and his sleeves rolled up, displaying three tattoos—the Virgin, a naked whore, and a sweet girl in a peasant blouse—was one of the hits of the Corcoran show, Martínez has moved on. After the irony of this series of confrontational paintings, he has returned to the desert, to the colors of sunset and sand, corrugated metal, votive candles. Chicanismo was but a step for him on the way to the study of deeper relations and a more personal style, a bridge of things from the social to the metaphysical.

California painters have also moved on from the didactic art of the sixties and seventies to a more personal art, but the relation of man to the Los Angeles landscape produces the car crashes of Carlos Almaraz and the grotesques in evening clothes of Gronk. Chicanismo remains a major theme in the work of Arturo Urista, a young painter working at Self-Help Graphics, but another young painter, Paul Botello, intends to expresses his "individual being, mankind's hopes." The muralists still work the walls of Los Angeles and San Francisco, but their function has been usurped by graffiti artists who paint huge nightmare murals on the cement walls of an informal open air gallery at the entrance to an abandoned streetcar tunnel in Los Angeles; social art has a new, irresponsible face in California, no longer chicano, now ritualistic, now *cholo*.

And in New York the painters can no longer find space in which to work. Manhattan lost out to Brooklyn, Long Island City, New Jersey. A style lasts a year, a few months; it can be as transitory as performance art. In New York the Latino painters must choose between the forms of "relinking." They can seek a stylistic return to Paris or Prague, to abstraction, neoexpressionism, superrealism, or surrealism. Or they can look for a way to paint themselves back to another place or people, back to Africa, Spain, Puerto Rico, Bogotá, Buenos Aires, Camagüey, Guanajuato, Guadalajara, Lima, Chimayó, or East L.A. There are no Latino painters or sculptors in New York. There is only motion, change, the maw of celebrity, business. In the New York art scene, Latinos are not hot, not out, not special, just there, a part of the crowd, standing in line. Those who will survive go to the hospitality of Chicago, and those who are lucky go home.

3.

In the translation from the game invented by Abner Doubleday to the ritual played by Latinos, baseball loses its sense of sport. It becomes much more like the bullfight, admired for the grace and character of the actor rather than for the outcome of the struggle. A Latino shortstop is not a baseball player, he is a performance artist, one for whom winning and losing matter less than the feeling expressed in the act of stretching, scooping, whirling, and throwing the ball beautifully across the grass.

Fernando Valenzuela, Don Drysdale, and Sandy Koufax played the same position on the same team, but the Anglos engaged in an entirely different activity. Koufax worked for seven or eight or nine innings, pitching consistently, carefully, with style and bravado, but with unerring attention to the mechanics of his business. Drysdale threw with a kid's abandon; he never lost sight of the fact that it was a sport, the most intense public fun a man could have. While he unwound his chubby arm, Fernando Valenzuela, with his pre-Columbian physique and unreliable eyes, looked heavenward, as if praying to the gods for speed, deception, and a piece of the strike zone. In contrast to Koufax and Drysdale, every move of Valenzuela's was part of a ritual offering to the muse; he did not play baseball, he expressed himself through the art of pitching.

The great Anglo players hit or pitch for average. Nolan Ryan can put a stadium to sleep while throwing a no-hitter. Joe DiMaggio came to glory through consistency. Lou Gehrig never missed a game until he was forced off the field by the disease that bears his name. Babe Ruth and Ted Williams connect to sixty and four hundred, respectively. In baseball one recalls numbers; in art beauty makes the mark. In baseball one remembers great seasons; in art we consider the life of the artist among our treasures. The greatest Latino baseball player got three thousand hits, but no one remembers him for that feat.

No other baseball player and very few practitioners of the art of life lived so well as the outfielder from Carolina, Puerto Rico. The color barrier had been broken when Roberto Clemente came up to the majors; he broke the cultural rules of the game: He was a sixties man wearing spikes, ethnically proud, racially unafraid, graceful afield and in his life. Clemente loved fast cars, fine clothes, and the poor. He was Martí, Manolete, Machito, and Muhammad Ali, and he could hit! He was not humble in the Anglo world: He said his name was Roberto; he refused ever to be called Bob.

Clemente was bringing relief to earthquake victims in Nicaragua when he was killed in the crash of a small plane on New Year's Eve at the end of 1972.

It was an extraordinary end, a famous death. Poets and statesmen die that way, not moody, hypchodriacal center fielders. After Roberto Clemente Latinos could play major league baseball in their own skin. The pattern of playing in the major leagues without wanting to be assimilated remains to this day. Latin America borrowed baseball, transformed it, and returned something of its own making, less like a contest than an exhibition: Latino shortstops go to their left better than anybody else in the game. In the double play, the Latino second basemen levitate like hummingbirds. Patience left the field in a pout with the arrival of Rubén Gómez, Juan Marichal, and Joaquín Andujar and never came back. Latino kids box, play soccer and American football, but in those games they are just immigrants or foreigners working in a northern field; in baseball Latinos have married into the family and changed the genetic pool.

José Canseco, a Cuban concocted by weightlifting and the Spanish dance, epitomizes the Latinization of baseball. Twenty or thirty years ago, Canseco would have been laughed off the field as a dandy, a bodybuilder in a baseball suit. Now, the fans sigh as he poses at the end of his swing, chin up, shoulders squared, tiny hips gathered under him, the bat no more than a twig at the end of his bulging forearms and great fists. But it is at the beginning of his swing, when the pitcher lets the ball go, that José Canseco brings the Latin translation to baseball in the United States, for he stands with his weight on his right foot, the bat held back and up, waving nervously, weightlessly. Then he extends his left foot and flexes his leg until the pointed toe hovers over the brown dust of the batter's box. At that moment, baseball is transformed; the batsman steps in time to understood music, dancing.

—

There must be music, there must be dancing, for nothing Latino exists in stillness or in silence, and the farther east one moves in the Americas the more excited, insistent, and important the music becomes.

Africa lives in this boisterous east. Middle Mexico was borne to war on the sounds of stately drums, a stone and sand society, south; the Mexica danced, but they were not airborne, like the Africans, like the Yaquis. The music of middle Mexico was played at a conqueror's cadence, as in Rome or America North.

Latino music plays nostalgia with the left hand, geography with the right. Every Latino sound crosses over from a crossover, hearkening back to its origin, even before the crossover of Africa and Spain. The Romans learned the rabbi's or the mullah's tune in Spain, beginning an infinite series, lacking only Bach, only Mozart.

"I don't want to put on a uniform and be a salsa boy," said Oscar Cartaya, who crossed over from Puerto Rico to California, from California to New

York, from acoustic bass to electronically amplified music, from working with Willie Colón and Celia Cruz to doing jazz charts for Spyro Gyra. "Electrified is easier," he said.

"Oh, wow! man. P.R. is too small. Go a hundred and one miles and you're in the water." Crossover. He learned guajiro music from his Cuban parents, jíbaro melodies from other musicians in Puerto Rico, standards and classical works from his teachers, and when he got to Los Angeles, to music school, "Everybody was doing like James Brown and I was doing 'Cuando calienta el sol. . . .' "

Cartaya has history in his tunes—even the melodies remember. He would have crossed over all the way, but for the holy nature of Latino music; in the five hundred years since the Spanish arrived in the hemisphere there has never been a secular song, and every drumbeat and wail on both sides of the Atlantic was a prayer before that. The Santería songs played on AM radio stations up and down the East Coast epitomize the nature of Latino music, for they connect the abstraction of music to the crossover religion's circuitous route through earthly manifestations to the Yoruba and Christian notations of a nonanthropomorphic god. That's a lot of ground to cover on a sunny afternoon drinking beer in front of a casita in the Bronx or Hialeah, but music has such magic; it bears spirits on palanquins of chords; God is in the progressions.

The religions underlying Latino music predate Christian notions of private communication between people and their gods. Ancient music treats publicly of the family of gods; it dances. Latinos are not alone, never alone. In this fundamental element of culture Latinos and Anglos occupy the opposing poles of existence: Concert music is the sound of reason played for an individual soul; dance music is the glue that holds the group together, family.

Crossover keeps the family healthy; it obeys the ancient prohibitions. Yet the music never becomes lonely. In an era of recorded music made in studios where each musician works through his individual headset and microphone, divorced from ensemble and audience, the last big touring bands play Latin rhythms for Latino dancers. Ritual music requires real priests. The soothsayers of the sixties were wrong; there can be no electronic global village, no electronic family; electronics make masses of individuals, vast privacies. Latinos pray together. In the family of music the dancer and the drummer both sweat, one a simulacrum of the other. The bandleader, the patriarch and priest of the gathering, leads them in the public performance of the unifying ritual. The gods, who have never heard of Calvin, allow the family of man to worship in wonderful ways; the sad separation of pleasure and prayer was a late occurrence, a revision of music, an attack on dancing, the rise to power of the lonely life of modern, individualistic man.

24

AN EXPERIMENT IN DEMOCRACY

Does the mere creation of civil government mean true freedom, if that government is exclusively created by Anglo-Saxons for Anglo-Saxons, and not by men for all men?

Eugenio María de Hostos

Politics has no purchase on Latinos, except for Cubans, who lived once on their island in a public way, as if it were Athens. All the rest have a later sense of freedom, a Christian sense, freedom in the soul instead of the agora. They are metaphysicians, the children of God; the public realm interests them less than home or heaven.

Latin America has no democratic tradition, as Dr. Lorenzo Pelly observed from his post on the border, but that is only part of the problem. Its warriors have a history of greed and an uncanny ability to rationalize murder, but they fought more for God than gold, more for glory than terrain. They did not practice politics, for metaphysicians do not believe people can be free except in dreams.

The Spaniards had no need to teach metaphysics in the Americas; they merely translated it. There was no freedom in the public realm in Tenochtitlán or on the islands where the Caribs dined. All was dreaming in the Americas—power and the ability to endure life according to the dictates of power. In the public realm, in Latin America, men gave orders or obeyed orders; there were no other relations; there was no discourse; politics did not exist. Only power operated in the public realm; without freedom, there could be nothing else.

For the powerless, the choice was between metaphysics and despair. To endure their lives they embraced metaphysics, adored metaphysics. Dreams consoled them in the private realm: Dreams made them free. Even as slaves they were free; even in dying they were free. They had no need for politics;

they were responsible for their dreams; they bore the burden of their thoughts. *¡Aguantar!,* they said. They cherished the ability to bear pain, to endure suffering; it showed that they were true metaphysicians, spiritual men, believing women, worthy of inner freedom, of conversations with the gods.

After a long time, some Latinos learned the idea of politics. They learned first in Cuba, the most secular nation, that freedom could be public. In Cuba, there was no liberator; the man on the white horse read to cigarmakers and wrote for newspapers; Martí was the product of politics and the maker of politics. He was not consoled by philosophy; he would not settle merely for separation from Spain.

In Cuba, the worst of men as well as the best understood the ancient nature of freedom: Jorge Valls was beaten for reading Plato. The man who ordered the beating almost certainly did not know about the Athenian concept of freedom, but animal instinct told him something: Latin American tyrants have always known that freedom must be confined to dreams. The Argentines who tortured Jacobo Timerman twenty years later accused him of being a communist and insulted him for being a Jew, but the crux of their argument with Timerman was his idea of politics and of the realm in which freedom belonged. He lacked the Christian sense of satisfaction with freedom in the soul; he was dangerous because he did not dream.

Before the Spanish intrusion it was a hemisphere mainly of theocracies, and under the Inquisition, they continued to be theocracies—only the names changed. The native peoples, never having lived a political life, did not know how to revolt, except in their souls; they could not imagine freedom in the public realm, and there was no one to teach them. Only the Cubans dared; all the rest endured.

After World War II, a different notion was born in the United States; a hint of political life, of freedom in the public realm, came into the Latino world. The generations of *aguantar* were ending. *"Respeto!"* someone said; "that is the key to our character." It was the first sign of a change from the sovereignty of metaphysics: *respeto,* the recognition of the importance of life in the public realm, of the possibility of interactions among free men, the concept of freedom in the here and now; a whisper of politics.

No more fundamental change has been initiated in the Latino character since village cultures were first consolidated into empires in Mesoamerica. With the shift of freedom from the private to the public realm, Latinos became political Anglos, inheritors of the great democratic legacy of duties and dissatisfactions. Their notion of what should be judged passed from the realm of thought to the realm of action; *zoon politikon* came to the barrio.

Such changes do not take place magically, in a moment. Only a few people abandoned the dreamy freedom of *aguantar,* and the stream of political and economic refugees constantly replenishes the community of docile persons who can be satisfied by the freedom to decide on good and evil in their souls. Latinos remain the least political group in the United States, the most likely to endure three bad jobs or life in Third World conditions in a colonia along the border, the most patriotic citizens and the least likely to vote. Only Latinos could have endured decades of farm labor using the torturous and deforming short hoe. It is another aspect of a condition Fidel Castro understands as well as anyone in the hemisphere: He wishes to bring Christian concepts of freedom back to Cuba, for he has enhanced the political sense of his people while denying them freedom in the public realm; he knows that nothing short of a return to metaphysics can save his regime.

In the United States, the task of those committed to social and economic justice for Latinos is exactly reversed: They must draw their people out of the refuge of metaphysics and family into the risky life of acting in the world. They must convince them that one can love God, live within the rigid rules of family, and still understand freedom in a worldly way. They have their Magna Carta, the Voting Rights Act. Now they must make Englishmen in the barrios.

I.

Su voto es su voz.[1]

William Velásquez

Active political participation can only be achieved by the removal of discriminatory election systems. Joaquín Avila

Although he was only forty-four years old when he died, in 1988, William C. (Willie) Velásquez had brought the Mexican-American concept of freedom out of the private realm into the light of the public world. Through his Southwest Voter Registration Education Project he had put an end to the docility born of dreaming for millions of Mexican-Americans.

Velásquez was not alone in this work. The Mexican American Youth Organization (MAYO), the Mexican American Unity Council, and La Raza Unida, all of which he helped to found, played a role, as did Rubén Salazar and César Chávez and Corky Gonzales. When Velásquez went into Rock Springs, Texas, to register voters and was told that he had better be gone by

---

[1] "Your vote is your voice."

sundown, Joaquín Avila[2] of MALDEF was beside him. And there were others; the Latino pantheon has many heroes, but none has been quite so effective as Willie Velásquez in transforming the political character of his people.

In 1974, Velásquez abandoned the radical politics of MAYO and La Raza Unida to join the Democratic party and found Southwest Voter (as it is generally known). It would have been just one more nonpartisan, nonprofit, ineffective organization dedicated to the empowerment of minorities through voting but for the mind of Willie Velásquez. He was a genuine intellectual, a political scientist who read the Greeks and immersed himself in British history, who urged Mexican-Americans to familiarize themselves with Díaz del Castillo and Aristotle. Velásquez was also a practical man who understood the benefits available to his people through the use of the best of Western civilization. His understanding of political philosophy was such that he recognized the place at which people could pass from the contemplative freedom of the private realm to a yearning for freedom to act in the public realm. He knew from the outset that Southwest Voter would have to operate at the grassroots level; he understood it as the Greek idea of politics practiced among people who know each other.

And that is how he worked, coaxing people out of the consolation of metaphysics into the public realm of politics. He found them in their churches and convinced them that they were free to act as well as to pray. He found them in their schools and taught them they were as capable of action as of thought. Velásquez did not limit the fields in which he worked to populations of philosophers; he understood that ordinary people wished to become immigrants rather than mere transporters, he knew that the new social contract initiated by immigrants was their passport to the public realm.

Like the Democrats with whom Southwest Voter was allied, he believed that "all politics is local." For people to dare to act in the public realm, to move from obeisance to affecting the world and bearing responsibility for it, they had to be able to visualize the effects of their actions. Possibility was the catalyst. Fix the streets, improve the schools, arrest the criminals, find work for the unemployed and better work for the underemployed, take good care of the children: That was politics, as Cleisthenes knew in ancient Greece and Willie Velásquez discovered while working toward an advanced degree in political science in San Antonio, Texas.

In the fourteen years during which Willie Velásquez headed Southwest Voter, from 1974 to 1984, the organization conducted over 1,150 voter registration campaigns in more than 200 communities in Arizona, Califor-

[2]See the Avila family in the Epilogue

nia, Colorado, New Mexico, and Texas. The number of Latinos registered to vote in those states grew to over 3 million, an increase of 98.6 percent. In the entire country, the number of Latino voters increased by over 2 million during the same period. Almost 72 percent of the increase came in the Southwest. In Texas, where most of Southwest Voter's efforts were concentrated, the increase was 125.4 percent.

Studies by the Southwest Voter Research Institute, also founded by Velásquez, show that the 98.6 percent increase in registered voters produced only a 60.9 percent increase in the number of voters cast by Latinos in the 1988 elections. The problem lay mainly in California, where a 95.6 percent increase in registered voters produced only 28.9 percent more votes. By comparison, Texas had a 114.7 percent jump in the number of votes cast by Latinos.

The difference between the Texas and California turnouts may be due to redistricting. Legal challenges by MALDEF and Southwest Voter over election districts in Texas led to a vast increase in the number of Latino elected officials, from 565 in 1973 to 1,611 in 1988. By contrast, California, with its at-large elections and gerrymandered districts, had more registered Latino voters than Texas, but only managed to elect 466 Latino officials in 1988.

California had institutionalized racism; since they couldn't elect people who would represent their interests, it made no sense for Latinos to vote in California. The California system worked according to design; it maintained the Latino understanding of freedom as part of the private realm; it kept them Mexican or Salvadoran or Nicaraguan in their relation to the world. The notion of a meaningful vote traveled from Athens across time to England and then to the United States. The last thing the California establishment wanted was millions of people with brown faces, liquid *l*s, rolling *r*s, and an Anglo sense of politics. Who would use the short hoe? Who would gut the chickens?

At the end of the 1980s, Joaquín Avila, who had followed Vilma Martínez as president and general counsel of MALDEF, set out alone, with no institutional help, to overturn the work of more than a century of the most sophisticated racism ever employed in the United States. He had not only the fact of the local laws to contend with, but the myth of California as a politically enlightened state.

Avila went from town to town, speaking at community meetings, explaining his willingness to sue the city government to demand fair representation under the Voting Rights Act. All he needed was a plaintiff, all he needed was whatever financial support, if any, the community could provide. And if they couldn't provide money, could they give him volunteers? Suing governments took a lot of hard work. He had a Harvard law degree, experience, computers: All he needed was a little help. If they won, he told them, the federal courts would award him a legal fee for his work. If he lost . . . He planned to win, to go through the state of California, city by city, town by town, overturning every unfair election law.

What he did not expect was the vindictiveness of the power structures in the towns he sued. In town after town, his victory was wounded by a lawsuit seeking to void or reduce his attorney's fees. The policy of the Anglo establishment was evident; the best way to stop Avila, perhaps the only way, was to break him.

They had misjudged Joaquín Avila, his wife, his family, and his friends. From the Watsonville case, which resulted in the historic Ninth Circuit Court decision, Avila moved through the state, taking on town after town. When MALDEF brought suit against Los Angeles County, seeking relief in the federal courts from the county's method of drawing districts to exclude Latino representation, Joaquín Avila was their expert in voting rights litigation. And beside him was Leobardo Estrada, the insightful demographer from UCLA, who could recite the numbers and then give social, political, and economic meaning to them.

On June 4, 1990, federal district court judge David V. Kenyon announced his opinion in the case: The Board of Supervisors of Los Angeles County had redrawn the districts in 1981 to maintain their incumbency despite the increasing percentage of Latinos in the county. It was, he ruled, unconstitutional. New district lines would have to be drawn and a new election held.

Less than a year later, Gloria Molina became the first Mexican-American supervisor in the history of Los Angeles County. She was forty-two years old, a Los Angeles City Council member who had served as deputy director of the U.S. Department of Health and Human Services during the Carter administration. For many of the people who had fought for a Latino district in the county, Molina was a second choice, at best. They had favored California state senator Art Torres.

Molina was an attractive candidate, a woman who had built her constituency on community affairs, an ally of Juana Beatriz Gutiérrez and the Mothers of East L.A. Ironically, she made it clear early on that she was not interested in the more profound question of empowerment of Latinos, the issue that had been the impetus for the court battle that led to her election. Molina cared for her people, she fought for them, but she was a soldier, not a philosopher; she would not be an instrument of profound change. With Gloria Molina, Latinos had a shrewd politician in a powerful position, but they did not have someone who envisioned them as citizens of Athens.

No matter whether Torres or Molina held the supervisor's job, Latinos had won a major victory. But the battle had just begun; California still had four hundred cities and towns with at-large voting or gerrymandered districts, and it was unlikely that the power brokers in the rest of the state would be willing to share control without a fight. Avila still had a lot of towns to visit, a lot of suits to file.

—

Across the country, in New York City, Latinos also fought over redistricting. The battle there was for seats in a newly expanded city council. The Latino population of the city had risen to 25 percent, according to the 1990 census. There was reason to hope. But after the fifty-one districts were defined, Latinos had a majority in only six. Even if they were able to elect their own choices in all six districts, the council would still not fairly reflect their presence in the city. They would have representation, but no power; six votes is not a lot to trade.

They had expected more. Dennis Rivera, president of Hospital Workers Local 1199, had become an important figure in the labor movement. New York had elected its first black mayor, the feeble gentleman David Dinkins. He had proclaimed "a gorgeous mosaic" in his administration, and named a Latina to the figurehead position of deputy mayor for economic development, but the reality was business as usual: Latinos had no access to the mayor and no influence on policy other than that wielded by political bosses like Ramon Velez in Hunt's Point. They had a borough president in the Bronx and a congressman to replace the disgraced Robert García in Washington, but that was all; they had found no strength in numbers.

Latino influence in New York City politics had never been strong. Puerto Ricans, almost all of whom voted in Puerto Rico, hardly voted at all in New York. In 1970, Herman Badillo, who was born in Caguas, Puerto Rico, was elected to the U.S. Congress, but his election was a manifestation of the power of the Kennedy Democrats in the city, not of Puerto Ricans. Badillo, who had been borough president of the Bronx, was a disappointment almost from the start. Anglos found him insufferably ambitious, blacks betrayed him at every turn, and Latinos thought him arrogant. Badillo wanted to be everything, hold every office, but he lacked both the subtlety and the ruthlessness of a successful ethnic politician; he made the mistake of communicating to his own constituency that they existed mainly for the use of Herman Badillo. He lost one election after another. He became an appointed official, an old Kennedy Democrat rewarded for past service. The appointments went sour. There were no more appointments; he remained a lonely liberal voice on the board of the state college system.

There had been a time when Herman Badillo was known as "the most prominent Puerto Rican leader in North America." The Democratic party had been interested in him, the power brokers thought he had something special, but Badillo had not understood that, in the Bronx, the only Latinos who voted were Englishmen. He was the last *cacique* in New York City.

In Florida, the Cubans, who had been worldly actors at home, gained an even more profound understanding of the true place of freedom when they went into exile. They voted. But it was not until 1989 that they were able to show the results of their powerful sense of politics. In a special election held to fill the seat of the late Claude Pepper in the U.S. Congress, Ileana Ros-Lehtinen, known affectionately and not so affectionately as the "darling of the Cuban community," easily defeated a Jewish Democrat with an aged constituency in Miami Beach. Ros made no secret of her views; she was tied to the farthest fringes of the political right through the Cuban American National Foundation (CANF) and through her husband, then U.S. Attorney in Miami, Dexter Lehtinen.

Her election was important to the CANF, which had been forced until then to do its anti-Castro business through PACs and promises, the back doors of Washington. With Ros-Lehtinen in office, the fanatical anti-Castro right finally had a member of Congress it really could call its own.

—

Although one was a Republican and the other a Democrat, the election of Latinas to important positions on both coasts and the election of Dan Morales as attorney general of the state of Texas showed that the transition to an Anglo understanding of politics was well under way. Gaining power, however, raised a new and potentially more difficult question. Andrew Hernández, who followed his friend and mentor Willie Velásquez as president of Southwest Voter, said, "The first step is access to power. The second step is how to exercise this power we are getting. The second step is harder—you must think of a larger vision than your own political interest. The challenge of the nineties is the exercise of political power—how to govern."

Hernández, an ordained minister who graduated from the divinity school at Southern Methodist University, was the first person hired by Velásquez at Southwest Voter. He is less flamboyant, but perhaps better suited to the needs of a community coming to power. He ponders the role of Latinos in the American polity; he dreams of more than gaining power; he concentrates on the responsibility. Hernández is an easy person to be with, a dieter given to sixty-pound swings, a man who ministers to strangers, *muy gente* (a genuine human being), and always well-spoken, always precise. He understands the theory of his work: "People must learn to make an investment in public life together." And he worries about the fragility of power.

Latinos in the United States have never known the kind of corruption that New York, Chicago, and Detroit have endured, but they do not have an admirable record in public office. While Henry B. González, the powerful head of the House Banking Committee from San Antonio, has been a paragon of political virtue during his long career, others have not performed so well. Lauro Cavazos, former secretary of education, one of the highest posts ever held by a Latino in the United States, was an utter failure. He had no ideas, he couldn't run his department, and he couldn't even make himself a forceful role model for Latino children. At about the time the Bush administration pushed him out of office, the secretary was under investigation for the misuse of airline tickets.

California State Senator Joseph Montoya was convicted of extortion and racketeering. U.S. district court judge Robert Aguilar was tried for racketeering and conspiracy, the first U.S. judge ever indicted under the RICO law. U.S. Representative Robert García of New York was convicted of extortion. Tony Coelho, who had been the most influential Latino in the U.S. Congress, resigned his seat to avoid investigation of his part in a junk bond deal. The greatest blow to Latino politics came in 1988: Henry Cisneros, the mayor of San Antonio and a man who had been seriously considered for the vice-presidential place on the Democratic ticket in 1984, said he would not run for reelection after the San Antonio *Express* revealed his extramarital affair with the wife of a local merchant.

The 1980s, once heralded as "The Decade of the Hispanic,"[3] especially in politics, were a disappointment. In absolute numbers few Latinos had been forced to resign from public office, but there were rumors of more to come, and the percentage was disproportionately high. Willie Velásquez had feared the appearance of the *patrón*. Andrew Hernández worried about how to govern. Had they foreseen something? Was it exceptionally difficult for minorities to exercise political power? The disgraced Latino politicians were not big city backroom hacks. Good men, promising men—the single most promising Latino politician in U.S. history—had fallen. Something had gone wrong on the way to Athens.

2. ORPHANS IN OFFICE

In Houston, they call Ben Reyes *el patrón*. Everybody has a story about the city councilman from the Latino side of town:

- "He romanticizes that angry Vietnam Vet stuff. You know how he got elected the first time? His mother was a powerful figure in local politics, a precinct judge. She knew everyone in the district. A lot of people owed her."
- "Ben had his district locked up so tight that people who didn't vote for him couldn't even get their mail delivered."

[3]The slogan, first associated with politics, was picked up by the Coors Brewing Co., which used the phrase in its advertising.

- "He once ran against a fellow named Richard Holguin. Ben's people spread the rumor that Holguin was actually an Anglo named Hogan. Holguin, who is very fair, spent the whole campaign explaining that he really was a Mexican. Reyes was elected."
- "You know the Jones Lumber Co. that he owns? He makes his money selling at exorbitant prices to guys who want contracts from the city."

Some of the stories about Reyes are probably true. The solid citizens of the next generation of Latino politics in Texas, the academics and the reformers, the Brooks Brothers Texicans, believe they are all true. They expect Ben Reyes to be indicted for something, and soon. His expensive BMW galls them; they find his good ole boy obscenities unseemly in a man who has been in government for more than twenty years. Reyes is too rough, too blunt, too shrewd; the shrapnel scars he brought home from Vietnam are vulgar—in a finely tailored charcoal gray business suit he looks dangerous, and in his denim jeans and jacket he looks like one of those goddamn cowboys who gets drunk on Saturday night and raises hell. The man is an anachronism, the newcomers imply, a Texas pol with a scarred brown face; he should be gotten rid of, and the sooner the better.

But no one would deny that Ben Reyes knows politics or power—or that he was there at the beginning, in the early seventies, when single-member districting gave Latinos a chance at election to the Texas legislature. He remembers how it was for him. "In most cases you've got nobody to follow, nobody to ask how the real politics works. You can read all the books in the world you want to read, but that's not the way it operates. You got to learn the good ole boy system.

"Hell, I was twenty-three years old when I first got elected and have probably been the foremost leader in this city for the last twenty years. And hell! that's a lot of responsibility for a guy like that. My dad was a sharecropper; my mom had about a sixth grade education, and she was the educated one in the family. I couldn't walk up to Dad and say, 'Hey, Dad, how do I deal with the guys up in the legislature?' He didn't know where it was, let alone what was going on up there.

"It was really hard to get crankin'. It's hard for all of us. You got no one that you can go to, no mentor that you can sit down and visit with, you know; 'Should I be talkin to this guy or be workin with this guy? Or should I take this offer or that offer? Should I take this job or that? Why is he doin' it?' That makes it real difficult for all of us. We make some tough decisions, and sometimes they're not the right decisions. There's a tremendous amount of temptation in politics after you become involved in it, especially with minorities.

"I've seen the mayor of Houston take a job away from the low bidder and give it to the second low bidder because the guy is a friend of hers. If a minority did that, you know, Jesus, they'd lynch us. She does it and they say, 'Well, he's affiliated with a guy who did a bad job on another job.' "

Reyes said he works sixty hours a week as a city councilman, for which he is paid $30,000 a year. He also runs a lumber company that grosses $7 million a year. Few minority officials are so lucky. "I think that's where Henry (Cisneros) was," he said. "Henry was absolutely one of the most successful, if not the most successful Hispanic politican in this country. Shit, he was scrapin', man, to pay the bills, to buy groceries. The whole time I'd run into him at meetings across the country. Shit! he was livin' off his speaking engagements."

Ben Reyes knows how people view him, and he is not shy about discussing it. "Some people call me a *patrón,*" he said. "Shit! I get blamed for things you wouldn't believe. They said I was developing a *patrón* system. I call it leadership development. You know, there's a difference. Again, that's the stage our people are in. We're in that infancy stage where you're gonna get called the names, where you're gonna have the problems. But if you look around, most of the major leadership in this city has either one time or another been my assistant or been an aide of mine. All the guys in the legislature, all the guys on the local benches, a lot of the good lawyers in town, people on the port commission."

In his "leadership development" work he spends a lot of time giving lessons in politics. In the state legislature, he has a simple solution to most problems: "I pick up the phone and call the Speaker."

There is nothing shy, nothing apologetic about Reyes. He is only too glad to describe his approach to politics: "A guy calls and says, 'I really need this for bettering my career. I'm good at transportation' or 'I'm good at appropriations. You know, I know a lot about money, I really need to get on the Appropriations Committee. How do we do it?'

"Then I tell him. 'The first thing, we gotta go help the Speaker, take care of the Speaker.'

"Right now, all the trading is for redistricting, so who do you have to help right now so that two years from now you're in a position to have an effect? Hell, the lieutenant governor appoints the goddam redistricting board. Now, I learned that the hard way the first time I did redistricting in 1973.

"The power's in the damned lieutenant governor and the Speaker. Well, the Speaker's got an opponent. I've already called him and said, 'Mr. Speaker, you know, you've got a lot of Hispanics over in your district.' I know how many he's got. They're Democrats; he's a Democrat. 'And dammit, whatever you need . . . You need some people that can speak Spanish and go walk door to door? We'll send 'em from Houston for you. You need some money? We'll get some business people to raise you five, ten thousand dollars, send it down, because we want you to be Speaker next time around.' So that when it does come time to do the redistricting, 'Mr. Speaker, you know that ole boy, Omar Martínez, ought to be on that redistricting committee. Be a good thing for him to do for Houston, because you know we need to get that next congressional district.' Shit! he owes you!

"And on the other side of the deal is the lieutenant governor. So I've already been to the lieutenant governor. 'Put us down for twenty-five thousand. We'll raise it. You know, block walk it. We'll put up your signs, whatever you need to get you elected lieutenant governor, we're gon' do it.' He knows. And we'll do it. And when that redistricting bill comes over to the Senate, where it really gets put together, we can slide over into the lieutenant governor's office: 'We really need that new district in Houston. We need another senate seat. You ought to help us, Mister Lieutenant Governor. Remember, we was there when it counted.' It's politics. We learned it the hard way.

"I got young people positioned everywhere. I'm teaching them. I got 'em in Washington; I got 'em in the post office; I got 'em in INS, kids that work with me. I got some of 'em at Georgetown right now that spend their summer workin' with me. You know, I take 'em to dig ditches. I take 'em to haul garbage. I take 'em to fix an old lady's porch. I take 'em to do that during the summer, and right now, they're some of the top students at Georgetown or at Yale, Harvard. We raise the money here to keep 'em in college. We're going even further now: We're looking at the next high-school class."

He goes on talking, a politician without end, Texas. The promise and the problems of Latino politics tear at each other inside him, ancient adversaries in a battle between two philosophies: One is Athens, the other is the *patrón*. Reyes is a liberal Democrat, a man who fought for prenatal health care, bilingual education, and food stamps. He believes in service to the people at the grass roots. But he is not Willie Velásquez; he stumbles over the distinction between service in pursuit of power and service as a means of teaching the proper realm of freedom. The academics and the reformers have missed the point about him: He is not an anachronism; he is simply not an Englishman.

The polar opposite of Ben Reyes no longer holds public office. His business is called Cisneros Asset Management now, and it is housed in beautifully appointed offices near River Walk in downtown San Antonio. In his comfortable study, something like an office, among dark woods, expensive fabrics, Henry Cisneros stands, limned by the lovely, considered light, a tall man, just entering middle age, attenuated as a statue of Don Quixote, but with Oriental elegance, as if he were a prince of the Mexica thrust forward in time.

If he chose to run for office again in San Antonio, he would be elected in a landslide. The secret, as his friend and political ally, Jorge Hanes, said, is *las viejitas*. They rule the Latino world, as everyone knows, and they are all in love with Henry. One can knock on a hundred doors on the west side or talk across a hundred chain link fences on the south side, and all the stern women, the wise women, the widows, grandmothers, matriarchs, *todas las viejitas*, have forgiven Henry. "Such things happen," they say; "he is human." He has confessed; *las viejitas* have given him absolution; the affair with the jewelry store owner's wife, *la gringa*, is in the past.

However, it was not the affair that led to the founding of Cisneros Asset Management. It was money. Although Henry Cisneros—the holder of three graduate degrees, including a masters degree in public administration from Harvard and a Ph. D. from George Washington University, the recipient of more than a dozen honorary degrees, a former White House fellow, and the mayor of San Antonio for four terms—has far too much dignity to speak of his own travail, he can speak of the forces that have made life nearly impossible for other Latinos in government.

"There are some inherent difficulties," he said. "The systems of politics, particularly in places like Texas, are not set up to admit to power people who are outside of the economic mainstream, so that, for example, a legislator in Texas makes $4,800 a year, a city councilman in San Antonio makes $20 a week, and if you're going to serve, then you have to have another job. Most Hispanics are not financially independent; therefore, you have to have another job; therefore, that job needs either to be in the mainstream in which case you're under a lot of pressure to make your politics match the politics of the economically dominant community or you have another position, which is not in the economic mainstream at all. You're a university professor or something of that nature, and you're poor and struggling to keep ends together, with all the stresses that implies for family, etc.

"You find yourself being admitted to the world of the banks and the corporations because you are a power broker, a leader in the community, legitimately so, but then you cannot, in terms of your own means, in any way, shape, or form, relate to that, and you find yourself very much at odds socially, very much at odds economically, and after a while it just doesn't get to be fair or right even.

"Willie Velásquez, for example, died, in part, because he didn't have the kind of medical insurance that would allow him to be checked soon enough, so the cancer went pretty far before he actually was checked, and then when he died, he left his family without the kind of insurance that would tide them over for any considerable period of time. It was just because he worked in an organization that was hand to mouth and one of the things that went by the board was benefits, insurance benefits.

"So that's one aspect of the difficulty. I think another aspect . . ." Something caught in him; it caused a hitch in the smooth delivery, the polished voice, the senatorial sound of "right reason." He had spoken so easily, exhibiting what one of his loving critics called "a cut and paste mind," and now he stopped, if only for an instant—to catch his thoughts? to return the memories to their proper places in the ordered mind of Henry Cisneros? There were so many rumors about him. He was beholden to Senator Lloyd Bentsen. Bentsen had set him up in business. He was going to change his party registration, become a Republican. If he wasn't going to become a Republican, why had a Republican president called upon him to brief the premier of the Soviet Union? So much was riding on him, even now, even out of office, out of politics. He considered every gesture. He was the former mayor of San Antonio who still mowed his own lawn; he was the prince of the Mexica, the son of a middle-class man, a federal employee, Councilman Henry who had ridden the city garbage trucks with the workers. But there had been no money. His youngest son had suffered from a heart ailment. There had been medical bills. The older children were preparing to go to college. Those bills were coming, too. He had no money; elected officials in Texas cannot make money honestly. He had never strayed, never. There was the woman, but it had not really been the woman. It was economics, the doctor bills and the tuition costs that had driven him out of office. The Anglos, the system, history had forced him out of the running.

He kept his angers locked away inside. He was cool, gracious; he spoke in paragraphs, a dark brown Englishman with Indian eyes who stood as straight and thin as a knife. He sipped at his coffee, caught his breath, and went on. "It's very difficult in our society to live in the middle, ideologically, philosophically, politically, that is to say. As much as you might try to represent the interests of the Hispanic community, you find yourself up against a system where you constantly have to compromise, because it's not possible to drive through a system of school finance that gives the kind of money that needs to be going into minority districts. Because you don't have the array of power in Texas yet to be able to do that.

"The question is, Where is the compromise point? You are, by definition, an instrument of compromise with some line of demarcation between those who have the luxury of being ideologically pure—on the left—and at the same time, not a believer in the ideology of the right, of business, of power. And so the person ends up a bridge, but a bridge takes a lot of wear and tear. Bridges are to be trampled on, trampled across, I should say. And so it takes a very strong sense of self, of mission, and of stamina, to play that role. It's difficult, and people frequently fall one way or the other. Very few just stay there for a long time as a bridge.

"It takes a rare person. Henry B. Gonzalez. In thirty years, he broke a lot of trail." The former mayor smiled; modesty became him. He knew.

Cisneros had fallen, but only temporarily; *las viejitas* were waiting to embrace him. Others fell for reasons of politics. As the Latinos of Texas came to understand themselves as actors in the public realm, they revised their view of elected officials. They began to do what Andrew Hernández expected of them: They held Latino elected officials accountable. One of the first to be tried by the new rules was H. Tati Santiesteban of El Paso, the third ranking member of the Texas Senate and one of the most powerful political figures in the state. He had been in office for twenty-three years when he ran for another senate term in 1990, and lost. In 57 of the 106 precincts that voted in the senate contest, the majority of the voters had Spanish surnames. Santiesteban carried only 30 of those precincts; an Anglo, Peggy Rosson, won the rest. And it was not a question of money. Santiesteban had four times as much money as his opponent, who couldn't even afford to open an official campaign headquarters.

The local newspapers opposed Santiesteban, accusing him of accepting consulting fees from the El Paso Electric Company when he was voting on issues that concerned electric utilities. There were other irregularities, commingled personal and campaign funds (legal under Texas law), flowers for a woman friend charged to his campaign, and so on. The El Paso *Times* said Santiesteban lost because he was arrogant; others said he was corrupt. But the real reason for his fall had to do with the shift in political consciousness of the majority of the electorate, from Mexican to Mexican-American.

In the Latino neighborhoods of the Lower Valley east of the city, he was Tati, which is a Yaqui[4] name, for Santiesteban is a first generation mestizo, the son of a Yaqui father and a Spanish mother. At his baptism his father wanted to name him Tati, but the priest said he could not have a Yaqui name, if he was to be baptized a Roman Catholic. His father consented, but the boy named Humberto was never called anything but Tati, not as a child, not as the first Latino president of the student body of the University of Texas, not as a member of the lower house, not even as the third most powerful senator in Texas.

No one was more charming than Tati. He was funny, with a wild Yaqui sense of humor and a Spanish correctness in his dress and manners; macho, a real *cabrón*,[5] as only the Yaquis can be. He had a spring-steel physique,

---

[4]The Yaquis are a famously fierce tribe, originally from northwestern Mexico, but now living partly in the United States. Yaqui troops, fighting under the command of Alvaro Obregón, who was from Sonora, inflicted terrible casualties on Pancho Villa's troops during several of the major battles of the Mexican Revolution of 1910. The Yaqui tribe was severely reduced in numbers when many of the men were forcibly deported to the Yucatán, where they died by the hundreds on the tropical plantations, reportedly under the whips of overseers brought from China.

[5]Often used to describe the Yaqui character, meaning pitiless, physically and emotionally tough, a real son of a bitch. In standard Spanish, however, *cabrón* means cuckold, goat.

straight black hair, cut and combed in the duck's tail style of his youth, and skin that grew more Indian, taking on the character of brown parchment, as he neared sixty. Campaigning at a party in the Lower Valley, east of El Paso, he was pure *patrón,* charming the ladies who had been up all night cooking taquitos, flautas, tostaditas, beef ribs, French bread, and beans for their Tati and his campaigners; meeting in an inner room of the house with the mayor of Socorro, an Anglo judge whose reelection campaign was in trouble, a candidate for Democratic county chairman, and other local politicians.

Beer was pumped out of kegs; a mariachi band played in the patio of the house. Tati moved through the crowd, a boy again, quick, in a dark blue suit, white shirt, black tie, and black, perfectly plain cowboy boots. The mariachis played a fanfare when it was time for Tati to speak. "I was born, raised, and I plan to die in El Paso," he said. "I'm just a human bean [he pronounced the word that way]. If I made some mistakes, I apologize. But I never took nothing from nobody. I'm a lawyer and I've been practicing law for a long time in El Paso. I'm running for our seat in the Senate, our power in Texas, the most power and influence we have ever had and the most anyone from El Paso has had in the history of the state of Texas."

Then he said that his mother told him when he was growing up, "Si quiere ser egual, debe ser mejor."[6]

He made a blatant appeal to racism, asking for the Latino vote, but he made it in English. An old man interrupted, asking if Tati really knew how to speak Spanish. The candidate smiled, and repeated the last part of the speech *en Español.*

Then he switched to a mix of Spanish and English: "Sixty-eight percent of the *habitantes de El Paso son raza,* 51 percent of the registered voters are *raza,* but north of the freeway, where there are 45,000 Hispanic registered voters, only 4,500 voted in the last election." Again and again, he urged them to vote. "After God," he said, "politics is the most important thing in your life."

The band played Dianas, the traditional musical applause, then Tati sang romantic songs, Mexican crooner's songs, "Perfidia," "Mujer." There were speeches, testimonies for Tati. A giant of a man, known as the "singing cop," gave a speech about Tati and concluded with a bellowing rendition of "Volver." It was Tati's evening. This was the precinct in which he would win by a two to one margin, his best. The evening ended with cake and champagne. Although it was the first time in twenty years that he had faced serious opposition, there was no doubt in the Lower Valley about the outcome of the election.

A few days later, on the grass, near the parking area at the Delta Sports Center, the coaches and managers of the adult leagues that play baseball there gathered to drink beer and talk to Tati. He could not have chosen a

[6]The old immigrant refrain, "If you want to be equal, you must be better."

better place to campaign. Each coach represented a team of twenty or more players and each league president represented at least twenty teams. The multiplier effect, assuming that most players were married, was at least fifteen hundred. Including parents and siblings and their families, Tati had a way to reach thousands of voters with a single Sunday afternoon visit. His field organizer, Chalío Acosta, had great influence with the baseball players. Chalío was political, as everyone knew, but he also had a powerful reputation for telling the truth. People said he did not accept money or political appointments in return for his work; he did what he believed was right. Any political campaign in the county that could enlist Chalío was guaranteed a good showing, if not a win.

Tati himself had no link to the managers; he was guided by Chalío, who acted as his advance man and spokesman. It would have been a rich afternoon for the candidate had the man with two nicknames, Uncle Willie and Memo, not appeared. If Chalío was the paragon of politics in the sports world, Memo Villarreal was the epitome of ethics. He was widely known as the most rigid follower of the rules of conduct in all the community. Memo was often asked to collect tickets at dances and sporting events, because no one could talk his way around Memo, not his friends, not his wife, not even his own mother. Memo was on the level, all the way. At the age of sixty-four, with almost no beard, a deeply creased face, red under the brown, Memo was filled with some rage he probably could not name. It drove him to drink and brutal honesty.

Memo looks for arguments, seeks third party endorsement for everything he says, even his assertion that he and all his brothers joined the navy during World War II. Since midmorning Memo had been drinking beer, but not from the kegs Tati's people had brought; he drank from cans he and his friends kept in a cooler of their own. "Tati thinks he can buy us for a couple of kegs of beer; that's all it takes. He hasn't been here since the first time we elected him to the senate, seventeen years ago. He went up for us, the people, for the Mejicanos." Up and down the line of beer drinkers Memo walked, following Tati and Chalío, a self-appointed truth squad.

"Now, you see what happens. Politics is a dirty game. It's all under the table. This is the most corrupt country in the world, not like Mexico where the *mordida* is right out in the open; here everything is under the goddamned table."

He sputtered, he slurred his words; people turned away from him. He found others. "These Mejicano politicians are all the same; they get up there with the money, and they don't give a damn about the *gente*. I don't have to vote for a Mejicano politician, because what has he done for us? A gringo, that's different, they have to do something for the Mejicano people, because we don't vote for them if they don't do nothing for us. *Pero* the Mejicano, he gets up there and gets the money and he doesn't do shit for the *gente*.

"So I'm voting for Peggy Rosson. She's a gringo, *pero* she'll do something for the people. I trust a gringo before a Mejicano any time, because the gringo will do for the Mejicano people, and the Mejicano, he'll do for the money."

Memo the ethicist and Chalío the politician faced each other near the keg of beer. It was the agora updated. Memo presented his evidence to the court, to the newcomers and youngsters, to those who knew the history and those who did not, to all the beer drinkers and gossipers who had gathered around them. "Look at the shithouse over there!" he began. "You know how long the fucking shithouse has been stopped up? You got to walk in there on your toes, like this. The floor is all covered, it's all stopped up. Some of us have to do it outside by the wall, and people are watching over there from the ballpark.

"You know how long the shithouse has been like that? How long, Chalío? Fifteen years, right? Fifteen years! The politicians come down here to look for our vote; we ask them about fixing up the fucking shithouse. They all promise. Fifteen years you can't use the fucking shithouse, you have to walk in on your toes like this. Oh, man, the politicians!

"You're damned right the gringo is who I'm voting for, not for Tati."

Through the entire attack Chalío stood quietly, looking down at the ground. After Memo finished, Chalío looked up once, past Memo to the useless cement-block toilet, then he turned and walked away. There had been rumors about Tati: He had no money; the IRS was after him; the furniture in his law office had been repossessed; he mistreated his gringa wife. None of those tales mattered very much. If the third most powerful senator in the state of Texas had known enough about politics to fix the shithouse at the Delta Sports Center, he would have been unbeatable.

3.

At the close of the 1988 Republican National Convention a thirty-three-year-old Latino from Orange County, California, spoke to his party and perhaps to the future of his people. "The Democratic candidate may speak Spanish," he said, "but he doesn't speak our language."

He was not a Cuban or a Nicaraguan in flight from the Sandinista government. He was the son of an Apostolic preacher, a Mexican-American who had spent his early childhood in migrant farm worker camps. According to the canon of American politics, he should have been a liberal Democrat, but Gaddi Vasquez had taken a long look at the two major parties when he was eighteen years old and decided that the values of the Republican party were much closer to those his parents had brought from Mexico.

He came from a family of strivers, classic immigrants, according to

Vasquez. The new social contract demanded by his parents and his grand-mother included a proviso that the lives of Gaddi and his brother not be "a sequel to theirs." The preacher's son wore a shirt and tie to high school classes. His sport was debate. He had all the external attributes of a timid, bookish boy, but the signals were wrong. He became a cop, a bookish cop who went to college at night, but a cop nevertheless, a man who carried a club and a gun and worked among thieves, prostitutes, drug runners, and killers.

The rise of Gaddi Vasquez from a patrol car to the county supervisor's office happened at phenomenal speed. He left the police force to work in the Riverside city manager's office. From there, he became assistant to an Orange County supervisor. He moved to the private sector as area manager for governmental relations at the local electric utility, but George Deukmejian, then governor of California, picked him out of that job after only four months and brought him to Sacramento as his aide. In 1987, a county supervisor's position came open, and Deukmejian gave the job to Vasquez.

He was the first Latino supervisor in the history of Orange County, but he had only a year to prepare for an election. His district was 85 percent Anglo and one of the wealthiest in the world: The median family income in the district when Vasquez ran for office was $180,000. He opened his campaign with no money and practically no name recognition. Vasquez worked so hard he had to be hospitalized for a heart problem during the campaign. He won, as he put it, "hands down."

For the first time, the Republican party outside of Florida had a young, attractive Latino who could win Anglo votes. He looked good, he spoke with an Apostolic preacher's fervor and a trained debater's edge, and he was scrupulously, obsessively honest: He would not permit his staff to accept gifts or meals from business contacts, even under conditions permitted by the county's ethical standards. He had a second telephone installed in his office so that he could keep his business and personal calls completely separate. He didn't smoke, drink, or use foul language, and he had married the one and only girl in his life. In Vasquez, the Republicans had something the Democrats dreamed of—a Latino who could run for statewide office, and win!

They groomed him; they hired advisors for him; they showed him off at every opportunity, at parades and fund raisers, at parties and conferences, at their national convention. He was a good Republican, but a mixed bag as a conservative. He argued that Republicans should support prenatal care, because it was fiscally conservative—cheaper to take care of the children earlier than later. When people complained about the day laborers who stood on the street looking for work, Vasquez responded with an echo of the argument MALDEF attorneys made in federal district court: "For crying out loud, they're looking for a job, a job nobody else wants." He prefers Latino to Hispanic, which he recognizes as a bureaucratic word; "Latino," he said, "is more ethnic, more encompassing." He makes jokes about the word "Hispanic," although it is the choice of the conservatives, the marketers.

People accuse Vasquez of dealing with Anglo and Latino audiences differently. He does not deny it. "I'm more comfortable sitting in a little *cocinita* on Fourth Street eating homemade Mexican food, eating tortillas with my hands.

"A lot of people, before they knew me, would say, 'A Republican, the guy must have been born with a silver spoon in his mouth. This guy's not a chicano. This guy's not a Mejicano. This guy's a *bolillo*[7] or a coconut, or whatever.' The fact of the matter is, once people hear my background, where I came from, the fact that I'm completely bilingual, immediately—you know, there's a certain terminology that I use in speeches that immediately tells people this guy is one of us and he knows what he's talking about—the Republican politics becomes a secondary issue. So, yes, I approach it differently when I talk to someone like that, because I'm speaking about me, about us."

Vasquez believes he has found the reasons for the movement of Latinos, especially Mexican-Americans, into the Republican party. It is the political issue he understands best, the key to his future. "The ideology of the Democratic party has changed," he said, "while the ideology of the traditional Latino community has remained intact. It's very basic: family, God, country, church, the barrio, the closeness. We're very antiabortion, very pro capital punishment, very, very law and order, and so on. That has created a gap, which was very evident in the 1988 campaign. I was on the road a lot, and you could almost touch the discomfort that Latinos had with Michael Dukakis and some of the positions he took. And that's where the line came from that he may speak Spanish, but he doesn't speak our language.

"Latinos should look to a government that is prepared to give a hand and not a handout. There is still a sense of not freeloading: If you're going to give me help, I'll go out and pick up papers or something."

It is the argument made by another Mexican-American Republican, Jorge Garza, the counselor at the Centro Campesino in Florida City, and by Henry Cisneros when he retailed the political cliché: Give a man a fish and you feed him for a day; teach him to fish and he can feed himself from then on. Vasquez believes it; he said that his own parents turned down welfare. He

---

[7]Roll, originally a mildly derogatory term for an Anglo, derived from the fact that Anglos eat bread or rolls while Mexicans traditionally eat tortillas, now also used for assimilated persons in which case it refers to the brown crust and white interior of the roll. "Coconut" refers to Latinos who are *vendidos* (sell outs), brown on the outside, white on the inside.

talks about "his inspiration," his grandmother, who was a widow at the age of thirty-two and raised six children. "She had a fighting spirit," he said, "a survivor's attitude."

All of the values Gaddi Vasquez ascribes to Latinos are borne out in studies done by SVRI, the research arm of Southwest Voter, and by the observations of the organizers from the Industrial Areas Foundation in the Southwest. As more Latinos move out of the barrios and into the suburbs, they bring their social values with them, but not their economic concerns. They marry Anglos, open businesses, move into middle-class occupations, and become Republicans. Vasquez points to his own brother, who is married to an Anglo woman, lives in an Anglo suburb, and has a secure job in the telephone company; he is, of course, a Republican.

Richard Rodriguez, whose autobiography angered so many Mexican-Americans, may have understood more about Latinos than the chicanos would like to admit. The language dies in the suburbs, in the intermarriages; only the values remain, and those are not liberal. The liberals want to hold on to the Latinos by creating Athens in the barrio. They teach freedom in the public realm, immigrant political values, dignity. But freedom is only a stage on the way to success in America. When the liberals have completed their work, the Republicans come to collect the best students; the Democrats do not know how.

4.

I want us to be like the Jews, able to vote against our own interests in pursuit of justice.   Andrew Hernández, SVREP

In the United States, interests may gain influence, but only factions, those great confluences of interests that we think of as political parties and movements, can truly take power. The problem for Latinos, who dream of political influence equal to their numbers, is that they are a large congeries of different, often competing, interests rather than a small faction. Interests, as James Madison wrote, can be balanced each against the other, effectively limiting their power. For that reason he preferred a state of balanced interests to one divided into great factions. It was a good enough notion for a small nation in which women, slaves, indentured servants, and people who did not own land were prohibited from voting, but in a country of a quarter of a billion citizens, nothing less than a faction has meaning.

Blacks and Latinos, who might have begun to form a faction, have been at each other's throats since the Mexican-American War. Black civil rights leaders have not welcomed Latinos for the simple reason that there are too few jobs, schools, hospitals, and so on to serve blacks, let alone another gigantic group of victims of racial, social, cultural, and economic discrimination. On the national level black civil rights organizations have had some success (17.8 percent of civilian federal jobs for 12.1 percent of the population) while Latinos, represented by the National Council of La Raza in Washington, have been tragically ineffective (5.1 percent of civilian federal jobs for over 9 percent of the population).

In a nation that remains uncommitted to the notion of redress for past errors, blacks and Latinos are pitted against each other, for there is not enough education, economic opportunity, health care, and so on to serve either group, let alone both. As a result, they must live by the rules of war rather than civility; they cannot form themselves into a coherent, powerful political force. The problem for Latinos, who would seem to be a faction by definition, is whether they act like a faction or a collection of competing interests, for the nature of factions in U.S. politics, as defined by Madison, has changed.

Recently, Americans from different factions have been able to unite around single issues or interests, such as abortion rights, school prayer, and so on. Latinos, who might otherwise have become a faction, are deeply affected by these issues, for their immigration is still incomplete. They are neither rich nor poor, neither metaphysicians nor political actors; no longer Mexicans or Bolivians or Cubans, but not yet Yanquis. All the world is an irony to them, never what it seems, like a translation from another language; they live by inference, divination, and luck; to survive they must sweat in two realms.

It is a simple matter to exploit Latinos. The marketer asks, "What cheese do they eat?" But politics presents more complex problems. The political leader has two questions: "What is their hope of Heaven?" and "What can they afford to put on the table for dinner?"

The twin questions of politics force almost every Latino to seek answers to the dilemma of living in two realms: "What good is Heaven without a few *tostones* for *abuela* or a little piece of something for the children to scrape up with a tortilla?' 'What good is a feast of *pernil*[7] or the most exquisitely filled *pupusas*[8] if by my sins I cause Jesus to suffer?"

If one were to take the essences of these two questions and draw a matrix of Latinos and issues, dividing the Latinos into country of origin, length of time in the United States, economic status, educational level, church mem-

[7]Roast pork, Puerto Rican style
[8]Corn turnover filled with cheese, meat or chicken; a Honduran or Salvadoran dish

bership, marital status, age, and gender, it might begin to describe the complexity of interests national Latino politics must overcome.

Some political leaders have argued that Latinos can come together around a few issues: bilingual education, entitlements, concern for newcomers, and so on. But they are dreaming. The matrix includes those who favor language maintenance, another segment that favors a transitional curriculum, and a third that opposes anything but the teaching of English. Conservatives have spoken out often in opposition to affirmative action programs,[9] which are at the core of the demands of the young Latino leftists and liberals. The United Farm Workers made a political deal to support the Immigration and Reform Act, because it was in the interest of the members of their union to limit the labor supply. When Nicolás Kanellos, not a Cuban, but a Puerto Rican married to a Mexican-American, went to Miami to accept an award for his aid to Latino literature, the Cuban right wing threatened to kill him with a bomb because they didn't like his politics, even though he had published many young Cuban writers.

If a Latino Democratic candidate came out in favor of abortion rights and an Anglo Republican sided with the right-to-life position, how would the members of COPS in San Antonio or EPISO in El Paso vote? In the churchyard after a Mothers of East L.A. meeting, the radical women, the bravest women gathered to speak of their opposition to abortion. On that issue alone any sophisticated candidate can fragment the Latino community according to the relative importance of Heaven and the dinnertable.

When Andrew Hernández said he wished Latinos would act like Jews and vote against their own interests, it was not only a prayer for liberalism but for power as well. In the simplest terms, American political power has two requirements: money and numbers. Among Latinos the two requirements are separated by a wall as high as history: The Cubans have the money, and the Mexican-Americans have the numbers. It is both a real division and a portent of the future.

The poorest Latinos have been, with the exception of political exiles, the newest arrivals, and more than 50 percent of the growth of the Latino population continues to be from new arrivals. According to Leobardo Estrada, adding in the high birthrate of the newest arrivals, they contribute something closer to 60 or even 65 percent of the growth. In the foreseeable future a great number of Latinos will continue to be newcomers and poor people, even as more and more of the true immigrants move into the middle class and out of the barrios. Economic differences will cause a deep, debilitating split in the national Latino population, dividing the faction initially into the two great families noted by Cervantes: the Haves and the Have-Nots. Then

---

[9]Compare this to Tati Santiesteban's advice: "Si quiere ser egual, debe ser mejor."

the families will be divided again and again, according to beliefs, dreams, and histories. And after all the interests have split the Latinos like a machete cleaving a coconut into bite-sized chunks of meat comes the question of *racismo;* in the meeting rooms where all the Latinos go to caucus, no one sees clearly.

Gaddi Vasquez's attack on Michael Dukakis, which drew applause from Richard Nixon and the other wisemen of the Republican party, could be applied by any Latino to any opposing political candidate. When he said Dukakis "may speak Spanish, but he does not speak our language," Vasquez thought he had delivered a coup to the Democratic campaign for Latino votes, but he had really only voiced the political dilemma of Latinos. Until then, all Latinos but the Cubans and a few Nicaraguan exiles had been conceded to the Democratic party. Vasquez unknowingly articulated the growing fragmentation of the bloc; he showed the way to balancing the interests within what might have been a faction, giving the lie to arguments about Latino political power having a decisive effect on the 1992 or 1996 elections.

Unless some great, unifying issue can be found to unite rich and poor, Africa and indigenous America, this world and the next, Latinos are unlikely to have national political power consonant with their numbers. The political experts in Washington and New York will find it more advantageous to pit them against each other than to suggest that candidates attempt to satisfy their needs. With the coming of the intimations of political power, if not yet real power, Latinos face a cruel dilemma: If they remain separate and distinct, they will become an island within the nation, a troublesome toy to the powerful majority; otherwise, they will eventually become assimilated into the great factions, a politically indistinct group, with an appetite for different cheeses and ideas, the largest insignificant minority in American history.

25

FOR WANT OF A FAMOUS DEATH

I.

In Tenochtitlán, in the time of the great, brief dynasty of Aztec kings, the hope of princes and parvenus was for a famous death. Tlacaélel, the uncle and advisor of kings, the monster whom the wise men and warriors called "conqueror of the world, embodiment of power on earth," taught them to sacrifice blood to the sun, to make war for the sake of the sun. He taught them above all to die famously, in battle or on the bloody stone altar, in the full light of the sun. If they died so, he promised them, if they died famously, they would live forever in the dwelling place of the sun, Heaven. The word in Náhuatl for this ideal state in which to die is the passive form of the verb *mati* (to know), which is *macho* (to be known).[1]

Tlacaélel did not invent machismo; he perverted one of the basic tenets of Native American conduct in order to create the invincible Aztec military machine. Elsewhere in North America, the Lakota used coup sticks to touch their enemies in battle solely for reasons of reputation. Most tribes carried trophies to make themselves known: scalps or feathers plucked from the tail of an eagle. Among the Navahos, Apaches and other Diné-speaking tribes, the beginning of a medicine cure is the fame of the shaman. In all the Americas, from the great potlatches of the Pacific Northwest to the rain

[1]The translation and definition is paraphrased from Miguel León-Portilla, *Aztec Thought and Culture.*

forests of the Amazon, the rule was to be known, to die a famous death. "Hoka-hey, Lakota," Crazy Horse told his magnificent light cavalry, "it's a great day to die!"

To die a famous death, to have one's last exploits painted on a buffaloskin robe or the side of a tepee; to be seen by the thousands gathered at the base of the Pyramid of the Sun in the most beautiful, most sophisticated city in the hemisphere, perhaps in the world, as a priest tore the heart from one's body; to be killed on the battlefield in full view of the thousands; to be known, to be remembered; to die immortal: These were the dreams of the Americas, the passports to Heaven.

Machismo was also a passport to higher status in this world, even among the Aztecs whose social classes were as rigid as those of ancient Athens. A warrior whose bravery was known, whose death was certain to be famous, could rise up through the social ranks of Tenochtitlán; he could become a nobleman on his way to Heaven.

In Tula and Boriquen, Montana and Monte Albán, the citizens of the Americas had developed societies based on the morality of machismo. As Sir Isaiah Berlin pointed out in his essay on "The Originality of Machiavelli," there are two distinct moralities, one Christian and one pagan. Christian morality includes "humility, kindness, scruples, unworldliness, faith in God, sanctity. . . ." The values of the pagan world are "courage, vigour, fortitude in adversity, public achievement, order, discipline, happiness, strength, justice, above all assertion of one's proper claims and the knowledge and power needed to secure their satisfaction." Although Machiavelli never denies that the Christian virtues are good, it is pagan morality or *virtú*, the pre-Christian concept, that he admires and suggests for the prince. *Virtú* is morality in the world as it is, applied to men as they are.

The machismo of the Americas, prior to the rise of the Aztec dynasty and the arrival of Christian morality, bore a close resemblance to *virtú*.[2] Without Tlacaélel or Jesus, some of the native societies might have evolved into an Athens or a Rome, or they might all have descended into superstition and madness. There is, of course, no way to know. What did happen was not social, philosophical, or religious in nature, but political; the pagan version of machismo was frustrated by the imperialism of the European conquerors. An oppressed people cannot express *virtú*, for the actions of the powerless have no meaning. A Taino chief telling his Roman Catholic captors he would prefer to die without converting to Christianity because he did not want to go to a heaven filled with priests was probably the last expression of pagan machismo in the Caribbean. His was a famous death; no one knows the

[2]Compare the original notion of machismo ("to be known") to a later version of morality, John Rawls's notion of publicity as the test of morality.

names or the circumstances of deaths of the hundreds of thousands of Tainos who died in the overtaxed fields and chimerical mines; *virtú* had been killed by the Spaniards, destroyed by the steel of Toledo and the Inquisition's dismissal of this world.

In Tenochtitlán, *virtú* was driven mad by Tlacaélel; a famous death no longer required courage or public-spiritedness, merely the wish to die. So many were killed, the blood ran so freely, that when Cuauhtémoc led the last resistance to the Spaniards his actions seemed more like Christian self-sacrifice than Aztec machismo.

There were still acts of machismo after the defeat of the Aztecs: The Sioux, Cherokees, Pawnees, Cheyenne, Kiowa, Apaches, Nez Perce, Yaquis, and others produced famous deaths as the Europeans and their African slaves and mercenaries killed them off or herded them onto reservations. It took hundreds of years to eradicate it completely, but the day the Spaniards landed in the hemisphere the existence of pagan *virtú* in the Americas was doomed. The expression of machismo as *virtú* was no longer possible, but the desire for a famous death remained in the psyche of the Native American and the great mestizaje that was to become the dominant population of the hemisphere.

The old machismo, the ethical core of America before the conquest, was transmogrified by the loss of the power to consummate the wish. Under Spanish rule, no native, no mestizo could do anything but obey. Dark-skinned people lost their identity. Individuals, families, whole tribes lost their names. Even the gods lost their names. And as the nameless, faceless, godless Latinos lost hope of a famous death, machismo suffered a terrible metamorphosis. Under the rule of despair, the public macho became secretive, the proud person felt ashamed, the steadfast one turned capricious, the civic-minded man could not even defend his own family; powerlessness transmuted the notion of a famous death into the dream of a famous killing. In the roiled soul of the conquered American, antipodal characteristics emerged; the man who could no longer protect his wife took to beating her; the wish to be brave inspired the bully; the hero got drunk. Machismo produced the great paradox of the conquest, for no oppressed native or mestizo could bear either to be what he seemed or to seem what he was; those who would be known, the lovers of *virtú,* were condemned to an ironic life.

2.

The Mexican mother . . . is often the real boss. . . . If not matriarchal in fact, the family has been shown to be matrifocal or at least egalitarian.

Rev. Rosendo Urrabazo, CMF

In its original form machismo prescribed a competition among men. The best record of it, described by his Aztec informants to Fray Bernardino de Sahagún at the beginning of the sixteenth century, is a poetic picture of *virtú*. The ideal Aztec life emphasized the outward manifestation of goodness, education for children and the ethics of moderation.

The decline of *virtú* in the Native American male, is prefigured in the myth of the good monk of Tula, Quetzalcóatl, and the evil Tezcatlipoca.[3] After Tezcatlipoca tricked him into getting drunk, the good monk lost his senses, carousing wildly and sexually abusing his own sister. The next morning, he saw the results of his behavior on his swollen, ugly face, which he hid behind a jade mask.

History followed the same pattern: The man who wished a famous death was shamed by the conquest, and then by his own response to the conquest. Juridical shame was followed by the shame of disapproval. Since he failed the test of publicity, he lived secretly, hidden behind the jade mask. In public, he was docile, the conquered, but in the secrecy of his house, behind the jade mask, he was a tyrant, he abused his own family. No one could quite understand him, no one could ever be completely certain of him, for the violent response to the conquest lay under the mask.

His answer to a shameful life was to endure *(aguantar)*, first the Aztec hegemony or the heavy hand of the Iroquois Confederation or the arrogance of the Caribs, then the Spanish conquest, and finally the imperialism of the United States. But *aguantar* does not mean surrender; it is not a bargain: The one who endures does not do so gladly; sullenness lives under the surface; the bowed head hides the rage of despair. Defeated by the stranger, the

---

[3]A more complete retelling of the myth appears on page 22. Quetzalcóatl is the plumed serpent of D. H. Lawrence; Tezcatlipoca is usually translated as "Smoking Mirror." Aztec names and phrases often appear laughable to English- or Spanish-speaking readers, because the language is concrete, depending upon *difrasismos*, dualities, to name abstract concepts: face and heart for character; flowers and song for poetry; night and wind for invisibility; jade and feathers for beauty; black and red ink for wisdom. The classic work on this subject is by Angel María Garibay K., *Llave de Náhuatl*.

macho does the only thing he can, he turns on those he loves—family, friends, acquaintances—but not always, not daily, only capriciously, only drunkenly, only when he is most ashamed.

The macho of the perverted code threatens his wife, he beats her, he beats his children, he betrays his friend, he abuses everyone he can, for he feels that he has been abused in the world and he is ashamed; he demands vengeance, but the vengeance he extracts only leaves him more ashamed.

Stories of machismo abound, among Mexican-Americans, Cubans, Puerto Ricans, Colombians, Dominicans; and it is not just the women who know, not just the women who complain, the men also suffer shame for their fathers, for the grandeur lost to the conquest, for the hope of a famous death mired in the bitter reaction to powerlessness. Lina Frescas Dobbs, the young economist just embarking on a political career in Texas, drew a classic picture of perverse machismo in her own life. She grew up in a housing project, the daughter of a small-time prize fighter who seldom beat his opponents, but often beat his wife. After he punched his wife in the face and broke her nose, she finally threw him out. With no man in the house and no child support payments, living in a state that was utterly heartless in its unwillingness to give a decent level of aid to families with dependent children, the single mother sent her children to Harvard, Yale, and Notre Dame. She took the ancient macho role; she was the public person; *virtú* was hers. The prizefighter lived in the pall of shame.

The pattern repeats itself in families from the Caribbean as well as Mexico. Robert Otero, a Puerto Rican, saw his father strangling his mother with her own braids, and attacked him. The journalist Mike Castro threatened his father as a means of defending his mother. A Dominican describes the alcoholism of a father who could not bear life in New York City, where his wife could find work and he could not. Cuban women in Miami argue that they have the highest divorce rate of any definable group in the United States, because their husbands (or ex-husbands) are domineering and unfaithful.

In its perverse form, machismo is neither male chauvinism nor courage. Some women who dote on their sons fear they are teaching them machismo by waiting on them, sparing them from household chores, and so on, but the connection between love and cruelty seems farfetched: The doting mother cannot be blamed for making both mamma's boys and machos. Nor does there appear to be a cause and effect relationship between macho fathers and their sons.

A novel by the late Arturo Islas, Jr., *The Rain God,* describes a macho father, one who demonstrates his machismo with bonecrushing bearhugs, crude sensibilities, and an affair with his wife's close friend. Islas, Jr., portrays the perfectly macho father in his novel as a crude man, a tough cop who is unable to understand an intellectually curious, physically weak son. Only the mother of the novel understands her son and defends him to his father.

When I read the novel, I wrote to Islas, Jr., telling him of my friendship with his father, of the gentleness his father had shown toward young people who were arrested, and of the love and pride his father had expressed about his son, who was a student at Stanford. It seemed to me that Islas, Jr., had written a novel of exorcism, an attempt to get rid of his own devils.

No response came from Arturo, Jr., but after a long time there was a letter from Art. He thanked me for the remembrances. He, too, recalled the afternoons we had spent together when he was still just a detective lieutenant. It amused him that I had taken over the police beat from Rubén Salazar with whom he had had the same conversation about "man's inhumanity to man."

When last I was home, I visited with Art Islas in his little house at the beginning of Waymore Street, only a block from the house in which my parents had lived. He was more than seventy-five years old, and his knees had given out, so he walked in a strange, bowlegged way, assisted by canes. When I walked up the path to his doorway, he came outside and gave me one of those bonecrushing *abrazos* his son had complained about, calling them "embraces without affection."

At first, we reminisced. We talked about Rudy Tellez and Rubén. He corrected my history of the town, speaking from the inside. Yes, he had broken the race barriers in the department. Yes, he had been hurt when they failed to make him chief of police. His list of allies surprised me; his list of enemies was as expected. After his wife and their grandchild went out, he told me that much of what his son had said of him in the novel was true. At the age of fifty, struck by the thought of middle age, he had had suffered a common crisis. His wife had found out and insisted that he sell their big house so that she would have money enough to take care of herself if their marriage broke up.

He sold the house to please her, but it hadn't been necessary. The toughest cop the town had ever known never considered leaving his wife, for he treasured her and his family; it was not machismo but middle age that blinded him. The whole period had been very difficult, he recalled. His voice quavered. He looked like my father around the eyes; they had the same cheekbones at seventy-five, the same blending of the color of the skin and the cornea. Perhaps it was all those years in the desert, the heat, then the chill of the swamp coolers, and the late afternoon sun. They had known each other, but not well; Sal, Rubén's father, and my father were friends, co-workers, and Art was from another world, an acquaintance, nothing more.

We talked a long time, through a tall drink and a refill. All the while a copy of his son's new book, *Migrant Souls,* lay on the coffee table. It was like an itch in an unseemly place. We glanced over at it, now and then, felt it, but

could not deal with it. Finally, I asked him about the first book; had it made
him angry? He let me stew for a moment in the discomfort of asking the
question, still the detective, ruling the silences; then he laughed:

They were friends, he said, father and son. Art, Jr., came home often. He
was really a very good writer; this new book was even better than the first
one. More than that, it was tough living on a policeman's pension; they
hadn't paid much, even to inspectors, when he was in the department, and
the pension was based on those old numbers. He said that Art, Jr., sent them
something now and then to help out. He was very pleased to accept the help
of his delicate son, the one who taught English at Stanford.

Arturo Islas, Jr., died soon afterward. He was hardly more than fifty years
old, and he had been plagued by ill health all his life. The second novel was
not so good as the first, which had been very good indeed. The second novel
lacked the anger of the first one, as if the writer had learned something about
his villainous model. The despicable macho, the toughest cop, had turned
out to be a throwback; his adversaries had been men, not women; he had
always been a public person; he had been the possessor of face and heart, the
difrasismo by which the Náhuas meant to say character; he had never surrendered, he had never been docile; *aguantar* was anathema to him.

The father's sense of order, of the moderating role of civilization did not
desert him in the streets or in his home. The toughest cop, nearly confined to
a chair now, with canes to help him walk the shortest distances, said that
once, however, he had wanted to kill a man with his bare hands. A child
molester had incited him to thoughts of violence; he still remembered the
crime, every detail of the body of the little girl who had been torn apart by
her killer. He regretted what he thought of now as his descent into the brutal,
postconquest form of machismo, but only a little. To die a famous death was
still possible in the minds of both Arturo Islases, father and son. Each in his
way overcame the shame of conquest; each lived according to the rules of
virtú.

The Aztecs had a public school for machismo, the *telpuchcalli,* where the
rules were codified. No system has existed since then; little boys learn the
rules at home, in school, and in the street. The lessons are life; most are
learned by a kind of cultural osmosis; some are demonstrated; only a few are
actually taught. As a young boy growing up in an almost entirely Latino
neighborhood, I learned some of the public rules. They were all ritualistic, in
retrospect a little mad, at the moment the height of normality. I remember
the lessons well. On a morehead[4] a few blocks south of El Paso High School
we found a nest of centipedes. My friend Luis, who was older and carried a
knife hidden in his shirt, scooped up the many-legged insects with an old tin

[4]The local name for a small mesa or cliff

can. We poked at them with sticks; Luis cut one in half with his knife. Then each of us tested himself by lying flat on the dry red clay of the morehead while a centipede crawled across his chest.

Other lessons were not so dramatic. Machismo is a quotidian business, the making of a man. The rules are unyielding, so that the interpretation of them is sometimes comic: a man can cry, he cannot whine; a man is strong, a woman is soft; a woman manipulates, a man demands; a man can fight, he cannot snitch; women scream, men sulk; mothers are holy, fathers fail the test. In the world of machismo there are no symmetries, honor magnifies every act. The orderly, awful notion of an eye for an eye is superseded by death for disrespect. Betrayal begets vengeance, always, without exception: The difference between a man and a priest is in the turning of the other cheek.

There is a catechism of machismo:

"Name the world!"
"God, family, country."

"Speak of yourself!"
"I am not alone."

"Are you afraid?"
"No."

"Does it hurt?"
"No."

"Can you bear it?"
"Yes."

"Do you dare?"
"Watch me."

"But this is dangerous."
"I was born to die."

Machismo is invisible to those who practice it; only observers can discern the act and intent. It is atavistic stuff, childhood memories, the adolescent refusing to die into the sensible life, fearing age, denying any but a famous death. Yet something cowardly lurks around the edges of machismo. It can easily turn ugly; all it takes is a run of bad luck, conquest.

Whether the man is writ large or the society is writ small, the issue always comes down to surrender and its consequences—the perversion of values and then shame. A conquered man has neither face nor heart: he cannot expect a famous death. Tezcatlipoca drives him to disgrace himself, and disgrace, in turn, drives him to life behind the mask; the souring of *virtú* causes a retreat from the public realm. But it need not always be so. Men rebel. Instead of falling into the ugly perversion of machismo, they become Jorge Valls or Arturo Islas, Jaime Inclán, Leobardo Estrada, Andrew Hernández, José Luis Morín, Joaquín Avila, Heriberto Cabrera, Ricardo Gutiérrez, Robert Navarro, Martín Espada. They do not surrender; they rebel against the dreamed freedoms of the private realm; they do politics.

Whoever is free to act, as these lives prove, bears responsibility for his actions; whoever bears responsibility for his actions has dignity; politics gives rough men that sense of power which enables them to be gentle. A PTA meeting, a block association campaign, a picket line, the human triumph of a secret ballot in a meaningful election; it does not require a revolution to overcome the perverting oppression of conquest; any symbol will do. But there must be something. The venerable rules of machismo require that a man have some effect in the world; that is the meaning of a famous death. For the lack of it men behave as if they were mad.

26

ESPIRITISMO: CONVERSATIONS WITH ERNESTO

Although my father-in-law Ernesto is only twenty-eight years old, he was born at the end of the nineteenth century, which makes him an interesting companion, a nice mixture of enthusiasms and venerability, but not always an easy man to deal with. When I announced my intentions toward his daughter, he asked, Do you know the history of this family? We are descended directly from one of the first men to write poetry in the Espanish language. The records exist! When Francisco Franco dies or the fascist son-of-a-bitch is overthrown, you will go to Toledo and see personally these records of the early poetry of Espain. Since long before this time, more than seven hundred years, more than a thousand years, we have been Espanish. And now you!

In retrospect, it may have been the accent that made him seem so stern. He never got as comfortable with English as Blanca did, even though he learned the grammar and gained quite a good vocabulary before he came to this country. The Germanic sounds of English, the stubby vowels and adenoidal consonants of New York, lay thickly on his palate, like the greasy food of Central Europe that congealed in the thousand delis of Manhattan, Brooklyn, and the Bronx. He strained to hear the music in the speech of his new country; he struggled to accommodate himself to the pace of hot jazz, motorcars, flappers, and stocks on margin. Was this a fit town for poets? he asked, a nation in need of socialists?

He died.

Was it really acute indigestion? I asked.

The subject did not interest him. What does a 28-year-old Latino care about death?

Ernesto chose to speak of other things—Esperanto; poetry, socialism, and Esperanto; always Esperanto. For the longest time I thought it was an affectation, intellectual social climbing, League-of-Nations liberalism.

Spirits do not explain. And we had no medium but Blanca, who always recalled his good looks, the way such a handsome young man could make everyone laugh, how the girls gathered around him. Ay, Ernesto!

But Esperanto? Blanca, now Blanche (it was better than Whitey), shrugged. A man does not talk politics with a child bride.

It came to me slowly over the decades that Ernesto had been a stubborn man, one who could haggle over epistemology the way some people haggle over fish. Assimilation is not the midpoint of anything, he said; language has no half-life. If not Espanish, then not English. Who do they think they are, these *other* immigrants! If we are to have an official language, an official culture, I say, perfect! *Adelante!*[1] But I will not go one step further than they. We will both learn a new language, Esperanto.

Of course, it was never going to be Esperanto. He knew that; Ernesto was a poet, but not a fool. The social contract in the United States could not be changed by a few Latinos demanding their rightful place. What was important, according to Ernesto, was not a new contract—any contract good enough for the people whose ancestors came over on the Mayflower was good enough for him—but the demand. To make demands was to do politics, and to do politics was to be one of nature's symmetries, a complete human being, one who enjoys freedom in the privacy of his dreams and in the ennobling daylight of publicity.

The United States never acceded to Ernesto's demand that his name be added to the existing contract, with no ethnic or linguistic asterisk. But he was permitted to make demands, which was, in itself, a new social contract, different from the one he had known in the old country. Ernesto knew that merely arriving in the United States meant nothing; only by making demands could he establish a beachhead—Esperanto made a person of him.

This fullness of being guided Ernesto during his brief life and the long years of observation and contemplation that followed. He became the owner of a point of view. Perhaps he knew (knows) something; in Tenochtitlán that was the definition of a wiseman, one who knows something. If Ernesto is such a man, it behooves us to learn what he thinks, which is not impossible. After all, what is a biographer but a medium hiding in a thicket of facts?

The rules of communing with spirits are simple and few:

[1]"Forward!"

- Spirits are not cynical. They recognize irony, but no longer have need of it.
- Spirits cannot be conjugated: Is and was are both wrong.
- Spirits do not ingest, digest, or excrete; nor do they reproduce. They are irritable, however; if they weren't irritable they wouldn't exist at all. Ask Ernesto.
- All spirits are classicists. They are like English majors, who stop reading new works when they die and become assistant professors. That's why the latest influences on Ernesto's thinking are Martí, Hostos, Flores Magón, and Vasconcelos; he missed Muñoz Marín by a few breaths.
- Spirits claim omniscience, not prescience, but the Latinos bend the rules a little.

Ernesto and I do not agree on every issue. For example, I tell him he is not a man of color, and he tells me that, in the United States, whoever speaks Spanish as a first language is a person of color. He has a point.

He thinks the organization called U.S. English is run by fascists, and I think it is run by fools. When he points out that the honorary chairman of the organization is S. I. Hayakawa, I nod and say that we're both right. It's good for the relationship.

We speak in English. I did not speak Spanish for twenty-five years out of respect for my father-in-law who referred to me as the singing criminal from the Rio Grande. Ernesto has always been very concerned with language. He did not think of Spanish as a private language and English as a public language, not in the shame-faced way that Richard Rodriguez distinguishes between the two. For him, English was merely the lingua franca of the land in which he lived. One could as well live a public life, in the public realm, speaking Spanish. He would have preferred it.

He learned English because no one else would learn Esperanto. He was a practical man, a shrewd businessman—for a socialist. The thought of sitting by in silence and poverty in the land where the streets were reputed to be paved with gold was not for him. Besides, he had the example of Bienvenida to guide him. Unlike her, Ernesto was not about to get lost on the subway.

However, he believes the alternative to Esperanto is bilingualism, not English. A bit of chauvinism comes into his thinking when he discusses the subject; he is quite willing for Latinos to be completely fluent in two or more languages (his French was excellent; he spoke almost without accent), while the Anglos know nothing but English. The advantage pleases him; he thinks of it as a kind of linguistic affirmative action. He whispers to his grandsons that in the rapidly growing Latin-American trade, the monolingual Anglos will be shown up for what they are—dumb.

Ernesto thought Latinos were on the way to a good alternative to Esperanto in the 1970s when the first chicano studies and Puerto Rican studies courses appeared in university catalogues. Nothing could have pleased him more. But he has changed his mind. He now thinks that culture, which had been the handmaiden of politics, can be an enemy of the public freedom. He sees far too many Latinos funneled into ethnic studies majors. Because so many ethnic studies courses are taught in Spanish, Ernesto claims it is theoretically possible for a person to get a degree from a college in the United States without knowing how to speak English.

Seeing this, he holds his head and wails the lamentation of a man who had hoped to make some trouble: Ay, Bienvenida! Yet again, Bienvenida!

Ernesto says that from his omniscient vantage it is not at all difficult to understand why the Anglo Establishment was so quick to allow Latinos to institute chicano and Puerto Rican Studies majors. It was an ideal way to remove them from competition for economic and social power, a trap. He believes the formation of islands within the universities is an act of repression, not accommodation. He says that these islands would be easier to deal with if they were called by their proper name, ghettos.

When I explain the notion of ethnic pride to him, I am glad that spirits have no weapons but their wits, because he gets very angry.

Pride! my son. When I go with my Espanish accent among these other immigrants—these English, Germans, Poles, Italians—and I wear a suit of good cloth and a shirt with a fresh collar, this is pride. But if I put on a sombrero or a beret [he pronounced the final consonant] and I hide my face from them, looking only in the mirror, is this the act of a proud man?

Esperanto is an accommodation. To build a prison of culture is suicide!

Apparently, he had not heard any of the arguments about the dominance of Western civilization in universities. When I spoke of the need to bring the West down from its intellectual pedestal, he responded with a series of questions, speaking each one very slowly.

Is it true that in Asia they do not have gravity? And that the influenza kills only the fair? In how many languages are the verbs indistinguishable from the nouns? Why is it of no interest to the non-Western mind to know whether we are truly here, and how we got here? And if we are here, how we should behave? In these diverse cultures of which you talk, is tomorrow truly the day before yesterday?

Don't be a fool, my son; the answer is Esperanto. The moment we say to the Anglo that he is the continent and we are satisfied to be islands, we are lost. After segregation, there are few survivors; it takes generations for the immune system to become strong enough to enable people who have lived in isolation to survive in the world. There is a politics of culture! Esperanto is politics. Ethnic studies, yes! But only ethnic studies, never! To encase oneself in the bubble of ethnic studies is to concede that the only freedom is the consolation of philosophy.

Who can eat dreams? Who can take a dream to court? We have come beyond dreaming. We must not go back!

"Aha!" I said, certain that I had found him out at last, "Then you favor assimilation."

What is assimilation? Who can be nothing? Even the dead are not nothing; we have a history. Similarly the living.

"There are mixed marriages," I said.

He responded with a shrug, The progeny of such marriages are always Latinos.

For the first time in more than a quarter of a century of debate I believed I had him in a corner. "That's an invitation to racism! Rednecks talk that way about blacks; Nazis talk that way about Jews! Do you mean to say that a person who has one drop of Latino blood is a Latino?"

Ojalá!

His petitioning of God was an act of self-respect so great that it began to bring him into focus. The colorless ectoplasm in the distant night of the eternal took shape. But the shape was strange, too large, too horizontal for a person. I feared some Buddhist error, my father-in-law turned into a beast, a camel; the shape looked a lot like a camel, the kind with a single hump.

"What are you?" I asked.

I was a man, he answered, but I did not know until I came here that in my life I suffered from strangerness. You know what this is?

Without waiting for my answer, he proceeded to tell me: Strangerness is to be without a home in the language, race, or culture of the nation in which one lives. This situation is almost unendurable, because it works against the most basic human conditions, which are society and the language that accompanies life in society. If we are to believe the theories of the materialists, language defines man and arises from the material condition, which is society. A person who cannot speak the language is therefore less than human.

Strangerness is to feel like a member of a different species. This quality of strangerness makes people more desperate to assimilate, thereby to enter human society, to join the human race. Probably strangerness could be cured by assimilation, but assimilation cannot be complete—hair, skin color, facial characteristics—history cannot be changed. No one can kill his dead grandmother.

After the language is forgotten, after the culture is converted, the sense of strangerness remains. You see, the genetic history of the person is worn on the surface of the body, like a badge; the strangerness is in the soul. So I say to you again, my son, Esperanto!

"Nostalgia!" I said.

Yes, he said, you begin to understand. Strangerness produces this nostalgia in a person. One becomes homesick for a language more even than for a place. We want to assimilate, but we cannot, so we are trapped in hope. And we want to be human, so we are also trapped in nostalgia.

It was not a camel, but a man standing beside his horse. I saw him sit down, as if to think over the problem of the stranger in the strange state of English.

"The suburb or the barrio?" I said, suddenly aggressive, like a holdup man asking someone to choose between his money and his life. He did not stir; he did not speak. Time moved slowly, like the trunk of a great tree adding to its girth. Ernesto would not be hurried.

There is no irony in the spirit world; everything is as it seems. Perhaps that is why Latinos are less afraid than other people when death comes near; they welcome the simplification. For here on earth, in the United States of America, the ironies of Latino life are overwhelming. Latinos are the first immigrants and the last, indivisible families of individuals, brown when they are white, poor when they are rich, the racist victims of racism, always on the rise while dying in a fall; they are required to forget even as they learn.

"Ernesto, Ernesto," I called, "What is the answer? To fight, to endure, to waste the generations in despair, to assimilate, to disappear? How should Latinos act in this inhospitable but not impossible land?" The intensity of the conversation brought everything into focus. I saw a man sitting beside a horse.

For a long time, perhaps a year or two, an instant in the spirit world, he sat with his chin on his fist, contemplating the future. Then this young man of more than ninety years mounted his grand Espanish horse. He was like the men the Aztecs saw, a *catzopine,* a man who wore barbs on his heels, but he was also one of them; he sang with them, he knew the rules of the sun; he ate tomatillos and chiles; he hunted in the green mountains of Boriquen; he swam rivers on the way north; he remembered prisons and crowded rooms. Very thin now, with his skin turned brown and the goatee of his grandfathers grown long and garbled with the gray of the gringo, he lifted his hand above his head, the long forefinger pointing upward toward the sky. For a decade, for generations he held that pose, and then he could wait no more: the rapture of youth came back into his face, his arm fell, reaching forward in an invitation to the millions, and he shouted, as only the immortal young can shout, *Adelante!*

27

EPILOGUE: TESTIMONIOS[1]

To enable the reader to measure the observations and theories in this book against a less edited reality, I have included brief oral histories of two families, one from the Caribbean and the other from the mainland. Neither family is ordinary. Joaquín Avila (Junior) is one of the heroic figures in the Mexican-American struggle for political and economic justice. The sensitivity of Miguell del Campillo to his environment is that of an artist; his cousin, Ivan Orta, is both sui generis and perfectly representative of the great pattern of immigration in the United States.

Although some members of both families have endured difficult times, all of them must be categorized, in the vocabulary of this book, as immigrants rather than transporters or sojourners or ghosts. They are racially mestizo, culturally Latino, politically ancient Athenian, and, above all, classically American. I am pleased to introduce them.

---

[1]All of the conversations were recorded. Margarita and Joaquín Avila and Zoraida and Francisco del Campillo spoke in Spanish. Sylvia Shorris transcribed and translated the recordings. All of the material has been edited for structure and length.

THE AVILA FAMILY

JOAQUÍN AVILA, SR.

I was an idler and a wanderer when I was young. I never did things right in the house, and they used to hit me and reproach me, my grandmother especially. But the more they would punish me, the more stubborn I got. I went to school, but only until the sixth year. I was the wiseguy. My brothers continued their studies; I was the only one who didn't. I got a job in a garage helping to paint automobiles, in Chihuahua.

I saw friends, though, earning more money and wearing nice clothes, and I said to myself, "I have to find a better job." I had ambition, I didn't want to just stay on in the garage. They used to pay us so little, two pesos a week. I used to give my family fifty centavos or one peso, and I was left with the rest.

By this time I was seventeen years old and got myself a job as a driver of small trucks. I did this for five years, bringing supplies to the mountains and bringing metals out of the mines. The work was somewhat dangerous, because in those days the roads were terrible. We had to cross rivers, and when it rained hard the rivers would overflow.

There were two social classes in Chihuahua, the very poor and the middle class (I'm not counting the upper class). I didn't belong to either one. My older brother liked social life; he was a member of different clubs and associations, but not me. I didn't have any real social life. I didn't like to dance, in the first place. In the second place, I liked to drink. Now, I drink very little, but in those days I did.

It was around that time that I met my wife. I think we loved each other very much, because I already owned two trucks, one was paid for and I was still paying for the other (so I was getting independent and bettering myself), but when she left, I sold everything I owned and came to the United States, too.

If I don't speak English now, I spoke even less then. I had never been in the U.S. before. I had never even had the urge to come up here. I was innocent, but I had to follow her. I had about $700 with me, from what I had sold. (In those days, $700 was a lot of money.) I grabbed a bus that made many stops, though I was trying to get an express that came directly to Los Angeles. I fell asleep somewhere in Arizona. I had money in my jacket, and I put my jacket on the seat next to me. What did I know? The upshot of it was that I arrived in Los Angeles with fifty-two cents. And not knowing anybody! This was in 1946, when I was twenty-one.

Well, I said, I just have to call her up. But nobody wanted to help me make the call. I would ask if they spoke Spanish and everybody would say, "No." Finally, a shoeshine boy got me a taxi and told the driver what had happened to me. The driver charged me fifty cents, so I had two cents left. *Two pennies!*

I got to the house where she was staying. I knocked on the door, and she answered. She couldn't believe her eyes when she saw me. She asked, "What are you doing here?"

I said, "I came to have a good time."

Then I told her I came to find her, but that I had no money. I couldn't go back because I was broke. Well, she was staying with some cousins, and one of them was a night worker in a foundry. He was a good person, a very good man, and he was so good to me. I told him my troubles, and he said, "Don't worry, my son is the foreman of the foundry, and I'll talk to him about you."

The next day he asked if I wanted to work days or nights, and I said I didn't care, either one was fine. So I started to work. Now, I had never even had a shovel in my hands. In those days, the foundry was fueled with coal, not like now with gas. I had to shovel the coal into the opening, into the cupola. Ay, ay, ay! But what could I do? I used to leave work all bent over. But in the Mexican style, I couldn't give up. I had to stick with it. It was only three days, and I felt like giving up, but I couldn't. I had to work.

But with the papers I had, I had to leave after one month. One of her uncles helped me to get my [working] papers, but first I lived in Tijuana for a year. Work was very scarce in Tijuana. There were times when I didn't eat. There were times when I slept and times when I couldn't sleep. Sometimes I slept on a park bench in Tijuana; sometimes there was just no work to be had. I would get just enough work to feed myself, but sometimes I couldn't. I would cry sometimes. And I would think to myself, "I'm going back to Chihuahua; what am I doing here? I'll get myself another girlfriend there."

But no, I really wanted to stay. Someone steered me to the Jai Alai in Tijuana, and that turned out to be great, from the tips alone. They used to pay twelve dollars, in silver,[2] per day. And there were nights I could make about thirty or thirty-five in tips. So I was doing okay. My job was such a good one that people would offer to buy it from me, but when we moved to the United States, I just passed it along to somebody I knew. Why should I make money on some poor working guy's troubles?

I went to the first place I had worked, the foundry, but they were on strike. I had to work, I had a wife, so I got factory jobs, whatever I could. We were living in Los Angeles, and we were struggling. I worked like that for about three months. My wife was working, too; she really helped out. In Mexico, she had a good job in a government office, but here she had to take what she could get. And what a difference!

[2]Mexican money, then set at four pesos to the U.S. dollar

I finally got a better job in a foundry. I didn't have a car (I didn't have a job, so why would I have a car?). I had to go on a trolley-car. I'd get up at three, have breakfast, make my lunch, and set out.[3]

I got to understand the foundry and I began to really like the work. Then we began to have a family, and I felt so proud. I had somebody to work hard for, my wife and son.

When the work dried up there, the boss told me he would talk to a friend of his who also had a foundry. The good thing was that this second foundry was much closer to home, about a twenty-minute walk. I stayed with them for thirteen or fourteen years. It was such a good place to work, and in those days, foundries paid the best wages.

Well, that's how life goes by. After a while, Jaime was born, then both boys began to grow, my work got better and I started to earn more money. But I suffered a lot at the beginning.

Then I worked for a third foundry, very close by, for about thirteen years. I knew that while Joaquín and Jaime were in school, I would never stop working hard. I knew I had to work for them.

Margarita [his wife, their mother] was the second teacher for the boys. She used to sit in this kitchen with one or the other until two in the morning sometimes, with their books. I used to get up at three to go to work, and I'd sometimes see them still sitting there. She helped them a lot, with their studies and their morale. I contributed with my work, of course.

We moved to this house when Jaime was newborn and Joaquín Junior was about three years old. We've lived here about thirty-seven years. The house we were living in before we moved here was about to be torn down for some factories, and we had to move out of there. We had to look for a place to rent because we didn't have enough money for a down payment. We had so many expenses and I didn't earn enough to buy a house.

Well, one day I said to Margarita, "Come on, let's go to the beach." While we were driving along, we saw an ad that said OPEN HOUSE. I said to her, "Let's go have a look."

This house wasn't finished inside. Only the outside was completed. I asked the real estate lady how much the house cost, and she told me that it was $4,200. (Houses were cheaper then.) You know how much we gave as a down payment? Five dollars. They saved it for us for five dollars!

The house had windows, but the floors were cement and very cold. I put in the electricity and the water, light, gas, everything. I would never move from this house because I love it so. It's my life. I live inside the house here, I don't live outside. I don't care about gangs or crime. I live happily here. I don't mix with them, and they don't bother me. I live in peace here. They've

[3]He explained later that foundry work began in the very early morning when it was still cool and ended before the heat of the day set in.

never really bothered us here. Once, some kids broke in, but it was just mischief. They took some cigarettes and ate some crackers and drank some soda.

To go back to the early days, my father was orphaned when he was very young, so he never knew his father or his mother; an aunt raised him. All I ever knew was his brother. On my mother's side, she was alone too; I did get to know my grandmother and grandfather, but she was the only daughter. So I didn't have a big family behind me. The family started to really develop with us.

I've noticed something about the Mexicans, maybe it's their ego. When they come from Mexico, they think it was worse there, even though they're worse off here. So they start, not speaking English, but losing their Spanish. They start using American slang or idioms, "you know" or "yeah." I worked for years with all kinds of immigrants. If you spoke to the Mexicans in Spanish, they wouldn't even answer; they wouldn't say yes or no. They just didn't want to talk Spanish.

I used to sit down with Joaquín, Jr., with the paper *La Opinión,* and he learned to read when he was about five or six, from reading *La Opinión.* The same with Jaime. In my house, we had to speak only Spanish. I knew they would learn English in school, but here it was only Spanish. And I think it paid off; it was good for them. To speak another language is to be more educated and to have more culture. It's beautiful to know four or five languages even, but I wouldn't let them forget their mother tongue.

Once Joaquín asked me, "Papa, why don't you become a citizen?" I told him I would think about it. He could have nagged me about it, but he never did. He and I talked about many things, but he didn't ask me the same question again.

I think you have to talk to your children about their roots, so they'll have an idea where they came from, what country their parents come from. You should tell them stories, anecdotes, and they begin to understand and to like history. Let's talk about Junior, for example. Mexican history is very beautiful to my son, to the extent that he gave his children the names of Mexican leaders. His oldest son is named for Zapata. His younger son is named Salvador Tiachka. Tiachka is an Indian name; it means the man who gives advice, a wise man. Everyone calls him Salvador, but my wife calls him Tiachka.[4]

Well, that's about all I can tell you about the trajectory of my life. At least it's the truth, just the way it happened. Why should I tell you or myself lies? I can't fool myself.

---

[4] Although Joaquín Avila speaks Spanish to the grandchildren whenever they visit, which is often, they answer in English.

MARGARITA AVILA

My mother had a very pretty voice, and she used to sing operas or operettas, and my father would sing back to her; they used to talk to each other that way. Sometimes they would be singing to each other and my mother would sit on my father's lap. They loved each other so much and communicated with each other so well that it impressed me when I was a child.

My father was a hard worker; he had no vices. He had a taxi when we lived in Chihuahua, and we lived very well. I remember because my sisters and I were the best-dressed children in school. We were five children, and I remember my mother had somebody to help her. My mother and father used to go out a lot—they used to love to go to the movies.

In Chihuahua then social life was very difficult. You had to have a new dress for every social occasion; you couldn't wear the same one. You had to wait five or six weeks before you could be seen in the same dress. So it was a very tight situation, very pretentious. Now I see it as extreme pretension. We were very middle-class, maybe slightly higher. I belonged to a social club. In those days, social clubs were all about parties and more parties. With all I had going on in my life, I didn't need too much more. Because my father had been liberal in terms of our education, we learned sports such as bicycle-riding, which were usually for boys. But my father was progressive in that way. And I was such a tomboy anyway, I was glad for the opportunity.

My sister and I took a commercial course in school so that we could become secretaries. We also studied English. When I first started to work, I worked in a secretarial pool that did work for Lázaro Cárdenas. When he would come to Chihuahua, his assistant would say to me, "Here, take these papers in to him for his signature, so you'll get to know him. Then you can ask him for whatever you want." I used to think, "What can I ask the general[5] for?" I was so embarrassed to be in his presence. But he was amiable and charming. I felt that he didn't so much bring me up to his level, but that he came down to mine.

Unfortunately, when I started to work, my father died. My mother became more strict, tougher. She couldn't be the soft little mother anymore, because my father's strength wasn't there anymore. But she didn't have to go to work. My oldest brother started to work (and to study). I was already working, and I helped out only a little, because I didn't earn very much.

Joaquín and I met at a *posada*[6] just before Christmas. We chatted all night, and then he asked me out and I agreed. But he stood me up. Two or three days later, he showed up at my door and asked if we could talk. I said, "I can't

[5]Cárdenas served as president of Mexico from 1934 to 1940.
[6]Christmas party

now. Come tomorrow." Well, he stood me up again. It was the first time anybody had stood me up; I used to stand up *my* dates.

Eventually, I paid him back. I left him waiting a few times. We were engaged later on, but he never liked to dance and I loved to dance. He would take me to a dance and leave me there.[7]

For a young person I think my era in Mexico was the best. There wasn't so much familiarity then; boyfriends didn't come to the house so much. It was harder to see each other. And there was more opportunity to flirt with other people. I think it was all so much nicer then, maybe because I was a romantic. He wanted to get married, but I wasn't ready. I wanted to know what was going on in the world, and I thought I'd get married when I was thirty years old. That was unusual for those times; my little sister thought she was a spinster when she was twenty-one.

The first time I came to the United States[8] was on a vacation. I was so impressed with the United States that I thought it was the maximum in every way and that the people were very honorable. When I got back to Chihuahua, I told my mother I wanted to move to the United States. I had already given up my government job, I had some savings, and I borrowed some money, so economically, I wasn't in bad shape. I was about twenty-one or twenty-two. My mother thought I was too young, but I didn't agree with her. I thought I was almost old.

I came to Los Angeles and he followed me. When I saw him arrive with two cents in his pocket, I got frightened. I didn't know what to think. Then I took him out for a walk and we got lost. We used the Sears Building for a landmark, but we lost sight of it and we wound up walking around for blocks and blocks. Eventually, we got to know the city. I was feeling lonely by then, so I agreed to get married.

It was the time of World War II, the end of the war, really. Seeing so many movies, I thought of myself as a heroine. I wanted to work in the war effort, in an airplane factory or something like that. I wound up working in a sewing machine factory. They asked if I had any experience, and I said, "Yes." They asked if I could come in tomorrow, and I said, "No, I want to start right now."

Well, I start to work. They seat me at a machine, and I have never worked at a sewing machine. A woman who worked next to me told me it was run by your knee. It sounded easy. When I sat down, the boss was standing right behind me. I started leaning forward and I had to put my feet on the pedal,

---

[7]He said, "I was never jealous. If she loved to dance, let her dance. When there's jealousy, there's no love."

[8]Margarita Avila was born in the United States, but returned to Chihuahua with her parents while she was still an infant.

and the machine went off, Ruh-h-h-h! I got so frightened I went over backward in my chair. Of course, the boss saw all this, and started to laugh. He joked, "Experienced?" I answered, very annoyed, "Yes."

I worked there for about a year. During that time I got married and got pregnant. Sometimes I would go in for a month to work, sometimes even for a day, but I didn't work regularly anymore after my son was born.

Joaquín started to read very young. One day he said to me, "Look, Mama, in this book it says that the world started many thousands of years ago, but here in the Bible it says that the earth was created in seven days." I couldn't answer things like these because I had never really studied the Bible. I had never read it, so I couldn't discuss it with him.

When my husband was going out to pay a bill, and he passed a toy store, he might buy a toy for the children instead of paying the bill,[9] but I never did that. I didn't buy them much. I thought the best thing I could give them was my time.

When they got a little older, we always had a dog. We wanted them to have what boys should have. But as far as their turning out so well, I think it was because they couldn't hide from me. I even told them when there was something they wanted to tell me, they should say, "I want to talk to my friend."

One of them said, "It's the same person as our mother." And I said, "No, there's a difference. If you tell your 'friend' something confidential, she won't tell your mother." I convinced them that they could trust their "friend," and believe me, they told me a lot of things. I nearly fainted from some of the things they told me.

Once, a neighbor complained that one of the boys had used dirty words to her son. I talked to my son and he told me what had really happened. When I got back to the neighbor, she said, "You're going to believe what your son tells you instead of what I say?"

I said, "Of course. I only know you a few minutes, but I know my son all his life."

When Joaquín started seeing girls, which is a time that mothers worry about, I felt concerned about disease or getting too seriously involved too

---

[9]He agreed: "For my children, I think I gave them what I didn't have. I never bought their love with toys, but because I never had much, I wanted them to have things. When they were young, I bought them an electric train set, a Lionel, and every year I would buy them accessories for the set. Then they grew up. One went to college, the other into the service, and I thought to myself, 'What do I do with this train set now?' Well, I used to play with it myself. Finally, I packed it away and years later gave it to Joaquín, Jr., for his son. Jaime had a girl at that time, so I gave it to Junior. And he keeps it in his garage in Fremont. It fills up most of the garage."

soon. I said to him, "Look, Son, I think a man is more of a man if he can control himself."

His answer was interesting. He said, "But you don't know how the girls are." And he told me things which surprised me.

When Jack[10] graduated, he was valedictorian. He had the highest marks. Jack got a scholarship to Yale. It was a change for him, a real culture shock. He was very homesick, though he didn't complain to us about it. We told him to call us whenever he wanted to, just call us collect. There were times, on Sundays, when he would call us, and we would talk as long as one hour. At first, he used to call us two or three times a week, then it became less often.

My oldest son is now forty, the younger is thirty-seven.[11] Jack is very patient, but when he gets angry. . . . It takes him a long time, but he finally explodes.[12] Only once did he get really angry at me, but I know he does lose his temper.

My other son, Jaime, is very different. He is not rancorous, but he gets mad often and then it's over. He hardly even remembers what made him angry. Jaime was more religious. Ever since he was a child, he was more attached to religion. When he was studying catechism for his First Communion, he used to hit the other boys because they weren't paying attention to the nuns. I would tell him to stop, but he would tell me that they weren't paying enough attention and they were laughing, and he wouldn't allow it. He has a very good heart. So the two boys are very different and very much alike, and they stick together.

Jaime changed his religion. He's now a Jehovah's Witness, and he's very involved in his religion.[13] He believes people should behave morally, and he helps them spiritually in any way he can. My other son helps them in other ways, legally and economically. That's why I say they're so different and so alike. Considering that they have such different careers and such different paths in life, they're both acting to achieve the same goal, to help people. The result is the same.

We made plenty of mistakes, too. But I have to say, if my sons are the way they are, it's because of how *they* are, what *they* believe. They have to take the

---

[10]She uses Joaquín, Jack, and Junior interchangeably.

[11]The interviews and conversations with the Avilas took place during 1988–89.

[12]Joaquín, Sr., said, "If something makes me angry, something important, I go off like a lit match, but in a few minutes I calm down. I go to the person who made me angry, and I ask for his forgiveness. I am not a rancorous person."

[13]Margarita and Joaquín Avila are both nominally Roman Catholic, but they do not attend church except for weddings and funerals. They do not give money to the church. Neither of them has been to confession for many years.

credit. It's something I can't explain. In the first place, when you're young, you don't listen to your elders. When I raised my sons, the thinking was that the child should be separated from his mother, not spend too much time with her. I don't agree; that's not the way. The best thing is to be very close to them, physically close, and affectionate with them.

When I first came to the United States, I was very impressed, but I soon found out that life is hard here. You work very hard, harder than in Mexico. I think life in general here is more difficult. But because I always wanted to be independent I didn't go back to Mexico. If I had gone back to Chihuahua, I would have just been my mother's daughter again, and I didn't want that.

All in all, I wouldn't like to go back; I prefer to go on living here, because now is when I will benefit from all the years I have worked. In this country, there are lovely travel plans for senior citizens, and I love to travel. I love to see other places.[14] But there are certain things that are wonderful here, just as there are bad things. Here we have so-called luxuries, but they really aren't. We need the washing machines and the televisions so that we can survive. For my part, I would rather have a maid to do all the housekeeping. Then I would go on a diet.

JOAQUÍN AVILA (JUNIOR)

I was born in Belvedere, in East L.A., in 1948. Then we moved to Compton in the early fifties. What I remember was that it was a wood frame house that just had the outside covering, and that if I stood in the living room I could see all the way to the kitchen, because there was just the inside skeleton. There were walls, but there wasn't any sheetrock attached to them. The area we lived in didn't have that many houses. There were open fields in some instances. There were no fences.

My dad had a variety of jobs, odd jobs initially, and then he started working in a foundry and that's where he stayed. My mom didn't work all the time. She stayed home with us for some of the time. I would go to this place called Elaine's of Hollywood with her, and my Mom would take me around and show me who her friends were and stuff like that. Whenever I would go in there, it would be nothing but rows and rows of sewing machines and all these women.

When I was growing up, I spent a lot of time in Chihuahua, summers. I had a good time. My grandfather was a watchmaker. He had a little shop in his house. When I would go there I would get to watch him, and he would give me a couple of watches and little spectacles and little tools to tinker

---

[14]She has traveled across the United States (e.g., to New York, New Haven, Boston, and Las Vegas) and through most of Asia, including Japan and China. Her husband, who dreams of returning to Mexico to live in a small town, does not accompany her on these trips.

[with]. When my cousins in Chihuahua used to get mad at me, they'd call me pocho. I wouldn't call it discomfort when we go back to Chihuahua, but there is a difference, a perception that we're pochos, almost like half-breeds living out here.

When I started going to school, the teachers could never pronounce Joaquín. The kindergarten teacher just called me Jack. Looking back, it wasn't very positive—people can't pronounce your name and then they give you another name, that's not very positive. How did it feel? Back then, it was just, "I hope I'm not creating a problem for you. Do whatever you think is right, just don't embarrass me in front of everyone."

One time when I was in elementary school we saw somebody who didn't belong on the block, a kid from someplace else. I was with one of my neighbors, and one of his older sisters asked, "*Es chicano? Es mayate? O es gabacho?*"[15] And I remember I didn't know what the difference was when she said that.

I guess it was in the fourth or fifth grade, after the *Brown v. Board* decision, that blacks started moving into Compton. It used to be a predominantly Anglo city—I remember going to theaters where it was really mostly Anglos and very few Mexicans. There were some theaters you wouldn't go to; you'd get harassed because you were Mexican. Some of the kids would start calling you names, then they'd start hitting you. Sometimes the theater owners—if you came in with friends who were Mexicans—wouldn't let you in.

I was an average student when I was in elementary school. I took that for my lot in life. In elementary school, they got me a little reflector telescope, one of these little cardboard things. I spent a lot of time looking at the stars. My uncle on my mother's side—he wasn't really a blood-related uncle, but we called him my uncle—who was a self-educated person, was working at Universal Studios as a film technician. Whenever he would come over, we would take out the telescope.

In later years, when I was in high school, when I started to become fairly serious about my education, my uncle would read *Scientific American* articles. You know how difficult they are. I would barely get through the first two paragraphs, and I would ask him to explain some of these articles. He provided a lot of guidance. Both of my parents did, and he did as well, in terms of emphasizing the importance of education. He played an important part in my whole educational process.

When I got into junior high school, I met a lot of other chicanos from other barrios, and some of them were what they called *pachucos*. I didn't belong to a gang, but I hung around with people from a couple of the gangs and I made some very good friends. I saw what the gangs were doing. When

[15]"Is he a chicano? Is he a black? Or is he a white?"

I was in the seventh and eighth grade, drugs started coming in—heroin. Some of my neighbors were into glue sniffing. I saw what the stuff was doing to some of my neighbors, so I stayed away from that aspect of it.

During the seventh and eighth grades my parents did have what I considered to be tight control over me. I could not go out beyond nine o'clock. They said I couldn't go out, and I wouldn't disobey them. Some of my friends, they'd be out all night at that age. They'd be ditching school. I never did that.

The people I grew up with spoke very little Spanish. The gang members and so on would use some words, *orale, esse, vato loco*. For cigarette, we said *frajo*, but not anything beyond that. I first heard the word "homeboys" in high school. We used to call them "homes." It was sort of ironic, because when I got to law school, I found out that there was an Oliver Wendell Holmes. So I used to say, "He's a Holmesboy." It took on a little different connotation.

I try not to back down from people or things. When I was growing up, in junior high school, you couldn't afford to, because if you did, you'd get picked on all the time. I'll never forget, my closest friend, who's no longer living, had a harelip, cleft palate; he couldn't talk very well and people would make fun of him. One individual was making fun of him a lot. He was older, not a typical ninth grader. My friend and I were walking down the street one day, and he pointed out this guy who had been making fun of him, so I walked up to the guy and said, "Look, you shouldn't be making fun of my friend." And the guy just started to fight. My friend had injured his hand, so he couldn't help me. I wound up with two black eyes and a bloody nose, but I didn't stop; I didn't stop fighting. In fact, we drew a crowd of people. I'll never forget, a bus even stopped. Anyway, if I had backed down and lived in that environment . . .

My interest in academic work came from a combination of things. The most important was my dad who was injured on the job and couldn't work anymore, couldn't work in the foundry because he had a slipped disc. He was a molder. He had worked for this company for I don't know how many years, and they just let him go. The only thing he could get was workman's compensation.

I went to summer school prior to going to high school, and I got good grades. The first year I took all of my studies very seriously. I did a lot of homework, hardly ever went out. I also ran track. I just started excelling. I maintained the interest in astronomy. My parents had bought me a larger telescope, a four-and-a-quarter inch reflector. They took me to the observatory and to some science classes at one of the local museums. We would spend a lot of time with the neighborhood kids looking at the stars, which I would say was very unusual for that neighborhood.

During school, I was working with the Neighborhood Youth Corps. I earned twenty or twenty-five dollars a week, and that would be my pocket change. It was part of Lyndon Johnson's Great Society program. They would provide money to schools to hire students to work out in the field or assist instructors with their work. I got connected to this reading instructor that I had for summer school. I worked after school in his program.

I worked hard in eleventh and twelfth grades. I was first in my class. Then I had a counselor who was very helpful, a guy by the name of Kenneth Washington. Mr. Washington suggested that I apply to some of the top schools. I got accepted to Yale.

My brother went to a different high school, Compton instead of Centennial. He went through some pretty rough periods, too, but his lasted longer. One of the important things that happened between me and my brother is that we were always being compared. We fought a lot, like any brothers do, I guess. The feeling that I get is that he's happy that I've gotten where I'm at. I don't know if there's any resentment. If there is, he hasn't told me.

He finished high school, then he went into the Marine Corps, and he got a medical discharge, because he was born with a hand on which the fingers were smaller. He got married, and he lives in the house next door to my parents. He's got a family, a sixteen-year-old girl. He works with Southern California Gas Company as a service technician. He's now a Jehovah's Witness, and for him it's probably the best thing that happened to him, because it provided a lot of direction. We were raised as Catholics, but not very strong Catholics; I don't think any of the males went to church. My dad didn't. My mom didn't.

I was really worried about him, because of his friends and what they were getting into and that he might be having some problems with the law eventually. After he got married and his wife became a Jehovah's Witness and he became a Jehovah's Witness, he became like a Puritan. He became very dogmatic. He has stopped trying to convert me now.

The summer before I went to Yale, my counselor received some materials from them. Because this was the first class in which Yale was accepting any significant numbers of public school students, they had an orientation session. They sent us off to Lawrenceville a prep school in New Jersey, for the summer. They paid everything. At Lawrenceville there were a lot of blacks and some white kids, but I don't really remember any other Latinos.

I had one roommate my first year who was a third- or fourth-generation Yale man, a blueblood: His name was listed in the social register; he could trace his family back to the pilgrims or whatever. I had another roommate who was from Oklahoma, whose father owned a jewelry store. He was Jewish; the other guy was Episcopalian. And there was me. I was a bursary[16] student, so I had to work in the cafeteria.

[16]Received economic aid

There were social adjustment problems. I think there were only two other chicanos at the school out of an undergraduate class of four thousand, so I felt isolated. Secondly, there was a great deal of elitism, snobbery, and racism, because many of the students who were there had gone to prep schools, and they were all white. Some people just didn't want to room with blacks. My roommates never told me to my face that they didn't want to room with me, but I'm sure the third- or fourth-generation person was probably making snide comments about me to his friends or his peers. After the first year we didn't have to room together, but I roomed with the guy from Oklahoma. We became pretty good friends.

Some of the people were insensitive. There was some racism among the students, and I told them about it. During my first year I contacted the other chicano students who were there and talked to them about forming a club of some sort. I found them through the directory, just looked for Spanish surnames. One of the chicanos was from El Paso. He dropped out. The other person just didn't feel he needed to join a club. Now, there were some other Spanish surnames, but not that many, less than a handful. They were Puerto Rican, but they were from the island. These were from wealthy families, and they saw Mexicans differently.

It was a complete cultural clash. You just had to adjust. You went to the residential colleges, to the freshman commons to eat. I missed Mexican food, that's for sure.

At Yale, I never really got into the education as much as I should have. It wasn't until the end of my sophomore and junior years that my grades really went up, but I never took as much interest in my studies as I did during my freshman year in high school. I became involved with the grape boycott in the late sixties when I was at Yale. I became more involved in student admissions, stuff like that. I didn't spend a lot of time on my studies.

The grape boycott was a full-time thing. I eventually became the coordinator for Connecticut. We would go to supermarkets, ask them to take grapes off the shelves. We would picket, help out farmworker families that came to Connecticut. There were other students that were involved, but they were not Latinos, not initially. By the time I was a senior, there were ten or twelve of us. Among the chicano classmates of mine I retain the connections, but not among the others. During my last three years there, I spent all my time with chicanos.

The end of my junior year, my uncle, the self-educated one, asked me what I was going to do after college, and I said I didn't know. He said, "If you don't know, maybe you better consider going to law school." I applied to various law schools, and I got into Harvard.

My first impression of law school was that it was very competitive. I didn't do well that first year. I studied a lot, and yet I barely passed my courses. I think it was just a matter of not having the right legal approach. My second and third years, I did well. I was politically active during those years, but not as active as I was during college. There wasn't time.

I got married my first year, and my wife joined me my second year up at Cambridge. I married a girl from Compton. When my wife came back with me my second year, I still spent a lot of time in libraries. Then I became involved with the Harvard *Civil Rights, Civil Liberties Law Review*. If I can point to a contributing factor to my improving grades, I think it was that involvement. In my third year, I became a case-and-comments editor, and I received a lot of feedback. It helped me a lot with my writing and my approach to legal issues.

When I was applying to law schools, I met a woman named Vilma Martínez, who was my predecessor at MALDEF. She encouraged me to apply to Columbia Law School. I didn't get accepted there, but we remained in contact. She was very much involved with the Mexican American Legal Defense [and Education] Fund, and when she became president and general counsel, she encouraged me to come and work for the organization.

Before I went to MALDEF, I went to the Alaska Supreme Court, where I had a clerkship for a year. In seventy-four to seventy-six I was a general staff attorney for MALDEF in San Francisco. I started traveling to Texas, focusing on voting rights cases. In seventy-six there was a new position, directing the voting rights program, and I was promoted to that. Subsequently, there was a vacancy for the associate counsel in Texas. So I moved to Texas in seventy-six. I liked the years I spent at MALDEF, although the last three years were tough because of the additional pressures I felt there.

We came out here to Fremont in seventy-four, and when I became president and general counsel in eighty-two, we decided to stay in this area. It's not by choice that we live in a white neighborhood. We decided to live in a neighborhood where there were good schools. The children identify themselves as Mexicans. But they don't connect to the culture by language. They know that they're different from their classmates, and the oldest one knows that there's discrimination against Hispanics.

He says the discrimination is very subtle. He'll say, "Well, you don't get invited to certain parties. You can hang around with some friends and you can't hang around with other people." It's very subtle, it's not like people telling you they don't want to hang around with you because you're Mexican, but he does feel it. He's expressed it to me several times.

He wants to go back to Compton, because that's where a lot of his relatives are. He feels less isolated when he goes to Compton and spends time with his cousins. In Compton, the areas he spends time in are the barrios. He likes Compton. Even though they're having all these killings, he feels more at ease. I want him to grow up in a neighborhood where people aren't shooting at each other, where one can feel relatively safe. Whether that's a black or a white or a brown community, to me personally, it doesn't make any difference.

I don't see any conflict between this [living in a predominately Anglo neighborhood] and the voting rights case (Watsonville). The reason why you have barrios in many instances has been because of economic segregation and deliberate residential segregation, and that's wrong. I think it's also important to have reinforcement of the culture as much as you can. For me personally, I don't feel I'm losing the culture. For my kids I think it's important to learn Spanish and not to be ashamed of what they are.

If you take the line of reasoning that I'm less Hispanic because I don't live in the barrio, I should be back in Compton, and if you take that line of reasoning all the way to the end, I should be one of the dropouts. If you don't want to move out of the low income area, that means you can't get a job, that means you're going to drop out of school, etcetera. I don't think that's a part of our culture. I think what should be part of our culture are the values, the language, and an emphasis on achieving, getting an education.

I'm not guided by culture. I see things more in terms of power relationships, and I know that Latinos have less power than their Anglo counterparts in this country. Whether it's due to culture or economics, to me it doesn't matter, I just know that it exists. One of the reasons why I'm involved in this whole area of political access is because the political process and the political institutions is where a lot of the power is, and we need to get that power so that we can start improving our own community in terms of education, economics, and so on.

Hopefully, this Watsonville suit will serve as an impetus for legislation at the state level. Watsonville came out of the Ninth Circuit Court of Appeals, and it covers nine states. It's a major, major step. It doesn't solve the problem, but it permits us to go after these discriminatory at-large election systems. We don't have to show intent. We have to show certain requirements, and if we meet those requirements, then it's a violation of the Voting Rights Act. Still, these cases can take anywhere from fifteen hundred to two thousand hours of work. With the Watsonville case, I myself spent twelve hundred hours on it. I think total attorney time in that case will range anywhere between twenty-one hundred and twenty-five hundred hours.

Since I don't get paid for these cases until we win, and it takes like a couple hundred hours to do an investigation before you can determine whether it's a good case or not, I have to delegate. If people in the community are really interested, they have to get together some resources, not money, but resources so I can guide them through the investigation process.

I was the first one out of all my cousins in the United States that went on to college. I would like my children to go on to college. I would like them to go on and have a happy life, a good family life, a good work environment. I would like them never to forget that they're Mexicans, never to forget where their parents and grandparents came from.

THE THIRD GENERATION

It's sad. It's scary. I get scared when I go outside to get the mail. I used to go outside and everything, but it just got too crazy, too many gangs, too many innocent people getting killed. Even if you just like wore a tie or sunglasses, you could get killed for that. Wrong color. Some people say they got killed for just wearing the wrong color sunglasses. It's just terrible. It's not getting any better. I mean, if President Reagan can't do anything, what makes you think Bush is going to do something?[17] This world is terrible.

When I was little there wasn't as much violence. I could go out and play and not worry about nobody bothering me, no kidnappings or anything. I was with people I trusted. I would go over so-and-so's house and nothing would happen, but now things are so crazy, you know sometimes people walk down the street and they never come back. I knew of a girl, she went down to her neighbor's house, she never came back. She ended up dead the next day.

The Crips are blue and the Bloods are red. It used to be they just fought with fists, but now they fight with machine guns. And it's not like one on one, it's like ten on one, ten on ten. It's like group on group. They fight to kill. They don't fight to hurt, they fight to kill. They don't care. It's like they kill somebody tomorrow, they don't care. It's like they're used to it, so they just kill again.

Girls get involved in gangs very much, but I wouldn't. It's too crazy. And sometimes if somebody's going to jump you, they just like leave you there, they don't even jump in and help you, and they're supposed to be like your friends, backing you up in the gang, but they'll just like leave you.

I'm seventeen. I'll be eighteen in April [1989]. I used to know a lot of people and a lot of things, two years ago. Sometimes I hear things now. I know different things. I don't worry about it. I don't put myself in a position where I'll get hurt. I just go about my business. I don't do things in Compton. I go to my cousin's house or something. I don't do nothing in Compton.

I've been to Norwalk once. That's farther from here. It was pretty nice and pretty quiet. I would like to move; Compton is just too crazy. We'll probably move when I get married. We're . . . they're going to move to Idaho. That's what they want to do. My dad wants to go really bad, but he's going to wait 'til like later.

---

[17]The conversation took place shortly before the 1988 presidential election.

I would like to live somewhere far from here, but not out of the state, not in the country. I don't like the country, it's too quiet. It's different. You have to work really hard out there. Say you're a farmer, you have your crops and all that; you have to feed all your animals. You have to drink goat's milk and that's gross. It's too quiet. You have to walk like twenty miles to get to the nearest gas station or something. But in the city, everybody's like for their-self. There's so much hate and so much rush—rushing here, rushing there—so much hate, but the country goes really slow. I would like to live in the city, but between, like in a rural/urban in-between, not too country, not too city, but just right, not too packed, but not too far away from each other.

When I was in junior high all my friends were black, and I always felt they were superior and this and that, so I started hanging around with them. I dressed like one. I wasn't proud to be a Mexican, you know, like, *I'm a Mexican, oh no!* I used to think Mexicans weren't nothing, I used to thought blacks were superior, you know. I guess because they walked around in big groups and all this and that, you know. I was in Ralph Bunche Junior High. It was mostly black, 70 percent black. The other kids were Mexican and maybe two or three Samoans. I had some friends who were Mexican, but I didn't hang around with them, because I didn't think they were anything. I didn't think they were important. I thought they were nerds or ugh! Mexican. I was telling myself, "I want to be black. I want to be black." So I used to hang around with black people when I thought I was black and all this.

I did little ridiculous things. I totally talked, you know, like slang, every-thing. I used to have a attitude. I used to like put my hair up high, like make it straight. You know, curl it. I used to buy all this like activator. I used to buy clothes for it and everything. I used to dress like it and everything. I wore like cords, tee shirts. Back then Pumas were in style, then Fila, then Booties and white socks and that. I'd you know chew my gum and like that and try and pop it all the time. The blacks acted like what I did was normal. They accepted me as being me.

Then I started getting older and my mind was maturing and all that and I said, "Why am I trying to be something I'm not. I should just be myself." Then by the tenth grade I started to realize different things. I should just be myself, Mexican.

Mexicans speak a different language, first of all, some do; second of all, different home styles, the way they're brought up, the way they cook—different cultures, two totally different cultures. The way they keep up their house, Mexicans have like a bunch of flowers or something in their front yard, sometimes they have dirt floors, like in Mexico. They have a lot of little kids. Black has kids, but not as much as Mexicans. Black, they have different ways, like in Africa they live like in huts or something. The food is different. We eat beans and rice and all that. That's not their everyday dish; they cook something else.

We all talk different. The blacks have like, "Child" and we have like *"O, mihija"* and *"hola"* and all this, you know. It's just different.

I wouldn't say Mexicans are more superior than the blacks. To me everybody's equal. Just because you're Mexican doesn't mean you have to get all into it, like being from a gang just to prove you're proud of your race. You can be proud of your race just to be proud. It feels good to know you're from somewhere.

I'm Mexican-American. I'm Mexican, but I wasn't born in Mexico. I'm not Caucasian. All my relatives are Mexican, plus I have a Mexican last name and everything, so I'm Mexican-American. Caucasian people are not from Mexico just like African people aren't from Mexico. It's just a difference, a whole difference.

I was bilingual when I was little. I used to speak Spanish and English, but unfortunately, it wasn't kept up. I could speak Spanish a little bit: *No se creas,* that means "I don't believe it." *Yo tengo una lápiz.*[18]

I've never been to Mexico. I would like to go really soon. All my relatives are there. I haven't seen nobody. I hardly know nobody. They live in Chihuahua, Mexico City, Guadalajara. Tijuana—I've been there. Tijuana was sad. I mean you think you don't have the richest house and you want more, but you should see what the people have. Sometimes they're like really poor. They sleep in boxes. Actually, it's really sad to see people living like that, but then there's a nice part. What really got me was the sad part, little kids coming up to cars begging for stuff and then they're selling little things they made. It's just really sad.

I go out with Mexicans. I used to like blacks. It doesn't matter to me, because I'm not prejudiced at all. I don't think anybody should be, because God created us all to be equal. But if a black comes up, that's fine with me as long as he treats me right and everything's right.

I don't try to be no cholo or anything because I don't have no feathers or big loops. Like Mexican girls wear really big loops so that they're chola, like in the girl gang, the Mexican gang. If I dressed that way, I would be rebelling. That's not the right way you're supposed to go. When you get into a gang, you're just asking for trouble. My hair's just me. I'm myself. My clothes I don't imitate nobody else; I'm myself.

I am sincere. I don't try to rule over people. I don't try to put people down. I care about people and what people think about me.

I work in a store in the Lakewood Mall. It's called Silverman's. I sell men's clothing, from leather to Cataricci pants, Carnegie sweaters, like really expensive stuff, really nice stuff. I like working, even though it is hard, but I enjoy it. I need to be responsible sometime, because I can't always be saying,

---

[18]The first sentence cannot be translated. *Creer* is not a reflexive verb. *No lo creo* means "I don't believe it!" The second sentence, "I have a pencil," contains a gender error.

"Daddy, I want this; Daddy, I want that." I gotta go out there and do for myself.

THE DEL CAMPILLO FAMILY

FRANCISCO DEL CAMPILLO

Well, my life was always a poor one; we were always poor. We were never of the powerful or moneyed class, or even of the middle class. We were poor people and at the age of five, I lost my father. My poor mother! Because my father, who had been a military man, had killed himself, she didn't get any pension. So she worked as a maid and a cook in a rich household. After I went to a public school, my mother managed to get me into the military, through the influence of Mrs. [Fulgencio] Batista.

When she needed an operation that's when we all went to work. We were three children. My older brother got me a job making deliveries because I had a bicycle. My sister became a hairdresser after a few years. I stayed with a cousin who had room for me in his apartment, while I worked in the store. This was all in the Vedado, a fancy residential part of Havana. It was where my mother and I both worked. So that's how we grew up, poor, but we never went to bed hungry.

Then came the revolution. I was about sixteen years old. Our father had been a military man, so my brother and I joined the militia for Fidel Castro. I actually joined an antiaircraft unit and took a hit in the knee.

At the age of nineteen, I got married; that was in 1961. Mige is really my son because I raised him as my own, and I really know him. He had already been born when his mother and I got married, but I was really his father. I consider the father to be the one who raises him and goes through everything with him. I hope I also gave him his values; I think I did. And I think I speak for him when I say that he considers me to be his father.

As time went by, we began to see things more clearly. As you get older, you start to see how things are really turning out and you begin to think. After our marriage, we started to work on leaving Cuba; we started to work on getting our papers in order. My sister-in-law was already in Miami, and she helped us leave by way of Spain. We were in Spain for two years. I got a job in a laundry, in maintenance and repair. They supplied hospitals and hotels. I was perfectly happy there, and they would have given me more money if I hadn't left, but my family was in the United States and that was where we were destined to be.

So after two years, we moved to New York; that was in 1964. I was lucky enough to get a job for General Motors at Tarrytown, but I was also unlucky enough to be let go during a big layoff. Everybody who had worked there less than ten years was let go.

Well, then we began thinking about Florida. My sister-in-law and her family went to Florida for a vacation and took my two sons with them. Well, my brother-in-law calls me one day and tells me, "I've found work here and I'm staying. What shall I do with the boys?"

So I told him, "I'm coming down, too." By then, I was working in a Bronx office-supply company, but I left my job without looking back. In Spain, I started the first new life, in New York the second, and down here, the third. I had to leave my mother and brother behind in Cuba, and the first new life was frightening, but by the third time, I wasn't too worried and we moved down here.

We were always frugal and never got ourselves into debt. We could have bought a house in 1976 that was a real bargain, just $500 down, but even if we had the money, we had to think about saving it in case some emergency came up. So I can't regret it now, even though if I had bought the place then it would have been so cheap now. Well, anyway, I got a good job, and Mige went to school here in Miami and did very well. Then he went to New York to study at Columbia University. We had to help him out, of course, so he could pay his room and board. My wife and I have always had to struggle one way or the other.

I always wanted to go out on my own, to have my own business, but I never had the money to take the gamble. Well, I finally decided to take the chance and I gave up my job to do freelance maintenance and repair work—all kinds, whatever came along. I made a living that way for a couple of years. I had good months and I had bad months. But it wasn't very steady, and we couldn't live that way. So I got my old job back. I'm a solderer and mechanic.

Finally, we realized that we were staying here in a stable situation. We're not rich but we can live decently and without problems. You know you have a salary to count on, to pay your rent, your utilities and so on. You save a lot of mental problems that way. When you're working for yourself [à la calle], you never know how much money you can count on. When I first started working for myself, I didn't even know about paying taxes and I didn't put any money aside. I wound up having to pay over a thousand dollars in back taxes. Now, I know better. I know about taxes and social security.

I've always been a homebody. I love my house. I get home at about five o'clock. I take off my shoes and get into my comfortable clothes. I sit here to watch television with my wife. Sometimes I drink a beer, not every day but when I feel like it. Then I take a bath. I try not to eat a big meal at night because it doesn't agree with me, but I snack, then I go to bed early.

That's what our life is like. It has a certain monotony and every day is the same, but I feel content here. The only thing that hurts me is that I don't have my mother [*la vieja*] nearby. She's still in Cuba. I did go to Cuba in 1980 to visit her. My brother is still there, too. After our visit, he got into some trouble because he had been seen with me. He had failed to notify the authorities that I was coming, so he was punished and sent to jail for a year, because he had not filled out the proper papers before I came.

I wanted to get my mother out, but it would have been too difficult for her to make the adjustment that it would take to get used to living with us. She has her friends and neighbors in Havana and my brother and sister. She can visit them whenever she wants to; she drops by in the mornings. Here, the lifestyle is very different, and she would feel lonely. I know some of my neighbors, of course, but not all. There isn't enough time for that; we all work too hard.

In Cuba, it's a slower pace. When you'd go out for a walk, everybody greeted you because you knew everyone. You would know whole blocks of neighbors. We know our neighbors here to say, "Hello, how's it going?" but no more. It was different in Cuba. There was more sharing. I have to admit that I miss that. I wish I still lived there. I tell my sons, "If Fidel falls, I'm going back," but I can't do that. Anyway, my sons have grown up here, and I guess I too am used to this style of life. I guess I really wouldn't go back there to live, but I would surely go for another visit.

Well, we have to get used to change in our lives, I guess. You know, when I was a boy, there was no television in our house. So I would go down to the stores that had them in the window and watch television there. When I got married, I bought a television for the house. So that's a difference in your life. My father-in-law had a little car and I used to drive it. I had never learned to drive, but I learned on that car. So there's always change in your life.

After two years in Spain, we arrived in New York, and after six months, I bought myself a car and a big color television. You know, in Cuba there was no color television. They had started getting set up for color but when Fidel came into power, it was dropped.

So that's my life, the tranquility of my home. Besides family life, I have two VCRs, and because I go to bed early, I record whatever I want to watch. I usually go to bed at ten o'clock, and I have a long-playing tape and I record whatever I want to see. I go to sleep, and the next day, if there's nothing on, I watch what I recorded.

ZORAIDA DEL CAMPILLO

I remember the day we left. It was the fifth of September. We spent the night in the airport because the plane had to be repaired. They kept telling us there would be a delay. Everybody was quiet and scared. We were afraid to talk to each other. Some people were able to go home and wait, but we couldn't because our house had been closed up, officially.

We were so nervous when we were leaving, because so many people had problems at the last minute. We didn't feel safe until we got off the plane in Madrid. Sometimes people even had a problem after they arrived at their destination. They stopped one man because they said his papers were forged. They put him in jail for a week, and you can imagine how worried his parents in Cuba were when they heard he hadn't arrived. Finally, he was let go with an apology; it turned out they had the wrong man.

So everyone was afraid, for the whole eight hours that it took to fly to Spain and even after that. I didn't feel lonely because I had left with my parents, my husband, and my children. The only family I left behind were a couple of uncles who were revolutionaries.

My sister wanted me to come out first, but I wouldn't hear of it. Either we got out together or we would stay in Cuba. There were so many people who got separated from their children and didn't see each other for years. I could have gotten out very easily by myself, and then waited for the rest of the family, but I wouldn't think of doing that. I wouldn't leave without my children. We had to leave together or not at all.

We lived in a suburb of Havana called Guanabacoa. My father was a doctor's assistant. He had wanted to become a doctor, but his parents couldn't afford to send him to medical school. He helped out people in our neighborhood when they were sick. They would say, "I need an injection, Alfredito." He was almost a doctor for our neighbors. Everybody trusted him. At night, he repaired radios and TVs for the extra money.

In Havana, people walked. If it was far, they would take a bus. My father had his own car, but we liked to walk. You'd see your friends and neighbors and say hello. It was the same in Spain. We could take the kids everywhere. It was the same in New York. But when we got here, there was such a difference. I don't drive a car, either, which makes it even harder for me.

I don't like Miami. I don't want to die in Miami. I like street life and there isn't any here. I like to walk to the store or to do my errands, and I like to see people. I like to walk everywhere and people are afraid to walk here, especially at night. Sure, the weather is nice here and it's cold in New York, but I don't care. I loved New York.

I work in a clothing factory about five blocks from here, but I get a ride there with a friend. I work on the floor, I don't do any sewing myself. I see to it that the work gets to the women, and they give it to me when they're finished. Then I pass it along to the next department, to be sized or whatever. I've been working there about three years. I like it all right.

Most of us in my factory are Cuban women and we're all good workers. We all get along. We eat together in the commissary. We have a stove and we can heat up our food. You know how Cubans are, they eat a lot, so most of the workers bring their own food. They bring rice, beans, whatever. They eat hot food, no sandwiches. They like to eat a real meal.

After work, I come here to my "part-time" job. I like to call it that. That's when I cook and clean. I call cooking my part-time job. I get home about three twenty-five and my husband about five. I make something for us and we eat. He goes to bed around nine. I do my real cooking in the morning. I get up at four-thirty because my husband takes a real lunch to work. He likes a big lunch, not a big dinner. I cook him meat, rice, beans, chicken. He loves his moros. That's his favorite, with rice.[19]

We always worked hard, sometimes at two jobs. And when Miguell had to spend two years at Columbia University, we had to help him out. It was hard, too. It was over a thousand dollars a year for his room and board. He would telephone us and say, "Mom, the money is due tomorrow." Sometimes Campillo would have to borrow the money and we would pay it back little by little. But it was important for Mige to study and think of his career. We did everything we could; Campillo took all the outside jobs he could get. We would do things like wallpapering people's houses; we did whatever we could. We used to run around like crazy people.

In Cuba, as far as material things went, we would buy a television set or record player after we saved enough money to buy it. Here, we do it with a credit card. I'm speaking of the working-class people, not the really poor people, of course. In Cuba, we would buy the cheapest we could find. Here we buy the most expensive. I guess that's why I loved this country as soon as we arrived in New York.

MIGUELL

Sometimes I wonder what it's like never to be an immigrant. I have friends who were born and raised here, and they have a different perspective and different views. My personality is completely shaped by this process of being an immigrant. It's fundamental. They don't have that, so I say, "How did they build their lives? They didn't go through any major crisis like this."

This friend of mine, he seems to be very happy and very content even though he's an intellectual. He can be like that because he always lived in the U.S. But I could never be like that; I always tend to worry about things, perhaps unnecessarily, because for so long I had to be so conscious. .

First, the idea of being born in one place and then you're told that you have to leave almost right away: Automatically, you stop growing into that place, that society in which you live. So I was growing up in Cuba and thinking about when is this day going to come when we go to the U.S., like this life that I'm living is not the real one; this is only until we go there. That was my feeling as a child, so a lot of my identity with the place was very superficial.

[19]Moros y christianos—white rice and black beans flavored with pork, a casserole

It was awful for me to walk into a high school in New York, having always been an A student and suddenly the teacher is calling my name and I was not understanding my name, so she thought I was not attending my classes. She mispronounced my name so tremendously it was not my name. Perhaps also my ears were not used to the phonetics of the English language. By the time she reported me I was wondering why she wasn't calling me. Finally, I got an explanation of what was going on here. But what that meant was I went from being an A student to not able to do anything. It was extremely shocking. It was horrifying.

At this point I was shaking on Sunday evenings, because I knew Monday was coming and I had to go back to school. That was very traumatic. So all these things, they really shape the way you are, so people who never went through this, I wonder what made them be the way they are. I just don't see these huge factors there. Their lives were more gradual; my life was intense by design—with very little choice.

At the beginning, in the U.S. at least, I remember, I felt very uncomfortable. And it was a most bizarre feeling, because I liked the idea of being here and I wanted to be part of it, but it was almost impossible. First, you don't speak the language and that's a big, big drawback. They'd send me out to physical education. In high school we played American football. I didn't know the rules. Well, they realized that. They explained them to me. In English!

I still didn't know the rules, so we go to the field and I'm doing all these horrible things, and they're screaming at me and I thought everyone is really angry at me and I don't know why. It was a nightmare. Later, you look back and you feel, I'm glad that this happened. Because of this I learned how to survive unusual situations. I know, for example, what's affecting people, the motive, because you learn to be perceptive to these things.

We were always poor, poor in Cuba, poor in Spain, and poor when we came here. I'm not saying like starving poor, but there were always these things that were missing, that we could not afford to have one way or another. So as a child, they start telling you when you go to the U.S. finally this is going to change. And it did, it got better, but not right away.

So this thing about postponement,[20] it becomes rather difficult. And then I had to do it in order to get educated. It was my own choice, so that was the ultimate test, because I had put up with that too long, but finally the time came when I wanted to go on and get a college education. I knew I had to once again do it. It's been the story of my life. That's why now at this point, I don't want to wait; I want to see if I can get that car.

---

[20]One evening, while driving to Miami Beach to have dinner at one of the new cafés in the art deco area of South Beach, near where Miguell lives, he had talked about the postponement of gratification and his desire to buy a convertible car. He was trying to save enough money to make a large down payment, keeping his monthly payments affordable.

I remember being a child in Cuba. I remember where I lived. The name of the town is Guanabacoa. It is a small city on the other side of the bay of Havana Harbor. It had a flare of Spain, the old houses, the tall ceilings, and the large windows. None of it was in good condition. It was a little rundown. For example, the houses were lacking paint; the colors were all faded. It always felt like things that I've seen here in this country with respect to Latin America: The image of the poor town that you get in the U.S., it always comes back to my neighborhood. Really, it hits me when you see, like a novel, that some Latin Americans have written—either you read it or you see a movie that's filmed about it. It always brings me back to that. It's like, I saw it. It was my neighborhood, that kind of thing.

The streets were narrow; the sidewalks were not complete; the lighting was not the best. My house was not an old house. It was my grandparents' house. There were no trees adorning the place for the sake of it. There were trees in the gardens but not on the sidewalks. And there were very few cars. My grandfather had one. It was, if I'm not mistaken, a Chevrolet 1948. It used to break down all the time, and we had to fix it, and I hated doing that. I didn't like that.

There were four cars in our block, the complete block. There was one Mercedes. I knew what a Mercedes was. It was pretty new; it was from the late sixties. That was the guy across the street. It was given or sold to him. His family were somehow connected to Castro—not in terms of blood, but in terms of participation in the revolution—so he ended up getting a great job in an oil refinery. But it was so funny—and I always think of this—the Mercedes stood there parked in front of his house. His house was in such bad shape. It was a wooden house, it was almost falling over, and there was a Mercedes there.

I did pretty well in school. The biggest difficulty for me was Spanish. I'm not good in languages. I hated the accents. I was so happy when I discovered English had no accents.

I was good in math and writing essays on political things. I would write these explanations why the revolution was the best. I remember writing about Che Guevara and the imperialist Yanquis, and we were going to destroy them and all that. It's so funny, because my family was trying to get out of there and I was writing these essays.

I had some problems once it became very evident that my family was going to emigrate. They tried to convince me to stay and let my family go. It was really funny, because of the way they tried to convince you. It's like this little story that I will never forget about this swimming pool of milk. This woman came to my school. She guaranteed me that in ten years—obviously, this never happened—Cuba was to produce more milk than Holland. There would be so much milk that the swimming pools . . . not only would there be a lot of swimming pools, which we didn't have, but they would be filled with milk.

No one in my family before me ever went to college. It's quite an uncomfortable position because it makes you a little different. It's not better, it's just different. Sometimes that can be rough, because they think that you're going to separate yourself from them. They have this view that you are of another social class, and it is a little scary. I don't enjoy it so much.

I always knew I was going to study. I always knew it was within me. I remember when I said to some people in my early days of college here in Miami, I was going to do my master's in either Georgetown or Columbia University, they would laugh: Obviously, you don't have a penny, you're not going to do this. But I was convinced. I didn't apply to any other schools. And I didn't have the money to apply. I remember, I borrowed thirty dollars to apply to Columbia University. I still owe that money. They wouldn't take it back.

I went to the School of International Affairs for the master's, which is a two-year program. I specialized in economic development, which all has to do with what I said in the beginning. If I had not been an immigrant that came from Cuba, probably I would have studied something else. Economic development has to do with the fact that I come from an underdeveloped society, the whole process that got me out of there, the revolution, trying to understand what happened that my life was cut up.

I knew New York was a city I loved, and I wanted to stay, but I had a girlfriend who was from France, a Vietnamese, another person who went through another episode, so she had adjusted to France very well and we were pretty serious at the time. She was thinking of coming here. She loved Miami. It didn't work. In the process, I had to get a job.

I'm the Coordinator of the Cuban/American Policy Center, which is a program of the Cuban/American National Council, which is funded by the Ford Foundation. I think it's a good job, but I never intended to work there. I don't have that image of me as a minority. I never understood it so well. I always thought that I was an immigrant, period. I did not develop this consciousness about being a minority who has to struggle to succeed. I always thought I have to struggle to succeed myself, not as a group, which is the story of most Cubans, I think. The idea of let's get together to succeed is only now being developed. Most Cubans did it individually.

I'm caught up in that in-between. It's very uncomfortable. It's a generation that's not totally Cuban, not totally American, but right in between, and you have to identify with the two sides. You never know which one you are.

I think when I have children, I would teach them Spanish; it's great to know another language. And they'll know my history, and they'll know where I come from, but they're Americans. I tell you, there are some kids who are born here, you ask them, What are you? And they say, Cuban. They don't know what Cuba is. You know, they've never been there, they probably never will go there, they don't speak Spanish well, and they say Cuban. And you go, What? That's not what I plan for my kids.

I get angry when people identify you as one of the two extremes, because it only shows me that they don't know the Cuban community. Anyone who would know a little bit about it would know that the majority is in between. Some people say the rich left Cuba, or they say the criminals left Cuba; the working people, they never left Cuba. And that's a lie. The rich left the first year and the criminals left twenty years later. In between, a lot of people left.

RAMÓN DEL CAMPILLO

I started going to school here. Miami Dade Junior High School, I went the full three years there. Then I got married, and I didn't make it to go to high school. I got married because I felt I had to get married; my wife got pregnant. My father had a talk with me and said, "You don't have to get married," and this and that. But I thought I was doing the right thing. I was seventeen years old. She was fourteen years old when she had the baby. We were very young. And we lasted, like a year and a half. And then, you know, we got divorced. You know, I kept on working; I didn't go back to school.

When I got married the first time, we lived with my parents-in-law. Her mom was divorced, so it was her mom, me, my wife, and the kid who lived there for a while until we got divorced. When I got divorced, I was working for the gas company, and I remember they gave me the worst jobs because I had to go to like Overtown to the worst sections, and then I would have to cut their gas off. It was a pretty good job, but when I got divorced, I lost the job. I wasn't doing anything. I was in the streets, you know, going around with my friends, doing nothing. I came back home to live with my parents. I had problems with my parents, too, because I didn't want to work. I didn't want to do anything. I was depressed, I guess. I wasn't thinking right. I was just racing my car, hanging out in the streets, you know.

Then I got married, two years later, with my wife now. We've been married for a long time already; we've been married four years. I started working with her father, in a lunch truck. We're not working right now, at the moment. He's going through some hard times himself. He just got divorced himself. I'm going to night school, trying to get my G.E.D. I went to the Miami North campus where they give the fireman course, and they told me that I could get the required diploma in the evenings, so I have to get my G.E.D. When I finish the course, they will give me the uniform, everything, and they'll try to get me a job, or if not, I'll go on my own, wherever there's an opening for a fireman. You work forty hours, which is two days, sleep there one night, and then I got five days of the week, you know. They start, I think, at $25,000.

Right now, I think it's one of the happiest times of my life, because everything is going so right for me. I got my plans, you know. I go to school every night, and I come home with so much knowledge. I'm learning so many things that I didn't know, and I'm doing good.

My wife, she's working late, like four o'clock, and I take care of the kid. Now we're gonna put her in a nursery school. My father-in-law will start working on the truck again, and I'll be with him again till I finish school.

To work on the lunch truck, we gotta get up at three thirty in the morning. We go load up the truck, that's why we start so early. That takes two, three hours. His routes, he has them in Hollywood, so we go all the way to Hollywood. His first stop, it's like at six forty-five. We got fifty-two stops altogether, and then we finish at about two o'clock.

He puts all the breakfast stuff first, where the tank heats up in the back. Then when breakfast is finished, he puts all the dinners and sandwiches for lunch next. It's mostly Cuban food. *Pastelitos de guayaba*—Americans, they love it—and cream cheese and guava. When we didn't have anymore, "Oh, you ran out already?" I guess those were their favorites. For lunch, Cuban rice, which is *moros* with pork and shrimp, yellow rice and shrimp, real food. We charge $2.50 for a large dinner, including the bread, the rice, the pork, and sometimes corn, or something else on the side. Everybody was complaining about the prices, too, even if it's cheap.

We sell almost everything during the day because he knows what the people want. When he was working every day, without missing a day, he would bring home like $600 or $700 a week. It would make, clean for him, after paying the food, $500, real good.

I like being Cuban. I don't know why. I want my daughter to speak Spanish, and I also want her to speak English. Right now, she's speaking Spanish a lot more than English. English, she knows little things from TV. I want her now, me and my wife were talking about it the other day, we want to start talking English around her a lot more because it's gonna help her more when she starts school. But we come here[21] or we go to my wife's folks, everybody speaks Spanish, and that's all she's learned up to now.

A lot of people live in Miami without speaking English. My father don't speak any English. My uncle, he don't speak any English, but he got work. He used to take kids to school on a bus. They can live here without speaking English. You see some of the retail stores, when they advertise, they say, "We speak English."

I never watch Spanish TV. I don't like it at all. I don't think they have any

[21]The interview was done in the home of his parents.

good programs or anything worthwhile watching. To tell you the truth, I don't like Spanish TV at all. I don't read the Spanish papers, either. I always buy the Sunday *Herald*. It's in English. It has a Spanish insert, but I never read it. On the radio, I sometimes listen to Cuban music. I like it. But that's about it. I don't listen to the talk stations, not [in] Spanish, not in English. I never got into them. I like to see the talk shows, especially David Letterman and Johnny Carson. I love to watch them because of the people they always have. It's very interesting.

I just finished filling out my application for my citizenship. My mom was telling me that July fourth they're gonna have in the Orange Bowl, like they did not so long ago, they're gonna fill it up and everybody's gonna swear the flag. Hopefully, I can go there to become a citizen, because that's another thing I'm gonna need to be a fireman. And I think all the jobs for the government, they require that.

Can you explain to me what a Republican is? I was going for Bush, so I guess I'm a Republican. I like Bush because he's been a real American all the time. He was in the war. The teacher was telling us he used to be a pilot in the war. He's been shot down about six times, so he's really been into the action. He's really an American because of that. You know, I like him because of that. He fought for his country. I think he's gonna be a real good president.

Castro, well, the only thing I know is everybody talks real bad about him because what he did, this and that. That's all I ever heard. I don't like Castro, but it's not important to me anymore, because even if Cuba won't be communist anymore, I wouldn't go back to Cuba. This will be my country. I like it. I love this place.

IVAN ORTA[22]

Ee-van in Spanish—I'm from Havana. Just when I'm coming, I work in some kind of restaurant, in the warehouse. It's a big restaurant that they have for foreign people, tourists. Not exactly in Havana, east of Havana, it's something outside the city, like you say here, Miami Beach.

I go to school, but not too much, only until eighth grade or something like this. Because I get a lot of trouble there because I got long hair, you know, the sixties. And if you got a long hair in the sixties, they don't want you to go to school. Yeah, because if you got a long hair, you are some kind of, in Cuba, they name *anti-socios*. I don't know what it is in English exactly.

I heard the Beatles, the Rolling Stones, things like this, and they said this is a crime, in Cuba. They said I could go out of school, some jobs, or maybe the army, military service for three years.

[22]Ivan Orta, Miguell del Campillo's cousin, insisted upon speaking English. He is a burly man with shoulder length hair and a ferocious black beard.

I decided to leave a long time ago. I think exactly when I saw that I can't hear the music that I want, when I can't say what I want to say, or my hair. I say, "This is no country for me." After that, so many things happen. We try to make our own business, you know, buy something from somebody they coming outside, some American tourists or something. And sell to the other guys in Cuba.

And sometimes the police get you and put you in jail, maybe one week, maybe two weeks. They cut your hair, and you go out and you grow your hair again. You know, it seems like never stops. And that's the way I must live. This was 1966, '65. But I can't do it until 1980.

I was married when I was seventeen years. I got my son who lives now in New York. He's a postman. I was divorced, like everybody who was married at seventeen years usually, eh? I was divorced six months after he was born, and I married my wife that she got two kids, one year before we come here, in 1978 or 1979. So I was single for a long time. I am forty-one now. Most of my married life is here in the United States.

I like music, but [I am] no musician. I got friends that were musicians in Cuba. It wasn't the music exactly that made me against the government. You understand? We get ten years old when the revolution came and everything, so it's different. Some of the Cubans think about what they got before or how free they are before Castro, things like this. We don't know nothing before Castro, was good or was bad. We don't know nothing about it. We know *now* it's bad. And in my case, many other persons think about what they don't have. They don't get pants, shirts, shoes, but it was mostly what we can do and what we can't do. Why can't I sit down outside? Why somebody can tell me what time I can wake up and what time go to bed?

I told you I left the school so fast but I start studying by myself. I don't know how you call it, you know, autodidact or something. I learn like this, I am so political, that I start to read, first, all the magazines, *Das Capital,* things like this. When I saw this, I said, this is not our case; this is never going to work. Nobody is going to work for nothing. This guy is crazy. In Cuba, I start to think about it, America. I start to go, and I say, nothing is coming with me from here; I get into a lot of trouble here; nothing is going to work for me here. That's what I put in my mind, me, like so many of my friends.

We came on the boat from Mariel and we get a lot of trouble because the kids of my wife, two kids, when we go to leave, the police said, "They can't go. Go alone." And they send us alone here. My wife don't see these kids for about five years or six years. Until we made American citizens, you remember the big one? On the Fourth of July? One year after that, they come. But for six years, she didn't see them because they said, "You want to go? Go alone."

When I got here, there was different reaction from different people. Everybody expected to meet somebody who is coming, with greased hair, maybe, dancing cha cha cha or something like this. When they saw somebody coming with long hair, you know, and they put some Cuban music on the radio, and I said, "I don't want to listen to that. I wasn't coming here to listen to that."

Maybe it was different, but my family was nice to me. I stayed at Miguell's house with his parents for about two or three months. Then my wife and me found jobs, different jobs; she was working at night, eleven at night to seven in the morning; I was working days. For a long time, we don't see each other, ten minutes maybe, you go to the job, I coming back. I have no car. In Cuba, usually you don't know nothing about driving. People that no have cars, don't drive.

I found a job with a Colombian guy with a coffee roaster. The guy is a big millionaire now, and he's in jail. I had to walk seven miles every day. Nobody gave me a ride. I worked about twelve hours daily. That's the reason mainly that I didn't see my wife. By the time I get back to my house it's nine o'clock.

After that, I get two jobs. I delivered Domino's Pizza at night. There's something in Cuba, snow cones. I prepared it, and put ice inside, and I go everywhere with my cart, after work.

I change my job for vending machines, and they call me, and I say, "That's okay, I drive all my life." The next day, I go for my driving test and get my license and I don't know nothing about it. And I told him, "I don't know nothing about driving." Cars, imagine trucks! He says, "Okay, I going to help you. Try to do it slowly." And I learned, I learned in fifteen days. He trained me to drive in the street, but I asked to not drive on the expressway at all. Some day, I would take the expressway.

In my second job, the vending machines, some American guy told me, "When you get to the top and you see you're not going to get more money, you looking for the next one." In Cuba, you'd say, "I'm going to stay here for forty years."

But here, the same guy is paying you the minimum wage for forty years, and the same guy don't give you nothing, no insurance, nothing.

Here, there was prejudice from different kinds. I think the American people had some prejudice over us, but mostly, it was the Cuban people. The Cuban people was discriminating against us. Cuban people said we are Marielitos. They feel that we are different from them. You see, it was a lot of people that are different, not like the ones before, different. We think so many things different. Cuba was a big country before the revolution, and we said, "Cuba was good, but not so good like you said."

In my house, it was only my TV set in the neighborhood, and all my friends were coming to my house to see my TV set. Was good, but not so good; good, if everybody got a TV set. Cuba was a good country, it was free, things like this, but not like we thought. So many young Cubans think about it—Cubans who come here when they are maybe three years old, or maybe they are born here but they think they are Cubans, I don't know why. I asked this guy why he thought so much of Cuba, and he said, "My father told me." I said, "Your father is a liar, you know." I know that everybody don't get a car in Cuba. I was only ten years old when the revolution came, but I know that it wasn't true. Everybody don't get a car in Cuba. They said the apples in Cuba were better than here, but Cuba don't have apples. The apples that they got in Cuba were from the United States. Things like this, you know.

I working now for three years a company for liquors and wine distribution. That's okay for me, for now. I get a lot of money there. It's good insurance, the benefits, vacation. I drive, I drive. I don't want it, now I must do every day.

You know, I get another driver supervisor. He's the big chief—Big George, we call him. He's a black guy who's about four hundred pounds. He talks with me too much, and he said to me, "You know why all the black people here like you? Because you try. You come and you don't know how can you say that? You asked. You say, 'How can I say this in English?' If we are rapping, you come and you clap. You try. You talk to us about gospel music."

The young Cubans, guys like Miguell, speak much better than me. So many of them go to the university. You know, it's different for them. They are Americans; they born here or coming here at three years, four years old. But most of them still think, Cuba. I tell the guys that tell me that Fidel is going down some day. Then you go to Cuba. You live in Cuba two days: One day to go there and the other day waiting for the plane to come back.

They don't want to think about it, but here I have my posters, the Beatles, Marilyn Monroe, the Rolling Stones. They're my favorites. You see all that music? We don't have Cuban music here. But this is no typical Cuban house.

Usually, the children prefer to talk to us in Spanish; they got only one year here. But with their friends, they talk English. I prefer to use both. Don't forget Spanish because you need it, but speak English with me, okay? I tell them every day, "This is your country now. You never going to live in another country. You'll never leave here. Better you be American. You think all your life you are Spanish, and you are not Spanish, you are nothing. And you go to ghetto. You live there for all your life, thinking you are Spanish, and you are not Spanish, you are nothing."

I don't believe in that. When I became American citizen, I go to my registration to vote. There is a Cuban lady and she is going to put the registration in Spanish. She is going to mark me down *Spanish*. I say to her, "I don't know any race, Spanish. I white, or I black, but not Spanish." She says,

"But you told me in Spanish." I said, "I told you in English. I know Spanish, but I told you in English." And she called the supervisor and everything. I wanted *white*, so he told her to put down white. Spanish no exist, or maybe only the people that come from Spain.

It's a bureaucratic invention that Spanish people go in there; they wanted to be Spanish, because they wanted to get welfare. They wanted to get special privilege when you go in some business, things like this. And I don't want it to be like this. I don't want nobody coming here and telling me, "I going to help you to do something." No, give me the job, give me the opportunity, and I do it. Don't tell me, "It's three jobs here: One for the nigger, one for the spic, and one for the American people." Don't tell me.

You know how I can take care of this job? Working more hard than him. It the only way I going to be a first-class citizen. I don't want to be second-class citizen—never. That's what I think about: I don't want to be second-class citizen; don't give me nothing for free. I work for it.

So many people think it more easy to say, "No, I Spanish. Give the job for me." That's what too many people see. I don't see this. I coming here to be like everybody: No less than nobody. But no more. Exactly like everybody else. We, the American people.

ACKNOWLEDGMENTS

This book is the work of many teachers, some of whose names and words appear on its pages. I would like to add the names of the others here. Some are old friends; others took time from their lives to tell me something for this book. I am grateful to them all: From early days, my classmates in the Douglas, Arizona, and El Paso schools; my neighbors, the Pera family; Rubito Hernández; Jesús Delgadillo; Rubén Blanco; Nacha Herrera; old friends from the El Paso *Herald-Post* and the *Times*; John Patrick; Carmen de la Vega and her sister, Rosario Nilsson; especially the Tellez family—Luz, Yvette, Steve, Keefer, and Rudy; for lessons in the high style, humor, and intellectual excitement of the Mexican mind, Sylvia's great friend and accomplice, the man from Chiapas, doctor, ambassador, Prince Edmundo Lassalle; for lessons in hospitality and publishing, Concepción Zea.

Many people helped once I began working on the book: Carlos Alvarez, David Behar, Moises Bujandra, César Caballero, Tulía María Caicedo, Ruth Capelle, Ramón Cernuda, Denise Chávez, Concilio de los Padres de District 4, Rita Davis, the de la Garza family, Mike Duran, María Eraña, Gloria Escobar, John Estrada, the Gelabert family, Alma González, Ray Gonzalez, Jorge Hanes, Mike Hernández, Jorge Hinojosa, Tom Holler, Victoria Horstmann, Felipe J. Préstamo, Marilyn Kalusin, Wilfredo Laboy, Sylvia Lema, Carlos Luis, Adrian Maciás, Eileen Madrid, Alicia Maldonado, Roberto Martínez, Susana Martínez, Tacho Mendiola, George Molinar, Alberto Moncada, Jonathon Moore, Douglas Mosier, Beatriz Nava, Becky Ochoa, Nereida Perez, Chevo Quiroga, Anita Rafky, Jorge Ramírez, Rev. Marcos Ramos, Luis Reyes,

Silvestre Reyes, Roberto Rivera, Mary Jean and Hal Roberts, Armando Rodríguez, Texas State Representative Ciro Rodríguez, Jesse Rodríguez, Primitivo Rodríguez, Margarita Roque, Dolores Sánchez, Gladys Sandlin, Cumanda Santos, Jerry Scott, Alan Shean, Marco Tulio Silva, Judy Stern Torres, Juan Tejeda, Lee Teran, Carmen Torres, Mercedes Toural, Rosa Urquiola, Councilman Frank D. Wing, Alice Valdez, Elizabeth Valdez, Tony Vásquez, Rubén Villalpando, Jesse Villarreal, and Michael Zamba.

The López and Rojas families, who came from Puerto Rico, settled in upstate New York, and made a good life for themselves and their children, taught me that the problem of moving to New York from rural Puerto Rico or from the cruelest neighborhoods of San Juan could be overcome. The young men of the family have moved to New York City to make their fortunes; Billy López, steady and careful, the planner, and Mike Rojas, excitable, imaginative, the fast-talking musician, writer, entrepreneur, are both destined to succeed in the city, each in his own way.

José Prince, whom I met through Jorge Valls, has proved to be a first rate sociologist (his profession) and the source of vast amounts of information, from the lyrics of sentimental songs to the most sophisticated aspects of Cuban culture and politics.

My thanks to the poet Norma Almquist for the months in which I lived as a writer should, in the loveliest cottage on Mount Washington.

Rina Tamayo, a Mexican woman working at the Chicano Studies Research Library at UCLA, helped me to understand the life of Zapotecan Indians living and working without papers in California. Lunches with her and Leo Estrada, the wise demographer, produced some of the best and liveliest conversation of the years I worked on the book.

David Blumenthal, Morton Coleman, John Davis, George Hambrick, Tom Kaufman, and Lourdes Nisce really did make this book possible, for which I am most grateful.

Lewis Lapham and Victor Navasky have been good friends and generous editors; I was pleased to be able to publish parts of this book in their magazines.

My friend, Roberta Pryor, who is sometimes my literary agent as well, knows something many people in publishing have forgotten, which is that writers need editors. Because of her, this book went to Starling Lawrence, who performed upon it that necessarily meticulous, occasionally magical act—he edited. And was nobly assisted in this by Richard Halstead, who never lost a page or failed to get a joke.

Much of this book is about Sylvia, who found roots in Mexico as she never could in New York; the love in the book was confirmed by her, and the thinking, when correct, was guided by her. She is a good teacher, but not quick; thirty-six years has not been nearly enough.

Brief Bibliography

Acosta, Oscar Zeta. *The Revolt of the Cockroach People.* San Francisco: Straight Arrow Books, 1973.

Aguilar Melantzón, Ricardo. *Madreselvas en flor.* Jalapa: Universidad Veracruzana, 1987.

Allman, T. D. *Miami.* New York: Atlantic Monthly Press, 1987.

Anaya, Rudolfo A. *A Chicano in China.* Albuquerque: University of New Mexico Press, 1986.

——. *Heart of Aztlán.* Albuquerque: University of New Mexico Press, 1976.

——. *Lord of the Dawn.* Albuquerque: University of New Mexico Press, 1987.

——. *Tortuga.* Albuquerque: University of New Mexico Press, 1979.

Anaya, Rudolfo A., ed. *Voces.* Albuquerque: University of New Mexico Press, 1987.

Anaya, Rudolfo A. and Francisco Lomeli. *Aztlán.* Albuquerque: El Norte Publications, 1989.

Anaya, Rudolfo A. and Antonio Márquez, eds. *Cuentos Chicanos.* Albuquerque: University of New Mexico Press, 1984.

Anguiano, Leonard. *El Quetzal Emplumece.* San Antonio: Mexican American Cultural Center, 1976.

Argueta, Manlio. *One Day of Life*. New York: Random House, 1983.

Asturias, Miguel Angel. *Week-end en Guatemala*. Buenos Aires: Editorial Losada, 1968.

Attwater, Donald. *A Dictionary of Saints*. Baltimore: Penguin, 1965.

Avila, Joaquín. *Mexican American Political Participation*. Fremont, Calif.: Self-published, 1989.

Bean, Frank and Marta Tienda. *The Hispanic Population of the United States*. New York: Russell Sage, 1987.

Benedict, Ruth. *Patterns of Culture*. Boston: Houghton Mifflin, 1934.

Bermudez, George S. "Beliefs, Boundaries and Burnout: The Threat of Burnout in the Hispanic Clinic Model for Delivery of Mental Health Services." Ph.D. diss. City University of New York, 1988.

Bonachea, Rolando E. and Nelson P. Valdés. *Cuba in Revolution*. New York: Anchor Books, 1972.

Burciaga, José Antonio. *Weedee Peepo*. Edinburg, Texas: Pan American University Press, 1988.

Candelaria, Nash. *The Day the Cisco Kid Shot John Wayne*. Tempe, Ariz.: Bilingual Press, 1988.

Casasola, Gustavo. *Historia Gráfica de la Revolución Mexicana*. Mexico: Trillas, 1960.

Castillo, Ana. *My Father Was a Toltec*. Novato, Calif.: West End Press, 1988.

Cervantes, Lorna Dee. *Emplumada*. Pittsburg: University of Pittsburg Press, 1981.

Cervantes M., Francisco. *Francisco Villa y la Revolución*. Mexico, D. F.: Ediciones Alonso, 1960

Chávez, Angelico. *The Short Stories of Fray Angelico Chávez*. Albuquerque: University of New Mexico Press, 1987.

Chávez, Denise. *The Last of the Menu Girls*. Houston: Arte Publico Press, 1987.

Chávez, John R. *The Lost Land*. Albuquerque: University of New Mexico Press, 1984.

Chavez, Linda. *Out of the Barrio*. New York: Basic Books, 1991.

Cisneros, Sandra. *The House on Mango Street*. Houston: Arte Publico Press, 1985.

———. *Woman Hollering Creek*. New York: Random House, 1991.

Cockcroft, James D. *Intellectual Precursors of the Mexican Revolution, 1900–1913*. Austin: University of Texas Press, 1969.

Cockcroft, James D. *Outlaws in the Promised Land*. New York: Grove Press, 1986.

Conover, Ted. *Coyotes*. New York: Random House, 1987.

Cortina, Rodolfo J. and Alberto Moncada, eds., *Hispanos en los Estados Unidos*. Madrid: Instituto de Cooperación Iberoamerican, 1988.

Cummins, Jim and Swain Merrill. *Bilingualism in Education*. New York: Longman, 1986.

de Alba, Alicia Gaspar. *Three Times a Woman*. Tempe, Ariz: Bilingual Press, 1989.

de la Garza, Rodolfo O. et al., eds. *The Mexican American Experience*. Austin: University of Texas Press, 1985.

de León, Arnoldo. *Ethnicity in the Sunbelt: A History of Mexican-Americans in Houston*. Houston: University of Houston, 1989.

del Rosario, Rubén. *Vocabulario Puertorriqueño*. Sharon, Conn.: Troutman Press, 1965.

Díaz, Guarione M., *Evaluation and Identification of Policy Issues in the Cuban Community*, Miami: Cuban National Planning Council, 1981.

Dihigo y López-Trigo, Ernesto. *Los Cubanismos en el Diccionario de la Real Academia Española*. Madrid: Comisión Permanente de la Asociación de Academias de la Lengua Española, 1974.

Draper, Theodore. *Castro's Revolution*. New York: Praeger, 1962.

Espada, Martín. *Rebellion is the Circle of a Lover's Hands*. Willimantic, Conn.: Curbstone Press, 1991.

————. *Trumpets from the Islands of their Eviction*. Tempe, Ariz.: Bilingual Press, 1987.

Fernández, Manuel, *Exilio y Esperanza*. Miami: Saeta Ediciones, 1987.

Fernández, Roberto G. *Raining Backwards*. Houston: Arte Publico Press, 1988.

Ferré, Rosario. *Sweet Diamond Dust*. New York: Ballantine, 1988.

Fitzpatrick, Joseph P. and Robert E. Gould. "Mental Illness Among Puerto Ricans in New York: Cultural Condition or Intercultural Misunderstanding?" In *On the Urban Scene*, ed. Morton Levitt and Ben Rubenstein. Detroit: Wayne State University Press, 1972.

Flores Magón, Ricardo. *La revolución Mexicana*. Mexico, D. F.: Grijalbo, 1970.

Foley, Douglas E. *From Peones to Politicos*. 2d ed. Austin: University of Texas Press, 1988.

Forbes, Jack D. *Aztecas del Norte*. New York: Fawcett, 1973.

Freire, Paulo. *Pedagogy of the Oppressed*. New York: Herder and Herder, 1972.

Galván, Roberto A. and Richard V. Teschner. *El Diccionario del Español Chicano*. Lincolnwood, Ill.: National Textbook Co., 1989.

Garcia, Mario T. *Desert Immigrants*. New Haven: Yale University Press, 1981.

———. *Mexican Americans*. New Haven: Yale University Press, 1989.

García, Nasario. *Recuerdos de los Viejitos*. Albuquerque: University of New Mexico Press, 1987.

Garibay K., Angel María. *Llave de Náhuatl*. Mexico, D.F.: Otumba, 1940.

———. *Historia de la Literatura Náhuatl*. Mexico, D.F.: Editorial Porrua, 1953–54.

Gilb, Dagoberto. *Winners on the Pass Line*. El Paso: Cinco Puntos Press, 1985.

Glazer, Nathan and Daniel P. Moynihan. *Beyond the Melting Pot*. Cambridge, Mass.: MIT. Press, 1970.

Goffman, Erving. *Asylums*. New York: Doubleday, 1961.

———. *The Presentation of Self in Everyday Life*. Garden City, New York: Doubleday, 1959.

Goldemberg, Isaac. *Hombre de Paso/Just Passing Through*. Hanover, N.H.: Ediciones del Norte, 1981.

———. *Tiempo al Tiempo*. Hanover, N.H.: Ediciones del Norte, 1984.

Gonzales, Manuel G. *The Hispanic Elite of the Southwest*. El Paso: Texas Western Press, 1989.

Gonzalez, Ray. *Twilights and Chants*. Golden, Colo.: James Andrews and Co. Inc., 1987.

González-Wippler, Migene. *Santería*. New York: Crown, 1973.

Grosjean, Francois. *Life with Two Languages*. Cambridge, Mass.: Harvard University Press 1982.

Guevara, Ernesto. *Che: Selected Works of Ernesto Guevara*. Cambridge, Mass.: MIT Press, 1969.

Gutiérrez, Gustavo. *A Theology of Liberation*. Maryknoll, N.Y.: 1973.

Handlin, Oscar. *The Newcomers*. Cambridge, Mass.: Harvard University Press, 1959.

Hayes-Bautista, David E. *Intellectual Framework for Multicltural Society*. Unpublished paper, 1989.

Hernández, Angela. *Desafío*. Santo Domingo, Dominican Republic: Editora Búho, 1985.

————. *Emergencia del Silencio*. Santo Domingo, Dominican Republic: Editora Universitaria, 1986.

————. *Las Mariposas No Temen a Los Cactus*. Santo Domingo, Dominican Republic: Editora Universitaria, 1988.

————. *Los Fantasmas Prefieren la Luz del Día*. Santo Domingo, Dominican Republic: Alas, 1986.

————. *Tizne y Cristal*. Santo Domingo, Dominican Republic: Alas, 1987.

Herrera-Sobek, María. *Three Times a Woman*. Tempe, Ariz.: Bilingual Press, 1989.

Herrera-Sobek, María and Helena María Viramontes. *Chicana Creativity and Criticism: Charting New Frontiers in American Literature*. Houston: Arte Publico Press, 1988.

Hinojosa, Rolando. *Klail City*. Houston: Arte Publico Press, 1987.

Inclán, Jaime E. "Hope after the Mourning: Puerto Rican Families in the Eighties." Unpublished paper, 1982.

————. "Interpersonal Relations among Puerto Rican Men: Or Why So Much Dominoes?" Unpublished paper, 1983.

————. "Some Differences between Poor First Generation and Middle-Class Second Generation Puerto Rican Families in Treatment." Unpublished paper [1983].

Inclán, Jaime, E. with Ernesto Ferran, Jr. "Poverty, Politics, and Family Therapy." Unpublished paper [1987].

Islas, Arturo. *The Rain God*. Palo Alto: Alexandrian Press, 1984.

————. *Migrant Souls*. New York: Morrow, 1990.

Jiménez, Francisco. *The Identification and Analysis of Chicano Literature*. New York: Bilingual Press, 1979.

Johnson, William Weber. *Heroic Mexico*. New York: Doubleday, 1968.

Kandell, Jonathan. *La Capital*. New York: Random House, 1988.

Kanellos, Nicolás, ed. *A Decade of Hispanic Literature from Revista Chicano-Riqueña*. Houston: Arte Publico Press, 1982.

Keen, Benjamin. *The Aztec Image*. New Brunswick: Rutgers University Press, 1971.

Krich, John. *El beisbol*. New York: Atlantic Monthly Press, 1989.

Kroeber, A. L. and Clyde Kluckhohn. *Culture*. New York: Vintage, 1952.

Langley, Lester D. *MexAmerica*. New York: Crown, 1988.

Laviera, Tato. *AmerRícan*. Houston: Arte Publico Press, 1985.

————. *Mainstream Ethics.* Houston: Arte Publico Press, 1988.

León, Victor. *Diccionario de Argot Español.* Madrid: Alianza Editorial, 1980.

León-Portilla, Miguel. *Aztec Thought and Culture.* Norman, Okla.: University of Oklahoma Press, 1963.

Lernoux, Penny. *Cry of the People.* Garden City, N.Y.: Doubleday, 1980.

————. *People of God.* New York: Viking, 1989.

Levine, Barry B., ed. *The Caribbean Exodus.* New York: Praeger, 1987.

Lévi-Strauss, Claude. *The Savage Mind.* London: Weidenfeld and Nicolson, 1966.

Lewis, Oscar. *LaVida.* New York: Random House, 1966.

López Morales, Humberto. *Poésia Cubana contemporanea.* New York: Las Americas Publishing, 1967.

Maldonado-Denis, Manuel. *Una Interpretación Histórico-social.* Mexico: Siglo Veintiuno Editores, 1972.

Mann, Evelyn S. *The Puerto Rican New Yorkers,* Parts I & II. New York City Department of City Planning, 1985.

Mann, Evelyn S. and Joseph J. Salvo. *Characteristics of New Hispanic Immigrants to New York City: A Comparison of Puerto Rican and Non-Puerto Rican Hispanics.* New York City Department of City Planning, 1984.

Mares, E. A. *I Returned and Saw Under the Sun.* Albuquerque: University of New Mexico Press, 1989.

Martí, José. *Selected Writings of José Martí.* New York: Noonday Press, 1954.

Martin, Patricia Preciado. *Days of Plenty Days of Want.* Tempe, Ariz.: Bilingual Press, 1988.

Martínez, Demetria. *Three Times a Woman.* Tempe, Ariz.: Bilingual Press, 1989.

Martínez, Oscar J. *Across Boundaries.* El Paso: Texas Western Press, 1986.

Martínez Palau, Silvio. *Made in USA.* Hanover, N.H.: Ediciones del Norte, 1986.

Mason, John and Gary Edwards. *Black Gods—Orisha Studies in the New World.* Brooklyn: The Yoruba Theological Archministry, 1985.

Matthews, Herbert L. *Fidel Castro.* New York: Simon & Schuster, 1969.

Mead, Margaret. *Continuities in Cultural Evolution.* New Haven: Yale University Press, 1964.

Méndez, Miguel. *The Dream of Santa María de las Piedras.* Translated by David William Foster. Tempe, Ariz.: Bilingual Press, 1989.

Meyer, Michael C. and William L. Sherman. *The Course of Mexican History*. New York: Oxford University Press, 1987.

Mohr, Nicholasa. *Nilda*. Houston: Arte Publico Press, 1986.

———. *Rituals of Survival: A Woman's Portfolio*. Houston: Arte Publico Press, 1985.

Moncada, Alberto. *NorteAmérica con Acento Hispano*. Madrid: Instituto de Cooperación Iberoamericana, 1988.

Montejano, David. *Anglos and Mexicans in the Making of Texas, 1836–1986*. Austin: University of Texas Press, 1987.

Montejo, Esteban. *Autobiography of a Runaway Slave*. New York: Random House, 1968.

Moore, Joan W. *Homeboys*. Philadelphia: Temple University Press, 1978.

Morales, Alejandro. *The Brick People*. Houston: Arte Publico Press, 1988.

———. *Death of an Anglo*. Translated by Judith Ginsberg. Tempe, Ariz.: Bilingual Press, 1988.

Morgan, Ted. *On Becoming American*. Boston: Houghton Mifflin, 1978.

Morison, Samuel Eliot. *The Oxford History of the American People*. New York, Oxford University Press, 1965.

Muñoz, Elías Miguel. *Crazy Love*. Houston: Arte Publico Press, 1988.

Murphy, Joseph M. *Santería*. Boston: Beacon Press, 1988.

Obregón, Alvaro. *Ocho mil kilometros en campaña*. 1917. Reprint. Mexico, D.F.: Fondo de Cultura Económica, 1959.

Parkes, Henry Bramford. *A History of Mexico*. Boston: Houghton Mifflin, 1938.

The People Shall Judge. Selected and edited by the staff, Social Sciences I, University of Chicago. Chicago: University of Chicago Press, 1949.

Polkinhorn, Harry, Alfredo Velasco, and Malcolm Lambert. *El libro de caló*. Floricanto Press, 1986.

Portes, Alejandro and Robert L. Bach. *Latin Journey*. Berkeley: University of California Press, 1985.

Quiñonez, Naomi. *Hummingbird Dream*. Los Angeles: West End Press, 1985.

Ramos, Marcos A. *Panorama del Protestantismo en Cuba*. San José, Costa Rica: Editorial Caribe 1986.

Rebolledo, Tey Diana. *Las Mujeres Hablan*. Alburquerque: El Norte Publications, 1988.

Ribes Tovar, Federico. *A Chronological History of Puerto Rico.* New York: Plus Ultra, 1973.

―――. *The Puerto Rican Woman.* New York: Plus Ultra, 1972.

Riding, Alan. *Distant Neighbors.* New York: Knopf, 1985.

Rivera, Tomás. *. . . y no se lo tragó la tierra.* Houston: Arte Publico Press, 1987.

Rodríguez, Joe. *Oddsplayer.* Houston: Arte Publico Press, 1989.

Rodriguez, Richard. *Hunger of Memory.* Boston: David R. Godine, 1982.

Rulfo, Juan, et al. *Inframundo.* Mexico, D.F.: Instituto Nacional de Bellas Artes, 1980.

Sahagún, Fray Bernardino de. *General History of the Things of New Spain, The Florentine Codex.* 12 vols. Translated by Arthur J. O. Anderson and Charles E. Dibble. Salt Lake City: University of Utah Press, 1950–1981.

Sale, Kirkpatrick. *The Conquest of Paradise.* New York: Knopf, 1990.

Sánchez, Luis Rafael. *La guaracha del macho camacho.* Barcelona: Argos-Vergara, 1982.

Santamaría, Francisco J., *Diccionario de Mejicanismos.* Mexico, D.F.: Editorial Porrua, 1983.

Silén, Iván. *Los paraguas amarillos.* Hanover, N.H.: Ediciones del Norte, 1983.

Silva Herzog, Jesús. *Breve Historia de la Revolución Mexicana.* Mexico, D.F.: Fondo de Cultura Económica, 1960.

Soto Vélez, Clemente. *The Blood That Keeps Singing.* Willimantic, Conn.: Curbstone Press, 1991.

Steiner, Stan. *The Islands.* New York: Harper & Row, 1974.

Taracena, Alfonso. *La verdadera revolución Mexicana.* Mexico, D.F.: Editorial Jus, 1960.

Thomas, Hugh. *Cuba.* New York: Harper & Row, 1971.

Ulibarri, Sabine R. *Governor Glu Glu and Other Stories.* Tempe, Ariz.: Bilingual Press, 1988.

Urribazo, Rosendo. *Machismo.* Ph.D. diss., Graduate Theological Union, University of California, Berkeley, 1987.

Valls, Jorge. *Coloquio del Azogamiento.* Miami: Saeta Ediciones, 1989.

―――. *Donde Estoy No Hay Luz y Está Enrejado.* Miami: Ediciones Hispamerican Books, 1984.

―――. *Twenty Years and Forty Days/Life in a Cuban Prison.* New York: Americas Watch, 1986.

Vicioso, Chiqui. *Un extraño ulular traia el viento*. Santo Domingo, Dominican Republic: Editora Alfa y Omega, n.d.

Villanueva, Alma Luz. *The Ultraviolet Sky*. Tempe, Ariz.: Bilingual Press, 1988.

Villarreal, José Antonio. *Pocho*. New York: Doubleday, 1959.

Villaseñor, Victor. *Rain of Gold*. Houston: Arte Publico Press, 1991.

Wagenheim, Kal and Olga Jimenez. *The Puerto Ricans*. New York: Praeger, 1973.

Wakefield, Dan. *Island in the City*. New York: Houghton Mifflin, 1957.

West, John O. *Mexican-American Folklore*. Little Rock, Ark.: August House, 1988.

Weyr, Thomas. *Hispanic U.S.A.* New York: Harper & Row, 1988.

Williams, Eric. *From Columbus to Castro*. London: Deutsch, 1970.

Womack, John, Jr. *Zapata and the Mexican Revolution*. New York: Knopf, 1969.

Yglesias, José. *In the Fist of the Revolution*. New York: Random House, 1968.

PERIODICALS

Various magazines and newspapers provided information both for the chapter on media and the rest of the book. Of these, *Hispanic Link,* published in Washington, D.C., deserves to be singled out. Although its readership is relatively small and each edition is only a few pages, *Hispanic Link,* with its unique national perspective, may be the single best source of information, in English or Spanish, about the ongoing activities of Latinos. *El Sol* (Magazine of the California Chicano News Media Association), edited by Mike Castro and published in Los Angeles, was also helpful, as were various articles by Andrew David Hernández, which have been appearing in the San Antonio *Light* since 1989, and the regular columns by Lisandro Perez, which appear in the Miami *Herald*. Joseph P. Fitzpatrick's "New York City and Its Puerto Rican 'Problem' " (The Catholic Mind, January–February 1960) was also useful.

Glossary of Words, Phrases, and Acronyms

abrazo embrace, hug

abuela grandmother

adelante forward

agringado "gringoized," Americanized

aguantar to bear, to endure, to hold one's ground

apuntelo charge it

aquí here

Arroz Moro rice with black beans and pork, a casserole

atrevimiento bold, daring

Aztlán a mythical place, the chthonian origin of the people known as the Aztecs

babalawo priest

bacalao codfish, usually dried

barrio district

bato see *vato*

BBAS Bilingual Bicultural Art School

bendición blessing

bodega a small grocery store

bolillo breadroll, an Anglo, a Latino who has sold out

botánica a store selling herbs, incense, statues, and books used in folk medicine

brujo witch

cacique chieftan

Cakchikel Mayan of Guatemala, also the language

Caló border dialect

campesinos country folk

CANC Cuban American National Council (social agency)

CANF Cuban American National Foundation (political organization)

Cantinflas stage name of the Mexican actor Mario Moreno; the name is said to derive from an insult often hurled at dull or imcompetent actors, comedians, and circus performers: Te inflas en la cantina (literally, You inflate yourself in the tavern.)

CARECEN provides legal aid to Central American refugees

Carib native of the Caribbean

casita outhouse (Mex.); small house

Cemí an idol representing a god of the Tainos

chalupa a fried corn tortilla containing meat, cheese, etc.

chapine bow-legged, a Guatemalan

charro cowboy

chico small

chingar fuck, violate, etc.

chofer chauffer

cholo punk, hoodlum

chula cute, cutie

chuparosas hummingbird (Mex.)

cocinera a cook

cocinita small restaurant featuring home cooking

colibrí hummingbird

colonia unincorporated settlement, usually without services

comida corrida lunch of the day, blue plate special

comida criolla homestyle cooking

comité committee

communidad de base grass roots group

coño vagina in Mexico; wow! or damn! in Spain and Cuba

COPS Communities Organized to Provide Services

coraje righteous anger

costurera seamstress

CRASH Community Resources Against Street Hoodlums

CRECE provides social services to Central American refugees

criollo a person of European descent

Cuauhtemoc Aztec prince, leader of rebellion against Cortés

curandero healer

CSO Community Service Organization

CYO Catholic Youth Organization

delito criminal or crime

dichos sayings, proverbs

diss show disrespect, insult

East Los Angeles a town in Los Angeles County

East L.A. informal, the east side of Los Angeles, the barrio

east Los Angeles the east side of Los Angeles, including East Los Angeles, the barrio

ejido cooperative (Mex.)

el labor the fields

EPISO El Paso Interreligious Sponsoring Organization

escritor writer

ESL English as a Second Language

ESOL English for Speakers of Other Languages

esse anyone of Mexican descent

facha baby bottle

familia family

flaco skinny

Fulano, Mengano, Zutano Tom, Dick, and Harry

gabacho Frenchified, any Anglo

gente people

gua gua bus in Cuba

guajiro peasant (Cuba)

guayabera loose-fitting shirt

güero fair-skinned

IAF Industrial Areas Foundation

INS U.S. Immigration and Naturalization Service

IRCA Immigration Reform and Control Act (1986)

ito suffix meaning small or dear, a sign of affection, especially common in dialogue in Mexico

jacal a shack made of adobe and thatch

jarabes Mexican dances

jíbaro peasant (Puerto Rico)

La Migra Border Patrol, INS

lechón suckling pig

LEP Limited English Proficiency

libertad liberty

loco crazy

Loisaida Lower East Side of Manhattan

Lucumi or **Lucummí** Santería

LULAC League of United Latin American Citizens

maduros fried ripe plantains

MALDEF Mexican American Legal Defense and Education Fund

MAPA Mexican American Political Association

mayate nigger

mayombe A syncretic religion of the Caribbean associated with black magic

Mejicano The spelling of the Spanish name of people whose ancestors lived in Mexico is "Mejicano" rather than "Mexicano." That is not an affectation; the spelling indicates an important distinction: "Mexicano," according to Francisco J. Santamaria, editor of the *Diccionario de Mejicanismos,* refers to one of the seven Náhuatl-speaking tribes. "Mejicano" refers to citizens of the Republic of Mexico or things pertaining to them. To distinguish in English between citizens of Mexico and citizens of the United States who are of Mexican descent, the hyphen helps: They are either Mexican or Mexican-American. I have tried to make the further distinction between Mejicanos, U.S. residents or citizens born in Mexico, and Mexican-Americans.

mestizo a person of mixed races

Mi casa es tu casa. My house is your house.

mojado wet

mole from *moler,* to grind; in Mexico, mole poblano, a sauce of ground spices, cocoa, and peanuts

mordida bribe

Moros y Cristianos Rice and beans

Motecuhzoma I Aztec emperor 1440–1469

Motecuhzoma II Aztec emperor 1502–1520

náhual alter ego

norteño a person from the northernmost states of Mexico, a northerner

Ojalá! God willing!

Orisha a Yoruba god

P.S. New York City Public School (followed by a number)

papa pope; potato (Mex.)

paracaidista parachutist, squatter

patojo baby

patria nation

patrón boss, patron, defender, model

pelado literally, hairless; lower class, a bum

pendejo a fool, a stupid person; literally, a female's pubic hair

pero but

placita a small plaza

pocho Mexican-American (derogatory)

pollo literally, chicken; slang for undocumented person

porquería trash

PRI Partido Revoluciónario Institucional

prieta dark-skinned woman

PRLDEF Puerto Rican Legal Defense and Education Fund

puta whore

Quetzalcóatl Aztec god, the culture bearer, D.H. Lawrence's plumed serpent

Quiché Mayans of Guatemala, also the language

quinceañera fifteenth birthday celebration

raza race, hence raza cosmica

respeto respect

ropa clothing

ropa vieja old clothes or shredded beef

rubio blond

Sábado Saturday

salsa literally, sauce; also the dance music

sancho the lover of an adulterous woman

Santería a syncretic religion of the Caribbean with Yoruba roots

Segundo Barrio Second Ward

sin without

socios the old boy network

sones Mexican dances

soy I am

SVREP Southwest Voter Registration and Education Project

Taino Native of the Caribbean, also the language

tecato heroin addict

techo roof

Tejano native of Texas, usually Mexican-American

telenovela soap opera

Tezcatlipoca Aztec god, warrior and trickster, "Smoking Mirror"

tierra earth

tirilongo see *vatoloco*

TMO The Metropolitan Organization

todo all

tostones fried plantains

traída girlfriend (El Salvador)

UFW United Farm Workers

vate poet; El Vate is Luis Muñoz Marín's nickname.

vato guy

vatoloco crazy guy, fearless, gang member

vendido sellout

vete! Go away!

veteranos veterans

vieja old woman

Yoruba a civilization of West Africa, also the language

INDEX